PROCEEDINGS OF THE

12th IEEE Computer Security Foundations Workshop

CSFW12

PROCEEDINGS OF THE

12th IEEE Computer Security Foundations Workshop

June 28 – 30, 1999

Mordano, Italy

Sponsored by The IEEE Computer Society Technical Committee on Security and Privacy

IEEE COMPUTER SOCIETY

Los Alamitos, California

Washington • Brussels • Tokyo

IEEE Computer Society Order Number PR00201
ISBN 0-7695-0201-6
ISBN 0-7695-0202-4 (case)
ISBN 0-7695-0203-2 (microfiche)
ISSN Number 1063-6900

Additional copies may be ordered from:

IEEE Computer Society
Customer Service Center
10662 Los Vaqueros Circle
P.O. Box 3014
Los Alamitos, CA 90720-1314
Tel: + 1-714-821-8380
Fax: + 1-714-821-4641
E-mail: cs.books@computer.org

IEEE Service Center
445 Hoes Lane
P.O. Box 1331
Piscataway, NJ 08855-1331
Tel: + 1-732-981-0060
Fax: + 1-732-981-9667
mis.custserv@computer.org

IEEE Computer Society
Asia/Pacific Office
Watanabe Bldg., 1-4-2
Minami-Aoyama
Minato-ku, Tokyo 107-0062
JAPAN
Tel: + 81-3-3408-3118
Fax: + 81-3-3408-3553
tokyo.ofc@computer.org

Editorial production by Bob Werner

Cover art production by Joe Daigle/Studio Productions

Printed in the United States of America by The Printing House

IEEE COMPUTER SOCIETY

Table of Contents

1999 IEEE Computer Security Foundations Workshop — CSFW12

Interaction and Composition

Logics for Authorization and Access Control

Advances in Automated Security Protocol Analysis

Noninterference Using Process Algebras

Preface

The Computer Security Foundations Workshop, created in 1988 as an initiative of the IEEE Computer Society Technical Committee on Security and Privacy, comes for the first time to continental Europe, after eleven years of increasing popularity among researchers in security all over the world. The workshop aims and scope are described at the web site www.csl.sri.com/csfw.

The present location is Hotel Panazza in Mordano, Italy, a peaceful small town, very close to Imola, where each year the Formula One San Marino Grand Prix is held. The hotel maintains the tradition of a quiet, relaxing place. It is made up of seventeenth century buildings, surrounded by a park, a romantic lake with swans and peacocks, a tennis court and two swimming pools, and a conference hall in a former church.

This year the number of submissions (47) is even higher than in the past, witnessing the vitality of the workshop and the interest in foundational aspects of security. Certainly, the particular nature of the workshop provides two main reasons for its success: attendance is limited to about forty people (by invitation only); and the atmosphere is rather informal, facilitating discussion and the exchange of opinions among the participants. One discontinuity with the past is that in place of the traditional croquet tournament, this year we will have a bocce tournament. I hope the regular attendees will not complain too much!

Many people have been involved in the organization of the workshop. Paul Syverson is responsible for the excellent program this year, assisted by the program committee members; Joshua Guttman is to be thanked for his careful preparation of the proceedings; Jonathan Millen for the many suggestions he gave me about organizational details. Finally, I want to thank the University of Bologna, Department of Computer Science, for local support.

Roberto Gorrieri
General Chair

Workshop Committee

General Chair
Roberto Gorrieri, University of Bologna, Italy

Program Chair
Paul Syverson, Naval Research Laboratory, USA

Publications Chair
Joshua Guttman, The MITRE Corporation, USA

Program Committee

Martin Abadi, Compaq Systems Research Center, USA
Simon Foley, University College Cork, Ireland
Dieter Gollmann, Microsoft Research, UK
Joshua Guttman, The MITRE Corporation, USA
Dahlia Malkhi, AT&T Labs — Research, USA
John McLean, Naval Research Laboratory, USA
John Mitchell, Stanford University, USA
Jonathan Millen, SRI International, USA
George Necula, University of California, Berkeley, USA
Peter Ryan, Defence Evaluation and Research Agency, UK
Pierangela Samarati, University of Milano, Italy
Fred Schneider, Cornell University, USA
Dennis Volpano, Naval Postgraduate School, USA
Aris Zakinthinos, Independent Consultant, Canada

Steering Committee

Simon Foley, University College, Cork, Ireland
Li Gong, JavaSoft, USA
Roberto Gorrieri, University of Bologna, Italy
Joshua Guttman, The MITRE Corporation, USA
John McLean, Naval Research Laboratory, USA
Catherine Meadows, Naval Research Laboratory, USA
Michael Merritt, AT&T Labs — Research, USA
Jonathan Millen, SRI International, USA
Ravi Sandhu, George Mason University, USA
Paul Syverson, Naval Research Laboratory, USA

Welcome

Formal Models

A Formal Framework and Evaluation Method for Network Denial of Service

Catherine Meadows
Code 5543
Naval Research Laboratory
Washington, DC 20375
meadows@itd.nrl.navy.mil

Abstract

Denial of service is becoming a growing concern. As our systems communicate more and more with others that we know less and less, they become increasingly vulnerable to hostile intruders who may take advantage of the very protocols intended for the establishment and authentication of communication to tie up our resources and disable our servers. Since these attacks occur before parties are authenticated to each other, we cannot rely upon enforcement of the appropriate access control policy to protect us (as is recommended in the classic work of Gligor and Millen in [5, 18, 19]). Instead we must build our defenses, as much as possible, into the protocols themselves. This paper shows how some principles that have already been used to make protocols more resistant to denial of service can be formalized, and indicates the ways in which existing cryptographic protocol analysis tools could be modified to operate within this formal framework.

1 Introduction

Denial of service is becoming a growing concern. As our systems communicate more and more with others that we know less and less, they become increasingly vulnerable to hostile intruders who may take advantage of the very protocols intended for the establishment and authentication of communication to tie up our resources and disable our servers. Since these attacks occur before parties are authenticated to each other, we cannot rely upon enforcement of the appropriate access control policy to protect us (as is recommended in the classic work of Gligor and Millen in [5, 18, 19]). Instead we must build our defenses, as much as possible, into the protocols themselves.

The SYN attack on TCP (see [24] for a more complete discussion) is a classic example of this type of attack. In TCP, a source host initiates the protocol by sending a SYN (synchronization/start) message to its destination. The destination host responds with a SYN ACK, and waits for am ACK of the SYN ACK. When it receives it, the connection is established. The destination host keeps track of unacknowledged SYN ACKs in a connection queue. When a SYN ACK is acknowledged, it is removed from the queue.

The SYN attack is simple. The attacker sends SYN messages with fake source addresses to its victim, which then sends back SYN ACK messages which are never acknowledged. As a result, the victim's connection queue fills up, and TCP services are denied to legitimate users.

Although the SYN attack makes use of the features of a particular protocol, it is easy to see how it could be generalized. An attacker initiates an authentication protocol with its intended victim, using a fake identity. At some point in the protocol, the attacker simply stops participating. The victim is left with an unmanageably large number of uncompleted protocols on its hands, and shuts down operations. The victim cannot defend against this attack by refusing connections from the attacker, since the attacker uses a fake identity, and sometimes a number of different fake identities.

Attacks like this can be foiled by the use of good authentication protocols. But two things need to be kept in mind. First of all, such a protocol must provide authentication from the very beginning. It is not enough that the destination host should be able to verify the origin of the SYN ACK ACK message. It must be able to verify the origin of the SYN message as well. This is in contrast to such definitions of protocol security as are found in [3], in which correctness is defined in terms of the guarantees that must hold if the entire protocol completes. Thus the requirements for protection against denial of service appear to be much stronger than usual authentication requirements.

On the other hand, strong authentication itself can be a hook for denial of service attacks, since the mechanisms used to provide it are computationally intense. For example, suppose that the SYN message was protected by a digital signature. An attacker could send a number of bogus SYN messages with incorrect signatures, and the victim would

1063-6900/99 $10.00 © 1999 IEEE

use up its resources in verifying the signatures instead of in storing the SYN messages in the connection queue. The results, however, would be similar.

The approach that has been taken to resolve these conflicting requirements has been to use weak authentication when the protocol is initiated, but stronger authentication as it completes. Thus the protocol provides protection against a weak attacker in its initial stages without leaving itself vulnerable to denial of service attacks that take advantage of strong authentication, while still ultimately protecting the protocol against spoofing by a strong attacker. This does not leave the protocol completely invulnerable against a denial of service attack by a strong opponent, but it means that that opponent will have to work much harder, having first to break the weak authentication mechanisms.

A classic example of this approach is offered by Photuris [10]. A Photuris exchange begins with an interchange of cookies. A cookie is a unique nonce computed from the names of the sending and receiving parties and local secret information available only to the sender. Thus only the sender can origniate a cookie that it will accept, and only the originator of a cookie can verify that is genuine. Also, the cookie generation and verification methods are required to be fast, to make them less vulnerable to denial of service attacks. After initiator and responder exchange cookies, both cookies are included in all further messages. When either party receives a message, it first verifies the cookie. With this it gets the assurance that the message must have been sent after the cookie was generated, and by someone who was able to see the cookie. Thus the receiver knows that, if no intruder with the capability to generate new messages out of recent messages is present, then the message is genuine. Once this level of assurance is attained, the receiver performs the rest of the verification to achieve a higher degree of assurance.

Cookies provide an add-on that can be used to make an existing protocol more resistant to denial of service. But it is also possible to use these same principals as the basis for the design of an entire protocol. This is what is done by Kent et al. in [11], in which a protocol is developed that uses signed Lamport hash chains [13] to play the role of cookies in providing the weak authentication, while digital signatures are used to provide the strong authentication. Since the hash chains are precomputed and pre-authenticated, a member of the chain can be inserted in a signed message without having to include an initial cookie exchange in the protocol. Thus the participants gain the weak assurance without having to include a pair of cookie exchange messages in each instance of the protocol. The strong assurance can then be gained within the same message by verifying the digital signature. A separate protocol is needed to set up the hash chains, but this needs to executed much less often.

As we can see, the assurance offered by these protocols can increase in two ways. First of all, it can increase monotonically as each message is sent. In the cookie exchange, the receiver of a cookie has no way of verifying that the cookie it receives is genuine, so no assurance is offered at this stage. As the remaining messages are received and verified, however, the amount of assurance increases. The other way in which the assurance can increase is as a message is verified, as in [11], in which all messages are both signed and include a chained hash. When a party receives a message, it can verify the chained hash to determine its freshness; then it can verify the digital signature to determine that the message is not only recent but authentic.

The level of difficulty of the protocol execution also increases with the level of assurance. The cookie exchanges in Photuris proceed with a very low degree of assurance; however, cookie generation is intended to be cheap, so the risk to denial of service is lessened. But the protection against denial of service provided by including cookies in the later messages is somewhat higher, and it gives the receivers of the messages the confidence necessary to proceed to the next, more expensive stage of the authentication. Likewise for the protocol in [11], verification of chained hashes is cheap compared to signature verification.

We see that the type of assurance we must attempt to gain here is somewhat different from that the type of results that we attempt to prove to show that a protocol satisfies its authentication goals. For an authentication protocol, we generally only need to prove that its requirements are satisfied when the protocol completes. Moreover, we attempt to prove that the protocol is sound against the attacks of a uniformly strong intruder. But in order to prove that a protocol is secure against denial of service attacks, we must show that it satisfies the necessary properties at each step of the way. Moreover, the assumptions about the intruder's strengths that we consider may vary as the protocol proceeds.

Thus the process of assuring that a protocol is secure against denial of service is potentially much more complex than the problem of assuring that a protocol satisfies its authentication requirements. However, the underlying process, showing that certain authentication goals are achieved in the face of attack by an intruder who possesses certain capabilities, is similar to that used to show that a protocol satisfies its authentication requirements. Thus it should be possible to apply many of the tools and techniques that have been developed for the verification of authentication properties to the analysis of denial of service. In this paper we provide a framework for evaluating a protocol for resistance to denial of service attacks in a way that is intended to allow us to make maximal use of these tools.

The remainder of the paper is organized as follows. In Section 2 we motivate and present the framework. In Section 3 we apply the framework to an example. In Section

4 we discuss the ways in which existing security protocol analysis tools and methods could be modified to verify protocols within this framework.

2 The Framework

Our construction of the framework begins with the observation that any point at which during a protocol execution at which a responder may accept a bogus message as genuine could be used to launch a denial of service attack. If a bogus initial message could be accepted as genuine, an attack such as the SYN attack would be possible, in which the target wastes its resources storing and responding to bogus messages. If a bogus intermediate message is accepted, this could cause the target to waste even more of its resources to get to that point in the protocol. Finally, if a bogus final message is accepted as genuine, this could give rise to a particularly insidious denial of service attack in which a principal believes that it has been provided a service (e.g. a key shared with another party) when in fact this service was not provided. We will refer to these types of attacks as *service spoofing* attacks. Similar concerns exist for the case of the initiator, although these are not as strong here, since a denial of service attack would in most cases require the initiator to initiate a large number of protocols, which the attacker then subverts. This is not impossible, but it is not certainly not as likely as the attacker initiating a large number of protocols.

The fact that a certain degree of guarantee must be achieved at each step of the way naturally leads us to Gong and Syverson's concept of *fail-stop* protocols [7]. Briefly, a protocol is fail-stop if any bogus message (that is, a replay or a message manufactured by the intruder) can be detected, and the protocol halts upon detection.

Fail-stop protocols have some of the desirable features of a denial-of-service-resistant protocol. However, in order to achieve the fail-stop property, they must make use of strong authentication right from the beginning. This makes fail-stop protocols potentially vulnerable to denial of service attacks in which the target is forced to use up resources verifying bogus messages. Thus we need to modify our concept of fail-stop in order to make it applicable to our needs. However, we will do so in the manner we suggested earlier in this paper, by modifying our notion of an intruder's capability.

2.1 Alice-and-Bob Specifications and Causal Sequencing

In this paper we will be making use of the popular "Alice-and-Bob" specification style. This has been criticized as confusing the description of what should happen with what actually does happen [6]. But in this case, a description of what does happen which can be made to correspond to a description of what should happen is exactly what we want, so much so that we are led to a formal definition of what we will call annotated Alice-and-Bob specifications.

Definition 1 *An* Alice-and-Bob *specification is a sequence of statements of the form* $A \rightarrow B : M$ *where* A *and* B *are processes and* M *is a message.*

Since we are interested in how messages are processed, as well as what messages are sent, we need to annotate our Alice-and-Bob specifications to include message processing steps.

Definition 2 *An* annotated *Alice-and-Bob specification is a sequence of statements of the form* $A \rightarrow B : T_1, ..., T_k \mid\mid M \mid\mid O_1, ..., O_n$ *where* A *and* B *are processes,* M *is a message, and* $T_1, ..., T_k$ *and* O_1, ..., O_n *are sequences of operations performed by* A *and* B*, respectively.*

The sequence $T_1, ..., T_k$ preceding the message in an annotated Alice-and-Bob specification represents the sequence of operations performed by A in producing M, while the sequence $O_1, ..., O_n$ represents the sequence of operations performed by B in processing and verifying M. We now look at the make-up of a line in an Alice-and-Bob protocol more closely.

Definition 3 *Let* $\mathbf{L} = A \rightarrow B : T_1, ..., T_k \mid\mid M \mid\mid O_1, ..., O_n$ *be a line in an annotated Alice-and-Bob specification. We say that* X *is an* event occurring in **L** *if*

1. *X is one of the T_i or O_j, or;*
2. *X is 'A sends M to B' or 'B receives M from A'.*

We say that the events $T_1, ..., T_k$ *and 'A sends M to B'* occur at A *and the events 'B receives M from A',* $O_1, ..., O_n$ occur at B. *There are two types of events:* normal events *and* verification events *(also called* verification operations*). Normal events can occur at either sender or receiver, and have only one outcome : success. Verification events occur only at the receiver. A verification operation can have two outcomes, success or failure. If the operation succeeds, then* B *engages in the next event in* **L***; if the operation fails,* B *stops does not engage in the next event, and stops participating in the protocol. We also attach at the end of each line a special event called an* accept event *which describes* B*'s deciding to proceed with the protocol after successfully verifying a message.*

For example, consider the case in which A computes a digital signature over B's name and a nonce, and sends the result to B, together with its own name and B's. The resulting annotated specification would look like this:

$A \rightarrow B$:
$computenonce_1$, $storenonce_1$, $storename_1$, $sign_1$ $||$
$A, B, S_A(B, N_A))$ $||$
$checkname_2$, $storenonce_2$, $storename_2$, $checksig_1$, $accept_1$

where *computenonce* denotes A's computing a nonce, *storenonce* and *storename* denote A (respectively, B)s storing its nonce and B's (respectively, A's), name for future reference, *sign* denotes A's computing a digital signature, *checkname* denotes the checking for the presence of B's name, and *checksig* denotes the checking of A's digital signature.

We now want to use our annotated Alice-and-Bob specifications to help us give our requirements for a cryptographic protocol. For this, as in [7], we use a notion very similar to Lamport's notion of causally-precedes [12]. The only difference between our notion and Lamport's is that Lamport was dealing with a situation in which, although messages could be delayed or lost, they were not spoofed, redirected, or altered by a hostile intruder. Thus, Lamport used the notion of causally-before to describe what actually happened in his environment, while we will merely use it to describe what we would like to happen in our environment.

For motivation, we first give Lamport's definition:

Definition 4 *Let S be a system of distributed processes that communicate by sending messages. Let E be a temporally ordered sequence of events in S, where E consists of internal events, sending of messages, and receiving of messages. If a and b are two events from E, then b is causally-after a if:*

1. *a and b occur at the same process, and a precedes b;*
2. *a is the sending of a message by one process, and b is the receiving of the same message by another process, or;*
3. *there is an event c such that c is causally-after a and b is causally-after c.*

We say that E_1 is *causally-after* E_2 if E_2 causally-precedes E_1.

We note that notions very similar to Lamport's have found fruitful application in the analysis of cryptographic protocols, most notably in the definition of strand spaces [4]. However, for our purposes, we will need something a little different. An Alice-and-Bob specification of a cryptographic protocol can be thought of as giving of a requirements specification in terms of what events *should* causally-precede others. We thus define *desirably-precedes* (or *desirably-after*), as follows:

Definition 5
1. *If $A \rightarrow B : R_1, ..., R_m \; || \; M \; || \; O_1, ..., O_n$ appears then the event in which B receives M desirably-precedes any of the O_i, and O_i desirably-precedes any of the O_j for which $i < j$;*
2. *If $A \rightarrow B : R_1, ..., R_m \; || \; M \; || \; O_1, ..., O_n$ appears then any R_i desirably-precedes the event in which A sends M and R_i desirably-precedes any of the R_j whenever $i < j$;*
3. *If $A \rightarrow B : R_1, ..., R_m \; || \; M \; || \; O_1, ..., O_n$ precedes $B \rightarrow Y : S_1, ..., S_p \; || \; N \; || \; T_1, ..., T_k$ then O_n desirably-precedes S_1;*
4. *If $A \rightarrow B : R_1, ..., R_m \; || \; M \; || \; O_1, ..., O_n$ appears then the event in which A sends M to B desirably-precedes the event in which B receives M from A, and;*
5. *If $\mathbf{E_1}$ desirably-precedes $\mathbf{E_2}$ and $\mathbf{E_2}$ desirably-precedes $\mathbf{E_3}$ then $\mathbf{E_1}$ desirably-precedes $\mathbf{E_3}$.*

Note that our definition of desirably-precedes assumes that a principal will not start creating a message it wants to send until it has finished processing all relevant messages it has received. This assumption is reasonable when we are attempting to avoid denial of service attacks : a principal should not risk wasting resources on creating a message until it has verified that the messages it has received are genuine.

2.2 Fail-Stop Protocols

A fail-stop protocol is one that provides a certain degree of security against attack. Thus, in order to define a fail-stop protocol, we need first to say what an attack is. But an attack describes a behavior of the implemented protocol that deviates from its requirements. An Alice-and-Bob specification describes the desired behavior very well; what we need to supply as well the derivation of an implementation of a protocol from an Alice-and-Bob specification as follows. This will allow us to make clear the difference between actual and required behavior.

Definition 6 *An implementation of an Alice-and-Bob specification is a set of programs, one for each participant in the protocol. We say that the program corresponding to* A *implements* A *and refer to it at* Pr(A). *Multiple copies of this program can exist and can be running on behalf of different principals.* **Pr**(A) *has the following properties:*

1. *For each instance of $A \rightarrow B : R_1, ..., R_m \; || \; M \; || \; O_1, ..., O_n$ in the protocol there are corresponding portion of* **Pr**(A) *describing A performing the operations $R_1, ..., R_m$ and sending the resulting message to B. When we can avoid confusion, we will refer to these as* **Pr**(A)*$[A \rightarrow B : M]$ and* **Pr**(A)*$[R_i]$.*

2. *For each instance of* $C \rightarrow A : R_1, ..., R_m \parallel M \parallel O_1, ..., O_n$*, there are corresponding portions of* **Pr**(A) *describing* A *receiving a message. performing the operations* $O_1, ..., O_n$ *on a received message, and halting if any of the verification operations fail. When we can avoid confusion, we will refer to these as* **Pr**(A)*[*$B \rightarrow A : M$*] and* **Pr**(A)*[*O_i*].*

3. *If both* E_1 *and* E_2 *occur at* A*, and* E_1 *desirably-precedes* E_2*, then* **Pr**(A)*[*E_1*] always executes before* **Pr**(A)*[*E_2*].*

We do not go any further into describing a procedure for deriving implementations from annotated Alice-and-Bob specifications, but we note that a number of tools, such as Casper [16] and the CAPSL-to-NRL translator [1] already exist that provide such a functionality by translating high-level Alice-and-Bob-style specifications into process algebra and state machine specifications.

Definition 7 *We say that the* event B receives M from A *in a cryptographic protocol has occurred if the program fragment* **Pr**(B)*[*$A \rightarrow B : M$*] has executed successfully. We say that* M *has been* interfered with *if the event* B *receives* M *from* A *occurs but some event desirably-preceding it did not.*

Note that the fact that B receives M from A occurs does not mean the B actually received M from A or anyone else. It simply means that B received a message at the point at which it was expecting the message M, and it is ready to perform a set of tests to determine whether the message was genuinely M. Thus although we use the term "interfered with" to be consistent with the language in [7], we note that it covers not only messages that were tampered with, but fake messages generated by an intruder.

We are now ready for the definition of fail-stop from [7], modified slightly to take into account our slightly different definition of an event.

Definition 8 *An Alice-and-Bob specification of a cryptographic protocol is* fail-stop *if, whenever a message is interfered with, then no accept event desirably-after the receiving of that message will occur.*

We have as yet said nothing yet about our assumptions about an intruder's capabilities. In most of the literature on cryptographic protocol analysis, the assumptions that are made about what an intruder can do are the same. An intruder is assumed to be able to read all traffic, delete and modify traffic, have access to system operations such as the encryption functions used, to be in collusion with some legitimate users of the system, and possibly have access to compromised session keys and other secrets from previous executions of the protocol. In our case, of course, we are interested in intruders with different capabilities:

Definition 9 *We define an* intruder action *to be an event engaged in by an intruder that affects messages received by legitimate participants in a protocol. We define an* intruder capability *to be a set of actions available to an intruder, partially ordered by set inclusion.*

We do not list the types of capabilities available to the intruder, since at this point we do not want to limit ourselves. However, examples would include such cases as an intruder who could send messages but not read messages that were not addressed to it, an intruder who could send and read messages but not block messages, an intruder who could send, read, and block messages, but could not replace the blocked messages with other messages in real time, and so forth. We might also want to include actions outside the usual intruder model, such as the ability to break certain classes of cryptosystems.

Definition 10 *Let* Γ *be a function from the set of events defined by an annotated Alice-and-Bob specification* P *to a set of intruder capabilities. We refer to* Γ *as an* intruder capability function. *We say that* P *is* fail-stop with respect to Γ *if, for each event* E *in the system, if an intruder of capability* $\Gamma(E)$ *interferes with any message desirably-causally-preceding* E*, then neither* E *nor any events desirably-after* E *will occur.*

The idea behind an intruder capability function is that, for each accept event E, an intruder of capability $\Gamma(E)$ should not be able to cause E to occur by using its capabilities to manipulate the system.

If we set $\Gamma(E)$ to be the usual intruder capability whenever E is an accept event, and the null capability for all other events, then the reader can verify that our definition of fail-stop is equivalent to Gong and Syverson's. In the case of denial of service, though, we may want Γ to be gradually increasing with respect to final verification events. For example, in the Photuris protocol, the intruder capability associated with the first accept events, which only concern the cookie exchange, would be the ability to read and block messages, but nothing else, while the intruder capability associated with the later events is greater. We would also want Γ to be gradually increasing with respect to any sequence of verification events on a single line of an annotated Alice-and-Bob specification, since the amount of assurance gained after each check done on a single message should increase the confidence in that message.

Intruder capability functions tell us only half the story, however. We also need a way of calculating the expense of executing each protocol step. In order to do this, we need to define a cost function.

Definition 11 *A* cost set $\mathbf{C}$ *is a partially ordered set with partial order* $<$ *together with a function* $+$ *from* $\mathbf{C} \times \mathbf{C}$ *to*

C *such that + is associative and commutative, and x + y ≥ max(x,y), along with an zero element 0 such that x = 0 + x = x + 0, for all x in* **C**.

Examples of cost could be things like time or money, in which case + is simple addition. Or it could be a rough estimate such as a division into "easy" or "hard," in which case $x + y$ is simply the maximum of x and y. In general, we would expect the cost of a verification event to express the expense of performing the verification, the cost of sending a message to express the expense involved in preparing that message, and the cost of accepting a message (that is, the cost of a final accept event) to be the cost of performing all the verification steps on that message, as well as the cost of sending the next message, if any.

Definition 12 *A function δ from the set of events defined by an annotated Alice-and-Bob specification P to a cost set C which is 0 on the accept events is called an* event cost function.

We now define two functions based on cost functions. One describes the cost of processing a single message in a protocol. The other describes the cost of a principal's reaching a given point in the protocol.

Definition 13 *Let P be an annotated Alice-and-Bob protocol, let C be a cost set, and let δ be an event cost function defined on P and C. We define the* message acceptance cost function associated with δ *to be the function δ' on events following the receipt of a message as follows:*

If the line $A \rightarrow B : O_1, ...O_k \parallel M \parallel V_1, ..., V_n$ appears in P, then for each event V_j:

$\delta'(V_j) = \delta(V_1) + ... + \delta(V_j)$.

We define the protocol engagement cost function associated with δ *to be the function Δ defined on accept events as follows:*

If the line $A \rightarrow B : O_1, ...O_k \parallel M \parallel V_1, ..., V_n$ appears in the protocol, where V_n is the accept event, then:

1. *If there are no lines $B \rightarrow X : O'_1, ...O'_k \parallel M' \parallel V'_1, ..., V'_n$ such that V_n immediately desirably-precedes O'_1, then $\Delta(V_n)$ is the sum of all the costs of all operations occurring at B desirably-preceding V_n;*

2. *If there is a line $B \rightarrow X : O'_1, ...O'_k \parallel M' \parallel V'_1, ..., V'_n$ such that V_n immediately desirably-precedes O'_1, then $\Delta(V_n)$ is the sum of the costs of all operations occurring at B desirably-preceding V_n, plus the sum of the costs of the O'_i,.*

Thus the message acceptance cost represents the cost of reaching a certain point in accepting a message, while the protocol engagement cost represents the total cost of accepting a message in terms of both the cost of processing it and the costs of any events that are necessarily engaged in as a result of accepting the message.

Our construction of message acceptance and protocol engagement costs reflects two ways in which denial of service attacks can proceed. One is by sending a principal a bogus message at any point in the protocol, and having the victim waste resources processing it. This is protected against by performing the relatively cheap verification events first upon receiving a message, and should be reflected in the message acceptance costs. In particular, we would like the costs to start out cheap, and only become more expensive towards the end of the message. The other is to persuade a principal to waste resources participating in a bogus instance of the protocol; this can be defended against by performing cheap verification and computation events early in the protocol, and should be reflected in the protocol engagement costs.

We are now ready to relate cost and intruder capability functions.

Definition 14 *Let C be a cost set and G an intruder capability set. We define a* tolerance relation defined by a protocol designer *to be the subset of $C \times G$ consisting of all pairs (c,g) such that the protocol designer is willing to tolerate a situation in which an effort of cost c that provides security against an intruder of capability g but no greater. We say that (c', g'), is* within the tolerance relation *if there is a (c,g) in the relation such that $c' \leq c$ and $g' \geq g$.*

We do not put any constraints on the tolerance relation, since we believe it may vary from situation to situation.

We can now describe the procedure for evaluating whether or not a protocol is secure against denial of service using the following steps:

1. Decide what your cost function is, and what you assume the various capabilities of the intruder can be.

2. Decide what your tolerance relation is: how much are you willing to spend to provide a certain level of security, and how much insecurity are you willing to put up with given a certain amount of cost?

3. Calculate an intruder capability function Γ such that:

   a) If E_1 is an event immediately preceding a verification event E_2, in a line of a protocol, then $(\delta'(E_2),\Gamma(E_1))$ is in the tolerance relation. This means, that, if M is the message received in the line in which E_1 and E_2 appear, the cost of getting to the point where E_2 succeeds or fails is $\delta'(E_2)$, and no intruder of capability $\Gamma(E_1)$ will have been able to successfully interfere with M after E_1 has finished executing.

   b) If E is an accept event, then $(\Delta(E),\Gamma(E))$ is in the tolerance relation.

4. Verify that the protocol is fail-stop with respect to Γ.

Note that Step 3a) allows us to reason about the ability of a protocol to prevent an intruder from mounting a denial-of-service attack by causing a legitimate principal to waste resources processing a message before it has been able to verify that it could not have been spoofed by an intruder of a certain capability. Step 3b) allows us to reason about the ability of a protocol to prevent an intruder from mounting a denial-of-service attack by causing a legitimate principal to waste resources participating in a protocol up to receiving a particular message and responding to it, before it has been able to verify that that message could not have been spoofed by an intruder of a certain capability.

3 Example: The Station-to-Station Protocol

In this section we show how we can apply our framework to the Station to Station protocol of Diffie, van Oorschot, and Wiener. This protocol was designed with message economy rather than denial of service in mind, so, not surprisingly, it turns out not to meet the demands of our framework. However, the framework can help us identify areas of weakness and suggest possible improvements from the denial of service perspective.

The protocol uses Diffie-Hellman for key generation and digital signatures for authentication. It involves a number of different operations, to which we assign costs as follows: exponentiation over a finite field during the protocol execution (expensive), represented by exp, exponentiation over a finite field which can be precomputed (medium), represented by $preexp$, computation and verification of digital signatures (expensive), represented by $sign$ and $checksig$, single key encryption and decryption (medium), represented by $encrypt$ and $decrypt$, checking for the presence of names and retrieving nonces (cheap), represented by $checkname$ and $retrievenonce$, and storing of names and nonces (medium), represented by $storename$ and $storenonce$. We define a + operation on costs by $X+Y$ = max(X, Y), where expensive > medium > cheap > 0.

Next, let $\mathbf{Z_P}$ be the integers modulo P for some P, let α be a generator of the multiplicative group of $\mathbf{Z_P}$, let α^x denote α raised to the x'th power mod P, let $K = \alpha^{X_B \cdot X_A} = \alpha^{X_A \cdot X_B}$, let E_K represent single key encryption with key K, and S_B denote a digital signature obtained using B's private key. We can now use our notation to describe the protocol as follows:

1. $A \to B$: $preexp_1$ ||
   α^{X_A} ||
   $storenonce_1, storename_1, accept_1$.

2. $B \to A$:
   $preexp_1, sign_1, exp_1, encrypt_1$ ||
   $\alpha^{X_B},\ E_K(S_B(\alpha^{X_B}, \alpha^{X_A}))$ ||
   $checkname_1,\ retrievenonce_1,\ exp_2,\ decrypt_1,\ checksig_1,\ accept_2$.

3. $A \to B$:
   $retrievenonce_2, sign_2,\ encrypt_2$ ||
   $E_K(S_A(\alpha^{X_A}, \alpha^{X_B}))$ ||
   $checkname_2,\ retrievenonce_2,\ decrypt_2,\ checksig_2,\ accept_4$.

Since we are dealing with a protocol that has already been developed, rather than designing one from scratch, we will proceed in an order somewhat different than that recommended in the last section. First, we will determine the values of the cost functions. Secondly, we determine the intruder capability function with respect to which the protocol is fail-stop. We will use this to determine a likely set of tolerance relations, and discuss their significance to the protocol.

We first note that protocol engagement cost function is $expensive$ for all accept events. For the first, the responder B must compute the Diffie-Hellman key and sign a message. For the second, the initiator A must check a signature, compute a Diffie-Hellman key and sign a message. For the third, B must check a signature. For the message acceptance cost functions, none is defined for the first message, since it contains no verification events. For the second the cost of B's checking the name is cheap, while the cost of B's performing the signature is expensive. Likewise for the third message: the cost of A's checking a name is cheap, while the cost of its checking a signature is expensive.

How does the intruder capability function fare for the accept events? Clearly, since the first message is not authenticated at all, it protects only against a very weak intruder, so best we can take $\Gamma(accept_1)$ to be is the intruder with the powers of a non-malicious network, or an intruder with the capability of sending a message. Any intruder who could create an acceptable-looking return address should be able to defeat the protocol at this point. We can take $\Gamma(accept_3)$ to the intruder with full powers (we have verified this using the NRL Protocol Analyzer). What is surprising, however, is $\Gamma(accept_2)$. We would expect this to also be an intruder with full powers, but as a matter of fact it is somewhat weaker. As was shown by Lowe in [15], the event $accept_2$ is vulnerable against the following attack, where I is the intruder, and I_Z is the intruder impersonating Z:

1. $A \to I_B\ :\ \alpha^{X_A}$
2. $I_C \to B\ :\ \alpha^{X_A}$
3. $B \to I_C\ : \alpha^{X_B},\ E_K(S_B(\alpha^{X_B}, \alpha^{X_A}))$
4. $I_B \to A : \alpha^{X_B},\ E_K(S_B(\alpha^{X_B}, \alpha^{X_A}))$

5. $A \rightarrow I_B\ : K(S_A(\alpha^{X_A}, \alpha^{X_B}))$

At this point A is convinced that it is sharing a key with B, although B knows nothing about this; if B received A's final message it would reject it, since it is expecting a response from C. Note that all this attack requires is an intruder with the ability to intercept messages intended for B, and to forward them to B as messages from C. It does not need to be capable of performing any cryptographic operations such as exponentiation or the checking of a digital signature.

Since this is an attack against the initiator, not the responder, it is potentially less useful for tying up resources; the victim must decide to initiate an instance of the protocol before the attack can be mounted. (Note that a successful denial-of-service attack using this vulnerability would require the initiator to start the protocol not once, but many times.) On the other hand, it can be thought of as a service spoofing attack, since A thinks it shares a key with B, when in fact it does not.

We now discuss what the values of Γ for the verification events. The first verification event is $checkname_1$. Since no verification is done before the name is checked, the associated Γ is the intruder with the powers of a non-malicious network. However, since no event except the reception of the message precedes $checkname_1$ at that line, and the cost of $checkname_1$ itself is quite low, the pair (c,g) computed should be well within any tolerance relation. The next verification event is $checksig_1$. The message acceptance cost of $checksig_1$ is expensive; however $\Gamma(decrypt_1)$, the immediately preceding event, is an intruder who is not able to forge B's return address and prevent messages from reaching their destinations, in other words a relatively weak intruder. This pair would probably not be within most tolerance relations. The next verification event is $checkname_2$. Again, the message acceptance cost of $checkname_2$ is cheap, while the assurance provided before $checkname_2$ is executed is against an intruder with the powers of a non-malicious network. Again, the associated pair (c,g) should be well within any tolerance relation. Finally, the last verification event is $checksig_2$. Again, the message acceptance cost of $checksig_2$ is expensive, but the assurance provided until $checksig_2$ has been executed successfully is relatively weak: it is only strong against an intruder who cannot forge A's address and prevent messages from reaching their destinations.

Thus the Station-to-Station protocol, as it stands, is vulnerable to denial of service attacks in several places. In the first message, an intruder who is capable of doing nothing more than sending messages could send a bogus message and cause the responder to waste resources responding to it. Likewise, since the only cheap interim checks on the last two messages are weak, an intruder who is capable of faking return addresses could cause either initiator or responder to waste resources in processing a bogus message. Finally, though less seriously, a somewhat more capable intruder could mount Lowe's attack and convince an initiator that it is sharing a key with a responder when it does not, and when the responder is not even expecting a message from the initiator.

There are a number of ways in which this protocol could be strengthened against denial of service attacks. First, a cookie exchange could be done initially, to introduce some weak authentication before the major message exchange starts, as is done in the IKE protocol [8], which uses a protocol based on the station-to-station protocol. Secondly, if cookies are included in second and third messages, checking them could provide weak authentication for these as well (as is also done by IKE). Weak authentication could also be provided by including both α^{X_A} and α^{X_B} in the second and third messages, so that either party Y could check for the presence of α^{X_Y} before proceeding with the more expensive verification steps. Finally, Lowe's attack could be prevented by including the identity of the intended receiver in the signed part of the message, as is recommended in [15].

4 Applicability of Existing Tools and Models

In this section, we consider how some of the existing tools and methods could be applied within our framework.

We begin with belief logics. To look at them, we would not expect belief logics such as BAN [2] to be very useful within our framework. They use an implicit model of the intruder, and guarantee properties such as freshness and authentication, not immunity against intruders of various strengths. However, like our framework, BAN and similar logics are used to analyze protocols incrementally; one sees what degree of security is provided by each message as it is processed. And, although the properties guaranteed by these logics are currently cast in terms of beliefs in the properties of keys and messages, not properties of the intruder, there does not seem to be any inherent reason why they could not be recast as statements about what capabilities the intruder is supposed to have. For example, consider a message that contains a fresh sub-element, such as a cookie. That message is authentic if we assume the the intruder is not able to read and modify messages in real time. On the other hand, a signed message containing a fresh sub-element is authenticated in the face of a stronger intruder.

We next consider tools that make use of state exploration techniques in some form or the other. These include model checkers such as FDR/Casper [16] or Murϕ [22], specialized tools such as the Interrogator [20] that provide much of the same capability but are fine-tuned for cryptographic protocol analysis, and tools such as the NRL Protocol Analyzer [17] that combine state exploration with a limited theorem-proving capability. What all of these tools have in common is that at some point their designers implemented the standard intruder model as part of the tool. Thus, in order to make use of our framework, it would be necessary to have the option to replace the standard intruder with intruders of different strengths. This should not be too difficult, since all these tools model the intruder as an independent state machine; all that is needed is to replace this state machine with another. Similarly, most uses of theorem provers to analyze cryptographic protocols (e.g. Paulson [23]), include an independent specification of an intruder; thus it should be straightforward to deal with intruders of various strengths for theorem provers as well as state exploration tools.

Another issue remains to be considered, however. Usually, when we attempt to prove security of cryptographic protocols, we examine only a handful or properties, e.g., that two parties always agree on a key, that the key is not a replay, that the key remains secret, and so forth. In the case of denial of service, we are attempting to prove at least one goal for each accept event (and thus for each message sent), as well as one goal for each verification event. Thus the work involved could be multiplied several times. The model checkers have an advantage here; since model checkers verify whether or not a program satisfies its specification, all the user has to do is write a specification in terms of all the security goals that are relevant to a particular intruder strength, and run the protocol together with that intruder. Thus it may be possible to proceed so that the amount of work really only increases by a factor equal to the number of intruder strengths involved.

In the case of tools such as theorem provers and the NRL Protocol Analyzer, in which goals are verified separately, the problem is a little more difficult. In this case it would probably be necessary to develop some standard lemmas involving different goals and intruders of different strengths to allow us to use the weaker results that we find to aid us in proving the stronger ones. This is an open area of research.

Finally, we consider the applicability of high-level protocol description languages, such as CAPSL [21] and Casper [16]. These languages are based on the popular Alice-and-Bob notation, so the most straightforward thing would appear to be to include the annotations that we have used in building our framework. But, as a matter of fact, this may not be necessary. Translators for these languages commonly infer the necessary operations directly from the specification; there is no reason that they should not also be able to derive a sequence of such operations that is optimal with respect to increasing cost, assuming that they are given the cost of each type of operation. Thus, all that would be needed to be added to the high-level specification would be an estimate of the cost of each type of operation; these could even be built into the translators when they are well understood.

5 Conclusion

We have developed a framework for reasoning about network denial of service, and indicated how existing tools and methods could be modified for reasoning within this framework. But there is still much work that remains to be done. Denial of service, unlike authentication, is a matter of degree. No protocol is completely immune against denial of service attacks. Moreover certain types of mechanisms, such as strong authentication, may make a protocol more resistant to one kind of attack but more vulnerable to other kinds. Things are made even more complicated by the fact that certain types of denial of service attacks may take advantage of other, previous, denial of service attacks. For example, an attack that requires an intruder to impersonate another principal may be easier to implement if that principal was disabled by a denial of service attack. This may include extending our model to cases in which intruder strengths may vary for different executions of a protocol. Thus, we need ways of measuring the degree to which a protocol is vulnerable to denial of service, and ways of using our measurements to reason about the different ways denial of service requirements can interact.

Another issue arises from the possible interaction of our framework with other classes of defenses against denial of service. For example, the SYN attack depends upon the necessary fact that principals must store state information when they participate in a protocol. There is no way to make this requirement go away, but it is possible to mitigate the bad effects by paying careful attention to such matters as how much state information is held, and for how long. We have not addressed this problem here, but others have begun applying formal techniques to its analysis [14]. It may turn out to be useful to pursue this matter further and see if our framework can be adapted and/or expanded to take into account countermeasures such as these. Another possibility for further investigation is the use of cryptographic "puzzles" to increase the difficulty of a clients' making any connection whether genuine or fake, thus making it more difficult for a malicious client to flood a server [9]. Here, the concept of increasing the client's work is still used, but the cryptographic functions are used directly to increase a client's workload instead of to provide authentication. It may be that, with some modification, our framework could be extended to handle this type of defense.

6 Acknowledgments

We would like to thank Stephen Brackin and the anonymous referees for their helpful comments on earlier versions of this paper. This work was supported by ONR.

References

[1] Stephen Brackin, Catherine Meadows, and Jonathan Millen. CAPSL interface for the NRL Protocol Analyze. In *Proceedings of ASSET'99*. IEEE Computer Society Press, March 1999.

[2] Michael Burrows, Martín Abadi, and Roger Needham. A Logic of Authentication. *ACM Transactions in Computer Systems*, 8(1):18–36, Feb. 1990.

[3] W. Diffie, P. C. van Oorschot, and M. J. Wiener. Authentication and authenticated key exchanges. *Designs, Codes, and Cryptography*, 1992.

[4] F. Javier Thayer Fabrega, Jonathan C. Herzog, and Joshua D. Guttman. Strand spaces: Why is a security protocol correct? In *Proceedings of the 1998 IEEE Symposium on Security and Privacy*, pages 160–171. IEEE Computer Society Press, May 1998.

[5] V. Gligor. A note on the denial-of-service problem. In *Proceedings of the 1983 Symposium on Security and Privacy*, pages 139–149. IEEE Computer Society Press, 1983.

[6] Dieter Gollmann. What do we mean by entity authentication? In *Proceedings of the 1996 IEEE Symposium on Research in Security and Privacy*, pages 46–54. IEEE Computer Society Press, 1996.

[7] Li Gong and Paul Syverson. Fail-stop protocols: An approach to designing secure protocols. In R. K. Iyer, M. Morganti, Fuchs W. K, and V. Gligor, editors, *Dependable Computing for Critical Applications 5*, pages 79–100. IEEE Computer Society, 1998.

[8] D. Harkins and D. Carrel. The Internet Key Exchange (IKE), version 8. draft-ietf-ipsec-isakmp-oakley-08.txt, June 1998.

[9] Ari Juels and John Brainard. Client puzzles: A cryptographic countermeasure against connection depeletion attacks. In *Proceedings of the 1999 Network and Distributed System Security Symposium (NDSS'99)*. Internet Society, March 1999. Available at http://-www.isoc.org/ndss99/proceedings/.

[10] P. Karn and W. Simpson. The Photuris session key management protocol. Internet draft: draft-simpson-photuris-17.txt, November 1997.

[11] S. T. Kent, D. Ellis, P. Helinek, K. Sirois, and N. Yuan. Internet routing infrastructure security countermeasures. BBN Report 8173, BBN, January 1996.

[12] L. Lamport. Times, clocks, and the ordering of events in a distributed system. *CACM*, 21(7):558–565, July 1978.

[13] L. Lamport. Password authentication with insecure communication. *Communications of the ACM*, pages 770–772, November 1981.

[14] Patrick Lincoln. personal communication, Sept. 1998.

[15] Gavin Lowe. Some new attacks upon security protocols. In *Proceedings of the 9th IEEE Computer Security Foundations Workshop*, pages 162–169. IEEE Computer Society, June 1996.

[16] Gavin Lowe. Casper, a compiler for the analysis of security protocols. In *Proceedings of 10th IEEE Computer Security Foundations Workshop*, pages 18–30. IEEE Computer Society Press, Jun 1997.

[17] Catherine Meadows. The NRL Protocol Analyzer: An overview. *Journal of Logic Programming*, 26(2):113–131, 1996.

[18] Jonathan Millen. A resource allocation model for denial of service. In *Proceedings of the 1992 IEEE Symposium on Security and Privacy*, pages 137–147. IEEE Computer Society Press, 1992.

[19] Jonathan Millen. Denial of service : A perspective. In F. Cristian, G. Le Lann, and T. Lunt, editors, *Dependable Computing for Critical Applications 4*, pages 93–108. Springer-Verlag, 1995.

[20] Jonathan Millen. The Interrogator model. In *Proceedings of the 1995 IEEE Symposium on Security and Privacy*, pages 251–260. IEEE Computer Society Press, May 1995.

[21] Jonathan K. Millen. CAPSL: Common Authentication Protocol Specification Language. Technical Report MP 97B48, The MITRE Corporation, 1997. See http://www.csl.sri.com/ millen/capsl.

[22] J. Mitchell, M. Mitchell, and U. Stern. Automated analysis of cryptographic protocols using Murϕ. In *Proceedings of the 1997 IEEE Symposium on Security and Privacy*, pages 141–151. IEEE Computer Society Press, May 1997.

[23] Lawrence C. Paulson. The inductive approach to verifying cryptographic protocols. *Journal of Computer Security*, 6:85–128, 1998.

[24] C. Schuba, I. Krsul, M. Kuhn, G. Spafford, A. Sundaram, and D. Zamboni. Analysis of a denial of service attack on TCP. In *Proceedings of the 1997 IEEE Symposium on Security and Privacy*, pages 208–223. IEEE Computer Society Press, May 1997.

I/O Automaton Models and Proofs for Shared-Key Communication Systems

Nancy Lynch
MIT Laboratory for Computer Science
Cambridge, MA 02139, USA
lynch@lcs.mit.edu

Abstract

The combination of two security protocols, a simple shared-key communication protocol and the Diffie-Hellman key distribution protocol, is modeled formally and proved correct. The modeling is based on the I/O automaton model for distributed algorithms, and the proofs are based on invariant assertions, simulation relations, and compositional reasoning. Arguments about the cryptosystems are handled separately from arguments about the protocols.

1. Introduction

Security protocols must satisfy important correctness requirements, which means that it is important to be able to think about them clearly and precisely. But they can also be large and complicated, which makes such reasoning difficult. One needs ways of decomposing the task into clearly separable pieces. This includes separating different types of concerns, for example, distributed algorithms issues, cryptosystem computability issues, probabilistic issues, and issues of accurate modeling of reality. It also includes decomposing the protocols using the normal techniques for decomposing distributed algorithms, based on levels of abstraction and parallel composition of interacting components.

This paper describes an experiment in modeling and analyzing security protocols, using *I/O automata* [14, 12] and the usual techniques that go along with them—a combination of invariant assertions, simulation relations, and compositional reasoning using traces. The aim of the experiment is to explore how these methods can help in decomposing the task of reasoning about security protocols. This model and these methods have been used successfully for decomposing the reasoning about many standard distributed algorithms (see, e.g., [12, 16, 13]), and about several distributed system designs (see, e.g., [6, 7, 9, 10]), so it is worth discovering what they can do for security protocols.

The experiment involves combining simple shared-key communication and key distribution protocols to implement private communication. In the case we describe in detail here, simple Diffie-Hellman key distribution [4] is used, the protocols tolerate only passive eavesdroppers, and only safety properties are considered. In another case in progress, discussed briefly here, the more complex Diffie-Oorschot-Weiner key distribution protocol [5], which tolerates adversaries that can intrude more actively, is studied. Later work will include liveness guarantees, formulated in terms of timing properties.

Our main guideline in studying these protocols is to try to *decompose the reasoning* as much as possible, identifying sub-problems that can be treated separately. (Although the examples in this paper are simple enough to be understood informally, we believe that understanding how best to decompose them is a good first step toward understanding how to decompose more complex examples.) The handling of each piece should be appropriately abstract. For example, in discussing protocol issues, cryptosystem computability issues should be summarized by assumptions saying that certain values are not "easily computable" from others; number-theoretic arguments about *why* these values are not (likely to be) easily computable should be treated at a lower level, as mechanisms to achieve the more abstract non-computability guarantees. Probabilistic issues should be treated separately, as far as possible. After dividing up the problems in this way, we expect that the main benefit of the I/O automaton-based methods will be in clarifying the distributed algorithm issues. Cryptosystem issues, for example, may be better treated by other means, for example, the inductive techniques of Paulson [15]. However, a general framework should provide a rigorous way of combining the different types of issues.

In treating the distributed algorithms themselves, we similarly try to decompose them as much as possible. The most obvious form of decomposition involves treating the two sub-protocols separately, then trying to paste them together using general theorems about automaton composition. Another form involves giving very high level automaton specifications for services, giving separate descriptions of implementing algorithms, and showing, by means of simula-

1063-6900/99 $10.00 © 1999 IEEE

tion relations, that the algorithms implement the services. Still another form involves first studying a protocol using a natural, simple cryptosystem, and later trying to show that its correctness properties extend to modified versions that use more elaborate cryptosystems. And still another form of decomposition involves combining adversaries that interact with separate protocols into a single "colluding" unit.

Because I/O automata are composed by means of shared actions, and because we are considering only safety properties in this paper, it is natural to describe external behavior of automata in terms of sets of *traces* (i.e., sequences of external actions). The simple trace semantics yields simple and powerful projection and pasting theorems (see, e.g., [12], p. 211), for the behavior of compositions of automata. However, in order to enable compositional reasoning about particular kinds of properties, the traces must contain all the information relevant for those properties. For example, in treating fault-tolerance properties such as *wait-free termination* and *f-failure termination* compositionally, in terms of traces, it is convenient to allow the traces to contain special *fail* input actions that signal the occurrence of failure events (see, e.g., [12, 13]). Sometimes it is convenient to consider different strengths of failure actions (e.g., the *good*, *bad*, and *ugly* failure actions in [7]). Also, in order to treat timing properties compositionally, it is useful to introduce timing information into the traces.

In the case of security protocols, important properties involve *lack of knowledge*. To treat this compositionally, one should include something about knowledge in the traces. Our approach here is to give explicit *learn* input actions and *reveal* output actions by which a component can learn new information and reveal its knowledge, and to constrain the component's behavior in terms of these actions.

Specifically, the paper contains the following. Section 2 contains math preliminaries. Section 3 presents a model for cryptosystems, which describe the data types encountered in the protocols, including (cleartext and ciphertext) messages, keys, and lower-level data from which keys are constructed. This data model also describes the functions that manipulate data, and the reachability (computability) relationships that say which values can be computed easily from which others. This model is similar to others in the literature. Section 7 then describes some "standard" types of automata that model certain components appearing in many systems—service environments, insecure channels, and eavesdroppers.

Section 11 gives I/O automaton specifications for the two main security services considered in this paper—private communication and key distribution. The specification for private communication is abstract: it talks only about communication and revealed information, and not about keys. Section 14 models and analyzes the implementation of private communication using an abstract key distribution service, and Section 19 treats the Diffie-Hellman implementation of key distribution. These protocols use particular cryptosystems, and the protocol proofs assume the limitations on easy computability expressed by those cryptosystems. The proofs are based on invariant assertions and on simulation relations relating the protocols to the specifications for the services they are intended to implement.

Section 24 shows what is involved in moving from a description of each of the two individual protocols in terms of its own natural cryptosystem to a description in terms of a common, richer cryptosystem. For example, the shared key protocol is initially analyzed in terms of abstract, unstructured keys taken from a simple "shared-key cryptosystem". However, when one combines this protocol with Diffie-Hellman, it is necessary to consider a version that uses structured keys, taken from a richer "structured-key cryptosystem".

Section 27 puts the pieces together, to get an implementation of private communication that uses shared-key communication with Diffie-Hellman key distribution. Most of this is accomplished automatically from the general projection and pasting theorems for I/O automata; special arguments must be made for combining the insecure channels used in the two protocols, and for combining the two adversaries into one. Section 30 gives a final discussion. Because of limited space, most of the proofs have been omitted from this version; the rest will appear in a technical report [].

Related work: Of the formal work on modeling and analyzing cryptographic protocols, the efforts that seem closest in spirit to ours are those of Abadi and of Paulson. Abadi has developed a framework for formal study of composable security protocols [2, 1], and Paulson has developed inductive reasoning methods, which appear valuable both for proving assertions and for determining cryptosystem reachability relationships [15]. Others have stated and proved invariant assertions for security protocols, though we do not know of other work on simulation relations for such protocols. We also do not know about other work using traces with explicit *learn* and *reveal* actions as an approach to compositional reasoning about security protocols. Wing and Cheiner are currently modeling security protocols using the approach of this paper, including verifying assertions using the PVS theorem prover.

Acknowledgments: I thank Ron Rivest for getting me started on this project and for some very helpful discussions about this project. Martin Abadi, Oleg Cheiner, Butler Lampson, Victor Luchangco, Anna Lysyanskaya, Dalia Malkhi, Mike Reiter, and Jeannette Wing provided useful comments and encouragement.

2. Mathematical Preliminaries

λ denotes the empty string. We use I/O automata as defined in [12]. Since we do not deal with liveness in this paper, the tasks are irrelevant. If A and B are I/O automata with the same external signature, then we say that A *implements* B provided that every trace of A is also a trace of B. Invariants and simulation relations are defined, for example, in [12].

3. Data Model

This section gives a basic model for the data types used in the protocols.

4. Cryptosystems

A *cryptosystem signature* $\mathcal{S}$ consists of:

- $TN_{\mathcal{S}}$, a set of *type names*.
- $FN_{\mathcal{S}}$, a set of *function names*.
- $domains_{\mathcal{S}}$, a mapping from $FN_{\mathcal{S}}$ to $(TN_{\mathcal{S}})^*$.
- $range_{\mathcal{S}}$, a mapping from $FN_{\mathcal{S}}$ to $TN_{\mathcal{S}}$.
- $EN_{\mathcal{S}} \subseteq FN_{\mathcal{S}}$, a set of *easy* function names.

A *constant name* is a function name f such that $domains_{\mathcal{S}}(f) = \lambda$. Let $CN_{\mathcal{S}} \subseteq FN_{\mathcal{S}}$ denote the set of constant names of $\mathcal{C}$. We omit the subscript $\mathcal{S}$ where no confusion seems likely. A *cryptosystem* $\mathcal{C}$ consists of:

- A cryptosystem signature $sig_{\mathcal{C}}$. We write $TN_{\mathcal{C}}$ as shorthand for $TN_{sig_{\mathcal{C}}}$, etc.
- $set_{\mathcal{C}}$, a mapping from $TN_{\mathcal{C}}$ to disjoint sets.
- $func_{\mathcal{C}}$, a mapping from $FN_{\mathcal{C}}$ to functions; We require that if $domain_{\mathcal{C}}(f) = (t_1, \ldots, t_k)$ and $range_{\mathcal{C}}(f) = t$ then $func_{\mathcal{C}}(f) : set_{\mathcal{C}}(t_1) \times \cdots \times set_{\mathcal{C}}(t_k) \longrightarrow set_{\mathcal{C}}(t)$.

We write $set_{\mathcal{C}}$ for $\bigcup_{t \in TN_{\mathcal{C}}} set_{\mathcal{C}}(t)$. We omit the subscript $\mathcal{C}$ where no confusion seems likely. If $X \cup \{y\} \subseteq set_{\mathcal{C}}$, we say that y is *easily reachable* from X in $\mathcal{C}$ provided that y is obtainable starting from elements of X, by applying only functions denoted by function names in $EN_{\mathcal{C}}$.

5. Term Cryptosystems

If $\mathcal{S}$ is a cryptosystem signature, then the *terms* of $\mathcal{S}$, and their *types*, are defined recursively, as follows:

1. If $c \in CN_{\mathcal{S}}$ and $range_{\mathcal{S}}(c) = t$, then c is a term and $type_{\mathcal{S}}(c) = t$.
2. If $f \in FN_{\mathcal{S}}$, $domains_{\mathcal{S}}(f) = t_1, t_2, \ldots, t_k$, where $k \geq 1$, $range_{\mathcal{S}}(f) = t$, and $e_1, \ldots, e_k$ are terms of types $t_1, \ldots, t_k$, respectively, then the expression $e = f(e_1, \ldots, e_k)$ is a term, and $type_{\mathcal{S}}(e) = t$.

Let $Terms_{\mathcal{S}}(t)$ denote the set of terms of $\mathcal{S}$ of type t. Let $Terms_{\mathcal{S}}$ denote the set of all terms of $\mathcal{S}$.

Some of the cryptosystems we consider are best understood as term algebras derived from cryptosystem signatures. In these cases, the values of the various types are, formally, equivalence classes of terms: An equivalence relation R on $Terms_{\mathcal{S}}$ is said to be a *congruence* provided that the following hold.

1. If eRe' then $type_{\mathcal{S}}(e) = type_{\mathcal{S}}(e')$.
2. Suppose that $f \in FN_{\mathcal{S}}$, $domains_{\mathcal{S}}(f) = t_1, t_2, \ldots, t_k$, where $k \geq 1$, $range_{\mathcal{S}}(f) = t$, $e_1, \ldots, e_k$ are terms of types $t_1, \ldots, t_k$, respectively, $e'_1, \ldots, e'_k$ are terms of types $t_1, \ldots, t_k$, respectively, and for all i, $1 \leq i \leq k$, $e_i R e'_i$. Then $f(e_1, \ldots, e_k) R f(e_1, \ldots, e_k)$.

Let $\mathcal{S}$ be a cryptosystem signature and R a congruence on $Terms_{\mathcal{S}}$. Then the *term cryptosystem* $\mathcal{C}$ for $\mathcal{S}$ and R is the unique cryptosystem satisfying:

- $sig_{\mathcal{C}} = \mathcal{S}$.
- If $t \in TN_{\mathcal{C}}$, then $set_{\mathcal{C}}(t)$ is the set of all R-equivalence classes of terms of type t in $Terms_{\mathcal{C}}$.
- If $f \in FN_{\mathcal{C}}$, $domain_{\mathcal{C}}(f) = (t_1, \ldots, t_k)$ and $range_{\mathcal{C}}(f) = t$ then $func_{\mathcal{C}}(f)$ is the function from $set_{\mathcal{C}}(t_1) \times \cdots \times set_{\mathcal{C}}(t_k)$ to $set_{\mathcal{C}}(t)$ defined as follows. Suppose that $e_i \in set_{\mathcal{C}}(t_i)$ for all i, $1 \leq i \leq k$. Then $func_{\mathcal{C}}(f)([e_1]_R, \ldots, [e_k]_R)$ is defined to be $[f(e_1, \ldots, e_k)]_R$. (Since R is a congruence, this is well-defined.)

We use the notation $R_{\mathcal{C}}$ for the congruence relation R of $\mathcal{C}$. If $e \in Terms_{\mathcal{C}}$, then we write $[e]_{\mathcal{C}}$ for the equivalence class of e with respect to $R_{\mathcal{C}}$. Also, if $E \subseteq Terms_{\mathcal{C}}$ then we write $[E]_{\mathcal{C}}$ for the set of equivalence classes $[e]_{\mathcal{C}}$ for $e \in E$.

6. Cryptosystem Examples

In this subsection we give the cryptosystems used later in the paper. The first kind of cryptosystem, a shared-key cryptosystem, is used in shared key communication. The second kind, a base-exponent cryptosystem, is used in the Diffie-Hellman protocol. The third kind, a structured-key cryptosystem, is essentially a combination of the two others. It is used when the two protocols are combined.

6.0.1 Shared-key cryptosystems

A *shared-key* cryptosystem $\mathcal{C}$ is a term cryptosystem. The signature $\mathcal{S} = sig_\mathcal{C}$ is defined as follows. $TN_\mathcal{S}$ consists of two type names: "M" for messages and "K" for keys. $FN_\mathcal{S}$ consists of:

- enc, with $domain(enc) = ($"M","K"$)$ and $range(enc) =$ "M".
- dec, with $domain(dec) = ($"M","K"$)$ and $range(dec) =$ "M".
- $MConsts_\mathcal{S}$, a set of message constant names, with $range(m) =$ "M" for all $m \in MConsts_\mathcal{S}$.
- $KConsts_\mathcal{S}$, a set of key constant names, with $range(k) =$ "K" for all $k \in KConsts_\mathcal{S}$.

$EN_\mathcal{S} = \{enc, dec\}$. The relation R is defined by means of all equations of the form:

- $dec(enc(m,k),k) = m$, where $m, k \in Terms_\mathcal{S}$, $type(m) =$ "M", $type(k) =$ "K".

Specifically, we want the smallest congruence relation on $Terms_\mathcal{S}$ that equates all terms that are related by the given equations.

6.0.2 Base-exponent cryptosystems

A *base-exponent* cryptosystem $\mathcal{C}$ is a term cryptosystem in which, letting $\mathcal{S} = sig_\mathcal{C}$: $TN_\mathcal{S}$ consists of two type names, "B" for bases and "X" for exponents. $FN_\mathcal{S}$ consists of:

- exp, with $domain(exp) = ($"B","X"$)$ and $range(exp) =$ "B".
- $BConsts_\mathcal{S}$, a set of base constant names, with $range(b) =$ "B" for all $b \in BConsts_\mathcal{S}$.
- $XConst1_\mathcal{S}$ and $XConst2_\mathcal{S}$, two disjoint sets of exponent constant names, with $domain(x) = \lambda$ and $range(x) =$ "X" for all $x \in XConst1_\mathcal{S} \cup XConst2_\mathcal{S}$.

$EN_\mathcal{S} = \{exp\} \cup BConsts_\mathcal{S}$. The relation R is defined by means of all equations of the form:

- $exp(exp(b,x),y) = exp(exp(b,y),x)$, where $b, x, y \in Terms_\mathcal{S}$, $type(b) =$ "B", $type(x) = type(y) =$ "X".

Define $B2_\mathcal{S}$ to be the set of all terms of the form $exp(exp(b,x),y)$, where $b \in BConsts_\mathcal{S}$, $x \in XConst1_\mathcal{S}$ and $y \in XConst2_\mathcal{S}$. An *augmented base-exponent* cryptosystem is a base-exponent cryptosystem together with a distinguished element $b0_\mathcal{S}$ of $BConsts_\mathcal{S}$.

6.0.3 Structured-key cryptosystems

A structured-key cryptosystem is a combination of a shared-key cryptosystem and a base-exponent cryptosystem, where certain terms of the base-exponent cryptosystem are identified with the keys. A *structured-key* cryptosystem $\mathcal{C}$ is a term cryptosystem in which, letting $\mathcal{S} = sig_\mathcal{C}$: $TN_\mathcal{S}$ consists of the type names "M", "B", and "X". $FN_\mathcal{S}$ consists of:

- enc, with $domain(enc) = ($"M","B"$)$ and $range(enc) =$ "M".
- dec, with $domain(dec) = ($"M","B"$)$ and $range(dec) =$ "M".
- exp, with $domain(exp) = ($"B","X"$)$ and $range(exp) =$ "B".
- $MConsts_\mathcal{S}$, a set of message constant names, with $range(m) =$ "M" for all $m \in MConsts_\mathcal{S}$.
- $BConsts_\mathcal{S}$, a set of base constant names, with $range(b) =$ "B" for all $b \in BConst$.
- $XConst1_\mathcal{S}$ and $XConst2_\mathcal{S}$, two disjoint sets of exponent constant names, with $range(x) =$ "X" for all $x \in XConst1_\mathcal{S} \cup XConst2_\mathcal{S}$.

$EN_\mathcal{S} = \{enc, dec, exp\} \cup BConsts_\mathcal{S}$. The relation R is defined by means of all equations of the form:

- $dec(enc(m,b),b) = m$, where $m, b \in Terms_\mathcal{S}$, $type(m) =$ "M", $type(b) =$ "B".
- $exp(exp(b,x),y) = exp(exp(b,y),x)$, where $b, x, y \in Terms_\mathcal{S}$, $type(b) =$ "B", $type(x) = type(y) =$ "X".

Once again, we write $B2_\mathcal{S}$ for the set of terms of the form $exp(exp(b,x),y)$, where $b \in BConsts_\mathcal{S}$, $x \in XConst1_\mathcal{S}$, and $y \in XConst2_\mathcal{S}$. An *augmented structured-key* cryptosystem is a structured-key cryptosystem together with a distinguished element $b0_\mathcal{S}$ of $BConsts_\mathcal{S}$.

7. Some Generally-Useful Automata

In this section, we give automaton models for some system components that will appear in many settings: environments for security services, insecure channels, and eavesdroppers. They are presented in a parameterized fashion so that they can be used in different contexts. We model these components as automata (rather than, e.g., by trace properties) for uniformity with the way we will model algorithms and system specs, and because this makes it possible to reason about them assertionally.

8. Environment Automata

Here we assume that U is a universal set of data values, A is an arbitrary finite set of adversary ports, that is, locations where information can be communicated to the adversary, and $N \subseteq U$. The environment automaton $Env(U, A, N)$ models any entities other than the channels from which an eavesdropper may learn information. It says that the environment is capable of communicating elements of U at any adversary port $a \in A$, but in fact does not communicate any elements of N.

$Env(U, A, N)$:

Signature:

Input:
None

Output:
$learn(u)_a$, $u \in U$, $a \in A$

States:

No variables

Transitions:

$learn(u)_a$
Precondition:
$u \notin N$
Effect:
none

9. Insecure Channel Automata

Here we assume that U is a universal set of data values, P is an arbitrary finite set of client ports, and A is an arbitrary finite set of adversary ports. The insecure channel admits *send* and *receive* actions for all elements of U and also has *eavesdrop* output actions, by which information in transit passes to an outsider. The insecure channel allows any message in transit to be communicated to an outsider.

$IC(U, P, A)$:

Signature:

Input:
$IC\text{-}send(u)_{p,q}$, $u \in U$, $p, q \in P$, $p \neq q$

Output:
$IC\text{-}receive(u)_{p,q}$, $u \in U$, $p, q \in P$, $p \neq q$
$eavesdrop(u)_{p,q,a}$, $u \in U$, $p, q \in P$, $p \neq q$, $a \in A$

States:

for every $p, q \in P$, $p \neq q$:
$buffer(p, q)$, a multiset of U, initially empty

Transitions:

$IC\text{-}send(u)_{p,q}$
Effect:
add u to $buffer(p, q)$

$IC\text{-}receive(u)_{p,q}$
Precondition:
$u \in buffer(p, q)$
Effect:
remove one copy of u from $buffer(p, q)$

$eavesdrop(u)_{p,q,a}$
Precondition:
$u \in buffer(p, q)$
Effect:
none

10. Eavesdropper Automata

Here we assume that $\mathcal{C}$ is a cryptosystem, P is an arbitrary finite set of client ports, and A is an arbitrary finite set of adversary ports. We define a model for an eavesdropper, as a nondeterministic automaton $Eve(\mathcal{C}, P, A)$. Eve simply remembers everything it learns and hears, and can reveal anything it has, at any time. It does this by maintaining a variable has, initially $\emptyset$. The value of has may change only in restricted ways: Namely, when $eavesdrop(u)_{p,q,a}$ or $learn(u)_a$ occurs, u gets added to has. When an internal $compute$ action occurs, the value resulting from applying an easy function (one in $EN_{\mathcal{C}}$) to values in has may be added to has. We restrict the $reveal(u)$ output so that $u \in has$, that is, Eve can only report a value that it has.

$Eve(\mathcal{C}, P, A)$:

Signature:

Input:
$eavesdrop(u)_{p,q,a}$, $u \in set_{\mathcal{C}}$, $p, q \in P$, $p \neq q$, $a \in A$
$learn(u)_a$, $u \in set_{\mathcal{C}}$, $a \in A$

Output:
$reveal(u)_a$, $u \in set_{\mathcal{C}}$, $a \in A$

Internal:
$compute(u, f)_a$, $f \in EN_{\mathcal{C}}$, $a \in A$

States:

$has \subseteq set_{\mathcal{C}}$, initially $\emptyset$

Transitions:

$eavesdrop(u)_{p,q,a}$
Effect:
$has := has \cup \{u\}$

$learn(u)_a$
Effect:
$has := has \cup \{u\}$

$reveal(u)_a$
Precondition:
$u \in has$
Effect:
none

$compute(u, f)_a$
Precondition:
$\{u_1, \ldots, u_k\} \subseteq s.has$
$u = f(u_1, \ldots, u_k)$
Effect:
$has := has \cup \{u\}$

11. The Services

In this section, we describe the two services that are implemented by the protocols in this paper. They are described as automata, which is convenient for assertional reasoning. The use of input and output actions provides convenient ways of composing these automata with others, and of describing what is preserved by implementation relationships. For simplicity, we write these specifications to describe only safety properties, although the same methods can be used to handle liveness properties, formulated as time bounds (see, e.g., [11, 12]).

12. Private Communication

This section contains a specification of the problem of achieving private communication among the members of a finite collection P of clients. The specification expresses three properties: (1) only messages that are sent are delivered, (2) messages are delivered at most once each, and (3) none of the messages is revealed by an "adversary". We describe the problem using a high-level I/O automaton specification $PC(U, P, M, A)$, where U is a universal set of data values, P is an arbitrary finite set of client ports, $M \subseteq U$ is a set of messages, and A is an arbitrary finite set of adversary ports. This specification does not mention distribution or keys; these aspects will appear in implementations of this specification, but not in the specification itself. The specification simply describes the desired properties, as an abstract machine. As usual for automaton specifications, the properties, listed separately above, are intermingled in one description.

$PC(U, P, M, A)$:

Signature:

Input:
  $PC\text{-}send(m)_{p,q}$, $m \in M, p, q \in P, p \neq q$

Output:
  $PC\text{-}receive(u)_{p,q}$, $u \in U, p, q \in P, p \neq q$
  $reveal(u)_a$, $u \in U, a \in A$

States:

for every pair $p, q \in P, p \neq q$:
  $buffer(p, q)$, a multiset of M

Transitions:

$PC\text{-}send(m)_{p,q}$
  Effect:
    add m to $buffer(p, q)$

$PC\text{-}receive(u)_{p,q}$
  Precondition:
    $u \in buffer(p, q)$
  Effect:
    remove one copy of u
      from $buffer(p, q)$

$reveal(u)_a$
  Precondition:
    $u \notin M$
  Effect:
    none

The first two properties listed above, which amount to at-most-once delivery of messages that were actually sent, are expressed by the transition definitions for $PC\text{-}send$ and $PC\text{-}receive$. The third property, privacy, is expressed by the constraint for $reveal$.

13. Key Distribution

This is a drastically simplified key distribution service, which distributes a single key to several participants. We do not model requests for the keys, but assume that the service generates the key spontaneously. The simplified key distribution problem is specified by the automaton $KD(U, P, K, A)$, where U is a universal set of data values, P is an arbitrary finite set of client ports, $K \subseteq U$ is a set of keys, and A is a finite set of adversary ports.

$KD(U, P, K, A)$:

Signature:

Input:
  none
Output:
  $grant(u)_p$, $u \in U, p \in P$
  $reveal(u)_a$, $u \in U, a \in A$

Internal:
  $choose\text{-}key$

States:

$chosen\text{-}key$, an element of $K \cup \{\bot\}$, initially $\bot$
$notified \subseteq P$, initially $\emptyset$

Transitions:

$choose\text{-}key$
  Precondition:
    $chosen\text{-}key = \bot$
  Effect:
    $chosen\text{-}key :=$
      choose $k \in K$

$reveal(u)_a$
  Precondition:
    $u \notin K$
  Effect:
    none

$grant(u)_p$
  Precondition:
    $chosen\text{-}key \neq \bot$
    $u = chosen\text{-}key$
    $p \notin notified$
  Effect:
    $notified :=$
      $notified \cup \{p\}$

14. Implementing Private Communication using Shared Keys

This section describes a straightforward shared-key communication protocol. The protocol simply uses a shared key, obtained from a key distribution service, to encode and decode messages. Throughout the section, we assume that $\mathcal{C}$ is a shared-key cryptosystem, P is a set (of clients) with at least 2 elements, and A is a nonempty finite set (of adversaries).

15. The Encoder and Decoder

We define parameterized encoder and decoder automata, parameterized by the shared-key cryptosystem $\mathcal{C}$, the set P

of clients, and elements $p, q \in P, p \neq q$. Note that, in the code for $IC\text{-}send(u)$, we are using the abbreviation enc for $func_{\mathcal{C}}(enc)$ – that is, we are suppressing mention of the particular cryptosystem $\mathcal{C}$.

$Enc(\mathcal{C}, P)_{p,q}$, **where** $p, q \in P, p \neq q$:

Signature:

Input:
$PC\text{-}send(m)_{p,q}$, $m \in [MConst_{\mathcal{C}}]$
$grant(u)_p$, $u \in set_{\mathcal{C}}$

Output:
$IC\text{-}send(u)_{p,q}$, $u \in set_{\mathcal{C}}$

States:

buffer, a multiset of elements of $[MConst_{\mathcal{C}}]$, initially empty
$shared\text{-}key \in [KConst_{\mathcal{C}}] \cup \{\bot\}$, initially $\bot$

Transitions:

$PC\text{-}send(m)_{p,q}$
Effect:
add m to *buffer*

$grant(u)_p$
Effect:
if $u \in [KConst_{\mathcal{C}}]$ then
$shared\text{-}key := u$

$IC\text{-}send(u)_{p,q}$
Precondition:
m is in *buffer*
$shared\text{-}key \neq \bot$
$u = enc(m, shared\text{-}key)$
Effect:
remove one copy of m
from *buffer*

More-or-less symmetrically, we have:

$Dec(\mathcal{C}, P)_{p,q}$, **where** $p, q \in P, p \neq q$:

Signature:

Input:
$IC\text{-}receive(u)_{p,q}$, $u \in set_{\mathcal{C}}$
$grant(u)_q$, $u \in set_{\mathcal{C}}$

Output:
$PC\text{-}receive(u)_{p,q}$, $u \in set_{\mathcal{C}}$

States:

buffer, a multiset of elements of $set_{\mathcal{C}}$("M"), initially empty
$shared\text{-}key \in [KConst_{\mathcal{C}}] \cup \{\bot\}$, initially $\bot$

Transitions:

$IC\text{-}receive(u)_{p,q}$
Effect:
if $u \in set_{\mathcal{C}}$("M") then
add u to *buffer*

$grant(u)_q$
Effect:
if $u \in [KConst_{\mathcal{C}}]$ then
$shared\text{-}key := u$

$PC\text{-}receive(u)_{p,q}$
Precondition:
m is in *buffer*
$shared\text{-}key \neq \bot$
$u = dec(m, shared\text{-}key)$
Effect:
remove one copy of m
from *buffer*

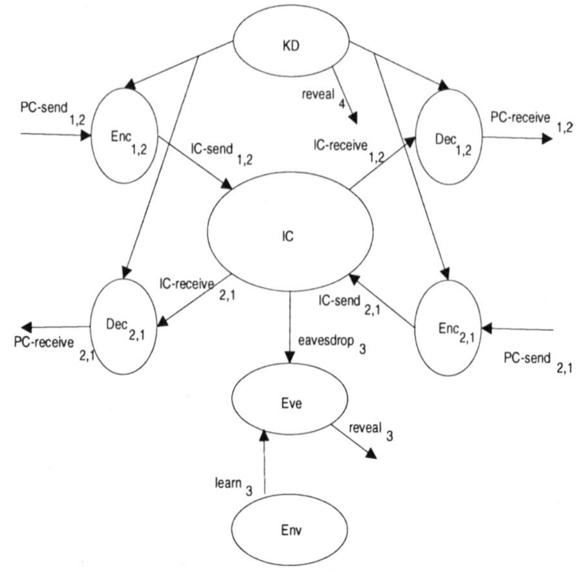

Figure 1. S_1; $P = \{1,2\}$, $A = \{3\}$; $A' = \{4\}$

16. The Complete Implementation

In the rest of this section, we assume: $U = set_{\mathcal{C}}$; $M = [MConst_{\mathcal{C}}]$; $K = [KConst_{\mathcal{C}}]$; $N = M \cup K$; U' is an arbitrary set with $K \subseteq U'$; A' is an arbitrary set, disjoint from A.

The implementation consists of encoder and decoder components, an insecure channel, eavesdropper and environment, plus a key distribution service. More precisely, the implementation, $S_1(\mathcal{C}, P, A, U', A')$, is obtained by composing the following automata and then hiding certain actions.

- $Enc(\mathcal{C}, P)_{p,q}$, $Dec(\mathcal{C}, P)_{p,q}$, $p, q \in P, p \neq q$.
- $IC(U, P, A)$, $Eve(\mathcal{C}, P, A)$, $Env(U, A, N)$.
- $KD(U', P, K, A')$, a key distribution service.

In this system, the eavesdropper Eve does not acquire any information directly from the KD component. Later, in Section 27, we combine this eavesdropper with another that arises in the key distribution service implementation.

To get $S_1(\mathcal{C}, P, A, U', A')$, we hide the following actions in the composition just defined: $eavesdrop_{p,q,a}$, $p, q \in P$, $a \in A$; $IC\text{-}send_{p,q}$, $IC\text{-}receive_{p,q}$, $p, q \in P$; $grant_p$, $p \in P$; $learn_a$, $a \in A$; $reveal_a$, $a \in A'$. We sometimes omit explicit mention of parameters of S_1, or of other systems and components, when we think that confusion is unlikely. Figure 1 contains an interaction diagram for S_1.

Our system model says that the eavesdropper learns no elements of $N = M \cup K$ from outside sources. That choice of N is fine for this protocol, but we do not now have a general prescription for how to choose "good" sets N for all protocols. ("Good" here means that the set should have a simple definition, should be large enough to include all values that the adversary could use to break the protocol, and should be small enough to exclude values produced by other protocols with which the given protocol is to be composed.)

17. Invariants

In system S_1, we use $Enc_{p,q}$, $Dec_{p,q}$, IC, Eve, and KD as "handles" to help in naming state variables in the composed state. This handle naming device for state variables is taken from Vaziri's work [17]. The first invariant says that the keys granted by the key distribution service are consistent.

Lemma 17.1 *In all reachable states of S_1, the following are true:*

1. *If $Enc_{p,q}.shared\text{-}key \neq \bot$ then $Enc_{p,q}.shared\text{-}key = KD.chosen\text{-}key$.*
2. *If $Dec_{p,q}.shared\text{-}key \neq \bot$ then $Dec_{p,q}.shared\text{-}key = KD.chosen\text{-}key$.*

The next invariant says that no N elements appear in $Eve.has$ or in the insecure channel.

Lemma 17.2 *In all reachable states of S_1, the following are true:*

1. *For all $p, q \in P$, $p \neq q$, and all $u \in N$, $u \notin IC.buffer(p, q)$.*
2. *If $u \in N$ then $u \notin Eve.has$.*

Lemma 17.3 *In all reachable states of S_1, the following are true:*

1. *If $u \in N$ then u is not easily reachable from $Eve.has \cup (U - N)$ in $\mathcal{C}$.*

The proofs of the first two of these invariants are straightforward inductive arguments. In some of the steps (e.g., the $IC\text{-}send$ steps in Part 1 of Lemma 17.2), facts about the cryptosystem are used (in this case, some inequivalence facts for terms). The third invariant follows from the second.

18. Implementation Proof

We show that S_1 implements $PC(U, P, M, A)$, using a simulation relation from S_1 to $PC(U, P, M, A)$. The relation F is defined by saying that $(s, t) \in F$ provided that the following condition holds:
For each $p, q \in P, p \neq q$, $t.buffer(p, q)$ is the multiset union of three multisets, A_1, A_2, A_3, of U, where:

1. $A_1 = s.Enc_{p,q}.buffer$.
2. $A_2 = dec(s.IC.buffer(p, q), s.KD.chosen\text{-}key)$ if $s.KD.chosen\text{-}key \neq \bot$ else $\emptyset$.
3. $A_3 = dec(s.Dec_{p,q}.buffer, s.KD.chosen\text{-}key)$ if $s.KD.chosen\text{-}key \neq \bot$ else $\emptyset$.

That is, each high-level multiset of messages in transit is obtained from the messages in the buffers at the encoder and decoder, plus those in transit in the low-level insecure channels. The messages in the insecure channels and in the decoder buffer must be decoded for the correspondence.

Theorem 18.1 *F is a simulation relation.*

Proof: By standard assertional methods for proving simulations, see, e.g., [12], p. 225. The invariants of the preceding section are used here. ∎

Theorem 18.2 *$S_1(\mathcal{C}, P, A, U', A')$ implements $PC(U, P, M, A)$.*

Proof: Follows from Theorem 18.1. ∎

19. Diffie-Hellman Key Distribution Protocol

This section describes the Diffie-Hellman key distribution protocol. Throughout the section, we assume $\mathcal{C}$ is an augmented base-exponent cryptosystem, $P = \{p1, p2\}$, and A is a nonempty set.

20. The Endpoint Automata

We define two symmetric automata, for the two elements of P.

$DH(\mathcal{C}, P)_{p1}$:

Signature:

Input:
$IC\text{-}receive(b)_{p2,p1}$, $b \in set_{\mathcal{C}}(\text{"}B\text{"})$
Output:
$IC\text{-}send(b)_{p1,p2}$, $b \in set_{\mathcal{C}}(\text{"}B\text{"})$
$grant(b)_{p1}$, $b \in set_{\mathcal{C}}(\text{"}B\text{"})$

Internal:
$choose\text{-}exp_{p1}$

States:

$chosen\text{-}exp \in [XConst1_{\mathcal{C}}] \cup \{\bot\}$, initially $\bot$
$base\text{-}sent$, a Boolean, initially $false$
$rcvd\text{-}base \in set_{\mathcal{C}}(\text{"}B\text{"}) \cup \{\bot\}$, initially $\bot$
$granted$, a Boolean, initially $false$

Derived variables:
$chosen\text{-}base \in set_{\mathcal{C}}(\text{"}B\text{"}) \cup \{\bot\}$, given by:
if $chosen\text{-}exp \neq \bot$ then $exp([b0_{\mathcal{C}}], chosen\text{-}exp)$ else $\bot$

Transitions:

$choose\text{-}exp_{p1}$
Precondition:
$chosen\text{-}exp = \perp$
Effect:
$chosen\text{-}exp :=$
choose $x \in [XConst1_C]$

$IC\text{-}send(b)_{p1,p2}$
Precondition:
$chosen\text{-}exp \neq \perp$
$b = chosen\text{-}base$
$base\text{-}sent = false$
Effect:
$base\text{-}sent := true$

$IC\text{-}receive(b)_{p2,p1}$
Effect:
$rcvd\text{-}base := b$

$grant(b)_{p1}$
Precondition:
$chosen\text{-}exp \neq \perp$
$rcvd\text{-}base \neq \perp$
$b = exp(rcvd\text{-}base, chosen\text{-}exp)$
$granted = false$
Effect:
$granted := true$

The automaton for $p2$ is the same, but interchanges uses of $p1$ and $p2$, and likewise of $XConst1$ and $XConst2$.

21. The Complete Implementation

In the rest of this section, we assume: $U = set_C$; $K = [B2_C]$; $X = [XConst1_C] \cup [XConst2_C]$; $N = K \cup X$.

The implementation consists of two endpoint automata, an insecure channel, an eavesdropper and an environment. Specifically, implementation $S_2(\mathcal{C}, P, A)$ is the composition of the following automata, with certain actions hidden:

- $DH(\mathcal{C}, P)_p$, $p \in P$, endpoint automata.
- $IC(U, P, A)$, $Eve(\mathcal{C}, P, A)$, $Env(U, A, N)$.

To get $S_2(\mathcal{C}, P, A)$, we hide: $eavesdrop_{p,q,a}$, $p, q \in P, p \neq q$, $a \in A$; $IC\text{-}send_{p,q}$, $IC\text{-}receive_{p,q}$, $p, q \in P$, $p \neq q$; $learn_a$, $a \in A$. Figure 2 contains an interaction diagram for S_2.

22. Invariants

In system S_2, we use $DH(p)$ for $p \in P$, IC, and Eve as handles to help in naming state variables in the composed state. The first invariant says that messages that have been received or are in transit are correct:

Lemma 22.1 *In all reachable states of S_2, the following are true:*

1. *If $DH(p).rcvd\text{-}base \neq \perp$ and $q \neq p$ then $DH(q).chosen\text{-}exp \neq \perp$, and $DH(q).rcvd\text{-}base = DH(p).chosen\text{-}base$.*
2. *If $u \in IC.buffer(p,q)$, then $DH(p).chosen\text{-}exp \neq \perp$, and $u = DH(p).chosen\text{-}base$.*

Lemma 22.2 *In all reachable states of S_2, the following are true:*

1. *For all $p, q \in P$, $p \neq q$, and all $u \in N$, $u \notin IC.buffer(p,q)$.*

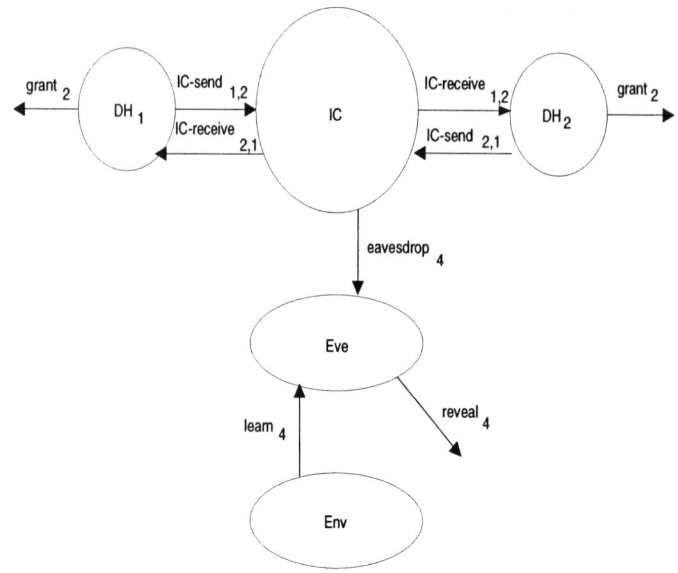

Figure 2. S_2; $P = \{1,2\}$; $A = \{4\}$

2. *If $u \in N$ then $u \notin Eve.has$.*

Lemma 22.3 *In all reachable states of S_2, the following are true:*

1. *If $u \in N$ then u is not easily reachable from $Eve.has \cup (U - N)$ in $\mathcal{C}$.*

23. Implementation Proof

We show that S_2 implements $KD(U, P, K, A)$ using a simulation relation. The relation F is defined by saying that $(s,t) \in F$ provided that:

1. If $s.DH(p).chosen\text{-}exp \neq \perp$ for all $p \in P$, then $t.chosen\text{-}key = exp(s.DH(p1).chosen\text{-}base, s.DH(p2).chosen\text{-}exp)$, and otherwise $t.chosen\text{-}key = \perp$.
2. $t.notified = \{p \in P : s.DH(p).granted\}$.

Theorem 23.1 *F is a simulation relation.*

Proof: By induction.
Base: Easy.
Inductive step: Consider (s, π, s') and t and consider cases. The most interesting cases are:

1. $\pi = choose\text{-}exp_p$.
   If $s.DH(q).chosen\text{-}exp = \perp$, where $q \neq p$ then this maps to the trivial one-state execution fragment t. The correspondence is trivially preserved (part 1 is vacuous). Otherwise, this corresponds to $choose\text{-}key$,

with a chosen value of $exp(s'.DH(p1).chosen\text{-}base, s'.DH(p2).chosen\text{-}exp)$. Enabling is straightforward, as is the preservation of the simulation.

2. $\pi = grant(b)_p$

   This corresponds to $grant(b)_p$ in the specification. The interesting fact to show here is the enabling, specifically, that the value $b = exp(s.DH(p).rcvd\text{-}base, s.DH(p).chosen\text{-}exp)$ is equal to $t.chosen\text{-}key$. But Lemma 22.1 implies that $b = exp(s.DH(q).chosen\text{-}base, s.DH(p).chosen\text{-}exp)$. and equations in the cryptosystem imply that this is equal to $exp(exp([b0], s.DH(p1).chosen\text{-}exp), s.DH(p2).chosen\text{-}exp)$. But the definition of F says that this is equal to $t.chosen\text{-}key$, as needed.

3. $\pi = reveal(u)_a$

   This corresponds to $reveal(u)_a$ in the specification. We must show that $u \notin K$. The precondition for $reveal(u)_a$ (in Eve) implies that $u \in s.Eve.has$. Lemma 22.2 implies that $u \notin N$, which implies that $u \notin K$.

∎

Theorem 23.2 *$S_2(\mathcal{C}, P, A)$ implements $KD(U, P, K, A)$.*

Proof: By Theorem 23.1. ∎

24. Algorithms Using Structured-Key Cryptosystems

In this section, we extend the implementations of private communication and of key distribution so that they use a structured-key cryptosystem, in place of a shared key cryptosystem or base-exponent cryptosystem. For the rest of the paper, fix $\mathcal{C}$ to be any augmented structured-key cryptosystem.

25. Private Communication

25.0.4 Notation and assumptions

We define a shared-key cryptosystem $\mathcal{C}'$ directly from $\mathcal{C}$, by saying that $MConst_{\mathcal{C}'} = MConst_{\mathcal{C}}$ and $KConst_{\mathcal{C}'} = B2_{\mathcal{C}}$. That is, we use the $B2$ terms in $\mathcal{C}$ as "names" for keys in $\mathcal{C}'$. In this subsection, we assume: P is an arbitrary set with at least 2 elements; A is an arbitrary set; $U = set_{\mathcal{C}}$; $M = [MConst_{\mathcal{C}}]$; $K = [B2_{\mathcal{C}}]$; $X = [XConst1_{\mathcal{C}}] \cup [XConst2_{\mathcal{C}}]$.

Also, W is the set of all elements $w \in set_{\mathcal{C}}(\text{“}M\text{”})$ that can be obtained as follows: In cryptosystem $\mathcal{C}$, w is obtained from an element $m \in set_{\mathcal{C}'}(\text{“}M\text{”})$ by applying some number of enc operations with second arguments in $set_{\mathcal{C}}(\text{“}B''\text{”}) - K$. (That is, w is obtained by "wrapping" the element.) Furthermore, $N = W \cup K \cup X$; $U' = U = set_{\mathcal{C}}$; A' is an arbitrary set, disjoint from A.

The most interesting part of this is the definition of W, which is intended to designate the elements of type "M" that are to be avoided. Set W must be sufficiently large to include all elements of type "M" that could help to compute elements that are supposed to remain unknown. But W must be sufficiently small to exclude elements that might be communicated in other protocols with which the present protocol is going to be composed. And, W must be defined reasonably simply. Coming up with a good choice of W seems at this point to be something of an art, similar to coming up with a good invariant.

The choice we have made above is one of several possibilities. We think it looks a little messy, especially because it does not fall into a formalized style that might suggest how similar definitions might be made for more complicated protocols. A simpler choice that would work for this paper would be $W = set_{\mathcal{C}}(\text{“}M\text{”})$, but that seems to be ruling out more than would be ideal. Another choice would be a smaller W, for instance the set of elements of U that are easily reachable from $M \cup (set_{\mathcal{C}}(\text{“}B''\text{”}) - K)$ in $\mathcal{C}$. We leave this for later work.

25.0.5 New encoder and decoder automata

The formal definitions of $Enc3$ and $Dec3$ are nearly identical to those of Enc and Dec. The difference is that the new automata use elements of type "B" in place of $KConst$. Of course, the parameters have new meanings, as defined just above.

25.0.6 New implementation

We define S_3 to be the algorithm from Section 14, but implemented using the structured-key cryptosystem $\mathcal{C}$ rather than a shared key cryptosystem. That is, $S_3(\mathcal{C}, P, A, U', A')$ is the composition of the following automata, with some actions hidden:

- $Enc3(\mathcal{C}, P)_{p,q}$ and $Dec3(\mathcal{C}, P)_{p,q}$, $p, q \in P$, $p \neq q$.
- $IC(U, P, A)$, $Eve(\mathcal{C}, P, A)$, $Env(U, A, N)$.
- $KD(U', P, K, A')$.

To get $S_3(\mathcal{C}, P, A, U', A')$, we hide: $eavesdrop_{p,q,a}$, $p, q \in P$, $a \in A$; $IC\text{-}send_{p,q}$, $IC\text{-}receive_{p,q}$, $p, q \in P$; $grant_p$, $p \in P$; $learn_a$, $a \in A$; $reveal_a$, $a \in A'$. We want to show that this system implements $PC(U, P, M, A)$.

25.0.7 Invariants

Lemma 25.1 *In all reachable states of S_3, the following are true:*

1. *For all p, $Enc3_{p,q}.shared\text{-}key \in K \cup \{\bot\}$.*
2. *For all p, $Dec3_{p,q}.shared\text{-}key \in K \cup \{\bot\}$.*
3. *For all p, q, if $u \in IC.buffer(p,q)$ then $u = enc(m,k)$, where $m \in M$ and $k \in K$.*
4. *For all p, q, all $x \in X$, $x \notin IC.buffer(p,q)$.*

Lemma 25.2 *In all reachable states of S_3, the following are true:*

1. *No element of X is in $Eve.has$.*
2. *Assume that $(M \cup K) \cap Eve.has = \emptyset$. If $w \in W \cap Eve.has$ and $v \in set_{C'}(\text{“}M\text{”})$ is easily reachable from $\{w\} \cup (set_C(\text{“}B''\text{”}) - K)$ in C, then $v \in Eve.has$.*

Part 2 of invariant 25.2 has a somewhat different style from those we have used so far. It basically says that if a “wrapped version” of an element of $set_{C'}(\text{“}M\text{”})$ is in has, then the actual element of $set_{C'}(\text{“}M\text{”})$ must also be there. Note that we did not give any invariants here saying that K elements or M elements do not appear in $Eve.has$, as we did in Section 17. This is because (in the interests of decomposition) we are trying to avoid proving facts that have already been proved for the more abstract version of the algorithm. Instead, we are trying to rely on the simulation relation, described in the next subsection, to give such facts.

25.0.8 Implementation proof

We prove the correctness of S_3 as a consequence of that of the analogous system $S_1(C', P, A, U', A')$. By our previous result about S_1, Theorem 18.2:

Lemma 25.3 *$S_1(C', P, A, U', A')$ implements $PC(set_{C'}, P, M, A)$.*

In order to prove correctness of $S_3(C, P, A, U', A')$, we would like to demonstrate a simulation relationship from $S_3(C, P, A, U', A')$ to $S_1(C', P, A, U', A')$. To do this, we first make the interfaces consistent, by defining $S_3'(C, P, A, U', A')$ from S_3 by hiding the actions $reveal(u)_a$, $u \in U - set_{C'}$.

Lemma 25.4 *If β is a trace of $S_3(C, P, A, U', A')$ then β with all $reveal(u)$ actions removed, $u \in U - set_{C'}$, is a trace of $S_3'(C', P, A, U', A')$.*

Now we define the relation F from $S_3'(C, P, A, U', A')$ to $S_1(C', P, A, U', A')$: $(s,t) \in F$ provided:

1. For all components except Eve, all state components are identical.
2. If $u \in set_{C'}$ and u is easily reachable from $s.Eve.has \cup (set_C - N)$ in C then u is easily reachable from $t.Eve.has \cup (set_{C'} - (M \cup K))$ in C'.

Theorem 25.5 *F is a simulation relation.*

Proof: For the initial condition, let s and t be the unique start states of $S_3'(C, P, A, U', A')$ and $S_1(C', P, A, U', A')$, respectively. We must check that $(s,t) \in F$. The key is to show that if $u \in set_{C'}$ and u is easily reachable from $U - (W \cup K \cup X)$ in C then u is easily reachable from $set_{C'} - (M \cup K)$ in C'. But properties of the cryptosystem imply that there is no such element u, so this is vacuously true. For the step condition, the most interesting cases are:

1. $\pi = reveal(u)_a$, $a \in A$

   We must show that $u \notin M$. So suppose for the sake of contradiction that $u \in M$. By the precondition, we know that $u \in s.Eve.has$. Since $u \in set_{C'}$, the definition of F implies that u is easily reachable from $t.Eve.has \cup (set_{C'} - (M \cup K))$ in C'. But Lemma 17.3 implies that no element of M is easily reachable from $t.Eve.has \cup (set_{C'} - (M \cup K))$ in C'. This yields the needed contradiction.

2. $\pi = compute(u, f)$

   This maps to the trivial fragment. We must argue that $(s', t) \in F$. It suffices to show that any element $u \in set_{C'}$ that is easily reachable from $s'.Eve.has \cup (U - N)$ is also easily reachable from $s.Eve.has \cup (U - N)$. But this follows from general properties of the $compute$ action in Eve.

3. $\pi = learn(u)_a$

   We consider two cases:

   (a) $u \in set_{C'}$

   Then the corresponding fragment consists of a single step, with the same action. To see that this is enabled, note that $u \notin N$, by the precondition in S_3'. In particular, $u \notin M \cup K$. This implies that $learn(u)$ is enabled in S_1.

   To show that $(s', t') \in F$, suppose that $v \in set_{C'}$ and v is easily reachable from $s'.Eve.has \cup (U - N)$ in C. Then since $u \in U - N$, we have also that v is easily reachable from $s.Eve.has \cup (U - N)$ in C. Then since $(s,t) \in F$, we have that v is easily reachable from $t.Eve.has \cup (set_{C'} - (M \cup K))$ in C', which implies that v is easily reachable from $t'.Eve.has \cup (set_{C'} - (M \cup K))$ in C'. This proves that $(s', t') \in F$.

(b) $u \in U - set_{\mathcal{C}'}$

Then the corresponding fragment consists of the single state t. We must show that $(s', t) \in F$. It suffices to show that any element $v \in set_{\mathcal{C}'}$ that is easily reachable from $s'.Eve.has \cup (U - N)$ in $\mathcal{C}$ is also easily reachable from $s.Eve.has \cup (U - N)$ in $\mathcal{C}$. But the precondition implies that $u \in U - N$, so $s'.Eve.has \cup (U - N) = s.Eve.has \cup (U - N)$, so this is obvious.

□

Theorem 25.6 *$S_3'(\mathcal{C}, P, A, U', A')$ implements $S_1(\mathcal{C}', P, A, U', A')$.*

Lemma 25.7 *If β is a trace of $S_3(\mathcal{C}, P, A, U', A')$ then β with all $reveal(u)$ actions removed, for $u \in U - set_{\mathcal{C}'}$, is a trace of $S_1(\mathcal{C}', P, A, U', A')$.*

Proof: By Theorem 25.6 and Lemma 25.4. □

Theorem 25.8 *$S_3(\mathcal{C}, P, A, U', A')$ implements $PC(U, P, M, A)$.*

Proof: By Lemmas 25.7 and 25.3. Let β be a trace of $S_3(\mathcal{C}, P, A, U', A')$. Then Lemma 25.7 implies that β_1 is a trace of $S_1(\mathcal{C}', P, A, U', A')$, where β_1 is equal to β with all $reveal(u)$ actions removed, for $u \in U - set_{\mathcal{C}'}$. Then Lemma 25.3 implies that β_1 is a trace of $PC(set_{\mathcal{C}'}, P, M, A)$. It follows that β_1 is a trace of $PC(set_{\mathcal{C}}, P, M, A)$. Now, since β differs from β_1 only by including some $reveal$ actions for elements in $U - set_{\mathcal{C}'}$, it follows that β is a trace of $PC(set_{\mathcal{C}}, P, M, A)$. □

The proofs of the results in this and the next subsection deal with specific cryptosystems. It would be interesting to extract general theorems that could be applied to get such results. Such theorems would involve some kind of notion of "embedding" of one cryptosystem in another, and statements articulating when a protocol that works with a cryptosystem also works with any cryptosystem in which that cryptosystem is embedded.

26. Key Distribution

26.0.9 Notation and assumptions

We define an augmented base-exponent cryptosystem $\mathcal{C}'$ directly from $\mathcal{C}$, by saying $BConst_{\mathcal{C}'} = BConst_{\mathcal{C}}$, $XConst1_{\mathcal{C}'} = XConst1_{\mathcal{C}}$, $XConst2_{\mathcal{C}'} = XConst2_{\mathcal{C}}$, and $b0_{\mathcal{C}'} = b0_{\mathcal{C}}$. In this subsection, we assume: $P = \{p1, p2\}$; A is an arbitrary set; $U = set_{\mathcal{C}}$; $K = [B2_{\mathcal{C}}]$; $X = [XConst1_{\mathcal{C}}] \cup [XConst2_{\mathcal{C}}]$; $N = K \cup X$.

26.0.10 New implementation

The new endpoint automata are syntactically the same as the old endpoint automata. The only difference is that the subscript $\mathcal{C}$ now refers to a structured-key cryptosystem. We define S_4 to be the algorithm from Section 19, but implemented using the structured-key cryptosystem $\mathcal{C}$ rather than a base-exponent cryptosystem. That is, $S_4(\mathcal{C}, P, A)$ is the composition of the following automata, with some actions hidden:

- $DH(\mathcal{C}, P)_p, p \in P$.
- $IC(U, P, A)$, $Eve(\mathcal{C}, P, A)$, $Env(U, A, N)$.

To get $S_4(\mathcal{C}, P, A)$, we hide: $eavesdrop_{p,q,a}, p, q \in P, a \in A$; $IC\text{-}send_{p,q}, IC\text{-}receive_{p,q}, p, q \in P$; $learn_a, a \in A$. We want to show that this system implements $KD(U, P, K, A)$.

We prove the correctness of S_4 as a consequence of that of the analogous system $S_2(\mathcal{C}', P, A)$. By our previous result about S_2, Theorem 23.2:

Lemma 26.1 *$S_2(\mathcal{C}', P, A)$ implements $KD(set_{\mathcal{C}'}, P, K, A)$.*

Lemma 26.2 *If β is a trace of $S_4(\mathcal{C}, P, A)$ then β with all $reveal(u)$ actions removed, for $u \in U - set_{\mathcal{C}'}$, is a trace of $S_4'(\mathcal{C}', P, A)$.*

Now we define the relation F from $S_4'(\mathcal{C}, P, A)$ to $S_2(\mathcal{C}', P, A)$: $(s, t) \in F$ provided:

1. For all components except Eve, all state components are identical.
2. If $u \in set_{\mathcal{C}'}$ and u is easily reachable from $s.Eve.has \cup (set_{\mathcal{C}} - N)$ in $\mathcal{C}$ then u is easily reachable from $t.Eve.has \cup (set_{\mathcal{C}'} - N)$ in $\mathcal{C}'$.

Theorem 26.3 *F is a simulation relation.*

Proof: Analogous to that of Theorem 25.5. □

Theorem 26.4 *$S_4'(\mathcal{C}, P, A)$ implements $S_2(\mathcal{C}', P, A)$.*

Lemma 26.5 *If β is a trace of $S_4(\mathcal{C}, P, A)$ then β with all $reveal(u)$ actions removed, for $u \in U - set_{\mathcal{C}'}$, is a trace of $S_2(\mathcal{C}', P, A)$.*

Theorem 26.6 *$S_4(\mathcal{C}, P, A)$ implements $KD(U, P, K, A)$.*

27. Putting the Pieces Together

Now we describe how to put the previous results together, to get an implementation of private communication that uses the shared-key communication protocol in combination with the Diffie-Hellman key distribution service. The first step combines the two protocols, but still keeps the insecure channels, eavesdroppers, and environments for the two algorithms separate. The second step combine the two channels into one and likewise for the eavesdroppers and the environments.

28. Composing Diffie-Hellman and Shared-Key Communication to get Private Communication

Recall that we have already fixed $\mathcal{C}$ to be an augmented structured-key cryptosystem. We now fix, for the rest of the paper: $U = set_{\mathcal{C}}$; $P = \{p1, p2\}$; $P' = \{p1', p2'\}$; A is an arbitrary set; $M = [MConst_{\mathcal{C}}]$; $K = [B2_{\mathcal{C}}]$; $X = [XConst1_{\mathcal{C}}] \cup [XConst2_{\mathcal{C}}]$; W is the set of elements of $set_{\mathcal{C}}(\text{"}M\text{"})$ that can be obtained from $set_{\mathcal{C}'}(\text{"}M\text{"}) \cup (set_{\mathcal{C}}(\text{"}B''\text{"}) - K)$ in $\mathcal{C}$ using enc; $N = W \cup K \cup X$; A' is an arbitrary set, disjoint from A. The combined system S_5 consists of the following pieces:

- $Enc3(\mathcal{C}, P)_{p,q}$, $Dec3(\mathcal{C}, P)_{p,q}$, $p, q \in P, p \neq q$.
- $DH5_p$, $p \in P$; each of these is a renamed version of $DH(\mathcal{C}, P)_p$, with the subscripts in $IC\text{-}send_{p,q}$ and $IC\text{-}receive_{q,p}$ actions renamed to their primed versions.
- $IC(U, P, A)$, $Eve(\mathcal{C}, P, A)$, $Env(U, A, N)$.
- $IC(U, P', A')$, $Eve(\mathcal{C}, P', A')$, $Env(U, A', N')$.

S_5 hides all the actions except for the $PC\text{-}send$, $PC\text{-}receive$, and $reveal_a$ actions for $a \in A$.

Figure 3 contains an interaction diagram for S_5.

Theorem 28.1 *S_5 implements $PC(U, P, M, A)$.*

Proof: This follows from Theorems 26.6 and 25.8, using general projection and pasting lemmas for I/O automata. □

29. Merging Channels, Adversaries, and Environments

The final implementation, S_6, is obtained from S_5 by merging the two separate insecure channels into one, and likewise for the two adversaries and the two environments.

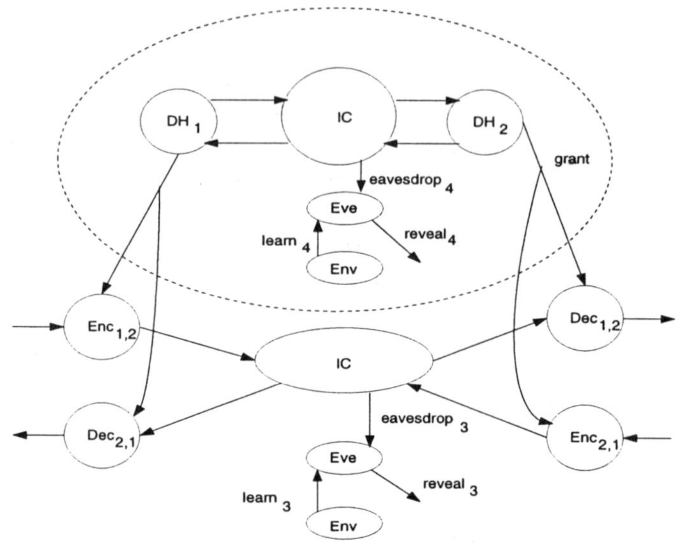

Figure 3. S_5

To do this, and yet keep the same interfaces, we extend the definitions of IC and Eve to allow two types of ports, primed and unprimed. Specifically, S_6 consists of:

- $Enc3(\mathcal{C}, P)_{p,q}$, $Dec3(\mathcal{C}, P)_{p,q}$, $p, q \in P, p \neq q$.
- $DH5_p$, $p \in P$.
- $IC(U, P, A, P', A')$.
- $Eve(\mathcal{C}, P, A, P', A')$.
- $Env(U, A \cup A', N \cup N')$.

Here, the extended IC is the same as $IC(U, P \cup P', A \cup A')$ but only has actions with subscripts p, q, a where either $p, q \in P$, $a \in A$ or $p, q \in P'$, $a \in A'$. Similarly for the extended Eve. Also, S_6 hides all actions except for the $PC\text{-}send$, $PC\text{-}receive$, and $reveal_a$ actions for $a \in A$.

The combined eavesdropper eavesdrops and learns on all adversary ports in $A \cup A'$, and can use all this information in calculating its has information, which resides in a single state component. The combined environment avoids communicating any information in $N \cup N'$. We claim that S_6 implements S_5, which implies that S_6 implements $PC(U, P, M, A)$. To prove this result, we define S_7, which is just like S_5 except that it combines the eavesdroppers, but not the channels or environments.

Lemma 29.1 *S_7 implements S_5.*

The essence of this lemma is that information that an eavesdropper can acquire in either protocol does not upset the requirements of the other protocol. It would be nice to show that $Eve(\mathcal{C}, P, A, P', A')$ implements $Eve(\mathcal{C}, P, A) \times Eve(\mathcal{C}, P', A')$. But this is not quite correct: the implementation relationship requires assumptions about the contexts in which the eavesdroppers run, (and also, the relationship does not preserve the *learn* actions). So we just prove an implementation relationship for the eavesdroppers in their contexts. However, it is clear that the argument uses only minimal information about the particular contexts, namely, what kind of information they can contribute in *eavesdrop* and *learn* actions; it should be possible to extract a general lemma stating these restrictions on contexts explicitly.

Proof: We use a simulation relation F from S_7 to S_5 defined so that $(s, t) \in F$ exactly if:

1. Everything except for *has* components is the same in s and t.
2. If $u \in s.has$ then u is easily reachable from $t.Eve(\mathcal{C}, P, A).has \cup (U - N)$ in $\mathcal{C}$.
3. If $u \in s.has$ then u is easily reachable from $t.Eve(\mathcal{C}, P', A').has \cup (U - N')$ in $\mathcal{C}$.

This mapping says, essentially, that any information that the combined eavesdropper acquires is something that either of the individual eavesdroppers could have acquired anyway. We show that this is a simulation. The initial conditions are immediate, because $s.has$ is empty. We consider steps:

1. $reveal(u)_a$, $a \in A$

   We know that $u \in s.has$. So by definition of F, we have that u is easily reachable from $t.Eve(\mathcal{C}, P, A).has \cup (U - N)$. Let this step correspond to a sequence of $learn_a$ and $compute_a$ actions sufficient to put u into $Eve(\mathcal{C}, P, A).has$, followed by the same $reveal(u)_a$ action. The sequence of learns and computes guarantees that the action is enabled in the spec.

2. $reveal(u)_a$, $a \in A'$

   Analogous to the previous case.

3. $learn(u)_a$, $a \in A \cup A'$

   Map this to the trivial execution fragment. By the precondition, this adds something in $U - (N \cup N')$ to $s.has$. But this is obviously easily reachable from $t.Eve(\mathcal{C}, P, A).has \cup (U - N)$ and from $t.Eve(\mathcal{C}, P', A').has \cup (U - N')$. So the correspondence is preserved.

4. $compute(u, f)_a$, $a \in A \cup A'$

   Map to the trivial fragment. The precondition implies that u is easily reachable from $s.has$. By the inductive step, all the elements of $s.has$ that are needed for this computation are easily reachable from $t.Eve(\mathcal{C}, P, A).has \cup (U - N)$ and from $t.Eve(\mathcal{C}, P', A').has \cup (U - N')$. So u is also easily reachable from $t.Eve(\mathcal{C}, P, A).has \cup (U - N)$ and from $t.Eve(\mathcal{C}, P', A').has \cup (U - N')$ (using one more step).

5. $eavesdrop(u)_a$, $a \in A$

   Then Lemma 25.1 implies that u is of the form $enc(m, k)$, $m \in M$, $k \in K$. Therefore, $u \in U - N'$. Let this correspond to the same action in the spec. We must show that $(s', t') \in F$. This means we must show that u is easily reachable from $t'.Eve(\mathcal{C}, P, A).has \cup (U - N)$ in $\mathcal{C}$ and u is easily reachable from $t'.Eve(\mathcal{C}, P', A').has \cup (U - N')$ in $\mathcal{C}$.

   By the effect of the action in the spec, $u \in t'.Eve(\mathcal{C}, P, A).has$, so u is obviously easily reachable from $t'.Eve(\mathcal{C}, P, A).has \cup (U - N)$ in $\mathcal{C}$. Also, since $u \in U - N'$, u is obviously easily reachable from $t'.Eve(\mathcal{C}, P', A').has \cup (U - N')$ in $\mathcal{C}$.

6. $eavesdrop(u)_a$, $a \in A'$

   Then u is of the form $exp(b0, x) \in U - N$ Let this correspond to the same action in the spec. We must show that $(s', t') \in F$. This means we must show that u is easily reachable from $t'.Eve(\mathcal{C}, P, A).has \cup (U - N)$ in $\mathcal{C}$ and u is easily reachable from $t'.Eve(\mathcal{C}, P', A').has \cup (U - N')$ in $\mathcal{C}$.

   By the effect of the action in the spec, $u \in t'.Eve(\mathcal{C}, P', A').has$, so u is obviously easily reachable from $t'.Eve(\mathcal{C}, P', A').has \cup (U - N')$ in $\mathcal{C}$. Since $u \in U - N$, u is obviously easily reachable from $t'.Eve(\mathcal{C}, P, A).has \cup (U - N)$ in $\mathcal{C}$.

□

Lemma 29.2 *S_6 implements S_7.*

The proof of Lemma 29.2 is easy, based on the following two lemmas:

Lemma 29.3 *$Env(U, A \cup A', N \cup N')$ implements $Env(U, A, N) \times Env(U, A', N')$.*

Lemma 29.4 *$IC(U, P, A, P', A')$ implements $IC(U, P, A) \times IC(U, P', A')$.*

This all yields:

Lemma 29.5 *S_6 implements S_5.*

Proof: By Lemmas 29.2 and 29.1. □

Theorem 29.6 *S_6 implements $PC(U, P, M, A)$.*

Proof: By Lemmas 29.5 and Theorem 28.1. □

30. Discussion

In this paper, we have modeled and analyzed the combination of simple shared key communication with Diffie-Hellman key distribution, in the presence of an eavesdropper adversary. Although this example is very simple, many kinds of decomposition are evident in its presentation. Understanding these in a simple context is a prerequisite for extending them to more complicated protocols.

We believe that this type of presentation is useful in clarifying protocol issues. It also helps in separating the protocol issues from other issues, such as cryptosystem reachability issues, which can be treated separately. It appears possible to decompose the presentation in this paper even more, for example, by defining a notion of embeddings of cryptosystems and obtaining the results of Section 24 as consequences of such theorems.

In work in progress, we are extending these ideas to more complex protocols like that of Diffie, Oorschot, and Weiner [5], which tolerate more active adversaries. So far, it appears that the modeling/analysis ideas of this paper scale well to the more complicated examples. Some issues that arise in modeling the protocol of [5] are: The cryptosystems are more complicated, so more complicated arguments need to be made about reachability; for example, the analogues of the set W defined in Section 25.0.4 become more complicated. Also, because the adversary has more active control of the communication system, it is convenient to combine them into a single automaton model. (The *has* component of that automaton is now used to decide what may be delivered to the client, as well as what may be revealed.) Also, the correctness guarantees are weaker—for instance, repeated deliveries of the same message, and deliveries to the wrong recipient, are possible. A more complicated key distribution service specification will also be needed, including key requests and granting of multiple keys.

The work of this paper has not mentioned liveness properties. For the simple case of this paper, with a passive eavesdropper, liveness claims are certainly possible. They can be incorporated easily into the model in the form of time bounds, and proved using the usual assertional methods for timing analysis, such as those appearing in [3, 11]. For more active adversaries, more sophisticated algorithms can also guarantee liveness properties, which could also be formulated as time bounds and proved similarly.

Another interesting research direction is the modular introduction of probabilistic considerations. We expect that it is possible to accomplish a great deal at a high level of abstraction, by simply assuming that certain low probability "bad" events do not occur. The low probability bad events could then be introduced separately, with general theorems used to limit their impact on system behavior. But such general theorems remain to be developed.

References

[1] M. Abadi. Protection in programming-language translations. In *Automata, Languages and Programming: 25th International Colloquium (ICALP'98)*, pages 868–883, July 1998. Also, Digital SRC Research Report 154 (April 1998), Palo Alto, CA.

[2] M. Abadi, C. Fournet, and G. Gonthier. Secure implementation of channel abstractions. In *Proceedings of the Thirteenth Annual IEEE Symposium on Logic in Computer Science*, pages 105–116, June 1998.

[3] H. Attiya and N. A. Lynch. Time bounds for real-time process control in the presence of timing uncertainty. *Information and Computation*, 110(1):183–232, April 1994.

[4] W. Diffie and M. Hellman. New directions in cryptography. *IEEE Transactions on Information Theory*, IT-22(6):644–656, November 1976.

[5] W. Diffie, P. C. van Oorschot, and M. J. Wiener. Authentification and authenticated key exchanges. *Designs, Codes and Cryptography*, 2:107–125, 1992.

[6] A. Fekete, M. F. Kaashoek, and N. Lynch. Implementing sequentially consistent shared objects using broadcast and point-to-point communication. *Journal of the ACM*, 45(1):35–69, January 1998.

[7] A. Fekete, N. Lynch, and A. Shvartsman. Specifying and using a partitionable group communication service. In *Proceedings of the Sixteenth Annual ACM Symposium on Principles of Distributed Computing*, pages 53–62, Santa Barbara, CA, August 1997. Expanded version in [8].

[8] A. Fekete, N. Lynch, and A. Shvartsman. Specifying and using a partitionable group communication service. Technical Memo MIT-LCS-TM-570, Laboratory for Computer Science, Massachusetts Institute of Technology, Cambridge, MA, 02139, 1997.

[9] J. Hickey, N. Lynch, and R. van Renesse. Specifications and proofs for ensemble layers. In *Fifth International Conference on Tools and Algorithms for the Construction and Analysis of Systems,(TACAS '99, Amsterdam, the Netherlands, March 1999)*, Lecture Notes in Computer Science. Springer-Verlag. To appear.

[10] B. Lampson and A. Shvartsman. POCS Course Notes (Principles of Computer Systems), 1997. Available online at ftp://theory.lcs.mit.edu/pub/classes/6.826/www/6.826-top.html.

[11] V. Luchangco. Using simulation techniques to prove timing properties. Master's thesis, Department of Electrical Engineering and Computer Science, Massachusetts Institute of Technology, Cambridge, MA 02139, June 1995.

[12] N. Lynch. *Distributed Algorithms*. Morgan Kaufmann Publishers, Inc., San Mateo, CA, March 1996.

[13] N. Lynch and S. Rajsbaum. On the Borowsky-Gafni simulation algorithm. In *Proceedings of the Fourth ISTCS: Israel Symposium on Theory of Computing and Systems*, pages 4–15, Jerusalem, Israel, June 1996. IEEE Computer Society. Also, short version appears in *Proceedings of the Fifteenth Annual ACM Symposium on Principles of Distributed Computing*, Philadelphia, PA, page 57, May 1996.

[14] N. A. Lynch and M. R. Tuttle. An introduction to input/output automata. *CWI-Quarterly*, 2(3):219–246, September 1989. Centrum voor Wiskunde en Informatica, Amsterdam, The Netherlands. Technical Memo MIT/LCS/TM-373, Laboratory for Computer Science, Massachusetts Institute of Technology, Cambridge, MA 02139, November 1988.

[15] L. C. Paulson. Inductive approach to verifying cryptographic protocols. *J. Comp. Security*, 1998.

[16] T. P. Petrov, A. Pogosyants, S. J. Garland, V. Luchangco, and N. A. Lynch. Computer-assisted verification of an algorithm for concurrent timestamps. In R. Gotzhein and J. Bredereke, editors, *Formal Description Techniques IX: Theory, Applications, and Tools* (FORTE/PSTV'96: Joint International Conference on Formal Description Techniques for Distributed Systems and Communication Protocols, and Protocol Specification, Testing, and Verification, Kaiserslautern, Germany, October 1996), pages 29–44. Chapman & Hall, 1996.

[17] M. Vaziri. Naming state variables of composite automata in IOA. Manuscript, Nov. 9, 1998.

Security Protocol Analysis: Notation, Transformation, and Simplification

Safe Simplifying Transformations for Security Protocols
or
Not Just the Needham Schroeder Public Key Protocol

Mei Lin Hui Gavin Lowe

Department of Mathematics and Computer Science, University of Leicester,
University Road, Leicester, LE1 7RH, UK
E-mail: {m.hui, gavin.lowe}@mcs.le.ac.uk

Abstract

Recent techniques for analyzing security protocols have tended to concentrate upon the small protocols that are typically found in the academic literature. However, there is a huge gulf between these and most large commercial protocols: the latter typically have many more fields, and much higher levels of nested encryption. As a result, existing techniques are difficult to apply directly to these large protocols.

In this paper we develop the notion of safe simplifying transformations*: transformations that have the property of preserving insecurities; the effect of such transformations is that if we can verify the transformed protocol, then we will have verified the original protocol. We identify a number of such safe simplifying transformations, and use them in the analysis of a commercial protocol.*

1. Introduction

Many security protocols have been suggested, with various goals, such as establishing a cryptographic key, or achieving authentication (where an agent becomes sure of the identity of the other agent taking part in the protocol). These protocols are supposed to succeed even in the presence of a malicious agent, called an *intruder*; this intruder is assumed to have complete control over the communications network, and so can intercept messages, and introduce new messages into the system using information from messages that have previously been seen. Unfortunately, a large proportion of the protocols that have been suggested do not succeed in their stated goals!

In recent years, a number of techniques have been developed for analysing protocols; the two main categories of such techniques are model checking techniques, where a model checker is used to search the state space of a small system running the protocol looking for attacks, and direct proofs, where the protocol is proved correct directly (possibly with the help of machine assistance), typically using some form of induction.

These techniques have proved successful at analysing the protocols that have appeared in the academic literature. Such protocols are normally small, typically having between two and seven messages, each message having between two and ten fields. However, most commercial protocols are considerably more complicated, typically containing several layers of nested encryptions, and significant amounts of redundancy. For example, the CyberCash Main Sequence Protocol—a protocol for carrying out commercial transactions over the Internet—is given in Appendix A.

This extra complexity of such protocols makes analysis much more difficult: for the model checkers, it leads to an explosion in the state space and the message space; for those doing direct proofs, the complexity just makes the protocol harder to understand, let alone verify it.

However, we will often have a strong feeling that much of the complexity of such a protocol could be removed without altering its security: for example, some of the fields and some of the nested encryption might appear to be irrelevant to security. If we could prove that this complexity is indeed not needed for the security of the protocol, then it would be enough to analyse the protocol with this complexity removed. This is the question we address in this paper. We identify a number of *simplifying transformations* on protocols that have the property that if there is an attack upon the original protocol (i.e. it is insecure), then there is also an attack upon the simplified protocol; we call transformations with this property "*safe*". This means that if we can verify the simplified protocol, we will have verified the original protocol.

The idea will be, starting from the original protocol, to apply as many safe simplifying transformations as possible, trying to avoid introducing new attacks, and then to analyse the simplified protocol. If the simplified protocol is secure, then so is the original; if, however, our analysis discloses

1063-6900/99 $10.00 © 1999 IEEE

an attack upon the simplified protocol, we have to consider whether there is a corresponding attack on the original protocol; if there *is* such an attack, then clearly the original protocol is flawed; otherwise, we have oversimplified, so we have to try again, learning from our mistakes.

Our approach is to identify a function f from the messages of the original protocol P_1 to the messages of the simplified protocol P_2, describing how messages are simplified. We then lift this function to traces (i.e. finite sequences of messages), by pointwise application. In order for the transformation to satisfy the condition outlined above, we require that if tr is a trace representing an attack upon P_1, then $f(tr)$ is an attack upon P_2. Proving this for a particular f will consist of two things: proving that for every trace tr of P_1, $f(tr)$ is a trace of P_2; and that if a trace tr constitutes an attack upon P_1, then $f(tr)$ constitutes an attack upon P_2.

In the next section, we give a model of a system running a protocol, along with an intruder who can interact with that system; we also formalize some security properties. In Section 3 we formalize the class of simplifying transformations that we are interested in, and show that if such a transformation satisfies two properties, then it is safe. In Section 4 we show that a number of useful transformations satisfy these properties, and in Section 5 we illustrate our techniques by applying them to the CyberCash Protocol, simplifying the protocol to a stage where we can applying standard analysis techniques. We sum up in Section 6.

2. The model

We will use the process algebra CSP [2, 9], to reason about security protocols, to formalize the simplifying transformations, and to verify that they satisfy the desired condition that if there is an attack on the original protocol, then there is an attack on the simplified protocol.

We use CSP because it is well suited for reasoning about systems of communicating agents. Further, it has been much used for security protocol analysis, and the translation from descriptions of protocols in "standard form" into CSP is well understood. Also, CSP has a well developed theory, which we may exploit. Finally, the transformations themselves are easy to formalize—they are simply CSP renamings! We should stress, though, that our results may be used to support *any* protocol analysis technique, not just those based around CSP.

In Section 2.1 we define the underlying space of messages; in Section 2.2 we describe how the honest agents are modelled in CSP, and in Section 2.3 we do the same for the intruder; then in Section 2.4 we formalize what we mean by an attack upon the protocol, thus formalizing the security properties that we are interested in.

2.1. Messages

Our model of a system running a protocol is based around a datatype $Message$, representing the messages that are sent or received by agents. We define the message space to be built up from some set $Atom$ of atomic values, by pairing, encryption and hashing. We define $Key \subseteq Atom$ to be those atoms used for encrypting and decrypting messages; we write K^{-1} for the inverse key of K. We let $HashFn$ be the set of cryptographic hash functions. The set $Message$ is defined by:

$$\begin{aligned} Message ::= \; & \textsc{Atom}\, Atom \mid \\ & \textsc{Pair}\, Message\; Message \mid \\ & \textsc{Encrypt}\, Message\; Key \mid \\ & \textsc{Hash}\, HashFn\; Message. \end{aligned}$$

We will use the syntactic sugar (M, M') for $\textsc{Pair}\, M\, M'$, $\{M\}_K$ for $\textsc{Encrypt}\, M\, K$, and $g(\!| M |\!)$ for $\textsc{Hash}\, g\, M$.

This datatype definition means that some messages are distinguished that we would like to identify, for example $((\textsc{Atom}\, A, \textsc{Atom}\, B), \textsc{Atom}\, C)$ and $(\textsc{Atom}\, A, (\textsc{Atom}\, B, \textsc{Atom}\, C))$: the definition does not capture the associativity of pairing. We therefore identify a *normal form* for messages, and will ensure that only messages in normal form are passed in the system[1]. The normal form will have all pairing associating to the right, for example $(\textsc{Atom}\, A, (\textsc{Atom}\, B, \textsc{Atom}\, C))$. This means that for any pair in normal form, the first element will not itself be a pair. We write $pair(M)$ if M is a pair (easily defined over the structure of the message space), and define a function to convert a message into normal form as follows:

$$\begin{aligned} NF &: Message \to Message, \\ NF(\textsc{Atom}\, A) &\mathrel{\hat{=}} \textsc{Atom}\, A, \\ NF((M_1, M_2), M_3) &\mathrel{\hat{=}} \text{let } (M_1', M_2') = NF(M_1, M_2) \\ &\qquad \text{in } (M_1', NF(M_2', M_3)), \\ NF(M_1, M_2) &= (NF(M_1), NF(M_2)), \\ &\qquad \text{if } \neg pair(M_1), \\ NF(\{M\}_K) &\mathrel{\hat{=}} \{NF(M)\}_K, \\ NF(g(\!| M |\!)) &= g(\!| NF(M) |\!). \end{aligned}$$

We define $NFMessage$ to be the set of all messages in normal form.

2.2. Honest agents

We will model each agent taking part in the protocol by a CSP process, using the following events:

[1] Having to define a normal form in this way is very much orthogonal to the main thrust of the paper, but is unfortunately necessary; the reader is advised not to be distracted too much by the details.

- events of the form $send.A.B.M$, representing agent A sending (normal form) message M, with intended recipient B;
- events of the form $receive.A.B.M$, representing agent B receiving message M, apparently from A;
- events of the form $claimSecret.A.B.M$, representing that A thinks that M is a secret shared only with B; if B is not the intruder, then the intruder should not learn M;
- events of the form $running.A.B.Ms$, representing that A thinks he is running the protocol with B; Ms is a sequence of messages, recording some details about the run in question;
- events of the form $finished.A.B.Ms$, representing that A thinks he has finished a run of the protocol with B; Ms is a sequence of messages, recording some details about the run in question.

Events of the first two forms are used for modelling the main communications of the protocol. The latter three forms will be used for writing specifications for the protocol; we discuss this further in Section 2.4.

Each honest agent can be represented by a CSP process, describing the way the agent sends and receives messages. The precise details will depend upon the protocol in question; a number of previous papers (e.g. [4, 6, 8, 11]) have described the translation from a protocol description in "standard form" to a CSP representation. However, it turns out that we don't need to assume anything else about the CSP representation of the honest agents (apart from the fact that such a representation exists)—our results apply to arbitrary CSP processes.

We write P_A for the CSP process representing the honest agent with identity A; this process will have the following alphabet:

$$\begin{array}{l} \{send.A.B.M \mid B \in Agent, M \in NFMessage\} \\ \cup \{receive.B.A.M \mid B \in Agent, M \in NFMessage\} \\ \cup \{claimSecret.A.M \mid M \in NFMessage\} \\ \cup \{running.A.B.Ms \mid \\ \qquad B \in Agent, Ms \in NFMessage^*\} \\ \cup \{finished.A.B.Ms \mid \\ \qquad B \in Agent, Ms \in NFMessage^*\}. \end{array}$$

2.3. The intruder

We now define the most general intruder who can interact with a system running the protocol. Following [11], the definition is based around a relation $\vdash$, which defines the ways in which the intruder can deduce new messages; we write $B \vdash M$ if message M can be deduced from the set of messages B; the relation is defined by the following six rules:

member $M \in B \Rightarrow B \vdash M$;

pairing $B \vdash M \wedge B \vdash M' \wedge \neg pair(M) \Rightarrow B \vdash (M, M')$;

splitting $B \vdash (M, M') \Rightarrow B \vdash M \wedge B \vdash M'$;

encryption $B \vdash M \wedge B \vdash \mathrm{ATOM}\,K \wedge K \in Key \Rightarrow B \vdash \{M\}_K$;

decryption $B \vdash \{M\}_K \wedge B \vdash \mathrm{ATOM}\,K^{-1} \Rightarrow B \vdash M$;

hashing $B \vdash M \wedge g \in HashFn \Rightarrow B \vdash g(\!|M|\!)$.

The intruder can create new messages by creating or splitting pairs, by encrypting or decrypting with keys he can produce, and by hashing.

Our model of the system will ensure that the intruder receives every message sent by an honest agent, and can then choose what messages are received by honest agents. A system with two honest agents, A and B, can therefore be pictured as below:

In effect, the intruder process also models the effect of the communication medium.

The intruder can be represented by a CSP process parameterized by the set S of messages that he either initially knew, or has subsequently seen (recall that the $send$ channel represents messages that are sent by honest agents and so are received by the intruder, and that the $receive$ channel represents messages that are received by honest agents and are sent by the intruder):

$$\begin{array}{l} INTRUDER(S) \mathrel{\hat{=}} \\ \quad \Box_{M \in Message}\ send?A?B!M \rightarrow \\ \qquad\qquad INTRUDER(S \cup \{M\}) \\ \quad \Box \\ \quad \Box_{M \in Message, S \vdash M}\ receive?A?B!M \rightarrow \\ \qquad\qquad INTRUDER(S) \\ \quad \Box \\ \quad \Box_{M \in Message, S \vdash M}\ leak.M \rightarrow INTRUDER(S). \end{array}$$

The intruder may:

- see messages sent by honest agents, and so learn the contents;
- send messages with contents that can be derived from his current knowledge, such messages being received by an honest agent;

- signal that he knows any message that can be derived from his current knowledge.

We assume that the intruder initially knows some set IK_0 of messages. The complete system is then represented by the CSP process:

$$SYSTEM \mathrel{\widehat{=}} \left(|||_{A \in Honest} P_A \right) \parallel INTRUDER(IK_0),$$

(where $Honest$ is the set of honest agents' identities) that is, the parallel composition of the honest agents and the intruder, synchronizing on their common events, i.e. the $send$ and $receive$ events.

2.4. Attacks

In this subsection we consider possible requirements of a protocol. We will produce various *trace specifications* representing different security properties that we would like systems running the protocol to satisfy. A trace specification is a predicate $SPEC(tr)$ whose free variable tr represents a trace. A process satisfies such a specification if $SPEC(tr)$ is true for all its traces:

$$P \textbf{ sat } SPEC \Leftrightarrow \forall tr \in traces(P) \bullet SPEC(tr).$$

Thus, we will be interested in whether $SYSTEM$ **sat** $SPEC$, for various specifications representing security properties.

First of all, we define a breach of secrecy to occur when an honest agent thinks a certain message (typically an atomic message) is secret, but the intruder learns it. We formalize secrecy by specifying that if an agent A performs a $claimSecret.A.B.M$ event (representing that A believes M to be a secret shared only with B), where B is not the intruder, then the intruder should never perform $leak.M$ (i.e. should never learn M):

$$\begin{array}{l} Secrecy(tr) \mathrel{\widehat{=}} \\ \quad \forall A \in Agent\,;\, B \in Honest \bullet \\ \qquad claimSecret.A.B.M \text{ in } tr \Rightarrow \neg leak.M \text{ in } tr. \end{array}$$

We now define some entity authentication specifications. As explained in [5], we believe that the term "authentication" refers to a collection of related requirements, rather than there being a single generic authentication specification. The following is one of the more common forms of authentication:

> Whenever A completes a run of the protocol, apparently with B, then B has previously been running the protocol, apparently with A, and the two agents agreed on some collection Ms of messages, and each such run of A corresponds to a *unique* run of B.

To formalize this requirement, we specify that the number of $finished$ events performed by A concerning B with some sequence of messages Ms must be no more than the number of corresponding $running$ events performed by B. We write this requirement as a trace specification, parameterized by the set $AgreementSet$ of sequences of messages upon which the agents should agree (for example, if it is required that the agents agree upon a key and a nonce, then the agreement set will be all sequences of the form $\langle K, N \rangle$ for keys K and nonces N):

$$\begin{array}{l} Agreement_{AgreementSet}(tr) \mathrel{\widehat{=}} \\ \quad \forall A \in Agent\,;\, B \in Honest\,;\, Ms \in AgreementSet \bullet \\ \qquad tr \downarrow finished.A.B.Ms \leq tr \downarrow running.B.A.Ms. \end{array}$$

If tr is a trace, and e is an event, then $tr \downarrow e$ represents the number of occurrences of e in tr. Of course, in order to ensure that this specification captures the requirements outlined above, we need to ensure that the $finished$ and $running$ events correctly capture the informally descriptions given to them above: the $finished$ events should be performed by honest agents when they complete a protocol run, and the $running$ event should be performed just before the last $send$ event; see [5] for more details.

We believe it would be completely straightforward to extend the results of this paper to other authentication specifications, such as the aliveness and non-injective agreement specifications of [5]. It might also be possible to deal with completely different specifications such as non-repudiation or anonymity.

3. Transformations on protocols

In this section we formalize how we represent transformations upon protocols; we then state a result, giving sufficient conditions for a transformation to be safe. Proofs are omitted due to lack of space; the interested reader is referred to [3].

3.1. Formalizing transformations

A transformation will be defined via a function

$$f : Message \to Message,$$

which defines how messages in the original protocol are replaced by messages in the simplified protocol. In the following, we will overload f to apply to several different types of arguments.

We lift the function f to events as follows:

$$\begin{array}{rcl} f(send.A.B.M) & \mathrel{\widehat{=}} & send.A.B.f(M), \\ f(receive.A.B.M) & \mathrel{\widehat{=}} & receive.A.B.f(M), \\ f(claimSecret.A.B.M) & \mathrel{\widehat{=}} & claimSecret.A.B.f(M), \end{array}$$

$$f(running.A.B.Ms) \mathrel{\hat=} running.A.B.f(Ms),$$
$$f(finished.A.B.Ms) \mathrel{\hat=} finished.A.B.f(Ms),$$

and lift it to traces by:

$$f(tr) \mathrel{\hat=} \langle f(e) \mid e \leftarrow tr \rangle.$$

We now define the CSP representation of an honest agent A in the transformed system, corresponding to the process P_A in the original system. We need a process that sends or receives the message $f(M)$ whenever the process P_A sends or receives M. We therefore define the new representation to be the process $f(P_A)$ (recall that the CSP process $f(P)$ is the process that acts like P, except where every event e is renamed to $f(e)$). This is certainly the right model for the honest agents when one considers only the sending and receiving of messages. Some protocols, however, involve more than just a straightforward sending and receiving of messages; for example, in many cases agents perform tests upon the messages they receive; in these cases, it's not immediately obvious how the simplifying transformations affect the protocol. This definition gives the answer: the behaviour of the agent in the transformed protocol is described by the process $f(P_A)$.

When we transform the protocol, we similarly have to transform the initial knowledge of the intruder; we will let IK_0' be this transformed initial knowledge. Below we will state various results relating IK_0 and IK_0': these results will tell us what initial knowledge (IK_0') we have to give the intruder in the transformed system, in order to prove properties of the original system for a particular choice (IK_0) of the intruder's initial knowledge there.

The complete transformed system is modelled, therefore, by:

$$SYSTEM' \mathrel{\hat=} \left(|||_{A \in Honest} f(P_A)\right) \parallel INTRUDER(IK_0').$$

3.2. A general result for safe transformations

We now present a general result that gives sufficient considerations under which a transformation is safe. In the next section we give particular examples of such transformations.

In order to show that a particular transformation f is safe, we need to show that if there is an attack upon $SYSTEM'$, then there is an attack upon $SYSTEM$. We begin by showing that if $tr \in traces(SYSTEM)$ then $f(tr) \in traces(SYSTEM')$; we then go on to consider attacks.

It turns out that we will need two conditions upon the transformation function f and the intruder's initial knowledge in the two systems. The first condition is that if the intruder can deduce a particular message M in the original protocol, then he can deduce the corresponding message $f(M)$ in the corresponding setting in the transformed protocol:

$$\forall B \in \mathbb{P}(NFMessage) ; M \in NFMessage \bullet \\ B \cup IK_0 \vdash M \Rightarrow f(B) \cup IK_0' \vdash f(M). \quad (1)$$

We call this property the *distribution* property. (This property is very similar to Roscoe's positive property from [10].)

The second condition is that if the intruder initially knows a particular message in the original system, then he knows the corresponding message in the transformed system:

$$f(IK_0) \subseteq IK_0'. \quad (2)$$

This property tells us how to choose the initial knowledge for the intruder in the transformed system, given his initial knowledge in the original system.

We now give our main theorem, which relates the traces of the two systems. The proof can be found in the full version of this paper [3].

Theorem 1 If the transformation function f satisfies equations (1) and (2), then

$$\forall tr \in traces(SYSTEM) \bullet \\ f(tr) \in traces(SYSTEM').$$

The above theorem shows that every trace of the original system is "matched" by one in the new system. We want to show that every *attack* on the original system is "matched" by one on the new system. We produce sufficient conditions such that if tr constitutes an attack upon the original protocol, then $f(tr)$ constitutes an attack on the transformed protocol. We begin with the secrecy specification:

Lemma 2 If a particular trace tr constitutes a breach of secrecy on the original protocol, then $f(tr)$ is a breach of secrecy on the simplified protocol:

$$\neg Secrecy(tr) \Rightarrow \neg Secrecy(f(tr)) .$$

This result shows that such transformations are safe for the secrecy property:

Corollary 3 If equations (1) and (2) are satisfied, then:

$$SYSTEM' \textbf{ sat } Secrecy \Rightarrow SYSTEM \textbf{ sat } Secrecy.$$

We now consider the agreement authentication specification. If the messages upon which agreement is intended in the original protocol is $AgreementSet$, then we should take the messages upon which agreement is intended in the transformed protocol to be $f(AgreementSet)$. Further, we require the following condition:

$$\forall Ms \in AgreementSet ; Ms' \in Message^* \bullet \\ Ms \neq Ms' \Rightarrow f(Ms) \neq f(Ms'). \qquad (3)$$

That is, f does not map a different sequence Ms' of messages to the same value as a member Ms of *AgreementSet*.

Lemma 4 If equation (3) is satisfied, then if a particular trace tr constitutes a failure of agreement authentication on the original protocol, then $f(tr)$ constitutes a failure of agreement authentication on the simplified protocol:

$$\neg Agreement_{AgreementSet}(tr) \Rightarrow \\ \neg Agreement_{f(AgreementSet)}(f(tr)).$$

The following corollary shows that such transformations are safe with respect to the agreement property:

Corollary 5 If equations (1), (2) and (3) are satisfied, then:

$$SYSTEM' \textbf{ sat } Agreement_{f(AgreementSet)} \Rightarrow \\ SYSTEM \textbf{ sat } Agreement_{AgreementSet} .$$

The reason for condition (3) about f can be explained by the following example: suppose the protocol aims to achieve agreement upon a key, so *AgreementSet* is the set of all singleton sequences of keys; and suppose the function f maps two different keys K_1 and K_2 to the same value, so $f(\langle K_1 \rangle) = f(\langle K_2 \rangle)$ and condition (3) is not satisfied; then there might be some attack on the original protocol where the two honest agents end up accepting these different keys K_1 and K_2, but this would not be recognized as an attack in the simplified protocol, because the two agents would use the same key $f(K_1) = f(K_2)$.

4. Examples of safe simplifying transformations

In this section we present a number of transformations that satisfy the conditions from the previous section, and are hence safe.

4.1. Removing encryptions

We begin by defining a transformation that removes some of the encryptions from the protocol. We identify a set *Encs* of encrypted messages such that all encrypted components $\{M\}_K$ from *Encs* that appear in the protocol should be replaced with the body M. We define the transformation function f as follows:

$$\begin{aligned} f(\text{ATOM } A) &\mathrel{\widehat{=}} \text{ATOM } A, \\ f(M, M') &\mathrel{\widehat{=}} NF(f(M), f(M')), \\ f(\{M\}_K) &\mathrel{\widehat{=}} \begin{cases} f(M), & \text{if } \{M\}_K \in Encs, \\ \{f(M)\}_K, & \text{otherwise,} \end{cases} \\ f(g(\!|M|\!)) &\mathrel{\widehat{=}} g(\!|f(M)|\!). \end{aligned}$$

The interesting case is the case for $\{M\}_K$ with $\{M\}_K \in Encs$, where the outermost encryption is stripped off; most of the other cases simply apply the function recursively; the "NF" in the definition for pairs is necessary to ensure that the messages returned by the function are in normal form.

We define the intruder's initial knowledge in the transformed protocol as the result of applying the simplifying function to his knowledge in the original protocol:

$$IK'_0 \mathrel{\widehat{=}} f(IK_0).$$

This clearly satisfies condition (2). In [3] we show that this transformation also satisfies the distribution property, condition (1). Hence, we can use Corollary 3 to deduce that this transformation is a safe transformation with respect to secrecy:

$$SYSTEM' \textbf{ sat } Secrecy \Rightarrow SYSTEM \textbf{ sat } Secrecy.$$

Further, f is clearly injective on atoms, so we can use Corollary 5 to deduce that this transformation is a safe transformation with respect to agreement on atoms:

If *AgreementSet* is a set of sequences of atoms, then

$$SYSTEM' \textbf{ sat } Agreement_{f(AgreementSet)} \Rightarrow \\ SYSTEM \textbf{ sat } Agreement_{AgreementSet}.$$

The way this simplifying transformation will be used in practice is to identify a particular encryption in the protocol description that we think is unnecessary, and to take f to be the function that removes this encryption; that is, we take *Encs* to be the set of all instances of the encrypted component in question. Note though, that if there is a second encrypted component in the protocol description whose instances are of the same type as the instances of the original encryption, then the instances of the second encrypted component are also in *Encs*, and so we must also strip off the encryptions on these instances.

4.2. Removing some atomic or hashed fields

We now define a transformation that completely removes some fields from the protocol. It turns out that we must restrict these fields to being either atoms that are not keys, or the application of hash functions. Formally, we let

$$Ms \subseteq Message$$

be the set of such messages, and assume:

$$\begin{array}{l}\forall M \in Ms \bullet \\ \quad (\exists A \in Atom \bullet M = \text{ATOM}\ A \wedge A \notin Key) \\ \quad \vee (\exists g \in HashFn\,;\, M' \in Msg \bullet M = g(\!| M' |\!)).\end{array}$$

In order to define this transformation, we need to specify how it acts upon a message that is to be removed, leaving an "empty message". The $Message$ datatype has no concept of an "empty message", so we model such "empty messages" by a distinguished atomic value nil $\in Atom$.

We define the transformation as follows:

$$\begin{array}{rcl} f(M) & \mathrel{\widehat{=}} & \text{ATOM nil}, \quad \text{if } M \in Ms, \\ f(\text{ATOM}\ A) & \mathrel{\widehat{=}} & \text{ATOM}\ A, \\ f(M, M') & \mathrel{\widehat{=}} & \begin{cases} f(M'), & \text{if } f(M) = \text{ATOM nil}, \\ f(M), & \text{if } f(M') = \text{ATOM nil}, \\ (f(M), f(M')), & \text{otherwise}, \end{cases} \\ f(\{M\}_K) & \mathrel{\widehat{=}} & \begin{cases} \text{ATOM nil}, & \text{if } f(M) = \text{ATOM nil}, \\ \{f(M)\}_K, & \text{otherwise}, \end{cases} \\ f(g(\!| M |\!)) & \mathrel{\widehat{=}} & \begin{cases} \text{ATOM nil}, & \text{if } f(M) = \text{ATOM nil}, \\ g(\!| f(M) |\!), & \text{otherwise}. \end{cases} \end{array}$$

We adopt a convention from functional programming languages such as Haskell, namely that the patterns in the definition are matched from top to bottom, so that a definition further down the page will be applied only if no earlier definition applies; this means that the line with the pattern "ATOM A" applies only to atoms that are not matched by the first line, i.e. only to atoms not in Ms.

For composite messages, the definition gets applied recursively to the subcomponents; if either member of a pair gets removed in this way, then we are left with the other member of the pair; if all of the body of an encryption or a hash function application gets removed, then the encryption or hash function is removed.

We define the intruder's initial knowledge in the transformed protocol by:

$$IK_0' \mathrel{\widehat{=}} f(IK_0) \cup \{\text{ATOM nil}\}.$$

Note that we assume the intruder can produce ATOM nil, i.e. an empty message.

Our definitions satisfy conditions (1) and (2). We hence deduce that this is a safe transformation with respect to secrecy. Note that the transformation is safe even if we remove a field that we are trying to prove is secret; however, in this case the secret will be renamed to ATOM nil, which is in the intruder's initial knowledge, and so this transformation will introduce a new attack: such a transformation is safe but stupid.

If all the values upon which agreement is intended are atoms, and none are removed, i.e.:

$$\begin{array}{l}\forall Ms' \in AgreementSet \bullet \forall M \text{ in } Ms' \bullet \\ \quad \exists A \in Atom \bullet M = \text{ATOM}\ A \wedge M \notin Ms,\end{array}$$

then the transformation satisfies condition (3), and so we deduce that this is a safe transformation with respect to agreement on such values. The above condition simply states that if you want to be sure that the protocol guarantees agreement on a particular field, then your simplification shouldn't remove that field!

In practice, we will use this transformation to remove *all* fields of a particular type: to remove one field we would have to define Ms to be all values with which that field could be instantiated, i.e. all values of that type; this would have the effect of removing all fields of the type.

4.3. Coalescing atoms

Our next transformation is one that coalesces certain pairs of atoms, replacing them by the first. We define the transformation with respect to a set of pairs of atoms:

$$Pairs : \mathbf{P}(Atom \times Atom),$$

the idea being that for each $(A, A') \in Pairs$, any occurrence of the pair $(\text{ATOM}\ A, \text{ATOM}\ A')$ is replaced by ATOM A.

We need the following condition upon $Pairs$:

$$\forall (A, A') \in Pairs \bullet IK_0' \cup \{\text{ATOM}\ A\} \vdash \text{ATOM}\ A', \quad (4)$$

that is, the atom removed can be deduced from the atom remaining and the intruder's initial knowledge. If we did not have this condition, then removing the atom A' would remove a possible source of information for the intruder. We will therefore tend to use this transformation in two situations: where the atom removed is in the intruder's initial knowledge, and where the atom removed is equal to the one remaining.

We formalize the transformation as follows:

$$\begin{array}{l} f(\text{ATOM}\ A) \mathrel{\widehat{=}} \text{ATOM}\ A, \\ f(\text{ATOM}\ A, \text{ATOM}\ A') \mathrel{\widehat{=}} \\ \quad \begin{cases} \text{ATOM}\ A, & \text{if } (A, A') \in Pairs, \\ (\text{ATOM}\ A, \text{ATOM}\ A'), & \text{otherwise}, \end{cases} \\ f(\text{ATOM}\ A, (\text{ATOM}\ A', M)) \mathrel{\widehat{=}} \\ \quad \begin{cases} f(\text{ATOM}\ A, M), & \text{if } (A, A') \in Pairs, \\ (\text{ATOM}\ A, f(\text{ATOM}\ A', M)), & \text{otherwise}, \end{cases} \\ f(M, M') \mathrel{\widehat{=}} (f(M), f(M')), \\ f(\{M\}_K) \mathrel{\widehat{=}} \{f(M)\}_K, \\ f(g(\!| M |\!)) \mathrel{\widehat{=}} g(\!| f(M) |\!). \end{array}$$

We define the intruder's initial knowledge in the transformed system by:

$$IK'_0 \mathrel{\widehat{=}} f(IK_0).$$

Our definitions satisfy conditions (1) and (2). Hence we deduce that this is a safe transformation with respect to secrecy. It is also a safe transformation with respect to the agreement property provided f is injective on the messages upon which agreement in intended.

4.4. Other transformations

We have defined a number of other safe transformations; the reader is referred to [3] for details:

- a transformation that removes some of the hash functions from the protocol; this transformation is very similar to that for removing encryptions;
- a transformation that uniformly renames atoms in protocol messages;
- a transformation that moves fields outside the body of encryptions;
- a transformation that swaps particular pairs of atoms when they appear next to one another; this transformation is very similar to that for coalescing atoms.

5. Case study: The CyberCash Main Sequence Protocol

We illustrate our simplifying transformations by applying them to the CyberCash Main Sequence Protocol. The protocol is designed to allow credit card purchases to take place securely between a customer and merchant, with the aid of CyberCash who acts as a trusted third party. The customer and merchant send details to CyberCash who verifies their involvement in the transaction.

A complete description of the protocol is included in Appendix A, taken from [1]; the following discussion should be read in conjunction with this protocol description.

5.1. Simplifying the protocol

The complete protocol contains dozens of fields, but very few seem directly relevant to the security of the protocol. Many fields are included solely for reasons of functionality (e.g. *CardCityOptional*). Our first simplification is therefore a "remove fields" simplification, to remove all atomic fields other than those that we believe are necessary: the fields that are retained are the price of the transaction according to each agent (*Amount* and $MerchantAmount$), the customer's credit card number ($CardNumber$), agents' identities, keys, and transaction numbers (which act as a kind of run identifier). (If we were testing whether the protocol guarantees timeliness, we would want to retain the timestamps.)

The protocol description contains many occurrences of the fields *PrSignedHash_* (also known as $Merchant$-*SignedHash_*) and $PrHash\_$. These seem to duplicate security already present, and so appear unnecessary. Several hashes of public keys are passed around by the protocol; these similarly seem to be unnecessary for the security of the protocol. Our second transformation is to remove all of these fields, using the transformation of Section 4.2 to remove atomic or hashed fields.

The next simplification is to remove all applications of the hash function $MD5$; this hash function is simply used to reduce the size of messages, for efficiency.

This still leaves nested encryption within *OpaqueCH1_* and $MerchantOpaqueCM1\_$: an encryption with a secret (asymmetric) key as a signature to ensure authentication, and an encryption with a symmetric shared key to ensure the secrecy of fields such as $CardNumber$. We can consider these two security properties separately, performing different simplifications for each: stripping off the signatures when testing for secrecy, and stripping off the symmetric key encryptions when testing for authentication.

In each of the resulting protocols, several data items are repeated within some encryptions. By swapping pairs of atoms around we can bring together like atoms, which can then be coalesced to a single atom. Doing this, produces fully simplified versions of the protocol as in Figure 1.

In order to make the simplifying transformations easier to apply (particularly the swapping and coalescing pairs transformations), we have produced tool support as an extension to Casper [6]. The tool takes in a description of the complete protocol and a specification of a sequence of transformations, and applies them in order.

5.2. Analysis of the simplified protocol

We have analyzed the simplified version of the Main Sequence Protocol using Casper and FDR [6], testing whether the protocol kept the customer's credit card number and the session keys secret, and testing whether the two agents were authenticated to one another with agreement on the amount of the transaction.

We found a rather weak authentication attack upon the protocol, where the intruder watches a run of the protocol up until message 4, intercepts this message, and then fakes the message 5 from what he has seen in previous messages. This applies to both the simplified protocol and the original protocol. The customer thinks he has completed the protocol run successfully, but the merchant thinks the run

Simplified version for secrecy analysis:

$$
\begin{array}{lll}
1. & M \rightarrow C & : MerchantCcId, MerchantAmount \\
2. & C \rightarrow M & : Id, MerchantAmount, MerchantCcId, Transaction, \{kcs\}_{PKCyberKey}, \\
& & \{Amount, CardNumber, MerchantCcId, Id, MerchantAmount, Transaction\}_{kcs} \\
3. & M \rightarrow CB & : MerchantCcId, MerchantTransaction, \{kcs\}_{PKCyberKey}, \\
& & \{Amount, CardNumber, MerchantCcId, Id, MerchantAmount, Transaction\}_{kcs}, \\
& & \{kms\}_{PKMerchantCyberKey}, \\
& & \{Id, MerchantAmount, MerchantCcId, MerchantTransaction, Transaction\}_{kms} \\
4. & CB \rightarrow M & : MerchantCcId, MerchantTransaction, \\
& & \{CardNumber, MerchantAmount, Id, MerchantId, Transaction\}_{kms}, \\
& & \{CardNumber, Amount\}_{kcs} \\
5. & M \rightarrow C & : MerchantCcId, MerchantAmount, Transaction, Id, \{CardNumber, Amount\}_{kcs} .
\end{array}
$$

Simplified version for authentication analysis:

$$
\begin{array}{lll}
1. & M \rightarrow C & : MerchantCcId, MerchantAmount \\
2. & C \rightarrow M & : Id, MerchantAmount, MerchantCcId, Transaction, \\
& & \{kcs\}_{PKCyberKey}, Amount, CardNumber, \\
& & \{Amount, CardNumber, MerchantCcId, Id, MerchantAmount, Transaction\}_{SK(C)} \\
3. & M \rightarrow CB & : MerchantCcId, MerchantTransaction, \{kcs\}_{PKCyberKey}, Amount, CardNumber, \\
& & \{Amount, CardNumber, MerchantCcId, Id, MerchantAmount, Transaction\}_{SK(C)} \\
& & \{kms\}_{PKMerchantCyberKey}, Id, MerchantAmount, MerchantCcId, Transaction, \\
& & \{Id, MerchantAmount, MerchantCcId, MerchantTransaction, Transaction\}_{SK(M)} \\
4. & CB \rightarrow M & : MerchantCcId, MerchantTransaction, \\
& & \{CardNumber, MerchantAmount, Id, MerchantId, Transaction\}_{kms}, \\
& & \{CardNumber, Amount\}_{kcs} \\
5. & M \rightarrow C & : MerchantCcId, MerchantAmount, Transaction, Id, \{CardNumber, Amount\}_{kcs} .
\end{array}
$$

Figure 1. Simplified versions of the CyberCash Main Sequence Protocol

was broken off after message 3. It is arguable whether this should be classified as an attack; however, it is certainly a behaviour that we should be aware of. This is an attack according to our definition of authentication [5], which is that when one agent completes a run of the protocol, the other agent should at least have progressed as far as the last message it sends. When we adapted our authentication specification appropriately, we were able to verify that whenever the customer completes a protocol run, the merchant has progressed at least as far as message 3.

We found another attack, because we oversimplified the protocol. We removed the field $MerchantCcId$, because we didn't realize that this was effectively the merchant's identity; unsurprisingly, this introduced an authentication attack. The simplifications were easily undone to realize that there was no corresponding attack on the original protocol, and hence that we had oversimplified (Steve Brackin has claimed that the fields Id and $MerchantCcId$ are actually identification numbers, rather than actual identities, in which case our attack can be extended to the full protocol; at the time of writing, we have been unable to verify this claim).

Failure to find an attack using a model checker does not (in the absence of arguments like those in [7, 10]) necessarily imply that the protocol is secure: there might be attacks upon systems running the protocol that are larger than those analysed. However, the model checking results certainly improve our confidence in the security of the protocol. A formal proof could be performed on the simplified protocol and, if successful, the results would also apply to the original protocol.

The overall effect of these simplifications is to reduce the protocol to a version which can be easily understood. The main aspects of the protocol have been retained to ensure it still fulfills its original function, yet it is simple enough to apply standard analysis techniques.

6. Conclusions

In this paper we have introduced the notion of *safe simplifying transformations*: transformations that have the property of preserving attacks. We have produced sufficient conditions for a transformation to be safe, and used this result to show that a number of transformations are indeed safe. We have illustrated these techniques by applying them to a large commercial protocol, simplifying this down to a size that can be modelled and analysed. Attacks that are found can be traced back to the original protocol to see if they are feasible.

We close by giving brief pointers to future work. We intend to apply this techniques to more commercial protocols, for example SET [12] and SSL [13]. Most complications in commercial protocols lie in the large number of fields and nested encryption within each message, we are able to simplify these with our current techniques. It is likely that such case studies will reveal further useful safe simplifying transformations.

We would like to extend this work to deal with other forms of authentication specification, and also other security properties such as non-repudiation.

One class of simplifying transformation that is not captured by the results of this paper is what we are terming *redirecting transformations*. In the simplified versions of the CyberCash protocol in Figure 1, the customer sends two encrypted components to the merchant in message 2, which the merchant simply forwards to CyberCash in message 3, without performing any checks upon them. It seems clear to us that sending these encrypted messages directly to CyberCash would give an equally secure protocol; in other words, we believe that redirecting these encrypted components would be a safe simplifying transformation.

Acknowledgements

This research was supported by grants from the UK Engineering and Physical Sciences Research Council, the US Office of Naval Research and the UK Defence Evaluation and Research Agency.

References

[1] S. Brackin. Automatic formal analysis of two large commercial protocols. In *Proceedings of the DIMACS Workshop on Design and Formal Verification of Security Protocols*, 1997. Available via URL: `http://dimacs.rutgers.edu/Workshops/Security/program2/program.html`.

[2] C. A. R. Hoare. *Communicating Sequential Processes*. Prentice Hall, 1985.

[3] M. L. Hui and G. Lowe. Safe simplifying transformations on security protocols. Technical Report 1999/1, University of Leicester, 1999. Available via URL: `http://www.mcs.le.ac.uk/~glowe/Security/Papers/simplify.ps`.

[4] G. Lowe. Breaking and fixing the Needham-Schroeder public-key protocol using FDR. In *Proceedings of TACAS*, volume 1055 of *Lecture Notes in Computer Science*, pages 147–166. Springer Verlag, 1996. Also in *Software—Concepts and Tools*, 17:93–102, 1996.

[5] G. Lowe. A hierarchy of authentication specifications. In *Proceedings of 10th IEEE Computer Security Foundations Workshop*, 1997.

[6] G. Lowe. Casper: A compiler for the analysis of security protocols. *Journal of Computer Security*, 6:53–84, 1998. World Wide Web home page at URL `http://www.mcs.le.ac.uk/~glowe/Security/Casper/index.html`.

[7] G. Lowe. Towards a completeness result for model checking of security protocols (extended abstract). In *11th Computer Security Foundations Workshop*, 1998.

[8] G. Lowe and B. Roscoe. Using CSP to detect errors in the TMN protocol. *IEEE Transactions on Software Engineering*, 23(10):659–669, 1997.

[9] A. W. Roscoe. *The Theory and Practice of Concurrency*. Prentice Hall, 1997.

[10] A. W. Roscoe. Proving security protocols with model checkers by data independence techniques. In *11th Computer Security Foundations Workshop*, pages 84–95, 1998.

[11] S. Schneider. Security properties and CSP. In *IEEE Computer Society Symposium on Security and Privacy*, Oakland, 1996.

[12] Secure Electronic Transaction (SET) specification. Available from `http://www.setco.org/download.html`, 1997.

[13] The SSL protocol. Available via `http://home.netscape.com/newsref/std/SSL.html`, 1996.

A. The CyberCash Main Sequence Protocol

A description of the CyberCash Main Sequence Protocol is in Figure 2; those fields whose names finish with an underscore are abbreviations, which are defined in Figures 3 and 4. This description is based upon Steve Brackin's description from [1].

1 $M \to C$: $Accepts, MerchantAmount, MerchantAmount2Optional, MerchantCcId, MerchantOrderId, MerchantDate, MerchantSwVersion, Note, Payload, PayloadNote, Type, UrlCancel, UrlFail, UrlPayTo, UrlSuccess, MD5(Payload), MerchantSignedHashKey\_, MerchantSignedHash\_$

2 $C \to M$: $CyberKey, Date, Id, MerchantCcId, MerchantDate, MerchantSignedHashKey\_, OrderId, ServiceCategory, Transaction, Type, PrHash\_, PrSignedHash\_, OpaqPrefixCH1\_, OpaqueCH1\_$

3 $M \to CB$: $CyberKey, MerchantCcId, MerchantCyberKey, MerchantDate, MerchantTransaction, ServiceCategory, OpaqPrefixCH1\_, OpaqueCH1\_, MerchantOpaqPrefixCM1\_, MerchantOpaqueCM1\_$

4 $CB \to M$: $MerchantCcId, MerchantTransaction, MerchantDate, ServiceCategory, MerchantOpaqueCM6\_, OpaqueCM6\_$

5 $M \to C$: $Date, MerchantCcId, MerchantDate, MerchantMessage, MerchantResponseCode, MerchantSwVersion, Id, ServiceCategory, Transaction, Type, PrHash\_, PrSignedHash\_, OpaqueCM6\_$

Figure 2. The CyberCash Main Sequence Protocol

$$MerchantSignedHashKey\_ \mathrel{\hat{=}} MD5(PK(M)),$$

$$MerchantSignedHash\_ \mathrel{\hat{=}} \{MD5(Accepts, MerchantDate, MerchantAmount, MerchantCcId, MerchantOrderId, MerchantSignedHashKey\_, Note, Type, UrlCancel, UrlFail, UrlPayto, UrlSuccess)\}_{SK(M)},$$

$$PrHash\_ \mathrel{\hat{=}} MD5(Accepts, Date, MerchantAmount, MerchantCcId, MerchantOrderId, MerchantSignedHashKey\_, Note, Type, UrlCancel, UrlFail, UrlPayTo, UrlSuccess),$$

$$PrSignedHash\_ \mathrel{\hat{=}} MerchantSignedHash\_,$$

$$OpaqPrefixCH1\_ \mathrel{\hat{=}} \{kcs\}_{PKCyberKey},$$

$$OpaqueCH1\_ \mathrel{\hat{=}} \{Amount, CardCIdOptional, CardCityOptional, CardCountryOptional, CardExpirationDate, CardName, CardNumber, CardOtherFieldsOptional, CardPostalCodeOptional, CardPrefixOptional, CardSalt, CardStateOptional, CardStreetOptional, CardType, SwVersion, MD5(PK(C)), SignatureCH1\_\}_{kcs},$$

$$SignatureCH1\_ \mathrel{\hat{=}} \{MD5(Amount, CardCIdOptional, CardCityOptional, CardCountryOptional, CardExpirationDate, CardName, CardNumber, CardOtherFieldsOptional, CardPostalCodeOptional, CardPrefixOptional, CardSalt, CardStateOptional, CardStreetOptional, CardType, CyberKey, Date, Id, MerchantCcId, MerchantSignedHashKey\_, OrderId, PrHash\_, PrSignedHash\_, SwVersion, Transaction, Type)\}_{SK(C)},$$

Figure 3. Abbreviations in the CyberCash Main Sequence Protocol

$MerchantOpaqPrefixCM1\_ \mathrel{\widehat{=}} \{kms\}_{PKMerchantCyberKey},$

$MerchantOpaqueCM1\_ \mathrel{\widehat{=}}$
$\{Date, DescriptionListOptional, Id, MerchantAmount, MerchantDba, MerchantLocationOptional,$
$MerchantMessage, MerchantSignedHashKey\_, MerchantSwMessageOptional,$
$MerchantSwServerOptional, MerchantSwVersion, MerchantUrlOptional, OrderId,$
$PrHash\_, PrSignedHash\_, RetrievalReferenceNumberOptional, ServerDateMerchantOptional,$
$TerminalIdFuture, Transaction, TransactionDescriptionOptional,$
$Type, MD5(PKMerchantCyberKey), MerchantSignatureCM1\_\}_{kms},$

$MerchantSignatureCM1\_ \mathrel{\widehat{=}}$
$\{MD5(CyberKey, Date, Id, MerchantAmount, MerchantCcId, MerchantCyberKey,$
$MerchantDate, MerchantTransaction, OrderId, PrHash\_, PrSignedHash\_,$
$ServerDateMerchantOptional, Transaction, Type)\}_{SK(M)},$

$MerchantOpaqueCM6\_ \mathrel{\widehat{=}}$
$\{AcquirerRefDataOptional, ActionCode, Addn1ResponseDataOptional, AuthorizationCode,$
$AvsInfoOptional, CardCIdOptional, CardCityOptional, CardCountryOptional,$
$CardExpirationDate, CardName, CardNumber, CardPostalCodeOptional, CardPrefixOptional,$
$CardStateOptional, CardStreetOptional, CardType, Date, DebuggingInfoOptional,$
$Id, MerchantMessage, MerchantSignedHashKey\_, MerchantSwMessageOptional,$
$MerchantSwSeverityOptional, OrderId, ProcessorErrorCodeFuture,$
$PrHash\_, PrSignedHash\_, MerchantResponseCode, ResponseDetailCodeFuture,$
$RetrievalReferenceNumberOptional, ServerDate, TerminalIdFuture, Transaction, Type\}_{kms},$

$OpaqueCM6\_ \mathrel{\widehat{=}}$
$\{Amount, AuthorizationCode, CardCIdOptional, CardCityOptional, CardCountryOptional,$
$CardExpirationDate, CardName, CardNumber, CardOtherFieldsOptional,$
$CardPostalCodeOptional, CardPrefixOptional, CardSalt, CardStateOptional,$
$CardStreetOptional, CardTypeOptional, MerchantDba, MerchantLocationOptional,$
$MerchantUrlOptional, Message, OrderId, ResponseCode, ServerDate,$
$SwMessageOptional, SwSeverityOptional, TransactionDescriptionOptional\}_{kcs}.$

Figure 4. Abbreviations in the CyberCash Main Sequence Protocol, continued

Decision Procedures for the Analysis of Cryptographic Protocols by Logics of Belief*

David MONNIAUX
Laboratoire d'Informatique de l'École Normale Supérieure †
&
SRI International, Computer Science Laboratory ‡

Abstract

Belief-logic deductions are used in the analysis of cryptographic protocols. We show a new method to decide such logics. In addition to the familiar BAN logic, it is also applicable to the more advanced versions of protocol security logics, and GNY in particular; and it employs an efficient forward-chaining algorithm the completeness and termination of which are proved. Theoretic proofs, implementation decisions and results are discussed.

1 Introduction

Cryptographic protocols are specifications for sequences of messages to be exchanged by machines on a possibly insecure network, such as the Internet, to establish private or authenticated communication. These protocols can be used to distribute sensitive information, such as classified material, credit card numbers or trade secrets, or to authenticate information.

Many cryptographic protocols have been found to be flawed; that is, there exists a way for an intruder that has gained partial or total control over the communication network and is able to read, suppress and forge messages to trick the communicating machines into revealing some sensitive information or believing they have an authenticated communication, whereas they are actually communicating with the intruder. Several tools and techniques have therefore been devised for analyzing and verifying the security of cryptographic protocols.

A common feature of these techniques, including ours, is that they address the design of the protocol rather than the strength of the underlying cryptographic algorithms, such as message digests or encryption primitives. For instance, it is assumed that one may decrypt a message encrypted with a public key only when possessing the corresponding private key.

Three main categories of approaches have been proposed:

Belief logics represent reasoning such as "if a message arrives encrypted with a key known only to me and machine M, and I did not send it originally, then it must have been sent by M". The first of these was the so-called BAN logic from Burrows, Abadi and Needham [3], which was followed by more expressive and elaborate extensions such as GNY (Gong, Needham and Yahalom [5, 6]) and SVO (Syverson and van Oorschot [17, 18]). One limitation of these logics is the need to annotate the protocols with logical assertions that are assumed to represent the intent of the sender of the message, as well as logical assumptions on the secrecy or freshness of certain pieces of information. Also, they cannot verify secrecy.

Partial model checking of a semantic model is a stronger method. Here a limited but wide set of possible attacks is generated and systematically tried against the protocol. The hope is that this set is wide enough so that any attack will be detected. Efficient implementations have been devised [9, 10, 13].

Theorem proving of properties of a semantic model is the strongest method. Formal proofs are sought for safety theorems on the protocols (in a certain model of what a protocol is). There are two approaches:

- using a generic proof assistant with specific procedures [14];
- using a specific analyzer like the NRL Protocol Analyzer [11].

Of course, a clear definition of the model that is considered is needed, and subtle points can have dramatic

*This work was partially funded by NSF grant CCR-9509931
†ENS-LIENS, 45, rue d'Ulm , 75230 PARIS cédex 5, FRANCE
‡SRI-CSL, 333 Ravenswood Ave., Menlo Park, CA 94025-3493, USA

$$\dfrac{\dfrac{A \triangleleft \star \{N_a\}_{-K_b}\,(2) \quad A \ni +K_b\,(a) \quad A \models \overset{+K_b}{\mapsto} K_b\,(b) \quad A \models \phi(N_a)\,(c)}{A \models B \mid\!\sim N_a}\,\text{I4} \qquad A \models \sharp(N_a)\,(d)}{A \models B \ni N_a}\,\text{I6}$$

Figure 1. A derivation in GNY logic.

effects on whether some methods are suitable or not, as shown in [7]. More specifically, the rewriting systems that very often quotient the space of messages have to be taken into account in the design of the proof method [7, 12]. Rewriting systems also have to be taken into account in analyses by GNY logic and will be dealt with in this paper.

The three approaches have increasing strength, but also roughly increasing cost, human-directed theorem proving being very costly in human time and model checking in computation times. All approaches can be effectively used in combination, starting with belief logics, which, although the weakest, are simple to use and can be very effective in detecting certain flaws. Their simplicity and low cost would be enhanced if their analysis could be automated with complete reliability; this is such a complete, provably reliable automation that we are presenting in this paper.

The purpose of this paper is to present a new method for automating belief-logic deductions. It is applicable to the more advanced versions of protocol security logics, and GNY in particular; and it employs an efficient forward-chaining algorithm the completeness and termination of which are proved.

There have been other efforts to automate belief-logic security analyses [1, 2, 8, 15]. Their approaches have been less satisfactory since they were either incomplete or nonterminating [15] or limited to BAN logic [8]; completeness and nontermination have sometimes not been explicitly addressed [1, 2]. Our method is complete, meaning that if a formula is provable from a set of hypotheses in a logic where our method is applicable, our method will find a suitable derivation (proof tree); and it is terminating, meaning that when the formula is not provable, our method will stop and give a negative answer. Also, our method yields results in a matter of seconds, comparable to the times of the incomplete procedure of [15].

1.1 A simple example of belief-logic analysis

1	$A \to B$	N_a
2	$B \to A$	$\{N_a\}_{-K_b}$
3	$A \to B$	$\{K_{ab}\}_{+K_b}$

This is to be understood as: in step 1, A sends a newly generated number N_a to B; B answers with the encryption of N_a by its private key $-K_b$; A answers with the encryption of a newly generated session key K_{ab} with B's public key $+K_b$.

To illustrate how belief-logic deductions work, we first show the "idealized" version of the protocol in GNY:

1	$B \triangleleft N_a$
2	$A \triangleleft \star \{N_a\}_{-K_b}$
3	$B \triangleleft \star \left(\{K_{ab}\}_{+K_b} \rightsquigarrow A \overset{K_{ab}}{\longleftrightarrow} B\right)$

The star means that the following term was not originated by the party who receives it. The statement after the wavy arrow in 3 is an annotation meaning that K_{ab} is intended to be a shared secret key for use between A and B.

We also need some assumptions, written as follows in GNY:

(a) $A \ni +K_b$ (A possesses $+K_b$)

(b) $A \models \overset{+B}{\mapsto} B$ (A believes that $+K_b$ is B's public key)

(c) $A \models \phi(N_a)$ (A believes N_a to be recognizable; that is, if A sees a message field that is supposed to be N_a, A can check whether it is or not)

(d) $A \models \sharp(N_a)$ (A believes N_a to be fresh; that is, to have been used for the first time in this run of the protocol)

Using GNY logic, we can derive the conclusion $A \models B \ni N_a$ (see fig. 1). This means that from the fact, coming from protocol step 2, that A sees the message consisting of the encryption of N_a by the private key for the public/private couple of keys K_b, from assumption a (A possesses the corresponding public key), from assumption b (B uses the private key of the couple K_b) and from assumption c (A believes that it can recognize N_a), we deduce using rule I4 that A is entitled to believe that B once said N_a. Then, using assumption d, which is that N_a is fresh (has never been used in another session before), we deduce that A is entitled to believe that B possesses N_a. See [6] for a complete list of the GNY inference rules and their designations.

The final goal of the protocol might be to cause B to believe that A believes that K_{ab} is the shared key ($A \models A \overset{K_{ab}}{\longleftrightarrow} B$). However, message 3 could have been forged by any intruder possessing $+K_b$, which is realistic since it is a public key, replacing K_{ab} by any key of his choice. The logic (correctly) fails to conclude that the protocol accomplishes this goal: this goal has no derivation in GNY logic from the above set of hypotheses.

2 Our method

The purpose of our method is, given a set of hypotheses Γ and a would-be conclusion t, to decide whether t is derivable from Γ in GNY logic. Additionally, if it is derivable, a derivation is output; if it is not, an attempt is made to suggest some additional hypotheses to the user.

2.1 Vocabulary

We place ourselves in a free algebra of terms. By a "rule", we mean a finite set of terms with variables $\{\mathcal{H}_1, \ldots, \mathcal{H}_n\}$ called the premisses and a term with variables $\mathcal{C}$ call the conclusion, traditionally represented as

$$\frac{\mathcal{H}_1 \quad \cdots \quad \mathcal{H}_n}{\mathcal{C}}$$

Applying that rule to hypotheses $H_1, \ldots, H_n$ to yield the conclusion C means finding a common unifier for $\{(H_1, \mathcal{H}_1), \ldots, (H_n, \mathcal{H}_n), (C, \mathcal{C})\}$. A derivation is a tree whose nodes are such applications, with its root the conclusion and its leaves the hypotheses.

There are two traditional methods to test whether a formula t admits a derivation from a set of hypotheses Γ in a system of rules $\vdash$ (which we note by $\boldsymbol{\Gamma \vdash t}$):

Forward chaining, that is starting from the hypotheses Γ, apply all the possible deduction rules to deduce new formulas, then start again with the union of the hypotheses and the new formulas, until the formula t is discovered;

Backward chaining, that is, starting from the purported conclusion, find all the rules and all the instantiations of the variables in them that yield that conclusion, then try recursively to prove the hypotheses of each of these rules with each of the instantiations; it is a kind of search with backtracking.

Both these methods suffer from the following problems:

- Both methods may never terminate if $\Gamma \nvdash t$.
- Some rules maybe unsuitable for a given method: for a forward (resp. backward) chaining method, if some variables in the conclusion (resp. premisses) are not found in the premisses (resp. conclusion), then the system has to instantiate them with all possible terms. In the opposite case, we say that the rule is **suitable for forward (resp. backward) chaining**.

There are two problems with the systems of rules like GNY:

- There exist infinite derivations;
- There are rules that are unsuitable for forward-chaining and rules that are unsuitable for forward-chaining.

Nevertheless, we will give a characterization of a class of systems of rules, to which GNY belongs, that are equivalent to systems suitable for forward-chaining; moreover, we have a convenient criterion ensuring termination.

2.2 The transformation

If we straightforwardly (and naively) implement the rules of BAN or GNY logic in a general-purpose automatic theorem prover, as it has been done [15], the prover is likely to search an infinite space of possible proofs, which means that the system doesn't terminate when the conclusion is not provable. Furthermore, even in cases of termination, the computation time might be prohibitive, due to lots of unfruitful search.

Our idea is that, given a logic of belief for authentication (abiding by certain restrictions given in the definitions below), we can construct another logic in which for any Γ and t the search space in which to look for a derivation of t from the set of hypotheses Γ is finite. The implementation just has to enumerate exhaustively this search space and test whether it contains such a derivation.

2.2.1 Classes of rules and normal derivations

We deal with two classes of rules[1]:

- **composition rules**, in which all the variables of the premisses are found in the conclusion (these rules are suitable for backward-chaining);
- **decomposition rules**, in which all the variables of the conclusion are found in the premisses (these rules are suitable for forward-chaining); for these rules, we distinguish the **principal premisses** (which can be one or more) and the optional **auxiliary premisses**; the variables in the auxiliary premisses are a subset of these in the principal premisses.

We consider a partition of the rules between these two classes. The intuition is that composition rules introduce

[1] This partition of the set of rules into two classes is very similar to that of [8], where they are called respectively *growing* and *shrinking rules*. This is also similar to the introduction and elimination rules of intuitionistic logic; see [4, p. 75]. Our theorem on normal derivations is thus similar to the normalization theorem of intuitionistic logic or Gentzen's Hauptsatz [4, p. 105].

constructors, like a pair, and decomposition rules break these constructors, as in taking the first projection of a pair.

Of course, several partitions abiding by the above criteria can exist; the choice for the partition that is implemented has to take into account issues like termination and complexity. For termination purposes, one may use a well-founded ordering so that for any decomposition rule, there exists at least one premiss so that the conclusion is strictly less than that premiss.

Informally, a decision procedure would have to backward-chain on the composition rules and to forward-chain on the decomposition rules.

We define the following criterion (called the **normal derivation criterion**) on systems of rules: we require that if there exists a derivation of $\Gamma \vdash t$ then there must also exist a **normal derivation** of $\Gamma \vdash t$. A derivation Δ of a conclusion $\Gamma \vdash t$ is said to be **normal** if there is no composition rule to be used as the root rule of the sub-derivation for a principal premise of a decomposition rule: for any decomposition rule used in Δ:

$$\frac{\dfrac{\vdots}{P_1}\,r_1 \quad \cdots \quad \dfrac{\vdots}{P_n}\,r_n \quad \overset{\vdots}{A_1} \quad \cdots \quad \overset{\vdots}{A_m}}{C}\,r$$

where the P_i are the principal hypotheses and the A_j the auxiliary hypotheses, none of the rules $r_1, \ldots, r_n$ is a composition rule. In the opposite case, we say that there is a **cut** at r.

Informally, that means that it must be possible to derive anything that is derivable without having to compose something and decompose it afterwards; for instance, in

$$\dfrac{\dfrac{\overset{\vdots\,\alpha}{P \ni X} \quad \overset{\vdots\,\beta}{P \ni Y}}{P \ni (X, Y)}\,\mathsf{P2}}{P \ni X}\,\mathsf{P3}$$

we compose a pair just to decompose it afterwards. This is a like a cut in logic and poses difficulty for automatic proof search because it requires invention (in the above example, the system would have had to guess a suitable value for Y).[2] Of course, the above derivation can be replaced by the following one:

$$\overset{\vdots\,\alpha}{P \ni X}$$

The possibility of such replacements is what we express in our criterion.

We will only deal with systems matching the normal derivation criterion. GNY logic doesn't match the criterion, that's why we'll have to supplement it with a few rules, yielding an equivalent system that matches the criterion.

2.2.2 The "goal" symbol

We introduce a special symbol, **goal**. $\boxdot X$ means that "we would like to compose X". We use it to internalize our decision strategy, which is that composition rules will only be applied when their conclusion is to be composed.

Our transformation turns the composition rule

$$\frac{\mathcal{H}_1 \cdots \mathcal{H}_n}{\mathcal{C}}$$

into a pair

$$\frac{\boxdot\mathcal{C} \quad \mathcal{H}_1 \cdots \mathcal{H}_n}{\mathcal{C}} \qquad \frac{\boxdot\mathcal{C}}{\boxdot\mathcal{H}_1 \cdots \boxdot\mathcal{H}_n}$$

and adds to the decomposition rule

$$\frac{\mathcal{D}_1 \cdots \mathcal{D}_m \quad \mathcal{K}_1 \cdots \mathcal{K}_n}{\mathcal{C}},$$

where the one or more $\mathcal{D}_i$ are principal premisses and the zero or more $\mathcal{K}_i$ are auxiliary premisses, the triggering rule

$$\frac{\mathcal{D}_1 \cdots \mathcal{D}_m}{\boxdot\mathcal{K}_1 \cdots \boxdot\mathcal{K}_n}.$$

Theorem 1 *For all system of rules $\vdash$ matching the conditions for the above transformation, calling $\vdash'$ the system of rules resulting from the transformation of $\vdash$, we have: for all set of hypotheses Γ and formula t,*

$$\Gamma \vdash t \iff \Gamma, \boxdot t \vdash' t;$$

furthermore, in that case a derivation of $\Gamma, \boxdot t \vdash' t$ can be obtained by forward-chaining.

The second claim is evident, given the structure of the rules in $\vdash'$ (all the rules in $\vdash'$ are suitable for forward-chaing). The right-to-left direction of the first claim comes from the fact that the rules whose conclusions are non-goal formulas are rules from the original system, weakened by adding extra hypotheses. The other direction is a consequence of the following lemma:

Lemma 2 *If $\Gamma \vdash t$ then $\boxdot t, \Gamma \vdash' t$; we then have $t \vdash' t$ if there exists a normal derivation $\Gamma \vdash t$ that does not end with a composition rule.*

[2] A stronger constraint is that when a composition rule is used to produce a principal premise of a decomposition rule, both rules can be removed (i.e., it is never necessary to compose some object to split it up afterwards); doing so until impossible yields a *normal derivation*. This is the case for BAN logic and the simple system of rules expressing the knowledge that is derivable from some piece of data by pairing, projection, encryption and decryption. However, this constraint is unnecessarily strong, and for instance fails to capture logics where this condition is not true for all composition-decomposition pairs, but where the remaining pairs can be transformed into a decomposition rule, such as GNY logic (see part 3.2). We call that last condition the **strong normal derivation criterion**.

The proof is by induction on the structure of a normal derivation of $\Gamma \vdash t$:

- for axioms, it is evident;
- if the bottom rule is a composition rule
$$\frac{\mathcal{H}_1 \cdots \mathcal{H}_n}{t},$$
because we have $\boxdot t$ we can apply the corresponding rule
$$\frac{\boxdot t \quad \mathcal{H}_1 \cdots \mathcal{H}_n}{t}$$
at the bottom of the derivations of $\boxdot\mathcal{H}_i, \Gamma \vdash' \mathcal{H}_i$ of the induction hypothesis; the $\boxdot\mathcal{H}_i$ are derived using
$$\frac{\boxdot\mathcal{C}}{\boxdot\mathcal{H}_1 \cdots \boxdot\mathcal{H}_n};$$
- if the bottom rule is a decomposition rule
$$\frac{\mathcal{D}_1 \cdots \mathcal{D}_m \quad \mathcal{K}_1 \cdots \mathcal{K}_n}{t}$$
then for any i the sub-derivation of $\mathcal{D}_i$ is normal and does not end with a composition rule (we act on a normal derivation); then we have $\Gamma \vdash' \mathcal{D}_i$; we then use the triggering rule
$$\frac{\mathcal{D}_1 \cdots \mathcal{D}_m}{\boxdot\mathcal{K}_1 \cdots \boxdot\mathcal{K}_n}$$
and the induction hypothesis to get the $\boxdot\mathcal{K}_i, \Gamma \vdash' \mathcal{K}_i$; we apply the original decomposition rule at the bottom of these.

3 Application to GNY logic

As the treatment of BAN logic by our method is very similar to that of GNY logic, and BAN is simpler, we deal here with GNY logic.

3.1 Definitions

The GNY logic [6], named after its authors, Li Gong [5], Roger Needham and Raphael Yahalom is a logic of belief similar to BAN, but which addresses some deficiencies in that latter one; among other things, it addresses unencrypted message parts and includes a notion of recognizability.

We use the rules from [6], plus the following rule, which was forgotten in the original paper

$$\frac{P \triangleleft (X \rightsquigarrow Y)}{P \triangleleft X} \text{ TZ}$$

that is, if a principal is told a message meaning something, it is told that message. This rule is necessary to do the analysis of the Needham-Shroeder protocol found in [6].

GNY logic has two peculiar features that need special treatment:

The rationality rule All the rules of the logic may be applied with any preceding chain of belief modality. That is, for all rule
$$\frac{\mathcal{H}_1 \quad \dots \quad \mathcal{H}_n}{\mathcal{C}}$$
and new principal variable name P, we have a rule
$$\frac{P \models \mathcal{H}_1 \quad \dots \quad P \models \mathcal{H}_n}{P \models \mathcal{C}}$$
We consider the closure of the rules by this meta-rule.

Rewrites The set of formulas is quotiented by the following rewrites (or simplifications):

- $\{\{X\}_K\}_K^{-1} \longrightarrow X$
- $\{\{X\}_{+K}\}_{-K} \longrightarrow X$

This system R is confluent and terminating, and we'll call the normal forms of formulas under these rewrites their **canonical forms**.

We will show in the next subsection that these features can be accommodated within our framework.

3.2 The set of rules and our additions

We first divide the rules of GNY logic into three categories:

Decomposition rules such as rule T3
$$\frac{\boxed{P \triangleleft \{X\}_K} \quad P \ni K}{P \triangleleft X}$$
The principal premiss is shown within a frame.

Composition rules such as rule P6
$$\frac{P \ni X \quad P \ni K}{P \ni \{X\}_K \quad P \ni \{X\}_K^{-1}}$$
These rules make a syntactically defined measure (see tab. 1) decrease.

Equivalence rules Equivalence rules such as F5
$$\frac{\boxed{P \models \sharp(+K)}}{P \models \sharp(-K)}$$
are handled like composition rules.

We then have to deal with the rewrites. These are problematic; for instance, we have

$$\cfrac{\cfrac{P \ni K \quad P \ni \{X\}_K}{P \ni \{\{X\}_K\}_K^{-1}} \text{ P6}}{P \ni X} \text{ simplification}$$

t	$\mathcal{M}(t)$
Beliefs and conveyance	
$P \mid\equiv X$	$\mathcal{M}(X)$
$P \lhd X$	$20 + \mathcal{M}(X)$
$P \ni X$	$\mathcal{M}(X)$
$P \mid\sim X$	$3 + \mathcal{M}(X)$
Properties of formulas	
$\sharp(X)$	$2 + \mathcal{M}(X)$
$\phi(X)$	$\mathcal{M}(X)$
Keys and secrets	
$P \overset{S}{\longleftrightarrow} Q$	0
$\overset{+P}{\mapsto} P$	0
$+K$	0
$-K$	0
Message constructors	
$\{X\}_K$	$3 + \mathcal{M}(X) + \mathcal{M}(K)$
$\{X\}_K^{-1}$	$3 + \mathcal{M}(X) + \mathcal{M}(K)$
(X, Y)	$1 + \mathcal{M}(X) + \mathcal{M}(Y)$
$F(X, Y)$	$2 + \mathcal{M}(X) + \mathcal{M}(Y)$
$H(X)$	$2 + \mathcal{M}(X)$
Jurisdiction	
$P \mid\Rightarrow X$	$1 + \mathcal{M}(X)$
$P \mid\Rightarrow P \mid\equiv \star$	0
$(X \rightsquigarrow C)$	$\mathcal{M}(X) + \mathcal{M}(C)$
Detection of replays	
$\star X$	$1 + \mathcal{M}(X)$
Proof direction	
$\boxdot X$	$1 + \mathcal{M}(X)$

Table 1. The measure $\mathcal{M}$ used, defined inductively on the formulas.

That is, we sometimes have to construct the decryption of a piece of data just to apply a simplification rule. We add a rule P6' standing for the former derivation:

$$\frac{\boxed{P \ni \{X\}_K} \quad P \ni K}{P \ni X}$$

We add similar rules in similar other cases, making up the $\vdash_+$ derivation system. $\vdash_+$ does not include rewrites. $\vdash_+$ is therefore made up of the rules found in [6], plus the following decomposition rules:

$$\frac{\boxed{P \ni \{X\}_K} \quad P \ni K}{P \ni X}\ \text{P6'}$$

$$\frac{\boxed{P \ni \{X\}_{+K}} \quad P \ni -K}{P \ni X}\ \text{P8'}$$

$$\frac{\boxed{P \mid\equiv \sharp(\{X\}_K)} \quad P \ni K}{P \mid\equiv \sharp(X)}\ \text{F2'}$$

$$\frac{\boxed{P \mid\equiv \sharp(\{X\}_{+K})} \quad P \ni -K}{P \mid\equiv \sharp(X)}\ \text{F4'}$$

$$\frac{\boxed{P \mid\equiv \phi(\{X\}_K)} \quad P \ni K}{P \mid\equiv \phi(X)}\ \text{R2'}$$

$$\frac{\boxed{P \mid\equiv \phi(\{X\}_{+K})} \quad P \ni -K}{P \mid\equiv \phi(X)}\ \text{R4'}$$

If $\vdash$ is GNY logic, consisting of the rules and the rewrites, we then state the following:

Property 3 *For all set of formulas Γ and formula t, $\Gamma \vdash t$ if and only if $C(\Gamma) \vdash C(t)$ where $C(f)$ denotes the canonical form under the rewrites of a formula or set of formulas.*

The proof is by induction on the structure of a derivation of $\Gamma \vdash t$. All pairs of rewrites and rules are considered; the only annoying cases are rules P6, P8, F2, F4, R2, R4; in these cases the sequence

$$\cfrac{\begin{array}{ccc} \vdots\ \Delta_1 & & \vdots\ \Delta_m \\ H_1 & \cdots & H_m \end{array}}{\cfrac{C'}{C}\ \text{rewrite}}\ R$$

gets collapsed into

$$\dfrac{\begin{array}{c}\vdots\ \Delta_1\\ H_1\end{array}\quad\cdots\quad\begin{array}{c}\vdots\ \Delta_m\\ H_m\end{array}}{C}\ R'.$$

We also have the following important property

Property 4 *$\vdash_+$ matches the normal derivation criterion.*

Again, the proof is by induction on the structure of the derivation, by considering all pairs of composition rules and decomposition rules. All pairs of composition and decomposition rules that constitute a cut (as defined in 2.2.1) can be collapsed. For instance

$$\dfrac{\dfrac{\begin{array}{c}\vdots\ \Delta_1\\ P \ni X\end{array}\quad\begin{array}{c}\vdots\ \Delta_2\\ P \ni K\end{array}}{P \ni \{X\}_K}\ \text{P6}\qquad\begin{array}{c}\vdots\ \Delta_3\\ P \ni K\end{array}}{P \ni X}\ \text{P6'}$$

is collapsed into

$$\begin{array}{c}\vdots\ \Delta_1\\ P \ni X\end{array}$$

3.3 Transformation into a forward-chaining system

We apply our transformation (section 2.2) to the $\vdash_+$ system of rules, getting the $\vdash'_+$ system of rules.

The measure $\mathcal{M}$ we've defined (see tab. 1) over the formulas of this logic, then satisfies the following strict decreasing property:

Property 5 *For each rule*

$$\frac{\mathcal{H}_1 \cdots \mathcal{H}_n}{\mathcal{C}}$$

of $\vdash'_+$, except the equivalence rules, we have:

$$\mathcal{M}(\mathcal{C}) \leq \max\{\mathcal{M}(\mathcal{H}_1), \ldots, \mathcal{M}(\mathcal{H}_n)\} - 1.$$

This property is very important, since it ensures the finiteness of the search space, as it is explained below, and thus the termination of the method. We chose the measure *ad hoc* for this.

At first sight, it would seem that because of the "rationality rule", an infinite number of rules exist in GNY; that is, for any rule

$$\frac{H_1 \ldots H_n}{C}$$

there exists the infinity of rules

$$\frac{S.H_1 \ldots S.H_n}{S.C}$$

where S is a sequence of "believes" modalities $P_i \models \ldots$. But in a given problem, only a finite number of these rules needs to be considered. This is a consequence of the above property: since the belief modalities weigh in the measure of the formulas, and the measure of the formulas always decreases in the derivation, then we can bound the length of the chains of belief modalities to be taken into account.

Theorem 6 *The following strategy:*

- *rewrite (by the rewriting system R) until normalization all formulas in $\Gamma \cup \{t\}$; we will assume in the next step that these formulas are normalized;*
- *initialize the system with a set $\Gamma \cup \{\boxdot t\}$;*
- *iteratively, apply all the possible rules to the formulas in the set and add the consequences to the set, until a fixpoint is reached;*
- *test whether t is in the set*

decides whether $\Gamma \vdash t$.

- It **terminates**, since the set of generated formulas is finitely bounded and we stop once we don't add any new formula. This set is finite because we only build a bounded number of derivations:
  - there exists a finite number of rules that can be applied, since there is a finite number of rules in the logic without the rationality rule and there is a upper bound on the depth of the modality chains generated by the rationality rule;
  - the number of steps (that is, applied rules) in such a derivation is bounded because:
    - the number of non-equivalence steps is bounded, because of property 5;
    - the number of equivalence steps is bounded too, because equivalence classes are finite and our system cannot derive already derived formulas;
- It is **complete** and **correct**, following from property 3 and theorem 1 (which applies because of property 4).

The reader should not be confused by the fact that no computation of measure happens in our algorithm. The measure is solely a construct for the proof of termination of the algorithm.

4 A practical implementation

We implemented the aforementioned algorithm as a program in ML[3]. As we achieved adequate performance using relatively simple optimizations, discussed below, we didn't feel the need for more ambitious and complex implementation techniques, like BBDs.

4.1 Our algorithm

Our algorithm proceeds by iterations up to a fixpoint (see Fig. 2). The iterated procedure takes a current set S and outputs a set $S' \supset S$. How to implement the rationality rule ? We could of course compute the aforementioned (section 3.3) bound on the length of the belief modality chains to be considered. A more clever tactic, which is used in our implementation, is the following: consider $P = \{p \in S \mid \exists X\ p \models X \in S\}$; for each $p \in P$, consider $S_p = \{X \mid p \models X \in S\}$ and apply Z recursively, yielding S'_p; then $S' = S \cup W(S) \cup \{p \models X \mid p \in P \wedge X \in S'_p\}$ where $W(S)$ is the set of all conclusions that one may get by applying each rule to elements of S.

A side-effect of this transformation from $\vdash$ to $\vdash_+$ is that in the case of failure, the system may give some crude clues as what extra assumptions would have been needed: just collect the formulas f so that $f \neq t$ and $\boxdot f$ but not f have been derived; some further filtering may be necessary to produce a reasonably small number of hints for the user.

Extracting $\vdash_+$ proofs from the $\vdash'_+$ proofs (which contain "goal" operators) yielded by that techniques is simple, and our implementation does so before pretty-printing the proofs. It is easy to see that, given a proof of $\Gamma, \boxdot t \vdash'_+ t$, one can extract a proof of $\Gamma \vdash_+ t$ by pruning out all branches whose root is a "goal" formula. One can get $\vdash$ proofs, that is, pure GNY proofs, by simply expanding the rules we added to GNY to form $\vdash_+$ into GNY proof trees.

4.2 Avoiding combinatorial explosion

In this subsection, we do not consider the rationality rule, which is discussed in the previous subsection.

Implementing a working forward-chaining strategy for this problem is not as trivial as it seems. For instance, trying all possible rules in the fashion that to try a n-ary rule you match it against all the n-tuples of already derived formulas, until it ends, leads to prohibitive costs (in our case, $n = 6$, which makes the number of matchings grow in D^7, where D is the number of derivable formulas).

A first optimization we tried was based on the fact that one need not test all possible n-tuples, but only ones containing at least one "new" formula; that is, a formula made during the last application of the rules. This is not sufficient, since it reduces only to D^6; experimentally, this is far too slow.

Our implementation is based on the fact that to instantiate all the variables in a rule, you need not consider all the hypotheses; especially, in the modified versions of the composition rules, only one "goal" hypothesis suffices; in the decomposition and trigger rules, only the principal premisses are needed. Expensive exhaustive searches for the fully instantiated hypotheses are replaced by a much faster binary search.

Our algorithm is in Fig. 2.

To refine that algorithm even more, the pattern matching over d-tuples is replaced by d successive pattern matchings, and any failure of one the k searches ends the search process with a negative answer.

Such an algorithm is at most in $D^{d+1}(\log D)^k$, where $d = 2$ and $k = 4$ in the case of GNY logic.

Another obvious improvement is to consider only tuples of premisses where at least one is new, that is, has been added at the last iteration.

Obviously, more clever implementation techniques using, for instance, BDD-like data structures, could be more

do
    for all rule R having d principal premisses
                        k auxiliary premisses
    do
        for all d-tuple D of "old" formulas
        do
            if D matches the principal premisses pattern
            then
                if the auxiliary premisses are in
                  the "old" formulas
                then put the conclusions into
                      the "new" formulas
    add the "new" formulas that were not already in
    the "old" formulas to the "old" formulas
until no more formulas are added

Figure 2. Practical GNY logic decision procedure.

[3] More precisely, it is written in Objective CAML, on which more information is available from `http://pauillac.inria.fr/ocaml`. A first ML program reads the set of GNY rules and outputs some other ML code expressing them, using the ML pattern matching facility. The resulting code, along with some parsing and control modules, is then compiled, resulting in an executable gnytool. gnytool takes an input of the protocol, the assumptions, and the purported conclusions, expressed in an ASCII syntax for GNY formulas, and outputs some pretty-printed LaTeX version of it, along with a pretty-printed version of the derivations produced for the proved conclusions. The total source code length is approximately 2700 lines long.

efficient. We didn't investigate these, since our implementation achieved good performances on realistic problems.

4.3 Example

We ran our automatic analyzer on, among other things, a version of the Needham-Shroeder protocol (tab. 2). This analysis took 0.3 second on a 400 Mhz Pentium-II machine[4], taking only 1.6 megabytes of memory, including the runtime system.

4.3.1 Assumptions

A $P \ni K_{ps}$

B $P \ni N_p$

C $P \models P \overset{K_{ps}}{\longleftrightarrow} S$

D $P \models \sharp(N_p)$

E $P \models \phi(Q)$

F $Q \ni K_{qs}$

G $Q \ni N_q$

H $Q \models Q \overset{K_{qs}}{\longleftrightarrow} S$

I $Q \models \sharp(N_q)$

J $Q \models \phi(N_q)$

K $P \models S \mid\!\Rightarrow P \overset{K}{\longleftrightarrow} Q$

L $P \models S \mid\!\Rightarrow S \models \star$

M $P \models Q \mid\!\Rightarrow Q \models \star$

N $Q \models S \mid\!\Rightarrow P \overset{K}{\longleftrightarrow} Q$

O $Q \models S \mid\!\Rightarrow S \models \star$

P $Q \models P \mid\!\Rightarrow P \models \star$

Q $S \ni K_{ps}$

R $S \ni K_{qs}$

S $S \ni K$

T $S \models P \overset{K_{ps}}{\longleftrightarrow} S$

U $S \models Q \overset{K_{qs}}{\longleftrightarrow} S$

V $S \models P \overset{K}{\longleftrightarrow} Q$

4.3.2 Goals

- $P \models P \overset{K}{\longleftrightarrow} Q$
- $P \ni N_q$

[4]Using `ocamlopt -inline 2` for compilation, with OCaml version 2.00

4.3.3 Derivation

obtained automatically
$P \models P \overset{K}{\longleftrightarrow} Q$,
  applying rule J1 to:
 $P \models S \mid\!\Rightarrow P \overset{K}{\longleftrightarrow} Q$,
  from hypothesis **K**.
 $P \models S \models P \overset{K}{\longleftrightarrow} Q$,
  applying rule J3 to:
 $P \models S \models S \models P \overset{K}{\longleftrightarrow} Q$,
  applying rule J2 to:
 $P \models S \mid\!\sim \left(\star \{(K, P)\}_{K_{qs}} \leadsto S \models P \overset{K}{\longleftrightarrow} Q\right)$,

⋮ ⋮ ⋮ ⋮ ⋮

This is an excerpt from the 100-line pretty-printed output[5] of the analysis.

4.4 Other examples

Following [3, part 4], we analyzed some properties of the Otway-Rees protocol; the analysis, on the same hardware, took 0.08 s.

A previous implementation using the same method, this time of BAN logic [3] inside the PVS theorem prover [16], using its forward-chaining capability, allowed us to check mechanically the results of [3], on:

- the Otway-Rees protocol,
- the Needham-Shroeder shared-keys protocol,
- the wide-mouthed frog protocol,
- the Kerberos protocol (let's note that there's a slight error in [3]: one has to add the reasonable hypothesis $A \models \sharp(N_a)$ to get $A \models B \models A \models A \overset{K_{ab}}{\longleftrightarrow} B$),
- the Needham-Shroeder public-key protocol (the rule

  $$\frac{P \models \langle X \rangle_Y \quad P \models \sharp(Y)}{P \models \sharp(\langle X \rangle_Y)}$$

  which is consistent with the informal semantics of the logic, has to be added to reach the conclusions given in [3]).

This implementation, being made in a general system, was of course significantly slower than the one we wrote for GNY, and the implementation of some of the GNY capabilities looked difficult in that context.

[5]The LaTeX macros used in the outputs of our implementation and in this paper are available from `http://www.csl.sri.com/~monniaux/download/ban-gny.sty.tar.gz`.

1	$P \rightarrow S$	$(\star P, \star Q, \star N_p)$
2	$S \rightarrow P$	$\left(\star\left\{\left(N_p, Q, \star K, \left(\star\{(K,P)\}_{K_{qs}} \rightsquigarrow S \models P \overset{K}{\leftrightarrow} Q\right)\right)\right\}_{K_{ps}} \rightsquigarrow S \models P \overset{K}{\leftrightarrow} Q\right)$
3	$P \rightarrow Q$	$\left(\star\{(\star K, \star P)\}_{K_{qs}} \rightsquigarrow S \models P \overset{K}{\leftrightarrow} Q\right)$
4	$Q \rightarrow P$	$\star\{\star N_q\}_K$
5	$P \rightarrow Q$	$\left(\star\{\star F(N_q)\}_K \rightsquigarrow P \models P \overset{K}{\leftrightarrow} Q\right)$

Table 2. The Needham-Shroeder protocol steps, in GNY logic

4.5 Generalization

How are the above techniques generalizable to other similar logics? The general method we've given: test whether $\Gamma \vdash t$ by generating all $\vdash'$-conclusions from $\Gamma \cup \{\boxdot t\}$ and testing whether t belongs to them, works as long as:

- $\vdash$ fulfills the normal derivation criterion;
- for any Λ, the set of formulas that are $\vdash'$-derivable from Λ is finite.

This second condition is ensured by the existence of a well-founded preorder $\preccurlyeq$ so that

- for any formula X, $X \prec \boxdot X$;
- for any decomposition rule
$$\frac{\mathcal{D}_1 \cdots \mathcal{D}_m \quad \mathcal{K}_1 \cdots \mathcal{K}_n}{\mathcal{C}},$$
whose set of variables is Ξ, and any instanciation ξ, for any $F \in \{\mathcal{C}[\xi/\Xi], \boxdot\mathcal{K}_1[\xi/\Xi], \ldots, \boxdot\mathcal{K}_n[\xi/\Xi]\}$ there exists $H \in \{\mathcal{D}_1[\xi/\Xi], \ldots, \mathcal{D}_m[\xi/\Xi]\}$ so that $F \prec H$.

For GNY logic, we chose $x \preccurlyeq y \iff \mathcal{M}(x) \leq \mathcal{M}(y)$.

5 Conclusions

We have a general framework for deciding authentication logics, encompassing BAN and GNY logics. This framework is flexible and likely to handle other similar logics.

Particularizing our method on well-known authentication logics, we implemented a decision procedure for BAN logic in a general-purpose forward-chaining system, which we used to mechanically check the results in the reference paper on this logic, and we implemented a special-purpose decision procedure for GNY logic. This latter system decided GNY problems found in related papers using little time (a fraction of a second) and memory space.

In our opinion, this tool can be integrated in a general environment for the analysis of cryptographic protocols, as a fast analysis that, applied first, before more expensive methods, can help detecting some bugs in protocol specifications, particularly unwanted assumptions.

Acknowledgements

We wish to thank Jonathan K. Millen for his valuable help in making the paper clearer, John Rushby for inviting us to his group at SRI International, the OCaml team and all the people working on LaTeX packages and related tools.

References

[1] S. H. Brackin. Deciding cryptographic protocol adequacy with HOL. In *IWHOLTP: 8th International Workshop on Higher Order Logic Theorem Proving and Its Applications*, volume 971 of *Lecture Notes in Computer Science*. Springer-Verlag, 1995.

[2] S. H. Brackin. Automatic formal analyses of cryptographic protocols. In *NISSC: 19th National Information Systems Security Conference*, pages I.181 – 193, Baltimore, MD, October 1996. National Institute of Standards and Technology and National Computer Security Center.

[3] M. Burrows, M. Abadi, and R. Needham. A logic of authentication. Technical Report 39, Digital Equipment Corporation, Systems Research Centre, Feb. 1989.

[4] J. Girard. *Proofs and Types*. Cambridge University Press, 1990. Translated and with appendices by Paul Taylor, Yves Lafont.

[5] L. Gong. *Cryptographic Protocols for Distributed Systems*. PhD thesis, University of Cambridge, Cambridge, England, April 1990.

[6] L. Gong, R. Needham, and R. Yahalom. Reasoning about belief in cryptographic protocols. In *IEEE Symposium on Research in Security and Privacy*, pages 234–248, Oakland, California, May 1990. IEEE Computer Society, IEEE Computer Society Press.

[7] J. W. Gray and J. McLean. Using Temporal Logic to Specify and Verify Cryptographic Protocols (progress report). In *America in the Age of Information, National Science and Technology Council Committee on Information and Communications Forum*, Bethesda, 1995.

[8] D. Kindred and J. M. Wing. Fast, automatic checking of security protocols. In *Second USENIX Workshop on Electronic Commerce*, pages 41–52, Oakland, California, Nov. 1996. USENIX.

[9] G. Lowe and B. Roscoe. Using CSP to detect Errors in the TMN Protocol. *IEEE Transactions on Software Engineering*, 23(10):659–669, 1997.

[10] W. Marrero, E. Clarke, and S. Jha. Model checking for security protocols. Technical Report CMU-SCS-97-139, Carnegie Mellon University, May 1997.

[11] C. Meadows. The NRL Protocol Analyzer: An Overview. *Journal of Logic Programming*, 1995. To appear.

[12] J. K. Millen and H.-P. Ko. Narrowing terminates for encryption. In *Computer Security Foundations Workshop*, 1996.

[13] J. Mitchell, M. Mitchell, and U. Stern. Automated analysis of cryptographic protocols using murphi. In *IEEE Symp. Security and Privacy*, pages 141–153, Oakland, 1997.

[14] L. C. Paulson. Proving properties of security protocols by induction. In *10th Computer Security Foundations Workshop*, pages 70–83. IEEE Computer Society Press, 1997.

[15] J. Schumann. Automatic verification of cryptographic protocols with SETHEO. In W. McCune, editor, *14th Conference on Automated Deduction (CADE)*, volume 1249 of *Lecture Notes in Computer Science*. Springer-Verlag, 1997.

[16] SRI International, Computer Science Laboratory. *Overview of the PVS Verification System.*

[17] P. Syverson. Adding time to a logic of authentication. In *1st ACM Conference on Computer and Communications Security*, pages 97–101, 1993.

[18] P. Syverson and P. C. van Oorschot. On unifying some cryptographic protocol logics. In *1994 IEEE Computer Society Symposium on Research in Security and Privacy*, pages 14–28, May 1994.

A Meta-notation for Protocol Analysis*

I. Cervesato N.A. Durgin P.D. Lincoln J.C. Mitchell A. Scedrov

Computer Science Lab
SRI International
Menlo Park, CA
lincoln@csl.sri.com

Computer Science Dept.
Stanford University
Stanford, CA 94305-9045
{iliano, nad, jcm}@cs.stanford.edu

Mathematics Dept.
University of Pennsylvania
Philadelphia, PA
andre@cis.upenn.edu

Abstract

Most formal approaches to security protocol analysis are based on a set of assumptions commonly referred to as the "Dolev-Yao model." In this paper, we use a multiset rewriting formalism, based on linear logic, to state the basic assumptions of this model. A characteristic of our formalism is the way that existential quantification provides a succinct way of choosing new values, such as new keys or nonces. We define a class of theories in this formalism that correspond to finite-length protocols, with a bounded initialization phase but allowing unboundedly many instances of each protocol role (e.g., client, server, initiator, or responder). Undecidability is proved for a restricted class of these protocols, and PSPACE*-completeness is claimed for a class further restricted to have no new data (nonces). Since it is a fragment of linear logic, we can use our notation directly as input to linear logic tools, allowing us to do proof search for attacks with relatively little programming effort, and to formally verify protocol transformations and optimizations.*

1 Introduction

In the literature on security protocol design and analysis, protocols are commonly described using an informal notation that leaves many properties of a protocol unspecified. For example, a short challenge-response section of a protocol might be written like this:

$$\begin{array}{ll} A \longrightarrow B: & \{n\}_K \\ B \longrightarrow A: & \{f(n)\}_K \end{array}$$

In this notation, a message of the form $\{x\}_y$ consists of a plaintext x encrypted with key y. In this example protocol, Alice chooses a random number n and sends its encryption to Bob. There is no specific indication of how Bob determines what to send in response, but we can see that Bob returns a message that contains the encryption of $f(n)$. By analogy with familiar protocols, we might assume that he decrypts the message he receives to determine n, then applies f to n and returns the result to Alice (encrypted with the same key).

As written, the protocol description only gives an intended trace or family of traces involving the honest principals. There is no standard way of determining the initial conditions or assumptions about shared information, nor can we see how the principals will respond to messages that differ from those explicitly written. For example, in the case at hand, we must explain in English that K is assumed to be a shared key and that n is generated by Alice. Otherwise, it is a perfectly reasonable interpretation of the two lines above that Alice and Bob initially share a number n. In this case, Alice might send $\{n\}_K$ to Bob, with Bob returning $\{f(n)\}_K$ to Alice only if he receives precisely $\{n\}_K$. While the two readings of the protocol give the same sequence of messages when no one interferes with network transmission, the effects are different if an intruder intercepts the message from Alice to Bob and replaces it with another message. For this reason, the notation commonly found in the literature does not provide a precise basis for security protocol analysis.

Most formal approaches to protocol analysis are based on a relatively abstract set of modeling assumptions, commonly referred to as the "Dolev-Yao model," which appear to have developed from positions taken by Needham and Schroeder [26] and a model presented by Dolev and Yao [11]. In this approach, messages are composed of indivisible abstract values, not sequences of bits, and encryption is modeled in an idealized way. Although the same basic modeling assumptions are used in theorem proving [27], model-checking methods [18, 20, 25, 28, 29] and symbolic search

*Partially supported by DoD MURI "Semantic Consistency in Information Exchange" as ONR Grant N00014-97-1-0505, and by NSF Grants CCR-9509931, CCR-9629754, and CCR-9800785 to various authors.

tools [17], there does not appear to be any standard presentation of the Dolev-Yao model as it is currently used in a variety of projects. One goal of this paper is to identify the modeling assumptions using the simplest formalism possible, so that the strengths and weaknesses of the Dolev-Yao model can be analyzed, apart from properties of logics or automated tools in which the model is commonly used.

While we began with the idea of creating a new formalism for this purpose, we naturally gravitated toward some form of rewriting, so that protocol execution could be carried out symbolically. In addition to rewriting to effect state transitions, we also needed a way to choose new values, such as nonces or keys. While this seems difficult to achieve directly in standard rewriting formalisms, the proof rules associated with existential quantification appears to be just what is required. Therefore, we have adopted a notation, first presented in [24], that may be regarded as either an extension of multiset rewriting (see, e.g., [3, 4]), with existential quantification, or a Horn fragment of linear logic [14]. A similar fragment of linear logic is used in [16] to represent real-time finite-state systems. Two other efforts using linear logic to model the state-transition aspect of protocols (but not existential quantification for nonces) are [8, 9].

Using this formalism, it is relatively straightforward to characterize the Dolev-Yao intruder and associated cryptographic assumptions. The formalism also seems appropriate for analyzing the complexity of protocol problems, and as a potential intermediate language for systems or approaches that might combine several different protocol analysis tools. We develop a format for presenting finite-length protocols, as the disjoint union of a set of initialization rules and sets of independent transition rules for each protocol participant. Using this form of protocol theory, we show that secrecy is an undecidable property even if data constructors, message depth, message width, number of distinct roles, role length, and depth of encryption are bounded by constants. If any of these restrictions are lifted, prior results, folklore, or a small amount of thought can be used to show undecidability, but we show even for the very small fragment with only nonces secrecy is undecidable. Finally, we have used a linear logic tool, *LLF* [5] in two ways. The first is to search executions of a protocol and intruder for protocol flaws. While symbolic search by a logic programming tool is not as efficient as optimized search by tools such as Murφ[10], this method does have the advantage that the input is substantially easier to prepare. The second use of LLF is to formally verify proofs of protocol optimizations. This provides a basis for simplifying search-based analysis and theorem-proving analysis of protocols.

2 Multiset rewriting with existential quantification

2.1 Protocol Notation

The notation we use involves *facts* and *transitions*. Our facts are first-order atomic formulas, and transitions are given by rewrite rules containing a precondition and postcondition. One important property of this formalism is that in applying a rule to a collection of facts, each fact that occurs in the precondition of the rule is removed. This gives us a direct way of representing state transitions, and provides the basis for the connection with linear logic. Another key property is that the postconditions of a rule may contain existentially quantified variables. Following the standard proof rules associated with existential quantification (in natural deduction or sequent-style systems), this provides a mechanism for choosing new values that are distinct from any other in the system.

More formally, our syntax involves terms, facts and rules. If we want to represent a system in this notation, we begin by choosing a vocabulary, or *first-order signature.* This is a standard notion from many-sorted algebra or first-order logic (see, e.g., [13, section 4.3].) As usual, the *terms* over a signature are the well-formed expressions produced by applying functions to arguments of the correct sort. A *fact* is a first-order atomic formula over the chosen signature. This means that a fact is the result of applying a predicate symbol to terms of the correct sorts. A *state* is a multiset of facts (all over the same signature).

A state transition is a *rule* written using two multisets of facts, and existential quantification, in the following syntactic form:

$$F_1, \ldots, F_k \longrightarrow \exists x_1 \ldots \exists x_j . G_1, \ldots, G_n$$

The meaning of this rule is that if some state S contains facts $F_1, \ldots F_k$, then one possible next state is the state S' that is similar to S, but with:

- facts $F_1, \ldots F_k$ removed,
- $G_1, \ldots G_m$ added, where $x_1 \ldots x_j$ are replaced by new symbols.

While existential quantification does not semantically imply there exist "new" values with certain properties, standard proof rules for manipulating existential quantifiers require introduction of fresh symbols (sometimes called Skolem constants), as described below.

If there are free variables in the rule $F_1, \ldots, F_k \longrightarrow \exists x_1 \ldots \exists x_j . G_1, \ldots, G_n$, these are treated as universally quantified throughout the rule. In an application of a rule, these variables may be replaced by any terms. To give a quick example, consider the following state, S, and rule, R:

$$
\begin{array}{rcl}
S & = & \{P(f(a)), P(b)\} \\
R & = & (\, P(x) \longrightarrow \exists z.\, Q(f(x), z)\,)
\end{array}
$$

One possible next state is obtained by instantiating the rule R to $P(f(a)) \longrightarrow \exists z.\, Q(f(f(a)), z)$. Applying this rule, we choose a new value, c, for z and replace $P(f(a))$ by $Q(f(f(a)), c)$. This gives us the state

$$S' = \{Q(f(f(a)), c), P(b)\}$$

The importance of existential quantification, for security protocols, is that it provides a direct mechanism for choosing a new value that is different from other values used in the execution of a system. Since many protocols involve choosing fresh nonces, fresh encryption keys, and so on, existential quantification seems like a useful primitive for describing security protocols.

The way that existential quantification is used in our formalism is based on the existential elimination rule from natural deduction. This proof rule is commonly written as follows.

$$
(\exists\ \textbf{elim}) \qquad \frac{\exists x.\phi \qquad \begin{array}{c}[y/x]\phi \\ \vdots \\ \psi\end{array}}{\psi} \qquad \begin{array}{l} y \text{ not free in any} \\ \text{other hypothesis}\end{array}
$$

If we have an existentially quantified axiom, $\exists x.\phi$, then this rule says that if we wish to prove some formula ψ, we can choose a new symbol y for the "x that is presumed to exist" and proceed to derive ψ from $[y/x]\phi$. The side condition "y not free in any other hypothesis in the proof of ψ" means that the only hypothesis in the proof of ψ that can contain y is the hypothesis $[y/x]\phi$.

2.2 Simplified Needham-Schroeder

As a means of explaining the Dolev-Yao intruder and encryption models using our notation, we begin with an overly simplified form of the Needham-Schroeder public-key protocol [26]. Without encryption, the core part of the Needham-Schroeder protocol proceeds as follows:

$$
\begin{array}{ccccl}
A & \longrightarrow & B & : & N_a \\
B & \longrightarrow & A & : & N_a, N_b \\
A & \longrightarrow & B & : & N_b
\end{array}
$$

where N_a and N_b are fresh nonces, chosen by Alice (A) and Bob (B), respectively.

We can describe this simplified protocol in our notation using the predicates A_i, B_i, N_i for $0 \leq i \leq 3$, with the following intuitive meaning:

$$
\begin{array}{ll}
A_i(\,\dots) & \text{Alice in local state } i \text{, with the indicated data} \\
B_i(\,\dots) & \text{Bob in local state } i \text{, with indicated data} \\
N_i(\,\dots) & \text{Network has message } i \text{, with indicated data}
\end{array}
$$

The data associated with the state of some principal, or a network message, will depend on the particular state or message. Each principal begins in local state 0, with no data. Therefore, predicates A_0 and B_0 are predicates with no arguments. When Alice chooses a nonce, she moves into local state 1. Therefore, predicate A_1 is a predicate of one argument, intended to be the nonce chosen by Alice. Similarly, predicate B_1 has two arguments, the data received from Alice in message one of the protocol and the nonce chosen by Bob for his response.

Using these predicates, we can state the protocol using four transition rules:

$$
\begin{array}{rcl}
A_0() & \longrightarrow & \exists x. A_1(x), N_1(x) \\
B_0(), N_1(x) & \longrightarrow & \exists y. B_1(x,y), N_2(x,y) \\
A_1(x), N_2(x,y) & \longrightarrow & A_2(x,y), N_3(y) \\
B_1(x,y), N_3(y) & \longrightarrow & B_2(x,y)
\end{array}
$$

Each rule corresponds to an action by a principal. In the first rule, Alice chooses a nonce, sends it on the network, and remembers the nonce by moving into a local state that retains the nonce value. In the second step, Bob receives a message on the network, chooses his own nonce, transmits it and saves it in his local state. In the third step, Alice receives Bob's message and replies, while in the fourth step Bob receives Alice's final message and changes state.

In Table 1 is a sample trace generated from these rules, beginning from state A_0, B_0. Spacing is used to separate the facts that participate in each step from those that do not.

2.3 Formalizing the intruder

There are two main parts of the Dolev-Yao model as commonly used in protocol analysis. The first is the set of possible intruder actions, applied nondeterministically throughout execution of the protocol. The second is a "black-box" model of encryption and decryption. We explain the intruder actions here, with the encryption model presented in Section 2.4.

The protocol adversary or "intruder" may nondeterministically choose among the following actions at each step:

- Read any message and block further transmission,
- Decompose a message into parts and remember them,
- Generate fresh data as needed,
- Compose a new message from known data and send.

By combining a read with resend, we can easily obtain the effect of passively reading a message without preventing another party from also receiving it.

$$
\begin{array}{rrcll}
B_0(), & A_0() & \longrightarrow & A_1(\mathsf{nA}), N_1(\mathsf{nA}), & B_0() \\
A_1(\mathsf{nA}), & B_0(), N_1(\mathsf{nA}) & \longrightarrow & B_1(\mathsf{nA},\mathsf{nB}), N_2(\mathsf{nA},\mathsf{nB}), & A_1(\mathsf{nA}) \\
B_1(\mathsf{nA},\mathsf{nB}), & A_1(\mathsf{nA}), N_2(\mathsf{nA},\mathsf{nB}) & \longrightarrow & A_2(\mathsf{nA},\mathsf{nB}), N_3(\mathsf{nB}), & B_1(\mathsf{nA},\mathsf{nB}) \\
A_2(\mathsf{nA},\mathsf{nB}), & B_1(\mathsf{nA},\mathsf{nB}), N_3(\mathsf{nB}) & \longrightarrow & B_2(\mathsf{nA},\mathsf{nB}), & A_2(\mathsf{nA},\mathsf{nB})
\end{array}
$$

Table 1. Sample trace of simplified Needham-Schroeder

In general, the intruder processes data in three phases. The first is to read and decompose data into parts. The second is to remember parts of messages, and the third is to compose a message from parts it remembers. We illustrate the basic form of the intruder actions using one unary network-message predicate N_1 and one binary network-message predicate N_2. Using predicates D for decomposable messages and M for the intruder "memory", the basic rules for intercepting, decomposing and remembering messages are

$$
\begin{array}{lcl}
N_1(x) & \longrightarrow & D(x) \\
N_2(x,y) & \longrightarrow & D(x,y) \\
D(x,y) & \longrightarrow & D(x), D(y) \\
D(z) & \longrightarrow & M(z)
\end{array}
$$

While the predicate D may appear to be an unnecessary intermediary here, a protocol with more complicated messages will lead to more interesting ways of destructuring messages. As noted in [7], it is important in proof search to separate the decomposition phase from the composition phase, which is accomplished here using separate D and C predicates. The rules for composing messages from parts are written using the C, for "composable", predicate as follows:

$$
\begin{array}{lcl}
M(x) & \longrightarrow & C(x), M(x) \\
C(x) & \longrightarrow & N_1(x) \\
C(x), C(y) & \longrightarrow & C(x,y) \\
C(x,y) & \longrightarrow & N_2(x,y)
\end{array}
$$

The rule for generating new data is

$$\longrightarrow \exists x.M(x)$$

The reason we need the last transition rule (which can be applied any time without any hypothesis) is that the intruder may need to choose new data in order to trick an honest participant in a protocol. This is illustrated in the following attack on the simplified (and obviously insecure) form of the Needham-Schroeder protocol.

For the simplified example at hand, we can compose rules to eliminate the D and C predicates as follows:

$$
\begin{array}{lcl}
N_1(x) & \longrightarrow & M(x) \\
M(x) & \longrightarrow & N_1(x), M(x) \\
N_2(x,y) & \longrightarrow & M(x), M(y) \\
M(x), M(y) & \longrightarrow & N_2(x,y), M(x), M(y) \\
N_3(x) & \longrightarrow & M(x) \\
M(x) & \longrightarrow & N_3(x), M(x)
\end{array}
$$

This reduces the number of steps in the trace, shown in Table 2, which has actions of the honest participants in the left column and actions of the intruder indented. For simplicity, duplicate copies of $M(\ )$ facts are not shown, since these have no effect on the execution of the protocol or intruder.

In this attack, the intruder intercepts messages between A and B, replacing data so that the two principals have a different view of the messages that have been exchanged. Specifically, the intruder replaces Alice's nonce nA by a value n chosen by the intruder. When Bob responds to the altered message, the intruder intercepts the result and replaces n by nA so that Alice receives the message she expects.

2.4 Modeling Perfect Encryption

The commonly used "black-box" model of encryption may be written in our multiset notation using the following vocabulary. For concreteness, we discuss public-key encryption. Symmetric or private-key encryption can be characterized similarly. We assume that plaintexts have sort plain and ciphertexts have sort cipher.

- Additional sorts: e_key, d_key
- Predicate: Key_pair(e_key, d_key)
- Function: enc : e_key × plain → cipher

We could also include a decryption function dec : d_key × cipher → plain. However, it seems simpler to write protocols using pattern-matching (encryption on the left-hand-side of a rule) to express decryption.

$B_0(), A_0()$	Initial configuration
$\longrightarrow A_1(\mathsf{nA}), N_1(\mathsf{nA}), B_0()$	Alice chooses nonce and sends
$\longrightarrow A_1(\mathsf{nA}), B_0(), M(\mathsf{nA})$	Intruder intercepts message nA
$\longrightarrow A_1(\mathsf{nA}), B_0(), M(\mathsf{nA}), M(n)$	Intruder generates fresh value n
$\longrightarrow A_1(\mathsf{nA}), N_1(n), B_0(), M(\mathsf{nA}), M(n)$	Intruder sends n to Bob
$\longrightarrow B_1(n, \mathsf{nB}), N_2(n, \mathsf{nB}), A_1(\mathsf{nA}), M(\mathsf{nA}), M(n)$	Bob receives, generates nonce, replies
$\longrightarrow A_1(\mathsf{nA}), B_1(n, \mathsf{nB}), M(\mathsf{nA}), M(n), M(\mathsf{nB})$	Intruder intercepts message with n
$\longrightarrow A_1(\mathsf{nA}), N_2(\mathsf{nA}, \mathsf{nB}), B_1(n, \mathsf{nB}), M(\mathsf{nA}), M(n), M(\mathsf{nB})$	Intruder sends message with nA
$\longrightarrow A_2(\mathsf{nA}, \mathsf{nB}), N_3(\mathsf{nB}), B_1(n, \mathsf{nB}), M(\mathsf{nA}), M(n), M(\mathsf{nB})$	Alice receives and responds
$\longrightarrow B_2(n, \mathsf{nB}), A_2(\mathsf{nA}, \mathsf{nB}), M(\mathsf{nA}), M(n), M(\mathsf{nB})$	Bob changes to final state, indicating successful completion of protocol

Table 2. Sample attack on simplified Needham-Schroeder

Example The core Needham-Schroeder protocol with encryption begins with each principal generating and publishing a key pair. Therefore the "local state 0" predicate for each principal will contain a key pair. For example, Bob's initial actions can be stated as the following rules:

$$\begin{array}{rcl} & \longrightarrow & \exists k : \mathsf{e\_key}.\, \exists k' : \mathsf{d\_key}.\, B_0(k), \\ & & \mathsf{Key\_pair}(k, k') \\ B_0(k) & \longrightarrow & \mathsf{Announce}(k), B_0(k) \end{array}$$

The first rule (without hypotheses) lets Bob generate a key pair, while the second announces the public key so that other principals can choose to communicate with Bob. Alice similarly chooses and publishes her public key. After doing so, she chooses a principal to communicate with from the set of announced public keys and transmits a message.

$$\begin{array}{rcl} A_0(k), \mathsf{Announce}(k') & \longrightarrow & \exists x.\ A_1(k, k', x), \\ & & N_1(\mathsf{enc}(k', \langle x, k \rangle)), \\ & & \mathsf{Announce}(k') \end{array}$$

The following transition rule then allows Bob to decrypt the message from Alice.

$$\begin{array}{rcl} B_0(k), N_1(\mathsf{enc}(k, \langle x, k' \rangle)) & \longrightarrow & \exists y.\ B_1(k, k', x, y), \\ & & N_2(\mathsf{enc}(k', \langle x, y \rangle)) \end{array}$$

A complete presentation with slightly more general initialization steps is given in Appendix A, for the interested reader.

Intruder To model the encryption capabilities of the intruder, we add a decomposition and a composition rule to the intruder model. The decomposition rule allows the intruder to decrypt a message (or part of a message) when the decryption key is known.

$$\begin{array}{l} D(\mathsf{enc}(k,x)),\ \mathsf{Key\_pair}(k, k'),\ M(k') \\ \quad \longrightarrow \ D(x),\ \mathsf{Key\_pair}(k, k'),\ M(k') \end{array}$$

The composition rule allows the intruder to encrypt a message with any encryption key known to the intruder.

$$M(k),\ C(x) \longrightarrow C(\mathsf{enc}(k,x)),\ M(k)$$

3 Bounded protocols

It is relatively straightforward to use the multiset rewriting framework summarized in the preceding section to describe finite-state and infinite-state systems. Using function symbols, it is possible to describe computation over unbounded data types. In particular, it is easy to encode counter machines or Turing machines, implying that implication is undecidable. However, the principal authentication and secrecy protocols of interest are all of bounded length (see [6] for a relevant survey).

In order to study finite-length protocols more carefully, we identify the syntactic form of a class of well-founded protocol theories, called simply *well-founded theories* in this paper.

3.1 Creation, consumption, persistence

Some preliminary definitions involve the ways that a fact may be created, preserved, or consumed by a rule. While multiple copies of some facts may be needed in some derivations, we are able to eliminate the need for multiple copies of certain facts.

Definition 1. A rule $l \to r$ in a theory $\mathcal{T}$ *creates* P facts if some $P(\vec{t})$ occurs more times in r than in l. A rule $l \to r$ in a theory $\mathcal{T}$ *preserves* P facts if every $P(\vec{t})$ occurs the same number of times in r and l. A rule $l \to r$ in a theory $\mathcal{T}$ *consumes* P facts if some fact $P(\vec{t})$ occurs more times in l than in r. A predicate P in a theory $\mathcal{T}$ is *persistent* if every rule in $\mathcal{T}$ which contains P either creates or preserves P facts.

To give an example, a rule of form

$$P(\vec{x}) \to P(\vec{y})$$

does not preserve P facts, since it can be used to create a fact $P(\vec{t})$ and consume a fact $P(\vec{s})$.

Since a persistent fact is never consumed by any rule, there is no need to generate more than one copy of a particular fact – as long as that fact is never needed twice by a single rule. By simple transformation, it is possible to eliminate the need for more than one copy of any persistent fact. For example, a rule of form:

$$P(\vec{x}), P(\vec{y}), \ldots \to Q(\vec{x}, \vec{y}), P(\vec{x}), P(\vec{y}), \ldots$$

(with P a persistent predicate) can be replaced by rules of form:

$$\begin{array}{lll} P(\vec{x}) & \to & P_1(\vec{x}), P(\vec{x}) \\ P(\vec{x}) & \to & P_2(\vec{x}), P(\vec{x}) \\ P_1(\vec{x}), P_2(\vec{y}), \ldots & \to & Q(\vec{x}, \vec{y}), P_1(\vec{x}), P_2(\vec{y}), \ldots \end{array}$$

where P_1 and P_2 are persistent predicates.

Definition 2. A rule $l \to r$ in a theory $\mathcal{T}$ is a *single-persistent rule* if all predicates that are persistent in theory $\mathcal{T}$ appear at most once in l. A theory $\mathcal{T}$ is a *uniform theory* if all rules in $\mathcal{T}$ are single-persistent rules.

Since any theory can be rewritten as a uniform theory, we will assume that all theories discussed from this point are uniform theories.

Definition 3. Let $\mathbf{P}$ be a set of predicates, each persistent in a uniform theory $\mathcal{T}$. Two states S and S' are *P-similar* (denoted $S \simeq_P S'$) if, after removing all duplicate persistent P facts from each state, they are equal multisets.

Lemma 1. *Given a uniform theory $\mathcal{T}$, $\mathbf{P}$ the set of predicates persistent in $\mathcal{T}$, σ a substitution, and R a rule that creates only persistent facts, if $S \overset{\mathcal{T}}{\twoheadrightarrow} T$ is a derivation which invokes σR more than once, then there exists a derivation $S \overset{\mathcal{T}}{\twoheadrightarrow} T'$ that invokes σR only once, with $T \simeq_P T'$.*

3.2 Protocol theories

In many protocols, there is an implicit or explicit initialization phase that distributes keys or establishes other shared information. We incorporate this into our formal definitions by letting a protocol theory consist of an initialization theory, together with the disjoint union of bounded subtheories that characterize the behavior of each protocol agent (role). In order to bound the entire protocol, we must assume that the initialization theory is bounded, and that initialization can be completed prior to the execution of the protocol steps proper.

Definition 4. A rule $R = l \to r$ *enables* a rule $l' \to r'$ if there exist σ, σ' such that some fact $P(\vec{t}) \in \sigma r$ is also in $\sigma' l'$. A theory $\mathcal{T}$ *precedes* a theory $\mathcal{R}$ if no rule in $\mathcal{R}$ enables a rule in $\mathcal{T}$.

In particular, if a theory $\mathcal{T}$ precedes a theory $\mathcal{R}$, then no predicates that appear in the left hand side of rules in $\mathcal{T}$ are created by rules that are in $\mathcal{R}$.

Definition 5. A theory $\mathcal{A}$ is a *well-founded principal theory* if it has an ordered set of predicates, called the *principal role states* and numbered $A_0, A_1, \ldots, A_k$ for some k, such that each rule $l \to r$ contains exactly one state predicate $A_i \in l$ and one state predicate $A_j \in r$, with $i < j$. We call the first role state, A_0, an *initial role state.*

By defining a principal theory in this way, we ensure that each application of a rule in $\mathcal{A}$ advances the state forward. Each instance of a principal role can only result in a finite number of steps in the derivation.

Definition 6. A theory $\mathcal{S} \subset \mathcal{T}$ is a *bounded sub-theory* if all rules R in $\mathcal{S}$ that create a fact fall into one of the following categories:

1. The facts created by R contain existentials.
2. The facts created by R are initial role states of $\mathcal{T}$.
3. The facts created by R are persistent in $\mathcal{T}$.

Definition 7. A theory $\mathcal{P}$ is a *well-founded protocol theory* if $\mathcal{P} = \mathcal{I} \uplus \mathcal{A} \uplus \mathcal{B} \uplus \mathcal{C} \ldots$ where $\mathcal{I}$ is a bounded sub-theory (called the *initialization theory*) and $\mathcal{A}, \mathcal{B}, \mathcal{C} \ldots$ are a finite number of well-founded principal theories, with $\mathcal{I}$ preceding $\mathcal{A}, \mathcal{B}, \mathcal{C} \ldots$.

The structure of protocol theories allows derivations to be broken down into two stages – the initialization stage, and the non-initialization (protocol run) stage. Any derivation in the theory can be reordered to contain all initialization steps before any non-initialization steps.

Lemma 2. *Given a well-founded protocol theory $\mathcal{P} = \mathcal{I} \uplus \mathbf{A}$, where $\mathcal{I}$ is the initialization theory, and $\mathbf{A}$ is the disjoint union of one or more principal theories, if $S \overset{\mathcal{P}}{\twoheadrightarrow} T$ is a derivation over $\mathcal{P}$, then there is a derivation $S \overset{\mathcal{I}}{\twoheadrightarrow} S'$ and $S' \overset{\mathbf{A}}{\twoheadrightarrow} T$, where all rules from $\mathcal{I}$ are applied before any rules from $\mathbf{A}$.*

3.3 Intruder theory

One motivation for using multiset rewriting for protocol analysis is that this framework allows us to use essentially the same theory for all adversaries for all protocols. In this subsection, we specify the properties of intruder theories that are needed to bound the number of intruder steps needed to produce a given message. As explained in [7], the actions of the standard intruder can be separated into two phases, one in which messages are decomposed into smaller parts, and one in which these parts are (re)assembled into a message that will be sent to some protocol agent. An additional detail is that we sometimes need to postpone decomposition of a specific fact until a later time, such as until a decryption key becomes available.

In determining the *size* of a fact, we count the predicate name, each function name, and each variable or constant symbol. For example, fact $P(A, B)$ has size 3, and fact $P(f(A, B), C)$ has size 5.

Definition 8. A rule $R = l \rightarrow r$ is a *composition rule* if the non-persistent facts in r have larger size than the facts in l. A rule $R = l \rightarrow r$ is a *decomposition rule* if the non-persistent facts in r have smaller size than the facts in l.

For example,

$$C(A), C(B) \rightarrow C(\langle A, B\rangle)$$

is a composition rule, and

$$D(\langle A, B\rangle) \rightarrow D(A), D(B)$$

is a decomposition rule.

For the intruder theories we will consider, we allow persistent facts to appear in both the left and right hand sides. So, in general a decomposition rule is of form:

$$D(\langle A, B\rangle), \vec{P}(\ldots) \rightarrow D(A), D(B), \vec{P'}(\ldots)$$

where $\vec{P}$ and $\vec{P'}$ are sets of persistent predicates, with $\vec{P} \subseteq \vec{P'}$ (and similarly for composition rules).

We also need to introduce more complicated decomposition rules, which we call "Decomposition rules with Auxiliary facts". These are pairs of rules of form:

$$D(t), \vec{P}(\ldots) \rightarrow \vec{P'}(\ldots), A(t)$$

and

$$A(t), \vec{Q}(\ldots) \rightarrow \vec{Q'}(\ldots), D(t')$$

where $\vec{P} \subseteq \vec{P'}$, $\vec{Q} \subseteq \vec{Q'}$, and $size(t') < size(t)$. Here, A represents an Auxiliary fact (which can appear only in a pair of rules of this form) which is used to amortize the decomposition of $D(t)$ into $D(t')$ across the two rules. Appendix A.3 shows an example of when this type of decomposition rule is needed, in order to allow for decrypting an old fact with a newly learned encryption key.

Definition 9. A theory $\mathcal{T}$ is a *two-phase* theory if its rules can be divided into three disjoint theories, $\mathcal{T} = \mathcal{I} \uplus \mathcal{C} \uplus \mathcal{D}$, where $\mathcal{I}$ is a bounded sub-theory preceding $\mathcal{C}$ and $\mathcal{D}$, $\mathcal{C}$ contains only composition rules, $\mathcal{D}$ contains only decomposition rules, and no rules in $\mathcal{C}$ precede any rules in $\mathcal{D}$.

Definition 10. A *normalized derivation* is a derivation where all rules from the decomposition theory are applied before any rules from the composition theory.

As also shown in [7] in a slightly different context, all derivations in a two-phase theory can be expressed as normalized derivations.

Lemma 3. *If a theory $\mathcal{T}$ is two-phase, and we limit the size of terms, and we limit the number of times each existential is instantiated, then there are a finite number of normalized derivations in the theory.*

3.4 Protocol and intruder

Definition 11. Given a well-founded protocol theory $\mathcal{P} = \mathcal{I} \uplus \mathbf{A}$ and a two-phase intruder theory $\mathcal{M}$, a *standard trace* is a derivation which has all steps from the initialization theory $\mathcal{I}$ first, then interleaves steps from the principal theories $\mathbf{A}$ with normalized derivations from the intruder theory $\mathcal{M}$.

Theorem 1. *Let $\mathcal{P}$ be any well-founded protocol theory and $\mathcal{M}$ be any two-phase intruder theory. If we bound the number of uses of each existential, and we bound the size of each term, then the set of standard traces of $\mathcal{P} \cup \mathcal{M}$ is finite.*

4 Intractability

There are many undecidable properties of arbitrary protocols. If we consider all possible systems that are definable using Horn logic as protocols, then undecidability follows easily from the undecidability of Horn-clause logic. In particular, it is possible to give finite descriptions of infinite-state systems using function symbols. For example, if we have 0 : nat and suc : nat $\rightarrow$ nat, then we can write expressions for arbitrarily many natural numbers. It is straightforward to go from there to various undecidability results based on counter machines. However, this kind of intractability result ignores the fact that most protocols used in practice have a fixed number of steps and communicate data of bounded complexity. If we restrict our attention to finite-length protocols, of the form identified in the previous section, then it does not seem possible to write protocols whose behavior is as complicated as arbitrary Turing machines. However, as shown in this section, there are nontrivial lower bounds if we combine protocols with an intruder. Throughout this section, we will restrict our attention to runs in which all terms have fewer than some fixed number of symbols and the protocol principals have bounded activity.

4.1 Protocols without nonces

Even without generating new data, determining a security property may require exponentially-many runs of a protocol and the decision problem is PSPACE-Complete. The first result, that there are protocols without nonces where the shortest insecure run is exponential, is illustrated by the following family of protocols, one for each integer k. The protocol for integer k assumes that a private symmetric key K is shared between principals $A, B_1, ..., B_k$ and C. (The same effect can occur achieved in a public key protocol, by first running secure key exchange steps.) In Table 3 we show the protocol for $k = 4$.

In this artificial protocol, A sends C a message containing $(0,0,0,0)$ but C will only respond to a message with $(1,1,1,1)$. However, principals $B_1, \ldots, B_k$ implement a k-bit increment on encrypted tuples. Therefore, if an intruder routes the initial message from A through $2^k - 1$ B principals in repeated runs of the protocol, C will expose the secret key. It is easy to see that unless an exponential number of messages are sent, the key K remains secret.

If we formulate security as a decision problem without requiring the faulty trace as output, it is easy to show that the problem is PSPACE-hard by straightforward reduction from linear-bounded Turing machines. An interesting aspect of the protocol above is that it shows that a protocol can be secure against polynomial-time attack, but considered insecure under Dolev-Yao assumptions.

4.2 Undecidability

4.2.1 Restricted protocol form

In general, it is convenient to write the steps of a protocol agent A in the form

$$\begin{array}{l} A_i(\ldots), N_j(\ldots), P(\ldots), Q(\ldots), \ldots \\ \rightarrow \vec{\exists} \ldots . A_k(\ldots), N_k(\ldots), P(\ldots), Q(\ldots), \ldots \end{array}$$

where $P(\ldots), Q(\ldots), \ldots$ are persistent facts appearing on the left and right of the rule. However, for the purpose of proving a stronger negative result, we restrict our attention to a simpler form of protocol step in this section. Specifically, we say a protocol theory is in *restricted form* if the constituent principal theories consist only of rules of the form

$$A_i(\ldots), N_j(\ldots) \rightarrow \vec{\exists} \ldots . A_k(\ldots), N_\ell(\ldots)$$

with one principal role state and one network message on the left and one principal role state and one network message on the right. As with all finite-length protocols, we assume the states of agent A are given by a finite list of predicates $A_1, \ldots, A_a$. We also assume that set of possible network messages are given by a finite list of predicates $N_1, \ldots, N_n$, with $i < k \leq a$ and $j < \ell \leq n$ in each rule of the form above.

Theorem 2. *Secrecy is undecidable for finite-length protocols of restricted form. More specifically, there is no algorithm for deciding whether a given protocol, run in combination with the standard intruder, allows the intruder to gain access to a given initial secret.*

The proof involves representing existential Horn theories as protocols, as described below. While space limitations prevent us from presenting the proof in detail, we will sketch the main ideas.

4.2.2 Representation of existential Horn theories

Given a set of existential Horn formulas, of the form described in Appendix B and repeated below, we can construct a protocol so that, when combined with the standard intruder theory, the intruder memory may contain formulas representing all consequences of the theory.

In order to do this, we must use the intruder in an essential way. Specifically, each agent can only execute a finite sequence of steps. Therefore, we use a separate agent for each Horn clause. The role of the intruder is to convert the final message sent by one agent to an initial message received by another agent. As a result of intruder actions, a datum may pass through an unbounded number of protocol steps.

At the same time, in order to represent the Horn theory faithfully, we cannot give the intruder complete access to all to atomic formulas used in a Horn clause. In particular, we cannot let the intruder combine data from different messages. For example, if one agent sends a message representing $P(a,b)$, we cannot allow the intruder to intercept this message and replace it with $P(b,a)$. However, it is easy to prevent this form of interference if we encrypt atomic formulas with a shared private key.

Putting these two ideas together, we represent an existential Horn clause theory by a protocol with one agent per clause. The agent A for a clause

$$\begin{array}{l} \forall x_1 \ldots \forall x_i[(\alpha_1 \wedge \ldots \wedge \alpha_k) \\ \quad \Longrightarrow \exists y_1 \ldots \exists y_j(\beta_1 \wedge \ldots \wedge \beta_\ell)] \end{array}$$

is

$$\begin{array}{l} A_0, N_{a_0}(\lceil \alpha_1 \wedge \ldots \wedge \alpha_k \rceil) \\ \rightarrow \exists y_1 \ldots \exists y_j . A_1, N_{a_1}(\lceil \beta_1 \wedge \ldots \wedge \beta_\ell \rceil) \end{array}$$

where the encoding $\lceil \alpha_1 \wedge \ldots \wedge \alpha_k \rceil$ of a conjunction of atomic formulas as a single atomic formula is described below.

There are several ways to represent a conjunction of atomic formulas as a single network message, containing only one predicate symbol, hidden from the adversary. One

$A \longrightarrow C:$	$(0,0,0,0)_K$
$C \longrightarrow A:$	if sent $(1,1,1,1)_K$then respond K
$B_1 \longrightarrow A:$	if sent $(x_1,x_2,x_3,0)_K$then respond $(x_1,x_2,x_3,1)_K$
$B_2 \longrightarrow A:$	if sent $(x_1,x_2,0,1)_K$then respond $(x_1,x_2,1,0)_K$
$B_3 \longrightarrow A:$	if sent $(x_1,0,1,1)_K$then respond $(x_1,1,0,0)_K$
$B_4 \longrightarrow A:$	if sent $(0,1,1,1)_K$then respond $(1,0,0,0)_K$

Table 3. Rules for exponential protocol, $k = 4$

way, intended to keep syntactic complication to a minimum, is to assume that for each k, we have a k-ary encryption function $\mathsf{Encrypt}_k$. For notational simplicity, we will suppress k in the description below. We also assume that for each sequence of predicates $P_1, \ldots, P_k$ that occurs together in the left or right hand side of is a given Horn clause, we have a constant symbol $P_1.P_2.\ldots.P_k$. (Although we have used a sequence of letters, numbers and subscripts to write out our name for this constant symbol, we assume it is an atomic constant symbol of the language.) Given these assumptions, we let

$$\begin{aligned}&\lceil P_1(t_{1,1}, \ldots t_{1,i_1} \wedge \ldots \wedge P_j(t_{j,1}, \ldots, t_{j,i_1})\rceil \\ &= \mathsf{Encrypt}(P_1.P_2.\ldots.P_k, t_{1,i_1}, \ldots, t_{j,1}, \ldots, t_{j,i_1})\end{aligned}$$

We assume that all encryption is done using the same key, the key is shared among honest participants, but not revealed to the intruder. (It suffices to have one principal executing several roles, using a private key.)

The final main idea in the representation of Horn theories is the way that a set of conjunctions may be combined to produce the conjunction of atomic formulas needed to apply another Horn clause. This is perhaps best illustrated by example.

Suppose that the existential Horn clause

$$\forall x \forall y[(P(x) \wedge Q(x,y) \wedge R(y)) \implies \exists z(P(z) \wedge Q(y,z)]$$

is part of the Horn theory we wish to represent by a protocol. In order to use this implication, the protocol must produce a message containing $\lceil (P(a) \wedge Q(a,b) \wedge R(b)\rceil$ for some a and b. However, the protocol agents that represent Horn clauses produce encodings of conjunctions of atomic formulas, and the atomic formulas here may come from different rules. Therefore, we need additional protocol agents that select atomic formulas out of conjunctions and combine them.

The process is very similar to the encoding of the intruder, except that protocol agents can manipulate encrypted values. For each conjunction form (including variables) that appears on the right-hand side of a Horn clause, such as $P(z) \wedge Q(y,z)$, we include *decomposition agents* of the form

$$A_0, N_0(\lceil P(z) \wedge Q(y,z)\rceil) \rightarrow A_1, N_1(\lceil P(z)\rceil)$$

and

$$B_0, N_0(\lceil P(z) \wedge Q(y,z)\rceil) \rightarrow B_1, N_1(\lceil Q(y,z)\rceil)$$

for predicates A_0, A_1, B_0, B_1 not used for other agents. We also need a *composition agent* for the left-hand-side of each original Horn clause. For the clause above, the agent will have states A_0, A_1, A_2 and A_3. At each step, the agent reads one of the atomic formulas in its target conjunction, sending out either a dummy message or, at the last step, a message containing the conjunction of atomic formulas needed. In order to assemble $\lceil (P(x) \wedge Q(x,y) \wedge R(y)\rceil$, we can use an agent A with the following steps:

$$\begin{aligned}&A_0, N_0(\lceil P(x)\rceil) \rightarrow A_1(\lceil P(x)\rceil), N_1() \\ &A_1(\lceil P(x)\rceil), N_2(\lceil Q(x,y)\rceil) \rightarrow \\ &\qquad A_2(\lceil P(x) \wedge Q(x,y)\rceil), N_3() \\ &A_2(\lceil P(x) \wedge Q(x,y)\rceil), N_4(\lceil R(y)\rceil) \rightarrow \\ &\quad A_3(), N_5(\lceil P(x) \wedge Q(x,y) \wedge R(y)\rceil)\end{aligned}$$

After this agent sends message N_5, the intruder can read the data $\lceil P(x) \wedge Q(x,y) \wedge R(y)\rceil$ contained in this message and forward it to the agent representing the Horn clause with hypothesis $P(x) \wedge Q(x,y) \wedge R(y)$.

In each of our examples, we have numbered the network messages $N_0, N_1, \ldots$, but it is possible to renumber them so that each message number has a fixed format.

5 Multiset rewriting and LLF

5.1 Linear logic and LLF

The multiset-rewriting notation used in this paper is the first-order Horn fragment of linear logic [14], with existential quantification. Specifically, each transition rule

$$A_1, \ldots, A_n \longrightarrow \exists \vec{x}. B_1, \ldots, B_m$$

can be written as a linear logic formula

$$A_1 \otimes \ldots \otimes A_n \multimap \exists \vec{x}. B_1 \otimes \ldots \otimes B_m$$

Under this correspondence, every derivation using multiset rewriting corresponds to a linear logic derivation, and conversely. This allows us to use linear logic tools for protocol analysis. In particular, we have used the linear logical framework *LLF* [5] to simulate the execution of protocols, detect attacks, and construct formal proofs about protocol transformations. Similar results could be obtained using other linear logic systems such as *Forum* [23] or *Lygon* [15], except that our proofs about protocol transformations rely on the proof-term representation of *LLF*, discussed below.

Since we will describe some aspects of the protocol proofs carried out using LLF, we give a brief overview of LLF. Although operators $\otimes$ and $\exists$ are not provided directly in LLF, it is possible to write rules as logically equivalent formulas using other linear logic connectives. Although the exact syntax is not overly important, we give an illustration since it provides an opportunity to illustrate an operational reading of linear logic formulas. As in other forms of logic, conjunction in hypotheses, $A \otimes B \multimap C$, is equivalent to nested implication, $A \multimap B \multimap C$. There is also a double-negation property of linear logic, with $(A \multimap \mathit{false}) \multimap \mathit{false}$ equivalent to A, that allows us to write existential quantification using negated universal quantification. In place of *false*, we use a propositional variable, which is implicitly universally quantified. This leads to a form of "continuation-passing" logic program, of the sort usually associated with double-negation in constructive logic. Using *loop* as our propositional variable, the formula $A_1 \otimes \ldots \otimes A_n \multimap \exists \vec{x}. B_1 \otimes \ldots \otimes B_m$ can be written as the clause

$$\begin{array}{ll} & A_1 \multimap \ldots \multimap A_n \\ \multimap & \forall \vec{x}.(B_1 \multimap \ldots \multimap B_m \multimap \mathit{loop}) \\ \multimap & \mathit{loop} \end{array}$$

Following conventional logic-programming notation, we often write this clause with the outer implications reversed:

$$\begin{array}{ll} \mathit{loop} & \circ\!- A_1 \\ & \ldots \\ & \circ\!- A_n \\ & \circ\!- \forall \vec{x}.(B_1 \multimap \ldots \multimap B_m \multimap \mathit{loop}) \end{array}$$

This formula may be read operationally as follows: "in order to make an iteration, consume $A_1, \ldots, A_n$, generate new constants $\vec{c}$ and substitute them for the variables $\vec{x}$, then assert the facts $B_1, \ldots, B_m$, and finally try another rule (clause)".

5.2 Protocol Formulation in LLF

The signature used to describe protocols uses different types for messages, keys, nonces, and so on. For example, we use type `key` for both public keys and principal names, which we identify. Nonces have type `atm`, for atomic message, while other messages have type `msg`. The function symbols `@` and `k2m` are used as type conversion functions from nonces and keys to messages, respectively. Composite messages are obtained from their parts using the infix `*` operator, and a message M encrypted with key K is written `crypt` M K. A key K is made public by a fact of the form `annKey` K. The inverse of a key K is specified as `inv` K.

Messages sent by a principal have the form `toNet` P N M, where P identifies the protocol, N is the message number within that protocol, and M is the message itself. Principals receive messages in packets of the form `fromNet` P N M. As we will see, both the network and the intruder can convert `toNet` assertions to `fromNet` assertions.

In actual LLF syntax, Alice's first step in the Needham-Schroeder protocol is written as follows:

```
nsA1: loop
       o- annKey B
       o- a0 A
       o- ({Na:atm}
             a1 A B (@ Na)
          -o toNet ns 1
             (crypt ((@ Na) * (@ (k2m A))) B)
          -o loop).
```

Here `nsA1` is a label, used to name this clause in traces, and `{Na:atm}` indicates a quantified variable `Na` of type `atm`.

5.3 Network and intruder

The network simply converts every `toNet` assertion into a `fromNet` assertion, so that each message sent to the network can be read as message from the network by other principals. The intruder can intercept a message and decompose it into its atomic constituents (of the form `@` N or `k2m` K). The intruder then builds up a message from these fragments and possibly newly generated data. Finally it sends it off in the form of a `fromNet` message.

5.4 An equivalence proof

As an example equivalence proof, we describe an optimization of our Needham-Schroeder model and prove the equivalence between the "standard" model with network and intruder and an optimized version in which the network is eliminated. Since the intruder can simulate the network, by decomposing and then recomposing each message, the two models are equivalent, in the sense that for every trace of the system with network and intruder, there is a corresponding trace of the system without the network in which all honest parties see exactly the same sequences of messages, and conversely.

We state the equivalence using standard logical notation. Specifically, we write $\Gamma \vdash A$ if there is a derivation $\mathcal{D}$ of this judgment of linear logic. Let NS, I, N, and $Init$ be the multisets of linear logic formulas representing the steps of the Needham-Schroeder protocol, the intruder, the network, and the initial facts, respectively. For any pair of principals A,B in $Init$, let ϕ_{AB} be the formula

$$\phi_{AB} = \exists x_a, x_b . A_2(A, B, x_a, x_b) \otimes B_2(B, A, x_a, x_b)$$

stating that the protocol between A and B runs to completion. We use this formula as an example goal for proof search; similar equivalences hold for other goals.

Theorem 3 (Equivalence). *If there is a derivation $\mathcal{D}$ of $(NS, I, N, Init) \vdash \phi_{AB}$, then there is a derivation $\mathcal{D}'$ of $(NS, I, Init) \vdash \phi_{AB}$. Moreover, it is the case that $\mathcal{D}$ and $\mathcal{D}'$ contain the same protocol steps in the same order.*

5.5 Formal proof in LLF

While LLF is not a complete proof checker, there is a precise sense in which LLF can be used to develop machine-checkable proofs. In comparison with proof methods using more standard logics, e.g. [27], LLF has some advantages and disadvantages. One advantage is that the constructive nature of proofs is immediately apparent: from an LLF proof of the equivalence above, we obtain an algorithm that transform a trace of one system into a trace of the other. This is in part a result of the way we formalize the equivalence, and in part a consequence of the constructive nature of our fragment of linear logic. A disadvantage of LLF is that it supports only a restricted fragment of linear logic. Moreover, we must write proofs in a certain style in order for LLF to be able to check their correctness.

Overview of the proof We wish to prove that for every trace, possibly relying on the network to carry messages to principals, there exist an equivalent trace where the network is never used. We do this by formulating two versions of the protocol. Traces of the system including a separate network have type `loop1`, while traces of the system without a network have type `loop2`. Our definition of *equivalent* traces is that there is no noticeable difference from the point of view of any honest participant in the protocol: they send and receive the same messages and apply the same transitions. The LLF formalization of this proof involves definition of a binary predicate `net2intr` which relates a derivation possibly involving the network (of type `loop1`), and a derivation that is network free (of type `loop2`). The arguments of this predicate are LLF terms corresponding to derivations and therefore representing traces. The proof of equivalence proceeds by induction on the structure of the derivation using the network, using a nested induction on the structure of the messages whenever we encounter a network transmission.

LLF proof checking The LLF equivalence proof consists of clauses that formalize each inductive case of the proof. While LLF checks the type of each clause, type checking does not guarantee that the proof is correct since (a) the LLF implementation does not guarantee that each case is covered, and (b) it does not check whether uses of the induction hypothesis are well-founded. However, we can prove an adequacy theorem which shows that any type-checked proof of a certain form must be a correct proof.

In order to state this result, we write $\Delta \vdash_{LLF} M : A$ for the judgment that the LLF term M has type A with respect to the (intuitionistic and linear) declarations in Δ. Let Δ_{NS} be the complete set of declarations used in the equivalence proof.

Theorem 4 (Adequacy of representation). *Let A and B be principals in Init, and ϕ_{AB} defined as above*

- *There is a bijection between derivations $\mathcal{D}$ of $(NS, I, N, Init) \vdash \phi_{AB}$ and LLF terms M such $\Delta_{NS} \vdash_{LLF} M :$ `loop1` is derivable,*
- *There is a bijection between derivations $\mathcal{D}'$ of $(NS, I, Init) \vdash \phi_{AB}$ and LLF terms M' such that $\Delta_{NS} \vdash_{LLF} M' :$ `loop2` is derivable,*
- *For every term M such that $\Delta_{NS} \vdash_{LLF} M :$ `loop1` is derivable, there exist terms M' and P such that $\Delta_{NS} \vdash_{LLF} M' :$ `loop2` and $\Delta_{NS} \vdash_{LLF} P :$ `net2intr` M M' are derivable.*

The terms M and M' above contain the same sequences of protocol steps, and the same `toNet` *and* `fromNet` *tokens, in the same order.*

6 Conclusion

We believe that a logic-based formalism as described in this paper, with existential quantification for choosing new values, provides a useful notation for examining the standard Dolev-Yao protocol security assumptions. Using this formalism, we can describe all protocols we have encountered by formulating a rewrite rule (or several related rules) for each step of each principal. In addition, we have developed standard theories (sets of rewrite rules) for initialization steps such as generating and announcing public keys, and for the nondeterministic Dolev-Yao intruder. This gives us a set of conventions for describing protocols and provides the basis for developing general theorems and techniques for protocol analysis.

There are several advantages and intentional disadvantages of the formalism used in this paper. The intent of the design is that this formalism provides exactly the primitives needed to formalize protocols, no more. This makes it possible to analyze protocols without having to confront complications that might be inherent in a formalism but not intrinsic to protocols themselves. In particular, we are able to prove lower bounds on protocol analysis that seem faithful to the notion of finite-length protocol. Since the formalism is based on linear logic, we have a direct method for describing state changes. In contrast, axiomatizing protocol traces in higher-order logic requires rather complex conditions to guarantee that when a principal moves from one state to another, the previous state is no longer available for further use. In comparison with using CSP [18, 28, 29] or Murφ [25], our notation allows us to describe unbounded runs of the protocol simply, recovering bounded instances of th protocol by restricting the uses of existential quantification. Perhaps the closest formalism is spi-calculus [1]. However, there are several characteristics of the underlying pi-calculus, such as creation of new channels, that are absent from our system, making it simpler to prove meta-theoretic results. Finally, we should make clear that the formalism presented in this paper is not intended to be a logic for specifying and reasoning about protocols, only a notation for defining the behavior of a protocol in the face of network intruder.

We have found the linear-logic tool *LLF* useful for reasoning about protocols. As a first step toward developing an algorithmic meta-theory of protocols, we have proved correctness of a protocol/intruder optimization using this tool. We expect to develop and verify additional optimizations and transformations. In addition to meta-results, *LLF* also seems useful for searching the possible runs of a protocol and intruder. While we do not expect pure *LLF* to be more efficient or more comprehensive than tools such as the NRL analyzer [21] that have been refined over many years, there is some benefit in the simplicity of the tool. If we can improve our search-strategy language to make it more effective in common cases, then this may lead to better understanding of general techniques that could be adopted in a variety of settings.

Finally, although not discussed in this paper, we believe that there may be some advantage in developing translations between the notation used here and other standard protocol formalisms. We believe the translation into Murφ is straightforward and easy to implement, as is a translation into process calculus with ν operator [12]. On this basis, we believe there may be practical translations into CSP, for example, based on choosing bounds on the number of new values that are to be generated in any run. It also seems feasible to translate protocol definition languages such as CASPER [19] and CAPSL [22] into this formalism, making it possible to use our framework as an intermediate language in some kind of federated protocol analysis environment.

Acknowledgments: Thanks to Grit Denker, Jon Millen, Mourad Debbabi, Mark Mitchell, Vitaly Shmatikov and Ulrich Stern for helpful discussions.

References

[1] M. Abadi and A. Gordon. A calculus for cryptographic protocols: the spi calculus. *Information and Computation*, 148(1):1–70, 1999.

[2] S. Abiteboul, R. Hull, and V. Vianu. *Foundations of Databases*. Addison-Wesley, 1995.

[3] J.-P. Banâtre and D. L. Métayer. Computing by multiset transformation. *Communcations of the ACM*, 36:98–111, 1993.

[4] G. Berry and G. Boudol. The chemical abstract machine. *Theoretical Computer Science*, 96:217–248, 1992.

[5] I. Cervesato and F. Pfenning. A linear logical framework. In E. Clarke, editor, *Proceedings of the Eleventh Annual Symposium on Logic in Computer Science — LICS'96*, pages 264–275, New Brunswick, NJ, July 1996. IEEE Computer Society Press.

[6] J. Clark and J. Jacob. A survey of authentication protocol literature. Web Draft Version 1.0 available from `www.cs.york.ac.uk/~jac/`, 1997.

[7] E. Clarke, S. Jha, and W. Marrero. Using state space exploration and a natural deduction style message derivation engine to verify security protocols. In *Proc. IFIP Working Conference on Programming Concepts and Methods (PROCOMET)*, 1998.

[8] K. Compton and S. Dexter. Proving authentication protocols in a fragment of linear logic. Manuscript, 1998.

[9] G. Denker, J. Meseguer, and C. Talcott. Protocol specification and analysis in Maude. In *Proc. of Workshop on Formal Methods and Security Protocols*, 1998.

[10] D. L. Dill, A. J. Drexler, A. J. Hu, and C. H. Yang. Protocol verification as a hardware design aid. In *IEEE International Conference on Computer Design: VLSI in Computers and Processors*, pages 522–5, 1992.

[11] D. Dolev and A. Yao. On the security of public-key protocols. *IEEE Transactions on Information Theory*, 2(29), 1983.

[12] N. Durgin and J. Mitchell. Analysis of security protocols. To appear in the Proceedings of the 1998 International Summer School of Marktoberdorf, 1999.

[13] H. Enderton. *A Mathematical Introduction to Logic*. Academic Press, 1972.

[14] J.-Y. Girard. Linear logic. *Theoretical Computer Science*, 50:1–102, 1987.

[15] J. Harland, D. Pym, and M. Winikoff. Programming in Lygon: An overview. In M. Wirsing and M. Nivat, editors, *Algebraic Methodology and Software Technology*, pages 391–405, Munich, Germany, July 1996. Springer-Verlag LNCS 1101.

[16] M. Kanovich, M. Okada, and A. Scedrov. Specifying real-time finite-state systems in linear logic. In *COTIC '98: Second Workshop on Concurrent Constraint Programming for Time-Critical Applications and Multi-Agent Systems*, Nice, France, 1998. Electronic Notes in Theoretical Computer Science, Volume 16, Issue 1. http://www.elsevier.nl/locate/entcs.

[17] R. Kemmerer, C. Meadows, and J. Millen. Three systems for cryptographic protocol analysis. *J. Cryptology*, 7(2):79–130, 1994.

[18] G. Lowe. Breaking and fixing the Needham-Schroeder public-key protocol using CSP and FDR. In *2nd International Workshop on Tools and Algorithms for the Construction and Analysis of Systems*. Springer-Verlag, 1996.

[19] G. Lowe. Casper: a compiler for the analysis of security protocols. In *Proc. 10th IEEE Computer Security Foundations Workshop*, pages 18–30, 1997.

[20] C. Meadows. Analyzing the Needham-Schroeder public-key protocol: a comparison of two approaches. In *Proc. European Symposium On Research In Computer Security*. Springer Verlag, 1996.

[21] C. Meadows. The NRL protocol analyzer: an overview. *J. Logic Programming*, 26(2):113–131, 1996.

[22] J. Millen. CAPSL: Common authentication protocol specification language. Technical Report MP 97B48, The MITRE Corporation, 1997.

[23] D. Miller. A multiple-conclusion specification logic. *Theoretical Computer Science*, 165(1):201–232, 1996.

[24] J. Mitchell. Analysis of security protocols. Slides for invited talk at CAV '98, available at `http://www.stanford.edu/~jcm`, July 1998.

[25] J. Mitchell, M. Mitchell, and U. Stern. Automated analysis of cryptographic protocols using Murφ. In *Proc. IEEE Symp. Security and Privacy*, pages 141–151, 1997.

[26] R. Needham and M. Schroeder. Using encryption for authentication in large networks of computers. *Communications of the ACM*, 21(12):993–999, 1978.

[27] L. Paulson. Proving properties of security protocols by induction. In *10th IEEE Computer Security Foundations Workshop*, pages 70–83, 1997.

[28] A. W. Roscoe. Modelling and verifying key-exchange protocols using CSP and FDR. In *8th IEEE Computer Security Foundations Workshop*, pages 98–107. IEEE Computer Soc Press, 1995.

[29] S. Schneider. Security properties and CSP. In *IEEE Symp. Security and Privacy*, 1996.

[30] M. Sipser. *Introduction to the Theory of Computation*. PWS Publishing, 1997.

A Example: Needham-Schroeder Public Key Protocol

As an example, we give the full theory of the three-step core of the Needham-Schroeder public-key protocol.

$$\begin{array}{lcll} A & \longrightarrow & B & : \{A, N_a\}_{K_b} \\ B & \longrightarrow & A & : \{N_a, N_b\}_{K_a} \\ A & \longrightarrow & B & : \{N_b\}_{K_b} \end{array}$$

Note that this is a simplified version of the protocol, where the use of a trusted server to distribute the public keys is omitted. This results in a particularly straightforward representation for the Initialization and Protocol Theories.

A.1 Initialization Theory

The Initialization Theory is shown in Table 4. Here, the predicate *GoodGuy* indicates an uncompromised principal, parameterized by its encryption and decryption (public and private) keys. For simplicity, we identify the principal with its public key (i.e. where "A" appears in the protocol, we use the public key "K_a"). The GOODGUY rule allows for the creation of an unlimited number of principals, each with a unique key pair, denoted by the predicate KP.

The BADKEY rule provides a mechanism for specifying an unlimited number of compromised key pairs, which appear to belong to valid principals, but whose private keys are known to the intruder. The predicate *BadKey* denotes these compromised key pairs.

ROLA and ROLB allow an unlimited number of sessions to be started for any principal to act in the role of either "Alice" (the initiator) or "Bob" (the responder). A_0 and B_0 denote the initial role state for the A and B roles, respectively, parameterized by the public key (principal) acting in that role.

Since we are omitting the trusted server from this example, we accomplish key distribution by having the principals announce their keys. The ANNK rule accomplishes this for the *GoodGuy* participants, while the ANNKB rule does the same for the *BadKey* pairs. Note that both rules generate a predicate *AnnK* indicating a public key that is available for communication, so from this point the valid participants can't distinguish the good guys from the bad guys.

Note that in this initialization theory, all predicates are persistent except for initial role states A_0 and B_0.

A.2 Protocol Theory

The protocol theories, shown in Table 4, are derived directly from the specification of the Needham-Schroeder protocol. Theory $\mathcal{A}$ corresponds to the role of "Alice", and theory $\mathcal{B}$ corresponds to "Bob".

In rule A1, which corresponds to the first line of the protocol, a principal k_e, in its initial state A_0, decides to talk to another principal k_e', whose key has been announced. A new nonce x is generated, along with a network message N_{S1} corresponding to the first message sent in the protocol, and the principal moves to the new state A1, remembering the values of x and k_e'. Note that since *AnnK* is persistent, it must also appear on the right hand side of the rule.

In step B1, corresponding to the second step of the protocol, a principal k_e, in the initial state B_0, responds to a

Initialization Theory $\mathcal{I}$:

GOODGUY:		$\to$	$\exists k_e.k_d.GoodGuy(k_e, k_d), KP(k_e, k_d)$
BADKEY:		$\to$	$\exists k_e.k_d.KP(k_e, k_d), BadKey(k_e, k_d)$
ROLA:	$GoodGuy(k_e, k_d)$	$\to$	$GoodGuy(k_e, k_d), A_0(k_e)$
ROLB:	$GoodGuy(k_e, k_d)$	$\to$	$GoodGuy(k_e, k_d), B_0(k_e)$
ANNK:	$GoodGuy(k_e, k_d)$	$\to$	$AnnK(k_e), GoodGuy(k_e, k_d)$
ANNKB:	$BadKey(k_e, k_d)$	$\to$	$AnnK(k_e), BadKey(k_e, k_d)$

Protocol Theories $\mathcal{A}$ and $\mathcal{B}$:

A1:	$AnnK(k_e'), A_0(k_e)$	$\to$	$\exists x.A_1(k_e, k_e', x), N_{S1}(enc(k_e', \langle x, k_e\rangle)), AnnK(k_e')$
A2:	$A_1(k_e, k_e', x), N_{R2}(enc(k_e, \langle x, y\rangle))$	$\to$	$A_2(k_e, k_e', x, y), N_{S3}(enc(k_e', y))$
B1:	$B_0(k_e), N_{R1}(enc(k_e, \langle x, k_e'\rangle)), AnnK(k_e')$	$\to$	$\exists y.B_1(k_e, k_e', x, y), N_{S2}(enc(k_e', \langle x, y\rangle)), AnnK(k_e')$
B2:	$B_1(k_e, k_e', x, y), N_{R3}(enc(k_e, y))$	$\to$	$B_2(k_e, k_e', x, y)$

Table 4. Needham Schroeder Theory

message on the network which is of the expected format (i.e. encrypted with k_e's public key, and with the identity of a participant whose key has been announced, embedded inside). k_e generates another nonce, and replies to the message, moving to a new state B_1 where all the information (the two nonces and the two principals) is remembered.

Similarly, A2 corresponds to the third line of the protocol, and B2 corresponds to the implicit step where the responder actually receives the final message.

Note that sent messages are denoted by N_{Si} and received messages are denoted by a corresponding predicate N_{Ri}. The intruder theory, described in the next section, can be thought of as providing a network that, at a minimum, transforms N_{Si}'s to N_{Ri}'s, so the protocol can execute.

A.3 Intruder Theory

The Intruder Theory is shown in Table 5. Here the M predicate denotes persistent facts known to the intruder, while D and C represent non-persistent facts which can be decomposed and composed into other facts.

LRNKB is an initialization rule that allows the intruder to learn any Bad Keys. Since *BadKey* predicates are generated only by the initialization theory, we know from Lemma 1 that this rule only needs to be applied once per derivation, per *BadKey* fact.

The REC and SND rules are used to connect the intruder to the network being used by the participants. The REC rule intercepts a message from the network and saves it as a decomposable fact. The SND rule sends composed facts onto the network.

The COMP rule allow the user to compose small terms into larger ones, while the DCMP rule allows for decomposition of large terms into smaller ones..

LRN converts a decomposable fact into intruder knowledge, and USE converts intruder knowledge into a composable fact.

The ENC and DEC rules allow the intruder to decrypt a message if it knows the private key, and to generate encrypted message from known public keys.

Note that LRNA and DECA are decomposition rules with auxilliary facts that handle a special case for encrypted messages. If the message can't be decrypted because the key isn't currently known, LRNA remembers the decrypted message with the special "Auxilliary" predicate, A. The DECA rule allows Auxilliary messages to be decrypted at a later time, if the decryption key becomes known.

Finally, GEN allows the intruder to generate new facts (i.e. nonces) as needed.

This Intruder Theory can be divided into Composition and Decomposition rules, as shown in Table 5. So, this is a Two-Phase Intruder Theory, as described in Section 3.3.

B Horn Clauses with Existential Quantification

An *existential Horn clause* is a closed first-order formula of the form

$$\forall x_1 \ldots \forall x_i[(\alpha_1 \wedge \ldots \wedge \alpha_k) \\ \Longrightarrow \exists y_1 \ldots \exists y_j(\beta_1 \wedge \ldots \wedge \beta_\ell)]$$

where $\alpha_1, \ldots, \alpha_k, \beta_1, \ldots, \beta_\ell$ are first-order atomic formulas. Without restriction on the form of the atomic formulas, undecidability of the implication problem for existen-

Initialization Rules:			
LRNKB:	$BadKey(k_e, k_d)$	$\rightarrow$	$M(k_e), M(k_d), BadKey(k_e, k_d)$
I/O Rules:			
REC:	$N_{Si}(x)$	$\rightarrow$	$D(x)$
SND:	$C(x)$	$\rightarrow$	$N_{Ri}(x)$
Decomposition Rules:			
DCMP:	$D(\langle x, y\rangle)$	$\rightarrow$	$D(x), D(y)$
LRN:	$D(x)$	$\rightarrow$	$M(x)$
DEC:	$M(k_d), KP(k_e, k_d), D(enc(k_e, x))$	$\rightarrow$	$M(k_d), KP(k_e, k_d), D(x), M(enc(k_e, x))$
LRNA:	$D(enc(k_e, x))$	$\rightarrow$	$M(enc(k_e, x)), A(enc(k_e, x))$
DECA:	$M(k_d), KP(k_e, k_d), A(enc(k_e, x))$	$\rightarrow$	$M(k_d), KP(k_e, k_d), D(x)$
Composition Rules:			
COMP:	$C(x), C(y)$	$\rightarrow$	$C(\langle x, y\rangle)$
USE:	$M(x)$	$\rightarrow$	$C(x), M(x)$
ENC:	$M(k_e), C(x)$	$\rightarrow$	$C(enc(k_e, x)), M(k_e)$
GEN:		$\rightarrow$	$\exists x.M(x)$

Table 5. Two-Phase Intruder Theory

tial Horn clauses follows immediately from the undecidability of Horn clauses without existential quantifiers. The problem of interest to us, however, is implication when the atomic formulas contain no function symbols.

The formulas we are interested in are a special case of database dependencies [2]. However, while database dependencies include existential quantification and do not involve function symbols, database dependencies also allow equality in the conclusions of Horn clauses. Since we do not use equality in our protocols (except by pattern matching in the hypotheses of rules), it is not immediately clear to us whether the following theorem is a consequence of standard results in database dependency theory.

Theorem 5. *The implication problem for existential Horn clauses without function symbols is undecidable. In particular, there is no algorithm for deciding whether a set of existential Horn clauses without function symbols implies a single atomic formula $A(b_1, \ldots, b_k)$ without function symbols or variables.*

This theorem has a straightforward direct proof based on axiomatizing a Cook's-theorem-style Turing machine tableau. Specifically, given any Turing machine, we write axioms of the form

$$\begin{aligned}&\forall x, y, z.[(\mathsf{Adj}(x, y) \wedge \mathsf{Adj}(y, z) \wedge \\ &\mathsf{Cont}(x, 0) \wedge \mathsf{Cont}(y, 1.q_i) \wedge \mathsf{Cont}(z, 1)) \\ &\implies \exists x', y', z'((\mathsf{Adj}(x', y') \wedge \mathsf{Adj}(y', z') \wedge \\ &\mathsf{Below}(x', x) \wedge \mathsf{Below}(y', y) \wedge \mathsf{Below}(z', z)) \wedge \\ &\mathsf{Cont}(x', 0.q_j) \wedge \mathsf{Cont}(y', 0) \wedge \mathsf{Cont}(z, 1))\end{aligned}$$

In this formula, the variables represent cells of the Turing machine tableau (i.e., cells of the tape at some stage of the computation); a nice picture of the tableau we use appears in [30, page 255]. The constants 0 and 1 indicate symbols in these cells, and constants of the form $0.q_i$ or $1.q_j$ indicate that the cell contains a symbol 0 or 1 and is the location of the tape head, with machine in state q_i or q_j (respectively). A fact $\mathsf{Adj}(x, y)$ means that cell x is adjacent to y, $\mathsf{Below}(x', x)$ that cell x' is below cell x, and $\mathsf{Cont}(x, c)$ that the cell x has contents described by constant c, possibly giving the machine state in addition to the symbol contained in the cell. The atomic formula $A(b_1, \ldots, b_k)$ mentioned in the statement of the theorem can be an atomic formula that is derivable by a rule that requires, in its hypothesis, that the Turing machine is in a halting state.

Strand Spaces

Mixed Strand Spaces*

F. Javier THAYER Fábrega Jonathan C. HERZOG
Joshua D. GUTTMAN

The MITRE Corporation
{jt, jherzog, guttman}@mitre.org

Abstract

Strand space analysis *[13, 12] is a method for stating and proving correctness properties for cryptographic protocols. In this paper we apply the same method to the related problem of mixed protocols, and show that a protocol can remain correct even when used in combination with a range of other protocols.*

We illustrate the method with the familiar Otway-Rees [10, 1] protocol. We identify a simple and easily verified characteristic of protocols, and show that the Otway-Rees protocol remains correct even when used in combination with other protocols that have this characteristic.

We also illustrate this method on the Neuman-Stubblebine protocol [9]. This protocol has two parts, an authentication protocol (I) in which a key distribution center creates and distributes a Kerberos-like key, and a re-authentication protocol (II) in which a client resubmits a ticket containing that key. The re-authentication protocol II is known to be flawed [2]. We show that in the presence of protocol II, there are also attacks against protocol I. We then define a variant of protocol II, and prove an authentication property of I that holds even in combination with the modified II.

1 Introduction

In [13, 12, 14], we proposed a general model for encryption protocols and used this model to study specific protocols. In those instances, we assumed that the protocols were being run in a "pure" environment: one in which the protocol is used in isolation. In such an environment, all activity would either be penetrator activity or the activity of a legitimate participant of that protocol.

In practice, however, no environment is "pure." Many different protocols may be in use at the same time, by the same parties, using the same communication channels. As noted in [5], there are at least three reasons that different protocols might use the same secret information:

- Certification is costly, so users will want to use as few certified keys as possible;
- Widespread use of cryptographic APIs will lead to multiple uses of key formats, and perhaps the keys themselves; and
- Smart cards have limited capacities, so cards that are used for multiple protocols might use the same key material for more than one protocol.

Re-use of key material is also a consideration in protocols with multiple parts, such as the Kerberos [6] and the Neuman-Stubblebine [9] protocols. One sub-protocol may be used to retrieve a ticket from a key distribution center, while a second sub-protocol is used to re-present that same ticket to a security-aware server. In such as case, the same secret key is used in two different ways.

In this paper we study the case of mixed protocols, where principals use secret material in more than one protocol. In such cases the two protocols can potentially interact, forming vulerabilities not present in either protocol alone. We apply the strand space model to such cases, and show that the same concepts and techniques as used to analyze the pure environment still apply in that of the mixed.

There have been previous attempts to reason rigorously about protocol interactions. For instance, Meadows [8] studies the Internet Key Exchange protocol, emphasizing the potential interactions among its specific sub-protocols. Gong and Syverson [3] define a (fairly restrictive) class of protocols such that any members of this class may be freely mixed without security failures.

However, our approach is somewhat different. We study a given protocol, which we refer to as the *primary* protocol, and identify some loosely syntactic conditions. We then show that any secondary protocol that meets these syntactic conditions may then freely mix with the primary protocol

*This work was supported by the National Security Agency through US Army CECOM contract DAAB 07-99-C-C201.

1063-6900/99 $10.00 © 1999 IEEE

without undermining its secrecy and authentication properties. As we shall see, this sort of result is quite natural given the strand space proof methods. These results fall out from a careful examination of the proofs that the primary protocol meets its security goals in isolation.

In the remainder of this paper, we start (Section 2) by providing a resumé of the strand space theory. We then expand the theory to accomodate the case of mixed protocols (Section 3). We then (Section 4) revisit to a familiar example, the Otway-Rees protocol, which we first studied in [12]. We reproduce some results from [12] in the new context of a mixed environment, and obtain a general contraint which must be met by the other protocols in the environment for Otway-Rees to maintain its correctness properties.

In Section 5, we turn to the Neuman-Stubblebine protocol [9], intended as an example of a protocol with multiple parts. The first part of the Neuman-Stubblebine protocol, called the authentication part, distributes a secret key and a Keberos-like ticket to a client. In the second part of the protocol, called the re-authentication part, the client uses that key and ticket to authenticate itself to a security-aware server.

We perform the same analysis as in Section 4 on the authentication part of the Neuman-Stubblebine protocol, and again obtain a general constraint on other protocols in the environment. We show that the re-authentication does not meet this constraint, and demonstrate one vulnerability that results. We then modify the re-authentication part and show that it meets the general constraint, and so maintains the security of the authentication part.

We end with a brief discussion (Section 6).

2 Strand Spaces

The following is a brief overview of the strand space model as developed in [13], [12], and [14]. Although some theorems and concepts from those two papers are reproduced here, the proofs and proof techniques are not. The reader is referred to those two documents for a more complete and formal exposition. Those already familiar with the strand space method may safely skip this section.

In brief, we introduce a structure called a *strand*, which represents both the abilities of the penetrator and the local experience of a legitimate principal. We then define a structure on strands, called a *bundle*, combines these local views to form a global view. We then define the penetrator, and show that the abilities of the penetrator obey strict bounds. We end with a few words on how these bounds can be used to prove correctness conditions.

More formally:

Definition 2.1 *Let* A *be the set of messages that can be sent between principals. We will call elements of* A terms.

A strand *is a sequence of message transmissions and receptions, where transmission of a term a is represented as $+a$ and reception of term a is represented as $-a$. We will often write a strand as $\langle \pm a_1, \pm a_2, \ldots \pm a_n \rangle$.*

A node *is any is any particular transmission or reception on a particular strand. We often write $\langle s, 1\rangle$ for the first node on a strand s, $\langle s, 2\rangle$ for the second, and so on.*

In the case of a legitimate participant, the strand represents those messages that the participant would send or receive as part of one particular run of the protocol. In the case of the penetrator, the strands represent atomic deductions from which more complex actions can be formed. Note that principals are represented only what they say and hear; the penetrator, however, can "say" anything that it can deduce.

Because strands are ordered sequences of message transmissions or receptions, it is meaningful to speak of when something is first said:

Definition 2.2 *Let I be a set of terms. Then a node n is an* entry point *to I if*

1. *the sign of n is positive (i.e. a message transmission),*
2. *the term of n is in I, and*
3. *the term of no previous node on the strand is in I.*

In other words, entry points are those nodes where the strand "enters" the set, i.e. transmits something in the set without having previously transmitted or receiving anything in the set. Entry points are useful for discussing the origins of messages.

We use a similar concept to discuss the first time a particular value is sent out as part of a larger message. To do so, assume that the *subterm* relation is defined on A: $t_1 \sqsubset t_2$ if t_1 is a subterm of t_2.

Definition 2.3 *A* term originates *on a node n iff n is an entry point to the set $I = \{t' : t \sqsubset t'\}$.*

We impose upon strands a graph structure with two types of edges: $\Rightarrow$ and $\rightarrow$. The first arrow represents immediate precedence on a strand:

Definition 2.4 *If n_i and n_{i+1} are consecutive nodes on an strand, we write $n_i \Rightarrow n_{i+1}$.*

The other edge represents inter-strand communication by transmission of terms. When one strands transmits a term, we allow another strand to receive that same term:

Definition 2.5 *If a node $n_1 = +a$ and node $n_2 = -a$, then we write $n_1 \rightarrow n_2$.*

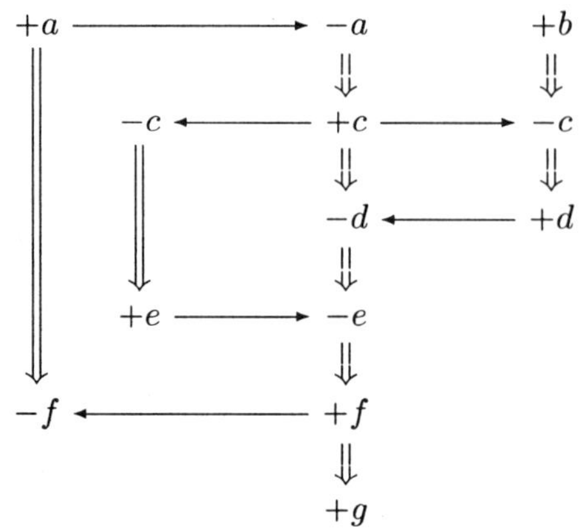

Figure 1. A Bundle

A *strand space*, which is any collection of strands, can be thought of as an ordered graph on the nodes of those strands($\mathcal{N}$) formed by the edges $\rightarrow$ and $\Rightarrow$. A *bundle* is a meaningful finite subgraph of $\langle \mathcal{N}, (\rightarrow \cup \Rightarrow) \rangle$. By "meaningful," we mean that it respects the laws of causality:

- Time flows in only one direction (the arrows of the bundle contain no loops), and
- Causal precedence is preserved. In other words, if an event occurs, then all other events necessary for that occurrence have also occurred. (Bundles are closed backward along arrows).

Definition 2.6 *Let $\mathcal{C} \subset (\rightarrow \cup \Rightarrow)$ be a set of edges, and let $\mathcal{N}_\mathcal{C}$ be the set of nodes incident with any edge in $\mathcal{C}$. $\mathcal{C}$ is a bundle if:*

1. *$\mathcal{C}$ is finite.*
2. *If $n_2 \in \mathcal{N}_\mathcal{C}$ and term(n_2) is negative, then there is a unique $n_1 \in \mathcal{C}$ such that $n_1 \rightarrow n_2$.*
3. *If $n_2 \in \mathcal{N}_\mathcal{C}$ and $n_1 \Rightarrow n_2$ then $n_1 \Rightarrow n_2 \in \mathcal{C}$.*
4. *$\mathcal{C}$ is acyclic.*

(For simplicy, we will often speak of a node being in $\mathcal{C}$ when it is in $\mathcal{N}_\mathcal{C}$.) Figure 1 illustrates an example bundle.

The concept of a bundle is an important one: all possible runs of a protocol can be represented as bundles, and almost all correctness properties can be stated as properties of bundles.

Bundles also have a very useful property:

Lemma 2.7 *Let $\mathcal{C}$ be a set of edges, and let $\preceq_\mathcal{C}$ be the transitive, reflexive closure of $\mathcal{C}$. If $\mathcal{C}$ is a bundle then $\preceq_\mathcal{C}$ is a partial order, i.e. a reflexive, transitive, antisymmetric relation. Then every non-empty set of the nodes of $\mathcal{C}$ have $\preceq_\mathcal{C}$-minimal elements.*

This is also important to our model. Almost all of our reasoning will use the concept of $\preceq_\mathcal{C}$-minimal elements: both entry points and origination points are $\preceq_\mathcal{C}$-minimal elements for sets of certain forms. Before we progress further, however, we add more structure to A and develop our model of the penetrator.

The set of terms A is assumed to be freely generated from two sets:

- $\mathsf{T} \subseteq \mathsf{A}$, which contains texts (the atomic messages), and
- $\mathsf{K} \subseteq \mathsf{A}$, which contains keys (and is disjoint from T),

By two operations:

- $\mathsf{encr} : \mathsf{K} \times \mathsf{A} \rightarrow \mathsf{A}$, which represents encryption, and
- $\mathsf{join} : \mathsf{A} \times \mathsf{A} \rightarrow \mathsf{A}$, which represents concatenation of terms.

We also define injective unary operator $\mathsf{inv} : \mathsf{K} \rightarrow \mathsf{K}$, which maps each member of a public/private key pair to the other, and a symmetric key to itself. We will follow custom and write $\mathsf{inv}(K)$ as K^{-1}, $\mathsf{encr}(K, m)$ as $\{m\}_K$, and $\mathsf{join}(a, b)$ as $a\, b$. If k is a set of keys, k^{-1} denotes the set of inverses of elements of k.

The freeness assumption is stronger than strictly necessary; we assume it here to simply exposition. In [12] we develop the model with weaker freeness assumptions, allowing such relations as associativity of join.

We define the subterm relationship $\sqsubset$ so that for $K \in \mathsf{K}$, $K \sqsubset \{g\}_K$ only if $K \sqsubset g$ already. Defining the subterm relationship in this way reflects an assumption about the penetrator's capabilities: that keys can be obtained from ciphertext only if they are embedded in the text that was encrypted. This might not always be the case—if, for instance, a dictionary attack is possible—but it is the assumption we will make here.

The powers that are available to the penetrator are characterized by two ingredients: a set of keys known initially to the penetrator, and a set of penetrator strands that allow the penetrator to generate new messages.

A *penetrator set* consists of a set of keys $\mathsf{K_P}$ which contains the keys initially known to the penetrator. Typically it would contain: all public keys; all private keys held by the penetrator or his accomplices; and all symmetric keys K_{px}, K_{xp} initially shared between the penetrator and principals playing by the protocol rules. It may also contain "lost keys" that became known to the penetrator previously.

The atomic actions available to the penetrator are encoded in a set of *penetrator strands*. They summarize his ability to discard messages, generate well known messages, piece messages together, and apply cryptographic operations using keys that become available to him. A protocol attack typically requires several of these atomic actions to be used in combination.

Definition 2.8 *A* penetrator strand *is one of the following:*

M. *Text message:* $\langle +t \rangle$ *where* $t \in \mathsf{T}$

F. *Flushing:* $\langle -g \rangle$

T. *Tee:* $\langle -g,\ +g,\ +g \rangle$

C. *Concatenation:* $\langle -g,\ -h,\ +g\,h \rangle$

S. *Separation into components:* $\langle -g\,h,\ +g,\ +h \rangle$

K. *Key:* $\langle +K \rangle$ *where* $K \in \mathsf{K_P}$.

E. *Encryption:* $\langle -K,\ -h,\ +\{h\}_K \rangle$.

D. *Decryption:* $\langle -K^{-1},\ -\{h\}_K,\ +h \rangle$.

Strands that are not penetrator strands are regular strands.

(This set of penetrator strands gives the penetrator powers similar to those in other approaches, e.g. [7, 11].) By explicitly listing the abilities of the penetrator, we gain an important ability ourselves. Because the actions available to the penetrator are independent of any particular protocol, we can prove bounds on the penetrator that are also protocol-independent. In particular, we often show that a set of terms is *honest*:

Definition 2.9 *A set* $I \subseteq \mathsf{A}$ *is* honest *relative to a bundle* $\mathcal{C}$ *if and only if whenever a penetrator node p is an entry point for I, p is an* **M** *node or a* **K** *node.*

In other words, a set is honest if elements of that set cannot be synthesized by the penetrator. They can be guessed—by way of a lucky **M** node or **K** node—but the penetrator cannot deduce them via a sequence of decryptions, encryptions, concatenations, or separations.

In applications, honest sets are usually taken to be sets of a particular form, called *ideals*:

Definition 2.10 *If* $\mathsf{k} \subseteq \mathsf{K}$, *a* k*-ideal of* A *is any set* $I \subset \mathsf{A}$ *such that for all* $h \in I$, $g \in \mathsf{A}$ *and* $K \in \mathsf{k}$

1. $h\,g, g\,h \in I$.
2. $\{h\}_K \in I$.

The smallest k*-ideal containing* h *is denoted* $I_{\mathsf{k}}[h]$. *If* $S \subseteq \mathsf{A}$, $I_{\mathsf{k}}[S]$ *is the smallest* k*-ideal containing* S.

Our main theorem interrelates the structure of ideals with the property of honesty:

Theorem 2.11 *Suppose* $\mathcal{C}$ *is a bundle over* A; $S \subseteq \mathsf{T} \cup \mathsf{K}$; $\mathsf{k} \subseteq \mathsf{K}$; *and* $\mathsf{K} \subseteq S \cup \mathsf{k}^{-1}$. *Then* $I_{\mathsf{k}}[S]$ *is honest.*

Intuitively, the set S usually contains some number of secrets. The set k usually contains keys which should be considered insecure. Hence, the ideal $I_{\mathsf{k}}[S]$ would represent all terms where a secret occurs in a vulnerable position, i.e. encrypted only with insecure keys. In this case, the theorem states that under certain weak conditions the penetrator will be unable to synthesize elements of the ideal. Hence, if legitimate principals never utter an element of the ideal, then the penetrator is unable to synthesize them:

Corollary 2.12 *Suppose* $\mathcal{C}$ *is a bundle,* $\mathsf{K} = S \cup \mathsf{k}^{-1}$ *and* $S \cap \mathsf{K_P} = \emptyset$. *If no regular node* $n \in \mathcal{C}$ *is an entry point for* $I_{\mathsf{k}}[S]$, *then no node in* $\mathcal{C}$ *is in* $I_{\mathsf{k}}[S]$.

Contrapositively, if the penetrator can deduce an element of the ideal, then some legitimate principal must have slipped and let an element loose:

Corollary 2.13 *Suppose* $\mathcal{C}$ *is a bundle,* $\mathsf{K} = S \cup \mathsf{k}^{-1}$ *and* $S \cap \mathsf{K_P} = \emptyset$. *If there exists a node* $m \in \mathcal{C}$ *such that* m *is in* $I_{\mathsf{k}}[S]$, *then there exists a regular node* $n \in \mathcal{C}$ *such that* n *is an entry point for* $I_{\mathsf{k}}[S]$.

(Note that these are facts about honest sets in general applied to ideals in particular.)

Suppose a key can be proven secret by the above theorem. Then the penetrator is also unable to create any terms that are encrypted with that key:

Theorem 2.14 *Suppose* $\mathcal{C}$ *is a bundle;* $\mathsf{K} = S \cup \mathsf{k}^{-1}$; $S \cap \mathsf{K_P} = \emptyset$; *and no regular node* $\in \mathcal{C}$ *is an entry point for* $I_{\mathsf{k}}[S]$. *Then any term of the form* $\{g\}_K$ *for* $K \in S$ *does not originate on a penetrator strand.*

These bounds are usually used in the following way: Suppose that one wishes to prove a correctness condition about a protocol. First, one forms a bundle that reflects the assumptions of the condition in question. Then the penetrator bounds can be used to prove that some other property about the bundle—the conclusion of the correctness condition—must follow.

For example, authentication conditions usually state that if a principal engages in one side of a protocol, then some other principal must have engaged in the other side of the protocol. In our model, local views of a protocol run are represented by regular strands, and global views of a protocol run are represented by bundles. The authentication condition then states that if a bundle contains one particular regular strand, then it must contain another regular strand of a certain form.

Secrecy conditions are more subtle. Because the penetrator is able to say anything that it can deduce, secrecy of a term is shown by proving that it is "unsayable." In particular, it is shown that no regular strand contains entry points to an honest set that contains the secret. Because the set is honest, no penetrator strand can contain an entry point either. Hence, no strand in the bundle is an entry point to the honest set, and therefore no node is in the set at all. Hence, the set—and in particular, the secret—cannot be said.

3 Multi-Protocol Strand Spaces

We use exactly the same notion of strand space [13, 12, 14]. In the case of mixed protocol environments, however, the regular strands may be those of more than one protocol. We identify one particular protocol for analysis and distinguish the strands of that protocol from all other regular strands:

Definition 3.1 *A mixed strand space is a strand space in which a subset of the regular strands is distinguished. We refer to elements in this set as* primary strands. *The regular strands which are not primary strands are called* secondary strands. *A node is a* primary *or a* secondary node *iff it is on a primary or a secondary strand.*

The intended interpretation of secondary strands is that they correspond to runs of other protocols.

When a strand space mixes protocols, it is typically crucial to correctness to ensure that no secondary strand originates values of some particular form.

Definition 3.2 *A set $I \subseteq \mathsf{A}$ is* unserved *in a strand space Σ if no entry point for I is on a secondary strand in Σ.*

A set $I \subseteq \mathsf{A}$ is strongly unserved *in a strand space Σ if, for every $t \in I$, t does not originate on any secondary strand in Σ.*

In other words, if a set is unserved, then no "original" instances of a set will occur on secondary strands. They may hear one element of the unserved set and then speak another element, but they may not utter any element of the set without hearing an element first.

The strongly unserved condition is the same in form as the unserved condition, but is strengthened from the set level to the term level. Whereas secondary strands can only speak an element of an unserved set after hearing any other element, they can speak a value in a strongly unserved set—even as a subterm of a larger message—only after receiving that same exact value as a component of some previous message.

4 Mixing Otway-Rees

In this section, we review the Otway-Rees Protocol described and analyzed in [12], of which a normal run is summarized in Figure 2. As in [12], assume the following:

- A set $\mathsf{T}_{\text{name}} \subseteq \mathsf{T}$ of names.

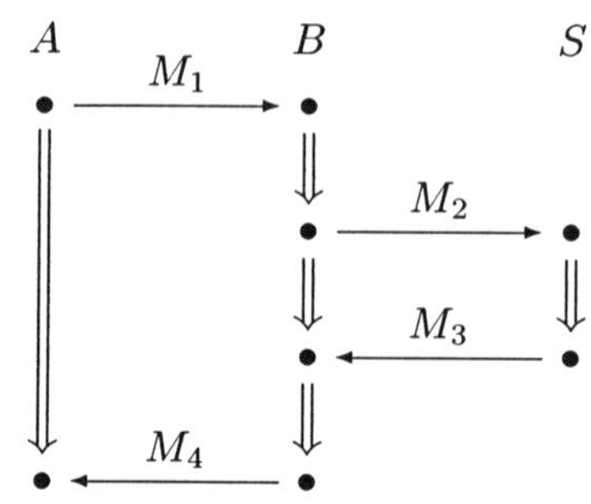

$$M_1 = M\,A\,B\,\{N_a\,M\,A\,B\}_{K_{AS}}$$
$$M_2 = M\,A\,B\,\{N_a\,M\,A\,B\}_{K_{AS}}\,\{N_b\,M\,A\,B\}_{K_{BS}}$$
$$M_3 = M\,\{N_a\,K_{AB}\}_{K_{AS}}\,\{N_b\,K_{AB}\}_{K_{BS}}$$
$$M_4 = M\,\{N_a\,K_{AB}\}_{K_{AS}}$$

Figure 2. Message Exchange in Otway-Rees

- A mapping $K : \mathsf{T}_{\text{name}} \to \mathsf{K}$. This is intended to denote the mapping which associates to each principal the key it shares with the server. In the literature on this protocol this mapping is usually written using subscripts $K(A) = K_{AS}$.

  We assume the mapping $A \mapsto K_{AS}$ is injective. We also assume $K_{AS} = K_{AS}^{-1}$, i.e. that the protocol is using symmetric cryptography.

  Let L be the set of long-term keys, i.e. the range of K.

We will adopt some conventions on variables for the remainder of this section:

- Variables A, B, C, X range over T_{name};
- Variables K, K' range over K;
- Variables N, M (or the same letters decorated with subscripts) range over $\mathsf{T} \setminus \mathsf{T}_{\text{name}}$, i.e. those texts that are not names.

Other letters such as G and H range over all of A. We would emphasize that N_a is just a variable, having no reliable connection to A, whereas K_{AS} is the result of applying the function K to the argument A. Thus, the latter reliably refers to the long-term key shared between A and S.

4.1 Otway-Rees Formalized

The primary strands for an Otway-Rees strand space may be read off Figure 2. There are only two fine points. First, we assume that the respondent never picks a nonce N_b that happens to be the same as the initiator's nonce N_a. The respondent cannot enforce this directly, because N_a occurs encrypted with the initiator's long term key; instead, we assume that a probabilistic mechanism enforces it (cf. [12, Section 5]). Second, we assume that the server always selects a session key with three properties: it is a symmetric key; it is unknown to the penetrator; and it is different from any long-term key. The server presumably relies on probabilistic mechanisms to ensure that the last two of these conditions are met.

Definition 4.1 *Let Σ be a strand space.*

1. Init$[A, B, N, M, K]$ *is the set of strands $s \in \Sigma$ whose trace is*

$$\langle + M\, A\, B\, \{N\, M\, A\, B\}_{K_{AS}}, \quad - M\, \{N\, K\}_{K_{AS}} \rangle$$

Σ_{init} *is the union of the range of* Init.

2. Resp$[A, B, N, M, K, H, H']$ *is defined when $N \not\sqsubset H$; its value then is the set of strands in Σ whose trace is*

$$\begin{array}{l}\langle - \; M\, A\, B\, H, \\ \;\; + \; M\, A\, B\, H\, \{N\, M\, A\, B\}_{K_{BS}}, \\ \;\; - \; M\, H'\, \{N\, K\}_{K_{BS}}, \\ \;\; + \; M\, H' \rangle\end{array}$$

Σ_{resp} *is the union of the range of* Resp.

3. Serv$[A, B, N_a, N_b, M, K]$ *is defined if $K \notin \mathsf{K}_{\mathcal{P}}$, $K \notin \{K_{AS} : A \in \mathsf{T}_{name}\}$ and $K = K^{-1}$; its value then is the set of strands in Σ whose trace is:*

$$\begin{array}{l}\langle - \; M\, A\, B\, \{N_a\, M\, A\, B\}_{K_{AS}}\, \{N_b\, M\, A\, B\}_{K_{BS}}, \\ \;\; + \; M\, \{N_a\, K\}_{K_{AS}}\, \{N_b\, K\}_{K_{BS}} \rangle\end{array}$$

Σ_{serv} *is the union of the range of* Serv.

Note that the sets $\Sigma_{\text{serv}}, \Sigma_{\text{init}}, \Sigma_{\text{resp}}$ are pairwise disjoint (cf [12], Lemma 5.2).

For the rest of this example, we will assume that the primary strands are the elements of $\Sigma_{\text{serv}} \cup \Sigma_{\text{init}} \cup \Sigma_{\text{resp}}$ and that the secondary strands are strands of other, unspecified protocols.

Definition 4.2 *Let $\mathsf{L}_0 \subseteq \mathsf{L}$.*

- $\mathsf{Ticket}(\mathsf{L}_0)$ *= the set of all terms of the form $\{N\, K'\}_K$ for $N \in \mathsf{T} \setminus \mathsf{T}_{name}$, $K' \in \mathsf{K}$, and $K \in \mathsf{L}_0$.*
- $\mathsf{Request}(\mathsf{L}_0)$ *= the set of all terms of the form $\{N\, M\, A\, B\}_K$ for $N, M \in \mathsf{T} \setminus \mathsf{T}_{name}$, $A, B \in \mathsf{T}_{name}$, and $K \in \mathsf{L}_0$.*
- $I(\mathsf{L}_0) = I_{\mathsf{k}}[\mathsf{L}_0]$*, where* $\mathsf{k} = (\mathsf{K} \setminus \mathsf{L}_0)$.

An Otway-Rees strand space Σ respects *a set U of principals if, letting $\mathsf{L}_0 = K(U)$ be the image of U under the "key of" mapping K:*

1. $\mathsf{L}_0 \cap \mathsf{K}_{\mathcal{P}} = \emptyset$;
2. $I(\mathsf{L}_0)$ *is unserved in* Σ;
3. $\mathsf{Ticket}(\mathsf{L}_0)$ *and* $\mathsf{Request}(\mathsf{L}_0)$ *are strongly unserved in* Σ.

Otway-Rees remains correct in a mixed protocol environment Σ, for a collection of users U, if Σ respects U. In this paper we will concentrate on a single aspect of the correctness of Otway-Rees, namely the authentication guarantee that Otway-Rees provides to its initiator. However, the secrecy property of Otway-Rees [12, Section 6] and the authentication guarantees it offers to the other participants [12, Section 7.2] may be modified in an equally straightforward way using the same assumptions on Σ.

4.2 Mixed Otway-Rees: Authentication

In this subsection we will prove the authentication guarantee that Otway-Rees provides to its initiator. The proofs are minor modifications of the proofs given in [12].

4.2.1 Preliminaries

We first need a pair of small lemmas. The first is specific to the case of mixed protocols; the second matches a result given in [12].

Proposition 4.3 *Consider a bundle $\mathcal{C}$ in Σ. Suppose $\mathsf{L}_0 \subseteq \mathsf{L}$ is such that $\mathsf{L}_0 \cap K_{\mathcal{P}} = \emptyset$ and $I(\mathsf{L}_0)$ is unserved in Σ. Then no term of the form $\{g\}_K$ for $K \in \mathsf{L}_0$ can originate on a penetrator node in $\mathcal{C}$.*

PROOF. To apply Corollary 2.14, with $S = \mathsf{L}_0$ and $\mathsf{k} = \mathsf{K} \setminus \mathsf{L}_0$, we must check that no regular node n is an entry point for $I_{\mathsf{k}}[S] = I(\mathsf{L}_0)$. By hypothesis, n cannot be a secondary node. n is thus a primary node. However, if n is primary, no long-term key can occur as a subterm of term(n), unless it occurs within the H-term of a responder strand. But in this case n is not an entry point for $I(\mathsf{L}_0)$. ■

We also need a case analysis for the locations at which a term in $\mathsf{Ticket}(\mathsf{L}_0)$ or $\mathsf{Request}(\mathsf{L}_0)$ can originate, assuming that they are originating on a primary strand. The proof matches that of [12, Proposition 7.2 and Corollary 7.3].

Proposition 4.4 *Let s be a primary strand of Σ.*

1. *Suppose $t = \{N\, K\}_{K_{XS}}$ originates on s. Then t and K originate on $\langle s, 2\rangle$, and either $s \in$ Serv$[A, X, N, N', M, K]$ or $s \in$ Serv$[X, B, N', N, M, K]$ for some A, B, N', M.*
2. *Suppose $t = \{N\, M\, A\, B\}_{K_{AS}}$ originates on s, and with $A \neq B$. Then t and N originate on $\langle s, 1\rangle$, and $s \in$ Init$[A, B, N, M, K]$ for some K.*

3. *Suppose* $t = \{N\, M\, A\, B\}_{K_{BS}}$ *originates on* s, *with* $A \neq B$. *Then* t *and* N *originate on* $\langle s, 2\rangle$, *and* $s \in \text{Resp}[A, B, N, M, K, H, H']$, *for some* K, H, *and* H'.

4.2.2 Initiator's Guarantee

The following theorem asserts that if a bundle contains a strand $s \in \Sigma_{\text{init}}$, then under the expected assumptions, there are primary strands $s_{\text{resp}} \in \Sigma_{\text{resp}}$ and $s_{\text{serv}} \in \Sigma_{\text{serv}}$ which agree on the initiator, responder, and M values.

Theorem 4.5 *Suppose* Σ *respects* U *and* $A, B \in U$. *Suppose* $\mathcal{C}$ *is a bundle in* Σ; $A \neq B$; *and* N_a *is uniquely originating in* $\mathcal{C}$.

If $s \in \text{Init}[A, B, N_a, M, K]$ *has* $\mathcal{C}$*-height 2, then for some* $N_b \in \mathsf{T}$ *there are primary strands:*

- $s_{serv} \in \text{Serv}[A, B, N_a, N_b, M, K]$ *of* $\mathcal{C}$*-height 2;*
- $s_{resp} \in \text{Resp}[A, B, N_b, M, K, H, H']$ *of* $\mathcal{C}$*-height at least 2, for some* K, H, *and* H'.

PROOF. The proof of this is similar to the proof of the initiator's guarantee for the unmixed Otway-Rees protocol. The novelty in this case is that we need to establish that a certain term originates on a primary node, whereas in the unmixed case it was sufficient to prove the term originated on a regular node. We will prove this by a sequence of steps. For the remainder of this section, fix Σ, U, $\mathcal{C}$ and s such that the assumptions hold. In particular, by the last assumption of the theorem,

$$\begin{aligned}\langle +\ & M\, A\, B\, \{N_a\, M\, A\, B\}_{K_{AS}},\\ &-\ M\, \{N_a\, K\}_{K_{AS}}\rangle\end{aligned}$$

is the $\mathcal{C}$-trace of a strand s.

Step 1 *There is an* $s_{serv} \in \Sigma_{serv}$ *with* $\mathcal{C}$*-height 2;* s_{serv} *is either of the form* $\text{Serv}[A, X, N_a, N_b, M_1, K]$ *or of the form* $\text{Serv}[X, A, N_b, N_a, M_1, K]$.

PROOF. We will apply Proposition 4.3 with $\mathsf{L}_0 = K(U)$, using Definition 4.2, Clauses 1 and 2; it follows $\{N_a\, K\}_{K_{AS}}$ does not originate on a penetrator node in $\mathcal{C}$. Because $\{N_a\, K\}_{K_{AS}} \in \mathsf{Ticket}(\mathsf{L}_0)$ and Σ respects U, by Definition 4.2, Clause 3, it must originate on a primary strand; the node at which it originates is in $\mathcal{C}$. By Proposition 4.4 Clause 1, this node is $\langle s_{\text{serv}}, 2\rangle$ where s_{serv} satisfies one of the conditions:

1. $s_{\text{serv}} \in \text{Serv}[A, X, N_a, N_b, M_1, K]$, or
2. $s_{\text{serv}} \in \text{Serv}[X, A, N_b, N_a, M_1, K]$. ■

Fix $s_{\text{serv}} \in \Sigma_{\text{serv}}$, X, and M_1 satisfying the conditions given in Step 1.

Step 2 $s_{serv} \in \text{Serv}[A, X, N_a, N_b, M_1, K]$.

PROOF. Suppose—in order to derive a contradiction—that $s_{\text{serv}} \in \text{Serv}[X, A, N_b, N_a, M_1, K]$ holds instead. Then $\{N_a\, M_1\, X\, A\}_{K_{AS}}$ is a subterm of $\text{term}(\langle s_{\text{serv}}, 1\rangle)$.

By Proposition 4.3 with $\mathsf{L}_0 = K(U)$ again, using Definition 4.2, Clauses 1 and 2, $\{N_a\, M_1\, A\, X\}_{K_{AS}}$ originates on a regular strand s_1.

Using Clause 3 $\{N_a\, M_1\, X\, A\}_{K_{AS}}$ originates on a primary strand s_1, and by Proposition 4.4, N_a originates on the same strand s_1.

But N_a also originates on the strand we began with, $s \in \text{Init}[A, B, N_a, M, K]$. Because N_a originates uniquely, $s = s_1$. Hence by Proposition 4.4, $X = A = B$, contradicting an assumption. ■

Step 3 $X = B$ *and* $M_1 = M$.

PROOF. Since $s_{\text{serv}} \in \text{Serv}[A, X, N_a, N_b, M_1, K]$, $\{N_a\, M_1\, A\, X\}_{K_{AS}} \sqsubset \text{term}(\langle s_{\text{serv}}, 1\rangle)$. By Proposition 4.3 with $\mathsf{L}_0 = K(U)$ again, using Definition 4.2, Clause 1, $\{N_a\, M_1\, A\, X\}_{K_{AS}}$ originates on a regular strand s_1. Using Definition 4.2, Clause 3, s_1 is a primary strand. By Proposition 4.4, N_a originates on the same strand s_1.

But N_a also originates on s. Because N_a originates uniquely, $s = s_1$. Thus $M_1 = M$ and $X = B$, and $s_{\text{serv}} \in \text{Serv}[A, B, N_a, N_b, M, K]$. ■

Step 4 *For some* K, H, *and* H', *there is a strand* $s_{resp} \in \text{Resp}[A, B, N_b, M, K, H, H']$ *of* $\mathcal{C}$*-height at least 2.*

PROOF. We again use Proposition 4.3 and Definition 4.2, Clause 3 to infer that $\{N_b\, M\, A\, B\}_{K_{BS}}$ originates on a primary node in $\mathcal{C}$. By Proposition 4.4, this node is the second on a strand $s_{\text{resp}} \in \text{Resp}[A, B, N_b, M, K, H, H']$ for some K, H, and H'. Since $\langle s_{\text{resp}}, 2\rangle \in \mathcal{C}$, it follows s_{resp} has $\mathcal{C}$-height at least 2. ■

5 Neuman-Stubblebine

An important kind of multiple-protocol environment are single protocols that contain multiple parts. Examples of such protocols—such as Kerberos [6], for example—are currently in widespread use. In this paper, we will demonstrate the analysis of such protocols on the Neuman-Stubblebine protocol [9].

The general structural elements needed to describe the protocol are very similar to those of Otway-Rees. In particular, we assume given an injective mapping $K : \mathsf{T}_{\text{name}} \to \mathsf{K}$ which associates to each name a symmetric long term key shared with a central server, and the set L of all long term keys defined to be the range of K. For $K \in \mathsf{L}$, $K^{-1} = K$.

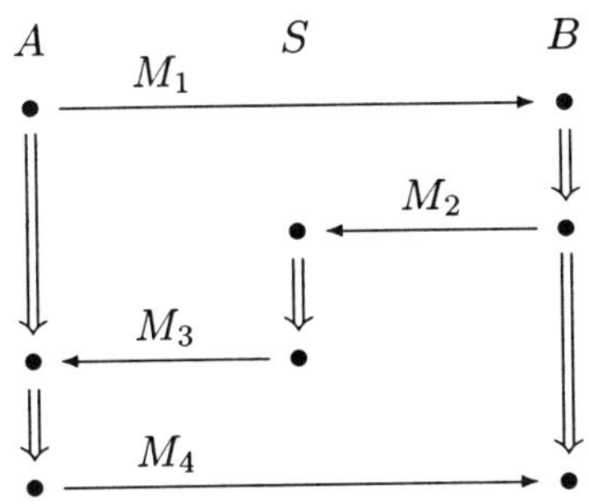

$$M_1 = A\, N_a$$

$$M_2 = B\,\{A\, N_a\, t_b\}_{K_{BS}}\, N_b$$

$$M_3 = \{B\, N_a\, K\, t_b\}_{K_{AS}}\, \{A\, K\, t_b\}_{K_{BS}}\, N_b$$

$$M_4 = \{A\, K\, t_b\}_{K_{BS}}\, \{N_b\}_K$$

Figure 3. Message Exchange in Neuman-Stubblebine

5.1 The Neuman-Stubblebine Protocol, Part I

The Neuman-Stubblebine protocol starts with an initial authentication protocol, summarized in Figure 3.

In this protocol, K is a unique key generated by the Key Distribution Center S, and t_b is an expiration time for the ticket $\{A\, K\, t_b\}_{K_{BS}}$. (We do not consider the issues of time and timestamps in our analysis.)

First, we define the primary strands to correspond to the three roles of the protocol:

Definition 5.1 *Let Σ be a strand space.*

1. $\mathsf{Init}[A, B, N_a, N_b, t_b, K, H]$ *is the set of strands $s \in \Sigma$ of the form:*

$$\langle +A\, N_a,\ -\{B\, N_a\, K\, t_b\}_{K_{AS}}\, H\, N_b,\ +H\{N_b\}_K\rangle$$

   Σ_{init} *is the union of the range of* Init.

2. $\mathsf{Resp}[A, B, N_a, N_b, t_b, K]$ *is the set of strands in Σ of the form:*

$$\langle -A\, N_a,\ +B\,\{A\, N_a\, t_b\}_{K_{BS}}\, N_b,\ -\{A\, K\, t_b\}_{K_{BS}}\, \{N_b\}_K\rangle$$

   Σ_{resp} *is the union of the range of* Resp.

3. $\mathsf{Serv}[A, B, N_a, N_b, t_b, K]$ *is defined if $K \notin \mathsf{K}_{\mathcal{P}} \cup \mathsf{L}$ and $K = K^{-1}$; its value then is the set of strands in Σ of the form:*

$$\langle -B\,\{A\, N_a\, t_b\}_{K_{BS}}\, N_b,\ +\{B\, N_a\, K\, t_b\}_{K_{AS}}\, \{A\, K\, t_b\}_{K_{BS}}\, N_b\rangle$$

   Σ_{serv} *is the union of the range of* Serv.

A NS space *is a strand space in which the primary strands are those in Σ_{init}, Σ_{resp}, or Σ_{serv}.*

We will not show that this protocol is correct in all respects. We use the Neuman-Stubblebine protocol as an illustrative example only, and so will instead focus on just one property: the authentication of initiator to responder.

The security of the Neuman-Stubblebine authentication protocol depends upon three types of terms:

1. *Tickets*, which are terms of the form $\{A\, K\, t_b\}_{K_{BS}}$. Tickets are how the secret key is distributed to the responder.

2. *Distributions*, or terms of the form $\{B\, N_a\, K\, t_b\}_{K_{AS}}$. The secret key is distributed to the initiator in terms of this form.

3. *Confirmations*, or terms of the form $\{N_b\}_K$. The initiator finishes the protocol by sending a confirmation to the responder.

We focus on the tickets, distributions, and confirmations built using actual long term keys and session keys; since we do not in general know what values these are, they appear in the definition as the parameters L_0 and S_0. As we use this definition, $\mathsf{k}_0 = \mathsf{L}_0 \cup \mathsf{S}_0$.

Definition 5.2 *Let $\mathsf{k}_0 \subset \mathsf{K}$, $\mathsf{L}_0 \subset \mathsf{L}$ and $\mathsf{S}_0 \subset \mathsf{K} \setminus \mathsf{L}$:*

1. $\mathsf{Ticket}(\mathsf{L}_0)$ *= the set of all terms of the form $\{X\, K\, t_x\}_{K'}$ for $X \in \mathsf{T}_{name}$, $K' \in \mathsf{L}_0$, $K \in \mathsf{K}$, and $t_x \in \mathsf{T} \setminus \mathsf{T}_{name}$.*

2. $\mathsf{Distribute}(\mathsf{L}_0, \mathsf{S}_0)$ *= the set of all terms of the form $\{X\, N\, K\, t_x\}_{K'}$ for $X \in \mathsf{T}_{name}$, $N, t_x \in \mathsf{T} \setminus \mathsf{T}_{name}$, $K' \in \mathsf{L}_0$, and $K \in \mathsf{S}_0$.*

3. $\mathsf{Confirm}(\mathsf{S}_0)$ *= the set of all terms of the form $\{N\}_K$ for $N \in \mathsf{T} \setminus \mathsf{T}_{name}$, and $K \in \mathsf{S}_0$.*

4. $I(\mathsf{k}_0) = I_{\mathsf{k}}[\mathsf{k}_0]$, *where* $\mathsf{k} = (\mathsf{K} \setminus \mathsf{k}_0)$.

5. $\mathsf{SK}(U)$ *= the set of K such that in Σ*

$$\exists A, B \in U\ .\ \mathsf{Serv}[A, B, *, *, *, K] \neq \emptyset$$

Clauses 1 though 3 formalize the terms of interest. Clause 4 is simply a notational convenience. Clause 5, on the other hand, allows us to define a particular set of keys. If we wish to prove a correctness condition about some arbitrary set U of principals, we not only need to consider their long term keys but also the secret keys $\mathsf{SK}(U)$ distributed to any two principals in U, as defined in clause 5.

Definition 5.3 *An NS strand space* Σ respects *a set of principals* U, *if, letting* $\mathsf{L}_0 = K(U)$ *and* $\mathsf{S}_0 = \mathsf{SK}(U)$:

1. $(\mathsf{L}_0 \cup \mathsf{S}_0) \cap \mathsf{K}_{\mathcal{P}} = \emptyset$;
2. $I(\mathsf{L}_0 \cup \mathsf{S}_0)$ *is unserved in* Σ;
3. $\mathsf{Ticket}(\mathsf{L}_0) \cup \mathsf{Distribute}(\mathsf{L}_0, \mathsf{S}_0) \cup \mathsf{Confirm}(\mathsf{S}_0)$ *is strongly unserved in* Σ.

Intuitively, a strand space respects a set of principals if it does not interfere with the way the Neuman-Stubblebine protocol uses long term keys, session keys, tickets, distributions and confirmations among members of that set. The long term keys and session keys for those principals must be uncompromised (Clause 1). Secondary strands cannot place any of the above keys in vulnerable positions (Clause 2). Lastly, the tickets, distributions, and confirmations relevant to the principals of interest cannot come from secondary strands (Clause 3). We do not prohibit secondary strands from making terms of those three forms, only from making term of those forms with values that might interfere with those of these principals. For instance, terms of the same forms could safely be constructed using a disjoint set of long term keys.

Before we examine the authentication property of interest, we apply Theorems 2.12 and 2.14 to show two preliminary lemmas: secrecy of keys, and non-synthesis of encrypted terms.

Fix a set of principals U, a NS space Σ, and a bundle $\mathcal{C}$. Let $\mathsf{L}_0 = K(U)$ and $\mathsf{S}_0 = \mathsf{SK}(U)$.

Lemma 5.4 *Suppose* $A, B \in U$, Σ *respects* U, *and* K *is uniquely originating. Let* $s_{serv} \in \mathrm{Serv}[A, B, *, *, *, K]$ *be in* $\mathcal{C}$. *For every node* $m \in \mathcal{C}$, $m \notin I(\{K, K_{AS}, K_{BS}\})$.

PROOF. Let $\mathsf{k}_0 = \{K, K_{AS}, K_{BS}\}$. By Corollary 2.12 with $S = \mathsf{k}_0$ and $\mathsf{k} = \mathsf{K} \setminus \mathsf{k}_0$, it is sufficient to show that no regular node is an entry point to $I(\mathsf{k}_0)$. Because $I(\mathsf{k}_0)$ is unserved, any regular node which is an entry point to the ideal must be a primary node.

By inspection, no term containing a key originates on any strand in Σ_{init} or Σ_{resp}. However, if $s' \in \Sigma_{\mathrm{serv}}$ then a key originates on node $\langle s', 2\rangle$. So suppose that $\langle s', 2\rangle$ is an entry point to $I(\mathsf{k}_0)$. Then $K \sqsubset \langle s', 2\rangle$, and since K_{AS}, $K_{BS} \not\sqsubset \langle s', 2\rangle$, K originates on s'.

Since K is uniquely originating, and it originates on s_{serv} as well as s', $s' = s_{\mathrm{serv}}$. Moreover, K does not occur in $\langle s, 2\rangle$ unencrypted or encrypted with anything but K_{AS} or K_{BS}. Hence s' does not contain an entry point into $I(\mathsf{k}_0)$, and so no primary strand is an entry point to $I(\mathsf{k}_0)$. ∎

Lemma 5.5 *Suppose* Σ *respects* U. *Then no term of the form* $\{g\}_K$ *for* $K \in \mathsf{L}_0$ *can originate on a penetrator node in* $\mathcal{C}$.

PROOF. (Similar to that of Proposition 4.3) Apply Corollary 2.14 with $S = \mathsf{L}_0$ and $\mathsf{k} = \mathsf{K} \setminus \mathsf{L}_0$, and confirm that no regular node is an entry point for $I(\mathsf{L}_0)$: Let n be a regular entry point for $I(\mathsf{L}_0)$. Since $I(\mathsf{L}_0) \subset I(\mathsf{L}_0 \cup \mathsf{S}_0)$ is unserved in Σ, n is not a secondary node. By observation, n is not a primary node. ∎

We can now prove the authentication condition under consideration:

Theorem 5.6 *Suppose* Σ *respects* U; $A, B \in U$; *and* K *is uniquely originating. Suppose* $\mathcal{C}$ *is a bundle in* Σ, *and* $s_1 \in \mathrm{Resp}[A, B, N_a, N_b, t_b, K]$ *has* $\mathcal{C}$*-height 3.*

Then some $s_3 \in \mathrm{Init}[A, B, *, N_b, t_b, K]$ *has* $\mathcal{C}$*-height 3.*

We prove this property by a series of intermediate steps. For those who are uninterested in the details, the statements of each step provide a sketch of the proof.

Step 1 *There is an* $s_2 \in \mathrm{Serv}[A, B, *, *, t_b, K]$ *with* $\mathcal{C}$*-height 2.*

PROOF. $\{A\,K\,t_b\}_{K_{BS}} \sqsubset \langle s_1, 3\rangle$. By Proposition 5.5, $\{A\,K\,t_b\}_{K_{BS}}$ originates on a regular node in $\mathcal{C}$. Because $\{A\,K\,t_b\}_{K_{BS}} \in \mathsf{Ticket}(\mathsf{L}_0)$, that regular node is a primary node n. By inspection, $n = \langle s_2, 2\rangle$ where $s_2 \in \mathrm{Serv}[A, B, *, *, t_b, K]$.

Step 2 *There is an* $s_3 \in \mathrm{Init}[X, Y, N_X, N_b, t_y, K]$ *with* $\mathcal{C}$*-height 3.*

PROOF. By Step 1, $K \in \mathsf{S}_0$. By Proposition 5.4 and Corollary 2.14, no term of the form $\{g\}_K$ originates on a penetrator strand. Hence, $\{N_b\}_K$, which is a subterm of $\langle s_1, 3\rangle$, originates on a regular node $n' \in \mathcal{C}$. Because $\{N_b\}_K \in \mathsf{Confirm}(\mathsf{S}_0)$, n' is a primary node. By inspection, $n' = \langle s_3, 3\rangle$ where $s_3 \in \mathrm{Init}[X, Y, N_X, N_b, t_y, K]$ for some X, Y, N_X, t_y.

Step 3 *There is an* $s_4 \in \mathrm{Serv}[X, Y, *, N_b, t_y, K]$ *with* $\mathcal{C}$*-height 2.*

PROOF. Letting $t = \{Y\,N_b\,K\,t_y\}_{K_{XS}}$, we see that $t \sqsubset \langle s_2, 2\rangle$. If $K_{XS} \notin \mathsf{L}_0$, then $t \in I(\mathsf{L}_0 \cup \mathsf{S}_0)$, contradicting Proposition 5.4. By Proposition 5.5, t originates on a regular node n''; because $t \in \mathsf{Distribute}(\mathsf{L}_0, \mathsf{S}_0)$, n'' is a primary node.

Inspecting the primary strands, we see that $n'' = \langle s_4, 2\rangle$ where $s_4 \in \mathrm{Serv}[X, Y, *, N_b, t_y, K]$.

Step 4 $s_2 = s_4$

PROOF. K is uniquely originating, and originates on both s_2 and s_4.

Step 5 $s_3 \in \text{Init}[A, B, *, N_b, t_b, K]$ *and* s_3 *has* $\mathcal{C}$*-height 3.*

PROOF. Since $s_2 \in \text{Serv}[A, B, *, N_b, t_b, K]$, $X = A$, $Y = B$, and $t_y = t_b$. In that case, $s_3 = \text{Init}[A, B, *, N_b, t_b, K]$, and it is already established that s_3 has $\mathcal{C}$-height 3.■

In other words, if the responder B finishes a run of the protocol apparently with A, then under the conditions given, A will have finished a run with B.

5.2 Part II (Re-Authentication)

Like Kerberos, this protocol is designed to secure other protocols in which the responder B—which typically provides some networked service—responds to requests from A but keeps no state itself. In such a case, A may need to issue several requests to B and so must re-authenticate itself each time. To that end the Neuman-Stubblebine protocol has a re-authentication part, in which A reuses the ticket issued to it in the initial protocol:

II_1 $A \to B:\ N'_a\{A\, K\, t_b\}_{K_{BS}}$

II_2 $B \to A:\ \{N'_a\}_K\, N'_b$

II_3 $A \to B:\ \{N'_b\}_K$

This re-authentication protocol is known to be flawed on its own [4]. However, it also introduces a potential attack on the initial authentication protocol as well. If B keeps no state—more specifically, if B does not track successful runs of the authentication part of the protocol—then the following attack can be accomplished by starting a run of the re-authentication protocol with B before the initial protocol has finished:

1. $Z(A) \to B:\ A\, N_a$
2. $B \to S:\ B\{A\, N_a\, t_b\}_{K_{BS}}\, N_b$
3. $S \to Z(A):\ \{B\, N_a\, K\, t_b\}_{K_{AS}}\, \{A\, K\, t_b\}_{K_{BS}} N_b$

II_1 $Z(A) \to B:\ N_b\, \{A\, K\, t_b\}_{K_{BS}}$

II_2 $B \to Z(A):\ \{N_b\}_K\, N'_b$

4. $Z(A) \to B:\ \{A\, K\, t_b\}_{K_{BS}} \{N_b\}_K$

The attack is possible because a term in $\text{Confirm}(\mathsf{S}_0)$ can now originate on a secondary strand (from the re-authentication part of the protocol). This attack does not seem to be known in the literature. However, it is a pure authentication attack; no session keys (for instance) are divulged.

A variant of the re-authentication part, however, satisfies the conditions of Lemmas 5.4, 5.5, and Theorem 5.6.

II'_1 $A \to B:\ N'_a\{A\, K\, t_b\}_{K_{BS}}$

II'_2 $B \to A:\ \{N'_a\, N'_b\}_K$

II'_3 $A \to B:\ \{A\, N'_b\}_K$

To formalize II', we add a "phantom" starting message in which the initiator receives a copy of message 3 from a run of protocol I. This serves merely to represent the state in which a principal stores the results of a run of I, until ready to begin a run of II'.

Definition 5.7 *Let* Σ *be a strand space.*

1. $\text{ReInit}[A, B, N'_a, N'_b, t_b, K, G, H]$ *is the set of strands in* Σ *of the form:*

$$\langle -\ \{B\, N_a\, K\, t_b\}_{K_{AS}}\, G\, H,\ +\ N'_a\, G,\ -\ \{N'_a\, N'_b\}_K,\ +\ \{A\, N'_b\}_K \rangle$$

where $N_a \in \mathsf{T}$ *and* $G, H \in \mathsf{A}$. Σ_{reinit} *is the union of the range of* ReInit.

2. $\text{ReResp}[A, B, N'_a, N'_b, t_b, K]$ *is the set of strands in* Σ *of the form:*

$$\langle -\ \{A\, K\, t_b\}_{K_{BS}}\, N'_a,\ +\ \{N'_a\, N'_b\}_K,\ -\ \{A\, N'_b\}_K \rangle$$

Σ_{reresp} *is the union of the range of* ReResp.

A NS+ space *is an infiltrated strand space in which all the regular strands are in* Σ_{init}, Σ_{resp}, Σ_{serv}, Σ_{reinit}, *or* Σ_{reresp}.

Observe that no node on these strands is an entry point to $I(\mathsf{L}_0 \cup \mathsf{k}_0)$. Likewise, $\text{Ticket}(\mathsf{L}_0) \cup \text{Distribute}(\mathsf{L}_0, \mathsf{S}_0) \cup \text{Confirm}(\mathsf{S}_0)$ is strongly unserved by these strands. Hence, we may infer that the modified re-authentication protocol does not interfere with the authentication property given in Theorem 5.6. Setting U to be the set containing A, B, for instance, yields:

Theorem 5.8 *Suppose* $\mathcal{C}$ *is a bundle in a NS+ space, and*

- $s_1 \in \text{Resp}[A, B, N_a, N_b, t_b, K]$ *has* $\mathcal{C}$*-height 3;*
- K_{AS}*,* K_{BS} *and* $K \notin \mathbf{K}_{\mathcal{P}}$*; and*
- K *is uniquely originating.*

Then $\mathcal{C}$ *contains* $s_3 \in \text{Init}[A, B, *, N_b, t_b, K]$ *with* $\mathcal{C}$*-height 2.*

6 Discussion

Cryptographic protocols are intended to accomplish very specific goals such as authentication or exchange of keys. Analysis of these protocols has usually centered around understanding how well the protocols achieve these stated goals when executed in isolation.

But in fact cryptographic protocols are never executed in isolation. Key exchange is useful only if the keys are then used for some further purpose, such as exchanging data confidentially. Authentication is meaningful only if some particular actions can be performed by the principals, that would not have been permitted had they not been authenticated. These further activities will typically involve the keys or secrets established by the protocol, so there is a risk that these later activities will interfere with the correctness of the base protocol. In many cases, the constraints of practical use mean that an "expensive" protocol is best combined with a "cheaper" protocol, as Kerberos and Neumann-Stubblebine combine one protocol that requires use of a Key Distribution Center with a cheaper re-authentication protocol. Thus, real life is necessarily a case of mixed protocols, even apart from the mixing of independently designed protocols that may be used for unrelated purposes.

In this paper we have developed the simple machinery necessary to reason about this problem within the strand space framework.

References

[1] Michael Burrows, Martín Abadi, and Roger Needham. A logic of authentication. *Proceedings of the Royal Society*, Series A, 426(1871):233–271, December 1989. Also appeared as SRC Research Report 39 and, in a shortened form, in ACM Transactions on Computer Systems 8, 1 (February 1990), 18-36.

[2] John Clark and Jeremy Jacob. A survey of authentication protocol literature: Version 1.0. University of York, Department of Computer Science, November 1997.

[3] Li Gong and Paul Syverson. Fail-stop protocols: An approach to designing secure protocols. In *5th International Working Conference on Dependable Computing for Critical Applications*, pages 44–55, September 1995.

[4] Tzonelih Hwang, Narn-Yoh Lee, Chuang-Ming Li, Ming-Yung Ko, and Yung-Hsiang Chen. Two attacks on Neuman-Stubblebine authentication protocols. *Information Processing Letters*, 53:103–107, 1995.

[5] John Kelsey, Bruce Schneier, and David Wagner. Protocol interactions and the chosen protocol attack. In *Security Protocols, International Workshop April 1997 Proceedings*, pages 91–104. Springer-Verlag, 1998.

[6] J. Kohl and C. Neuman. The Kerberos network authentication service (v5). RFC 1510, September 1993.

[7] Gavin Lowe. Casper: A compiler for the analysis of security protocols. In *10th Computer Security Foundations Workshop Proceedings*, pages 18–30. IEEE Computer Society Press, 1997.

[8] Catherine Meadows. Analysis of the Internet Key Exchange protocol using the NRL protocol analyzer. In *Proceedings, 1999 IEEE Symposium on Security and Privacy*. IEEE Computer Society Press, May 1999.

[9] B. Clifford Neuman and Stuart G. Stubblebine. A note on the use of timestamps as nonces. *Operating Systems Review*, 27(2):10–14, April 1993.

[10] D. Otway and O. Rees. Efficient and timely mutual authentication. *Operating Systems Review*, 21(1):8–10, January 1987.

[11] Lawrence C. Paulson. Proving properties of security protocols by induction. In *10th IEEE Computer Security Foundations Workshop*, pages 70–83. IEEE Computer Society Press, 1997.

[12] F. Javier THAYER Fábrega, Jonathan C. Herzog, and Joshua D. Guttman. Honest ideals on strand spaces. In *Proceedings of the 11th IEEE Computer Security Foundations Workshop*. IEEE Computer Society Press, June 1998.

[13] F. Javier THAYER Fábrega, Jonathan C. Herzog, and Joshua D. Guttman. Strand spaces: Why is a security protocol correct? In *1998 IEEE Symposium on Security and Privacy*. IEEE Computer Society Press, May 1998.

[14] F. Javier THAYER Fábrega, Jonathan C. Herzog, and Joshua D. Guttman. Strand spaces: Proving security protocols correct. *Journal of Computer Security*, 1999. Forthcoming.

Honest Functions and their Application to the Analysis of Cryptographic Protocols

Alfred P. Maneki
National Security Agency

Abstract

In ([1], [2]) Guttman, et al, have introduced "strand spaces" as a technique for describing and analyzing cryptographic protocols (i.e. schemes for exchanging messages between legitimate agents in a communications system for purposes of authentication or establishing session keys). The strands of such a protocol are directly mapped to traces of the messages which are transmitted and received by each agent. Strands may also be associated with the possible traces of a penetrator. Guttman, et al, use simple graph theoretic constructions to describe the underlying relations between legitimate agents and the penetrator. These researchers also develop an "algebra" for the set of all possible messages which may be transmitted in a given cryptographic protocol. They have successfully used strand spaces to prove correctness properties of several cryptographic protocols.

In this paper we extend the theory of strand spaces to include a broad class of cryptographic protocols which could not be analyzed in the original framework provided by Guttman, et al. This class includes the TMN(Roscose's version) and SSHV2 protocols, i.e. protocols which use the exclusive-or and exponential functions for message generation. In an intuitive manner we define the class of "honest" functions and extend the theory to include these functions. We conclude this paper with an analysis of the TMN protocol.

1 Introduction

The analysis of cryptographic protocols in communications systems (i.e., schemes for openly exchanging messages to generate cryptographic keys, or to authenticate the legitimate parties in a communications session), has received considerable attention in recent years. In particular, researchers have experienced considerable difficulties in constructing theoretical frameworks and automated tools for uncovering weaknesses in cryptographic protocols which employ commutative algebraic operations such as the "exclusive-or" function of binary vectors and the exponentiation of integers in a prime number field[3]. The recent debut of strand spaces([1], [2]) should prove to be a most useful approach for the analysis of cryptographic protocols because their theory successfully unifies a number of previously developed algebraic techniques. Although strand space theory did not initially provide the framework for properly describing the exclusive-or and the exponential functions, we have always believed that this theory was flexible enough so that it could be extended to include most of the concepts that are relevant to cryptographic protocols.

In this paper we provide the first extension of strand space theory. In our research, we began by considering the abstract properties of the exclusive-or and exponential functions and generalized these properties into a class of "honest" functions. We were then faced with the problem of consistently incorporating the class of honest functions into the strand space framework. To test the correctness of this extended strand space hierarchy we applied it to Roscoe's strengthened version of the TMN protocol[5] (which involves the use of the exclusive-or function). Another useful outcome of this research was the delineation of the finer points contrasting the application of strand space theory to protocols employing asymmetric cryptographic keys as opposed to protocols using symmetric keys only. Unfortunately, we are forced to assume that the reader of this paper has some familiarity with strand space theory. However, in section 2, we present an overview of strand space theory including relevant definitions and major theorems. In section 3 we define the class of honest functions and present the extension of the theory to include this class. In section 4 we devote considerable attention to the exclusive-or function, because of its importance in cryptography and because of the difficulties that it has posed to researchers in the analysis of cryptographic protocols. In section 5 we apply honest functions to verify the confidentiality properties of the TMN protocol. In section 6 we develop some surprising results concerning the authentication guarantees for the TMN protocol. Finally, in section 7, we arrive at several observations about the utility of strand space theory and outline areas of future research.

2 Strand Space Concepts, Terminology and Theorems

This section is included only for the purposes of review and completeness. Readers who are unacquainted with the theory of strand spaces should consult[1].

We will denote by A the "algebra" of terms or messages which can be exchanged in a protocol. In a protocol, we use +*t* to represent the sending of a term by a party and -*t* to represent the receiving of a term by another party. The symbols +*t*, -*t* are referred to as signed terms. We denote by $(\pm A)^*$ the set of all finite sequences of signed terms.

Definition 2.1 A strand space is a set Σ with a trace mapping

$$tr : \Sigma \rightarrow (\pm A)^*$$

The elements of Σ are called strands.

Definition 2.2 For a fixed strand space Σ:

1. a node is a pair (s, i) with $s \in \Sigma$ and i an integer satisfying $1 \leq i \leq$ length(tr(s)). The set of nodes is denoted by $\mathcal{N}$. We will say the node (s, i) belongs to the strand s.

2. If $n = (s, i) \in \mathcal{N}$ then $term(n) = (tr(s))_i$, i.e., the ith signed term of the trace of s.

3. If $n_1, n_2 \in \mathcal{N}, n_1 \rightarrow n_2$ means $term(n_1) = +a$ and $term(n_2) = -a$.

4. If $n_1, n_2 \in \mathcal{N}, n_1 \Rightarrow n_2$ means n_1, n_2 occur on the same strand with $n_1 = (s, i)$ and $n_2 = (s, i+1)$.

5. The node graph of $\mathcal{N}$ is the graph whose vertices are the nodes in $\mathcal{N}$ and whose edges are defined by relations 3 and 4 above.

A bundle in a strand space is a finite subgraph of the node graph $\mathcal{N}$.

Definition 2.3 Let C be a set of edges, and let $\mathcal{N}_C$ be the set of nodes incident with any edge in C. C is a bundle if:

1. C is finite.

2. If $n_1 \in \mathcal{N}_C$ and $term(n_1)$ is negative, then there is a unique n_2 such that $n_2 \rightarrow n_1 \in C$.

3. If $n_1 \in \mathcal{N}_C$ and $n_2 \Rightarrow n_1$ then $n_2 \Rightarrow n_1 \in C$.

4. C is acyclic.

Definition 2.4 If C is a bundle and $s \in \Sigma$, then the C-height of s, denoted by $height_C(s)$, is the largest $i \leq length(tr(s))$ such that $s \in \Sigma$ and $(s, i) \in C$. C contains s if $height_C(s) = length(tr(s))$.

Definition 2.5 If s is a strand and C a bundle, the C-trace of s is the restriction of $tr(s)$ to the integer interval $\{1, \ldots, height_C(s)\}$. A partial C-trace of s is the restriction of $tr(s)$ to any interval $\{1, \ldots, k\}$ for $k \leq height_C(s)$.

Definition 2.6 Suppose that S is a set of edges, i.e., a subset of the union of $\rightarrow$ and $\Rightarrow$ and let $\mathcal{N}_S$ be the set of nodes incident with any edge in S. Then $<_S$ is the transitive closure of S and $\leq_S$ is the reflexive, transitive closure of S.

Each relation is a subset of $\mathcal{N}_S \times \mathcal{N}_S$. Moreover, $n <_S n'$ means that there is a sequence of one or more edges (of either kind) belonging to S leading from n to n'. Similarly, $n \leq_S n'$ means that there is a sequence of zero or more edges belong to S leading from n to n'.

Lemma 2.7 Suppose C is a bundle. Then $\leq_C$ is a partial order; i.e., a reflexive, anti-symmetric, transitive relation. Every non-empty subset of nodes in C has $\leq_C$ minimal members.

Definition 2.8 Let A be a term algebra containing disjoint subsets K (cryptographic keys) and T (atomic text messages). We further specialize A by defining three operators:

$$\begin{array}{ll} encr: & \mathrm{K} \times \mathrm{A} \rightarrow \mathrm{A} \\ inv: & \mathrm{K} \rightarrow \mathrm{K} \\ join: & \mathrm{A} \times \mathrm{A} \rightarrow \mathrm{A} \end{array}$$

For convenience we denote $encr(K, m)$ by $\{m\}_K$; $inv(K)$ by K^{-1}; $join(a, b)$ by ab. These three operators represent message construction and message encryption in cryptographic protocols. We denote by E the set of all ciphers (i.e. the range of *encr*) and by C the set of concatenations (i.e. the range of *join*). The elements of $\mathrm{K} \cup \mathrm{T} \cup \mathrm{E}$ are the "simple" elements of A.

Definition 2.9 If $k \subseteq \mathrm{K}$, then a k-ideal of A is a subset I of A such that for all $h \in I, g \in \mathrm{A}$, and $K \in k$

1. $hg, gh \in I$
2. $\{h\}_K \in I$

The smallest k-ideal containing h is denoted by $I_k[h]$. A similar definition applies to $I_k[S]$ where $S \subseteq \mathrm{A}$.

Definition 2.10 h is a subterm of g, written $h \sqsubset g$, is defined as $g \in I_k[h]$.

Proposition 2.11 $\sqsubset$ is a transitive, reflexive relation. Moreover, if $h, g \in \mathrm{A}$ and $K \in \mathrm{K}$ then

1. $h \sqsubset hg$ and $g \sqsubset hg$
2. $h \sqsubset \{h\}_K$

Lemma 2.12 The sets K, T, E, and C are pairwise disjoint.

The proof of Lemma 2.12 is based on certain axioms which we have not included in this section. (see axioms 3.4 and 3.5 [1]).

The notion of an "honest ideal" is mainly concerned with a formal description of the capabilities of a penetrator. Since the penetrator is considered as a possible legitimate party in a communications system, the penetrator's capabilities may be described as a set of strands corresponding to the following traces:

Definition 2.13 A penetrator trace is one for the following:

M. $Text\ message : < +t >$ where $t \in \mathrm{T}$
F. $Flushing : < -g >$
T. $Tee : < -g, +g, +g >$
C. $Concatenation : < -g, -h, +gh >$
S. $Separation\ into\ components : < -gh, +g, +h >$
K. $Key : < +K >\ where\ K \in \mathrm{K}_p$

E. $Encryption : < -K, -h, +\{h\}_K >$

D. $Decryption : < -K^{-1}, -\{h\}_K, +h >$

Definition 2.14 Suppose Σ is a strand space and $\mathcal{N}$ the set of nodes of Σ. An unsigned term t originates on $n \in \mathcal{N}$ if and only if $term(n)$ is positive, $t \sqsubset term(n)$; and whenever n' precedes n on the same stand, $t \not\sqsubset term(n')$. An unsigned term t is uniquely originating if t originates on a unique $n \in \mathcal{N}$.

Definition 2.15 A node m is an entry point for $I \subseteq \mathrm{A}$ if and only if $term(m)$ is positive, $term(m) \in I$ and for all nodes m' which precede m on the same strand, $term(m') \notin I$.

Proposition 2.16 Suppose C is a bundle over A. If m is minimal in $\{m \in C : term(m) \in I\}$, then m is an entry point for I.

Definition 2.17 A set $I \subseteq A$ is honest relevant to a bundle C if and only if whenever a penetrator node p is an entry point of I, p is an **M** node or a **K** node.

Theorem 2.18 Suppose C is a bundle over A; $S \subseteq \mathrm{T} \cup \mathrm{K}$; $k \subseteq \mathrm{K}$; and $\mathrm{K} \subseteq \mathrm{S} \cup k^{-1}$. Then $I_k[S]$ is honest relative to C.

Corollary 2.19 Suppose C is a bundle, $\mathrm{K} = S \cup k^{-1}$ and $S \cap \mathrm{K_p} = \emptyset$. If $term(m) \in I_k[S]$ for some $m \in C$, then for some regular node $n \in C, n$ is an entry point for $I_k[S]$.

Corollary 2.20 Suppose C is a bundle, $\mathrm{K} = S \cup k^{-1}, S \cap \mathrm{K_p} = \emptyset$ and no regular node $\in C$ is an entry point for $I_k[S]$. Then any term of the form $\{g\}_K$ for $K \in S$ does not originate on a penetrator strand.

3 Honest Functions

Let B be a subset of the term algebra A. Suppose $f : B^n \to \mathrm{K}$ such that each element $y = f(x_1, \ldots, x_n)$ has so many inverse images that it is impossible to identify the "correct" (unique for a run of the protocol) pre-image for each y; or f is a one-to-one mapping where $f^{-1}(y)$ is not easily computed. For such functions f we define two new penetrator traces of types **B** and $\mathbf{B_f}$.

$$\mathbf{B}. < +b > \ where\ b \in B_p \subseteq B$$

$$\mathbf{B_f}. < -x_1, \ldots, -x_n, +y = f(x_1, \ldots, x_n) >$$

The penetrator trace **B** is analogous to the penetrator trace **K**. Just as the penetrator may be expected to know certain elements of K (i.e. elements of $\mathrm{K_p}$), the penetrator may also be expected to know certain elements of B (i.e., elements of B_p). The penetrator trace $\mathbf{B_f}$ simply characterizes the penetrator's ability to compute y, given $x_1, \ldots, x_n$. In strand space theory these notions are formalized in the following definitions:

Definition 3.1 The function f is defined to be honest with respect to the fixed pre-image $(x_1, \ldots, x_n)$ and relative to the bundle C, if whenever $f(x_1, \ldots, x_n)$ originates on a penetrator node in C, the only penetrator strands which contain $(x_1, \ldots, x_n)$ in their subterms are of type **B**.

Remark 3.2 In other words, an honest function f is a mapping such that a penetrator who knows y is in the range of f can only guess at the fixed values $(x_1, \ldots, x_n)$ which produce y.

Axiom 3.3 For the sets C and E as defined in Definition 2.8 we assume that

$$B \cap \mathrm{C} = B \cap \mathrm{E} = \emptyset.$$

Remark 3.4 We do not assume that $B \cap \mathrm{K} = \emptyset$ or $B \cap \mathrm{T} = \emptyset$. As we will see in the TMN protocol, B will be defined as a subset of K. The restrictions on B given in Axiom 3.3 are needed to prove the analogous result corresponding to Th 2.18. It appears unlikely that we will ever need to consider the case $B \subseteq \mathrm{T}$. However, there is no reason to require that $B \cap \mathrm{T} = \emptyset$.

Definition 3.5 When necessary, a term is simple if it is an element of $\mathrm{K} \cup \mathrm{T} \cup \mathrm{E} \cup B$. (Compare Definition 2.3 above).

Definition 3.6 For the sake of convenience we list all of the penetrator traces from Definition 2.13 along with the penetrator traces that are defined for honest functions:

M. $Text\ message : < +t >$ where $t \in \mathrm{T}$

F. $Flushing : < -g >$

T. $Tee : < -g, +g, +g >$

C. $Concatenation : < -g, -h, +gh >$

S. $Separation\ into\ components : < -gh, +g, +h >$

K. $Key : < +K > \ where\ K \in \mathrm{K}_p$

E. $Encryption : < -K, -h, +\{h\}_K >$

D. $Decryption : < -K^{-1}, -\{h\}_K, +h >$

B. $Domain : < +b > \ where\ b \in \mathrm{B}_p$

$\mathbf{B_f}$. $Function : < -x_1, \ldots, -x_n, +y = f(x_1, \ldots, x_n) >$

Definition 3.7 As in Remark 3.4, where $B \cap \mathrm{K} = B \cap \mathrm{T} = \emptyset$, a set $I \subseteq \mathrm{A}$ is honest relative to a bundle C if and only if whenever a penetrator node p is an entry point for I, it is an **M** node, **K** node or a **B** node. (Compare to Definition 2.17).

Theorem 3.8 (Analogous to Th 2.18) Suppose C is a bundle over A; $S \subseteq \mathrm{T} \cup \mathrm{K} \cup B$; $k \subseteq \mathrm{K}$; $\mathrm{K} \subseteq S \cup k^{-1}$. Let f be an honest function with respect to the fixed pre-image $(x_1, \ldots, x_n)$ and the bundle C. Suppose also that whenever y originates on a penetrator node in C, $y \in I_k[S]$ implies $x_1, \ldots, x_n \in I_k[s]$. Then the ideal $I_k[S]$ is honest.

Proof: The proof of Th 2.18 applies to all penetrator traces not of type **B** or $\mathbf{B_f}$. It is sufficient to prove that a penetrator node of type $\mathbf{B_f}$, where f is an honest function satisfying the hypothesis of Th 3.8, is not an entry point for the ideal $I_k[S]$. By the definition of entry point for an ideal, the only node in the penetrator strand of type $\mathbf{B_f}$ which would be an entry point for $I_k[S]$ is $(+y, n+1)$. However the condition $y \in I_k[S]$ implies $x_1, \ldots, x_n \in I_k[S]$ is equivalent to the condition that there exists $1 \leq j \leq n$ such that $x_j \notin I_k[S]$ implies $y = f(x_1, \ldots, x_n) \notin I_k[S]$. This is precisely the condition $(+y, n+1)$ is not an entry point for $I_k[S]$.□

Remark 3.9 In Theorem 3.8, we may assume that some of the x_j values are text and the remainder are elements of the domain B; i.e. $f : \mathrm{T}^{n_1} \times B^{n_2} \to \mathrm{K}$ where $n_1 + n_2 = n$.

The next two corollaries follow easily from Theorem 3.8. They may be proved in an analogous manner as the proofs for Corollaries 2.19 and 2.20. See [1].

Corollary 3.10 Assuming that $B \cap \mathrm{K} = B \cap \mathrm{T} = \emptyset$, suppose C is a bundle; $\mathrm{K} = (S \setminus B) \cup k^{-1}$ and $S \cap \mathrm{K}_p = S \cap B_p = \emptyset$. If $term(m) \in I_k[S]$ for some $m \in C$, then for some regular node $n \in C$, n is an entry point for $I_k[S]$.

Corollary 3.11 Again assuming that $B \cap \mathrm{K} = B \cap \mathrm{T} = \emptyset$, suppose C is a bundle; $\mathrm{K} = (S \setminus B) \cup k^{-1}; S \cap \mathrm{K}_p = S \cap B_p = \emptyset$ and no regular node $\in C$ is an entry point for $I_k[S]$. Then any term of the form $\{g\}_K$ for $K \in S$ does not originate on a penetrator strand.

4 The Exclusive-Or Function

In cryptography, the Boolean valued exclusive-or function ($false \oplus true = true \oplus false = true, false \oplus false = true \oplus true = false$) has many applications. For our purposes we will consider the case in which the domain B of section 3 is taken as the set K_1 of symmetric keys in K. Let us consider the function $f : \mathrm{K}_1^n \to \mathrm{K}_1$ in which $f(x_1, \ldots, x_n) = x_1 \oplus \ldots \oplus x_n$. In the literature the exclusive-or function is also referred to as the bit-wise mod 2 sum function since $x_1, \ldots, x_n$ may be represented as binary vectors of fixed length.

In this section we derive properties of this honest function f and show how cryptographic protocols employing this particular function may be analyzed.

Remark 4.1 The function $y = x_1 \oplus \ldots \oplus x_n$ is an honest function since each y has many pre-images, i.e., for each y there is a unique x_n whenever $x_1, \ldots, x_{n-1}$ are given arbitrary values. Refer to the paragraph preceding definition 3.1.

Definition 4.2 For the function f of 3.1 replace the trace $\mathbf{B_f}$ by the trace **Sum** where

$$\textbf{Sum}. < -x_1, \ldots, -x_n, +y >$$

and define n additional traces

$$\textbf{Sum}_\textbf{j}. < -x_1, \ldots, -x_{j-1}, -y, -x_{j+1}, \ldots, -x_n, +x_j >$$

for $j = 1, 2, \ldots, n$.

Corollary 4.3 Suppose C is a bundle over A; $S \subseteq \mathrm{T} \cup \mathrm{K}; k \subseteq \mathrm{K}; \mathrm{K} \subseteq S \cup k^{-1}$. Let $f : \mathrm{K}_1{}^n \to \mathrm{K}_1$ be the mod 2 sum function and let the penetrator traces $\{\textbf{Sum}_\textbf{j} : 1 \leq j \leq n\}$ be appended to the penetrator traces of Defn 3.6. Suppose also that whenever $y = x_1 \oplus \ldots \oplus x_n$ originates on a penetrator node in C, $y \in I_k[S]$ implies $x_1, \ldots x_n \in I_k[S]$. Finally suppose that for $1 \leq j \leq n$ when x_j originates on a penetrator node in C, $x_j \in I_k[S]$ implies $x_1, \ldots, x_{j-1}, y, x_{j+1}, \ldots, x_n \in I_k[S]$. Then the ideal $I_k[S]$ is honest.

Proof is similar to proof of Theorem 3.8.

Remark 4.4 Theorem 3.8 applies to an arbitrary honest function to the extent that no additional penetrator traces can be defined for that function. As we saw in the case of the mod 2 sum function, there are n additional penetrator traces which can be defined. Therefore, when evaluating a cryptographic protocol which uses an honest function, we must pay careful attention to any other relevant penetrator traces that may be defined for the function. Recall that each penetrator trace represents an action that can be performed by the penetrator. We must then state and prove a specific corollary to Theorem 3.8 taking into account these additional penetrator traces. Such a corollary places additional restrictions on the relation between the function's variables, the value of the function when evaluated on those variables, and the underlying ideal. However, these restrictions enrich the strand space model for the cryptographic protocol providing us with much more realistic theorems about secrecy and authentication.

5 The TMN Protocol(Roscoe's version)

In this section we apply the theory of honest functions to Roscoe's strengthened version of the TNM Protocol[5]. For this TMN Protocol, the honest function is $\oplus$ with n=2 [5].

In [5] the TMN Protocol is described as follows:

$A \to S \quad M_1 = \{m_1\ B\ r_a\ S_A\}_{pks}$
$S \to B \quad M_2 = Areq$
$B \to S \quad M_3 = \{m_3\ A\ r_b\ S_B\}_{pks}$
$S \to A \quad M_4 = r_a \oplus r_b$

In this protocol, A, B are names (elements of T_{name}) of legitimate parties. The texts m_1, m_3 designate message numbers of the protocol. The texts S_A, S_B are secret to A, B respectively but are known to the server. In step 4, $\oplus$ is used to denote the bitwise exclusive-or of keys r_a, r_b. In the asymmetric key pair (pks, pks^{-1}), pks is public, while pks^{-1} is known only to the server S. In this protocol the function $\oplus$ is defined on the set K_1 of symmetric keys, with $r_a \oplus r_b$ as a member of K_1 even though $\oplus$ is traditionally thought of as an encryption/decryption operator. (See section 4)

As we have observed in Remark 4.4, careful attention must be given to the choice of penetrator strands relevant to the honest functions used in any protocol. In this example, we choose to append only the penetrator trace **Sum**, since $r_a \oplus r_b$ is known to all parties and since the penetrator has no a priori knowledge of either r_a or r_b.

To apply Theorem 3.8, we define $S = \{r_a, r_b, S_A, S_B, pks^{-1}\}$ and $k = \mathrm{K} \setminus \{r_a, r_b, pks\}$. Then clearly, the condition $\mathrm{K} \subseteq S \cup k^{-1}$ is satisfied since $pks \in k^{-1}$. Note also that the condition if $r_a \oplus r_b$ originates on a penetrator node in C, then $r_a \oplus r_b \in I_k[S]$ implies $r_a, r_b \in I_k[S]$ is satisfied since we are assuming that $r_a, r_b \notin \mathrm{K}_p$. Thus, according to Theorem 3.8, $I_k[S]$ is an honest ideal, establishing the secrecy result for the TMN protocol.

6 The TMN Protocol: Authentication Guarantees

The TMN protocol, as stated in Section 5, provides no authentication guarantees for A or B since a penetrator may retransmit an arbitrary value for the message $r_a \oplus r_b$. Therefore, in this section we will consider a TMN protocol which includes two additional message exchanges in which the parties A and B transmit their identities encrypted with the session key. This extended TMN protocol is defined as follows:

Definition 6.1

$A \rightarrow S \quad M_1 = \{m_1\ B\ r_a\ S_A\}_{pks}$
$S \rightarrow B \quad M_2 = Areq$
$B \rightarrow S \quad M_3 = \{m_3\ A\ r_b\ S_B\}_{pks}$
$S \rightarrow A \quad M_4 = r_a \oplus r_b$
$A \rightarrow B \quad M_5 = \{A\}_{r_b}$
$B \rightarrow A \quad M_6 = \{B\}_{r_b}$

For the infiltrated TMN strand space $(\Sigma, P)_{TMN}$ (where P denotes the penetrator strands including **SUM** for $n = 2$), we define the pairwise disjoint sets of regular strands as follows:

Definition 6.2

$$\begin{aligned} Init[A, B, m_1, r, r', S] &= \\ \{s \in \Sigma : tr(s) &= \\ < +\{m_1\ B\ r\ S\}_{pks}, -(r \oplus r'), +\{A\}_{r'}, \quad -\{B\}_{r'} >\} \end{aligned}$$

$$\begin{aligned} Resp[A, B, m_3, r', S'] &= \\ \{s \in \Sigma : tr(s) &= \\ < -Areq, +\{m_3\ B\ r'\ S'\}_{pks}, -\{A\}_{r'}, \quad +\{B\}_{r'} >\} \end{aligned}$$

$$\begin{aligned} Serv[A, B, r, r', m_1, m_3, S, S', H, H'] &= \\ \{s \in \Sigma : tr(s) &= \\ < -\{H\}_{pks}, +Areq, -\{H'\}_{pks}, +(r \oplus r') >\} \end{aligned}$$

We define Σ_{init} = union of the range of $Init$; Σ_{resp} = union of the range of $Resp$; Σ_{serv} = union of the range of $Serv$; P = { TMN penetrator strands including **SUM** with $n = 2$ }. Finally the infiltrated TMN strand space can be written $(\Sigma, P)_{TMN} = \Sigma_{init} \cup \Sigma_{resp} \cup \Sigma_{serv} \cup P$.

The next proposition follows directly from Corollary 2.19.

Proposition 6.3 If C is a bundle in $(\Sigma, P)_{TMN}$ and $(H, H') \subseteq A$ are such that $S_A \sqsubset H$ and $S_B \sqsubset H'$, and if the non-symmetric key K is such that $\{H\}_K$ or $\{H'\}_K$ originates on a penetrator node then $K = pks^{-1}$.

Proof. Let $S = (S_A, S_B, pks^{-1})$ and $k = \mathrm{K} \setminus \{pks\}$. Since $pks \in k^{-1}$ and since $pks^{-1} \in S$, it follows that $\mathrm{K} = S \cup k^{-1}$. We apply Cor 2.19 with $term(m) = H = XS_A \in I_k[S]$. From Cor 2.19 the only entry point for the ideal $I_k[S]$ is a regular node. Therefore $K = pks^{-1}$. A similar argument is made for $\{H'\}_K$.□

Intuitively, since we assume that $pks^{-1} \notin \mathrm{K}_p$ Prop 6.3 states that no key $\in \mathrm{K}$ except pks^{-1} can be used to recover H and H', i.e. to recover S_A and S_B respectively.

Proposition 6.4 If $\{H\}_{pks}$ originates on a regular strand S then
If $s \in \Sigma_{init}$ then $H = m_1\ B\ r_a\ S_A$
If $s \in \Sigma_{resp}$ then $H = m_3\ B\ r_b\ S_B$.

Proof. The conclusion of this proposition follows immediately from Def 6.2.

Theorem 6.5 (Server's Authentication Guarantee). Suppose C is a bundle in $(\Sigma, P)_{TMN}; A \neq B; r_a, r_b$ uniquely originate on regular strands in $C; S_A, S_B$ originate on regular strands in C; and $pks^{-1} \notin \mathrm{K}_p$. Then if $s \in Serv[A, B, *, *, m_1, m_3, S, S', H, H']$ of C-height 3 then there exists $s_{init} \in Init[A, B, m_1, r, *, S]$ of C-height 1 and $s_{resp} \in Resp[A, B, m_3, r', S']$ of C-height 2.

Proof. By hypothesis, let

$$tr(s_{serv}) =< -\{H\}_{pks}, +Areq, -\{H'\}_{pks} > .$$

Since $pks^{-1} \notin \mathrm{K}_p$, there exist regular nodes (s, i) and (s', i') such that $\{H\}_{pks}$ originates on (s, i) and $\{H'\}_{pks}$ originates on (s', i'). Since $m_1 \sqsubset H, (s, i)$ must be a node on an initiator strand with $i = 1$. Therefore by Prop 6.4, there exist $s_{init} \in Init[A, B, m_1, r, *, S]$ of C-height 1. Similarly, since $m_3 \sqsubset H', (s', i')$ must be a node in a responder strand with $i' = 3$. By Prop 6.4 there exists a strand $s_{resp} \in Resp[A, B, m_3, r', S']$ of C-height 3. □

Prop 6.6 Let $(r_a \oplus r_b)$ originate uniquely on a regular strand. Let $\{g\}_K$ originate on a regular strand S with $K \neq pks$. If $s \in \Sigma_{init}$ then $g = A$ and $K = r_a$ and if $s \in \Sigma_{resp}$ then $g = B$ and $K = r_b$. If $(r_a \oplus r_b)$ uniquely originates on s, then $s \in \Sigma_{serv}$.

Proof. The conclusion of this proposition follows immediately from Defn 6.2.

From our discussion in Section 5, proving the secrecy result for the TMN protocol, it follows immediately that:

Prop 6.7 Let C be a bundle in $(\Sigma, P)_{TMN}$. If r, r', and $(r \oplus r')$ are symmetric keys in K_1 and if $(r \oplus r')$ originates on a penetrator node in C, then $r, r' \in \mathrm{K}_p$. By symmetry, if r originates on a penetrator node in C, then $r', (r \oplus r') \in \mathrm{K}_p$. If r' originates on a penetrator node in C, then $r, (r \oplus r') \in \mathrm{K}_p$.

We may readily observe that in the TMN protocol, both the initiator and responder cannot directly authenticate the server, since any party may send $(r \oplus r')$ to A and $Areq$ to B at any time. However, if A and B authenticate each other by correctly decrypting $\{A\}_{r_b}$ in step 5 and $\{B\}_{r_b}$ in step 6, they are assured of the server's authenticity. It is most unlikely for a penetrator to guess the correct value of r_b.

Theorem 6.8 (Initiator's Guarantee).

Suppose C is a bundle in $(\Sigma, P)_{TMN}; A \neq B; r_a, r_b$ uniquely originate on regular nodes in C; $pks^{-1} \notin \mathrm{K}_p$. If $s \in Init[A, B, m_1, r, r', S]$ has C-height 4, then there exists $s_{resp} \in Resp[A, B, m_3, r', S']$ of C-height 4.

Proof. By hypothesis, let $tr(s_{init}) =$
$< +\{m_1 B r_a S_A\}_{pks}, -(r_a \oplus r_b), +\{A\}_{r_b}, -\{B\}_{r_b} >$.

Since r_b originates uniquely on a regular node, there exists a node (s, i) such that $\{g\}_{r_b}$ originates on (s, i). By Prop 6.6, and since $A \neq B$ we have $s \in Resp[A, B, m_3, r', S']$ and $i = 4$.□

Theorem 6.9 (Responder's Guarantee).

Suppose C is a bundle in $(\Sigma, P)_{TMN}; A \neq B; r_a, r_b$ uniquely originate on regular nodes in $C; pks^{-1} \notin \mathrm{K}_p$. If $s \in Resp[A, B, m_3, r', S']$ of C-height 4 then there exists $s_{init} \in Init[A, B, m_1, r, r', S]$ of C-height 3.

Proof. By hypothesis, let $tr(s_{resp}) =$

$$< -Areq, +\{m_3\, B\, r'\, S'\}_{pks}, -\{A\}_{r_b}, +\{B\}_{r_b} > .$$

Since r_b originates uniquely on a regular node, there exists a node (s, i) such that $\{g\}_{r_b}$ originates on (s, i). By Prop 6.6, and since $A \neq B$ we have $s \in Init[A, B, m_1, r, r', S]$ and $i = 3$.□

7 Conclusions and Further Research

From our research, we are able to conclude that the strand space model permits straight-forward generalizations to include consideration of a broad class of cryptographic protocols. While the initial work of Guttman, et al, ([1], [2]) did not include structures for the algebraic functions frequently employed in these protocols, their research did point the way to the honest functions which we have developed in this paper.

From our experience the application of strand space techniques to the analysis of any cryptographic protocol may easily be described in the following way:

1. Ensure that all aspects of message generation can be described in the context of strand spaces.

2. Carefully determine the traces that are relevant for the penetrator.

3. List the traces for the legitimate parties in the protocol.

4. State the relevant secrecy and authentication theorems which are to be proved.

We believe that when protocol analysis is approached in this way flaws in the protocol may be detected. In the case of the TMN protocol the fact that neither A nor B could authenticate the server became readily apparent when we attempted to establish the authentication guarantees for A and B.

We cannot over-emphasize our belief that strand spaces provide an intuitive and non-automated approach to protocol analysis. While we do not argue with the utility of automated tools, we maintain that protocol analysis will remain in the domain of careful and creative intellectual endeavors for a long time to come.

In future investigations we will continue to apply strand spaces to other cryptographic protocols, extending the underlying theory as it becomes necessary.

8 Acknowledgements

The author takes this opportunity to express his appreciation for the assistance of Joshua Guttman, Javier Thayer Fábrega, Jonathan Herzog(MITRE), Sylvan Pinsky(NSA), and Will Harkness(NSA retired). These individuals have given freely of their time to review and critique the ongoing research of this author. In preparing section 2 we have quoted extensively from the work of [1]. Pinsky has been most supportive and encouraging as we have pursued this research. Finally we express our gratitude for the assistance of Pinsky and Harkness in preparing this manuscript. While we wish to credit these individuals for their contribution to this work all errors in judgement or fact remain the responsibility of this author.

References

[1] F. Javier Thayer Fábrega, Jonathan C. Herzog, and Joshua D. Guttman. Honest Ideals on Strand Spaces. In Joshua Guttman, editor, *Proceedings of the 11th Computer Security Foundations Workshop*, pages 66–77, Rockport, MA, June 1998. IEEE Computer Society.

[2] F. Javier Thayer Fábrega, Jonathan C. Herzog, and Joshua D. Guttman. Strand Spaces: Why is a security protocol correct? In *Proceedings of the 1998 IEEE Symposium on Security and Privacy*, pages 160–171. IEEE Computer Press, 1998.

[3] C. Meadows. The NRL Protocol Analyzer: An overview. In *Journal of Logic Programming*, volume 2 of *26*, Feb. 1996.

[4] C. Meadows, R. Kemmerer, and J. Millen. Three Systems for Cryptographic Protocol Analysis. In *Journal of Cryptology*, volume 2 of 7, pages 79–130, 1994.

[5] A. W. Roscoe. Intensional Specifications of Security Protocols. In Joshua Guttman, editor, *Proceeding of the 9th Computer Security Foundations Workshop*, pages 28–38, Kenmare, County Kerry, Ireland, June 1996. IEEE Computer Society.

Panel: Formalization and Proof of Secrecy Properties

Formalization and Proof of Secrecy Properties

Dennis Volpano
Computer Science Department
Naval Postgraduate School
Monterey, CA 93943, USA
volpano@cs.nps.navy.mil

After looking at the security literature, you will find secrecy is formalized in different ways, depending on the application. Applications have threat models that influence our choice of secrecy properties. A property may be reasonable in one context and completely unsatisfactory in another if other threats exist.

The primary goal of this panel is to foster discussion on what sorts of secrecy properties are appropriate for different applications and to investigate what they have in common. We also want to explore what is meant by secrecy in different contexts. Perhaps there is enough overlap among our threat models that we can begin to identify some key secrecy properties for wider application. Currently, secrecy is treated in rather ad hoc ways. With some agreement among calculi for expressing protocols and systems, we might even be able to use one another's proof techniques for proving secrecy!

Four experts were invited as panelists. Two panelists, Riccardo Focardi and Martín Abadi, represent formalizations of secrecy as demanded by secure systems that aim to prohibit various channels, or insecure information flows. More specifically, they represent noninterference-based secrecy. The other two panelists, Cathy Meadows and Jon Millen, represent formalizations of secrecy for protocols based on the Dolev-Yao threat model [2]. Below are some specific questions that were asked of each of the panelists:

1. Secrecy is sometimes formulated as a "safety" property in protocol analysis where one is concerned with whether an intruder learns a specific value (a secret). Such a criterion is inadequate for guaranteeing secure information flow in systems where secrets can always be encoded or transmitted in covert ways. Leaks arising by indirect flows from within a process executing a protocol seem as dangerous as those caused by message exchange with an adversary. This is especially true of crypto protocols whose implementations normally admit cryptanalytic attacks. So why does protocol analysis adopt a different criterion?
2. Is there a secrecy property for protocols and systems? Is it noninterference (NI) based? One key problem is encryption. It blows NI-based formulations apart. How can we cope with it? Do we assume perfect encryption and fiddle with notions of equivalence until we get the "desired effect"? Or do we use techniques that are more sensitive to the computational complexity of compromising secrets?
3. Can we study protocol secrecy within the same framework as that used for information flow in a concurrent setting? If not, why?
4. Suppose Mallory imitates Bob in a key establishment protocol with Alice, to get Alice to accept a key that Mallory knows. Is this a failure of secrecy because Alice incorrectly believes that the key is known only to Bob and herself?

Panelists were asked to try to respond to these questions or provide questions that they feel are more appropriate. Their responses are given in the following sections. Thanks to the panelists for participating.

1. Martín Abadi's Reply

Suppose that we wish to require that a protocol preserve the secrecy of one of its parameters, x. The protocol should not leak any information about x—in other words, the value of x should not interfere with the behavior of the protocol that the environment can observe. The parameter x may denote the identity of one of the participants or the sensitive data that is sent encrypted after a key exchange. In general, we cannot express this secrecy property as a predicate on behaviors. On the other hand, representing the protocol as a process $P(x)$, we may express the secrecy property by saying that $P(M)$ and $P(N)$ are equivalent (or indistinguishable), for all possible values M and N for x. Here we say that two processes P_1 and P_2 are equivalent when no third process Q can distinguish running in parallel with

1063-6900/99 $10.00 © 1999 IEEE

P_1 from running in parallel in P_2. This notion of process equivalence (testing equivalence) has been applied to several classes of processes and with several concepts of distinguishability, sometimes accounting for cryptographic operations.

Approaches based on predicates on behaviors rely on a rather different definition of secrecy, which can be traced back to the influential work of Dolev and Yao. According to that definition, a process preserves the secrecy of a piece of data M if the process never sends M in clear on the network, or anything that would permit the computation of M, even in interaction with an attacker.

Neither definition of secrecy implies the other. The first one concerns a process with a free variable x, while the second one concerns a process and a term with no free variables. With the first definition, we can say that $P(x)$ preserves the secrecy of the value of x even when this value may be a boolean; with the second one, it does not make much sense to talk about a secret boolean. In addition, the first definition rules out implicit information flows, while the second one does not. While the exact relations between the definitions remain unclear, I believe that the first one represents a more compelling criterion, and that the second one is a useful approximation that fits better into some formal frameworks.

2. Riccardo Focardi's Reply

Non-Interference (NI) has been introduced with the aim of formalizing security policies in systems. In particular, given two groups of users A and B, the requirement "A must not interfere with B" basically imposes that what is done by users in A cannot modify in any way the behaviour of the users in B. As a consequence, we obtain that the information which is known by users in A can never be revealed to users belonging to B. This gives us a strong notion of secrecy (in systems). For example, through NI requirements, we can easily formalize a multilevel security policy by requiring that users at a certain confidentiality level do not interfere with users at a lower level.

Indeed, NI is a general concept that can also be profitably applied in other settings, as it simply verifies if someone is able to induce a new (potentially dangerous) behaviour. As an example, NI has already been successfully exploited for the automatic verification of cryptographic protocols. Usually, when we consider a cryptographic protocol, we would like to be guaranteed that no enemy is able to introduce any "undesirable behaviours". This is exactly what NI requires. For example, for secrecy an "undesirable behaviour" is represented by the leaking of (secret) information which is detectable by simply observing the state of the enemy.

This reflects the power and the limitations of the use of NI-based properties in the analysis of security protocols:

- On one hand, the generality of NI makes it possible to detect in the same analysis completely different attacks (e.g., secrecy and authentication). This could increase the probability of finding new attacks, since we do not need to fix in advance the specific security property to be checked;
- On the other hand, this kind of analysis requires an additional effort in identifying which are the "undesirable behaviours", i.e., which of the revealed behaviours are attacks and which are not. However, when it is possible to reveal an attack by observing few well-defined events, e.g., in secrecy analyses, this task becomes trivial.

Finally, NI seems to be a good unifying approach to computer and network security. As a matter of fact, after the underlying model has been enriched (in some way) in order to deal with cryptography, NI can be used to analyze protocol secrecy within the same framework as that used for information flow in systems.

3. Cathy Meadows' Reply

Most of the work that has been done on applying formal methods to cryptographic protocols has relied upon the Dolev-Yao model, in which both intruders and honest participants have access to a finite number of well-defined operations obeying a finite set of algebraic rules. In this model the secrecy problem reduces to the problem of determining whether or not an intruder can learn a specific word by combining the set of operations available to it with the set of operations performed by the legitimate participants in the protocol. This is a very simple notion of secrecy: the intruder either learns the word or doesn't. Thus it avoids dealing with the question of whether or not the intruder can learn information about a word or key that would help in cryptanalysis, whether or not the intruder learns relationships between words (for example the relationship between a message and its sender), and whether a conspirator can encode secret information in the execution of the protocol. On the other hand, the Dolev-Yao model gives the protocol analyst a powerful tool for understanding a wide range of authentication properties that can be guaranteed by a cryptographic protocol.

This is in marked contrast to the notion of secrecy used in information flow, in which it is attempted to determine whether one untrusted process H could pass information to another untrusted process L by determining whether or not H has any effect on the system that is visible to L. Not only is this a much more subtle notion of secrecy than the Dolev-Yao version, relying on knowledge of possible as well as actual behavior, but the trust model is different: in the Dolev-Yao model the holders of secrets are trusted, while in the information flow model the holder of secrets H is untrusted, and it is up to the system to provide the guarantee that H does not reveal information.

Since the models satisfy such different requirements, it is difficult to "defend" one against the other. However, it does make sense to ask how they could be made to work together in a system that must satisfy multilevel security requirements and also engage in authentication protocols. For example, we might want to consider a system in which a subject is trusted to engage properly in a cryptographic protocol, but may or may not be trusted not to leak information via covert channels.

In order to understand how the two notions of security can be made to work together, we may want to look at another notion of security for systems: the type provided by access control policies. In the access control model, as in the Dolev-Yao model, the system consists of a set of principals (subjects), some of whom may be dishonest, a set of objects, and a finite set of operations that may be performed on the objects, such as creation, deletion, and the granting and removing of access rights. As in the Dolev-Yao model, the notion of secrecy is simple; it boils down to determining whether or not a subject can gain read access to an object. And, also as in the Dolev-Yao model, it is possible to use the finite set of operations to model a wide range of access control policies and requirements.

A number of attempts have been made to unify access control models with information-flow type models, with some success. The Bell-Lapadula model was perhaps the first; it foundered on the question of downgrading. The ability to downgrade data is necessary, but it also violates a straightfoward information flow policy, since it is an obvious flow from High to Low. Intransitive noninterference policies attempt to rectify this situation by allowing information to flow only through certain channels, such as downgraders. Other work, such as that of Simon Foley [3], has concentrated on developing a framework that allows complex structures of information flow requirements.

An approach like the above would allow us to integrate cryptographic protocol analysis into the information flow model, but at the possible price of ignoring information flow risks that could arise from deliberate information leakage during the execution of the protocol. For this we might want to look at work that has been done in the cryptographic community to address this very problem - known as "subliminal channels" in this context [1]. However, this work introduces an added expense: the introduction of a trusted warden to verify the absence of subliminal messages. Moreover, most of the existing work is applicable only to zero knowledge protocols, which have seen few practial applications. However, a closer look at this work may give us ideas for applying it to more generally applicable protocols and to integrating it with information flow models.

4. Jon Millen's Reply

It may seem odd that an apparently primitive concept like "secrecy" could be formalized in several different ways within a single application area such as cryptographic protocol analysis. But we already have a precedent for a multiplicity of models of secrecy in the analysis of secure operating systems. Figures 1 and 2 show the analogy between the two subjects. It is suggested that there is a good reason for having more than one model, and that similar reasoning applies to both areas.

The pyramid pictures illustrate the progression from simple, basic policies to a more detailed analysis that focuses on localized subsystems. The more focused analysis requires more detail in the system model. In both environments, a really thorough treatment of secrecy has to bring in Shannon's information theory, which implies probabilistic considerations.

There is a fundamental difficulty in applying noninterference to encryption, namely the fact that changes in plaintext cause changes in ciphertext. In a probabilistic context, one can rephrase secrecy as an inability to distinguish secret information from randomly generated text.

References

[1] Mike Burmester, Yvo Desmedt, Toshiya Itoh, Kouichi Sakurai, Hiroka Shizuya, and Moti Yung, A progress report on subliminal-free channnels, In Ross Anderson, editor, *Information Hiding - First International Workshop*, Springer Verlag Lecture Notes in Computer Science 1174, pp. 157–168, June 1996.

[2] Dolev, D. and Yao, A., On the Security of Public Key Protocols, *IEEE Transactions on Information Theory*, 29, 2, pp. 198–208, 1983.

[3] Simon Foley, A taxonomy of information flow policies and models, *Proc 1991 IEEE Computer Society Symposium on Research in Security and Privacy*, IEEE Computer Society Press, pp. 98–108., May 1991.

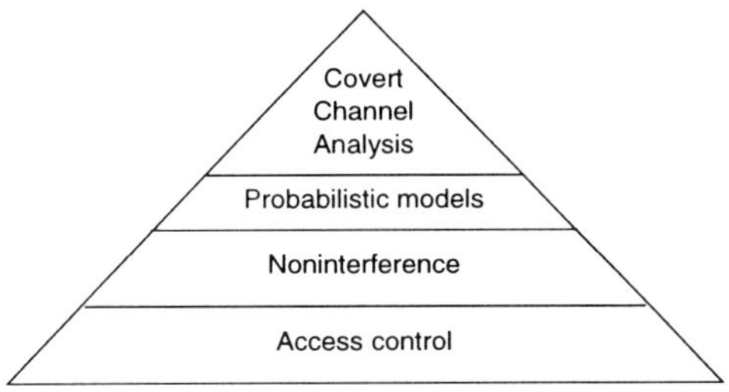

Figure 1. Secure Operating System Analysis

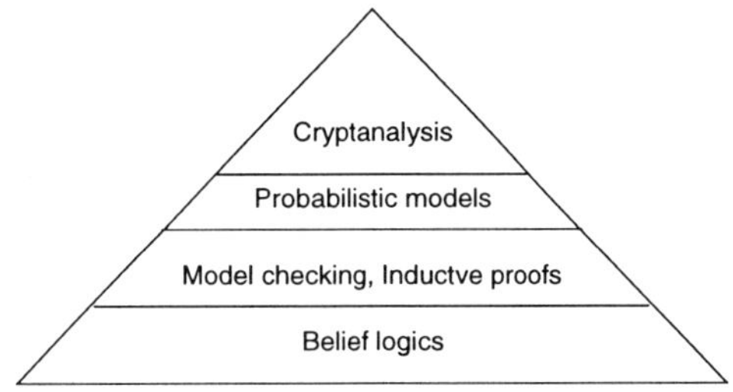

Figure 2. Cryptographic Protocol Analysis

Local Names

Authentication via Localized Names *

Chiara Bodei, Pierpaolo Degano
Dipartimento di Informatica, Università di Pisa
Corso Italia, 40, I-56125 Pisa, Italy
{chiara,degano}@di.unipi.it

Riccardo Focardi
Dipartimento di Informatica, Università Ca' Foscari di Venezia
Via Torino 155, I-30173 Venezia, Italy
focardi@dsi.unive.it

Corrado Priami
Dipartimento Scientifico Tecnologico, Università di Verona
Ca' Vignal 2, Strada Le Grazie, 1, I-37134 Verona, Italy
priami@sci.univr.it

Abstract

We address the problem of message authentication using the π-calculus, which has been given an operational semantics in [2] that provides each sequential process of a system with its own local space of names. We exploit here that semantics and its localized names to guarantee by construction that a message has been generated by a given entity. Therefore, our proposal can be seen as a reference for the analysis of "real" protocols. As an example, we study the way authentication is ensured by encrypting messages in the spi-calculus [1].

1. Introduction

Authentication is one of the main issues in security. It can have different purposes depending on the specific application considered. For example, *entity authentication* is related to the verification of an entity's claimed identity [8], while *message authentication* should make it possible for the receiver of a message to ascertain its origin [20]. In recent years there have been some formalizations of these different aspects of authentication (see, e.g., [3, 1, 11, 19, 5]). These formalizations are crucial for proofs of authentication properties, that sometimes have been automatized (see, e.g., [7, 14, 10, 9, 4]). A typical approach presented in the literature is the following. First, a protocol is specified in a certain formal model. Then the protocol is shown to enjoy the desired properties, regardless of its operating environment, that can be unreliable, and can even harbour an hostile intruder.

We use here a basic calculus for modelling concurrent and mobile agents, whose semantics offers a built-in mechanism that guarantees message authentication. This is the main contribution of our paper, because it enables us to abstract from the various implementations/specifications of authentication mechanisms, and to obtain idealized protocols which are "secure by construction". Our protocols, or rather their specifications can then be seen as a reference for proving the correctness of "real protocols". The actual proofs can be carried out following the approach and using the tools mentioned above. Additionally, our built-in authentication mechanism suggests a further proof technique, that we shall briefly discuss in the conclusions.

The essence of concurrent and mobile computation can be studied in a pure form using the π-calculus [12], a foundational calculus based on the notion of naming. Systems are specified as expressions of the calculus, called *processes*. These are obtained by combining via a few operators (parallel composition, nondeterministic choice, declarations) the basic actions of sending and of receiving names between processes along channels. Names represent values, or messages, and also channels. Since processes exchange names in communications, the interconnection structure of

*This work has been partially supported by by the MURST Progetto *Tecniche Formali per la Specifica, l'Analisi, la Verifica, la Sintesi e la Trasformazione di Sistemi Software*. The first two authors have been also partially supported by the CNR Progetto Strategico *Modelli e Metodi per la Matematica e l'Ingegneria*.

a network can vary dynamically. Recently, Abadi and Gordon [1] defined the *spi*-calculus by enriching the π-calculus with a primitive of encryption. The resulting calculus is particularly suited to security issues, among which authentication.

In [2] the π-calculus has been equipped with a structural operational semantics which endows each sequential process P in the whole system with its own *local* environment, i.e., P has its *local* space of names and its *local* name manager that generates a fresh name, whenever necessary. In this proposal, when a name is communicated, say from P to Q, it arrives at destination equipped with the so-called *relative address*: it represents the path between P and Q in (an abstract view of) the network (think to it as an abstract version of a logic IP address). The relative address encodes the information needed to point back to the local environment of P where the name has been installed as fresh, in the style of static chains that are used to solve non local references in sequential languages with nested environments [17]. The names enriched with relative addresses are called *localized.* The reference to the generator of a name is maintained during all the communications by an operator of *address composition*, which updates the relative addresses of the names transmitted. Names generated by different environments are thus certainly kept distinct. Note that address composition is *not* available to the users of the π-calculus, i.e. it *cannot* occur in a process. Rather it is used by the abstract machine of the π-calculus only, defined by its semantics.

We propose here to use this semantics, and its straightforward extension to the *spi*-calculus, to study authentication. As a matter of fact, the semantics itself provides us with a built-in primitive that enables the receiver of a message to ascertain its origin. The key point is that the relative address of a message uniquely identifies its originator, even after the message has been maliciously intercepted and forwarded.

We write the primitive for authentication as $[x \overset{@}{=} A]P$, where x is a name and A is a process. Intuitively, the execution of the process P starts only when the check $[x \overset{@}{=} A]$ succeeds, and this happens if and only if x has been originated by A. [1] In other words, the interpreter of the calculus (i.e. the semantic rules, *not* the user!) checks whether the local environment to which x belongs is the one of A.

A communication protocol that guarantees authentication by construction is now easy to define, by using the plain handshaking communication of the π-calculus and the primitive sketched above. Suppose that a process A sends a (fresh) message M to B along a public channel c. In the π-calculus syntax they have the following form:

$$A = (\nu M)\overline{c}M.A'$$

and

$$B = c(x).[x \overset{@}{=} A]B'(x),$$

where the operator (νM) declares M to be a fresh name, different from all the others in the whole system; $\overline{c}M$ stands for sending M along c; $c(x)$ is an input action that paired in a communication with an output $\overline{c}z$ has the effect of binding x to z within its residual yielding $[z \overset{@}{=} A]B'(z)$. If we put A, B and also an intruder E in parallel, $A \mid B \mid E$, the effect is to guarantee that the residual of B is indeed $B'(M)$. Note that the intruder might as well intercept the message M originated by A, but it cannot modify any of its parts, because relative addresses are manipulated by the semantics only. Also, there is no need for c to be a channel private to A and B.

The definition of the semantics of [2] is very detailed, and quite long. We omit large parts of it, referring the interested reader to its original presentation. We only describe it intuitively in Sect. 3, and recall in Sect. 4 the basic definitions of localized names and of their management. The SOS rules for the π-calculus and a few auxiliary notions are in the Appendix. The example above is worked out in detail in Sect. 3 and any intrusion shown to fail.

Our solution assumes that the implementation of the communication primitive has a reliable mechanism to control and manage relative addresses. In some real cases this is possible, e.g., if the network management system filters every access of a user to the network. This may be not the case in many other situations. Yet, our solution may help checking the correctness of different implementations, e.g. those based on cryptography. A remarkable example of a process algebra with cryptographic features is given by the *spi*-calculus [1], over which the mechanism of handling names locally carries easily. We can then verify if a cryptography-based protocol ensures authentication, by checking a version of it containing also the primitive $[x \overset{@}{=} A]$: the original formulation and the extended one should exhibit the same behaviour. This check of specifications against implementations, is much in the style of the congruence-based technique proposed in [1]. We shall not present it in detail. We only show in Sect. 5 the needed extensions to model in our framework the primitives for encryption and decryption and we show on an example how an attack is revealed.

2. The π-calculus

In this section we briefly recall the π-calculus [12], a model of concurrent communicating processes based on the notion of *naming*. We give only its intuitive semantics; the formal semantics of the calculus is in Appendix A.

[1]For the sake of readability we write here the operands in a simplified form; in the full notation, the name x is equipped with a relative address, that is checked for equality against the address of A (for details, see below).

Definition 2.1 (syntax) *Let $\mathcal{N}$ be a countable, infinite set of* names *ranged over by $a, b, \ldots, x, y, \ldots$, and let τ be a distinguished element such that $\mathcal{N} \cap \{\tau\} = \emptyset$.* Processes *(denoted by $P, Q, R, \ldots \in \mathcal{P}$), are built from names according to the syntax*

$$P \ ::= \ \mathbf{0} \mid \pi.P \mid P + P \mid P|P \mid (\nu x)P \mid [x = y]P \mid A(y_1, \ldots, y_k)$$

where π may either be $x(y)$ for input, *or $\overline{x}y$ for* output *or τ for* silent *moves and A is an agent identifier. Hereafter, the trailing $\mathbf{0}$ will be omitted (i.e. π will stand for $\pi.\mathbf{0}$).*

Intuitively, $\mathbf{0}$ represents the null process which can do nothing. The prefix π is the first atomic action that the process $\pi.P$ can perform. After the execution of π the process $\pi.P$ behaves like P. The input prefix $x(y)$ binds the name y in the prefixed process as follows: when a name z is received along the link named x, all the (free) occurrences of y in the prefixed process P are substituted with z. This models an input on link x. [2] The output prefix $\overline{x}z$ does not bind the name z which is sent along x. The silent prefix τ denotes an action which is invisible to an external observer of the system. Summation denotes nondeterministic choice. The process $P_1 + P_2$ behaves like either P_1 or P_2. The operator $|$ describes parallel composition of processes. The components of $P_1|P_2$ may act independently; also, an output action of P_1 (resp. P_2) at any output port $\overline{x}$ may synchronize with an input action of P_2 (resp. P_1) at x to create a silent action denoting the communication. The value sent by P_1 replaces the relevant occurrences of the placeholder y in P_2 (see the comment above on input). The operator (νx) acts as a static declaration (i.e. a binder for) the name x in the process P that it prefixes. In other words, x is a unique name in P which is different from all the external names. The agent $(\nu x)P$ behaves as P except that actions at ports $\overline{x}$ and x are prohibited. However communications along link x of components *within* P are allowed since the result is a silent action. When a private name x is sent as (bound) output on a public channel y the effect is to vanish the (νx) operator, as in $Q = (\nu x)\overline{y}x.P \xrightarrow{\overline{y}(x)} P$. The intuition behind this operation is to make the name x, which is private to Q, available to the environment of P. Since the operator (νx) can be interpreted as a declaration, the bound output enlarges its scope and guarantees that the name x is fresh. (For this reason a bound output is sometimes referred to as *scope extrusion* in the literature.) For example, the generation of a session key can be modelled by an action of this kind. Matching $[x = y]P$ is an `if-then` operator: process P is activated only if $x = y$. Finally, each agent identifier A has a unique defining equation of the form $A(y_1, \ldots, y_k) = P$. The equation $A(y_1, \ldots, y_k) = P$ is akin to the definition of function: it is invocated by $A(z_1, \ldots, z_k)$ and triggers the substitution of the actual parameter z_i for the corresponding formal parameter y_i.

The operational semantics of the calculus is defined in a logical style by inducing on the syntax of the processes. This approach is usually called structural operational semantics (SOS, for short). There are also static rules that make equivalent syntactical different terms, like commutativity of choices or avoidance of declaration of unused names. These rules define a structural congruence $\equiv_P$ that simplifies the semantic rules. E.g. the processes $[x = x]P$ and P behave exactly in the same way, and this can be expressed through the static structural rule $[x = x]P \equiv_P P$. For more details see the Appendix A.

[2]This is the so-called *late* semantics, because the binding of y takes place at communication time, opposed to the *early* semantics [13] that we do not consider here.

3. The Authentication Primitive

We recall here the basic ideas of [2] which extend the standard semantics of the π-calculus of [12], in that it handles names locally. The resulting operational semantics provides us with an authentication primitive that can be used to specify protocols which guarantee authentication "by construction".

Consider for a while the binary parallel composition as the main operator of the π-calculus, stipulating that it is neither associative nor commutative. Then, build abstract syntax trees of processes as binary trees, called *trees of (sequential) processes* as follows. Given a process P, the nodes of its tree correspond to the occurrences of the parallel operator in P, and its leaves are the sequential components of P. For an example, see Fig. 1.

Assume now that the left (resp. right) branches of a tree of sequential processes denote the left (resp. right) component of parallel compositions, and label their arcs with tag $||_0$ (resp. $||_1$). Therefore, any sequential component of a process is uniquely identified by a string ϑ over $\{||_0, ||_1\}^*$. The string corresponds to a path from the root, the top-level $|$ of the whole process, to a leaf. Intuitively, ϑ is the address of the sequential component relative to the root of the binary tree. The space of names of a whole process is then partitioned into local environments associated each with its sequential sub-process. Consider two different sequential processes, say G and R, that have generated two syntactically equal names, say n. Suppose now that G sends its n to R. It is necessary to distinguish between the two different instances of n. In order to do this, in the local environment of R, the name generated by G will be enriched with the *address* of G *relative* to R, which points back from R to the local environment of G. The relative address can be decomposed into two parts according to the minimal common predecessor P of G and R in the tree. A relative address

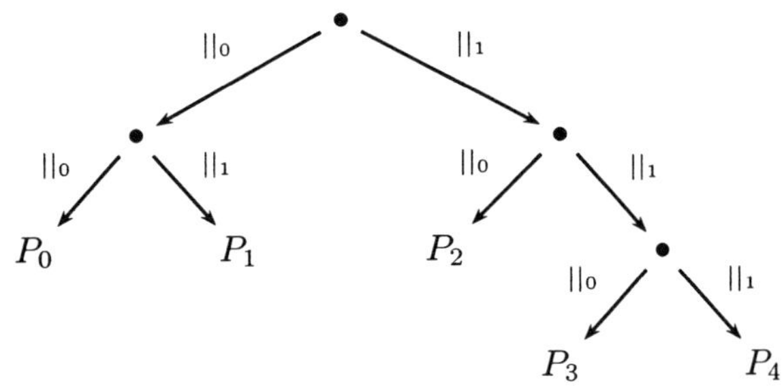

Figure 1. The tree of (sequential) processes of $(P_0|P_1)|(P_2|(P_3|P_4))$.

is then a string $\vartheta \bullet \vartheta' \in \{||_0, ||_1\}^* \bullet \{||_0, ||_1\}^*$, where ϑ represents the path from P to R, and ϑ' the path from P to G. Let G and R respectively be the processes P_3 and P_1 of Fig. 1. The address of P_3 relative to P_1 is $||_0||_1 \bullet ||_1||_1||_0$ (read the path upwards from P_1 to the root and reverse, then downwards to P_3). Relative addresses are inductively built while deducing transitions.

A slightly more complex situation arises when a process receives a name and sends it to another process. The name must arrive at the new receiver with the address of the generator (*not* of the sender) relative to the new receiver (think to an intruder that simply forwards an intercepted message). As an example assume that, in Fig. 1, P_1 sends to P_2 a name generated by P_3 (i.e. with relative address $||_0||_1 \bullet ||_1||_1||_0$). The rules for communication determine the address of P_1 relative to P_2, i.e. $||_1||_0 \bullet ||_0||_1$, and compose it with the address of the communicated name in order to derive the new relative address. This is done through the address composition operation $\star$ which is defined in the next section: $||_1||_0 \bullet ||_0||_1 \star ||_0||_1 \bullet ||_1||_1||_0 = ||_1||_0 \bullet ||_0$.

We can now intuitively present our authentication primitive $[x \overset{@}{=} A]$. It is akin to the matching operator of the π-calculus. The process $[x \overset{@}{=} A]P$ enables P only if the relative addresses of the two localized names x and A are exactly the same, i.e. only if x has been generated by A. [3] It is now simple to ascertain the origin of a message.

Consider again the example presented in the Introduction, on which we show in detail how our authentication primitive works. The protocol P is:

$$\begin{aligned} P &= A \mid (B \mid E) \\ A &= (\nu M)\bar{c}M.A' \\ B &= c(x).[x \overset{@}{=} A]B'(x) \end{aligned}$$

Now we show the role that localized names play, and how we guarantee by construction that B' is executed only if the message bound to x has been originated by A, i.e., if the message received on channel c is indeed M. Assume, for simplicity, that the name of A used by B in the authentication check is indeed the relative address $||_1||_0 \bullet ||_0$ pointing from B to A. As said above, this relative address encodes the "site" hosting A, thus it gives the identity of the process from which B is expecting to receive a message on channel c. In order to analyze the behaviour of the protocol in an hostile environment, we consider a generic enemy E, as powerful as possible. We now consider the following two possible message exchanges:

$$\begin{aligned} \text{Message } 1 &\;:\; A \to B : M \\ \text{Message } 2 &\;:\; E \to B : N \end{aligned}$$

The first message represents the correct exchange of message M from A to B. The second one is an attempt of E to send a different message N to B. The enemy E could actually be of the following form:

$$E = (\nu N)\bar{c}N.E' + \langle \text{other evil actions} \rangle.$$

The names M and N are received by B prefixed by the relative address corresponding to the respective originators.

Fig. 2 shows the two message exchanges. In particular we see that M is received by B as $||_1||_0 \bullet ||_0 M$ while N becomes $||_0 \bullet ||_1 N$. It is now immediate to see that only in the first case B will evolve to $B(M)$ while in the latter it will stop. This is so because only $||_1||_0 \bullet ||_0 M$ matches with the address of A. Every attempt of the enemy of introducing new messages on c is filtered out by the authentication primitive.

A further interesting case arises when the enemy intercepts M and forwards it to B. We will show in the following section that our mechanism accepts the message, as it is authentic.

4. Address Composition

Here we recall the definition of relative addresses and show how these are updated when names are communi-

[3] We assume that a process knows which are the other processes around, and which are the relative addresses of their local environments. Note also that x is a name while A is a process: we do not distinguish them here for the sake of presentation.

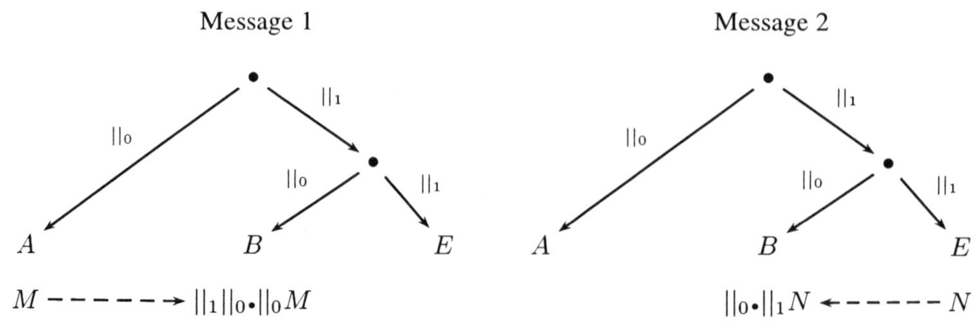

Figure 2. The process B detects that the message $\|_1\|_0 \bullet \|_0 M$ is authentic while the message $\|_0 \bullet \|_1 N$ comes from the enemy E.

cated. More intuition, the full definitions and the statements of their correctness are in [2].

Definition 4.1 (relative addresses)
Let $\vartheta, \vartheta'_i, \vartheta_i \in \{\|_0, \|_1\}^*$, let ϵ be the empty string, and let $\oplus$ be sum modulo 2. Then, the set of relative addresses *is*

$$\mathcal{A} = \{\vartheta_0 \bullet \vartheta_1 : \vartheta_i = \|_j \vartheta'_i \Rightarrow \vartheta_{i\oplus 1} = \|_{j\oplus 1} \vartheta'_{i\oplus 1}, i, j = 0, 1\}.$$

As we said in the previous section, we use relative addresses to encode paths between pairs of nodes of binary trees of processes, like the one in Fig. 1. Note that the condition $\|_0 \vartheta'_0 \bullet \|_1 \vartheta'_1$ (and $\|_1 \vartheta'_0 \bullet \|_0 \vartheta'_1$) makes it explicit that the two components of the relative address describe the two distinct paths going out from the *same* node in a binary tree. This node is the minimal common predecessor of the generator of a name and its user. We now define address composition. It is a partial operation, defined only when relative addresses can indeed be composed. We make sure that this is always the case when we apply it. Fig. 3 depicts the cases in which we will use the address composition $\star$, that discards the dashed paths.

Definition 4.2 (address composition) *Address composition $\star : (\mathcal{A} \times \mathcal{A}) \rightharpoonup \mathcal{A}$ is defined by the following three exhaustive cases:*

1. $\vartheta_0 \bullet \vartheta \star \vartheta_2 \vartheta \bullet \vartheta_3 = \vartheta_2 \vartheta_0 \bullet \vartheta_3$ *with* $\vartheta_2 \neq \epsilon$
2. $\vartheta_0 \bullet \vartheta_1 \vartheta \star \vartheta \bullet \vartheta_3 = \vartheta_0 \bullet \vartheta_1 \vartheta_3$ *with* $\vartheta_1 \neq \epsilon$
3. $\vartheta' \vartheta_0 \bullet \vartheta \star \vartheta \bullet \vartheta' \vartheta_3 = \vartheta_0 \bullet \vartheta_3$

Let G be the generator of a name, and S be the process which receives the name and sends it to the process R. Moreover, let $\vartheta_S \bullet \vartheta_G$ and $\vartheta_R \bullet \vartheta'_S$ be the addresses of G relative to S, and of S relative to R, respectively. Then, our address composition is correct because $\vartheta_R \bullet \vartheta'_S \star \vartheta_S \bullet \vartheta_G$ is the address of G relative to R (see Theorem 4.7 of [2]).

We extend below the syntax of the π-calculus with localized names. In the following definition we assume to have all the standard names of the π-calculus, including τ, and to represent a localized name as a natural number n, prefixed by a relative address, i.e. these names will have the form $\vartheta_0 \bullet \vartheta_1 n$. Actually, there is an additional extension that provides each sequential process with its own name generator. For the sake of readability, we ignore name generators here, and we refer the reader to the Appendix B for their definition. We only mention that technically a name generator keeps track of the last local name n originated so far, and produces on demand $n+1$ as the new local name. (This may explain our use of natural numbers as local names, which however is not a limitation at all.) As a matter of fact, a new name is needed whenever the scope of a declaration (νx) is enlarged. This happens when a process P extrudes its local name x and makes it available to another process, say Q. In this case, the name x is replaced in (the residual of) P by the newly generated name $n+1$, localized to the environment of P by prefixing it with the empty relative address $\epsilon \bullet \epsilon$. When communicated to Q, this name receives the correct relative address $\vartheta_0 \bullet \vartheta_1$, as sketched above.

Definition 4.3 *Let $\mathcal{N}' = \mathcal{A} \cdot \mathbf{Z} \cup \mathcal{N} \cup \{\tau\}$ be the set of* localized names, *ranged over by $r, s, u, \ldots$, possibly indexed, where $\mathbf{Z}$ is the set of non-zero integer numbers, and "$\cdot$" is the operator of language concatenation.*
The new syntax of the π-calculus is obtained from the one in Def. 2.1, with r, s in place of x, y. In particular, π can either be $r(s)$ or $\overline{r}s$ or τ and a restricted name can be s.

Note that a free name, i.e., a name known to all the processes, is an element of $\mathcal{N}$ (the second set forming $\mathcal{N}'$) and carries no relative address.

We recall below how the operation of address composition is exploited to update the addresses of localized names when they are sent from one site to another (note that free

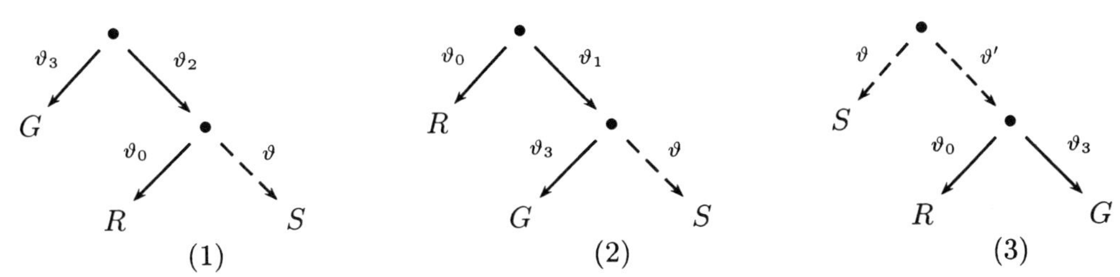

Figure 3. The three possible placements of the generator (G), the sender (S), and the receiver (R) of a name.

names, like a below, are not affected by the $\star$ operator).

Definition 4.4 *Let $r = \vartheta_r \bullet \vartheta'_r n$ (resp. a) be a name. A name r exported to the relative address $\vartheta \bullet \vartheta'$ is $\vartheta \bullet \vartheta' \star r = (\vartheta \bullet \vartheta' \star \vartheta_r \bullet \vartheta'_r)n$ (resp. $\vartheta \bullet \vartheta' \star a = a$).*

An example of address composition may help. We reconsider the protocol of the previous section and we analyze the case of a different enemy that, masquerading as B (written $E(B)$), intercepts M and forwards it to B:

$$\begin{array}{lcl} \text{Message 3} & : & A \rightarrow E(B) : M \\ \text{Message 4} & : & E \rightarrow B : M \end{array}$$

Since E does not modify M we would like to accept the message in B even if it has been forwarded by E. Address composition maintains the identity of messages, so we accept indeed this behaviour. In detail, $E(B)$ receives M as $||_1||_1 \bullet ||_0 M$. When E forwards it to B, the message is composed with the address of E relative to B, $||_0 \bullet ||_1$, yielding $||_0 \bullet ||_1 \star ||_1||_1 \bullet ||_0 M$. By applying the rule (1) of Def. 4.2 we see that the message is received by B as $||_1||_0 \bullet ||_0 M$ and that it is accepted as it is authentic.

5. Implementing Authentication

As we have shown above, our primitive allows processes to obtain authentication in a direct and "secure" way. It thus permits to completely abstract from the underlying mechanisms which are necessary to guarantee authentication. However, if we want to implement it, the interpreter itself of the calculus (or of a language based on it) must control and manage relative addresses in a highly reliable manner. E.g., this is the case for intranets.

Unfortunately, this may be not the case in many other situations. Typically, in a wide-area network setting, the network is completely insecure, i.e., users may have a complete access to the net management system and there is no reliable way of filtering these accesses. In our terminology, a malicious user could change the relative addresses of localized names making them unreliable, and our authentication primitive completely useless.

In these situations the "standard" approach to guarantee authentication (and security in general) is to use cryptography. The *spi*-calculus [1] is an extension of the π-calculus with cryptographic primitives. They make the formal definitions of protocols compact and elegant, and facilitate the proof that protocols guarantee authentication.

We use below our proposal to analyze the cryptographic "implementation" of authentication mechanisms specified in the *spi*-calculus. To do this, we first carry on the *spi*-calculus the semantics of [2] used so far. This step is quite easy, because the *spi*-calculus has the π-calculus as "core" language. We then observe if a particular authentication protocol is indeed able to "implement" our authentication primitive, i.e., if the cryptographic protocol is as strong in detecting names with an "incorrect" relative address as our secure-by-construction authentication protocol is.

Lack of space prevents us from giving all the definitions in detail; we only present them intuitively. We first extend our calculus with the shared-key cryptographic primitives of the *spi*-calculus: [4]

- $\{M\}_K$ represents the encryption of message M with key K;
- *case* x *of* $\{y\}_K$ *in* P represents the decryption of message x through key K; the result of the decryption is put in y. It can be read as follows: "if x is of the form $\{M\}_K$ then $P[M/y]$ is executed (i.e., P where M replaces all the free occurrences of y); otherwise it is stuck".

The management of localized names extends easily to the encryption and decryption primitives. The first raises no problems, because $\{M\}_K$ is a *new* name, local to the process that encrypts M, say P. Technically, one has only to

[4] In the following items, both M and K can in fact be localized names; for better supporting intuition, we prefer to write M and K instead of following pedantically our conventions that impose to use names r and u.

make sure that this new name never clashes with those produced by the name generator. The two localized names M and K are frozen just like they were at encryption time, and their own relative addresses are not changed when the encrypted message is sent through the net; actually, these relative addresses *cannot* be updated. Since $\{M\}_K$ is a new name, its relative address, say $\vartheta_0 \bullet \vartheta_1$, will always point to the process P that made the encryption. In this way, when decrypting $\{M\}_K$ the semantic rules recover the correct addresses for M and K by simply composing the actual address of $\{M\}_K$, $\vartheta_0 \bullet \vartheta_0$, with the (frozen) relative addresses of M and K, respectively.

We do not give an operational rule for encryption since it constructs a local name in quite a standard way. Instead, a static definition of structural congruence suffices, that identifies two syntactically different, but semantically equivalent processes, just as it is the case with the rule for structural congruence $[x = x]P \equiv_P P$. For decryption we stipulate the following (again M should be a localized name r; see the preceding footnote):

$$case\ \vartheta_0 \bullet \vartheta_1 \{M\}_u\ of\ \{y\}_{\vartheta_0 \bullet \vartheta_1 \star u}\ in\ P \equiv_P P[\vartheta_0 \bullet \vartheta_1 \star M/y].$$

The intuition is that we can decrypt a message $\{M\}_u$ only if we use the key $s = \vartheta_0 \bullet \vartheta_1 \star u$ which is exactly how the frozen key u should appear to the receiver of the encrypted message. When the two names s and u, although starting from different sites, do refer to the same key, the semantic rules decrypt the message and update its relative address by composing $\vartheta_0 \bullet \vartheta_1$ with M. The congruence rule equates then the process at the left, where the match succeeds, and P, where $\vartheta_0 \bullet \vartheta_1 \star M$ replaces y.

We now show an example of a correct run of the Wide Mouthed Frog key exchange protocol. Consider its simplified version analyzed in [1]. The two processes A and B share keys K_{AS} and K_{BS} with a trusted server S. In order to establish a secure channel with B, A sends a fresh key K_{AB} encrypted with K_{AS} to the server S. Then, the server decrypts the key and forwards it to B, this time encrypted with K_{BS}. Now B has the key K_{AB} and A can send a message M encrypted with K_{AB} to B. The protocol should guarantee that when B receives M, such a message has been indeed originated by A.

The protocol is composed of the following three messages:

Message 1	$A \to S$:	$\{K_{AB}\}_{K_{AS}}$
Message 2	$S \to B$:	$\{K_{AB}\}_{K_{BS}}$
Message 3	$A \to B$:	$\{M\}_{K_{AB}}$

Its specification in our calculus with localized names is:

$$\begin{aligned} P &= (\nu K_{AS})(\nu K_{BS})(\ (A|B) \mid S) \\ A &= (\nu K_{AB})(\nu M)(\overline{c_{AS}}\{K_{AB}\}_{K_{AS}}.\overline{c_{AB}}\{M\}_{K_{AB}}) \\ S &= c_{AS}(x).case\ x\ of\ \{y\}_{K_{AS}}\ in\ \overline{c_{BS}}\{y\}_{K_{BS}} \\ B &= c_{BS}(x).case\ x\ of\ \{y\}_{K_{BS}}\ in \\ &\quad\ c_{AB}(z).case\ z\ of\ \{r\}_y\ in\ B'(r) \end{aligned}$$

Not surprisingly, the specification is in the style of [1]. Indeed the localized name mechanism is not visible at this level, and we are not using yet our authentication primitive. Fig. 4 shows how the localized names are handled in a correct execution of the protocol P. Note that K_{AS} and K_{BS} are standard names, belonging to $\mathcal{N}$. Indeed, they are restricted in P but never extruded and therefore they never assume the form of localized names. So the keys have no relative address; of course, no problem would arise if they were localized names and carry a relative address, instead.

After the reception of message 2, B decrypts the received message $||_0||_1 \bullet ||_1\{||_1 \bullet ||_0||_0 K_{AB}\}_{K_{BS}}$. This means computing

$$case\ ||_0||_1 \bullet ||_1\{||_1 \bullet ||_0||_0 K_{AB}\}_{K_{BS}}\ of\ \{y\}_{K_{BS}}\ in\ c_{AB}(z). \\ case\ z\ of\ \{r\}_y\ in\ B'(r),$$

where $||_0||_1 \bullet ||_1 K_{BS} = K_{BS}$ because the key is a standard name in $\mathcal{N}$ (see Def. 4.4). The variable y is then set to

$$||_0||_1 \bullet ||_1 \star ||_1 \bullet ||_0||_0 K_{AB},$$

that results in $||_1 \bullet ||_0 K_{AB}$, by the rule (3) of Def. 4.2. This is indeed the correct reference to the key K_{AB} generated by A and installed in its local environment. In the last message B receives $||_1 \bullet ||_0\{M\}_{K_{AB}}$, and succeeds in decrypting it with $||_1 \bullet ||_0 K_{AB}$, obtaining $||_1 \bullet ||_0 M$. The addresses of M and of A relative to B are equal, so M is indeed authentic. This characterizes a "correct" execution.

It is well-known that an attack can take place over two sessions of the protocol above. Basically, it occurs when the enemy replays some messages of the first session in the second one. We follow below the formalization of [1], where this attack is analyzed. Note that in the single session illustrated above no problem arises instead, even if an enemy intercepts the message sent by A and then forwards it to B. Indeed the message received is the right one, because no one can alterate it.

Now, we show that the attack above is immediately detected by an observer that can compare localized name, e.g. by using our authentication primitive $[x \overset{@}{=} A]$. For the sake of readability, we call A' and B' the two instances of A and B in the second session where A' is trying to send the

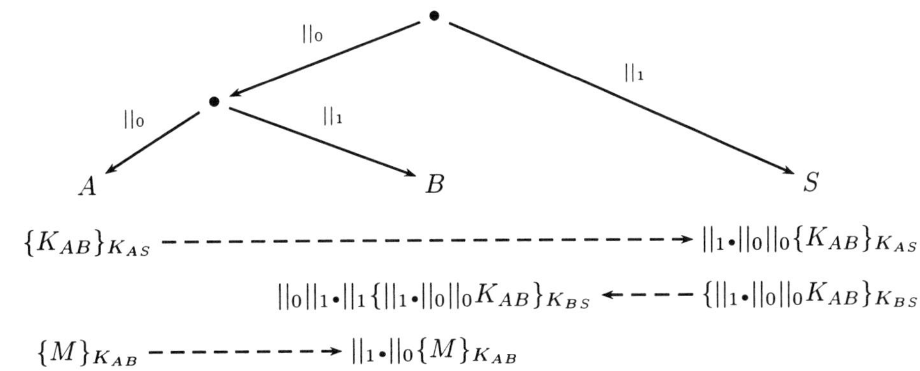

Figure 4. A correct execution of the Wide Mouthed Frog protocol

message M' to B' using the session key K'_{AB}:

$$\begin{array}{llll} \text{Message 1} & A \to S & : & \{K_{AB}\}_{K_{AS}} \\ \text{Message 2} & S \to B & : & \{K_{AB}\}_{K_{BS}} \\ & \langle E \text{ eavesdrops Message 2} \rangle & & \\ \text{Message 3} & A \to B & : & \{M\}_{K_{AB}} \\ & \langle E \text{ eavesdrops Message 3} \rangle & & \\ \text{Message 1}' & A' \to S & : & \{K'_{AB}\}_{K_{AS}} \\ \text{Message 2}' & E(S) \to B' & : & \{K_{AB}\}_{K_{BS}} \\ \text{Message 3}' & E(A') \to B' & : & \{M\}_{K_{AB}} \end{array}$$

The enemy eavesdrops the first session and then replays messages 2 and 3 in the second session (messages 2′ and 3′). The result is that B' receives a copy of M instead of one of M'.

The specification of the protocol is:

$$P' \;=\; (\nu K_{AS})(\nu K_{BS})(\,(A \mid A) \mid (B \mid B)\,) \mid (S \mid E)$$

Note that A generates both M and K_{AB} as fresh names. So when we consider $A \mid A$, the two A's originate two different messages, say M and M', and two different keys, say K_{AB} and K'_{AB}. We need to modify S so that it can serve more sessions:

$$S \;=\; c_{AS}(x).\mathit{case}\ x\ \mathit{of}\ \{y\}_{K_{AS}}\ \mathit{in}\ \overline{c_{BS}}\{y\}_{K_{BS}}.S$$

and we specify the enemy as:

$$E \;=\; c_{BS}(x).c_{AB}(y).\overline{c_{BS}}x.\overline{c_{AB}}y.$$

Note that the names c_{AB}, c_{AS} and c_{BS} are free, i.e., known to all the processes of P'.

Now we can observe the attack sequence in Fig. 5. Note in particular that when B' decrypts $||_1||_1\bullet||_0||_0\{M\}_{K_{AB}}$, it obtains $||_1||_1\bullet||_0||_0 M$ which is a message originated from A and not from A', as it should be. Indeed, the address of A' relative to B' is $||_1||_1\bullet||_0||_1$, and the attack is detected.

6. Conclusions and Future Work

We defined a primitive that guarantees message authentication over public channels. It is based on a semantics of the π-calculus where names, representing messages or channels, are localized, whenever needed. Localized names have a reference to their creator and the semantic rules update them, after a communication. This reference is the relative address of a message M. The authentication primitive compares it with the address of a process A. The check succeeds and authenticates the message M only if the process A originated M.

The same mechanism can also be applied in case one is interested in making sure which principal encrypted the message received, under the hypothesis that the same entity also generated the message or has been delegated to send it. This is a somehow weaker form of authentication than the one considered in this paper, which assumes that a key can be used by its trusted owners, only. We make use of this restricted version of authentication in the discussion below.

Note that our authentication primitive does not transform a public channel into a private one. It neither guarantees that the received messages have not been intercepted nor eavesdropped, i.e., it does not guarantee secrecy. Indeed, our primitive corresponds neither to a private channel in the basic π-calculus, nor to a cryptographic one in the *spi*-calculus. These appear to be too strong to model authentication alone, as they guarantee also secrecy.

As discussed in the paper, our primitive may be not implementable directly. Indeed, one should have a low-level, highly reliable mechanism to manage localized names, which is quite unrealistic in many cases. Nevertheless, our proposal can help reasoning on authentication and security from an abstract point of view. We briefly exemplified this using the *spi*-calculus. We plan to apply the proof techniques presented in [1] to our model. The idea is to define a

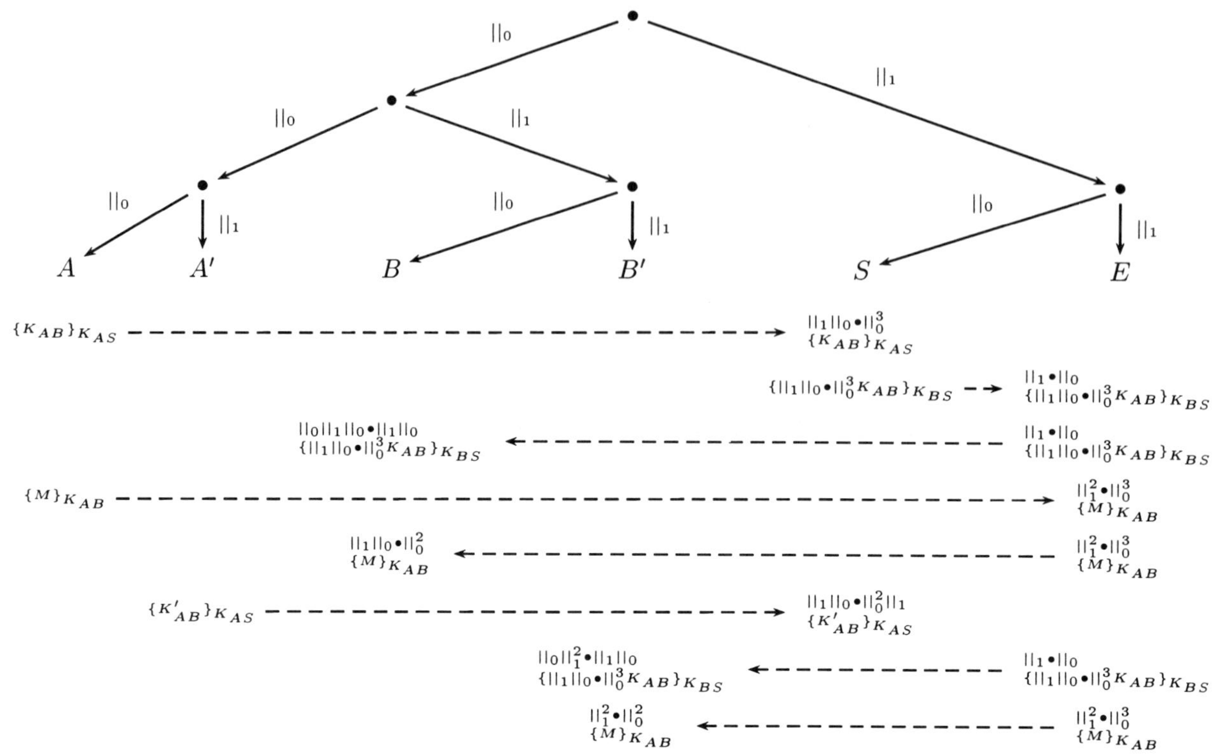

Figure 5. An attack on the Wide Mouthed Frog protocol; where $||_i^k$ stands for a sequence of k tags $||_i$.

suitable equivalence $\approx$ on our processes, and then check if a certain protocol guarantees authentication by comparing it with its corresponding "secure by construction" version. This secure version is easily got by adding the authentication primitive at the end of the protocol, i.e., where the message which should be authentic is derived. As an example, the process B in the Wide Mouthed Frog protocol becomes:

$$\begin{aligned} B' \;=\; & c_{BS}(x).\mathit{case}\ x\ \mathit{of}\ \{y\}_{K_{BS}}\ \mathit{in} \\ & c_{AB}(z).\mathit{case}\ z\ \mathit{of}\ \{w\}_y\ \mathit{in}\ [w \overset{@}{=} A]B''(w) \end{aligned}$$

which makes the protocol secure by construction. So, if we establish that

$$(A|B)|S \approx (A|B')|S,$$

we are guaranteed that also the original protocol $(A|B)|S$ is secure.

The authentication property studied in [1] seems slightly stronger than ours: it requires that if A has to send a message to B, then this should be the only message that B accepts at the end of (a successful run of) the protocol. Our approach to authentication relaxes this requirement. As a matter of fact, we only ask that the message received by B has been indeed originated by the process A. We have shown on an example how this feature can be exploited to reveal replay attacks. Further investigation is needed for comparing Abadi's requirement and property with ours.

Besides the technique mentioned above, our authentication primitive could support proofs of correctness that are split in a sequence of "small" steps. A simple example follows. Consider the transmission of an encrypted message M on a public channel in the *spi*-calculus:

$$\begin{aligned} P \;=\; & (\nu K_{AB})(\ (\nu M)\bar{c}\{M\}_{K_{AB}}\ | \\ & c(x).\mathit{case}\ x\ \mathit{of}\ \{y\}_{K_{AB}}\ \mathit{in}\ B'(y)\ ), \end{aligned}$$

that enables $B'(y)$ only if $y = M$. Its secure version is:

$$\begin{aligned} P' \;=\; & (\nu K_{AB})(\ (\nu M)\bar{c}\{M\}_{K_{AB}}\ | \\ & c(x).\mathit{case}\ x\ \mathit{of}\ \{y\}_{K_{AB}}\ \mathit{in}\ [y \overset{@}{=} A]B'(y)\ ) \end{aligned}$$

where we assume A to be (the address of) the process $(\nu M)\bar{c}\{M\}_{K_{AB}}$. Instead of checking P against P', we could prove it is equivalent to

$$\begin{aligned} P'' \;=\; & (\nu K_{AB})\ (\nu M)(\bar{c}\{M\}_{K_{AB}}\ | \\ & c(x).[x \overset{@}{=} A]\mathit{case}\ x\ \mathit{of}\ \{y\}_{K_{AB}}\ \mathit{in}\ B'(y)\ ) \end{aligned}$$

The check $P'' \approx P$ seems easier to prove than $P' \approx P$. Indeed, P'' makes explicit that P uses encryption to guarantee authentication: when B receives a message encrypted with K_{AB}, it knows that the encryption (not the encrypted message!) was originated by A. This constitutes the first step of the equivalence proof where we are still not interested in "what is encrypted". The next step consists of proving the equivalence $P'' \approx P'$, by observing that the only message which is encrypted with K_{AB} is actually originated by A. The steps above rely on the fact that K_{AB} is private to A and B, and exploit the weak notion of authentication mentioned above. Of course, devising the intermediate processes, like P'' above, could be non trivial, but we are confident that also their generation could be mechanized.

The idea of exploiting locations for the analysis of authentication comes from [6], where however entities are bound to physical addresses of the net. Here we relaxed the rigidity of that mapping, by introducing a sort of "identifiers of sites" represented by relative addresses. As a matter of fact, the actual placement of a process on a site can be recovered by composing our localized names (akin to the environment function of sequential languages) with allocation tables (similar to a store). Actually, [6] models a wider notion of authentication, that we plan to investigate next.

We feel that our authentication primitive also works when processes migrate while executing a communication protocol. Our claim is supported by [2], where the localized semantics of the (first order) π-calculus is extended to the Higher Order π-calculus [18], that describes explicitly code mobility, by permitting also processes to be exchanged in communications.

Finally, we feel confident that our proposal scales up, because many real languages for concurrency, like Facile [21], PICT [16], CML [15], are built on top of a core process calculus like the one we use here. Of course a great deal of work is still necessary to make our theoretical proposal applicable in real cases.

References

[1] M. Abadi and A. D. Gordon. "A Calculus for Cryptographic Protocols: The Spi Calculus". *Information and Computation 148*, 1:1–70, January 1999.

[2] C. Bodei, P. Degano, and C. Priami. "Names of Mobile Agents Handled Locally". To appear in *Theoretical Computer Science*. Also available at http://www.di.unipi.it/~chiara/publ-40/TCS.ps. Extended abstract in: *Proceedings of ICALP'96*, LNCS 1099, Springer-Verlag.

[3] M. Burrows, M. Abadi, and R. Needham. "A Logic of Authentication". *ACM Transactions on Computer Systems*, pages 18–36, Feb. 1990.

[4] A. Durante, R. Focardi, and R. Gorrieri. "CVS: A Compiler for the Analysis of Cryptographic Protocols". In *this volume*, 1999.

[5] F. J. T. Fabrega, J. C. Herzog, and J. D. Guttman. "Strand Spaces: Why is a Security Protocol Correct?". In *Proceedings of the 1998 Symposium on Security and Privacy*. IEEE Computer Society Press, May 1998.

[6] R. Focardi. "Using Entity Locations for the Analysis of Authentication Protocols". In *Proceedings of Sixth Italian Conference on Theoretical Computer Science (ICTCS'98)*, November 1998.

[7] R. Focardi, A. Ghelli, and R. Gorrieri. "Using Non Interference for the Analysis of Security Protocols ". In *Proceeding of the DIMACS Workshop on Design and Formal Verification of Security Protocols (H. Orman and C. Meadows Ed.)*, DIMACS Center, Rutgers University, September 1997.

[8] I. O. for Standardization. Information technology - Security techniques - Entity authentication machanism; Part 1: General model. ISO/IEC 9798-1, Second Edition, September 1991.

[9] R. Kemmerer, C. Meadows, and J. Millen. "Three systems for cryptographic protocol analysis". *J. Cryptology*, 7(2):79–130, 1994.

[10] G. Lowe. "Breaking and Fixing the Needham-Schroeder Public-key Protocol using FDR". In *Proceedings of Second International Workshop on Tools and Algorithms for the Construction and Analysis of Systems (TACAS'96)*, pages 146–166, Passau (Germany), March 1996. Springer-Verlag, LNCS 1055.

[11] G. Lowe. "A Hierarchy of Authentication Specification". In *Proceedings of the 10th Computer Security Foundation Workshop*. IEEE press, 1997.

[12] R. Milner, J. Parrow, and D. Walker. "A Calculus of Mobile Processes (I and II)". *Information and Computation*, 100(1):1–77, 1992.

[13] R. Milner, J. Parrow, and D. Walker. "Modal Logics for Mobile Processes". *Theoretical Computer Science*, 114:149–171, 1993.

[14] J. C. Mitchell, M. Mitchell, and U. Stern. "Automated Analysis of Cryptographic Protocols Using Murϕ". In *Proceedings of the 1997 IEEE Symposium on Research in Security and Privacy*, pages 141–153. IEEE Computer Society Press, 1997.

[15] F. Nielson and H. R. Nielson. "From CML to its Process Algebra". *Theoretical Computer Science*, 155:179–219, 1996.

[16] B. Pierce and D. Turner. "PICT: A programming language based on the pi-calculus". Technical report available electronically, 1995.

[17] T. Pratt. *Programming Languages: Design and Implementation.* Prentice Hall, 1984.

[18] D. Sangiorgi. *"Expressing Mobility in Process Algebras: First-Order and Higher-Order Paradigms"*. PhD thesis, University of Edinburgh, 1992.

[19] S. Schneider. "Verifying authentication protocols in CSP". *IEEE Transactions on Software Engineering*, 24(9), September 1998.

[20] B. Schneier. *Applied Cryptography.* John Wiley & Sons, Inc., 1996. second edition.

[21] B. Thomsen, L. Leth, S. Prasad, T.-M. Kuo, A. Kramer, F. Knabe, and A. Giacalone. "Facile Antigua Release Programming Guide". Technical Report ECRC-93-20, European Computer-Industry Research Centre, 1993.

A. The π-calculus

The late operational semantics of the π-calculus is defined in *SOS* (Structural Operational Semantics) style, and the labels of transitions are τ for silent actions, $x(y)$ for input, $\overline{x}y$ for free output, and $\overline{x}(y)$ for bound output. We will use μ as a metavariable for the labels of transitions (it is distinct from π, the metavariable for prefixes, though it coincides in three cases).

We recall the notion of free names $fn(\mu)$, bound names $bn(\mu)$, and names $names(\mu) = fn(\mu) \cup bn(\mu)$ of a label μ. Two functions, *sbj* and *obj*, are also defined giving the subject and the object of input and output actions, respectively.

μ	*Kind*	$fn(\mu)$	$bn(\mu)$	$sbj(\mu)$	$obj(\mu)$
τ	Silent move	$\emptyset$	$\emptyset$	$\emptyset$	$\emptyset$
$\overline{x}y$	Free output	$\{x, y\}$	$\emptyset$	$\{x\}$	$\{y\}$
$\overline{x}(y)$	Bound output	$\{x\}$	$\{y\}$	$\{x\}$	$\{y\}$
$x(y)$	Input	$\{x\}$	$\{y\}$	$\{x\}$	$\{y\}$

Functions *fn*, *bn* and *names* are extended in the obvious way to processes.

Below we assume the *structural congruence* $\equiv_P$ on processes, defined as the least congruence satisfying the following clauses:

- $P \equiv_P Q$ if P and Q are α-equivalent,
- $(\mathcal{P}/_{\equiv_P}, +, \mathbf{0})$ and $(\mathcal{P}/_{\equiv_P}, |, \mathbf{0})$ are commutative monoids,
- $[x = x]P \equiv_P P$,
- $(\nu x)(\nu y)P \equiv_P (\nu y)(\nu x)P$, $(\nu x)P \equiv_P P$ if $x \notin fn(P)$, $(\nu x)(P \mid Q) \equiv_P (\nu x)P \mid Q$ if $x \notin fn(Q)$, and
- $A(a_1, \ldots, a_k) \equiv_P P\{a_1/y_1, \ldots, a_k/y_k\}$, if $A(y_1, \ldots, y_k) = P$.

A *variant* of $P \xrightarrow{\mu}_L Q$ is a transition which only differs in that P and Q have been replaced by structurally congruent processes, and μ has been α-converted, where a name bound in μ includes Q in its scope.

Table 1 shows the late transition system of the π-calculus. The transition in the conclusion of each rule, as well as in the axiom, stands for all its variants.

B. Handling names locally

We recall the late operational semantics of the π-calculus of [2], which creates and handles names locally.

Definition B.1 *Let $\mathcal{N}' = \mathcal{A} \cdot \mathbf{Z} \cup \mathcal{N} \cup \{\tau\}$ be the set of* localized names, *ranged over by $r, s, u, \ldots$, possibly indexed, where $\mathbf{Z}$ is the set of non-zero integer numbers, and "$\cdot$" is the operator of language concatenation.*
The new syntax of the π-calculus is obtained from the one in Def. 2.1, with r, s in place of x, y. In particular, π can either be $r(s)$ or $\overline{r}s$ or τ and a restricted name can be s. Furthermore, we only assume on the new processes the least congruence induced by the monoidal laws for $+$, and the laws for matching and constant invocation.

$$act : \mu.P \xrightarrow{\mu}_L P$$

$$par : \frac{P \xrightarrow{\mu}_L P'}{P|Q \xrightarrow{\mu}_L P'|Q}, bn(\mu) \cap fn(Q) = \emptyset \qquad sum : \frac{P \xrightarrow{\mu}_L P'}{P+Q \xrightarrow{\mu}_L P'}$$

$$res : \frac{P \xrightarrow{\mu}_L P'}{(\nu x)P \xrightarrow{\mu}_L (\nu x)P'}, x \notin names(\mu) \qquad open : \frac{P \xrightarrow{\overline{x}y}_L P'}{(\nu y)P \xrightarrow{\overline{x}(y)}_L P'}, y \neq x$$

$$close : \frac{P \xrightarrow{\overline{x}(y)}_L P', Q \xrightarrow{x(y)}_L Q'}{P|Q \xrightarrow{\tau}_L (\nu y)(P'|Q')} \qquad com : \frac{P \xrightarrow{\overline{x}y}_L P', Q \xrightarrow{x(z)}_L Q'}{P|Q \xrightarrow{\tau}_L P'|Q'\{y/z\}}$$

Table 1. Late proved transition system of π-calculus.

We now lift the composition of addresses defined in Sect. 4 to exportation of names.

Definition B.2 *Let $r = \vartheta_r \bullet \vartheta'_r n$ (resp. a) be a name. A name r exported to the relative address $\vartheta \bullet \vartheta'$ is $\vartheta \bullet \vartheta' \star r = (\vartheta \bullet \vartheta' \star \vartheta_r \bullet \vartheta'_r)n$ (resp. $\vartheta \bullet \vartheta' \star a = a$).*

Below, we extend the needed notions to processes with localized names implemented as a family of operators $n \Rightarrow$ (with $n \geq 1$).

Definition B.3 *Let P be a process and n be a non-zero natural number. The* extended processes *(denoted by $t, t_i, t' \ldots \in \mathcal{T}$), are defined according to the syntax*

$$t ::= n \Rightarrow P | \; (\nu s)t \mid t|t$$

where P is as in Def. B.1. We assume on $\mathcal{T}$ the least congruence $\equiv$ which satisfies the following clauses

- $n \Rightarrow (\nu\, s)P \equiv (\nu\, s)n \Rightarrow P$ *and*
- $n \Rightarrow (P|Q) \equiv (n \Rightarrow P)|(n \Rightarrow Q)$.

The computations of a process $P \in \mathcal{P}$ start from the extended process $1 \Rightarrow P$.

The standard notions on names (free, bound) are carried over extended processes in the obvious way. We also need a new notion of substitution to correctly update localized names.

Definition B.4 *Let $\{-/-\}$ be the standard substitution. Then the* routed substitution $\{\!| - / - |\!\}$ *is defined by induction as follows:*

1. $(n \Rightarrow P)\{\!|u'/u|\!\} = n \Rightarrow P\{\!|u'/u|\!\}$
2. $((\nu\, s)t)\{\!|u'/u|\!\} = \begin{cases} (\nu\, -u)(t\{\!|-u/u'|\!\})\{\!|u'/u|\!\} & \\ & \textit{if } u' = s \\ (\nu\, s)t & \textit{if } u = s \\ (\nu\, s)(t\{\!|u'/u|\!\}) & \textit{otherwise} \end{cases}$
3. $(t_0|t_1)\{\!|u'/u|\!\} = t_0\{\!|u'_0/u_0|\!\}|t_1\{\!|u'_1/u_1|\!\}$,
   where $u'_i = ||_i \bullet \star u'$ and $u_i = ||_i \bullet \star u$, for $i = 0, 1$
4. $\mathbf{0}\{\!|u'/u|\!\} = \mathbf{0}$
5. $(\tau.P)\{\!|u'/u|\!\} = \tau.P\{\!|u'/u|\!\}$
6. $(\overline{r}s.P)\{\!|u'/u|\!\} = (\overline{r}s)\{u'/u\}.P\{\!|u'/u|\!\}$
7. $(r(s).P)\{\!|u'/u|\!\} = \begin{cases} r\{u'/u\}(-u).P\{\!|-u/u'|\!\}\{\!|u'/u|\!\} & \\ & \textit{if } u' = s \\ r\{u'/u\}(s).P & \textit{if } u = s \\ r\{u'/u\}(s).(P\{\!|u'/u|\!\}) & \textit{otherwise} \end{cases}$
8. $(P+Q)\{\!|u'/u|\!\} = P\{\!|u'/u|\!\} + Q\{\!|u'/u|\!\}$
9. $[r = s]P\{\!|u'/u|\!\} = [r\{u'/u\} = s\{u'/u\}]P\{\!|u'/u|\!\}$
10. $A(r_1, \ldots, r_k)\{\!|u'/u|\!\} = A(r_1\{u'/u\}, \ldots, r_k\{u'/u\})$

We use the above definition to implement a selective substitution that works on a given sub-process of a whole term.

Definition B.5 *Let t be an extended process and $\vartheta \in \{||_0, ||_1\}^*$. Then, the* selective rooted substitution *$t\{\!|/|\!\}_{@\vartheta}$ is defined by induction as*

- $(t_0|t_1)\{\!|r/s|\!\}_{@\vartheta} = \begin{cases} t_0\{\!|r/s|\!\}_{@\vartheta'}|t_1 & \textit{if } \vartheta = ||_0\vartheta' \\ t_0|t_1\{\!|r/s|\!\}_{@\vartheta'} & \textit{if } \vartheta = ||_1\vartheta' \end{cases}$
- $t\{\!|r/s|\!\}_{@\epsilon} = t\{\!|r/s|\!\}$

The selective increment *of counters $t\{n+1 \Rightarrow /n \Rightarrow\}_{@\vartheta}$ is defined as follows, by stipulating that $(n+1 \Rightarrow)$ and $(n \Rightarrow)$ are considered as tokens*

- $(t_0|t_1)\{n+1 \Rightarrow /n \Rightarrow\}_{@||_i\vartheta} = t_i\{n+1 \Rightarrow /n \Rightarrow\}_{@\vartheta}$
- $t\{n+1 \Rightarrow /n \Rightarrow\}_{@\epsilon} = t\{n+1 \Rightarrow /n \Rightarrow\}$.

The late transition system for the π-calculus with localized names is in Tab. 2. Note that our rules have *no global* conditions on names.

$$Out : n\Rightarrow \overline{r}s.P \xrightarrow{\overline{r}s} n\Rightarrow P \qquad In : n\Rightarrow r(s).P \xrightarrow{r(\bullet n)} (n+1)\Rightarrow P\{\!|\bullet n/s|\!\}$$

$$Tau : n\Rightarrow \tau.P \xrightarrow{\tau} n\Rightarrow P$$

$$Par_0 : \frac{t_0 \xrightarrow{\mu@\vartheta} t_0'}{t_0|t_1 \xrightarrow{\mu@||_0\vartheta} t_0'|t_1} \qquad Par_1 : \frac{t_1 \xrightarrow{\mu@\vartheta} t_1'}{t_0|t_1 \xrightarrow{\mu@||_1\vartheta} t_0|t_1'} \qquad Sum : \frac{n\Rightarrow P \xrightarrow{\mu@\vartheta} t'}{n\Rightarrow (P+Q) \xrightarrow{\mu@\vartheta} t'}$$

$$Res : \frac{t \xrightarrow{\mu@\vartheta} t'}{(\nu u)t \xrightarrow{\mu@\vartheta} (\nu u)t'},\ \mu \neq \tau \Rightarrow \begin{cases} u \notin \{r, s\} \\ r = \bullet\vartheta \star sbj(\mu) \\ s = \bullet\vartheta \star obj(\mu) \end{cases}$$

$$Com_0 : \frac{t_0 \xrightarrow{\overline{r_0}s_0@\vartheta_0} t_0',\ t_1 \xrightarrow{r_1(\bullet m)@\vartheta_1} t_1'}{t_0|t_1 \xrightarrow{\tau} t_0'|t_1'\{\!|s_1/\bullet m|\!\}_{@\vartheta_1}},\ \begin{cases} s_1 = ||_1\vartheta_1\bullet||_0\vartheta_0 \star s_0 \\ r_1 = ||_1\vartheta_1\bullet||_0\vartheta_0 \star r_0 \end{cases}$$

$$Com_1 : \frac{t_0 \xrightarrow{r_1(\bullet m)@\vartheta_1} t_0',\ t_1 \xrightarrow{\overline{r_0}s_0@\vartheta_0} t_1'}{t_0|t_1 \xrightarrow{\tau} t_0'\{\!|s_1/\bullet m|\!\}_{@\vartheta_1}|t_1'},\ \begin{cases} s_1 = ||_0\vartheta_1\bullet||_1\vartheta_0 \star s_0 \\ r_1 = ||_0\vartheta_1\bullet||_1\vartheta_0 \star r_0 \end{cases}$$

$$Open : \frac{t \xrightarrow{\overline{r}s@\vartheta} t'}{(\nu u)t \xrightarrow{\overline{r}(\bullet n)@\vartheta} (t'\{n+1\Rightarrow /n\Rightarrow\}_{@\vartheta})\{\!|\bullet\vartheta n/u|\!\}},\ \begin{cases} u = \bullet\vartheta \star s \\ r \neq s \end{cases}$$

$$Close_0 : \frac{t_0 \xrightarrow{\overline{r_0}(s_0)@\vartheta_0} t_0',\ t_1 \xrightarrow{r_1(\bullet m)@\vartheta_1} t_1'}{t_0|t_1 \xrightarrow{\tau} (\nu u)(t_0'|t_1'\{\!|s_1/\bullet m|\!\}_{@\vartheta_1})},\ \begin{cases} s_1 = ||_1\vartheta_1\bullet||_0\vartheta_0 \star s_0 \\ r_1 = ||_1\vartheta_1\bullet||_0\vartheta_0 \star r_0 \\ u = \bullet||_0\vartheta_0 \star s_0 \end{cases}$$

$$Close_1 : \frac{t_0 \xrightarrow{r_1(\bullet m)@\vartheta_1} t_0',\ t_1 \xrightarrow{\overline{r_0}(s_0)@\vartheta_0} t_1'}{t_0|t_1 \xrightarrow{\tau} (\nu u)(t_0'\{\!|s_1/\bullet m|\!\}_{@\vartheta_1}|t_1')},\ \begin{cases} s_1 = ||_0\vartheta_1\bullet||_1\vartheta_0 \star s_0 \\ r_1 = ||_0\vartheta_1\bullet||_1\vartheta_0 \star r_0 \\ u = \bullet||_1\vartheta_0 \star s_0 \end{cases}$$

Table 2. Late transition system of the π-calculus with localized names.

A Logic for SDSI's Linked Local Name Spaces
Preliminary Version*

Joseph Y. Halpern
Cornell University
Dept. of Computer Science
Ithaca, NY 14853
halpern@cs.cornell.edu

Ron van der Meyden
School of Computing Sciences
University of Technology, Sydney
PO Box 123, Broadway N.S.W. 2007
Australia
ron@socs.uts.edu.au

Abstract

Abadi has introduced a logic to explicate the meaning of local names in SDSI, the Simple Distributed Security Infrastructure proposed by Rivest and Lampson. Abadi's logic does not correspond precisely to SDSI, however; it draws conclusions about local names that do not follow from SDSI's name resolution algorithm. Moreover, its semantics is somewhat unintuitive. This paper presents the Logic of Local Name Containment, which does not suffer from these deficiencies. It has a clear semantics and provides a tight characterization of SDSI name resolution. The semantics is shown to be closely related to that of logic programs, leading to an approach to the efficient implementation of queries concerning local names. A complete axiomatization of the logic is also provided.

1 Introduction

Rivest and Lampson [12] introduced SDSI—a Simple Distributed Security Infrastructure—to facilitate the construction of secure systems. In SDSI, principals (agents) are identified with public keys. In addition to principals, SDSI allows other names, such as `poker-buddies`. Rather than having a global name space, these names are interpreted *locally*, by each principal. That is, each principal associates with each name a set of principals. Of course, the interpretation of a name such as `poker-buddies` may be different for each agent. However, a principal can "export" his bindings to other principals. Thus, Ron may receive a message from the principal he names `Joe` describing a set of principals Joe associates with `poker-buddies`. Ron may then refer to this set of principals by the expression `Joe's poker-buddies`.

Rivest and Lampson [12] give an operational account of local names; they provide a name-resolution algorithm that, given a principal k and a name $\mathtt{n}$, computes the set of principals associated with $\mathtt{n}$ according to k. Abadi [1] has provided a logic that, among other things, gives a more semantic account of local names. According to Abadi, its purpose "is to explain local names in a general, self-contained way, without requiring reference to particular implementations." Abadi shows that the SDSI name-resolution algorithm can be captured in terms of a collection of sound proof rules in his logic.

Abadi's focus is on axioms. He constructs a semantics, not with the goal of capturing the intended meaning of his constructs, but rather, with the goal of showing that certain formulas are not derivable from his axioms. (In particular, he shows that *false* is not derivable, showing that his axioms are consistent.) While adequate for Abadi's restricted goals, his semantics validates some formulas that we certainly would not expect to be valid. One consequence of this is that, while he is able to pinpoint some potential concerns with the logic, the resolution of these concerns is less satisfactory. For example, he observes that adding two seemingly reasonable axioms to his logic allows us to reach quite an unreasonable conclusion. However, it is not obvious from the semantic intuitions provided by Abadi which (if either) of the axioms is unreasonable, or why it is unreasonable. Moreover, while he proves that this particular unreasonable conclusion is not derivable in his framework, as we show, a closely related (and equally unreasonable) conclusion is in fact valid. This means we have no assurance that it or other similar formulas cannot be derived from Abadi's axioms.

We very much subscribe to Abadi's goal of using a logic to give a general account of naming. In this paper, we pro-

*This work was supported in part by NSF under grant IRI-96-25901 and by a UTS internal research grant.

vide a logic whose syntax is very similar to Abadi's, but whose semantics is quite different and, we believe, captures better the meaning we intend the constructs to have. Nevertheless, all but one of Abadi's name space axioms are sound in our system.

We remark that, in a sense, our task is much easier than Abadi's, since we give the constructs in the logic a somewhat narrower reading than he does. Abadi tends to intertwine and occasionally identify issues of naming with issues of rights and delegation. (Such an identification is also implicitly made to some extent in designs such as PolicyMaker [4].) We believe that it is important to treat these issues separately. Such a separation allows us to both give a cleaner semantics for each of the relevant notions and to clarify a number of subtleties. This paper focuses on naming, which we carefully separate from the other issues; a companion paper [8] considers authority and delegation.

We believe that our approach has a number of significant advantages:

- We can still simulate the SDSI's name resolution algorithm; Abadi's extra axiom is unnecessary. In fact, our logic captures SDSI's name resolution more accurately than Abadi's. Abadi's logic can draw conclusions that SDSI's name resolution cannot; our logic, in a precise sense, draws exactly the same conclusions as SDSI's name resolution algorithm.
- According to our semantic intuition, one of Abadi's proposed additional axioms is in fact quite unreasonable; it does not hold under our semantics, and it is quite clear why.
- We are able to provide a sound and complete axiomatization of our logic. Thus, unlike Abadi, we have a proof system that corresponds precisely to our semantics. This will allow us to prove stronger results than Abadi's about formulas that cannot be derived in our framework.
- Our logic is closely related to Logic Programming. This allows us to translate queries about names to Logic Programming queries, and thus use all the well-developed Logic Programming technology to deal with such queries.
- Our approach opens the road to a number of generalizations, which allow us to deal with issues like permission, authority, and delegation [8].

The rest of this paper is organized as follows. In Section 2, we review Abadi's logic and, in the process, describe SDSI's naming scheme. We also point out what we see as the problems with Abadi's approach. In Section 3, we give the syntax and semantics of our logic, and present a complete axiomatization. In Section 4 we show that our logic provides a tight characterization of SDSI name resolution. Section 5 deals with the connection between our account of SDSI name resolution and logic programming, and Section 6 concerns `Self`, an additional construct considered by Abadi. Section 7 concludes.

2 SDSI's Name Spaces and Abadi's Logic

In this section, we briefly review SDSI's naming scheme and Abadi's logic, and discuss our criticism of Abadi's logic. Like Abadi, we are basing our discussion on SDSI 1.1 [12].

2.1 SDSI's Name Spaces

SDSI has *local names* and a set of reserved names, which we refer to as *global names*. Both are associated with sets of principals, but the set of principals associated with a local name depends on the principal, while the set of principals associated with a global name does not. We denote the set of global names by G with generic element $\mathtt{g}$, the set of local names by N with generic element $\mathtt{n}$, and the set of keys (principals) by K with generic element $\mathtt{k}$. We assume that all these sets are pairwise disjoint. *Global identifiers* are either keys or global names.[1]

The elements of $K \cup G \cup N$ are said to be *simple names*. We form *principal expressions* from simple names inductively: Simple names are principal expressions, and if $\mathtt{p}_1, \ldots, \mathtt{p}_m$ are principal expressions, then so is $(\mathtt{ref}\ {:}\mathtt{p}_1, \ldots, \mathtt{p}_m)$, which is more typically written as $\mathtt{p}_1$'s $\cdots \mathtt{p}_{m-1}$'s $\mathtt{p}_m$.[2] Abadi's semantics (and ours) makes `ref` associative, in that (p's q)'s r, p's q's r, and p's (q's r) are all the same. In light of this, we can ignore parenthesization when writing such expressions. We remark for future reference that SDSI has a special global name denoted "DNS!!", which represents the root of the DNS (Internet mail) hierarchy; this allows us to express an email address such as `bob@fudge.com` as DNS!!'s com's fudge's bob.

SDSI allows a principal to issue *certificates* of the form $\mathtt{n} \longmapsto \mathtt{p}$, signed with its key. If k issues such a certificate, it has the effect of binding local name n in k's name space to the principals denoted by the principal expression p.[3] Notice that only principals issue certificates, and that these certificates bind a local name (not a global name) to some set of principals. In general, a local name may be bound to a unique principal, no principal, or many principals. SDSI allows a principal k to issue certificates $\mathtt{n} \longmapsto \mathtt{p}_1$ and $\mathtt{n} \longmapsto$

[1] Note that Abadi uses G for global identifier; thus, his G corresponds to our $G \cup K$.

[2] Like Abadi, we allow m to be 0, taking `(ref:)` to be the current principal. In Section 6, we follow Abadi by considering an expression `Self` that represents `(ref:)`.

[3] SDSI also allows other forms of binding that we do not consider here. Our notation is also a simplification of that used by SDSI.

p_2. This has the effect of binding n to (at least) the principals denoted by p_1 and p_2.

SDSI provides a name-resolution algorithm for computing the set of names bound to a principal. The core of the algorithm consists of a nondeterministic procedure REF2. For ease of exposition, we take REF2 to have four arguments: a principal k, a function c that associates with each principal k′ a set of bindings (intuitively, ones that correspond to certificates signed by k′), a function β which associates with each global name g a set of principals (intuitively, the ones bound to g), and a principal expression p. REF2(k,β,c,p) returns the principal(s) bound to p in k's name space, given the bindings β and the certificates c. REF2 is nondeterministic; the set of possible outputs of REF2 is taken to be the set of principals bound to p in k's name space. REF2 is described in Figure 1.[4]

2.2 Abadi's Logic: Syntax, Semantics, and Axiomatization

The formulas in Abadi's logic are formed by starting with a set of primitive propositions and formulas of the form $p \longmapsto p'$, where p and p′ are principal expressions. More complicated formulas are formed by closing off under conjunction, negation, and formulas of the form p *says* ϕ, where ϕ is a formula.

Abadi views $p \longmapsto p'$ as meaning that p is "bound to" p′. He considers two possible interpretations of "bound to". The first is equality; however, he rejects this as being inappropriate. (In particular, it does not satisfy some of his axioms.) The second is that $p \longmapsto p'$ means p′ "speaks-for" p, in the sense discussed in [2, 11]. Roughly speaking, this says that any message certified by p′ should be viewed as also having been certified by p. While the "speaking-for" interpretation is the one favored by Abadi, he does not commit to it. Note that under Abadi's "speaking-for" interpretation, it makes sense to write $p \longmapsto p'$ for arbitrary principal expressions p and p′. However, SDSI allows only local (simple) names to be bound to principal expressions. We shall make a similar restriction in our logic (and, indeed, under our semantic interpretation of binding, it would not make sense to allow an arbitrary principal expression to be bound to another one.)

The "speaks-for" interpretation intertwines issues of delegation with those of naming. As we suggested in the introduction, we believe these issues should be separated. We shall give $\longmapsto$ a different interpretation that we believe is simpler and more in the spirit of binding. We believe that the "speaks-for" relation of [2, 11] should have quite different semantics than that of binding names to principals. (We hope to return to this issue in future work.)

Abadi interprets p *says* ϕ as "the principal denoted by p makes a statement that implies ϕ". In the case where p is a key (i.e., principal) k, this could mean that k signs a statement saying ϕ. Under our more restrictive interpretation, this is exactly how we interpret our analogue to *says*.

In any case, note that Abadi translates SDSI's local name n being bound to p as $n \longmapsto p$ and captures k signing a certificate saying n is bound to p by the formula k *says* $n \longmapsto p$. For future reference, it is worth noting that, in order to capture the binding of names to principals, no use is made of primitive propositions.

Abadi's interprets formulas in his logic with respect to a tuple $(\mathcal{W}, \alpha, \rho, \mu)$. The function α maps global identifiers $(G \cup K)$ to subsets of $\mathcal{W}$. The function ρ maps $N \times \mathcal{W}$ to subsets of $\mathcal{W}$. Finally, μ associates with each world (principal) k and primitive proposition p a truth value $\mu(p, \mathrm{k})$.

Abadi does not provide any intuition for his semantics, but suggests that $\mathcal{W}$ should be thought of as a set of possible worlds, as in modal logic. However, he also suggests [private communication, 1999] that his semantics was motivated by the work of Grove and Halpern [7], in which the corresponding set contains *pairs* consisting of a world and an agent. Some of Abadi's definitions make more intuitive sense if we think of $\mathcal{W}$ as a set of agents, while others make more sense if we think of $\mathcal{W}$ as a set of worlds. We elaborate on this point below.

Given $\mathrm{k} \in \mathcal{W}$ and $\mathrm{p} \in P$, Abadi defines $[\![\mathrm{p}]\!]_\mathrm{k}$ inductively, as follows:

- $[\![\mathrm{g}]\!]_\mathrm{k} = \alpha(\mathrm{g})$, for $\mathrm{g} \in G \cup K$
- $[\![\mathrm{n}]\!]_\mathrm{k} = \rho(\mathrm{n}, \mathrm{k})$ for $\mathrm{n} \in N$
- $[\![\mathrm{p}_1\text{'s }\mathrm{p}_2]\!]_\mathrm{k} = \cup\{[\![\mathrm{p}_2]\!]_{\mathrm{k}'} : \mathrm{k}' \in [\![\mathrm{p}_1]\!]_\mathrm{k}\}$

Here we have used a notation corresponding to the interpretation of the "worlds" in $\mathcal{W}$ as agents. Using this interpretation we may think of $[\![\mathrm{p}]\!]_\mathrm{k}$ as the set of principals bound to principal expression p according to k. The clause for $[\![\mathrm{p}_1\text{'s }\mathrm{p}_2]\!]_\mathrm{k}$ then says that if k′ is one of the principals referred to by k as p_1, then k uses p_1's p_2 to refer to any principal referred to by k′ as p_2.

[4] Our version of REF2 is similar, although not identical, to Abadi's. Like Abadi's, it is simpler than that in [12], in that we do not deal with a number of issues, such as quoting or encrypted objects, dealt with by SDSI. Our presentation of REF2 differs from Abadi's mainly in its treatment of global names. Abadi assumes that REF2 takes only two arguments, o and p, where o is either a global identifier (i.e., an element of $G \cup K$) or `current principal`, denoted cp. Although he does not write c explicitly as an argument, he does assume that there is a set he denotes assumptions(o) that includes bindings corresponding to signed certificates. In addition, it includes bindings for cp. We do not have a distinguished current principal; rather, if the current principal is k, then for uniformity we assume that all of the current principal's bindings are also described by the bindings in c(k). More significantly, if g is a global name, then Abadi's REF2(o,g) would return g, while ours would return some principal k to which g is bound in β. Our approach seems more consistent with the SDSI presentation of REF2, but this difference is minor, and all of Abadi's results hold for our presentation of REF2.

```
REF2(k,β,c,p)
  if p ∈ K then return(p)
  else if p ∈ G
     then if β(p) = ∅ then fail
          else return(k') for some k' ∈ β(p)
  else if p is a local name n in N
     then if c(k) = ∅ then fail
          else for some n ⟼ q ∈ c(k) return(REF2(k,β,c,q))
  else if p is of the form q's r
     then return(REF2(REF2(k,β,c,q),β,c,r))
```

Figure 1. Procedure REF2

Abadi also defines what it means for a formula ϕ to be true at world $\mathrm{k} \in \mathcal{W}$, written $\mathrm{k} \models \phi$, inductively, by

- $\mathrm{k} \models p$ iff $\mu(p, \mathrm{k}) = \mathbf{true}$, if p is a primitive proposition
- $\mathrm{k} \models \phi \wedge \psi$ iff $\mathrm{k} \models \phi$ and $\mathrm{k} \models \psi$
- $\mathrm{k} \models \neg\phi$ iff $\mathrm{k} \not\models \phi$
- $\mathrm{k} \models \mathrm{p} \longmapsto \mathrm{p}'$ iff $[\![\mathrm{p}]\!]_{\mathrm{k}} \subseteq [\![\mathrm{p}']\!]_{\mathrm{k}}$
- $\mathrm{k} \models \mathrm{p}\ \mathit{says}\ \phi$ iff $\mathrm{k}' \models \phi$ for all $\mathrm{k}' \in [\![\mathrm{p}]\!]_{\mathrm{k}}$.

These clauses defining $\models$ are quite intuitive if one interprets $\mathcal{W}$ to be a set of worlds and considers $[\![\mathrm{p}]\!]_{\mathrm{k}}$ to be the set of worlds consistent with what principal p has said at world k. In particular, under this interpretation, the clause for *says* can be read as stating that p *says* ϕ if ϕ holds in all worlds consistent with what p has said. The clause for $\longmapsto$ also has quite a plausible reading under the "speaks-for" interpretation of this construct: it states that p′ speaks for p if all worlds consistent with what p has said are consistent with what p′ has said, i.e., p is constrained to speak consistently with what p′ has said. However, it seems rather difficult to extend this intuitive reading to encompass the inductive definition of $[\![\mathrm{p}]\!]_{\mathrm{k}}$. In particular, it is far from clear to us what intuitive understanding to assign to the clause for $[\![\mathrm{p}_1\text{'s }\mathrm{p}_2]\!]_{\mathrm{k}}$ on this reading.

On the other hand, note that if we interpret the worlds as agents, then we can think of $\mathrm{k} \models \phi$ as saying that ϕ is true when local names are interpreted according to agent k. But this reading of the clauses, when combined with the intuitive reading of $[\![\mathrm{p}]\!]_{\mathrm{k}}$ as the set of principals that k refers to using p, also has its difficulties. Intuitively, when n is bound to p in principal k's local name space, the principals that k refers to using p should be a subset of the principals that k refers to using n. Abadi interprets n being bound to p as $\mathrm{n} \longmapsto \mathrm{p}$, this holds with respect to principal k when $[\![\mathrm{p}]\!]_{\mathrm{k}}$ is a *superset* of $[\![\mathrm{n}]\!]_{\mathrm{k}}$. This is precisely the opposite of what we would expect. Thus, neither the interpretation of $\mathcal{W}$ as a set of worlds nor the interpretation of $\mathcal{W}$ as a set of agents gives a fully satisfactory justification for Abadi's semantics. As we shall see, in our semantics, the interpretation of a principal expression p according to an agent will be a set of agents, but we use the reverse of Abadi's containment to represent binding.

Abadi provides an axiom system for his logic, which has three components:

1. The standard axioms and rules of propositional logic.
2. The standard axiom and rule for modal logic for the *says* operator:

$$(\mathrm{p}\ \mathit{says}\ (\phi \Rightarrow \psi)) \Rightarrow ((\mathrm{p}\ \mathit{says}\ \phi) \Rightarrow (\mathrm{p}\ \mathit{says}\ \psi))$$

$$\frac{\phi}{\mathrm{p}\ \mathit{says}\ \phi}$$

3. New axioms dealing with linked local name spaces, shown in Figure 2.

He shows that this axiomatization is sound, but conjectures it is not complete.

2.3 Name Resolution in Abadi's Logic

Abadi proves a number of interesting results relating his logic to SDSI. First, he shows that in a precise sense his logic can simulate REF2. He provides a collection of name-resolution rules *NR* (which we present in the full paper [10]) and proves the following results:[5]

[5]The results stated here are a variant of those stated in Abadi's paper, since our version of REF2 differs slightly from his. Nevertheless, the proofs of the results are essentially identical.

Reflexivity:	$\mathrm{p} \longmapsto \mathrm{p}$
Transitivity:	$(\mathrm{p} \longmapsto \mathrm{q}) \Rightarrow ((\mathrm{q} \longmapsto \mathrm{r}) \Rightarrow (\mathrm{p} \longmapsto \mathrm{r}))$
Left-monotonicity:	$(\mathrm{p} \longmapsto \mathrm{q}) \Rightarrow ((\mathrm{p's\ r}) \longmapsto (\mathrm{q's\ r}))$
Globality:	$(\mathrm{p's\ g}) \longmapsto \mathrm{g}$ if g is a global identifier
Associativity:	$((\mathrm{p's\ q})\mathrm{'s\ r}) \longmapsto (\mathrm{p's\ (q's\ r)})$
	$(\mathrm{p's\ (q's\ r)}) \longmapsto ((\mathrm{p's\ q})\mathrm{'s\ r})$
Linking:	$(\mathrm{p}\ \mathit{says}\ (\mathrm{n} \longmapsto \mathrm{r}) \Rightarrow ((\mathrm{p's\ n}) \longmapsto (\mathrm{p's\ r}))$ if n is a local name
Speaking-for:	$(\mathrm{p} \longmapsto \mathrm{q}) \Rightarrow ((\mathrm{q}\ \mathit{says}\ \phi) \Rightarrow \mathrm{p}\ \mathit{says}\ \phi)$

Figure 2. Abadi's axioms for linked local name spaces

Proposition 2.1: *Given a collection of c of bindings corresponding to signed certificates and a set β of bindings of global names to keys, let E be the conjunction of the formulas* k *says* $\mathrm{n} \longmapsto \mathrm{q}$ *for each certificate* $\mathrm{n} \longmapsto \mathrm{q} \in c(\mathrm{k})$ *and the formulas* $\mathrm{g} \longmapsto \mathrm{k}$ *for each* $\mathrm{k} \in \beta(\mathrm{g})$. *Then* $E \Rightarrow ((\mathrm{k's\ p}) \longmapsto \mathrm{k}_1)$ *is provable with the name resolution rules NR if and only if* $\mathrm{REF2}(\mathrm{k}, \beta, c, \mathrm{p})$ *yields* k_1.

Proposition 2.2: *The name resolution rules are sound with respect to the logic. That is, given E as in Proposition 2.1 and any principal expression* p, *if* $E \Rightarrow (\mathrm{p} \longmapsto \mathrm{k})$ *is provable using NR then* $E \Rightarrow (\mathrm{p} \longmapsto \mathrm{k})$ *is also provable in the logic.*

These results show that any bindings of names to principals that can be deduced using REF2 can also be deduced using Abadi's logic. However, Abadi shows that his logic is actually more powerful than REF2, by giving two examples of conclusions that can be deduced from his logic but not using REF2:

Example 2.3 : Using the Globality, Associativity, and Transitivity axioms, if k and k' are keys, we immediately get $\mathrm{k's\ (Lampson's\ k')} \longmapsto \mathrm{k}'$. This result does not follow from the REF2 algorithm. That is, $\mathrm{REF2}(\mathrm{k}, \beta, c, \mathrm{Lampson's\ k'})$ does not necessarily yield k' for arbitrary c and β (in particular, it will not do so if Lampson is not bound to anything in c). ∎

Example 2.4 : Suppose c consists of the four certificates that correspond to the following formulas: k *says* $(\mathrm{Lampson} \longmapsto \mathrm{k}_1)$, k *says* $(\mathrm{Lampson} \longmapsto \mathrm{k}_2)$, k_1 *says* $(\mathrm{Ron} \longmapsto \mathrm{Rivest})$, and k_2 *says* $(\mathrm{Rivest} \longmapsto \mathrm{k}_3)$ (where k, k_1, k_2, and k_3 are keys). Using the Speaking-for axiom, it is not hard to show that we can conclude that $\mathrm{k's\ (Lampson's\ Ron)} \longmapsto \mathrm{k}_3$. It is easy to show that REF2 cannot reach this conclusion; that is, $\mathrm{REF2}(\mathrm{k}, \beta, c, \mathrm{Lampson's\ Ron})$ does not yield k_3 for any β. ∎

In reference to Example 2.3, Abadi [1] says that "it is not clear whether [these conclusions] are harmful, and they might in fact be useful". In general, he views it as a feature of his logic that it allows reasoning about names without knowing their bindings [private communication, 1999]. While we agree that, in general, reasoning about names without knowing their bindings is a powerful feature, we believe it is important to make clear exactly which conclusions are desirable and which are not. This is what a good semantics can provide. Under our semantics, neither of these two conclusions are valid. In fact, our logic draws precisely the same conclusions as REF2. Of course, the conclusions of Examples 2.3 and 2.4 are valid under Abadi's semantics but, as we observed earlier, Abadi's semantics is not really meant to be used as a guide to which conclusions are acceptable (and, indeed, as we shall see, it validates a number of conclusions that do not seem so acceptable).

Abadi also considers the effect of extending his axiom system. In particular, he considers adding the following two axioms:

- the converse of Globality: $\mathrm{g} \longmapsto (\mathrm{p's\ g})$
- a generalization of Linking: $(\mathrm{p}\ \mathit{says}\ (\mathrm{p}_1 \longmapsto \mathrm{p}_2)) \Rightarrow (\mathrm{p's\ p}_1 \longmapsto \mathrm{p's\ p}_2)$, for an arbitrary principal p.

The generalization of Linking is in fact sound under Abadi's semantics. The converse of Globality is not, but only because we may have $[\![\mathrm{p}]\!]_{\mathrm{k}} = \emptyset$. Note that $[\![\mathrm{p}]\!]_{\mathrm{k}} = \emptyset$ iff $\mathrm{k} \models \mathrm{p}$ *says false*; thus, the following variant of the converse of Globability is sound under Abadi's semantics: $\neg(\mathrm{p}\ \mathit{says\ false}) \Rightarrow (\mathrm{g} \longmapsto (\mathrm{p's\ g}))$.

This is quite relevant to our purposes because Abadi shows that if we added the two axioms above to his system, then from k *says* $(\mathrm{DNS!!} \longmapsto \mathrm{k})$, we can conclude $\mathrm{DNS!!} \longmapsto \mathrm{k}$. Thus, just from k saying that DNS!! is bound to k, it follows that DNS!! is indeed bound to k. This is particularly disconcerting under Abadi's "speaks-for" interpretation, where $\mathrm{DNS!!} \longmapsto \mathrm{k}$ becomes "k speaks for DNS!!". We certainly do not want an arbitrary principal to speak for the name server!

Abadi proves a result showing that such conclusions are not derivable from hypotheses of a certain type in his logic (which does not have these two axioms).

Proposition 2.5: [1] *Let* k *and* k' *be distinct global names; let* ϕ *be a formula of the form* $(\mathrm{k}'\ says\ (\mathrm{n}_1 \longmapsto \mathrm{p}_1)) \wedge \ldots \wedge (\mathrm{k}'\ says\ (\mathrm{n}_k \longmapsto \mathrm{p}_k))$*, where* $\mathrm{n}_1, \ldots, \mathrm{n}_k$ *are local names and* $\mathrm{p}_1, \ldots, \mathrm{p}_k$ *are principal expressions; let* ψ *be a formula of the form* $(\mathrm{k}\ says\ \psi_1) \wedge \ldots \wedge (\mathrm{k}\ says\ \psi_m)$*, where* $\psi_1, \ldots, \psi_m$ *are arbitrary formulas. Then* $\phi \wedge \psi \Rightarrow (\mathrm{k}' \longmapsto \mathrm{k})$ *is not valid.*[6]

While Proposition 2.5 provides some assurance that undesirable formulas are not derivable in the logic, it does not provide much. Indeed, if we allow the ψ to include the formula $\neg(\mathrm{k}'\ says\ false)$, then the result no longer holds. In fact, it follows from our earlier discussion that the formula

$$(\mathrm{k}\ says\ (\mathtt{DNS!!} \longmapsto \mathrm{k})) \wedge \neg(\mathrm{k}\ says\ false) \Rightarrow (\mathtt{DNS!!} \longmapsto \mathrm{k})$$

is valid. Moreover, it does not seem so unreasonable to allow conjuncts such as $\neg(\mathrm{k}\ says\ false)$ as part of ψ. We certainly want to be able to use the logic to be able to say that if a principal's statements are not blatantly inconsistent, then certain conclusions follow.

3 The Logic of Local Name Containment

In this section we propose the Logic of Local Name Containment (henceforth LLNC) as an alternative to Abadi's logic. LLNC interprets local names as sets of principals and interprets SDSI certificates as stating containment relationships between these sets. We define the syntax in Section 3.1. In Section 3.2 we describe two distinct semantics for the logic. Section 3.3 presents a complete axiomatization.

3.1 Syntax

LLNC has syntactic elements that are closely related to the syntactic elements of Abadi's logic. However, our notation differs slightly from Abadi's to help emphasize some of the differences in intuition.

Again, we start with keys K, global names G, and local names N, and form principal expressions from them. For technical reasons, we make the (quite reasonable) assumption that K is a finite set. The formulas of our language are formed as follows:

- If p and q are principal expressions then $\mathrm{p} \longmapsto \mathrm{q}$ is a formula.
- If $\mathrm{k} \in K$ and ϕ is a formula then $\mathrm{k}\ cert\ \phi$ is a formula.
- If ϕ_1 and ϕ_2 are formulas, then so are $\neg\phi_1$ and $\phi_1 \wedge \phi_2$. As usual, $\phi_1 \vee \phi_2$ is an abbreviation for $\neg(\neg\phi_1 \wedge \neg\phi_2)$ and $\phi_1 \Rightarrow \phi_2$ is an abbreviation for $\neg\phi_1 \vee \phi_2$.

We write $\mathcal{L}$ for the set of all formulas. (For simplicity, we omit primitive propositions, although we could easily add them. They play no role in Abadi's account of SDSI names, nor will they in ours.)

We read the expression $\mathrm{p} \longmapsto \mathrm{q}$ as "p contains q"; we intend for it to capture the fact that all the keys bound to q are also bound to p. However, our intuitions about the meaning of $\mathrm{p} \longmapsto \mathrm{q}$ are quite different from Abadi's. In particular, we do not wish to interpret $\mathrm{p} \longmapsto \mathrm{q}$ as "q speaks for p." We consider the "speaks for" relation as being about rights and delegation, which requires a more sophisticated semantics than we wish to consider here. (See [8] for a logic for reasoning about rights and delegation.) The expression $\mathrm{p} \longmapsto \mathrm{q}$ should be understood as simply asserting a containment relationship between the denotations of principal expressions p and q; this is exactly what our semantics will enforce.

We read the expression $\mathrm{k}\ cert\ \phi$ as "k has certified that ϕ." This corresponds roughly to Abadi's $\mathrm{k}\ says\ \phi$. There are two significant differences, however. For one thing, we do not allow arbitrary principal expressions on the left-hand side; only keys may certify a formula ϕ. For another, our interpretation of *cert* is more restrictive than Abadi's *says*, in that *cert* is treated quite syntactically; it refers to an actual certificate issued by a principal, while *says* considers logical consequences of such certificates. As a consequence, whereas *says* satisfies standard properties of modal operators (e.g., closure under logical consequence), *cert* does not.

3.2 Semantics

Our semantics is designed to model the SDSI principle that principals bind names in their local name space to values by issuing certificates. The interpretation of a local name depends on the principal and the certificates that have been issued. As the principal may rely on others for its interpretation of local names, the certificates issued by other principals also play a role. The interpretation of global names and keys will be independent of both the principal and the certificates that have been issued.

A *world* is a pair $w = (\beta, c)$, where $\beta : G \to \mathcal{P}(K)$ and $c : K \to \mathcal{P}^{fin}(\mathcal{L})$, where $\mathcal{P}(X)$ (resp., $\mathcal{P}^{fin}(X)$) denotes the set of subsets (resp., finite subsets) of X. Intuitively, the function β interprets global (or fixed) names as sets of keys. The intended interpretation of the function c is that it associates with every key k the set of formulas $c(\mathrm{k})$ that have been certified using this key. That is, if $\phi \in c(\mathrm{k})$ then,

[6] Abadi's result actually says "$\phi \wedge \psi \Rightarrow (\mathrm{k}' \longmapsto \mathrm{k})$ is not derivable"; since his axiomatization is sound, but not necessarily complete, the claim that it is not valid is stronger, and that is what Abadi's proof shows.

intuitively, a certificate asserting ϕ has been signed using k.[7]

Formulas of the logic will be interpreted in a world with respect to a key. Intuitively, this key indicates the principal from whose perspective we interpret principal expressions.

To interpret local names, we introduce an additional semantic construct. A *local name assigment* will be a function $l : K \times N \to \mathcal{P}(K)$ associating each key and local name with a set of keys. Intuitively, $l(\mathrm{k}, \mathrm{n})$ is the set of keys represented by principal k's local name n. We write LNA for the set of all local name assignments.

Given a world $w = (\beta, c)$, a local name assignment l, and a key k, we may assign to each principal expression p an interpretation $[\![\mathrm{p}]\!]_{w,l,\mathrm{k}}$, a set of keys. The definition is much like that of Abadi's $[\![p]\!]_{\mathrm{K}}$:

- $[\![\mathrm{k}']\!]_{w,l,\mathrm{k}} = \{\mathrm{k}'\}$, if $\mathrm{k}' \in K$ is a key,
- $[\![\mathrm{g}]\!]_{w,l,\mathrm{k}} = \beta(\mathrm{g})$, if $\mathrm{g} \in G$ is a global name,
- $[\![\mathrm{n}]\!]_{w,l,\mathrm{k}} = l(\mathrm{k}, \mathrm{n})$, if $\mathrm{n} \in N$ is a local name,
- $[\![\mathrm{p's\ q}]\!]_{w,l,\mathrm{k}} = \bigcup\{[\![\mathrm{q}]\!]_{w,l,\mathrm{k}'} \mid \mathrm{k}' \in [\![\mathrm{p}]\!]_{w,l,\mathrm{k}}\}$, for principal expressions $\mathrm{p}, \mathrm{q} \in P$.

We now define what it means for a formula ϕ to be true at a world $w = (\beta, c)$ with respect to a local name assignment l and key k, written $w, l, \mathrm{k} \models \phi$, by induction on the structure of ϕ.[8]

- $w, l, \mathrm{k} \models \mathrm{p} \longmapsto \mathrm{q}$ if $[\![\mathrm{p}]\!]_{w,l,\mathrm{k}} \supseteq [\![\mathrm{q}]\!]_{w,l,\mathrm{k}}$
- $w, l, \mathrm{k} \models \mathrm{k}'$ *cert* ϕ if $\phi \in c(\mathrm{k}')$
- $w, l, \mathrm{k} \models \neg\phi_1$ if not $w, l, \mathrm{k} \models \phi_1$
- $w, l, \mathrm{k} \models \phi_1 \wedge \phi_2$ if $w, l, \mathrm{k} \models \phi_1$ and $w, l, \mathrm{k} \models \phi_2$.

Note that the semantics of *cert* reinforces its syntactic nature. To determine if k′ *cert* ϕ is true at (w, l, k), we check whether a certificate has been issued in world w by k′ certifying ϕ. Moreover, as we shall see, while we allow any formula to be certified by k, the only formulas whose certification has a nontrivial semantic impact are those of the form $\mathrm{n} \longmapsto \mathrm{p}$, where n is a local name. We return to this issue below.

We do not consider all pairs w, l as being appropriate on the left-hand side of $\models$. If $w = (\beta, c)$, we expect the local name assignment l to respect the certificates that have been issued in c. That is, if $c(\mathrm{k})$ includes the binding $\mathrm{n} \longmapsto \mathrm{p}$, we would expect that $l(\mathrm{k}, \mathrm{n})$ would include all the keys bound to p in k's name space. The question is whether there can be other keys bound to n in k's name space beyond those forced by the certificates. How we answer this question depends on our intuitions for c. For example, we could view c as the set of certificates received by one of the principals. This would be particularly appropriate if we wanted to reason about the knowledge and belief of the agents, an extension we plan to explore in future work. With this viewpoint, we could view l as consisting of all the bindings, including ones that the principal does not know about. Thus, l would at least have all the bindings forced by c, but perhaps others as well. Alternatively, we could view c as consisting of all the certificates that have been issued. In this case, we would want l to be in some sense *minimal*, and have no bindings beyond those forced by the certificates in c. We now present two different semantics, which reflect each of these two intuitions. We then show that, as far as validity is concerned, the semantics are equivalent; that is, they have the same proof theory.

A local name assignment l is *consistent* with a world $w = (\beta, c)$ if, for all keys k, local names n, and principal expressions p, if the formula $\mathrm{n} \longmapsto \mathrm{p}$ is in $c(\mathrm{k})$, then $w, l, \mathrm{k} \models \mathrm{n} \longmapsto \mathrm{p}$. Intuitively, assignments that are not consistent with a world provide an inappropriate basis for the interpretation of local names, since the certificates issued by principals are not necessarily reflected in their local bindings. We obtain our first semantics, called the *open* semantics, by restricting to consistent local name assignments. We write $w, l, \mathrm{k} \models_o \phi$ if $w, l, \mathrm{k} \models \phi$ and l is consistent with w. The formula ϕ is *o-satisfiable* if there exists a triple w, l, k such that $w, l, \mathrm{k} \models_o \phi$ and ϕ is *o-valid*, denoted $\models_o \phi$, if there does not exist a triple w, l, k such that $w, l, \mathrm{k} \models_o \neg\phi$.

Although our syntax allows k to certify arbitrary formulas, it is easy to see that, according to the semantics just introduced (as well as the one we are about to introduce), only the certification of formulas of the form $\mathrm{n} \longmapsto \mathrm{p}$ has any impact on consistency; all other formulas certified by k are ignored. There is a good reason for this restriction. We are implicitly assuming that when k′ certifies $\mathrm{n} \longmapsto \mathrm{p}$, that very act causes all the keys bound to p to also be bound to n in k's name space. Thus, if $\mathrm{n} \longmapsto \mathrm{p} \in c(\mathrm{k})$, then we want $\mathrm{n} \longmapsto \mathrm{p}$ to be true in (w, l, k). But if k certifies a formula like k_1's $\mathrm{n} \longmapsto \mathrm{k}_3$ where $\mathrm{k}_1 \neq \mathrm{k}$, then we cannot conclude that this formula is true in (w, l, k) unless we are prepared to make additional assumptions about k's truthfulness. We feel that if such assumptions are to be made, then they should be modeled explicitly in the logic, not hidden in the semantics.

It does seem reasonable to extend the notion of l being consistent with w to require that if k certifies a formula ψ which is a Boolean combination of formulas of the form $\mathrm{n} \longmapsto \mathrm{p}$ then $(w, l, \mathrm{k}) \models \psi$. In fact, nothing would change in our results if we did this for formulas ψ that are conjunctions of formulas of the form $\mathrm{n} \longmapsto \mathrm{p}$ and $\neg(\mathrm{n} \longmapsto \mathrm{p})$.

[7] We make the simplifying assumption that certificates do not have expiration dates. It is not difficult to extend the logic to take into account certificate expiration.

[8] Note that our semantics is thus in the spirit of that of Grove and Halpern [7], in that the truth of a formula depends on both an agent and some features of the world (captured by w and l).

However, once we allow more general Boolean combinations (in particular, once we allow disjunctions), there will be problems making sense out of the intuition of our next semantics, that "no bindings beyond those forced by the certificates in c". We consider this issue next.

According to the open semantics, it is possible for a local name $\mathtt{n}$ of principal $\mathtt{k}_1$ to be bound to a key $\mathtt{k}_2$ even when no certificate concerning $\mathtt{n}$ has been issued. Arguably, this is not in accordance with the intentions of SDSI. To better capture these intentions, we define a second semantics, that restricts the name bindings to those forced by the certificates issued.

To do so, we first establish that the open semantics satisfies a kind of "minimal model" result. Define the ordering $\leq$ on the space LNA of local name assignments by $l_1 \leq l_2$ if $l_1(\mathtt{k},\mathtt{n}) \subseteq l_2(\mathtt{k},\mathtt{n})$ for all $\mathtt{k} \in K$ and $\mathtt{n} \in N$. It is readily seen that LNA is given the structure of a complete lattice [3] by this relation. Say that a local name assignment l is *minimal* in a set of local name assignments L if $l \in L$ and $l \leq l'$ for all $l' \in L$.

Theorem 3.1: *Given a world w, there exists a unique local name assignment l_w minimal in the set of all local name assignments consistent with w. Moreover, if $\mathtt{p}$ is a principal expression and $\mathtt{k}_1$ and $\mathtt{k}_2$ are keys, then $w, l_w, \mathtt{k}_1 \models_o \mathtt{p} \longmapsto \mathtt{k}_2$ iff, for all local name assignments l consistent with w, we have $w, l, \mathtt{k}_1 \models_o \mathtt{p} \longmapsto \mathtt{k}_2$.*

The proof of this result (which, like that of all the other theorems in this extended abstract, can be found in the full paper [10]) uses standard techniques from the theory of fixed points.

We now define our second semantics, called the *closed semantics*. It attempts to capture the intuition that the only bindings in l should be those required by the certificates in c, using the minimal assignment promised by Theorem 3.1. We write $w, \mathtt{k} \models_c \phi$ if $w, l_w, \mathtt{k} \models \phi$. We say that ϕ is *c-satisfiable* if there exists a world w and key $\mathtt{k}$ such that $w, \mathtt{k} \models_c \phi$ and that ϕ is *c-valid*, denoted $\models_c \phi$, if $w, \mathtt{k} \models_c \phi$ for all worlds w and principals $\mathtt{k}$. Note that by Theorem 3.1, the assignment l_w is consistent with w, so c-satisfiability implies o-satisfiability. Thus, if $\models_o \phi$ then $\models_c \phi$. As the following result shows, somewhat surprisingly, the converse holds as well.

Theorem 3.2: *The same formulas are c-valid and o-valid; i.e., for all formulas ϕ, we have $\models_o \phi$ iff $\models_c \phi$.*

3.3 A Complete Axiomatization

Theorem 3.2 shows that the same formulas are o-valid and c-valid. Thus, both the open semantics and the closed semantics can be characterized by the same axiomatization, which is described in Figure 3.

Theorem 3.3: *The axiom system in Figure 3 is a sound and complete axiomatization of LLNC, with respect to both the open and closed semantics.*

It is interesting to compare our axioms to Abadi's. Although we interpret $\longmapsto$ as superset and he interprets it as subset, Reflexivity, Transitivity, Left-Monotonicity, and Associativity, hold in both cases, for essentially the same reasons. The switch from subset to superset means that the Converse of Globality holds in our case. Globality does not hold in general because the denotation of $\mathtt{p}$'s $\mathtt{g}$ may be empty if the denotation of $\mathtt{p}$ is empty (as we observed, this is also why the Converse of Globality does not hold in general for Abadi). In fact, for our logic, $\mathtt{p}$'s $\mathtt{g} \longmapsto \mathtt{g}$ whenever the denotation of $\mathtt{p}$ is nonempty. Key Globality is a special case of this, and it turns out to be all we need for completeness.[9]

Key Linking is our analogue of Abadi's Linking axiom. Of course, we use *cert* whereas Abadi uses *says*; in addition, only keys can certify formulas for us. While this axiom shows that there are some similarities between *cert* and *says*, there are some significant differences. We have no analogue of Abadi's Speaking-for axiom and, unlike *says*, *cert* does not satisfy the standard axiom and rule of modal logic: $(\mathtt{k}\ cert\ (\phi \Rightarrow \psi)) \wedge (\mathtt{k}\ cert\ \phi)$ does not imply $\mathtt{k}\ cert\ \psi$ and $\mathtt{k}\ cert\ \phi$ is not valid even if ϕ is valid. Interestingly, Abadi does not use these properties of Speaking-for in proving that his name resolution rules *NR*, used to capture REF2, are sound. As a result, (with very minor changes) we can show that the name resolution rules are also sound for LLNC, and hence we can prove analogues of Propositions 2.1 and 2.2. However, we can actually prove a much stronger result: whereas Abadi's logic is able to draw conclusions about bindings that do not follow from REF2, LLNC captures REF2 exactly (see Theorem 4.1).

We have two axioms that do not appear in Abadi's axiomatization: Key-Distinctness and Witnesses. Key-Distinctness just captures the fact that we interpret keys as themselves. The two axioms that make up Witnesses essentially capture our interpretation of $\longmapsto$ as containment. They tell us that facts about containment of principal expressions can be reduced to facts about principals. For example, the first one says that if $\mathtt{p}$ does not contain $\mathtt{q}$, then there is a principal bound to $\mathtt{q}$ that is not bound to $\mathtt{p}$. Although the exact statement of these axioms depends on our assumption that the set of keys is finite, somewhat analogous axioms would be required even if the set of keys were infinite.

Considering the two contentious axioms discussed by Abadi, we find that Converse of Globality is valid, as we observed earlier. The generalization of Linking considered

[9] We have essentially only two types of ways of saying that the denotation of $\mathtt{p}$ is nonempty. One is if $\mathtt{p}$'s $\mathtt{q} \longmapsto \mathtt{k}$ holds, for some name $\mathtt{q}$ and some key $\mathtt{k}$, and the other is if $\neg(\mathtt{q} \longmapsto \mathtt{p})$ holds, for some name $\mathtt{q}$. In both these cases, the fact that $\mathtt{p}$'s $\mathtt{g} \longmapsto \mathtt{g}$ follows from Key Globality, using Witnesses.

Propositional Logic:	All instances of propositional tautologies
Reflexivity:	$\mathtt{p} \longmapsto \mathtt{p}$
Transitivity:	$(\mathtt{p} \longmapsto \mathtt{q}) \Rightarrow ((\mathtt{q} \longmapsto \mathtt{r}) \Rightarrow (\mathtt{p} \longmapsto \mathtt{r}))$
Left-monotonicity:	$(\mathtt{p} \longmapsto \mathtt{q}) \Rightarrow ((\mathtt{p's\ r}) \longmapsto (\mathtt{q's\ r}))$
Associativity:	$((\mathtt{p's\ q})\mathtt{'s\ r}) \longmapsto (\mathtt{p's\ (q's\ r)})$ $(\mathtt{p's\ (q's\ r)}) \longmapsto ((\mathtt{p's\ q})\mathtt{'s\ r})$
Key Globality:	$(\mathtt{k's\ g}) \longmapsto \mathtt{g}$ if $\mathtt{k} \in K$ and $\mathtt{g} \in G \cup K$
Converse of Globality:	$\mathtt{g} \longmapsto (\mathtt{p's\ g})$ if $\mathtt{g} \in K \cup G$
Key Linking:	$(\mathtt{k}\ cert\ (\mathtt{n} \longmapsto \mathtt{r})) \Rightarrow ((\mathtt{k's\ n}) \longmapsto (\mathtt{k's\ r}))$ if $\mathtt{n}$ is a local name
Key Distinctness:	$\neg(\mathtt{k}_1 \longmapsto \mathtt{k}_2)$ if $\mathtt{k}_1$ and $\mathtt{k}_2$ are distinct keys
Witnesses:	$\neg(\mathtt{p} \longmapsto \mathtt{q}) \Rightarrow \vee_{\mathtt{k} \in K}(\neg(\mathtt{p} \longmapsto \mathtt{k}) \wedge (\mathtt{q} \longmapsto \mathtt{k}))$ $(\mathtt{p's\ q}) \longmapsto \mathtt{k}_1 \Rightarrow \vee_{\mathtt{k} \in K}((\mathtt{p} \longmapsto \mathtt{k}) \wedge (\mathtt{k's\ q} \longmapsto \mathtt{k}_1))$
Modus Ponens:	From ϕ and $\phi \Rightarrow \psi$ infer ψ.

Figure 3. Axioms of LLNC

by Abadi, restricted to be syntactically well formed, amounts to

$$(\mathtt{k}\ cert\ (\mathtt{p}_1 \longmapsto \mathtt{p}_2)) \Rightarrow (\mathtt{k's\ p}_1 \longmapsto \mathtt{k's\ p}_2).$$

In general, this is not valid, since our semantics ignores certificates stating $\mathtt{p}_1 \longmapsto \mathtt{p}_2$ when $\mathtt{p}_1$ is not a local name. Thus, we avoid the "unreasonable" conclusions that can be drawn from these axioms. In particular, it does not follow in our logic that $(\mathtt{k}\ cert\ (\mathtt{DNS!!} \longmapsto \mathtt{k})) \Rightarrow \mathtt{DNS!!} \longmapsto \mathtt{k}$. However, the reason it does not follow in LLNC is quite different from the reason it does not follow in Abadi's logic: since DNS!! is a global name, a certificate such as $\mathtt{k}\ cert\ (\mathtt{DNS!!} \longmapsto \mathtt{k})$ has no impact on the interpretation of global names. This captures the intuition that k should not be trusted when making assertions about bindings not under its control. If we were willing to trust k on everything, then concluding that k is bound to DNS!! after k certifies that it is would not seem so unreasonable.

The following formula is also not valid in LLNC:

$$(\neg(\mathtt{k}\ cert\ false) \wedge (\mathtt{k}\ cert\ (\mathtt{DNS!!} \longmapsto \mathtt{k}))) \Rightarrow \mathtt{DNS!!} \longmapsto \mathtt{k}.$$

(This formula corresponds to the one that we noted earlier is valid in Abadi's logic.) Failure to issue a certificate stating *false* has no more impact on global names than does any other behavior of k. Nor would a precondition asserting that the interpretation of k is non-empty validate the formula, since this is true in every world. We can in fact prove the following generalization of Abadi's Proposition 2.5, which provides a stronger statement of the safety of our logic than Abadi's result.

Proposition 3.4: *Let Γ be any boolean combination of formulas of the form $\mathtt{k}$ cert ϕ, and let Δ be any boolean combination of formulas of the form $\mathtt{p} \longmapsto \mathtt{q}$ where neither $\mathtt{p}$ nor $\mathtt{q}$ contains a local name. Then $\models_c \Gamma \Rightarrow \Delta$ iff $\models_c \Delta$.*

Informally, Proposition 3.4 says that facts about global names are completely independent of facts about certificates; issuing certificates can have no impact on the global name assignment. As we observed earlier, the analogous result does *not* hold for Abadi's logic.

4 Name Resolution in LLNC

In this section, we show that LLNC captures REF2 exactly. Indeed, we show that it does so for several distinct semantic interpretations. Define the order $\geq$ on worlds by $(\beta', c') \geq (\beta, c)$ if

1. $\beta'(\mathtt{g}) \supseteq \beta(\mathtt{g})$ for all global names g, and
2. $c'(\mathtt{k}) \supseteq c(\mathtt{k})$ for all keys k.

That is, $w' \geq w$ when w' contains more certificates than w and the bindings to global names in w are a subset of those in w'.

Theorem 4.1: *Suppose $\mathtt{k}_1, \mathtt{k}_2$ are principals, $w = (\beta, c)$ is a world, and $\mathtt{p}$ is a principal expression. Let the formula E_w consist of the conjunction of the formulas $\mathtt{g} \longmapsto \mathtt{k}$ for all global names $\mathtt{g}$ occurring in $\mathtt{p}$ and keys $\mathtt{k} \in \beta(\mathtt{g})$ and the formulas $\mathtt{k}$ cert ϕ for all keys $\mathtt{k}$ and formulas $\phi \in c(\mathtt{k})$. The following are equivalent:*

1. $\mathtt{k}_1 \in \mathrm{REF2}(\mathtt{k}_2, \beta, c, \mathtt{p})$,
2. $w, \mathtt{k}_2 \models_c \mathtt{p} \longmapsto \mathtt{k}_1$,
3. $w', \mathtt{k}_2 \models_c \mathtt{p} \longmapsto \mathtt{k}_1$ *for all worlds* $w' \geq w$,
4. $\models_c E_w \Rightarrow (\mathtt{k}_2\mathtt{'s\ p} \longmapsto \mathtt{k}_1)$
5. $\models_o E_w \Rightarrow (\mathtt{k}_2\mathtt{'s\ p} \longmapsto \mathtt{k}_1)$

The equivalence between (1) and (2) in this theorem tells us that REF2 is sound and complete with respect to key binding, according to the semantics of LLNC. That is, REF2($\texttt{k}, \beta, c, \texttt{p}$) yields $\texttt{k}'$ iff $\texttt{p} \longmapsto \texttt{k}'$ is forced to be true by the bindings of global names in β and the certificates in c. Moreover, the equivalence between (2) and (3) (and also between (4) and (5)) shows that in any world where all the certificates in c have been issued (and perhaps others) $\texttt{p} \longmapsto \texttt{k}'$ will be true in k's name space. These equivalences emphasize that we get the same conclusions whether we view the information given by (β, c) as representing all the bindings or view it as partial information (perhaps one principal's view) of all the bindings that have in fact been created.

It is instructive to understand why the formulas considered in Examples 2.3 and 2.4, which give conclusions in Abadi's logic beyond those derivable by REF2, are not valid in LLNC. It is easy to see why the formula k's (Lampson's k') $\longmapsto$ k' from Example 2.3 (which, by Associativity and Transitivity, is equivalent to (k's Lampson)'s k' $\longmapsto$ k') is not valid in LLNC. This is simply because Globality does not hold in general. Now consider the formula in Example 2.4. The proof that this is valid in Abadi's logic uses the Speaking-for axiom, which does not hold for us (if we replace *says* by *cert*). To see that it is not valid in LLNC, consider a world $w = (\beta, c)$ containing only the certificates forced by the formulas (i.e., $c(\texttt{k}) = \{\texttt{Lampson} \longmapsto \texttt{k}_1, \texttt{Lampson} \longmapsto \texttt{k}_2\}$, $c(\texttt{k}_1) = \{\texttt{Ron} \longmapsto \texttt{Rivest}\}$, $c(\texttt{k}_2) = \{\texttt{Rivest} \longmapsto \texttt{k}_3\}$). Then it is easy to see that $w, \texttt{k} \not\models$ k's (Lampson's Ron) $\longmapsto$ $\texttt{k}_3$, since $[\![\text{k's (Lampson's Ron)}]\!]_{w,l_w,\texttt{k}} = \emptyset$ whereas $[\![\texttt{k}_3]\!]_{w,l_w,\texttt{k}} = \{\texttt{k}_3\}$.

5 Logic Programming Implementations of Name Resolution Queries

The reader familiar with the theory of logic programming may have noted a close resemblance of the results and constructions of the preceding sections to the (now standard) fixpoint semantics for logic programs developed originally by van Emden and Kowalski [5]. Indeed, it is possible to translate our semantics into the framework of logic programming. In fact, we provide a translation that does not require the use of function symbols and thus produces a *Datalog* program, a restricted type of logic program that has significant computational advantages over unrestricted logic programs. Our translation allows us to take advantage of the significant body of research on the optimization of Datalog programs [13, 14].

The idea is to translate queries to formulas in a first-order language over a vocabulary V which consists of a constant symbol for each element in $K \cup G \cup N$ and a ternary predicate symbol name. Intuitively, $\texttt{name}(x, y, z)$ says that, in the local name space of key x, the name y is bound to key z.

Using name, for each principal expression p and pair of variables x, y, we define a first-order formula $\tau_{x,y}(\texttt{p})$ that, intuitively, corresponds to the assertion "$y \in [\![\texttt{p}]\!]_x$," by induction on the structure of p:

1. $\tau_{x,y}(\texttt{p}) = \texttt{name}(x, \texttt{p}, y)$ when $\texttt{p} \in K \cup G \cup N$.
2. $\tau_{x,y}(\text{q's r}) = \exists z(\tau_{x,z}(\texttt{q}) \wedge \tau_{z,y}(\texttt{r}))$, where $z \neq x, y$.

For each world $w = (\beta, c)$, we can then define a theory (set of sentences) Σ_w that characterizes w; Σ_w consists of the following sentences:

1. a sentence $\texttt{name}(\texttt{k}_1, \texttt{k}_2, \texttt{k}_2)$, for each pair of keys $\texttt{k}_1, \texttt{k}_2 \in K$, and
2. the sentence $\texttt{name}(\texttt{k}_1, \texttt{g}, \texttt{k}_2)$, for each pair of keys $\texttt{k}_1, \texttt{k}_2 \in K$ and global name $\texttt{g} \in G$ such that $\texttt{k}_2 \in \beta(\texttt{g})$,
3. the sentence $\forall y(\tau_{\texttt{k},y}(\texttt{q}) \Rightarrow \texttt{name}(\texttt{k}, \texttt{n}, y))$, for each key k and binding $\texttt{n} \longmapsto \texttt{q}$ in $c(\texttt{k})$.

Recall that a *Herbrand structure* $M = (U, I)$ over the vocabulary V has as its domain $U = K \cup G \cup N$ and the interpretation I is such that $I(c) = c$ for each constant $c \in K \cup G \cup N$. Herbrand structures over V differ in their interpretation of the predicate name. We can put a partial order over the Herbrand structures over V by defining $M_1 = (U, I_1) \preceq M_2 = (U, I_2)$ iff $I_1(\texttt{name}) \subseteq I_2(\texttt{name})$. That is, $M_1 \preceq M_2$ if the interpretation of the name relation in M_1 has at least as many triples as its interpretation in M_2. It turns out that Herbrand models of Σ_w minimal with respect to $\preceq$ correspond to the minimal name assignments for w.

Theorem 5.1: *There is a minimal Herbrand model M_w of Σ_w and $M_w \models \tau_{\texttt{k}_1,\texttt{k}_2}(\texttt{p})$ iff $w, l_w, \texttt{k}_1 \models \texttt{p} \longmapsto \texttt{k}_2$.*

The theory Σ_w is a *definite Horn theory*, so corresponds to a logic program. As we explain in the full paper, as an immediate consequence of Theorem 5.1, we obtain efficient implementations of several types of queries, corresponding to different choices of bound and free variables in the predicate "name". We may even form complex queries not corresponding in any direct way to the capacities of the procedure REF2. Examples of this include the following:

1. the query $\texttt{name}(\texttt{k}_1, \texttt{n}, \texttt{k}_2)$ returns "yes" if $\texttt{k}_2$ is bound to the local name n according to $\texttt{k}_1$;
2. the query $\texttt{name}(X, \texttt{n}, \texttt{k})$ returns the set of keys X such that k is in n according to X;
3. the query $\texttt{name}(\texttt{k}_1, \texttt{n}, X) \wedge \texttt{name}(\texttt{k}_2, \texttt{n}, X)$ returns the set of keys X that $\texttt{k}_1$ and $\texttt{k}_2$ agree to be associated with local name n.

6 Self

Abadi considers an extension of his logic obtained by adding a special basic principal expression `Self`, intended to represent SDSI's expression `(ref:)`. (We remark that `Self` is essentially the same as I in the logic of naming considered in [7].) Intuitively, `Self` denotes the current principal. The semantics given to `Self` by Abadi extends the definition of the set of principals associated with a principal expression by taking $[\![\mathtt{Self}]\!]_a = \{a\}$ for each $a \in \mathcal{W}$. This suffices to validate the following axioms.

$$\text{Identity}: \quad \begin{array}{ll} (\mathtt{Self's\ p}) \longmapsto \mathtt{p} & \mathtt{p} \longmapsto (\mathtt{Self's\ p}) \\ (\mathtt{p's\ Self}) \longmapsto \mathtt{p} & \mathtt{p} \longmapsto (\mathtt{p's\ Self}) \end{array}$$

These axioms very reasonably capture the intuitions that `Self` refers to the current principal.

However, not all consequences of this semantics for `Self` are so reasonable. For example, the following is valid under Abadi's semantics:

$$\begin{array}{l} (\mathtt{k}_P \ \mathit{says}\ \mathtt{US} \longmapsto \mathtt{Self}) \wedge (\mathtt{k}_P \ \mathit{says}\ \mathtt{US} \longmapsto \mathtt{k}_{VP}) \\ \Rightarrow \mathtt{k}_P \ \mathit{says}\ ((\mathtt{US}\ \mathit{says\ false}) \vee (\mathtt{Self} \longmapsto \mathtt{k}_{VP})) \end{array}$$

Interpreting $\mathtt{k}_P$ as the key of the president of the US and $\mathtt{k}_{VP}$ the key of the vice-president, this is clearly unreasonable. It should not follow from the fact the the president says that both he and the vice-president speak for the US that according to the president, either the US speaks nonsense or the vice president speaks for the president.

Abadi's suggested semantics for `Self` works much better in the context of the logic LLNC. Suppose we extend this logic to include `Self`, and like Abadi, define $[\![\mathtt{Self}]\!]_k = \{k\}$ for keys $k \in K$. This again validates the Identity axioms above. In addition, we get the following axiom:

$$(\mathtt{Self} \longmapsto \mathtt{k}) \Leftrightarrow (\mathtt{k} \longmapsto \mathtt{Self})$$

where `k` is a key. However, we do not get a conclusion comparable to that for the example above. From $\mathtt{k}_P\ \mathit{cert}\ \mathtt{US} \longmapsto \mathtt{Self}$ and $\mathtt{k}_P\ \mathit{cert}\ \mathtt{US} \longmapsto \mathtt{k}_{VP}$ it follows that $[\![\mathtt{US}]\!]_{\mathtt{k}_P} \supseteq \{\mathtt{k}_P, \mathtt{k}_{VP}\}$. Thus, we have neither $[\![\mathtt{US}]\!]_{\mathtt{k}_P} = \emptyset$ nor $\{\mathtt{k}_{VP}\} \supseteq [\![\mathtt{US}]\!]_{\mathtt{k}_P}$, which would be required to get a conclusion similar to that drawn by Abadi's logic.

7 Conclusions

We have introduced a logic LLNC for reasoning about SDSI's local name spaces and have argued that it has some significant advantages over Abadi's logic. Among other things, it provides a complete characterization of SDSI's REF2, has an elegant complete axiomatization, and its connections with Logic Programming lead to efficient implementations of many queries of interest.

We believe that some of the dimensions in which Abadi's logic differs from SDSI warrant further investigation. For example, under some sensible interpretations, the conclusions reached by Abadi's logic in Example 2.4 are quite reasonable. One such interpretation is that while local names may be bound to more than one key, they are intended to denote a single individual. If `k` knows that $\mathtt{k}_1$ and $\mathtt{k}_2$ are two keys used by the one individual Lampson, and Lampson uses $\mathtt{k}_1$ to certify that his local name `Ron` is bound to the name `Rivest`, and also uses his key $\mathtt{k}_2$ to certify that his local name `Rivest` is bound to $\mathtt{k}_3$, then it is very reasonable to conclude that `k`'s `Lampson`'s `Ron` is bound to $\mathtt{k}_3$. Another interpretation supporting this conclusion would be that *says* aggregates the certificates issued using a number of distinct keys (possibly belonging to distinct individuals) much in the way that the notion of *distributed knowledge* [6] from the literature on reasoning about knowledge aggregates the knowledge of a collection of agents. We believe that our semantic framework, which unlike Abadi's, makes the set of certificates issued explicit, provides an appropriate basis for the study of such issues.

Our semantic framework also lends itself to a number of generalizations, which we are currently exploring. These include reasoning about the beliefs of principals and reasoning about permission, authority, and delegation. We hope to report on this work shortly.

References

[1] M. Abadi. On sdsi's linked local name spaces. *Journal of Computer Security*, 6(1-2):3–21, 1998.

[2] M. Abadi, M. Burrows, B. Lampson, and G. D. Plotkin. A calculus for access control in distributed systems. *ACM Trans. Prog. Lang. Syst.*, 15(4):706–734, 1993.

[3] G. Birkhoff. *Lattice Theory*. American Mathematical Society, Providence, R.I., 3rd edition edition, 1967.

[4] M. Blaze, J. Feigenbaum, and J. Lacy. Decentralized trust management. In *Proceedings 1996 IEEE Symposium on Security and Privacy*, pages 164–173, 1996.

[5] M. Emden and R. A. Kowalski. The semantics of predicate logic as a programming language. *J. ACM*, 23(4):733–742, 1976.

[6] R. Fagin, J. Y. Halpern, Y. Moses, and M. Y. Vardi. *Reasoning about Knowledge*. MIT Press, Cambridge, Mass., 1995.

[7] A. J. Grove and J. Y. Halpern. Naming and identity in propositional logics, Part I: the propositional case. *Journal of Logic and Computation*, 3(4):345–378, 1993.

[8] J. Halpern, R. van der Meyden, and F. Schneider. A logical framework for trust management. manuscript, 1999.

[9] J. Y. Halpern and R. van der Meyden. A logic for sdsi's linked local name spaces. In *12th IEEE Computer Security Foundations Workshop*, 1999.

[10] J. Y. Halpern and R. van der Meyden. A logic for sdsi's linked local name spaces. Available at http://www.cs.cornell.edu/home/halpern, 1999.

[11] B. Lampson, M. Abadi, M. Burrows, and E. Wobber. Authentication in distributed systems: Theory and practice. *ACM Trans. Comput. Syst.*, 10(4):265–310, 1992.

[12] R. Rivest and B. Lampson. SDSI — a simple distributed security infrastructure. at `http://theory.lcs.mit.edu/~cis/sdsi.html`, 1996.

[13] J. D. Ullman. *Principles of Database and Knowledge Base Systems, volume I.* Computer Science Press, 1988.

[14] J. D. Ullman. *Principles of Database and Knowledge Base Systems, volume II: The New Technologies*. Computer Science Press, 1989.

Interaction and Composition

Trusted System Construction

Colin O'Halloran
Systems Assurance Group
DERA, Malvern, UK
C.OHalloran@eris.dera.gov.uk

Abstract

Any system constructed today is likely to be constructed from COTS components. Encapsulation of these components using software wrappers promises to enable trusted systems to be constructed. These systems are complex and it is difficult to impose security without compromising operational effectiveness. The key problem which this paper addresses is to analyse encapsulations of COTS components to demonstrate the system is both secure and usable. Any foundation must be able to deal with the conflicting requirements of operational effectiveness and security especially with respect to COTS components. The approach is illustrated using the X windowing system.

1. Introduction

There is a perception that COTS technology has the potential to deliver greater performance and value for money to customers, especially in the defence world. The customers of COTS products have little ability to control the development of commercial products, so there is a problem of demonstrating that a system comprised of COTS components is secure. In a paper on the security risks associated with using COTS [16], eight risk management activities were identified: formulating a well-defined and relevant security policy; taking a holistic perspective; confining untrusted components; partitioning a system; contingency anticipation; flaw remediation; support; and awareness.

In [1] a holistic view of securing a COTS component was taken by performing a security vulnerability analysis of the component's operation within a system and considering how it could compromise that system. That analysis identified a series of security properties the component had to satisfy in order for it to work securely in its particular role. In this paper an approach to formulating a well-defined relevant security policy, based on a security vulnerability analysis is discussed, along with how this relates to confining untrusted COTS components.

2. An outline of the approach

The pace of commercial computing technology is so fast that some elements have a lifetime as little as two years, far less that the expected in-service life of any military system. This poses the problem of maintaining a stable environment in which COTS components can be substituted while allowing the system to evolve without re-certification from scratch. If evolution is not addressed then the user is at risk of the whole system being rendered obsolete by the future unavailability of a single commercial component.

It has been shown that COTS components, such as X windows, in the Open Systems world can be re-used (although it is not necessarily straightforward). Large information systems need to be flexible to deal with changing organisations and environments. COTS components with well-defined Application Programming Interfaces (APIs) and an enforceable portability policy are essential to make the system flexible.

Unfortunately even Open System components do not necessarily conform completely to Open System standards. However work within the Open Systems Software and the Systems Assurance Groups at DERA Malvern has been concerned with revealing APIs for languages such as C, Java and Ada. This means that techniques developed for portability can be applied to COTS components to ensure there are no hidden ways in which the component can interact with its environment. These APIs can then be encapsulated and policed to enforce critical properties. This means that even if a component contains a trojan horse, it can only communicate with its environment through the identified interface, which allows countermeasures to be taken. This approach is analogous to the confinement mechanisms for the Java sandbox model.

The next problem is to formulate a well-defined and relevant security policy. This is defined in [16] as "What is the appropriate way to confine an untrusted program so that it can do everything it needs to do to meet the user's expectation, but nothing else?". In the framework described above, this problem can be re-expressed as - "how should the untrusted component's interface be policed so that it can do everything it needs to do to meet the user's expectation, but nothing else?".

The problem with answering the above question is that it depends upon the user's expectation and the context in which the component is operating. To solve this problem an approach is required to determine that the user's expectations are met without compromising security. It is very easy to impose security controls which make a system difficult or impossible to use, therefore an analytical model is necessary to develop an appropriate security policy. The flexibility to be able to address both security and functionality is the observation that security failures arise from a series of actions rather than a single event.

To illustrate the analytical approach, the X windowing system is used as a concrete example because it is particularly vulnerable to security attacks, it is relatively complex and its usefulness can be significantly reduced by ill-considered security controls.

3. The X window system

The X window system provides some text based UNIX style operating systems, such as Solaris, with a graphical interface. This is achieved using a connection based client-server architecture, where the X server controls the user's interactions with their monitor(s). In other words, an X client that has connected to computer *C*'s X server, can only access *C*'s keyboard, mouse or monitor(s) via this server, as shown in Figure 1.

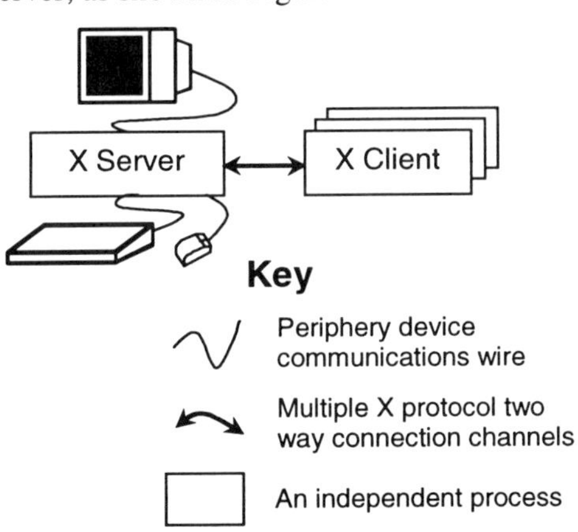

Figure 1 : X client-server model

The X window system was designed to be used over a local-area-network (LAN), so an X server does not differentiate between clients on the local (host) computer and those on a remote computer. However, the X server does require each client to authenticate itself, thus giving some control over which applications on the network are allowed to connect to the X server. For example, an X server that uses the host based connection mechanism stores a list of hosts that are allowed to connect to the server. So an application can connect to the server if: either it's host is contained in the server's host list; or it is on the same host as the server.

3.1 X's resources and properties

The X server provides various resources (e.g. windows and fonts) that are identified by unique resource numbers, called *resource ids*. A window resource is special as it may have properties associated with it, such as it's name. This allows the window manager to, for example, place an appropriate string in the window's title bar. Note that the window manager knows that a particular property is the window's name, because the property is tagged with an identification number called an atom.

3.2 The Broadway X window system

In 1996 the X consortium analysed the X design for security issues [**2**], which led to a redesign of the X server. The latest release of the X server (X11R6.3), known as Broadway [**3**], completed this redesign. It introduced several new extensions that together enable X functionality to be added to world-wide-web (WWW) pages. The security extension [**4**, **5**] underpins the ability to manage windows within a WWW page, by providing a mechanism for determining which clients can belong to the WWW page [**6**].

The Broadway security extension introduces the idea of an untrusted client and therefore an untrusted server resource, where an untrusted client can only access untrusted resources within the X server. Previously, all clients of the X server have been implicitly trusted, as they have been able to modify any resource within the server. Clients of a Broadway X server which use the security extensions are partitioned into a trusted and an untrusted group. This raises some interesting questions about what the untrusted clients should be allowed to do. For example, should an untrusted client be able to grab an image of a trusted clients window? The security extensions answer is no, and it achieves this by:

- preventing an untrusted client from directly grabbing the image of a trusted client's window;
- preventing an untrusted client from having a transparent window;
- filling obscured regions of the window being grabbed with a server dependent pattern.

In general, the security extension aims to prevent untrusted clients from accessing a trusted client's resources and properties without its permission.

The Broadway server has radically changed the direction of X, and is the last X server that the X consortium are going to produce. It has yet to be adopted by the industry as a whole and may only be partially adopted. Therefore it is not wise to rely on any of the extra security facilities it provides. Even if these facilities could be relied upon, they are not sufficient to provide an adequate solution to the problem presented in the next section. This is because the security mechanisms are too coarse.

3.3 Vulnerabilities of an X Window System

The increased use of the computer networks in the late 1980's provided the stimulus for looking at the vulnerabilities of the X window system. In particular:

- What prevents a remote computer from opening a connection to an X server?

The X server can require an authentication certificate to be sent to it before allowing a connection to the server. The most common mechanism is the MIT-MAGIC-COOKIE-1, where access is determined by a shared "cookie", which is passed unencrypted across the network. Alternatively, the host based acceptance criteria can be used, i.e. does the incoming connection come from a trusted host, but this is vulnerable to an IP spoofing attack.

- What prevents a (remote) client from monitoring or controlling an X server?

The paper "X, Spies and Videotape" [7] demonstrated that once an X connection was accepted, the client process could easily monitor or control the rest of the X system.

The potential security threats to an X application will vary from system to system due to the different contexts in which it is used. To retain the flexibility of an application, while ensuring it is secure, it is necessary to identify security threats by means of a vulnerability analysis. An X application can have its vulnerabilities analysed by, for example, a "message failure mode analysis" [1]. This is analogous to analysing the safety vulnerabilities by means of a hazard analysis. For example, the result of analysing a simple X file transfer client produced the following vulnerabilities:

- degrading the performance of the client's interface, e.g. by crashing or drowning it, or the server, with requests;
- modification of the client's interface, e.g. by re-labelling a button;
- spoofing the client's interface, e.g. by overlaying a similar intruder window.

A countermeasure for the first vulnerability relies on quotas, that is limiting the amount of resource available to a hostile client or remote host. For example sending multiple connection requests to an X server would affect the performance of its existing clients, perhaps bringing them to a halt.

The next two vulnerabilities can only be exploited by a series of interactions between a hostile client and the X server. Only one of these interactions, from each such sequence, needs to be blocked in order to provide an appropriate countermeasure. Which interaction should be blocked by wrapper software should be determined by its impact on the functionality of the client. An analytical model is needed if every sequence of interactions is to be determined.

4. An analytical model

4.1 The X Protocol

In this section a model of the interactions between an X server and its clients is developed in a machine readable dialect of CSP, called CSP_M [13] (a brief review of the language CSP_M is given in the appendix to this paper). The model provides a sound basis for validating configurations of an X windows system against functional and non-functional requirements.

Once the connection to the X server is successfully opened, the first thing most applications do is create one or more windows. The **CreateWindow** request is more complicated than most X protocol requests, but all requests have the same structure: a block of data consisting of an opcode; some number of fixed length parameters; and sometimes a variable length parameter.

If all this information for a single request was used in a model then analysis would be complex. For the purpose of analysing an X system with respect to security and usability, only information which is dependent upon other clients in X is of interest. For example **CreateWindow** has essentially 10 parameters most of which are concerned with the "look and feel" of the window to be created. For the purpose of analysing the propagation of information from other clients and their windows there is only one parameter of interest, the identity of the parent window.

The justification for this view is that security arises from the control of capabilities (assuming that he security mechanisms which control the capabilities are not bypassed). In X a capability is a request plus the information about the identities of entities such as a window. For example, without the identity of the parent window the protocol request **CreateWindow** cannot create the appropriate window. The information about the parent's identity is the only parameter of interest, all the other parameters are within the power of the client to generate.

Requests and replies to that request are represented by rules within the analytical model. In general a rule will be of the form

X Protocol Request

$$\frac{\text{Arguments of the X request}}{\text{name of request and reply to request}}$$

This means that the rule can only be used when the arguments of the X request are known to the client and then the fact that the request has been generated is recorded along with the reply from the X server. Any new information about the status of other client's resources, contained within the reply, is learnt by the requesting client and can be used as an argument for another request. In this way an inference system is generated which, based on a client's initial knowledge, can be used to analyse what that client can deduce about other clients. If a request does not generate a reply then only the fact that the request was made is recorded. For example the X request **CreateWindow** is modelled by the rules

$$\frac{parent.legal\_wins}{createwindow.legal\_wins}$$

and

$$\frac{parent.forbid\_wins}{createwindow.forbid\_wins}$$

which given a window identifier will record the fact that the request has been made. The parent identifier can either be one that the client is entitled to know, or knowledge of the identifier is forbidden - but the client has learnt it beforehand anyway. Nothing else is learnt by the client since the server does not generate a reply to this request.

These rules are modelled in the CSP functional language as a set of pairs, each pair consists of a set representing arguments to a request, above the line, and a set containing the reply and request name, below the line. For example

```
Create_Window =
{
({parent.legal_wins},{create_window.legal_wins}),
({parent.forbid_wins},{create_window.forbid_wins})
}
```

is a set of pairs each of which is a singleton set. Each parent identifier is a singleton set because in this case the request has only one argument, a set such as {x, y} would denote a request with two arguments. The arguments are collected together as a set rather than a list because individual arguments become enabled in no particular order since a client will learn information from the X Server in no fixed order.

The rule for creating a window models that the parent of a created window is either legally known to the creating client or forbidden. Nothing else of relevance is learnt from the X server, but the fact that the request was made is recorded. Appending the fact that the request was made with legal or forbidden knowledge is done in order to address the situation where learning about forbidden windows is not an issue, but acting on that knowledge is.

To modify some other client's X window requires knowledge of that window's identifier. A direct method for discovering the identity of a window is to use **QueryTree.** The rule which models **QueryTree** has only one relevant argument, the identity of the window to be queried. All windows on a particular screen have the same root, therefore the worst is assumed. The request will reveal the root window and therefore gives knowledge of forbidden windows as well.

```
Query_Tree =
        {({legal_wins},{query_tree,forbid_wins}) }
```

The rule does not deal with the case where the argument above the line is forbidden window information because the client cannot learn anything more than this. This rule specifies that there are two results: the fact that the request has been made; and that the client learns forbidden information from it.

Each part of the X protocol can be specified in a similar way to define the whole protocol as the union of the individual rules. The model requires only about 120 rules to be defined. X events are modelled within a single rule specifying when a client can observe events generated at a window. If a client can observe one event then it can observe all events.

4.2 An inference engine

In section 4.1 a discussion of how the X protocol can be modelled as rules was given. Given knowledge about a client's resources enables requests to be made, sometimes gaining more knowledge. In this context the hostile client is modelled as an inference engine.

The client inference engine is broken down into processes each of which attempts to infer one piece of X information. These individual processes are then composed in parallel synchronising over the information contained in the rules modelling the X protocol. The technical details of how the hostile client is modelled are given in appendix B.

The same inference engine can be used for different sets of rules for other Application Programming Interfaces, APIs. The arguments for a service within an API will appear above the line of a rule. The effect of calling the service, on the knowledge of the calling application, will appear below the line. In this way the inferences an entity can make within its environment of APIs can be modelled.

At higher levels of structure network nodes or business domains can also be modelled using the same inference engine. Wherever there is a natural level of encapsulation and identifiable capabilities, through which the encapsulation can interact with its environment, this inference engine with suitable rules can be used.

5. Analytical activities

The model described in section 4 is only significant if something useful can be done with it. The intention is to use it to discover potential attacks which will lead to the vulnerabilities identified in a security vulnerability analysis. These attacks will be a trace of requests with replies leading to further requests until the vulnerability arises. Countermeasures in the form of controls on what requests can be made in order to break the chain of requests can then be modelled to determine whether all potential attacks have been dealt with. If blocking a particular request has an unacceptable impact on the functionality of the system then another request in the trace can be blocked and an assessment made of whether both functionality and security can be achieved.

5.1 Refinement

To check the model against specified vulnerabilities the concept of refinement will be used. In CSP two processes P and Q can be composed together using non-deterministic choice, denoted `|~|` in the machine readable dialect of CSP called CSP_M. The non-deterministic choice between two processes means that the environment has no say in whether the overall process behaves like P or behaves like Q, hence its other name of internal choice. The reason for the choice is hidden to an observer and is arbitrary.

The process P can be used in any place where P `|~|` Q would work, since there is nothing to stop P `|~|` Q from behaving like P every time anyway. If R is such that R = R `|~|` P then P is more deterministic than R or P refines R, this is denoted by R `[=` P in CSP_M. This gives the basic notion of when one CSP process is better than another and is the notion of refinement used in this paper and automatically checked by the FDR tool [13]. FDR (Failures Divergence Refinement) is a refinement checker which reads a file containing processes constructed in CSP_M. FDR allows a user to check assertions about a process by exploring all of the states of a process necessary to verify these. The checks for FDR to perform can be pre-loaded into FDR by including lines such as

```
assert SPEC [T=  IMP
```

which represents the check that the process IMP is a trace refinement of the process SPEC. Using the operational semantics of CSP both SPEC and IMP are represented by augmented finite state transition systems, thus allowing state explorations to check the refinement assertion. If the refinement fails then FDR will produce the shortest trace which is a counter example to the refinement assertion. This feature is crucially important to the analysis activities described in this paper.

Checking security and functional properties for a model of an X windowing system will involve a large number of states. The use of parallelism in the model helps make it conceptually simple but causes a combinatorial explosion in the number of states which must be explored. Without some method to compress the state exploration the FDR tool would be useless for our purposes. Fortunately a function has been incorporated into FDR for this purpose: **chase**(P) behaves like P except that whenever P reaches a state where it can perform a hidden (or internal) tau action, **chase** will force FDR to execute tau actions until no more are possible. The other behaviour paths are not explored. There can be many tau paths out of the same state, in this case **chase** will arbitrarily choose one and ignore the others.

The **chase** function does not necessarily preserve the semantics of the process it is applied to, it therefore has to be used with care. Fortunately the model of X which has been constructed is amenable to hiding communications on the "enabled" channel and then chasing them. The semantics of the model are preserved because the order in which arguments to the X functions are enabled is irrelevant, therefore choosing one order over another by **chase** after they have been hidden is sound.

5.2 Analysis

Recall that the kind of security properties which are of interest are concerned with finding out from the X server information, such as the identity of a classified client's window, which could then be used to spy or modify the targeted window. The ability to reason about this kind of information has already been built into the model via the set "Critical_info" which when discovered is signaled via the channel "Misuse", see appendix B. To check the security properties, embodied in the set "Critical_info", the events communicated via the channel "enabled" must be hidden and chased (if the state exploration is to be tractable).

```
X_System = chase( X\{|enabled|} )
```

This leaves a process with only communications with the server and along the "Misuse" channel visible. The refinement check is therefore

```
STOP [T= X_System\{|server_reply|}
```

The refinement will succeed if the process "X_System", with only communications along the channel "Misuse" visible, is a refinement of STOP which is equivalent to saying that it is STOP. This means that there is no possible way for the client to find out the information necessary to misuse X's capabilities. If the refinement fails then FDR will return the shortest trace which demonstrates how the refinement fails, that is it provides a security attack which ends with the client gaining the necessary information. This trace can then be used to modify the X system to prevent that attack. Unfortunately, as the discussion about QueryTree demonstrated, a formal model and sophisticated model checking of FDR is not required to find an attack on an X windows system. The model and refinement checks become useful when encapsulation and capability control are used to secure X.

To model an encapsulated X system with capability controls it is necessary to build the CSP process "X_pair(i)" again. First a channel is defined

```
channel proxy_chan
```

This channel is used by a process called Proxy(i) which represents a proxy which mediates interactions between the server and a particular client. How the proxy is defined depends upon the results of the analysis. An example of an obvious but draconian definition of the proxy might be the following.

```
Proxy(i) =
member(i,Critical_info) & server_reply.block -> Proxy(i)
[]
not member(i,Critical_info) &
                    proxy_chan.i -> server_reply.i -> Proxy(i)
```

This process blocks any X requests that will reveal critical information to the client, but pass on any requests that will not compromise security. This is too restrictive, its impact on the functionality of X would probably make all but the simplest of X clients secure but ineffective, therefore analysis of all potential attacks is justified in order to define a weaker proxy which is still provides security. Whatever the final form of the proxy process the encapsulated server can be defined independently.

```
Encapsulated_Server(i) =
Proxy(i) [proxy_chan<->server_reply] Server(i)
```

The encapsulated server defined by placing the proxy in front of the server and linking the channels "proxy_chan" and "server_reply" as an common internal communication. This leaves the encapsulated server with just its channel "server_reply" visible and allows it to block requests for critical information. The new process "X_pair" is defined by parallel composition sharing the events in the alphabet of the server while allowing other events in "Client(i)" free to engage with the environment.

```
X_pair(i) =
Client(i) [|Alpha_Server(i)|] Encapsulated_Server(i)
```

The rest of the construction is as in appendix B since the proxy looks like the X server now with the communication between the proxy and the actual server hidden to the environment making it an internal communication. The assertion

```
STOP [T= X_System\{|server_reply|}
```

can now be checked by FDR to determine that the candidate proxy provides security. In this way the formal model can be used as an aid to designing secure usable X windowing systems.

6. The X proxy security mechanism (implementing the model)

6.1 The design

The formal model developed in section 5 is of limited value unless the model can be grounded in the architecture and implementation of a real X windowing system, this section addresses that problem. The X proxy capability control process encapsulates the X server as shown in figure 2; where the X server's port is blocked, by configuring the operating system (or hardware), to all clients except that of the proxy. Also, as X is based on a client-server architecture, this proxy effectively encapsulates each of the X server's client-connections.

This corresponds to the linked parallel composition of the processes "Proxy" and "Server" defined previously.

Encapsulated_Server =
Proxy(i) [proxy_chan<->server_reply] Server(i)

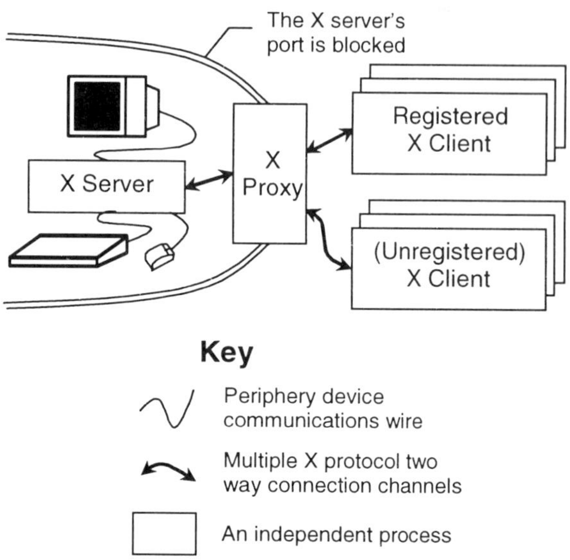

Figure 2 : X proxy client-server model

By this means all client communications with the X Server are mediated by the Proxy. What cannot be seen from figure 2 is that each client can have a different proxy between it and the server. This means that different security policies implemented by the proxy can in principle be defined for each client. However a set of clients within a particular application class, such as office or internet applications, would in practice have one proxy for that class. The proxy defined as a CSP process is just a simple state machine. It is relatively straightforward to "compile" this state machine description into the policy part of the X proxy implementation. For higher assurance we have investigated describing the state machine in terms of preconditions and postconditions and then formally refining the specification to an Ada program [19]. This is sound because the refinement relation for CSP and sequential program refinement coincide.

6.2 Implementation issues

A typical X client has in excess of 1,000 X protocol messages passing between the server and client during the start-up phase and will have to cope with at least 10 events per second (e.g. for typing or drawing) during operation. Any implementation of the security mechanism presented cannot afford to have anything more than a few milliseconds delay on checking that a given request or event is allowed. The proof of concept is implemented in Java and interpreted, hence it does not meet this requirement. However, it is fast enough to show that a production version of the security mechanism which was compiled, rather than interpreted, would meet the requirement. In appropriate situations the X proxy would be more efficient by the client side of the implementation being distributed amongst client machines.

7. Analysis issues

The security threats to a system depend upon its use and its environment. A threat, or vulnerability, in one situation will not be a threat, or vulnerability, in another. For example the vulnerabilities of a Command and Control System in a concrete bunker will be different from a distributed Command and Control System deployed in a battlefield.

A system only has to be secure enough for the anticipated threats, not absolutely secure. Indeed absolute security is impossible in practice because it can never be known that all possible scenarios for a security breach have been anticipated.

Admitting that a system can never be absolutely secure, especially when operational concerns are paramount, is uncomfortable but no different from the situation in the safety community. A system can never be 100% safe, there will be risk in operating most systems. For example an inherently unstable fly-by-wire aircraft is, compared to conventional aircraft, unsafe to fly. The extra risks involved in flying such an aircraft are justified by its increased manouverablity and operational effectiveness. It can however be shown to be safe enough in the context of anticipated hazards. If an unanticipated hazard presents itself then the system or its use is changed to address this new hazard.

The situation in the security world should fundamentally be no different. A great deal of care and attention should be devoted to identifying security threats or vulnerabilities. If this is not done then trade-offs between operational effectiveness and security cannot be made on a rational basis. The tendency is to reduce operational effectiveness in favour of security which has led to secure unusable systems.

If a threat or vulnerability analysis has been performed then it is believed that the modelling activity discussed in this paper is relatively straightforward. Only actual usage will prove whether this is correct, but the rules describing the X system were straightforward (although tedious) to write down. The reason this was true is because the vulnerability analysis identified the information of interest which the rules had to capture. In a different context the vulnerability analysis might lead to slightly different rules. A vulnerability analysis used for other kinds of encapsulated components could be used to define the rules which would model the components capabilities. In the same way as described in this paper the model would help in determining how these capabilities should be controlled.

The rules as they stand could be used to analyse patterns of interaction for the purpose of assessing information flow. However the number of rules for X Windows would probably make this intractable. For a smaller number of interactions information flow analysis could be assessed using FDR, but if this was important then a different approach would probably be more appropriate.

The inference approach, to assessing how an encapsulated component's capabilities should be controlled, could be supported using logical inference tools. The advantage of using CSP is that the encapsulation proxy and other system components can be modelled in a natural way, especially if they are distributed. Languages such as CCS could also be used, but it is not clear whether the present tool support for such languages could be used as effectively as FDR at the present time.

Initial investigations have been completed into the applicability of this approach to analysing network vulnerabilities. Nodes are a natural encapsulation within a network. There are well defined interfaces between a node and the rest of the network. These interfaces provide a means of analysing the network with respect to possible security attacks.

A small number of experiments have been performed which confirm the expectation that the technique is capable of detecting network vulnerabilities. The technique is capable of finding ALL possible attacks including, crucially, non-intuitive attacks. Furthermore, by posing a number of well chosen questions, a classification of all possible attacks can, in principle, be obtained.

Control of interactions in the network in the manner described in this paper does not seem very promising. This is because network security experts have indicated that existing networks have many easy to exploit vulnerabilities which cannot be removed without blocking highly desirable legitimate network activity. It has therefore been decided that the most productive exploitation route for the network vulnerability analysis work is to develop it to support intrusion detection.

Misuse Detection Systems (MDS) rely upon knowledge of possible attack scenarios for a network. However rather than use such knowledge to statically reconfigure the network (and thereby excessively restrict legitimate network usage) and MDS monitors system activities and flags a possible intrusion when a line of attack emerges. In the same way as the X analysis shaped the specification of the proxy's behaviour, the network analysis will shape the specification of the behaviour of a MDS.

8. Conclusions

The X windowing system is a widely used COTS product which was designed for use in open communities assuming no malicious clients. It is however being used in environments where that assumption is invalid and security counter measures are either non-existent or require special bespoke implementations of X, thus invalidating the advantages of using COTS products.

X has been used in this paper to illustrate a general approach to addressing some of the security issues of COTS discussed in [16]. Each client is untrusted, but its actions are controlled by a software wrapper or encapsulation. An analytical model has been developed in order to determine what sequence of interactions a client has to perform in order to reveal one of the system level vulnerabilities identified earlier. Using this information a proxy can be defined which breaks this chain by blocking one of the interactions, allowing the interaction with the least impact on the functionality to be chosen. For example an untrusted word processor application would not need to modify another client's window, but an application displaying a consistent air-sea picture distributed over several machines would. These two clients need different proxies to be identified and checked using the analytical model.

For a general COTS component the interface it uses to interact with its environment must be identified before it can be encapsulated. Techniques originally developed for portability at DERA have been developed for application to COTS components to ensure there are no hidden ways in which the component can interact with its environment. Once these interfaces have been identified they must be policed. Work into this general problem is being sponsored by DARPA [18]. The aim of the program is to generate software wrappers which can be inserted into COTS and legacy systems to add security and survivability.

If wrappers for COTS and legacy systems can be produced under this DARPA programme the problem of how these wrappers should control interactions to achieve both security and functionality remains. The analytical model presented in this paper can also be used for the general COTS problem. The model for X dealt with over 120 possible interactions defined by the X protocol, demonstrating that real APIs can be dealt with. The X server is just the environment with which the client interacts with, a similar model could be built for a COTS component and its environment. Building such a model for a COTS component and its environment would address the problem of how software wrappers should police the component in order to achieve security without unduly compromising the operational effectiveness of a system.

The critical properties to be enforced on an open system constructed from COTS could be safety properties [14]. Indeed X windows is used in some weapon systems and can interact with embedded software onboard a piece of Ordnance. The encapsulation and high assurance policing techniques described in this paper would be applicable in situations where safety depended upon blocking the inadvertent actions of untrusted X clients.

9. Acknowledgements

This work was supported by the European Union Espirit Project No. 20072 "Design for Validation" (DeVa) and the MoD CRP programme TG10 TA5.1. The formal modelling owed much to Bill Roscoe and his students' work on security protocols. The author is also grateful to his colleagues Nick Moffat and Anthony Smith for reviewing and improving the paper.

10. References

[1] C. O'Halloran and M. A. Smith, *An approach to securing an X application*, in DeVa – ESPIRT Long Term Research Project No. 20072 – 1st Year Report, pages 233-252, December 1996. http://www.newcastle.research.ec.org/deva/papers/2.2I.ps

[2] D P Wiggins, *Analysis of the X Protocol for Security Concerns*, X Consortium Inc, 10 May 1996, available as part of the Broadway distribution, ftp://sunsite.doc.ic.ac.uk/packages/X11R6.3/xc/doc/hardcopy/Xserver/analysis.PS.Z

[3] *X Window System, Version 11 Release 6.3 Release Notes*, X Consortium Inc, 23 Dec 1996, available as part of the Broadway distribution, ftp://sunsite.doc.ic.ac.uk/packages/X11R6.3/xc/RELNOTES.(PS/TXT)

[4] D P Wiggins, *Security Extension Specification*, X Consortium Inc, 15 Nov 1996, available as part of the Broadway distribution, ftp://sunsite.doc.ic.ac.uk/packages/X11R6.3/xc/doc/hardcopy/Xext/security.PS.Z

[5] D P Wiggins, *Security Extension Server Design*, X Consortium Inc, 20 Dec 1996, available as part of the Broadway distribution, ftp://sunsite.doc.ic.ac.uk/packages/X11R6.3/xc/doc/hardcopy/Xserver/secint.PS.Z

[6] K S Keithley, *Application Group Extension to the X Protocol*, X Consortium Inc, 27 Sept 1996, available as part of the Broadway distribution, ftp://sunsite.doc.ic.ac.uk/packages/X11R6.3/xc/doc/hardcopy/Xext/AppGroup.PS.Z

[7] D. Ross, "X, Spies and Videotape", *Proceedings of the European X Window System Conference*, (London , UK), Published by CEP consultants, pp 186-191, 1990.

[8] J. Steiner, C. Newman and J. Schiller, "Xkerberos: An Authentication Service for Open Network Systems", *Proceedings of the Winter USENIX 1988 Conference*, 1988.

[9] P. W. Core, *Strategic issues relating to dynamic component architectures*, DRA Report.

[10] J. Cazin, C. O'Halloran, C. T. Sennett, and P. Girard, "Formal Validation of Software for Secure Systems", *Journal of Defence Science*, 1996.

[11] J. Dobson, "Modelling real-world issues for dependable software", *High-integrity Software* (Ed. Chris Sennett), Pitman Computer Systems Series 1989, ISBN 0273030000.

[12] C. A. R. Hoare, *Communicating Sequential Processes*, Prentice-Hall International, 1985.

[13] A. W. Roscoe, *The Theory and Practice of Concurrency*, Prentice Hall series in computer science, 1998.

[14] C. O'Halloran, *Controlling the risk of COTS via Application Programming Interfaces*, proceedings IEE colloquium on COTS and Safety Critical Systems, Digest No: 97/013, 1997.

[15] A. W. Roscoe and M.H. Goldsmith, *The perfect "spy" for model-checking cryptoprotocols* , Proceeding of DIMACS workshop on the design and formal verification of crytographic protocols, 1997.

[16] U. Lindqvist and E. Jonsson, *A Map of Security Risks Associated with Using COTS,* pp. 60-66 Computer, Vol. 31, No. 6, 1998.

[17] C. O'Halloran, *Assessing Safety Critical COTS systems*, proceedings of the 1999 Safety Critical Systems Symposium, 1999.

[18] G. Koob, *Wrappers and Composition*, http://www.arpa.mil/ito/research/wc/background.html

[19] C. O'Halloran, *Don't Verify, Abstract*, Proceedings of the 13th conference on Automated Software Engineering, ASE98, 1998

Appendix A. The Language CSP_M

CSP_M is the machine readable dialect of CSP, used to define both the specification and implementation of models verified by FDR. It is very close to pure CSP and it is embedded in a Gofer/Haskell like functional programming language, which augments its utility substantially. Below is a summary of syntax of CSP_M.

`channel channel_id : ChannelType` is a CSP_M declaration of a channel, the name of the channel is `channel_id` and it communicates values of type `ChannelType`.

`STOP` is the simplest CSP process; it never engages in any action, and never terminates.

`a -> P` is the most basic program constructor. It waits to perform the event a and after this has occurred subsequently behaves as process `P`. The same notation is used for outputs `(c!v -> P)`, inputs `(c?x -> P(x))` and simple communication `(c.x -> P(x))` of values along named channels.

"boolean expression" `& a -> P` is the process which behaves as `a -> P` if the "boolean expression" is true.

`P |-| Q` represents the non-deterministic or internal choice between `P` and `Q`.

`P [] Q` represents the external or deterministic choice between `P` and `Q`. It will, at first, offer the initial actions of both `P` and `Q` to its environment; its subsequent behaviour is like `P` if the initial action chosen was possible only for `P` and like `Q` if the action selected `Q`. If both `P` and `Q` have common initial actions, its subsequent behaviour is non-deterministic (like `|-|`). `STOP [] P` is the same as `P`.

`[] x : X @ x -> P` represents replicated external choice.

`P \ A` is the CSP hiding operator. This process behaves as `P` except that events in set `A` are hidden from the environment and are solely (and internally) determined by `P`; the environment can neither observe nor influence them. `P\{|channel|}` hides all communications along the channel

`P [ | A | ] Q` represents shared parallel (concurrent) composition. `P` and `Q` evolve separately, except that events from A occur only when `P` and `Q` agree (i.e. synchronise) to perform them.

`P [Alphabet1 || Alphabet2] Q` represents alphabetised parallel composition. Any events in `P` which are not in Alphabet1 are blocked from occurring and similarly for `Q`. `P` and `Q` evolve separately except or events in the intersection of Alphabet1 and Alphabet 2 occur only when `P` and `Q` agree (i.e. synchronise) to perform them.

`|| i : Indexing_set @ [A(i)] P(i)` represents alphabetized parallel composition. for example `|| i : {1,2,3} @ [A(i)] P(i)` is equivalent to

```
(P(1) [A(1) || A(2)] P(2))
[Union(A(1),A(2))|| A(3)]
P(3)
```

`P [[ channel1<-> channel2 ]]Q` represents linked parallel composition. The two processes communicate via a common new hidden channel resulting from a re-naming of channel1 and channel2.

`chase(P)` The process `P` with the 'chase' operator applied to it. As a consequence, internal events, called tau-events, in `P`, are give priority over all other events. Where there is an option to perform several tau-events, one of them is chosen arbitrarily.

Appendix B. A CSP_M model of the X client and server

The inference rules described in 4.1 require an inference engine to use them. In this section an inference engine is defined in terms of a hostile client. In order to analyse the potential attacks which can be made by a hostile client, the types of information necessary to control requests in X must be specified. The information might be an X resource, or the name of an X request whose use the analyst wishes to be informed of. The set of items of information which are of interest is defined.

Critical_info

A channel called "Misuse" communicates to the environment what critical information has arisen.

channel Misuse : Critical_info

Another channel, called "enabled", is defined. It records which pieces of X information are available to be used as inputs for X requests such as "**QueryTree**".

channel enabled : {{i | i <- Xinfo}}

A channel "server_reply" is defined in order to model the X server communicating an interaction with a particular client.

channel server_reply : {{ i | I < -Xinfo }}

With these definitions a process can be defined in the machine readable syntax of CSP (CSP_M) to model a client's behaviour, in terms of an inference engine. The purpose of the inference engine is to gain information necessary to misuse requests in X. Two processes are defined, Client(i) and Client(i)'. Client(i) represents a client ignorant of some information 'i'. Client(i)' represents the same client aware of the information 'i'.

Client(i) =
[] (X,Y):{ (X,Y) | (X,Y) <- Xprotocol, ismember(i,Y) }

```
@ enabled.X -> ( server_reply.Y ->Client'(i)
                 []
                 server_reply.block -> Client(i) )
```

The client process is parameterised by either some X resource information or the name of an X request. The process Client(i) initially offers to engage in the set of arguments above the line, for a rule in the set "Xprotocol", whenever 'i' is in the set below the line. The process then waits for the environment to either communicate the information it was after from the server, or block that request. In this initial model the server cannot block a request, this option is built in to the model in order to allow encapsulation of the X server in a subsequent model. If a request is blocked then the process returns to its initial state of knowledge and the use of X requests, that require this information, is thus disabled. If the X server communicates 'i', then the process evolves to a new state (denoted by Client'(i)) where the X information 'i' will be available as an argument to other X requests in "Xprotocol".

The process Client'(i) offers a number of options to the environment: either to synchronise on a set of arguments to a rule; or if the information which has been learnt is one of the pieces of critical information, then it signals this to the analyst via the channel "Misuse" to indicate violation of a security policy. In all cases the process returns back to its original state to allow the information it has learnt to be used for other rules in "Xprotocol" and gain more information for potential misuse. The process Client'(i) is expressed in CSP_M as follows:

```
Client'(i) =
[] X : { (X,Y) | (X,Y) <- Xprotocol, member(i,X) }
    @ enabled.X -> Client'(i)
  []
  member(i,Critical_info) & Misuse.i -> Client'(i)
```

Note that there is no communication with the X server in this process because it exists only to enable other X requests to be used to obtain more information from the X server, or detect when critical information has been obtained. The actual client does however communicate with the X server, therefore a process is defined to model the server.

```
Server(i) = server_reply.{i} -> Server(i)
```

In fact at the moment the server is irrelevant to the model, it does exactly what the client says it should do. The reason it is defined is to provide something to encapsulate or confine in a subsequent model. In a real system a software wrapper would be placed around both the client and the server, so it is that client's view of the server which is being encapsulated. A different client running at the same time could well be encapsulated differently because its security vulnerabilities were different.

Before processes are composed together in parallel, an alphabet needs to be specified to control how processes co-operate and evolve together.

```
Alpha_Server(i) = { server_reply.{i} | member(i,Xinfo) }
```

```
Alpha(i) =
Union(
{Misuse.i | member(i,Critical_info)},
{enabled.(X,Y) | (X,Y) <- Xprotocol, member(i,X) or
member(i,Y)},
Alpha_Server(i)
    )
```

For a given piece of X information the alphabet indexed by that information, 'i', is the critical information for misuse, any request which uses or delivers it, and communication of it from the server.

Care needs to be taken when composing in parallel replicated copies of Client(i), for each 'i'. If the event "enabled.X" represents a client's initial knowledge then it must be allowed to occur without synchronising with its environment. If the event "enabled.X" does not represent a client's initial knowledge then the event must wait for the information to be learnt from the X server and hence synchronise with the environment if it is learnt.

For example, the request **QueryTree** requires a client to know a window identity before the identity of parent and child windows can be requested. If this is part of the client's initial knowledge then this request can occur without waiting for anything else. If the client is initially ignorant of this knowledge then the client has to wait for the required window identifier to be learnt by using other requests and its current knowledge.

B.1 The overall X model

Using the previously defined indexed alphabets the client and server can be placed in parallel.

```
X_pair(i) = Client(i) [| Alpha_Server(i) |] Server(i)
```

This new process constrains the client and server to evolve together with respect to the information 'i' which the client requests from the server. All the other events in "Alpha(i)" can occur without synchronising with "Server(i)", without this freedom the process "Server(i)" would block any other event apart from those that it wanted to do causing deadlock. To prevent this kind of deadlock being introduced into the overall model, a set representing any initial information the client has is defined. This will allow X requests which deliver this information to be used to evolve the process "Client(i)" to a state corresponding to its initial knowledge.

```
Initial_info
```

The overall X system can now be defined using the replicated alphabetized parallel operator.

X = (|| i: diff(Xinfo,Initial_info)@ [Alpha(i)] X_pair(i))

This process replicates the client/server pairs for each piece of X information in "Xinfo" except for those in "Initial_info" for the reasons discussed previously. Each replicated process, indexed by 'i', co-operates on those events specified by "Alpha(i)". The process 'X' evolves by enabling those X rules in "XProtocol" which deliver items of information in "Initial_info". The process 'X' can then use this initial knowledge as inputs into other X rules requesting further information from the X server. Whenever a piece of critical information is discovered, a signal is sent down the channel "Misuse" to alert an analyst that a potential misuse of the X system can occur.

Secure Composition of Insecure Components

Peter Sewell
Computer Laboratory,
University of Cambridge,
England
Peter.Sewell@cl.cam.ac.uk

Jan Vitek
Object Systems Group,
Université de Genève,
Switzerland
Jan.Vitek@cui.unige.ch

Abstract

Software systems are becoming heterogeneous: instead of a small number of large programs from well-established sources, a user's desktop may now consist of many smaller components that interact in intricate ways. Some components will be downloaded from the network from sources that are only partially trusted. A user would like to know that a number of security properties hold, e.g. that personal data is not leaked to the net, but it is typically infeasible to verify that such components are well-behaved. Instead, they must be executed in a secure environment, or wrapper, *that provides fine-grain control of the allowable interactions between them, and between components and other system resources.*

In this paper we study such wrappers, focusing on how they can be expressed in a way that enables their security properties to be stated and proved rigorously. We introduce a model programming language, the box-π calculus, that supports composition of software components and the enforcement of security policies. Several example wrappers are expressed using the calculus; we explore the delicate security properties they guarantee.

1 Introduction

Software systems are evolving. Increasingly, monolithic applications are being replaced with assemblages of software components coming from different sources. Instead of a small number of large programs from well-established suppliers, nowadays a user's desktop is made up of many smaller applications and software modules that interact in intricate ways to carry out a variety of information processing tasks. Moreover, whereas it used to be that a software base was fairly static and often controlled by a system administrator, it is now easy to download code from the network; technologies such as Java even allow an application program to be extended with new components while the program is running.

In such fluid operating environments, traditional security mechanisms and policies appear almost irrelevant. While passwords and access control mechanisms are adequate to protect the integrity of the computer system as whole, they utterly fail to address the issue of protecting the user from downloaded code being run from her account [19, 13, 27]. Approaches such as the Java sandbox that promise security by isolation are not satisfactory either: components can interact freely or not at all [35, 14]. What is needed is much finer-grained protection mechanisms that take into account the interconnection of software components and the specific security requirements of individual users.

We give a small motivating example (based on a true story) involving a fictional character, Karen, performing some financial computation. To manage her accounts she downloads a software package called *Quickest* from a company Q. Karen does not want any information about her to be leaked without her consent, so she would like to run Quickest in an environment that does not allow it access to the Internet (she has observed that it sometimes uploads information – presumably for marketing purposes – to Q). On the other hand she often needs stock quotes, for which she must allow net access. At present she runs two instances of Quickest, one on an isolated PC, with her financial records, and one connected, used to obtain stock quotes. She transfers data from the second to the first only on floppy disc, thereby manually ensuring that no information flows in the converse direction.

Karen would like to dispose of the isolated PC, using a software solution to prevent her personal data being leaked to the net. Now, Quickest is a large piece of commercial software that was not programmed by Karen. The source code is not available to her and its internal behaviour is complex and inaccessible; ensuring the desired properties by program analysis will not be feasible. Instead she must run the two copies of the package in secure software environments that allow control of the information flow between them and between each package and the net.

More generally, she will wish to run many packages, each trusted in different ways, and will want to be able to dynamically control the interactions between them and between these packages and other resources – the net, regions of the local disc, the terminal, audio and video capture devices etc. In some cases she will wish to log the data sent from one to another; in others she will wish to limit the allowed bandwidth (e.g. to disallow audio and video channels). In general her notion of what data is to be considered "sensitive" is likely to be context dependent. In a Web browser, she may choose to consider her e-mail address as a secret that should be protected from broadcast to junk mail lists, while the same e-mail will not be treated specially in her text editor.

While it is not feasible to analyse or modify large third-party software packages, it *is* possible to intercept the communications between a package and the other parts of the system, interposing code at the boundaries of the different software components [20, 11, 7, 13]. It is thus possible to monitor or control the operations that these components are able to invoke, and the data that is exchanged between them. We call a code fragment that encapsulates untrusted components a *security wrapper* or *wrapper* for short.

Clearly the task of writing wrappers should not be left solely to the end-user. Rather we envision wrappers as reusable software components, users should then only have to pick the most appropriate wrappers, customize them with some parameters and install them. All of this process should be dynamic: wrappers must be no harder to add to a running system than new applications. A user will require a clear description of the security properties that a wrapper guarantees. Moreover, wrappers should compose with a clear notion of which properties are preserved.

The goal of this work is to study such secure environments, focusing on how they can be expressed in a way that enables their security properties to be stated and proved rigorously. It appears that there is a wide range of rather delicate properties, making hard for designers to develop sufficiently clear intuitions without such rigour. Moreover the wrappers, although critical, may be rather small pieces of software, making it feasible to prove properties about them, or about mild idealisations.

To express and reason about wrappers we require a small programming language, with a well-defined semantics, that allows the composition of software components to be expressed straightforwardly and also supports the enforcement of security policies. Such a language, the box-π calculus, is introduced in §2. We begin with a simple example, a wrapper $\mathcal{W}_1$ written in the calculus. It encapsulates a single component and controls its interactions with the environment, limiting them to two channels in and out. $\mathcal{W}_1$ is written as a unary context:

$$\begin{aligned} \mathcal{W}_1[\_] \stackrel{def}{=} (\boldsymbol{\nu}\, a)(\ & a[\_] \\ & \mid !\, in^{\uparrow} y.\overline{in}^{a} y \\ & \mid !\, out^{a} y.\overline{out}^{\uparrow} y) \end{aligned}$$

This creates a box with a new name a, installing in parallel with it two forwarders – one that receives messages from the environment on channel in and sends them to the wrapped program, and one that receives messages from the wrapped program on channel out and sends them to the environment. An arbitrary program P (possibly malicious) can be wrapped to give $\mathcal{W}_1[P]$; the design of the calculus and of $\mathcal{W}_1$ ensures that no matter how P behaves the wrapped program $\mathcal{W}_1[P]$ can only interact with its environment on the two channels in and out. This could be achieved simply by forbidding *all* interaction between P and the outside world, a rather unsatisfactory wrapper — $\mathcal{W}_1$ is also *honest*, in that it faithfully forwards messages on in and out. These informal properties are made precise in Propositions 2 and 5 below. We also discuss the sense in which wrapping a *well-behaved* P has no effect on its behaviour. $\mathcal{W}_1$ is atypical in that it has no behaviour except the forwarding of legitimate messages – other reasonable unary wrappers may perform some kind of logging, or have a control interface for the wrapper. The honesty property that should hold for any reasonable wrapper is therefore somewhat delicate; to state it (and our other security properties) we make extensive use of a labelled transition semantics for the calculus.

The wrapper $\mathcal{W}_1$ controls interaction between a single component and its environment. Our second main example goes further towards solving Karen's problem, allowing control of the interaction between components. $\mathcal{W}_2$ (defined in §3) is a binary wrapper that encapsulates two components P and Q as $\mathcal{W}_2[P, Q]$, allowing each to interact with the environment in a limited way but also allowing information to flow from P to Q (but not vice versa) along a directed communication channel. Making this precise is the subject of §5.

Both $\mathcal{W}_1$ and $\mathcal{W}_2$ are chosen to be as simple as possible, in particular with fixed interfaces for components to interact with each other and with the environment. Generalising this to arbitrary interfaces and to wrappers taking any number of components should be straightforward but complicates the notation; other generalisations are discussed in the conclusion.

Overview We begin in the next section (§2) by introducing the calculus and giving its operational semantics. A number of wrappers are defined in §3, including one which logs traffic. The basic properties of honesty and well-behaviour are introduced in §4. Information flows between wrapped components are studied in §5, then we conclude in §6 with discussion of related and future work. This paper describes work in progress – Sections 4 and 5 contain a number of conjectures which are yet to be proved, but which we hope will stimulate discussion.

2 A Boxed π Calculus

The language – known as the *box-π calculus* – that we use for studying encapsulation properties must allow interacting components to be composed. The components will typically be executing concurrently, introducing nondeterminism. It is therefore natural to base the language on a process calculus. The box-π calculus lies in a large design space of distributed calculi that build on the π-calculus of Milner, Parrow and Walker [24]. Related calculi have been used by a number of authors, e.g. in [2, 4, 6, 9, 10, 12, 17, 16, 28, 30, 31, 33, 34, 36, 37]. A brief overview of the design space can be found in [32]; here we highlight the main design choices for box-π, deferring comparison with related work to §6.

The calculus is based on asynchronous message passing, with components interacting only by the exchange of unordered asynchronous messages. Box-π has an asynchronous π-calculus as a subcalculus – we build on a large body of work studying such calculi, notably [18, 8, 5]. They are known to be very expressive, supporting many programming idioms including functions and objects, and are Turing-complete; a box-π process may therefore perform arbitrary internal computation.

To π we must add primitives for constraining communication – in standard π-calculi, if one process can send a message to another then the only way to prevent information flowing in the reverse direction is to impose a type system, which (as observed above) is not appropriate here. We therefore add a boxing primitive. Boxes may be nested, giving hierarchical protection domains; communication across box boundaries is strictly limited. Underlying the calculus design is the principle that *each box should be able to control all interactions of its children, both with the outside world and with each other* [36]. Communication is therefore allowed only between a box and its parent, or within the process running in a particular box. In particular, two sibling boxes cannot interact without the assistance of their parent. To enable a box to interact with a particular child, boxes are named, analogously to π channel names. The security properties of our wrappers depend on the ability to create fresh box names.

Turning to the values that may be communicated, it is convenient to allow arbitrary tuples of names (or other tuples). Note that we do *not* allow communication of process terms. Moreover, no primitives for movement of boxes are provided. The calculus is therefore entirely first order, which is important for the tractable theory of behaviour (the labelled transition semantics) that we require to state and prove security properties. The calculus is also untyped – we wish to consider the wrapping of ill-understood, probably buggy and possibly malicious programs.

2.1 Syntax

The syntax of the calculus is as follows:

Names We take an infinite set $\mathcal{N}$ of *names*, ranged over by lower-case roman letters n, m, x, y, z etc. (except i, j, k, o, p, u, v). Both boxes and communication channels are named; names also play the role of variables, as in the π-calculus.

Values and Patterns Processes will interact by communicating values which are deconstructed by pattern-matching upon reception. Values u, v can be names or tuples, with patterns p correspondingly tuple-structured:

u, v	$::=$	x	name
		$\langle v_1 \mathinner{..} v_k \rangle$	tuple ($k \geq 0$)
p	$::=$	$\_$	wildcard
		x	name pattern
		$\langle p_1 \mathinner{..} p_k \rangle$	tuple pattern ($k \geq 0$, no repeated names)

Processes The main syntactic category is that of *processes*, ranged over by P, Q. We introduce the primitives in three groups.

Boxes A box $n[P]$ has a name n, it can contain an arbitrary process P. Box names are not necessarily unique – the process $n[0] \mid n[0]$ consists of two distinct boxes named n, both containing an empty process, in parallel.

P	$::=$	$n[P]$	box named n containing P
		$P \mid P'$	P and P' in parallel
		0	the nil process
		$\ldots$	

Communication The standard asynchronous π-calculus communication primitives are $\overline{x}v$, indicating an output of value v on the channel named x, and $xp.P$, a process that will receive a value output on channel x, binding it to p in P. Here we refine these with a tag indicating the direction of the communication in the box hierarchy. An *input tag* ι can be either $\star$, for input within a box, $\uparrow$, for input from the parent box, or a name n, for input from a sub-box named n. An *output tag* o can be any of these, similarly. For technical reasons we must also allow an output tag to be $\overline{\uparrow}$, indicating an output received from the parent that has not yet interacted with an input, or $\overline{n}$, indicating an output received from child

n that has not yet interacted. The communication primitives are then

$$
\begin{array}{lll}
P & ::= & \ldots \\
 & & \overline{x}^o v \qquad \text{output } v \text{ on channel } x \text{ to } o \\
 & & x^\iota p.P \qquad \text{input on channel } x \text{ from } \iota \\
 & & !\, x^\iota p.P \qquad \text{replicated input} \\
 & & \ldots
\end{array}
$$

The replicated input $!\, x^\iota p.P$ behaves essentially as infinitely many copies of $x^\iota p.P$ in parallel. This gives computational power, allowing e.g. recursion to be encoded simply, while keeping the theory simple. In $x^\iota p.P$ and $!\, x^\iota p.P$ the names occurring in the pattern p bind in P.

New name creation Both box and channel names can be created fresh, with the standard π-calculus $(\nu\, x)P$ operator. This declares any free instances of x within P to be instances of a globally fresh name.

$$
\begin{array}{lll}
P & ::= & \ldots \\
 & & (\nu\, x)P \qquad \text{new name creation}
\end{array}
$$

In $(\nu\, x)P$ the x binds in P. We work up to alpha conversion of bound names throughout, writing the free name function, defined in the obvious way for values, tags and processes, as fn(_).

2.2 Reduction

The simplest semantic definition of the calculus is a *reduction semantics*, a one-step reduction relation $P \rightarrow P'$ indicating that P can perform one step of internal computation to become P'. We first define the complement $\overline{\iota}$ of a tag ι in the obvious way, with $\overline{\star} = \star$ and $\overline{\overline{\iota}} = \iota$. We write $\{{}^v/_p\}P$ for the result of substituting appropriate parts of the value v for the names of the pattern p in P. Note that this may be undefined, either because the value does not match the pattern or because the syntax does not allow arbitrary values in all the places where free names can occur. We define structural congruence $\equiv$ as the least congruence relation such that the axioms below hold. This allows the parts of a redex to be brought syntactically adjacent.

$$
\begin{array}{rcll}
P \mid 0 & \equiv & P & \\
P \mid Q & \equiv & Q \mid P & \\
(P \mid Q) \mid R & \equiv & P \mid (Q \mid R) & \\
(\nu\, x)(\nu\, y)P & \equiv & (\nu\, y)(\nu\, x)P & \\
(\nu\, x)(P \mid Q) & \equiv & P \mid (\nu\, x)Q & x \notin \text{fn}(P) \\
(\nu\, x)n[P] & \equiv & n[(\nu\, x)P] & x \neq n
\end{array}
$$

The reduction relation is now the least relation over processes satisfying the axioms and rules below. The (Red Comm) and (Red Repl) axioms are subject to the condition that $\{{}^v/_p\}P$ is well-defined.

$$
\begin{array}{ll}
n[\overline{x}^{\uparrow} v \mid Q] \rightarrow \overline{x}^{\overline{n}} v \mid n[Q] & \text{(Red Up)} \\
\overline{x}^{n} v \mid n[Q] \rightarrow n[\overline{x}^{\overline{\uparrow}} v \mid Q] & \text{(Red Down)} \\
\overline{x}^{\overline{\iota}} v \mid x^\iota p.P \rightarrow \{{}^v/_p\}P & \text{(Red Comm)} \\
\overline{x}^{\overline{\iota}} v \mid !\, x^\iota p.P \rightarrow !\, x^\iota p.P \mid \{{}^v/_p\}P & \text{(Red Repl)} \\
P \rightarrow Q \ \Rightarrow\ P \mid R \rightarrow Q \mid R & \text{(Red Par)} \\
P \rightarrow Q \ \Rightarrow\ (\nu\, x)P \rightarrow (\nu\, x)Q & \text{(Red Res)} \\
P \rightarrow Q \ \Rightarrow\ n[P] \rightarrow n[Q] & \text{(Red Box)} \\
P \equiv P' \rightarrow Q' \equiv Q \ \Rightarrow\ P \rightarrow Q & \text{(Red Struct)}
\end{array}
$$

The (Red Up) axiom allows an output to the parent of a box to cross the enclosing box boundary. Similarly, the (Red Down) axiom allows an output to a child box n to cross the boundary of n. The (Red Comm) axiom then allows synchronisation between a complementary output and input within the same box. The (Red Repl) axiom is similar, but preserves the replicated input in the resulting state.

Communications across box boundaries thus take two reduction steps, for example in the following upwards and downwards communications.

$$
\begin{array}{rcl}
n[\overline{x}^{\uparrow} v] \mid x^{n} p.P & \rightarrow & n[0] \mid \overline{x}^{\overline{n}} v \mid x^{n} p.P \\
 & \rightarrow & n[0] \mid \{{}^v/_p\}P
\end{array}
$$

$$
\begin{array}{rcl}
\overline{x}^{n} v \mid n[x^{\uparrow} p.P] & \rightarrow & n[\overline{x}^{\overline{\uparrow}} v \mid x^{\uparrow} p.P] \\
 & \rightarrow & n[\{{}^v/_p\}P]
\end{array}
$$

This removes the need for 3-way synchronisations between a box, an output and an input (as in [36]), simplifying both the semantics and the implementation model.

2.3 Labelled Transitions

The reduction semantics defines only the internal computation of processes. The statements of our security properties must involve the interactions of processes with their environments, requiring more structure: a *labelled transition relation* characterising the potential inputs and outputs of a process. We give a labelled semantics for box-π in an explicitly-indexed early style, defined inductively on process structure by an SOS. The *labels* are

$$
\begin{array}{lll}
\ell & ::= & \tau \qquad \text{internal action} \\
 & & \overline{x}^o v \qquad \text{output action} \\
 & & x^\gamma v \qquad \text{input action}
\end{array}
$$

where γ ranges over all output tags except $\overline{\uparrow}$. The labelled transitions can be divided into those involved in moving messages across box boundaries and those involved in communications between outputs and inputs. The movement labels are

$\overline{x}^{\uparrow} v$ (sending to the parent)
$\overline{x}^{n} v$ (sending to child n)
$x^{\overline{n}} v$ (box n receiving from its parent)

$$\frac{}{\overline{x}^{o}v \xrightarrow{\overline{x}^{o}v} 0}\ \text{(Out)} \qquad \frac{}{x^{\iota}p.P \xrightarrow{x^{\iota}v} \{^{v}/_{p}\}P}\ \text{(In)} \qquad \frac{}{!\,x^{\iota}p.P \xrightarrow{x^{\iota}v} !\,x^{\iota}p.P \mid \{^{v}/_{p}\}P}\ \text{(Repl)}$$

$$\frac{A \vdash P \xrightarrow{\overline{x}^{\overline{\gamma}}v} P' \quad A \vdash Q \xrightarrow{x^{\gamma}v} Q'}{A \vdash P \mid Q \xrightarrow{\tau} (\boldsymbol{\nu}\,\mathrm{fn}(x,v) - A)(P' \mid Q')}\ \text{(Comm)} \qquad \frac{P \xrightarrow{\ell} P'}{P \mid Q \xrightarrow{\ell} P' \mid Q}\ \text{(Par)}$$

$$\frac{A \vdash P \xrightarrow{\overline{x}^{\uparrow}v} P'}{A \vdash n[P] \xrightarrow{\tau} (\boldsymbol{\nu}\,\mathrm{fn}(x,v) - A)(\overline{x}^{\overline{n}}v \mid n[P'])}\ \text{(Box-1)} \qquad \frac{}{n[P] \xrightarrow{x^{\overline{n}}v} n[\overline{x}^{\overline{\uparrow}}v \mid P]}\ \text{(Box-2)} \qquad \frac{P \xrightarrow{\tau} P'}{n[P] \xrightarrow{\tau} n[P']}\ \text{(Box-3)}$$

$$\frac{A, x \vdash P \xrightarrow{\ell} P'}{A \vdash (\boldsymbol{\nu}\,x)P \xrightarrow{\ell} (\boldsymbol{\nu}\,x)P'}\ \text{(Res-1)} \qquad \frac{A, x \vdash P \xrightarrow{\overline{y}^{o}v} P'}{A \vdash (\boldsymbol{\nu}\,x)P \xrightarrow{\overline{y}^{o}v} P'}\ \text{(Res-2)} \qquad \frac{P \xrightarrow{\ell} P' \quad P' \equiv P''}{P \xrightarrow{\ell} P''}\ \text{(Struct Right)}$$

The (Res-1) rule is subject to $x \notin \mathrm{fn}(\ell)$, the (Res-2) rule is subject to $x \in \mathrm{fn}(v) - \mathrm{fn}(y, o)$ if $\neg\mathrm{mv}(o)$ and to $x \in \mathrm{fn}(y, v) - \mathrm{fn}(o)$ otherwise. The indexing $A \vdash$ has beeen elided in rules where it is not involved in any interesting way. In all rules with conclusion of the form $A \vdash P \xrightarrow{\ell} Q$ there is an implicit side condition $\mathrm{fn}(P) \subseteq A$. In the (In) and (Repl) axioms there is an implicit side condition that $\{^{v}/_{p}\}P$ is well-defined. Symmetric versions of (Par) and (Comm) are elided.

Figure 1. Box-π Labelled Transitions

Say $\mathrm{mv}(o)$ is true if o is of the form n or $\uparrow$. The communication labels are

- $\overline{x}^{\star}v$ (local output)
- $x^{\star}v$ (local input)
- $\overline{x}^{\overline{n}}v$ (output received from child n)
- $x^{n}v$ (input a message received from child n)
- $\overline{x}^{\overline{\uparrow}}v$ (output received from parent)
- $x^{\uparrow}v$ (input a message received from parent)

Labels will synchronise in the pairs given:

$\overline{x}^{\star}v$	$x^{\star}v$
$\overline{x}^{\overline{n}}v$	$x^{n}v$
$\overline{x}^{\overline{\uparrow}}v$	$x^{\uparrow}v$
$\overline{x}^{n}v$	$x^{\overline{n}}v$

The labelled transition relation has the form

$$A \vdash P \xrightarrow{\ell} Q$$

where A is a finite set of names and $\mathrm{fn}(P) \subseteq A$; it should be read as 'in a state where the names A may be known to P and its environment, process P can do ℓ to become Q'. The relation is defined as the smallest relation satisfying the rules in Figure 1. We write A, x for $A \cup \{x\}$ where x is assumed not to be in A, and A, p for the union of A and the names occurring in the pattern p, where these are assumed disjoint. For the subcalculus without new-binding the labelled transition rules are straightforward — instances of the reduction rule (Red Up) correspond to uses of (Box-1), (Out), and (Par); instances of (Red Down) correspond to uses of (Comm), (Out), and (Box-2); instances of (Red Comm) correspond to uses of (Comm), (Out), and (In). The addition of new-binding introduces several subtleties, some inherited from the π-calculus and some related to scope extrusion and intrusion across box boundaries. We discuss the latter briefly.

The (Red Down) rule involves synchronisation on the box name n but *not* on the channel name x — there are reductions such as

$$((\boldsymbol{\nu}\,x)\overline{x}^{n}z) \mid n[0] \quad\rightarrow\quad (\boldsymbol{\nu}\,x)n[\overline{x}^{\overline{\uparrow}}z]$$

in which a new-bound name enters a box boundary. To correctly match this with a τ-transition the side-condition for (Res-2) for labels with output tag n requires the bound name to occur either in channel or value position, and the (Comm) rule reintroduces the x binder on the right hand side.

Similarly, the (Red Up) rule allows new-bound names in channel position to exit a box boundary, for example in

$$n[(\boldsymbol{\nu}\,x)\overline{x}^{\uparrow}z] \quad\rightarrow\quad (\boldsymbol{\nu}\,x)(\overline{x}^{\overline{n}}z \mid n[0])$$

The (Res-2) condition for output tag $\uparrow$ again requires the bound name to occur either in channel or value position, here the (Box-1) rule reintroduces the x binder on the right hand side.

Reductions generated by (Red Comm) involve synchronisation both on the tags and on the channel name. The (Res-2) condition for output tags $\star$, $\overline{\uparrow}$ and $\overline{n}$ is analogous to the standard π-calculus (Open) rule; requiring the bound name to occur in the value but not in the tag or channel. The (Comm) rule for these output tags is analogous to the standard π rule — in particular, here it is guaranteed that $x \in A$ (see Lemma 10).

Some auxiliary notation is useful. For a sequence of labels $\ell_1 \ldots \ell_k$ we write

$$A \vdash P_1 \xrightarrow{\ell_1} \ldots \xrightarrow{\ell_k} P_{k+1}$$

to mean $\exists P_2, \ldots, P_k \;.\; \forall i \in 1..k \;.\; A_i \vdash P_i \xrightarrow{\ell_i} P_{i+1}$, where $A_i = A \cup \bigcup_{j \in 1..i} \mathrm{fn}(\ell_j)$. If $\ell \neq \tau$ we write $A \vdash P \stackrel{\hat{\ell}}{\Longrightarrow} P'$ for $A \vdash P \xrightarrow{\tau}^* \xrightarrow{\ell} \xrightarrow{\tau}^* P'$; if $\ell = \tau$ then $A \vdash P \stackrel{\hat{\ell}}{\Longrightarrow} P'$ is defined as $A \vdash P \xrightarrow{\tau}^* P'$.

The two semantics coincide in the following sense.

Theorem 1 *If* $\mathrm{fn}(P) \subseteq A$ *then* $A \vdash P \xrightarrow{\tau} Q$ *iff* $P \rightarrow Q$.

This give confidence that the labelled semantics carries enough information. The proof is somewhat delicate — it is sketched in Appendix A; full details can be found in the forthcoming technical report.

2.4 Bisimulation

The statements of some relationships between the behaviour of a wrapped and an unwrapped program require an operational equivalence relation. As box-π is asynchronous, an appropriate notion can be based on the *weak asynchronous bisimulation* of [5]. Consider a family S of relations indexed by finite sets of names such that each S_A is a symmetric relation over $\{ P \mid \mathrm{fn}(P) \subseteq A \}$. Say S is a *weak asynchronous bisimulation* if

- $P \; S_A \; Q$, $A \vdash P \xrightarrow{\ell} P'$ and ℓ is an output or τ transition imply $\exists Q' \;.\; A \vdash Q \stackrel{\hat{\ell}}{\Longrightarrow} Q' \wedge P' \; S_{A \cup \mathrm{fn}(\ell)} \; Q'$, and
- $P \; S_A \; Q$, $A \vdash P \xrightarrow{x^\gamma v} P'$ imply either $\exists Q' \;.\; A \vdash Q \stackrel{x^\gamma v}{\Longrightarrow} Q' \wedge P' \; S_{A \cup \mathrm{fn}(x^\gamma v)} \; Q'$ or $\exists Q' \;.\; A \vdash Q \Longrightarrow Q' \wedge P' \; S_{A \cup \mathrm{fn}(x^\gamma v)} \; (Q' \mid \overline{x}^\gamma v)$.

We write $\approx$ for the union of all weak asynchronous bisimulations. (This definition has not been thoroughly tested – in particular, it has not been proved to be a congruence.)

3 Security Wrappers

This section gives three example wrappers. The first encapsulates a single component, restricting its interactions with the outside world to communications obeying a certain protocol. The second is similar, but also writes a log of all such communications. The third wrapper encapsulates two components, allowing each to interact with the outside world in a limited way but also allowing information to flow from the first to the second (but not vice versa).

A wrapper design must be in the context of some fixed protocol which components should use for communication with their environment and with each other. For the first two wrappers we fix two channel names, in and out, for components to receive and send messages respectively. Moreover, we assume that components will always be executed within some box and should be communicating with the parent box. A trivial component that receives values v and then copies pairs $\langle v\, v\rangle$ to the output would be written as

$$!\, in^{\uparrow} y.\overline{out}^{\uparrow} \langle y\, y\rangle$$

A malicious component might also write data to another illicit output channel available in the environment, e.g.

$$!\, in^{\uparrow} y.(\overline{net}^{\uparrow} y \mid \overline{out}^{\uparrow} \langle y\, y\rangle)$$

or eavesdrop on communications between other parts of the system, e.g.

$$!\, c^{\star} y.(\overline{net}^{\uparrow} c \mid \overline{c}^{\star} y)$$

We can express whether a component obeys the protocol in terms of the labelled transition semantics – say P is *well-behaved* for a unary wrapper iff whenever $A \vdash P \xrightarrow{l_1..l_k} Q$ then the l_j are of the form $in^{\uparrow} v$, $\overline{out}^{\uparrow} v$, or τ.

A Filtering Wrapper A filter is a wrapper that simply restricts the communication abilities of a process. We consider a static filter that allows interaction on two channels *in* and *out* only.

$$\begin{array}{rcll} \mathcal{W}_1[\text{-}] & \stackrel{def}{=} & (\nu\, a)(& a[\text{-}] \\ & & & \mid\, !\, in^{\uparrow} y.\overline{in}^{a} y \\ & & & \mid\, !\, out^{a} y.\overline{out}^{\uparrow} y\;) \end{array}$$

$\mathcal{W}_1$ executes its component within a freshly-named box, installing forwarders to move legitimate messages across the boundary. Note that this and further wrappers are non-binding contexts – equivalently, we assume wherever we apply $\mathcal{W}_1$ to a process P that the new-bound a does not occur free in P (in an implementation this could be ensured either probabilistically or with a linear-time scan of P). Irrespective of the behaviour of P, $\mathcal{W}_1[P]$ does obey the protocol – this can be stated clearly using the labelled transition semantics:

Proposition 2 *For any program* P *with* $a \notin \mathrm{fn}(P)$, *if* $A \vdash \mathcal{W}_1[P] \xrightarrow{l_1..l_k} Q$ *then the* l_j *are of the form* $in^{\uparrow} v$, $\overline{out}^{\uparrow} v$, *or* τ.

The proof is via an explicit characterisation of the states reachable by labelled transitions of $\mathcal{W}_1[P]$. A sketch of this, and of the other properties of $\mathcal{W}_1$, can be found in Appendix B; full details can be found in the forthcoming technical report. We say a unary wrapper with this property is *pure*.

The Logging Wrapper The filter can be extended to maintain a log of all communications of a process, sending copies on a channel *log* to the environment:

$$\begin{array}{rcl}\mathcal{L}[\text{-}] & \stackrel{def}{=} & (\nu\, a)(\;\; a[\text{-}] \\ & & \quad \mid\, !\, in^{\uparrow}y.(\overline{log}^{\uparrow}y \mid \overline{in}^{a}y) \\ & & \quad \mid\, !\, out^{a}y.(\overline{log}^{\uparrow}y \mid \overline{out}^{\uparrow}y)\;)\end{array}$$

A wrapped program $\mathcal{L}[P]$ again can interact only in limited ways.

Proposition 3 *For any program P with $a \notin \text{fn}(P)$, if $A \vdash \mathcal{L}[P] \stackrel{l_1..l_n}{\longrightarrow} Q$ then the l_j are of the form $in^{\uparrow}v$, $\overline{out}^{\uparrow}v$, $\overline{log}^{\uparrow}v$, or τ.*

A Pipeline Wrapper A pipeline wrapper allows a controlled flow of information between two components. We give a binary wrapper $\mathcal{W}_2$ that takes two processes. In an execution of $\mathcal{W}_2[Q_1, Q_2]$ the two wrapped processes Q_i can interact with the environment as before, on channels in_i and out_i. In addition, Q_1 can send messages to Q_2 on a channel mid. The pipeline implemented here is unordered.

$$\begin{array}{rcl}\mathcal{W}_2[\text{-}_1, \text{-}_2] & \stackrel{def}{=} & (\nu\, a_1, a_2)(\;\; a_1[\text{-}_1] \mid a_2[\text{-}_2] \\ & & \quad \mid\, !\, {in_1}^{\uparrow}y.\overline{in_1}^{a_1}y \\ & & \quad \mid\, !\, {in_2}^{\uparrow}y.\overline{in_2}^{a_2}y \\ & & \quad \mid\, !\, {out_1}^{a_1}y.\overline{out_1}^{\uparrow}y \\ & & \quad \mid\, !\, {out_2}^{a_2}y.\overline{out_2}^{\uparrow}y \\ & & \quad \mid\, !\, mid^{a_1}y.\overline{mid}^{a_2}y\;)\end{array}$$

As before $\mathcal{W}_2$ is a non-binding context – we assume, wherever we apply it to two processes P_1, P_2, that $\{a_1, a_2\} \cap \text{fn}(P_1, P_2) = \emptyset$. Say a binary wrapper $\mathcal{C}$ is pure iff for any programs P_1, P_2, (satisfying the appropriate free name condition – for $\mathcal{W}_2$ that with $\{a_1, a_2\} \cap \text{fn}(P_1, P_2) = \emptyset$), if $A \vdash \mathcal{C}[P_1, P_2] \stackrel{l_1..l_k}{\longrightarrow} Q$ then the l_j are of the form ${in_i}^{\uparrow}v$, $\overline{out_i}^{\uparrow}v$, or τ.

Proposition 4 *$\mathcal{W}_2$ is pure.*

For an example of a blocked attempt by the second process to send a value to the first, suppose $P_2 = \overline{mid}^{\uparrow}v$. We have

$$\begin{array}{l}\mathcal{W}_2[P_1, \overline{mid}^{\uparrow}v] = (\nu\, a_1, a_2)(a_1[P_1] \mid a_2[\overline{mid}^{\uparrow}v] \mid R) \\ \qquad \rightarrow (\nu\, a_1, a_2)(a_1[P_1] \mid a_2[0] \mid \overline{mid}^{a_2}v \mid R)\end{array}$$

where R is the parallel composition of forwarders. The output $\overline{mid}^{a_2}v$ in the final state cannot interact further – not with the environment, as a_2 is restricted, and not with the forwarder $!\, mid^{a_1}y.\overline{mid}^{a_2}y$, as $a_1 \neq a_2$.

These wrappers all assume a rather simple fixed protocol. It would be straightforward to generalise to arbitrary sets of channels instead of in, out and mid. It would also be straightforward to allow n-ary wrappers, encapsulating many components and allowing information to flow only on a given preorder between them. Other generalisations are discussed in the conclusion.

4 Honesty and Composition

The properties of wrappers stated in the previous section are very weak. For example, the unary wrapper

$$\mathcal{C}[\text{-}] \stackrel{def}{=} 0$$

is also pure, but is useless. In this section we identify the class of *honest* wrappers that are guaranteed to forward legitimate messages. This gives the authors of components a clear statement of (some of) the properties of the environment that can be relied upon.

An initial attempt might be to take $\mathcal{W}_1$ as a specification, defining a unary wrapper $\mathcal{C}$ to be honest iff for any program P the processes $\mathcal{C}[P]$ and $\mathcal{W}_1[P]$ are operationally equivalent. This is unsatisfactory – it rules out wrappers such as $\mathcal{L}$, and it does not give a very clear statement of the properties that may be assumed of an honest wrapper.

A better attempt might be to say that a unary wrapper $\mathcal{C}$ is honest iff for any well-behaved P the processes $\mathcal{C}[P]$ and P are operationally equivalent. This would be unsatisfactory in two ways. Firstly, some intuitively sound wrappers have additional interactions with the environment – e.g. the logging outputs of $\mathcal{L}$ – and so would not be considered honest by this definition. Secondly, this definition would not constrain the behaviour of wrappers for non-well-behaved P at all – if a component P attempted, in error, a single illicit communication then $\mathcal{C}[P]$ might behave arbitrarily.

To address these points we give explicit definitions of honesty, first for unary wrappers and then for binary, in the style of weak asynchronous bisimulation. Consider a family $\mathcal{R}$ indexed by finite sets of names such that each $\mathcal{R}_A$ is a relation over $\{\, P \mid \text{fn}(P) \subseteq A \,\}$. Say $\mathcal{R}$ is an *h-bisimulation* if, whenever $C\ \mathcal{R}_A\ Q$ then:

1. if $A \vdash C \stackrel{\ell}{\longrightarrow} C'$ for $\ell = \overline{out}^{\uparrow}v, \tau$ then $A \vdash Q \stackrel{\hat{\ell}}{\Longrightarrow} Q' \wedge C'\ \mathcal{R}_{A \cup \text{fn}(\ell)}\ Q'$

2. if $A \vdash C \stackrel{in^{\uparrow}v}{\longrightarrow} C'$ then either $A \vdash Q \stackrel{in^{\uparrow}v}{\Longrightarrow} Q'$ and $C'\ \mathcal{R}_{A \cup \text{fn}(in, v)}\ Q'$ or $A \vdash Q \Longrightarrow Q'$ and $C'\ \mathcal{R}_{A \cup \text{fn}(in, v)}\ Q' \mid \overline{in}^{\uparrow}v$

3. if $A \vdash C \xrightarrow{\ell} C'$ for any other label then $C' \; R_{A \cup \mathrm{fn}(\ell)} \; Q$

together with symmetric versions of clauses 1 and 2. Say a unary wrapper $\mathcal{C}$ is *honest* if for any program P (satisfying the appropriate free name condition) and any $A \supseteq \mathrm{fn}(\mathcal{C}[P])$ there is an h-bisimulation R with $\mathcal{C}[P] \; R_A \; P$.

Loosely, clauses 1, 2 and the symmetric versions ensure that legitimate communications and internal reductions must be weakly matched. Clause 3 ensures that if the wrapper performs some additional communication then this does not affect the state as seen by the wrapped process.

Proposition 5 *The unary wrappers $\mathcal{W}_1$ and $\mathcal{L}$ are honest.*

We give some examples of dishonest wrappers. Take

$$\mathcal{C}[\_] \stackrel{def}{=} (\nu \, a)a[\_]$$

This is not honest – a transition $A \vdash P \xrightarrow{\overline{out}^{\uparrow} v} P'$ cannot be matched by $\mathcal{C}[P]$, violating the symmetric version of clause 1. Now consider

$$\mathcal{C}[\_] \stackrel{def}{=} \_$$

This wrapper is also dishonest as $\mathcal{C}[P]$ can perform actions not in the protocol that essentially affect the state of P. For example, take $P = x^{\star}y.\overline{out}^{\uparrow}\langle\rangle$. Suppose $\mathcal{C}[P] \; R_A \; P$ for an h-bisimulation R. We have $A \vdash \mathcal{C}[P] \xrightarrow{x^{\star}\langle\rangle} \overline{out}^{\uparrow}\langle\rangle$ so by clause 3 $\overline{out}^{\uparrow}\langle\rangle \; R_A \; P$, but then clause 1 cannot hold – the left hand side can perform an $\overline{out}^{\uparrow}\langle\rangle$ transition that cannot be matched be the right hand side.

Composition of Wrappers The protocol for communication between a component and a unary wrapper is designed so that wrappers may be nested. We conjecture that the composition of any honest unary wrappers is honest.

Conjecture 6 *If $\mathcal{C}_1$ and $\mathcal{C}_2$ are honest unary wrappers then $\mathcal{C}_1 \circ \mathcal{C}_2$ is honest.*

Analogous results for non-unary wrappers would require wrappers with more complex interfaces so that the input, output and mid channels could be connected correctly.

A desirable property of a pure wrapper is that it should not affect the behaviour of any well-behaved component — one might expect for any pure and honest $\mathcal{C}$ and well-behaved P that $\mathcal{C}[P] \approx_A P$ (where $A \supseteq \mathrm{fn}(\mathcal{C}[P])$). Unfortunately this does not hold, even for $\mathcal{W}_1$, as the wrapper can make input transitions that cannot be matched. One can check $\mathcal{W}_1[0] \not\approx_A 0$, yet 0 is well-behaved. In practice one would expect the environment of a wrapper to not be able to detect these inputs, but to make this precise would require an operational equivalence relativised to such 'well-behaved' environments.

A simpler property would be that multiple wrappings have no effect. We conjecture that $\mathcal{W}_1$ is idempotent, i.e. that $\mathcal{W}_1[\mathcal{W}_1[P]]$ and $\mathcal{W}_1[P]$ have the same behaviour (up to weak asynchronous bisimulation):

Conjecture 7 *For any program P with $a \notin \mathrm{fn}(P)$ and $A \supseteq \mathrm{fn}(\mathcal{W}_1[P])$ we have $\mathcal{W}_1[P] \approx_A \mathcal{W}_1[\mathcal{W}_1[P]]$.*

Honesty for Binary Wrappers must take into account the *mid* communication. Consider a family R indexed by finite sets of names such that each R_A is a relation between terms and pairs of terms, all with free names contained in A. Say R is a *binary h-bisimulation* if, whenever $C \; R_A \; (Q_1, Q_2)$ the clauses below hold. The key difference with the unary definition is clause 7; the other clauses are routine, albeit notationally complex.

1. if $A \vdash C \xrightarrow{\overline{out_i}^{\uparrow} v} C'$ then $A \vdash Q_i \xRightarrow{\overline{out_i}^{\uparrow} v} Q_i'$, $A \vdash Q_{3-i} \Longrightarrow Q_{3-i}'$ and $C' \; R_{A \cup \mathrm{fn}(v)} \; (Q_1', Q_2')$.

2. if $A \vdash C \xrightarrow{in_i^{\uparrow} v} C'$ then $A \vdash Q_{3-i} \Longrightarrow Q_{3-i}'$ and either $A \vdash Q_i \xRightarrow{in_i^{\uparrow} v} Q_i' \wedge C' \; R_{A \cup \mathrm{fn}(v)} \; (Q_1', Q_2')$ or $A \vdash Q_i \Longrightarrow Q_i'' \wedge C' \; R_{A \cup \mathrm{fn}(v)} \; (Q_1', Q_2')$, where $Q_i' = Q_i'' \mid \overline{in}^{\uparrow} v$.

3. if $A \vdash C \xrightarrow{\tau} C'$ then $A \vdash Q_1 \Longrightarrow Q_1'$, $A \vdash Q_2 \Longrightarrow Q_2'$ and $C' \; R_A \; (Q_1', Q_2')$.

4. if $A \vdash C \xrightarrow{\ell} C'$ for any other label then $C' \; R_{A \cup \mathrm{fn}(\ell)} \; (Q_1, Q_2)$

5. if $A \vdash Q_i \xrightarrow{\ell} Q_i'$ for $\ell = \overline{out_i}^{\uparrow} v, \tau$ then $A \vdash C \xRightarrow{\hat{\ell}} C'$, and $C' \; R_{A \cup \mathrm{fn}(\ell)} \; (Q_1', Q_2')$, where $Q_{3-i}' = Q_{3-i}$.

6. if $A \vdash Q_i \xrightarrow{in_i^{\uparrow} v} Q_i'$ then either $A \vdash C \xRightarrow{in_i^{\uparrow} v} C' \wedge C' \; R_{A \cup \mathrm{fn}(v)} \; (Q_1', Q_2')$ or $A \vdash C \Longrightarrow C' \wedge C' \mid \overline{in}^{\uparrow} v \; R_{A \cup \mathrm{fn}(v)} \; (Q_1', Q_2')$, where $Q_{3-i}' = Q_{3-i}$.

7. if $A \vdash Q_1 \xrightarrow{\overline{mid}^{\uparrow} v} Q_1'$ then $A \vdash C \Longrightarrow C' \wedge C' \; R_{A \cup \mathrm{fn}(v)} \; (Q_1', Q_2 \mid \overline{mid}^{\uparrow} v)$.

A binary wrapper $\mathcal{C}$ is honest if for all P_1, P_2 (satisfying the appropriate free name condition) and any $A \supseteq \mathrm{fn}(\mathcal{C}[P_1, P_2])$ there exists a binary h-bisimulation R with $\mathcal{C}[P_1, P_2] \; R_A \; (P_1, P_2)$.

Conjecture 8 *$\mathcal{W}_2$ is honest.*

5 Constrained Interaction Between Components

In our motivating example Karen required fine-grain control over the information flows between components – in the binary case, allowing unidirectional flow. By examining the code for $\mathcal{W}_2$ it is intuitively clear that it achieves this, preventing information flowing from Q to P within $\mathcal{W}_2[P, Q]$. When one comes to make this intuition precise, however, it becomes far from clear exactly what behavioural properties $\mathcal{W}_2$ guarantees that make it a satisfactory wrapper from the user's point of view (who should not have to examine the wrapper code). Honesty is one, but it does not prohibit bad flows. In this section we give a number of candidate properties, stating four precisely and the others informally. We conjecture that all are satisfied by $\mathcal{W}_2$ but that none are equivalent. None are entirely satisfactory; we hope to provoke discussion of exactly what guarantees should be desired by users and by component designers. For simplicity, only pure binary wrappers $\mathcal{C}$ are considered – recall that for a pure binary $\mathcal{C}$ the labelled transitions of $\mathcal{C}[P_1, P_2]$ will only be of the forms $in_i{\uparrow}v$, $\overline{out_i}{\uparrow}v$ and τ.

New-name directionality As we are using a calculus with creation of new names, we can test a wrapper by supplying a new name to the second component, on in_2, and observing whether it can ever be output by the first component on out_1. Say $\mathcal{C}$ is *directional for new names* if whenever

$$A \vdash \mathcal{C}[P_1, P_2] \xrightarrow{\ell_1} \ldots \xrightarrow{\ell_j} \xrightarrow{in_2{\uparrow}u} \xrightarrow{\ell'_1} \ldots \xrightarrow{\ell'_k} \xrightarrow{\overline{out_1}{\uparrow}u'} P$$

with $x \in \mathrm{fn}(u)$, but x is new, i.e. $x \notin A \cup \mathrm{fn}(\ell_1 \ldots \ell_j)$, and x is not subsequently input to the first component, i.e.

$$x \notin \bigcup_{i \in 1..k \wedge \ell'_i = in_1{\uparrow}v} \mathrm{fn}(v)$$

then x is not output by the first component, i.e. $x \notin \mathrm{fn}(u')$. This property does not prevent all information flow, however – a variant of $\mathcal{W}_2$ containing a reverse-forwarder that only forwards particular values, such as

$$!\,mid^{a_2}y.\mathbf{if}\ y \in \{0, 1\}\ \mathbf{then}\ \overline{mid}^{a_1}y$$

could still satisfy it. (Here 0 and 1 are free names, which must therefore be in A.)

Note that a binary wrapper $\mathcal{C}$ is intended only to limit information flow *within* $\mathcal{C}[P_1, P_2]$. We do not wish to place any constraint on the environment of the wrapper, for example forbidding the environment to copy values received from out_2 to in_1. Such a restriction could only be imposed by draconian measures, e.g. by waiting for P_1 to terminate before starting P_2, that would not be acceptable to the desktop user. Many programs are essentially non-terminating; if they are executing concurrently then the user cannot be prevented from reading the output of one and copying it to the other. In many circumstances this should be explicitly supported by the desktop cut-and-paste, perhaps with a warning signal.

Permutation Our second property formalises the intuition that if no observable behaviour due to P_1 depends on the behaviour of P_2 then in any trace it should be possible to move the actions associated with P_1 before all actions associated with P_2. Say $\mathcal{C}$ has the *permutation property* if whenever

$$A \vdash \mathcal{C}[P_1, P_2] \stackrel{\ell_1}{\Longrightarrow} \ldots \stackrel{\ell_k}{\Longrightarrow} P$$

with $\ell_i \neq \tau$ there exists a permutation π of $\{1, \ldots, k\}$ such that

$$A \vdash \mathcal{C}[P_1, P_2] \stackrel{\ell_{\pi(1)}}{\Longrightarrow} \ldots \stackrel{\ell_{\pi(k)}}{\Longrightarrow} P$$

and no in_1 or out_1 transition occurs after any in_2 or out_2 transition in $\ell_{\pi(1)} \ldots \ell_{\pi(k)}$. For an example wrapper without this property, consider

$$\begin{aligned} \mathcal{C}[\_1, \_2] \stackrel{def}{=} (\boldsymbol{\nu}\, a_1, a_2)(\, & a_1[\_1] \mid a_2[\_2] \\ & \mid\ !\,in_2{\uparrow}y.(\overline{in_2}^{a_2}y \mid\ !\,in_1{\uparrow}y.\overline{in_1}^{a_1}y) \\ & \mid\ !\,out_1{}^{a_1}y.\overline{out_1}{\uparrow}y \\ & \mid\ !\,out_2{}^{a_2}y.\overline{out_2}{\uparrow}y \\ & \mid\ !\,mid^{a_1}y.\overline{mid}^{a_2}y) \end{aligned}$$

Here the in_1 messages are not forwarded until at least one in_2 input is received from the environment. Nonetheless, in some sense there is still no information flow from the second component to the first.

The new-name directionality and permutation properties are expressed purely in terms of the externally observable behaviour of $\mathcal{C}[P, Q]$ (in fact, they are properties of its trace set, a very extensional semantics). Note, however, that the intuitive statement that information does not flow from Q to P depends on an understanding of the internal computation of P and Q that is not present in the reduction or labelled transition relations (given only that $\mathcal{C}[P, Q] \rightarrow^* R$ there is no way to associate subterms of R with an 'origin' in $\mathcal{C}$, P or Q). Our next two properties involve a more intensional semantics in which output and input processes are tagged with sets of colours. The semantics propagates colours in interaction steps, thereby tracking the dependencies of reductions.

Coloured Reductions Take a set col of colours (disjoint from $\mathcal{N}$), and let c and d range over subsets of col. We define a coloured box-π calculus by annotating all outputs and inputs with sets of colours:

$$P \ ::= \ \mathsf{c}{:}\overline{x}^{o}v \mid \mathsf{c}{:}x^{\iota}p.P \mid \mathsf{c}{:}!\,x^{\iota}p.P \mid n[P] \mid 0 \mid P \mid P' \mid (\nu\, x)P$$

If P is a coloured term we write $|P|$ for the term of the original syntax obtained by erasing all annotations. Conversely, for a term P of the original syntax $\mathsf{c} \circ P$ denotes the term with every particle coloured by c. For a coloured P we write $\mathsf{c} \bullet P$ for the coloured term which is as P but with c unioned to every set of colours occurring in it. We write cd for the union $\mathsf{c} \cup \mathsf{d}$. The reduction relation now takes the form $P \rightarrow_{\mathsf{c}} Q$, where P and Q are coloured terms and c is a set of colours indicating what this reduction depends upon. It is defined as follows, in which structural congruence is defined by the same axioms as before.

$n[\mathsf{c}{:}\overline{x}^{\uparrow}v \mid Q] \rightarrow_{\mathsf{c}} \mathsf{c}{:}\overline{x}^{\overline{n}}v \mid n[Q]$	(C Red Up)
$\mathsf{c}{:}\overline{x}^{n}v \mid n[Q] \rightarrow_{\mathsf{c}} n[\mathsf{c}{:}\overline{x}^{\uparrow}v \mid Q]$	(C Red Down)
$\mathsf{c}{:}\overline{x}^{\overline{\iota}}v \mid \mathsf{d}{:}x^{\iota}p.P \rightarrow_{\mathsf{cd}} \mathsf{cd} \bullet(\{^{v}/_{p}\}P)$	(C Red Comm)
$\mathsf{c}{:}\overline{x}^{\overline{\iota}}v \mid \mathsf{d}{:}!\,x^{\iota}p.P \rightarrow_{\mathsf{cd}}$ $\mathsf{d}{:}!\,x^{\iota}p.P \mid \mathsf{cd} \bullet(\{^{v}/_{p}\}P)$	(C Red Repl)
$P \rightarrow_{\mathsf{c}} Q \ \Rightarrow \ P \mid R \rightarrow_{\mathsf{c}} Q \mid R$	(C Red Par)
$P \rightarrow_{\mathsf{c}} Q \ \Rightarrow \ (\nu\, x)P \rightarrow_{\mathsf{c}} (\nu\, x)Q$	(C Red Res)
$P \rightarrow_{\mathsf{c}} Q \ \Rightarrow \ n[P] \rightarrow_{\mathsf{c}} n[Q]$	(C Red Box)
$P \equiv P' \rightarrow_{\mathsf{c}} Q' \equiv Q \ \Rightarrow \ P \rightarrow_{\mathsf{c}} Q$	(C Red Struct)

The coloured calculus has the same essential behaviour as the original calculus:

Proposition 9 *For any coloured P we have $|P| \rightarrow Q$ iff $\exists \mathsf{c}, P' \,.\, P \rightarrow_{\mathsf{c}} P' \wedge |P'| = Q$.*

Mediation We can now capture the intuition that all interaction between wrapped components should be mediated by the wrapper. We consider coloured reduction sequences of a wrapper $\mathcal{C}$ and two components P_1, P_2 from an initial state in which each is coloured differently. Let gr, bl and rd be distinct singleton subsets $\{\mathsf{green}\}$, $\{\mathsf{blue}\}$, $\{\mathsf{red}\}$ of col. Suppose

$$(\mathsf{gr} \circ \mathcal{C})[\mathsf{bl} \circ P_1, \mathsf{rd} \circ P_2] \mid \mathsf{bl} \circ I_1 \mid \mathsf{rd} \circ I_2 \rightarrow_{\mathsf{c}_1} \ldots \rightarrow_{\mathsf{c}_k} Q$$

where each I_i is a parallel composition of messages on in_i, i.e. of terms of the form $\overline{in_i}^{\uparrow} v$. Say $\mathcal{C}$ is *mediating* iff whenever $\mathsf{red} \in \mathsf{c}_j$ and $\mathsf{blue} \in \mathsf{c}_j$ then $\mathsf{green} \in \mathsf{c}_j$.

Colour flow The coloured semantics can also be used to express the property that no output on out_1 should depend on the second wrapped component. Say $\mathcal{C}$ has the *colour directionality* property if whenever there is a reduction sequence as above and $Q \equiv (\nu\, A)(\mathsf{c}{:}\overline{out_1}^{\uparrow} v \mid Q')$ then $\mathsf{red} \notin \mathsf{c}$.

For an example wrapper that we conjecture has the permutation property but not the colour directionality property, consider a version of $\mathcal{W}_2$ that has an extra parallel component $out_2{}^{a_2}y.(\overline{out_2}^{\uparrow} y \mid out_1{}^{a_1}y.\overline{out_1}^{\uparrow} y)$. This establishes an additional one-shot forwarder for out_1 after forwarding a message on out_2.

These statements of mediation and coloured directionality share a defect: the use of a reduction semantics makes it awkward to consider inputs of values containing new names that have previously been output by the wrapped components. To address this one would need a coloured labelled transition semantics, allowing e.g. a refined colour directionality property to be stated as follows. Whenever

$$A \vdash (\mathsf{gr} \circ \mathcal{C})[\mathsf{bl} \circ P_1, \mathsf{rd} \circ P_2] \xrightarrow{\ell_1}_{\mathsf{c}_1} \ldots \xrightarrow{\ell_k}_{\mathsf{c}_k},$$

if the inputs are properly coloured (i.e. for each $i \in 1..k$ we have $\ell_i = in_1^{\uparrow} v \implies \mathsf{c}_i = \mathsf{blue}$ and $\ell_i = in_2^{\uparrow} v \implies \mathsf{c}_i = \mathsf{red}$), then for each $i \in 1..k$ the out_1 outputs should be properly coloured, i.e.

$$\ell_i = \overline{out_1}^{\uparrow} v \implies \mathsf{red} \notin \mathsf{c}_i$$

Causality A very strong directionality property that one might ask for – perhaps the strongest – would be that in an execution of $\mathcal{C}[P_1, P_2]$ no output on out_1 can be *causally dependent* on any action of P_2. Casual semantics for process calculi have been much studied, often under the name 'true concurrency semantics' – see [40] for an overview. It would be interesting to give a causal semantics to the box π calculus. There is a trade-off here, however – such a semantics would be rather complex; it would have to be understood in order to understand any property stated using it. The coloured reduction semantics can be considered as an more tractable approximation to real causality.

Another point is that a causal property is sometimes too strong – a usable wrapper may have to allow low-bandwidth communication in the reverse direction, perhaps not carrying any data values, to permit acknowledgement messages. A causal property would then not hold, while a modified colour flow property would.

6 Conclusion

The code base of modern systems is becoming increasingly diverse. Whereas previously a typical system would involve a small number of monolithic applications, obtained from trusted organisations, now users routinely download components from partially trusted or untrusted sources. Downloaded or mobile code fragments are commonly run under the user's authority to grant access to system resources and permit interaction with other software components. This presents obvious security risks for the secrecy and integrity of the user's data.

In this paper we have developed a theory of security wrappers. These are small programs that can regulate the interactions between untrusted software components, enforcing dynamic and flexible security policies. We have presented a minimal concurrent programming language for studying the problem, the box-π calculus, and proved a basic metatheoretic result: that a reduction and labelled transition semantics coincide. We have expressed a number of security wrappers in the calculus and begun an investigation of the security properties that wrappers should provide.

6.1 Related Work

There is an extensive literature on information flow properties of various kinds. Much of it is in the context of multilevel security, in which one has a fixed lattice of security levels and is concerned with properties which state that a component (expressed purely semantically, e.g. as a set of traces) respects the levels. The theory could be applied during the design of the components of a large multi-user system (with a relatively static security policy) by proving that the components obey particular properties. A concise introduction can be found in the survey of McLean [23]. The problem of designing and understanding wrappers appears to be rather different – we have focussed on the protection required by a single user executing a variety of partially-trusted components obtained from third parties. This requires flexible protection mechanisms – a static assignment of security levels would be inadequate – and cannot depend on static analysis of the components. Related work on dynamic enforcement of policies has been presented by Schneider [29].

Other recent work has studied type systems that ensure security properties, e.g. the type systems of Volpano, Irvine and Smith [38, 39], the SLam calculus of Heintze and Riecke [15], the systems allowing declassification of Myers and Liskov [26, 25], the type systems of Riely and Hennessy [17, 16, 28], and work on proof-carrying code [27]. If the producers of components that one uses all adopt such systems then they may become very effective. Until then, however, and until type systems can provide the flexible policies required, partially trusted code will in practice either be run dangerously or be wrapped.

In this paper we have made extensive use of techniques from process calculi and operational semantics. These are beginning to provide fruitful ways of studying problems in security and distributed systems, including the analysis of security protocols, for example in [3, 1, 22], and more general secure language design, including work on the Ambient calculus [9, 10], the Secure Join calculus [2], the mobile agent calculi in [17, 16, 28, 30, 31, 33, 34], and the Seal calculus of [36, 37]. These works have studied several different problems, using a variety of calculi designed for the purpose. Common to all is the use of a reduction or labelled-transition operational semantics, providing clear rigorous semantics to the rather high-level constructs involved. One distinguishing feature of the present work is that we do not consider any mobility primitives, allowing us to use a tractable early labelled transition system. This appears to be important for the statement of the delicate security properties of wrappers.

6.2 Future Directions

This paper opens up a number of directions that we would like to pursue. Most immediately, it gives several conjectures that should be proved or refuted, and we would like a better understanding of the properties of binary wrappers. There are then extensions for typing, to richer interfaces, and with mobility primitives.

Typing We are primarily interested in components for which it is infeasible to statically determine whether they are well-behaved. Nonetheless, for simple components one could conservatively ensure well-behaviour with a standard type system, most simply taking types

$$T \quad ::= \quad \mathbf{box} \mid \langle T_1..T_k \rangle \mid \updownarrow T$$

where $\updownarrow T$ is the type of channel names that can be used to communicate values of type T, together with the obvious inference rules. If P is well-typed with respect to a typing context $in : \updownarrow S,\ out : \updownarrow T$ for types S and T containing no instances of $\updownarrow$ then one would expect P to be well-behaved for unary wrappers.

Richer interfaces The wrappers of §3 allowed the encapsulated components to interact only on very simple interfaces. Ultimately, we would like to understand wrappers with more realistic interfaces. For example, in a mild extension of box-π one can express a wrapper that encapsulates k components, allows internal flow along an arbitrary preorder, and permits each component to open and close windows for character IO. Suppose $p_1, \ldots, p_k$ is a list of distinct names, and $\geq$ is a preorder over them giving the allowable information flow. Define a k-ary wrapper as follows.

$$\begin{array}{l} \mathcal{C}[\_1, \ldots, \_k] \stackrel{def}{=} \\ \quad (\boldsymbol{\nu}\, p_1, \ldots, p_k)(\\ \quad\quad p_1[\_1] \mid \ldots \mid p_k[\_k] \\ \quad\quad \mid\, !\, fwd^{(m)}(n\ z\ y).\mathbf{if}\ m \geq n\ \mathbf{then}\ \overline{z}^n y \text{ else } 0 \\ \quad\quad \mid \text{BWINDOW}) \end{array}$$

where

$$\begin{array}{lll}\text{BWINDOW} & \stackrel{def}{=} & !\,openwindow^{(m)}(s\,x).\\ & & \overline{openwindow}^{\uparrow}\langle s\,x\rangle\\ & & \mid x^{\uparrow}(getc\;putc\;close).\\ & & \quad \overline{x}^{m}\langle getc\;putc\;close\rangle\\ & & \quad \mid !\,getc^{m}y.(\overline{getc}^{\uparrow}y \mid y^{\uparrow}c.\overline{y}^{m}c)\\ & & \quad \mid !\,putc^{m}(c\,y).(\overline{putc}^{\uparrow}\langle c\,y\rangle \mid y^{\uparrow}.\overline{y}^{m})\\ & & \quad \mid !\,close^{m}y.(\overline{close}^{\uparrow}y \mid y^{\uparrow}.\overline{y}^{m})\end{array}$$

This uses an additional input tag – a process $x^{(n)}p.P$ will input from any child box, binding the name of the box to n in P. The BWINDOW part of $\mathcal{C}$ receives requests for a new window from the encapsulated components and forwards them to the OS. It then receives the interface for the new window from the OS, forwarding it down to the component and also setting up forwarders for the interface channels. Making the security properties of $\mathcal{C}$ precise is at present a challenging problem. One would like to extend $\mathcal{C}$ further by adding an interface allowing the user to dynamically add and remove pairs from $\geq$.

Covert channels It should be noted that none of the semantic models that we use for the box-π calculus make any commitment to the precise details of scheduling processes. The properties expressed using these semantics therefore cannot address timing-based covert channels such as those mentioned by Lampson [21]. Certain other covert channels, in particular those involving system IO and disc access, could be addressed by expressing models of the IO and disc systems in the calculus, further enriching the wrapper interfaces.

Mobility The original motivation for this work involved downloadable or mobile code and mobile agents. To explicitly model the dynamic configuration of wrappers and applications the calculus must be extended with mobility primitives, while keeping both a tractable semantics and the principle that each box controls the interactions and movements of its contents [36].

Acknowledgements Sewell was supported by EPSRC grant GR/L 62290 *Calculi for Interactive Systems: Theory and Experiment*. The authors would like to thank Ciarán Bryce for his comments.

Appendix

A Coincidence of the Two Semantics

This appendix sketches the proof of equivalence of the labelled transition semantics and the reduction semantics. It is divided into three parts, the first giving basic properties of the labelled transition system, the second showing that any reduction can be matched by a τ-transition and the third showing the converse.

Basic Properties of the LTS The first lemmas are all proved by induction on derivations of transitions.

Lemma 10 *If* $A \vdash P \xrightarrow{\ell} Q$ *then*

1. $\text{fn}(P) \subseteq A$ *and* $\text{fn}(Q) \subseteq \text{fn}(P, \ell)$.
2. *if* $\ell = \overline{x}^{o}v$ *then* $\text{fn}(\ell) \cap A \subseteq \text{fn}(P)$, $\text{fn}(o) \subseteq \text{fn}(P)$, *and moreover if* $\neg\text{mv}(o)$ *then* $x \in \text{fn}(P)$.
3. *if* $\ell = x^{\gamma}v$ *then* $\text{fn}(\gamma) \subseteq \text{fn}(P)$. *Moreover, if* $\gamma \neq \overline{n}$ *then* $x \in \text{fn}(P)$.

Lemma 11 (Strengthening) *If* $A, B \vdash P \xrightarrow{\ell} P'$ *and* $B \cap \text{fn}(P, \ell) = \emptyset$ *then* $A \vdash P \xrightarrow{\ell} P'$.

Lemma 12 (Injective Substitution) *If* $A \vdash P \xrightarrow{\ell} P'$, *and* $f : A \to B$ *and* $g : (\text{fn}(\ell) - A) \to (\mathcal{N} - B)$ *are injective, then* $B \vdash fP \xrightarrow{(f+g)\ell} (f+g)P'$.

Lemma 13 (Shifting)

1. $(A \vdash P \xrightarrow{z^{\iota}v} P' \wedge x \in \text{fn}(v) - A)$ *iff* $(A, x \vdash P \xrightarrow{z^{\iota}v} P' \wedge x \in \text{fn}(v) - \text{fn}(P))$.
2. $(A \vdash P \xrightarrow{z^{\overline{n}}v} P' \wedge x \in \text{fn}(z, v) - A)$ *iff* $(A, x \vdash P \xrightarrow{z^{\overline{n}}v} P' \wedge x \in \text{fn}(z, v) - \text{fn}(P))$

As we are working up to alpha conversion some care is required when analysing transitions. We need the following lemma for transitions of an input or restricted process, together with analogous but less interesting results for the other process constructors.

Lemma 14

1. $A \vdash x^{\iota}p.P \xrightarrow{\ell} Q$ *iff there exists* v *such that* $\text{fn}(x^{\iota}p.P) \subseteq A$, $\ell = x^{\iota}v$, $\{^{v}/_{p}\}P$ *is defined and* $Q \equiv \{^{v}/_{p}\}P$.
2. $A \vdash (\boldsymbol{\nu}\, x)P \xrightarrow{\ell} Q$ *iff either*

(a) *there exists* $\hat{x} \notin A \cup \mathrm{fn}(\ell) \cup (\mathrm{fn}(P) - x)$ *and* $\hat{Q}$ *such that* $A, \hat{x} \vdash \{^{\hat{x}}/_x\}P \xrightarrow{\ell} \hat{Q}$ *and* $Q \equiv (\boldsymbol{\nu}\,\hat{x})\hat{Q}$.

(b) *there exists* y, o, v, $\hat{Q}$ *and* $\hat{x} \notin A \cup \mathrm{fn}(y,o) \cup (\mathrm{fn}(P) - x)$ *such that* $\ell = \overline{y}^o v$, $A, \hat{x} \vdash \{^{\hat{x}}/_x\}P \xrightarrow{\overline{y}^o v} \hat{Q}$, $\hat{x} \in \mathrm{fn}(v)$, $\neg\mathrm{mv}(o)$ *and* $Q \equiv \hat{Q}$.

(c) *there exists* y, o, v, $\hat{Q}$ *and* $\hat{x} \notin A \cup \mathrm{fn}(o) \cup (\mathrm{fn}(P) - x)$ *such that* $\ell = \overline{y}^o v$, $A, \hat{x} \vdash \{^{\hat{x}}/_x\}P \xrightarrow{\overline{y}^o v} \hat{Q}$, $\hat{x} \in \mathrm{fn}(y, v)$, $\mathrm{mv}(o)$ *and* $Q \equiv \hat{Q}$.

Reductions Imply Transitions This direction of the equivalence has two main parts: we must show that transitions are invariant under structural congruence and construct τ-transitions for each reduction axiom.

Proposition 15 *If* $P' \equiv P$ *then* $A \vdash P' \xrightarrow{\ell} Q$ *iff* $A \vdash P \xrightarrow{\ell} Q$.

Proof A lengthy induction on the size of derivation of $P' \equiv P$. □

Lemma 16 *If* $\mathrm{fn}(P) \subseteq A$ *and* $P \to Q$ *then* $A \vdash P \xrightarrow{\tau} Q$.

Proof Induction on derivations of $P \to Q$, constructing derivations of τ-transitions for the reduction axioms (Red Up), (Red Down), (Red Comm) and (Red Repl), and using Proposition 15 for the (Red Struct) case. □

Transitions Imply Reductions For the converse direction we first show that if a process has an output or input transition then it contains a corresponding output, input or box subterm.

Lemma 17 *If* $A \vdash P \xrightarrow{\overline{z}^o v} P'$ *then* $P \equiv (\boldsymbol{\nu}\,\mathrm{fn}(z, v) - A)(\overline{z}^o v \mid P')$

Lemma 18 *If* $A \vdash Q \xrightarrow{x^\iota v} Q'$ *then there exist* B, p, Q_1 *and* Q_2 *such that* $B \cap (A \cup \mathrm{fn}(x^\iota v)) = \{\}$ *and either* $Q \equiv (\boldsymbol{\nu}\,B)(x^\iota p.Q_1 \mid Q_2)$ *and* $Q' \equiv (\boldsymbol{\nu}\,B)(\{^v/_p\}Q_1 \mid Q_2)$ *or* $Q \equiv (\boldsymbol{\nu}\,B)(!\,x^\iota p.Q_1 \mid Q_2)$ *and* $Q' \equiv (\boldsymbol{\nu}\,B)(\{^v/_p\}Q_1 \mid !\,x^\iota p.Q_1 \mid Q_2)$.

Lemma 19 *If* $A \vdash Q \xrightarrow{x^{\overline{n}} v} Q'$ *then there exist* B, Q_1 *and* Q_2 *such that* $B \cap (A \cup \mathrm{fn}(x^{\overline{n}} v)) = \{\}$, $Q \equiv (\boldsymbol{\nu}\,B)(n[Q_1] \mid Q_2)$ *and* $Q' \equiv (\boldsymbol{\nu}\,B)(n[(\overline{x}^{\uparrow} v \mid Q_1)] \mid Q_2)$.

Lemma 20 *If* $A \vdash P \xrightarrow{\tau} Q$ *then* $P \to Q$.

Proof Induction on derivations of $A \vdash P \xrightarrow{\tau} Q$, using the preceding three lemmas for the (Trans Box-1) and (Trans Comm) rules. □

The proof of Theorem 1, i.e. that if $\mathrm{fn}(P) \subseteq A$ then $A \vdash P \xrightarrow{\tau} Q$ iff $P \to Q$, is now immediate from Lemmas 16 and 20.

B Properties of $\mathcal{W}_1$

Explicit Characterisation The simple security properties of $\mathcal{W}_1$ are proved using an explicit characterisation of the states and labelled transitions of $\mathcal{W}_1[P]$. If N is a finite set of names, a is a name and $\mathcal{A}$ and Q are processes define

$$[\![a; N; \mathcal{A}; Q]\!] \stackrel{def}{=} (\boldsymbol{\nu}\,N \cup \{a\})(\ \mathcal{A} \mid a[Q] \mid !\,in^{\uparrow} y.\overline{in}^a y \mid !\,out^a y.\overline{out}^{\uparrow} y\ )$$

Say the 4-tuple a, N, $\mathcal{A}$, Q is *good* if N, $\{a\}$, and $\{in, out\}$ are pairwise disjoint, $\mathcal{A}$ is a parallel composition of outputs of the forms

$$\overline{out}^a v,\ \overline{out}^{\uparrow} v,\ \overline{in}^a v,\ \overline{x}^a v \text{ where } x \notin \{out, a\}$$

with $a \notin \mathrm{fn}(v)$ in each case, and Q is a process with $a \notin \mathrm{fn}(Q)$. Say a process P is good if $P \equiv [\![a; N; \mathcal{A}; Q]\!]$ for some good a, N, $\mathcal{A}$, Q.

Lemma 21 *If* $a \notin \mathrm{fn}(P)$ *then* $\mathcal{W}_1[P] \equiv [\![a; \emptyset; 0; P]\!]$, *hence* $\mathcal{W}_1[P]$ *is good.*

We define a transition relation $A \vdash P \stackrel{\ell}{\rightharpoonup} Q$ as the least satisfying the rules in Figure 2.

Lemma 22 *For all good* P *we have* $A \vdash P \xrightarrow{\ell} P'$ *iff* $A \vdash P \stackrel{\ell}{\rightharpoonup} P'$. *Moreover, if* $A \vdash P \stackrel{\ell}{\rightharpoonup} P'$ *then* P' *is good.*

Purity Proposition 2 can now be proved by induction on k using Lemma 22.

Honesty Proposition 5, that the unary wrapper $\mathcal{W}_1$ is honest, can be proved by giving an explicit h-bisimulation. Define

$$\langle\!\langle a; N; \mathcal{A}; Q \rangle\!\rangle \stackrel{def}{=} (\boldsymbol{\nu}\,N)(Q \mid \{\!\!|\ \overline{out}^{\uparrow} v \mid \overline{out}^{a} v \in \mathcal{A}\ |\!\!\} \mid \{\!\!|\ \overline{out}^{\uparrow} v \mid \overline{out}^{\uparrow} v \in \mathcal{A}\ |\!\!\} \mid \{\!\!|\ \overline{x}^{\uparrow} v \mid \overline{x}^{a} v \in \mathcal{A} \wedge x \neq out\ |\!\!\} \mid \{\!\!|\ \overline{in}^{\uparrow} v \mid \overline{in}^{a} v \in \mathcal{A}\ |\!\!\}\ )$$

$$
\begin{array}{rrcll}
 & A \vdash [\![a;N;\mathcal{A};Q]\!] & \xrightarrow{in^{\uparrow}v} & [\![a;N;\mathcal{A} \mid \overline{in}^{a} v;Q]\!] & \mathrm{fn}(v) \cap (N \cup \{a\}) = \emptyset \\
 & A \vdash [\![a;N;\mathcal{A} \mid \overline{in}^{a} v;Q]\!] & \xrightarrow{\tau} & [\![a;N;\mathcal{A};Q \mid \overline{in}^{\uparrow} v]\!] & \\
A,N,a \vdash Q \xrightarrow{\overline{out}^{\uparrow}v} Q' & A \vdash [\![a;N;\mathcal{A};Q]\!] & \xrightarrow{\tau} & [\![a;N,\mathrm{fn}(v)-(A,N,a);\mathcal{A} \mid \overline{out}^{a} v;Q']\!] & \\
A,N,a \vdash Q \xrightarrow{\overline{x}^{\uparrow}v} Q' & A \vdash [\![a;N;\mathcal{A};Q]\!] & \xrightarrow{\tau} & [\![a;N,\mathrm{fn}(x,v)-(A,N,a);\mathcal{A} \mid \overline{x}^{a} v;Q']\!] & \\
 & A \vdash [\![a;N;\mathcal{A} \mid \overline{out}^{a} v;Q]\!] & \xrightarrow{\tau} & [\![a;N;\mathcal{A} \mid \overline{out}^{\uparrow} v;Q]\!] & \\
 & A \vdash [\![a;N;\mathcal{A} \mid \overline{out}^{\uparrow} v;Q]\!] & \xrightarrow{\overline{out}^{\uparrow}v} & [\![a;N-\mathrm{fn}(v);\mathcal{A};Q]\!] & \\
A,N,a \vdash Q \xrightarrow{\tau} Q' & A \vdash [\![a;N;\mathcal{A};Q]\!] & \xrightarrow{\tau} & [\![a;N;\mathcal{A};Q']\!] & \\
A \vdash P \xrightarrow{\ell} P' \equiv P'' & A \vdash P & \xrightarrow{\ell} & P'' &
\end{array}
$$

For all rules we have a sidecondition that the 4-tuple in the left hand side of the conclusion is good and that the free names of the process on the left hand side of the conclusion are contained in A. For the fourth rule we have a side condition that $x \neq out$.

Figure 2. Explicit Characterisation of the Transitions of $\mathcal{W}_1[P]$

Now take the family of relations below.

$$
\begin{array}{l}
R_A = \equiv \circ \{ [\![a;N;\mathcal{A};Q]\!], \langle\!\langle a;N;\mathcal{A};Q \rangle\!\rangle \quad | \\
\qquad a;N;\mathcal{A};Q \text{ good and } \mathrm{fn}([\![a;N;\mathcal{A};Q]\!]) \subseteq A \} \circ \equiv
\end{array}
$$

One can check that for any P with $a \notin \mathrm{fn}(P)$ and $A \supseteq \mathrm{fn}(\mathcal{W}_1[P])$ we have $\mathcal{W}_1[P] \; R_A \; P$ and that R is an h-bisimulation.

References

[1] M. Abadi. Secrecy by typing in security protocols. In *TACS '97 (open lecture), LNCS 1281*, pages 611–638, Sept. 1997.

[2] M. Abadi, C. Fournet, and G. Gonthier. Secure implementation of channel abstractions. In *LICS 98 (Indiana)*, pages 105–116. IEEE, Computer Society Press, July 1998.

[3] M. Abadi and A. D. Gordon. A calculus for cryptographic protocols: The spi calculus. In *Proceedings of the Fourth ACM Conference on Computer and Communications Security, Zürich*, pages 36–47. ACM Press, Apr. 1997.

[4] R. M. Amadio. An asynchronous model of locality, failure, and process mobility. In *Proc. COORDINATION 97, LNCS 1282*, 1997.

[5] R. M. Amadio, I. Castellani, and D. Sangiorgi. On bisimulations for the asynchronous π-calculus. In U. Montanari and V. Sassone, editors, *CONCUR '96*, volume 1119 of *Lecture Notes in Computer Science*, pages 147–162. Springer-Verlag, 1996.

[6] R. M. Amadio and S. Prasad. Localities and failures. In P. S. Thiagarajan, editor, *Proceedings of* 14th *FST and TCS Conference, FST-TCS'94. LNCS 880*, pages 205–216. Springer-Verlag, 1994.

[7] G. Back, P. Tullmann, L. Stoller, W. C. Hsieh, and J. Lepreau. Java operating systems: Design and implementation. Technical Report UUCS-98-015, University of Utah, Department of Computer Science, Aug. 6, 1998.

[8] G. Boudol. Asynchrony and the π-calculus (note). Rapport de Recherche 1702, INRIA Sofia-Antipolis, May 1992.

[9] L. Cardelli and A. D. Gordon. Mobile ambients. In *Proc. of Foundations of Software Science and Computation Structures (FoSSaCS), ETAPS'98, LNCS 1378*, pages 140–155, Mar. 1998.

[10] L. Cardelli and A. D. Gordon. Types for mobile ambients. In *Proceedings of the 26th ACM Symposium on Principles of Programming Languages*, 1999.

[11] B. Ford, M. Hibler, J. Lepreau, P. Tullman, G. Back, and S. Clawson. Microkernels meet recursive virtual machines. In USENIX, editor, *2nd Symposium on Operating Systems Design and Implementation (OSDI '96), October 28–31, 1996. Seattle, WA*, pages 137–151, Berkeley, CA, USA, Oct. 1996. USENIX.

[12] C. Fournet, G. Gonthier, J.-J. Lévy, L. Maranget, and D. Rémy. A calculus of mobile agents. In *Proceedings of CONCUR '96. LNCS 1119*, pages 406–421. Springer-Verlag, Aug. 1996.

[13] I. Goldberg, D. Wagner, R. Thomas, and E. A. Brewer. A secure environment for untrusted helper applications. In *Sixth USENIX Security Symposium*, San Jose, California, July 1996.

[14] L. Gong. Java security architecture (JDK 1.2). Technical report, JavaSoft, July 1997. Revision 0.5.

[15] N. Heintze and J. G. Riecke. The SLam calculus: Programming with secrecy and integrity. In *Proceedings of the 25th POPL*, Jan. 1998.

[16] M. Hennessy and J. Riely. Resource access control in systems of mobile agents. In *Workshop on High-Level Concurrent Languages*, 1998. Full version as University of Sussex technical report CSTR 98/02.

[17] M. Hennessy and J. Riely. Type-safe execution of mobile agents in anonymous networks. In *Workshop on Mobile Object Systems, (satellite of ECOOP '98)*, 1998. Full version as University of Sussex technical report CSTR 98/03.

[18] K. Honda and M. Tokoro. An object calculus for asynchronous communication. In P. America, editor, *Proceedings of ECOOP '91, LNCS 512*, pages 133–147, July 1991.

[19] N. Islam, R. Anand, T. Jaeger, and J. R. Rao. A flexible security system for using Internet content. *IEEE Software*, 14(5):52–59, Sept./Oct. 1997.

[20] M. B. Jones. Interposition agents: Transparently interposing user code at the system interface. In J. Vitek and C. Jensen, editors, *Secure Internet Programing: Security Issues for Mobile and Distributed Objects*. Springer Verlag, 1999.

[21] B. W. Lampson. A note on the confinement problem. *Communications of the ACM*, 16(10):613–615, 1973.

[22] G. Lowe and B. Roscoe. Using CSP to detect Errors in the TMN Protocol. *IEEE Transactions on Software Engineering*, 23(10):659–669, 1997.

[23] J. McLean. Security models. In J. Marciniak, editor, *Encyclopedia of Software Engineering*. Wiley & Sons, 1994.

[24] R. Milner, J. Parrow, and D. Walker. A calculus of mobile processes, Parts I + II. *Information and Computation*, 100(1):1–77, 1992.

[25] A. C. Myers. Jflow: Practical static information flow control. In *Proceedings of the 26th ACM Symposium on Principles of Programming Languages (POPL 99)*, 1999.

[26] A. C. Myers and B. Liskov. Complete, safe information flow with decentralized labels. In *Proceedings of the 1998 IEEE Symposium on Security and Privacy, Oakland, California*, pages 186–197, 1998.

[27] G. C. Necula and P. Lee. Safe, untrusted agents using proof-carrying code. In G. Vigna, editor, *Mobile Agents and Security*, volume 1419 of *LNCS*, pages 61–91. SV, 1998.

[28] J. Riely and M. Hennessy. A typed language for distributed mobile processes. In *Proceedings of the 25th POPL*, Jan. 1998.

[29] F. B. Schneider. Enforceable security policies. Technical Report TR 98-1664, Computer Science Department, Cornell University, Ithaca, New York, Jan. 1998.

[30] P. Sewell. Global/local subtyping for a distributed π-calculus. Technical Report 435, University of Cambridge, Aug. 1997. Available from `http://www.cl.cam.ac.uk/users/pes20/`.

[31] P. Sewell. Global/local subtyping and capability inference for a distributed π-calculus. In *Proceedings of ICALP '98, LNCS 1443*, pages 695–706, 1998.

[32] P. Sewell. A brief introduction to applied π, Jan. 1999. Lecture notes for the Mathfit Instructional Meeting on Recent Advances in Semantics and Types for Concurrency: Theory and Practice, July 1998. Available from `http://www.cl.cam.ac.uk/users/pes20/`.

[33] P. Sewell, P. T. Wojciechowski, and B. C. Pierce. Location independence for mobile agents. In *Workshop on Internet Programming Languages, Chicago*, May 1998.

[34] P. Sewell, P. T. Wojciechowski, and B. C. Pierce. Location-independent communication for mobile agents: a two-level architecture. Submitted for publication. Draft available from `http://www.cl.cam.ac.uk/users/pes20/`, 1998.

[35] J. Vitek and C. Bryce. Secure mobile code: the javaseal experiment. Manuscript, 1999.

[36] J. Vitek and G. Castagna. Towards a calculus of mobile computations. In *Workshop on Internet Programming Languages, Chicago*, May 1998.

[37] J. Vitek and G. Castagna. Mobile Agents and Hostile Hosts. In *Journées Francophones des Langaages Applicatifs (JFLA99)*, Morizine, France, Feb 1999.

[38] D. Volpano, C. Irvine, and G. Smith. A sound type system for secure flow analysis. *Journal of Computer Security*, 4:167–187, May 1996.

[39] D. Volpano and G. Smith. Confinement properties for programming languages. *SIGACT News*, 29(3):33–42, Sept. 1998.

[40] G. Winskel and M. Nielsen. Models for concurrency. In Abramsky, Gabbay, and Maibaum, editors, *Handbook of Logic in Computer Science*, volume IV, pages 1–148. Oxford University Press, 1995.

Security Function Interactions

Pierre Bieber
ONERA CERT
2, avenue Edouard Belin
31055 Toulouse Cedex France
email: Pierre.Bieber@cert.fr

Abstract

We use a compositional framework to model security architectures involving heterogeneous and distributed security functions. Our goal is to assist the ITSEC evaluation of suitability, binding and vulnerability of a set of security functions. We propose constraints that security functions should guarantee in order to interact consistently and securely with other functions. To illustrate these notions we study the interactions of various components of a secure LAN.

Introduction

When designing a security architecture for a distributed application it is very likely that no security function can take into account every security objectives. Hence the global security of such an application will depend on various security functions. Multiple instances of the same security function could be used to perform the same controls on various components of the distributed system. And various kinds of functions are needed when there are different kind of security objectives such as authentication and access control.

If the system under construction has to be evaluated according to ITSEC criteria [3] each of the functions included in the security architecture should be shown correct with respect to security. In order to achieve an asssurance-correctness level higher than $E4$, a security function should be related with an existing security model.

But developing correct security functions is not enough, it is also important to show that, when put together, these security functions guarantee the global security objectives of the distributed system. For that purpose, ITSEC assurance-effectiveness evaluation is based on various analyses that the system developper should conduct, among them we have:

- A suitability analysis that links the security functions with the threats. The goal of this analysis is to show how a security function counter a given set of threats.
- A binding analysis that investigates the ability of the security functions to work together in a way that is mutually supportive and provides an integrated whole.
- A vulnerability assessment that, among other things, should study the existing ways to deactivate, bypass or circumvent security functions.

The corresponding documentation is notoriously difficult to write or to evaluate. So we believe that there is a need for technical guidelines that go beyond what is offered by the Information Technology Security Evaluation Manual (ITSEM) [4]. We think that a model that describes how functions can interact in a distributed system could be useful. The suitability analysis might be conducted by studying the interactions between a security function and the functions describing the controled entities that might perform unallowed actions. The binding analysis could consist of the study of the consistency of security function interactions. Ways to bypass a security function could also be assessed by studying the interactions between that security function and the remaining functions of the system.

In this paper, we show how to use a compositional specification framework in order to assist ITSEC assurance-effectiveness evaluation. We first describe the distributed security architecture of a secure LAN. Then, in the second section, we present a framework to compose formal specifications. In the third section we use the framework to model the interactions between various access control devices of the secure LAN. Finally, we propose constraints on specifications to be composed in order to check that their composition is both consistent and secure.

1 SMAC Security Functions

In the following of the paper we consider the security functions of a secure LAN based on the SMAC protocol,

1063-6900/99 $10.00 © 1999 IEEE

see [5]. Each host of the network has its Ethernet port connected to an Access Control Switch (ACS) that can cut the connection to the communication medium. Each ACS controls its host attempts to send or receive messages according to an authorisation. Authorisations are distributed to the ACS by a Central Security Server (CSS), that is responsible for the enforcement of the network security policy. An instance of network security policy could state that hosts may only communicate with other hosts in the same security domain. The CSS uses a security sub-network (SSN) to exchange authorisation information with ACS components.

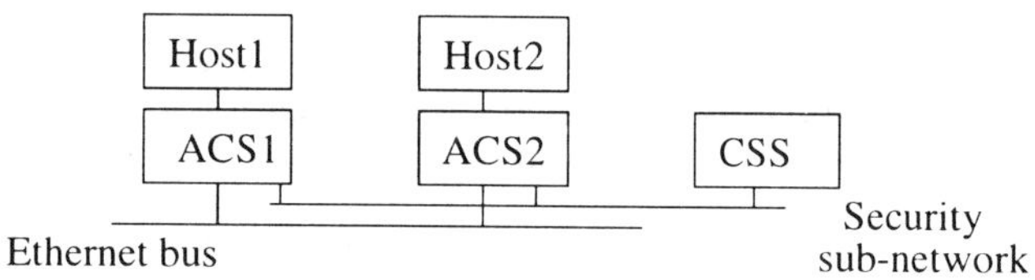

Figure 1. Secure LAN

1.1 Specification Semantics

A specification $Spec = (Sig, Behav)$ contains a signature $Sig = (Dom,\ ATT,\ Action)$ that gives the vocabulary of the component and $Behav = (ActDefs,\ Properties)$ that is a description of its behaviour. ATT is a set of attributes and Dom is the value domain, a state belonging to $State$ is a function that associates a value with each attribute. $Action$ is a set of actions the component can execute. Following specification notations as the B-method Abstract Machine Notation (see [1]) we propose to describe the behaviour of the system in two ways : an imperative one that defines a transition function over states and a declarative one that defines temporal properties that hold on these states.

The imperative definition of a system behaviour is given by $ActDefs = (init,\ step,\ run)$ where $init$ is the name of the initial state, $step$ models the transition function over states associated with an action symbol, $step(ac, cs)$ computes the state reached when action ac is performed in state cs and run is a transition function associated with sequences of actions. $run(\alpha_1, cs)$ computes the state reached when the list of actions α_1 is performed in state cs. If α_1 is empty then the state reached is cs. Otherwise, α_1 is made of action ac and sub-list α_0, α_0 is performed in cs and then action ac is performed. This means that actions in an action list are performed in reverse order.

$State = ATT \rightarrow Dom,$
$init : State,$
$step : Action \times State \rightarrow State,$
$run : list[Action] \times State \rightarrow State,$

$$run(\alpha_1, cs) = \begin{cases} cs & \text{if } \alpha_1 = null \\ step(ac, run(cs, \alpha_0)) & \text{if } \alpha_1 = ac.\alpha_0 \end{cases}$$

$Always : (State \rightarrow boolean) \rightarrow boolean,$
$Always(P) \equiv \forall \alpha : P(run(init, \alpha)),$

The declarative definition of a system behaviour is given by $Properties$, a collection of formulae containing temporal operators and predicates. A predicate is a function from states to boolean. In this paper, we only consider temporal operator $Always(P)$ meaning that P holds in the states reached by applying any list of actions in the initial state.

1.2 SMAC Security Function Specifications

In order to illustrate the formal definitions we just gave we present the formal specification of SMAC security functions.

The specification of an ACS component contains two boolean attributes: in that means that the entity is using the communication medium, ok meaning that the entity is authorised to use it. We consider four actions, use meaning that the entity begins to use the medium, $release$ meaning that the entity stops to use the medium, $granted$ meaning that the entity receives an authorisation message and $forbidden$ meaning that the entity receives a revocation message. The properties satisfied by an entity behaviour is that, in every state, if the entity uses the medium then it is authorised to.

Specification
  ACS
Attributes
  $in, ok : boolean;$
Initialisation
  $init = in, ok := 0, 0;$
Actions
  $use = in := 1$ if $ok;$
  $release = in := 0;$
  $granted = ok := 1;$
  $forbidden = in, ok := 0, 0$ if $\neg in;$
Properties
  $Always(in \Rightarrow ok)$

We use an abbreviated notation to describe the specification, it is trivial to derive the definitions of ATT, Dom and $Actions$ from this notation. To describe actions in a compact fashion, we use guarded substitutions. $guard$ associates a state predicate with each action and sub associates a multiple substitution with each action, such a substitution is a partial function from the set of attributes to the value domain. $step(ac, cs)$ is equal to cs overridden with $sub(ac)$ (noted $cs \oplus sub(ac)$) if predicate $guard(ac)$ holds in state cs otherwise $step(action, cs)$ is equal to cs. The state $cs \oplus sub(ac)$ associates the same value than cs with an attribute if it does not belong to the domain of $sub(ac)$ and it associates the same value than $sub(ac)$ otherwise.

$guard : Action \rightarrow State \rightarrow boolean,$
$partialState = ATT \nrightarrow Dom$
$sub : Action \rightarrow partialState,$

$$step(ac, cs) = \begin{cases} cs \oplus sub(ac) & \text{if } guard(ac)(cs) \\ cs & \text{otherwise} \end{cases}$$

Similarly, we use a logic style notation to denote predicates in an abbreviated fashion, for instance we use $in \Rightarrow ok$ instead of the corresponding function that associates 1 with the states cs where $(cs(in) \Rightarrow cs(ok))$ is true and 0 otherwise.

CSS describes how authorisations are distributed to the ACS instances. CSS has two boolean attributes ok_H (resp. ok_L) meaning that High-level (resp. Low level) hosts are granted the permission to use the communication medium, action $grant_H$ (resp. $grant_L$) authorizes High-level (resp. Low-level) hosts to use the medium. The specification guarantees that it is never the case that High-level and Low-level hosts are simultaneously granted the right to access to the medium.

Specification
  CSS
Attributes
  $ok_H, ok_L : boolean,$
Initial state
  $ok_H, ok_L := 0, 0;$
Actions
  $grant_H = ok_H, ok_L := 1, 0;$
  $grant_L = ok_H, ok_L := 0, 1;$
Properties
  $Always(\neg(ok_H \wedge ok_L))$

The SSN component describes the service offered by the sub-network dedicated to authorisation transport. We provide a simple model of authorisation transmission that assumes that this transmission is instantaneous. Specification SSN has only one attribute ok that is true whenever the current message is an authorisation and false if the message is a revocation. Action $transmit\_ok$ models the transmission of an authorisation and $transmit\_nok$ models the transmission of a revocation.

Specification
  SSN
Attributes
  $ok : boolean;$
Initialisation
  $init = ok := 0;$
Actions
  $transmit\_ok = ok := 1;$
  $transmit\_nok = ok := 0;$

Before trying to compose these specifications, we should prove for each of them that the declarative and imperative descriptions are consistent. For instance, for the ACS specification, we should check, according to the definition of the $Always$ operator, that in the initial state $(in \Rightarrow ok)$ is true and we should also prove that actions use, $release$, $forbidden$ and $granted$ preserve this state predicate.

2 A Specification Composition Framework

We would like to combine the specification of the ACS component with that of CSS in order to model a LAN guaranteeing that hosts in different security domains cannot communicate. We propose to connect ACS and CSS through the specification of the service offered by component SSN. The result of the composition of ACS and CSS is a new specification called $OneACS$ that could be regarded as the description of the security service offered by a secure LAN with one host. We then compose several instances of this specification together in order to model a secure LAN with several hosts.

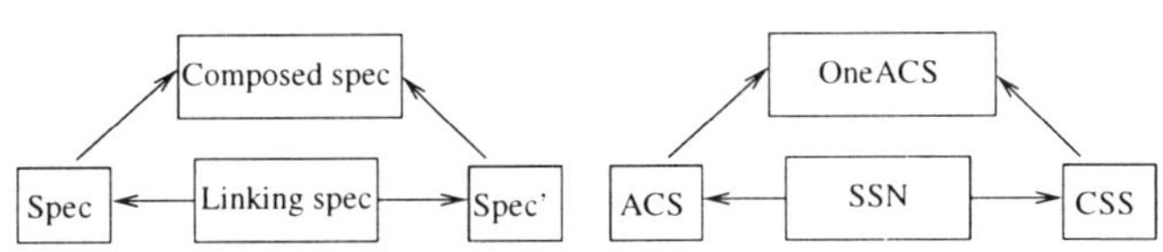

Figure 2. Specification composition

We follow the framewok defined by V. Wiels [12, 14] that uses Fiadeiro and Maibaum works on the combination of temporal logic and category theory [6]. In this framework, both component specifications ($Spec$ and $Spec'$) are connected through a linking specification $Lspec$ by a morphism. Such a morphism relates specification $Lspec$ and $Spec$ if the behaviour of $Spec$ is a refinement of the behaviour of $Lspec$ (i.e. every property enforced by the linking specification $Lspec$ should also be satisfied by $Spec$).

The composition rule defines the composed specification $Cspec$ and two morphims relating $Spec$ and $Spec'$ with $Cspec$. This rule states that the composed specification is a minimal refinement of both $Spec$ and $Spec'$ (i.e. no superfluous details are added to $Spec$ or $Spec'$ in order to build $Cspec$). A formal counterpart of this composition rule in terms of a categoric operation called push-out was given by Fiadeiro and Maibaum in [6] and V. Wiels in [14].

2.1 Signature Connection

A signature morphism connects the vocabularies of two specifications: attributes and actions of one specification are mapped onto attributes and actions of the other specification. In the following we assume that connected specifications share the same value domain.

ACS	SSN	CSS
in		
use		
$release$		ok_L
ok	ok	ok_H
$granted$	$transmit\_ok$	$grant\_H$
$forbidden$	$transmit\_nok$	$grant\_L$

Figure 3. Morphisms connecting SSN with ACS and CSS

We connect SSN and CSS with a morphism that relates ok with ok_H, $transmit\_ok$ with $grant\_H$ and $transmit\_nok$ with $grant\_L$. Similarly, SSN is connected to ACS with a morphism that relates ok with ok, $transmit\_ok$ with $granted$ and $transmit\_nok$ with $forbidden$. Linking attribute ok with ok_H means that the host controled by this ACS is authorised to use the medium at the same time that High-level hosts.

We call shared attributes and shared actions the members of the range of the signature morphism. For instance, ok is a shared attribute, $grant$ and $forbidden$ are shared actions whereas in is a private attribute and use, $release$ are private actions.

2.2 Property connection

We use the signature morphism in order to relate $Properties$ enforced by two connected specifications. A formula is related with the same formula where attributes were replaced with their image by the signature morphism. For instance, the image of formula $Always(\neg(ok_H \wedge ok_L))$ by the two morphisms shown in figure 3 is $Always(\neg(ok \wedge nok))$. More formally, the image by morphism m, connecting $Lspec$ and $Spec$, of predicate P is a predicate that takes in state cs of $State$ the same value than P in state cs_l of $State_l$ whenever cs_l is the state equivalent to cs with respect to m ($MorphPred$ property). Two states are equivalent with respect to m whenever these states associate the same value to attributes of ATT_l and their image by m (eqv property).

$eqv =$
$cs_l \sim_m cs \Leftrightarrow \forall at : ATT_l, cs_l(at) = cs(m(at)),$
$MorphPred(m) =$
$\forall cs_l : State_l, cs : State, P : State_l \to boolean$
$cs_l \sim_m cs \Rightarrow P(cs_l) = m(P)(cs),$

Furthermore to be correct, the morphism should be a refinement relation that preserves temporal properties: if P is an invariant in $Lspec$ then $m(P)$ should be an invariant in $Spec$.
$Ref(m) = \forall P : Pred_l, Always(P) \Rightarrow Always(m(P)),$

2.3 Composed Specification

$Cspec$ is the result of the composition of specifications $Spec$ and $Spec'$ related to $Lspec$ by two morphisms. Two renaming morphisms connecting the signature of $Spec$ and $Spec'$ with the signature of $Cspec$ are defined. Private attributes and actions of $Spec$ and of $Spec'$ are renamed in order to avoid name collisions. For instance, the new name is the original attribute or action name prefixed with its specification name. Shared attributes and actions of $Spec$ and $Spec'$ are renamed with the same name. For instance, the new name is the name of the shared action or attribute in $Lspec$.

We call $OneACS$ the result of the composition of ACS and CSS using the morphisms presented in figure 3. The two renaming morphisms that relate attribute and action names of ACS and CSS with attribute and action names of $OneACS$ are summarised in the table shown in figure 4:

ACS	$OneACS$	CSS
in	$ACS.in$	
use	$ACS.use$	
$release$	$ACS.release$ $CSS.ok_L$	ok_L
ok	ok	ok_H
$granted$	$transmit\_ok$	$grant\_H$
$forbidden$	$transmit\_nok$	$grant\_L$

Figure 4. Morphisms connecting ACS and CSS with $OneACS$

Renaming morphisms can be used directly to compute the definition of $Cspec$ actions that are connected to a private action of $Spec$ or $Spec'$. It is sufficient to rename all the attributes in the corresponding $Spec$ action definition. In the case of $Cspec$ actions connected to shared actions in $Spec$ and $Spec'$, a substitution is defined that associates attributes with the same value that correponding actions in $Spec$ and $Spec'$. The guard of a shared action is the conjunction of the image by the renaming morphisms of the guards of the corresponding actions in $Spec$ and $Spec'$. The property enforced by $Cspec$ is the conjunction of the image by the renaming morphisms of the properties of $Spec$ and $Spec'$.

3 Using the compositional framework

3.1 One User Secure LAN

The specification $OneACS$ describes a LAN with a unique host that is controled by an ACS communicating with CSS. The specifcation has three attributes: $ACS.in$ that is true whenever the host is using the Ethernet medium, ok_H that is true when High-level hosts are authorised to use the medium and $CSS.ok_L$ that is true when Low-level hosts are authorised to use the medium.

Action $ACS.use$ (resp. $ACS.release$) is obtained by renaming attributes in action use (resp. $release$). The guard of action $transmit\_ok$ (resp. $transmit\_ok$) is obtained by renaming attributes in the conjunction of the guards of $granted$ and $grant_H$ (resp. $forbidden$ and $grant_L$). The substitution of action $transmit\_ok$ (resp. $transmit\_ok$) is obtained by renaming attributes in the union of the substitutions of $granted$ and $grant_H$ (resp. $forbidden$ and $grant_L$).

Similarly, the properties that are enforced by $OneACS$ is obtained by renaming the conjunction of the properties of ACS and CSS.

Specification
  $OneACS$
Attributs
  $ACS.in, ok_H, CSS.ok_L$: $boolean$;
Initial state
  $init = ACS.in, ok_H, CSS.ok_L := 0, 0, 0$;
Actions
  $ACS.use = ACS.in := 1$ if ok_H;
  $ACS.release = ACS.in := 0$;
  $transmit\_ok = ok_H, CSS.ok_L := 1, 0$;
  $transmit\_nok = ACS.in, ok_H, CSS.ok_L := 0, 0, 1$
    if $\neg ACS.in$;
Properties
  $Always(ACS.in \Rightarrow ok_H)$
  $Always(\neg(ok_H \wedge CSS.ok_L))$

It is generally not compulsory to compute the definition of the composed specification actions because we are mainly interested in the properties that are satisfied by these actions. In the case of $OneACS$ we can derive that whenever the host is using the Ethernet medium then attribute $CSS.ok_L$ is false ($Always(ACS.in \Rightarrow \neg CSS.ok_L)$).

3.2 Multiuser Secure LAN

We now want to model a LAN with several users. For that purpose, we consider several instances of the ACS specification called ACS, ACS_2 and ACS_3. ACS is controling a High-level host whereas ACS_2 and ACS_3 are controling Low-level hosts.

ACS_i	SSN	CSS
in		
use		
$release$		ok_H
ok	ok	ok_L
$granted$	$transmit\_ok$	$grant\_L$
$forbidden$	$transmit\_nok$	$grant\_H$

Figure 5. Morphisms connecting SSN with ACS_i and CSS, for $i = 2, 3$

For each ACS_i we build a composed specification $OneACS_i$ by connecting ACS_i to CSS through SSN. $OneACS$ is obtained by using exactly the same connection morphisms that we used in the previous chapter. For $OneACS_2$ and $OneACS_3$ we use the morphisms described in figure 5.

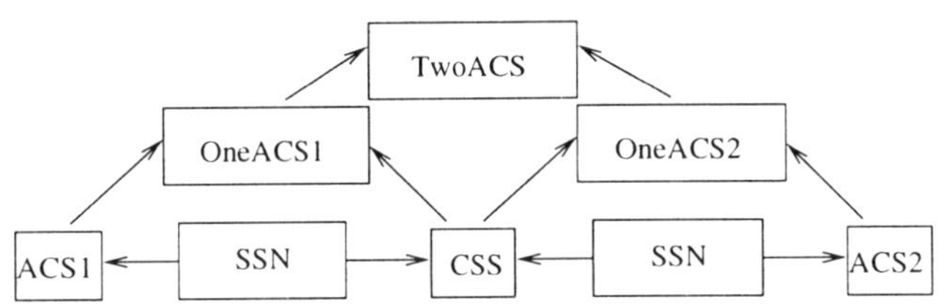

Figure 6. Two user LAN specification

To model a LAN with several users we compose several $OneACS_i$ specifications using CSS as the shared specification. For instance, to model a secure LAN with two users, we will use specifications $OneACS$ and $OneACS_2$ that model the dialogue between one user and the CSS and we use CSS as a shared specification to model the fact that there is a unique CSS component. The connection morphism used between CSS and $OneACS_i$ is the morphism that is computed to produce $OneACS_i$. As this morphism is a correct refinement relation by construction, there is no need to check the correct morphism constraints.

The specification $TwoACS$ is the result of the composition of $OneACS$ and $OneACS_2$.

Specification
  $TwoACS$
Attributes
  $ACS.in, ACS_2.in, ok_H, ok_L$: $boolean$;
Initial state
  $init = ACS.in, ok_H, ACS_2.in, ok_L := 0, 0, 0, 0$;

$OneACS$	CSS	$OneACS_2$
$ACS.in$		$ACS_2.in$
$ACS.use$		$ACS_2.use$
$ACS.release$		$ACS_2.release$
$CSS.ok_L$	ok_L	ok
ok	ok_H	$CSS.ok_H$
$granted$	$grant\_H$	$forbidden$
$forbidden$	$grant\_L$	$granted$

Figure 7. Morphisms connecting CSS with $OneACS$ and $OneACS_2$

Actions
$ACS.use = ACS.in := 1$ if ok_H;
$ACS_2.use = ACS_2.in := 1$ if ok_L;
$ACS.release = ACS.in := 0$;
$ACS_2.release = ACS_2.in := 0$;
$grant_H = ACS_2.in, ok_H, ok_L := 0, 1, 0$ if $\neg ACS_2.in$;
$grant_L = ACS.in, ok_H, ok_L := 0, 0, 1$ if $\neg ACS.in$;
Properties
$Always(ACS.in \Rightarrow ok_H)$
$Always(ACS_2.in \Rightarrow ok_L)$
$Always(\neg(ok_H \wedge ok_L))$

The image by the morphisms described in figure 7 of $Always(\neg(ok_H \wedge CSS.ok_L))$ (a property enforced by $OneACS$) and of $Always\ (\neg(ok_L \wedge CSS.ok_H))$ (a property enforced by $OneACS_2$) is $Always(\ \neg(ok_H \wedge ok_L))$. The image by the morphisms of $Always(\ ACS.in \Rightarrow ok_H)$ and $Always(\ ACS_2.in \Rightarrow ok_L)$ is unchanged. Hence formulae $Always(\ ACS.in \Rightarrow ok_H)$, $Always(\ ACS_2.in \Rightarrow ok_L)$ and $Always(\ \neg(ok_H \wedge ok_L))$ belong to the properties of specification $TwoACS$. So, we can derive that $TwoACS$ guarantees property $Always(\ \neg(ACS.in \wedge ACS_2.in))$, i.e. it is never the case that the hosts controled by ACS and ACS_2 access the Ethernet medium at the same time.

If we want to add a third host to the network, we would just have to compose specification $TwoACS$ and $OneACS_3$ with CSS as the shared specification. The morphism relating CSS and $OneACS_3$ is the one used to build $OneACS_3$ and the identity morphism is used to relate CSS and $TwoACS$. The resulting specification would enforce property $Always(ACS_3.in \Rightarrow ok_L)$ and we could conclude that entities controled by ACS_2 or ACS_3 never use the Ethernet medium at the same time than ACS.

4 Suitability and Circumvention analysis

In the previous section we have established that the various security functions of SMAC (CSS, SSN and ACS instances) are consistent with respect to the global security property that SMAC should enforce. This was performed by studying properties enforced by the composition of security functions. This result could be provided to the evaluators in the context of an ITSEC "binding analysis" as we described it in the introduction of the paper.

To perform the "suitability analysis" of security functions we propose to compose specifications of the controled entities with a specification of the security functions. Then we can study whether the properties enforced by the security functions are preserved in the composed specification.

In the case of SMAC, it would be interesting to compose the specification of the service offered by the access control devices with the specification of the service usually offered to the hosts by a conventional Ethernet medium. So we could compose specification $TwoACS$ that we defined in the previous section and $TwoHost$ that would be obtained by composing the specification of two hosts connected by an Ethernet medium. Specification $TwoHosts$ would certainly contain, for each host, a transmission attribute stating whether the host is sending or receiving a message and actions starting and ending a transmission.

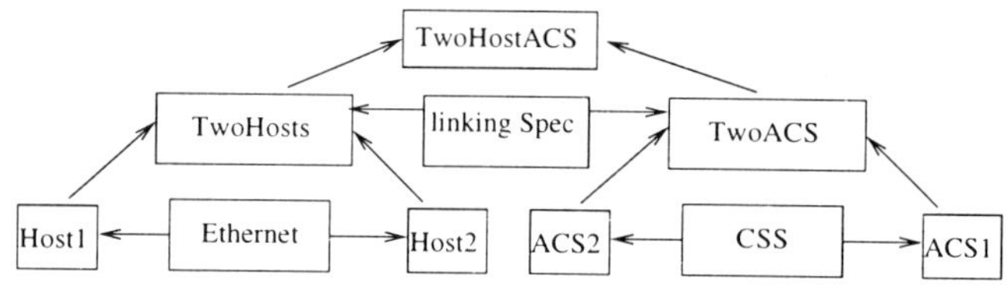

Figure 8. Composition of TwoHosts and TwoACS

If we use the compositional framework defined in the previous sections, we would have to describe a component that models the link between $TwoACS$ and $TwoHosts$. For instance, the linking specification could contain attributes called $ACS_1.in$, $ACS_2.in$ and actions $ACS_i.use$ and $ACS_i.release$, with the same definitions than in specification $TwoACS$. Then we could define morphisms that connect $ACS_i.use$ and $ACS_i.release$ actions of the linking specification with transmission actions of $TwoHost$ and the morphism could connect $ACS_i.in$ with the transmission status attribute. We call $TwoHostACS$ the resulting specification.

Let's recall that, if the two morphisms relating $Lspec$ with $Spec$ and $Spec'$ are correct, then the composed specification $Cspec$ guarantees the properties (with apropriate renaming of attributes) of both components $Spec$ and $Spec'$. So, if the morphisms relating the linking specification with both $TwoACS$ and $TwoHost$ are correct, the transmission actions performed by the hosts cannot invalidate the security properties guaranteed by ACS. Hence hosts cannot have an influence on the value of the global security property.

So, it seems that a good part of the suitability analysis can be performed very easily if we are able to show that the morphisms used to build specification $TwoHostACS$ are correctly defined. In the next section we investigate what are the constraints that should be checked on these morphisms to show that they are correct.

4.1 Composition Constraints

In the second section we have assumed that a correct morphism m relating $Lspec$ and $Spec$ should be a refinement relation between $Lspec$ and $Spec$. This implies that details added in the actions of $Spec$ should not affect the value of the image of invariant properties from $Lspec$. We note $Actions$ the set of actions of $Spec$ and $Actions_l$ the set of actions from $Lspec$. We can prove (see theorem 1 in annex) that m is a correct morphism if for any state reached by running a list of mixed shared and private actions in $Actions$ there is run of shared actions from $Actions_l$ that leads to an equivalent state with respect to m. We call this property weak non-interference $WNInt$ because it looks like the non-interference information flow control property (see [8, 9]) that aims at preventing highly confidential actions to interfere with public actions in order to leak confidential data. $WNInt$ is weaker than non-interference because it does not require the list of shared actions in $Actions_l$ to be obtained by removing all the private actions from the list of mixed shared and private actions in $Actions$.
$WNInt(m) =$
$\forall \alpha, \exists \alpha_l, run(\alpha_l, init_l) \sim_m run(\alpha, init)$

To prove that a morphism enforces non-interference it is sufficient to prove the three following properties (see theorem 2 in annex for a proof of this assertion):

1. Initial states should be equivalent with respect to m.
   $EqvInit(m) = init_l \sim_m init.$

2. The state reached by applying action $m(ac_l)$ in cs should be equivalent to cs_l or to the state reached by applying ac_l in cs_l whenever cs_l and cs are equivalent with respect to m.
   $EqvShared(m) = \forall ac_l, \forall cs_l, \forall cs, cs_l \sim_m cs \Rightarrow$
   $step(ac_l, cs_l) \sim_m step(m(ac_l), cs)$
   $\vee\ cs_l \sim_m step(m(ac_l), cs).$

3. If ac_1 is a private action, the state reached by applying ac_1 in cs should be equivalent to cs_l whenever cs_l and cs are equivalent with respect to m.
   $EqvPriv(m) = \forall ac_1, \forall cs_l, \forall cs, ac_1 \notin range(m)$
   $\wedge\ cs_l \sim_m cs \Rightarrow cs_l \sim_m step(ac_1, cs)$

To verify that a morphism is refinement relation one should check $EqvInit$ and the three following constraints that look like the usual refinement proof obligations (see theorem 3 and 4 in the annex for a proof of this property):

1. Shared attributes should never appear in the substitution of private actions.
   $NoPrivAlt(m) = \forall ac, \forall at,$
   $ac \notin range(m) \Rightarrow m(at) \notin domain(sub(ac))$

2. The guard of an action should be weaker than the guard of its refinement.
   $StrGuard(m) =$
   $\forall ac_l, \forall cs,$
   $guard(m(ac_l))(cs) \Rightarrow m(guard(ac_l))(cs),$

3. The substitution of an action and its refinement should agree on the values of refined attributes.
   $WidSub(m) = \forall ac_l, \forall at,$
   $sub(ac_l)(at) = sub(m(ac_l))(m(at)),$

The morphisms defined in figure 3 connecting SSN with CSS and ACS are refinement relations because:

- Initially, ok and ok_H are false (verification of $EqvInit$).
- Shared attribute ok does not appear in the substitution of private actions use and $release$ (verification of $NoPrivAlt$).
- The guards of $transmit\_ok$, $granted$ and $grant_H$ are equal to $true$. The guards of $transmit\_nok$ and $grant_L$ are equal to $true$. The guard of $forbidden$ is $\neg in$, it implies the guard of $transmit\_nok$ (verification of $StrGuard$).
- $grant_H$ associates the same value with ok_H than $transmit\_ok$ or $granted$ associates with ok (verification $WidSub$).

When we build $TwoHostACS$, shared attributes ok_H and ok_L can be considered as security attributes. We have required that private attributes ($ACS.in$ and $ACS_2.in$) should not interfere with these security attributes. This means that an entity controled by an ACS cannot alter security attributes in order to circumvent the access controls. Furthermore, in the composed specification $TwoHostACS$, hosts controled by ACS or ACS_2 cannot interact directly as only security actions ($grant_H$ and $grant_L$) are shared.

4.2 Composition Constraints for Secure Interactions

Because $WNInt$ is a weaker property than the non interference property as defined in [8], hosts controled by ACS or ACS_2 could interact indirectly. For instance, shared action $grant_H$ depends on the value of a private attribute because its guard is equal to $\neg ACS_2.in$. So, while ACS_2 does not stop using the medium, action $grant_H$ guard is false and ACS is denied access to the medium. This avoids that an authorisation change could interrupt an ongoing communication. But a malicious entity controled by ACS could modulate the amount of time it uses the medium to exchange data with another malicious entity controled by ACS_2, this would be a threat to confidentiality. It could also use the medium forever, this could be a threat to availability.

To correct this, we use another information flow control property called causal dependency that was introduced in [2]. This property extends $WNInt$, it requires that any pair of list of shared and private actions that agree on the list of shared actions should also agree on the value of shared attributes (property $CDep$). Two lists of actions agree on their shared actions if the projection function prj_m associate them with the same shared action list.

$$prj_m(\alpha) = \begin{cases} null & \text{if } \alpha = null \\ prj_m(\alpha_2) & \text{if } \alpha = ac_2.\alpha_2 \\ & \wedge ac_2 \notin range(m) \\ ac_2.prj_m(\alpha_2) & \text{if } \alpha = ac_2.\alpha_2 \\ & \wedge ac_2 \in range(m) \end{cases}$$

$Eqv_2 =$
$cs \simeq_m cs' \Leftrightarrow (\forall at \in ATT_l, cs(m(at)) = cs'(m(at)))$
$CDep(m) = \forall \alpha, \alpha' \in Actions,$
$prj_m(\alpha) = prj_m(\alpha') \Rightarrow run(\alpha) \simeq_m run(\alpha')$

This property can detect the possible indirect interaction between hosts controled by ACS components because the morphism relating SSN and ACS does not enforce the causal dependency property. We consider two actions where the ACS is first granted access, then it uses the Ethernet medium and in α it releases the medium whereas in α' it does not release it, finally the ACS receives a revocation message (recall that in the semantics defined in section 2.1 action lists are executed starting by the last action):
$\alpha = forbidden.release.use.granted$
$\alpha' = forbidden.use.granted$
$prj_m(\alpha) = forbidden.granted = prj_m(\alpha')$
$run(\alpha)(ok) = 0 \wedge run(\alpha')(ok) = 1$
Although α and α' agree on shared actions they associate a different value to shared attribute ok.

In order to prove $CDep$ it is sufficient to prove the usual constraints $EqvInit$, $NoPrivAlt$, $StrGuard$, $WidSub$ and to prove that if two states are equivalent with respect to shared attributes then the value of the guard of any shared action should be equal in the two states (constraint $DepGuard$). A stronger constraint would require that private attributes do not appear in the guard of a shared action.
$DepGuard(m) = \forall cs, cs'_1, ac_l,$
$cs \simeq_m cs'_1 \Rightarrow guard(m(ac_l))(cs) = guard(m(ac_l))(cs'_1)$

In the SMAC protocol [5] the ACS instances should maintain another shared attribute that contains the amount of time that an entity is entitled to use the medium. In SMAC, an authorisation change can interrupt a communication if the reserved amount of time has elapsed.

5 Conclusion

In this paper we presented a compositional framework to help us validate security architectures. We illustrated the framework by modelling a secure LAN and studying the consistency of various security functions performing access controls (ACS, CSS and SSN).

In a related work [10], Fiadeiro and Maibaum introduced the COMMUNITY language that is similar to the specification notation we considered. They propose constraints on the morphisms similar to $EqvInit$, $NoPrivAlt$, $StrGuard$ and $WidSub$.

An interesting aspect of our work is that we related these constraints on morphisms with information flow control properties as non-interference or causal dependency. This seems to be useful to understand how various functions in a distributed architecture should interact. In the general case, preservation of the properties of the functions is just needed so we can use the weak non-interference property to control the interaction between shared and private actions. But when we compose security function with a untrusted function the causal dependency property migh be used to detect possible indirect dependencies that could help the untrusted function to bypass the security function controls.

Originally information flow control properties were devised to counter covert channels where two entities communicate by using a shared resource in an indirect fashion. Covert channels are generally considered to be a threat to confidentiality because malicious entities might bypass the access controls in order to transmit secret data. We consider that information flow control properties could be used to detect a broader class of threats related to the circumvention of security functions.

A lot of work was performed on the composition of secure systems (see for instance [11]). The goal of these works is to propose an information flow property that would still hold when systems are combined. It is well known that the composition of two system that both enforce non-interference does not necessarily enforce non-interference. Our goal is quite different, we are interested in security properties that can be stated as invariants (a similar assumption is taken in [13]) and we study how to compose specifications guaranteeing such security properties. We do not use Causal dependency as a security property that a component should enforce, we rather use it as a constraint on the interactions between several components. We use causal dependency in order to show that a security function cannot be circumvented. In [7] Todd Fine proposes a compositional framework based on the temporal logic of actions. One difference with the framework we use is that, thanks to the linking specification, we can compose specifications with distinct vocabularies. This feature is particularly useful when you wish to build a system by composing already developed components.

Acknowledgements

This study was funded by DGA/STTC. I would like to thank Virginie Wiels for helpful comments about previous drafts of this paper.

References

[1] J.R. Abrial. *The B-book: assigning programs to meaning*. Cambridge University Press, 1996.

[2] P. Bieber and F. Cuppens. A Logical View of Secure Dependencies. *Journal of Computer Security*, 1(1):99–129, 1992.

[3] European Economic Community. Information Technology Security Evaluation Criteria (ITSEC). Technical report, 1990.

[4] European Economic Community. Information Technology Security Evaluation Manual (ITSEM). Technical report, 1993.

[5] B. d'Ausbourg and P. Siron. A Secure Medium Access Control protocol: security versus performances. In *Proceedings of ESORICS'94*, number 875 in LNCS. Springer-Verlag, 1994.

[6] J. Fiadeiro and T. Maibaum. Temporal theories as modularisation units for concurrent system specification. *Formal Aspects of Computing*, 4(3):239–272, 1992.

[7] T. Fine. A Framework for Composition. In *Conference on Computer Assurance (COMPASS)*, Gaithersburg, 1996.

[8] J. Goguen and J. Meseguer. Unwinding and Inference Control. In *IEEE Symposium on Security and Privacy*, Oakland, 1984.

[9] J. Haigh and W. Young. Extending the Noninterference Version of MLS for SAT. In *IEEE Symposium on Security and Privacy*, Oakland, 1986.

[10] J. Fiadeiro and T. Maibaum. Categorical Semantics of Parallel Program Design. *Science of Computer Programming*, 28(2-3):111–138, 1997.

[11] D. McCullough. Noninterference and the Composability of Security Properties. In *IEEE Symposium on Security and Privacy*, Oakland, 1988.

[12] P. Michel and V. Wiels. A Framework for Modular Formal Specification and Verification. In *Proceedings of FME'97*, number 1313 in LNCS. Springer-Verlag, 1997.

[13] F. Schneider. Enforceable Security Policies. Technical report, Cornell, 1998.

[14] V. Wiels. *Modularité pour la conception et la validation formelles de systèmes*. PhD thesis, ENSAE, 1997.

Annex: Proofs

Theorem 1 $\forall m,\ MorphPred(m) \wedge WNInt(m) \Rightarrow Ref(m)$

Proof sketch of Theorem 1

1. $WNInt(m) \models$ $run(\alpha_l, init_l) \sim_m run(\alpha, init)$, by definition of $WNInt$ and instanciation

2. $MorphPred(m), run(\alpha_l, init_l) \sim_m run(\alpha, init) \models m(P)(run(\alpha, init)) \Leftrightarrow P(run(\alpha_l, init_l))$, by definition of $MorphPred$

3. $Always(P) \models P(run(\alpha_l, init_l))$ by definition of $Always$ and instanciation

4. $MorpPred(m), WNInt(m), Always(P) \models$ $m(P)(run(\alpha, init))$ from 1, 2 and 3.

5. $MorphPred(m),\ WNInt(m) \models Ref(m)$, from 4 and generalisation.

Theorem 2 $\forall m,\ EqvInit(m) \wedge EqvShared(m) \wedge EqvPriv(m) \Rightarrow WNInt(m)$

Proof sketch of Theorem 2

1. $\alpha = null \models run(\alpha, init) = init$, by definition of run

2. $\alpha = null, EqvInit(m) \models$ $run(null, init_l) \sim_m run(\alpha, init)$, by definition of $EqvInit$

3. $\alpha = null$, $EqvInit(m) \models$ $\exists \alpha_l, run(\alpha_l, init_l) \sim_m run(\alpha, init)$, from 2 and instanciation

4. $EqvShared(m)$, $ac = m(ac_l) \models$ $run(\alpha_l, init_l) \sim_m run(\alpha, init)$ $\Rightarrow$ $step(ac_l, run(\alpha_l, init_l) \sim_m step(ac, run(\alpha, init))$ $\vee$ $run(\alpha_l, init_l) \sim_m step(ac, run(\alpha, init))$, by definition of $EqvShared$

5. $EqvShared(m)$, $ac = m(ac_l) \models$ $run(\alpha_l, init_l) \sim_m run(\alpha, init) \Rightarrow$ $run(ac_l.\alpha_l, init_l) \sim_m run(ac.\alpha, init))$ $\vee\, run(\alpha_l, init_l) \sim_m run(ac.\alpha, init)$, from 4 and def of run

6. $EqvPriv(m)$, $ac \notin range(m) \models$ $run(\alpha_l, init_l) \sim_m run(\alpha, init) \Rightarrow$ $run(\alpha_l, init_l) \sim_m step(ac, run(\alpha, init))$, by def of $EqvPriv$

7. $EqvPriv(m)$, $ac \notin range(m) \models$ $run(\alpha_l, init_l) \sim_m run(\alpha, init) \Rightarrow$ $run(\alpha_l, init_l) \sim_m run(ac.\alpha, init))$, from 6 and def of run

8. $\alpha = ac.\alpha'$, $EqvShared(m)$, $EqvPriv(m)$, $run(\alpha_l, init_l) \sim_m run(\alpha', init) \models$ $\exists \alpha_l, run(\alpha_l, init_l) \sim_m run(\alpha, init)$ from 5 and 7

9. $EqvInit(m)$, $EqvShared(m)$, $EqvPriv(m) \models \exists \alpha_l$, $run(\alpha_l, init_l) \sim_m run(\alpha, init)$, from 3 and 8 by induction on α

Theorem 3 $\forall m, NoPrivAlt(m) \Rightarrow EqvPriv(m)$

Proof sketch of Theorem 3

1. $cs_l \sim_m cs \models cs_l(at) = cs(m(at))$, by def of eqv

2. $cs_l \sim_m cs$, $\neg guard(ac)(cs) \models cs_l(at) = step(ca_1, cs)(m(at))$ by 1 and def of $step$

3. $cs_l \sim_m cs$, $guard(ac)(cs)$, $NoPrivAlt(m)$, $ac \notin range(m) \models cs_l(at) = (cs \oplus sub(ac))(m(at))$, by 1 and def of $NoPrivAlt$

4. $cs_l \sim_m cs$, $guard(ac)(cs)$, $NoPrivAlt(m)$, $ac \notin range(m) \models cs_l(at) = step(ac, cs)(m(at))$, by 3 and def of $step$

5. $cs_l \sim_m cs$, $NoPrivAlt(m)$, $ac \notin range(m) \models$ $cs_l \sim_m step(ac, cs)$, by 2, 4 and def of eqv

6. $NoPrivAlt(m) \models EqvPriv(m)$, by 5 and def of $EqvPriv$

Theorem 4 $\forall m, MorphPred(m) \wedge StrGuard(m) \wedge WidSub(m) \Rightarrow EqvShared(m)$

Proof sketch of Theorem 4

1. $cs_l \sim_m cs \models cs_l(at) = cs(m(at))$,by def of eqv

2. $cs_l \sim_m cs$, $\neg guard(ac_l)(cs_l)$, $\neg guard(m(ac_l))(cs)$ $\models$ $step(ac_l, cs_l)(at) = step(m(ac_l), cs)(m(at))$, by 1 and def of $step$

3. $cs_l \sim_m cs$, $\neg guard(ac_l)(cs_l)$, $guard(m(ac_l))(cs)$, $MorphPred(m) \models \neg m(guard(ac_l))(cs)$, by def of $MorphPred$

4. $cs_l \sim_m cs$, $\neg guard(ac_l)(cs_l)$, $guard(m(ac_l))(cs)$, $MorphPred(m)$, $StrGuard(m) \models false$, by 1, 3 and def of $StrGuard$

5. $cs_l \sim_m cs$, $\neg guard(ac_l)(cs_l)$, $guard(m(ac_l))(cs)$, $MorphPred(m)$, $StrGuard(m) \models$ $step(ac_l, cs_l)(at) = step(m(ac_l), cs)(m(at))$, by 4

6. $cs_l \sim_m cs$, $guard(ac_l)(cs_l)$, $\neg guard(m(ac_l))(cs)$ $\models cs_l(at) = step(m(ac_l), cs)(m(at))$.by 1 and def of$step$

7. $cs_l \sim_m cs$, $WidSub(m) \models (cs_l \oplus sub(ac_l))(at) = (cs \oplus sub(m(ac_l)))(m(at))$, by 1 and def of $WidSub$

8. $cs_l \sim_m cs$, $guard(ac_l)(cs_l)$, $guard(m(ac_l))(cs)$, $WidSub(m) \models step(ac_l, cs_l)(at) = step(m(ac_l), cs)(m(at))$. by 7 and def of $step$

9. $cs_l \sim_m cs$, $MorphPred(m)$, $StrGuard(m)$, $WidSub(m) \models step(ac_l, cs_l)(at) = step(m(ac_l), cs)(m(at))$ $\vee\, cs_l(at) = step(m(ac_l), cs)(m(at))$, by 2, 5, 6, 8

10. $MorphPred(m)$, $StrGuard(m)$, $WidSub(m) \models$ $EqvShared(m)$, by def of $EqvShared$

Logics for Authorization and Access Control

A Logic-based Knowledge Representation for Authorization with Delegation (Extended Abstract)*

Ninghui Li
Computer Science
New York University
251 Mercer Street
New York, NY 10012, USA
ninghui@cs.nyu.edu

Joan Feigenbaum
AT&T Labs – Research
Room C203
180 Park Avenue
Florham Park, NJ 07932, USA
jf@research.att.com
http://www.research.att.com/~jf

Benjamin N. Grosof
IBM T.J. Watson Research Center
P.O.Box 704,
Yorktown Heights, NY 10598, USA
grosof@us.ibm.com
http://www.research.ibm.com/people/g/grosof

Abstract

We introduce Delegation Logic (DL), a logic-based knowledge representation (i.e., language) that deals with authorization in large-scale, open, distributed systems. Of central importance in any system for deciding whether requests should be authorized in such a system are delegation of authority, negation of authority, and conflicts between authorities. DL's approach to these issues and to the interplay among them borrows from previous work on delegation and trust management in the computer-security literature and previous work on negation and conflict handling in the logic-programming and non-monotonic reasoning literature, but it departs from previous work in some crucial ways. In this introductory paper, we present the syntax and semantics of DL and explain our novel design choices. This first paper focuses on delegation, including explicit treatment of delegation depth and delegation to complex principals; a forthcoming companion paper focuses on negation.

Compared to previous logic-based approaches to authorization, DL provides a novel combination of features: it is based on logic programs, expresses delegation depth explicitly, and supports a wide variety of complex principals (including but not limited to k-out-of-n thresholds). Compared to previous approaches to trust management, DL provides another novel feature: a concept of proof-of-compliance that is not entirely ad-hoc and that is based on model-theoretic semantics (just as usual logic programs have a model-theoretic semantics). DL's approach is also novel in that it combines the above features with smooth extensibility to non-monotonicity, negation, and prioritized conflict handling. This extensibility is accomplished by building on the well-understood foundation of DL's logic-program knowledge representation.

Keywords: Authorization, delegation, trust management, security policy, non-monotonicity, conflict handling, knowledge representation, logic programs.

1 Introduction

In today's Internet, there are a large and growing number of scenarios that require authorization decisions. By an *authorization* decision, we mean one in which one party submits a *request*, possibly supported by one or more *credentials*, that must comply with another party's *policy* if it is to be granted. Scenarios that require authorization decisions

*This extended abstract appeared in the Proceedings of the 12th IEEE Computer Security Foundations Workshop, July 1999. An expanded, Research Report version of this paper is available via the IBM Research Report server website (http://www.research.ibm.com, then navigate) or via the authors.

include content advising [23], mobile-code execution [11], public-key infrastructure [6, 27, 16, 9, 24], and privacy protection [20, 18].

Electronic commerce is one class of services in which authorization decisions play a prominent role. Merchants and customers both have valuable resources at risk and must have appropriate policies in place before authorizing access to these resources. An interesting aspect of e-commerce is that security policies and business policies are not always clearly separable. If a merchant requires that electronic checks for more than a certain amount be signed by at least two members of a set of trusted parties, is that a "security policy" or a "business policy"? It would be desirable for one authorization mechanism to be able to handle both.

Authorization in Internet services is significantly different from authorization in centralized systems or even in distributed systems that are closed or relatively small. In these older settings, authorization of a request is traditionally divided into two tasks: *authentication* and *access control*. Authentication answers the question "who made the request?," and access control answers the question "is the requester authorized to perform the requested action?" Following the "trust-management approach," first put forth by Blaze *et al.* [4, 5], we argue that this traditional view of authorization is inadequate. Reasons include:

- **What to protect?**: In a traditional client/server computing environment, valuable resources usually belong to servers, and it is when a client requests access to a valuable resource that the server uses an authorization procedure to decide whether or not to trust the client. In today's Internet (or any large, open, distributed system), users access many servers, make many different types of requests, and have valuable resources of their own (*e.g.*, personal information, electronic cash); indeed "client" is no longer the right metaphor. Such a user cannot trust all of the servers it interacts with, and authorization mechanisms have to protect the users' resources as well as those of the servers.

- **Whom to protect against?**: In a large, far-flung network, there are many more potential requesters than there are in a smaller, more homogeneous (albeit distributed) system. Some services, *e.g.*, Internet merchants, cannot know in advance who the potential requesters are. Similarly, users cannot know in advance which services they will want to use and which requests they will make. Thus, authorization mechanisms must rely on delegation and on third-party credential-issuers more than ever before.

- **Who stores authorization information?**: Traditionally, authorization information, *e.g.*, an access control list, is stored and managed by the service. Internet services evolve rapidly, and thus the set of potential actions and the users who may request them are not known in advance; this implies that authorization information will be created, stored, and managed in a dynamic, distributed fashion. Users are often expected to gather all credentials needed to authorize an action and present them along with the request. Since these credentials are not always under the control of the service that makes the authorization decision, there is a danger that they could be altered or stolen. Thus, public-key signatures (or, more generally, mechanisms for verifying the provenance of credentials) must be part of the authorization framework.

For these and other reasons, dividing authorization into authentication and access control is no longer appropriate. "Who made this request?" may not be a meaningful question – the authorizer may not even know the requester, and thus the identity or name of the requester may not help in the authorization decision. The goal of a growing body of work on *trust management* [4, 5, 9, 7, 3] is to find a more flexible, more "distributed" approach to authorization. The trust-management literature approaches the basic authorization question directly: "Does the set C of *credentials* prove that the *request* r *complies* with the set of local security *policies* P?" The *trust-management engine* is a separate system component that takes (r, C, P) as input and outputs a decision about whether compliance with policy has been proven.

Furthermore, trust-management adopts a "peer model" of authorization. Every entity can be both a requester and an authorizer. To be an authorizer, it maintains policies and is the ultimate source of authority for its authorization decisions. As a requester, it must maintain credentials (*e.g.*, public-key certificates, credit card numbers, and membership certificates) or be prepared to retrieve or obtain them when it wants access to a protected resource. When submitting a request to an authorizer, the requester also submits a set of credentials that purport to justify that the requested action is permissible. An authorizer may directly authorize certain requesters to take certain actions (and may not even try to "authenticate" these requesters by resolving their "identities"), but more typically it will *delegate* this responsibility to credential issuers that it trusts to have the required domain expertise as well as relationships with potential requesters.

Basic issues that must be addressed in the design of a trust-management engine include the definition of "proof of compliance," the extent to which policies and credentials should be programmable, and the language or notation in which they should be expressed.

In this paper, we propose the authorization language Delegation Logic (DL) as a trust-management engine. Its notable features include:

- A definition of "proof of compliance" that is founded on well-understood principles of logic programming and knowledge representation. Specifically, DL starts with the notion of proof embodied in Datalog definite ordinary logic programs [17].[1] DL then extends this with several features tailored to authorization.

- A rigorous and expressive treatment of delegation, including explicit linguistic support for delegation depth and for a wide variety of complex principals.

- The ability to handle "non-monotonic" policies. These are policies that deal explicitly with "negative evidence" and specify types of requests that do *not* comply. Important examples include hot-lists of "revoked" credentials and resolution of conflicting advice from different, but apparently both trustworthy, sources.

"Non-monotonic" here means in the sense of logic-based knowledge representation (KR).[2]

In combining both of these properties, DL departs sharply from earlier trust-management engines, some key points of which we now review. PolicyMaker, which was introduced in [4] and was the first system to call itself a "trust-management engine," uses an *ad-hoc* (albeit rigorously analyzed [5]) notion of "proof of compliance" and handles only monotonic policies. KeyNote [3] is a second-generation system based on most, but not all, of the same design principles as PolicyMaker; in particular, KeyNote uses an *ad-hoc* notion of proof of compliance (derived from the one used in PolicyMaker), and it does not handle non-monotonic policies. Unlike PolicyMaker, KeyNote takes an integrated approach to the design of the compliance-checking algorithm and the design of the programming language in which credentials and policies are expressed. DL also takes an integrated approach to these two aspects of authorization. REFEREE [7] handles nomonotonic policies, but it uses an *ad hoc* proof system that was never rigorously analyzed. SPKI [9] handles limited forms of non-monotonicity, but the "proof of compliance" notion (to the extent that one is specified in [9]) is *ad-hoc*.

[1] For review of standard concepts and results in logic programming, see [2], for example. "Ordinary" logic programs (LP's) correspond essentially to pure Prolog, but without the limitation to Prolog's particular inferencing procedure. These are also known as "general" LP's (a misleading name, since there are many further generalizations of them) and as "normal" LP's. "Definite" means without negation. "Datalog" means without function symbols of more than zero arity. "Arity" means number of parameters.

[2] A KR $\mathcal{K}$ is (logically) *monotonic* when its entailment relationship (*i.e.*, what it sanctions as conclusions) has the following property: if the set of premises (e.g., rules) $\mathcal{P}_2$ is a superset of the set of premises $\mathcal{P}_1$, then the set of conclusions entailed by $\mathcal{P}_2$ according to $\mathcal{K}$ is a superset of the set of conclusions entailed by $\mathcal{P}_1$. If a KR is not monotonic, it is called *non-monotonic*. Non-monotonicity means that adding premises can lead to retracting previously-sanctioned conclusions.

The outline of the rest of the paper is as follows. In section 2, we give an overview of DL. In section 3, we give the syntax and semantics of the monotonic case of DL, called D1LP. In section 4, we give an example of D1LP's usage. In section 5, we give an overview of our expressive extension to handle negation and prioritized conflict, called D2LP. A forthcoming companion paper gives details about D2LP. In section 6, we briefly discuss related work and future work.

2 Overview of DL

Our use of a logic-program knowledge representation as the foundation of our authorization language (a.k.a. "trust-management engine") offers several attractions: computational tractability[3], wide practical deployment, semantics shared with other practically important rule systems, relative algorithmic simplicity, yet considerable expressive power.

We chose Datalog definite ordinary logic programs (OLP's) as the starting point for DL. (More generally, however, we could started from other variants of logic-based knowledge representation, e.g., OLP's without the Datalog restriction.) DL extends Datalog definite OLP's along two dimensions that are crucial to authorization: delegation and non-monotonic reasoning. The resulting notion of "proof of compliance" is easier to justify than the *ad-hoc* notions used in PolicyMaker, KeyNote, REFEREE, and SPKI, because it is an extension of the well-studied, logic-programming framework.

As in much of the related literature, *e.g.,* [1, 19, 25], we use the term *principal* to mean an "entity" or "party" to an authorization decision. For example, a principal may make a request, issue a credential, or make a decision. Each authorization decision must involve a distinguished principal that functions as the "trust root" of the decision; this principal is referred to as `Local`.[4] DL supports the specification of sets of principals, via thresholds and lists, as well as *dynamic* sets of the form "all principals that satisfy the following predicate." DL principals express beliefs by making *direct statements* and *delegation statements*.

The DL framework provides a uniform representation for requests, policies, and credentials. Information in DL is represented as rules and facts that are built out of statement expressions. A request in DL corresponds to a query. *E.g.*, a simple query might be to ask whether the ground statement `"Local says is_key(12345,Bob)"` is true. More generally, a request can be a complex expression of statements; these expressions are called *statement formulas* and

[3] Under commonly met restrictions (*e.g.*, no logical functions of non-zero arity, a bounded number of logical variables per rule), inferencing, *i.e.*, rule-set execution, in LPs can be computed in worst-case polynomial-time. By contrast, classical logic (*e.g.*, first-order logic), is NP-complete under these restrictions and semi-decidable without these restrictions.

[4] `Local` plays the role that `POLICY` plays in PolicyMaker.

are defined in the next section. All of the policies and credentials that the receiving principal uses in evaluating the request form a DL program P. The DL semantics defines a unique minimal model for P, and the request is authorized if and only if it is in this model. The DL semantics provide the definition of "proof of compliance." This use of model-theoretic semantics is a novel feature of DL and a clear departure from the approaches taken by other trust-management engines.

Delegation is one of the two major concepts with which we extended Datalog definite OLP's to form DL, and it is the main technical focus of this paper. Distinguishing features of DL's approach to delegation include:

- Delegations have arbitrary but specified depth. For example, by using a depth-2 delegation statement, a principal A may delegate trust about a certain class of actions to principal B and allow B to delegate to others but *not* allow these others to delegate further.

- Delegations to complex principal structures are allowed. For example, a principal A may delegate trust about a certain class of purchases to all principals that satisfy the predicate `GoodTaste()`.

The other major concept that we added to Datalog definite OLP's to form DL is non-monotonicity. DL uses explicit negation to allow a policy to say what is forbidden, negation-as-failure to allow a policy to draw conclusions when there is no information about something, and priorities to handle conflicts among policies.

We use DL to denote our general approach to trust management. The monotonic version of DL (*i.e.*, Datalog definite OLP's plus our delegation mechanism) is called D1LP, and the non-monotonic version (*i.e.*, with negation and prioritized conflict handling) is called D2LP. This first paper focuses on D1LP, and only gives an overview of D2LP; a forthcoming companion paper focuses on D2LP.

Compared to previous logic-based approaches to authorization, DL provides a novel combination of features: it is based on logic programs, expresses delegation depth explicitly, and supports a wide variety of complex principals (including but not limited to k-out-of-n thresholds). Compared to previous approaches to trust management, DL provides another novel feature: a concept of proof-of-compliance that is not entirely *ad-hoc* and that is based on model-theoretic semantics (just as usual logic programs have a model-theoretic semantics). DL's approach is also novel in that it combines the above features with smooth extensibility to non-monotonicity, negation, and prioritized conflict handling. This extensibility is accomplished by building on the well-understood foundation of DL's logic-program knowledge representation.

3 Syntax and Semantics of D1LP

In this section, we formally define D1LP's syntax and semantics.

3.1 Syntax

1. The *alphabet* of D1LP consists of three disjoint sets, the *constants*, the *variables*, and the *predicate symbols*. The set of *principals* is a subset of the constants and the set of *principal variables* is a subset of the variables. Variables start with '_' ("underscore").[5] The special variable symbol '_' means a new variable whose name doesn't matter. A *term* is either a variable or a constant. Note that we prohibit function symbols with non-zero arity: this is the *Datalog* restriction. This restriction helps enable finiteness of the semantics and of computing inferences (a.k.a. entailments).

2. A *base atom* is an expression of the form

$$pred(t_1, ..., t_n)$$

where $pred$ is a predicate symbol and each t_i is a term.

3. A *direct statement* is an expression of the form

$$X \texttt{ says } p$$

where X is either a principal or a principal variable, "`says`" is a keyword, and p is a base atom. X is called the *subject* of this direct statement. A base atom encodes a trust belief or a security action, and a direct statement represents a belief of the subject.

4. A *threshold structure* takes one of the following forms:

   - $\texttt{threshold}(k, \{(A_1, w_1), \ldots, (A_n, w_n)\})$

     where "`threshold`" is a keyword, k and the w_i's are positive integers, the A_i's are principals, and $A_i \neq A_j$ for $i \neq j$. The w_i's are called *weights*. The set
     $\{(A_1, w_1), \ldots, (A_n, w_n)\}$
     is called a *principal-weight pair set* (abbreviated *P-W set*). If $w_i = 1$, then (A_i, w_i) can be written as A_i. A threshold structure supports something if the sum of all the weights of those principals that support it is greater than or equal to k.

   - $\texttt{threshold}(k, Prin \texttt{ says } pred/x)$

     where "`threshold`" and k are the same

[5] In Prolog, variables can also start with upper-case letters, and all constants start with lower-case letters. We want to allow constants to start with upper-case letters, and we restrict variables to start with underscore.

as above, $Prin$ is a principal, $pred$ is a predicate symbol, and x is the arity (number of parameters) of $pred$. The arity x should be either 1 or 2. When $x = 1$, "$Prin$ says $pred/1$" defines a P-W set that gives weight 1 to all principals A such that "$Prin$ says $pred(A)$" is true. When $x = 2$, "$Prin$ says $pred/2$" defines a P-W set, where the corresponding weight for any principal A is the greatest positive integer w such that "$Prin$ says $pred(A, w)$" is true. These are called *dynamic threshold structures*.

5. A *principal structure* takes one of the following forms:

   - A — where A is a principal
   - TS — where TS is a threshold structure
   - PS_1, PS_2 — where PS_1 and PS_2 are principal structures. This is the conjunction of two principal structures. If both PS_1 and PS_2 support a base atom p, then PS_1, PS_2 also supports p.
   - $PS_1; PS_2$ — where PS_1 and PS_2 are principal structures. This is the disjunction of two principal structures. If either PS_1 or PS_2 supports a base atom p, then $PS_1; PS_2$ also supports p.
   - $\{PS\}$ — where PS is a principal structure

   In a principal structure, conjunction(',') takes precedence over disjunction(';'). A *principal list* is the special case of a principal structure that has the form $\{A_1, \ldots, A_n\}$, where each A_i is a principal. A *principal set* is the special case of a principal list in which there are no repetitions, *i.e.*, in which $A_i \neq A_j$ for $i \neq j$.

6. A *delegation statement* takes the form

   X `delegates` p^d `to` PS

   where X is either a principal or a principal variable, `delegates` and `to` are keywords, p is a base atom, d is either a positive integer or the asterisk symbol '$*$', and PS is a principal structure. X is called the *subject*, d is called the *delegation depth*, and PS is called the *delegatee*. For example,

   ```
   Alice delegates is_key(_,_)^2 to Bob
   ```

   is a delegation statement. Intuitively, it means:

   ```
   Alice says is_key(_Key_X,_X)
      if Bob says is_key(_Key_X,_X).
   ```

   In this example, Alice trusts Bob in making direct statements about the predicate `is_key`. Alice may also trust Bob in judging other people's ability to make direct statements about `is_key`, *i.e.*, Alice trusts anyone Bob trusts. In this case, the delegation depth is 2. Similarly, delegation depth can also be greater than 2. A

   delegation depth '$*$' means unlimited depth.

7. A *statement* is either a direct statement or a delegation statement. In the semantics of D1LP, the role of "statement" is similar to the role of "atom" in ordinary LP's.

8. A *statement formula* takes one of the following forms:

   - S — where S is a statement.
   - F_1, F_2 — meaning (F_1 and F_2), where F_1 and F_2 are statement formulas,
   - $F_1; F_2$ — meaning (F_1 or F_2), where F_1 and F_2 are statement formulas,
   - (F) — where F is a statement formula.

   In a statement formula, the operator ',' (and) takes precedence over the operator ';' (or).

9. A *clause*, also known as a *rule*, takes the form:

   S `if` F.

   where S is a statement and F is a statement formula in which no dynamic threshold structures appear. S is called the *head* of the clause, and F is called the *body* of the clause. The body may be empty; if it is, the "`if`" part of the clause may be omitted. A clause with an empty body is also called a *fact*. Permitting dynamic threshold structures in the body in effect introduces logical non-monotonicity, which is why we prohibit it in D1LP. However, when we introduce negation-as-failure in D2LP, this restriction will be dropped.

   There are two special principals that can be used in the body of a clause: "`I`" and "`Local`". "`I`" refers to the subject of the head. It is the default subject for all statements in the body and may optionally be omitted. For example, when Alice believes

   ```
   Bob says p if q, I says r.
   ```

   this is shorthand for Alice believing

   ```
   Bob says p
      if Bob says q, Bob says r.
   ```

   "`Local`" refers to the principal that is using this statement and trying to make an authorization decision, *i.e.*, the current trust root. For example, when Alice believes "`Bob says p if Local says q.`", and Alice believes (that `Alice says`) "`q`", then Alice can conclude that "`Bob says p.`"

   Multi-agent logics of belief (or of knowledge) express beliefs from the viewpoints of multiple agents. DL can be viewed as expressing beliefs from the viewpoints of multiple agents. However, in DL, there is a single, distinguished viewpoint: that of the principal `Local`. Every DL rule or statement is implicitly regarded as a belief of `Local`. In other words, DL is *used* from one principal's viewpoint: *i.e.*, `Local`'s. Let `Local` be the agent Alice. When Alice believes

```
Bob says is_key(Key_M, M)
    if CA says is_key(Key_M, M).
```

this means that "If I (Alice) believe that `CA says is_key(Key_M, M)`, then I (Alice) can believe that `Bob says is_key(Key_M, M)`." The direct statements "`CA says is_key(Key_M, M)`" and "`Bob says is_key(Key_M, M)`" actually mean "Alice believes `CA says is_key(Key_M, M)`" and "Alice believes `Bob says is_key(Key_M, M)`." It doesn't matter whether "`Bob says is_key(Key_M, M)`" is believed by other principals, even Bob himself.

10. A *program* is a finite set of clauses. This is also known as a *logic program (LP)* or as a *rule set*.

As usual, an expression (*e.g.*, term, base atom, statement, clause, or program) is called *ground* if it does not contain any variables.

3.2 Semantics

In this subsection, we define the set of statements that are sanctioned as conclusions by a D1LP. Formally, this set of conclusions is defined as the *minimal model* of the D1LP. This model assigns a truth value ($true$ or $false$) to each ground statement. The value $true$ means that the statement is an entailed conclusion; $false$ means that it is not an entailed conclusion. These conclusions represent the beliefs of the principal that is the trust root, *i.e.*, `Local`.

Let $\mathcal{P}$ be a given D1LP.

Our semantics is defined via a series of steps. First, we define a language $\mathcal{LO}_\mathcal{P}$ that expresses definite OLP's (definite logic programs [17]). By contrast, we write the original input (D1LP) language of $\mathcal{P}$ as $\mathcal{LI}_\mathcal{P}$. Second, we define a translation that maps $\mathcal{P}$ to a ground definite OLP $\mathcal{O}$ in $\mathcal{LO}_\mathcal{P}$. Third, we define the minimal model of $\mathcal{P}$ as the correspondent (under this translation) of $\mathcal{O}$'s minimal model in the usual OLP semantics [17].

We begin by defining $\mathcal{LO}_\mathcal{P}$. Let N be the number of all principals in $\mathcal{P}$, $MaxDepth$ be the greatest integer used as a delegation depth in $\mathcal{P}$, and $MaxArity$ be the maximum arity of any predicate in $\mathcal{P}$. The language $\mathcal{LO}_\mathcal{P}$ has two important predicates: $holds$ and $delegates$. The predicate $holds$ takes four parameters:

$$holds(subject, pred, [params], length)$$

Here, the domain of $subject$ is the set of all principals appearing in $\mathcal{P}$, which we write as $Principals$. The domain of $pred$ is the set of all the predicate symbols appearing in $\mathcal{P}$. The domain of $[params]$ is all the length-l lists of constants that appear in $\mathcal{P}$, where $0 \leq l \leq MaxArity$. The domain of $length$ is integers $[1..N]$.

A ground atom of the predicate $holds$ represents a ground direct statement

$$subject \texttt{ says } pred(params)$$

Intuitively, $length$ represents the number of delegation steps that is enough to derive the corresponding direct statement. When $length = 1$, it means this direct statement can be derived directly without the use of delegation. We need not consider cases in which this length exceeds the number N of principals.

The predicate $delegates$ takes six parameters:

$$delegates(subject, pred, [params],$$

$$depth, delegatee, length)$$

Here, $subject$, $pred$, $params$, and $length$ are as above. The domain of $depth$ is $[1..MaxDepth] \cup \{*\}$. The domain of $delegatee$ is the set of all principal sets, which we write as $2^{Principals}$. Recall that there are N principals altogether, and thus $2^{Principals}$ is finite. Notice that only principal sets, rather than more general principal structures, are permitted as $delegatee$ here. The reason this suffices to represent $\mathcal{P}$ will become clear soon.

A ground atom of the predicate $delegates$ represents a delegation statement

$$subject \texttt{ delegates } pred(params)\hat{\ }depth \texttt{ to } delegatee$$

We define $\mathcal{LO}_\mathcal{P}$ to include (in addition to $holds$ and $delegates$) several "built-in" predicates and functions, as follows. The predicates $=$, $\leq$, $\geq$, $<$, $>$, and the functions $+$, $-$, and $\min$, are defined on the domain $[1..max(N, MaxDepth)] \cup \{*\}$. The predicates $\subseteq$ and $\supseteq$ are defined on the domain of principal sets $2^{Principals}$. "Built-in" is used in the Prolog sense: the predicates and functions are interpreted (in the semantics and in inferencing) as having pre-defined behavior. The behavior of "$*$" is similar to ∞, *e.g.*, for any integer l in $[1, ..., max(N, MaxDepth)]$: $l < *$, $* - l = *$, $* = *$, and $\min(*, l) = l$. Notice that, technically, $\mathcal{LO}_\mathcal{P}$ is *many-sorted*, in that the domains of some parameters of the predicates (in particular, of $holds$ and $delegates$) are typed. This also is a straightforward and commonly-made extension of the usual OLP formalism. See, for example, [17].

The *Herbrand base* of $\mathcal{LO}_\mathcal{P}$ is the set of all ground atoms in $\mathcal{LO}_\mathcal{P}$. Because all the domains used above are finite, the Herbrand base of $\mathcal{LO}_\mathcal{P}$ is also finite. An *interpretation* of

$\mathcal{LO}_\mathcal{P}$ is an assignment of truth values (*true* and *false*) to the Herbrand base of $\mathcal{LO}_\mathcal{P}$. Such an interpretation can also be viewed as a set of true ground atoms, *i.e.*, as a *conclusion set*.

Given an interpretation I of $\mathcal{LO}_\mathcal{P}$ and a principal structure PS, we define PS^I, the *normal form of a principal structure* under (*i.e.*, relative to) I, as follows. A principal structure PS^I is in normal form when it is of the form: "$PS_1^I; PS_2^I; ...; PS_r^I$," where each PS_i^I is a principal set and, for any $i \neq j$, $PS_i^I \not\subseteq PS_j^I$. One can view PS as a negation-free formula in propositional logic; PS's normal form PS^I is then the result of converting that propositional-logic formula into its reduced disjunctive normal form (DNF). Here, the reduced DNF is logically equivalent (in propositional logic) to PS given I. "Reduced" means that there is no subsumption: neither within a conjunct (*i.e.*, no repetitions of principals) nor between conjuncts (*i.e.*, no conjunct is a subset of another conjunct). For dynamic threshold structures like "threshold(k, $Prin$ says $pred/x$)," the interpretation I determines the P-W set defined by $Prin$ and $pred$. A threshold structure

threshold(k, $\{(A_1, w_1), (A_2, w_2), \ldots, (A_n, w_n)\}$)

is converted to the disjunction of all minimal subsets of $\{A_1, \ldots, A_n\}$ whose corresponding weights sum to be greater than or equal to k. For example,

threshold($3, \{(A, 2), (B, 1), (C, 1), (D, 1)\}$)

is converted to

$$\{A, B\}; \{A, C\}; \{A, D\}; \{B, C, D\}.$$

After two principal structures have been transformed, their conjunction and disjunction are convertible to normal form using methods similar to the usual ones used in propositional logic.

Equipped with the definitions of $\mathcal{LO}_\mathcal{P}$ and PS^I, we are ready next to give the main definition of the translation. Given an interpretation I of $\mathcal{LO}_\mathcal{P}$, the translation $Trans^I$ maps $\mathcal{P}$ into a definite OLP $\mathcal{O}^I$ in the language $\mathcal{LO}_\mathcal{P}$, *i.e.*, $\mathcal{O}^I = Trans^I(\mathcal{P})$. We define $Trans^I$ via four steps.

Semantically, we treat a rule containing variables as shorthand for the set of all its ground instances. This is standard in the logic programming literature. We write $\mathcal{P}^{instd}$ to stand for the LP that results when each rule r in $\mathcal{P}$ is replaced by the set of all its possible *ground instantiations*, *i.e.*, by all of the ground clauses that can be obtained by replacing r's variables with constants (or "instantiating" them).

The first step of $Trans^I$ is to replace $\mathcal{P}$ by $\mathcal{P}^{instd}$.

The second step of $Trans^I$ is to replace all the delegation statements in $\mathcal{P}^{instd}$ by those that delegate to principal sets, as follows. Let PS^I be written as $PS_1^I; PS_2^I; ...; PS_r^I$; each PS_i^I is a principal set.

- Rewrite head delegation statements.
  Replace every clause of the form
  A delegates $s\hat{}d$ to PS if F.
  by the r clauses:
  $\{$ A delegates $s\hat{}d$ to PS_i^I if F. $| \; i = 1..r$ $\}$.

- Rewrite body delegation statements.
  Replace every delegation statement
  A delegates $s\hat{}d$ to PS
  that occurs in the body of a clause, by the conjunction of the r delegation statements:
  A delegates $s\hat{}d$ to PS_1^I,
  A delegates $s\hat{}d$ to PS_2^I,
  ...,
  A delegates $s\hat{}d$ to PS_r^I.

Let T_2^I denote the program after the above transformations.

The third step of $Trans^I$ takes T_2^I as input and translates it to an OLP T_3^I in the language $\mathcal{LO}_\mathcal{P}$, as follows.

- For any direct statement
  A says $pred(params)$
  in the body of a clause, change it to:
  $holds(A, pred, [params], N)$.

- For any direct statement
  A says $pred(params)$
  in the head of a clause, change it to:
  $holds(A, pred, [params], 1)$.

- For any delegation statement
  A delegates $pred(params)\hat{}d$ to PS
  in the body of a clause, change it to:
  $delegates(A, pred, [params], d, PS, N)$

- For any delegation statement
  A delegates $pred(params)\hat{}d$ to PS
  in the head of a clause, change it to:
  $delegates(A, pred, [params], d, PS, 1)$.

Here, as before, N is the number of principals in $\mathcal{P}$. Intuitively, if a statement in the head is deduced, then it is deduced directly (length 1); if a statement can be deduced within any length, it is true.

The result of these changes is T_3^I.

The fourth step of $Trans^I$ is to add a further collection of clauses to T_3^I; the resulting OLP program is $\mathcal{O}^I$ in the language $\mathcal{LO}_\mathcal{P}$. Intuitively, these additional clauses represent all instances of several *meta-rules of deduction involving delegation*. Because the relevant domains are finite, there are a finite number of such instances.

Let A be a principal; BS be a principal set $\{B_1, \ldots, B_n\}$; CS be another principal set; d and d_0 be delegation depths (*i.e.*, elements of $[1..MaxDepth] \cup \{*\}$); and, l and l_0 be lengths (*i.e.*, elements of $[1..N]$). Let $pred$

and $[params]$ be as above (recall the definition of *holds*). Below, "length" means delegation-path length.

The additional clauses are as follows.

1. Every ground clause that has the form:
   $holds(A, pred, [params], l)$
   `if` $holds(A, pred, [params], l_0)$,
   $l \geq l_0$.
   Intuitively, this represents the deduction meta-rule that: If a direct statement is deducible within length l_0, then the direct statement is deducible within any longer length $l \geq l_0$.

2. Every ground clause that has the form:
   $delegates(A, pred, [params], d, CS, l)$
   `if` $delegates(A, pred, [params], d_0, BS, l_0)$,
   $d \leq d_0,\ l \geq l_0,\ CS \supseteq BS$.
   Intuitively, this represents the deduction meta-rule that: If a delegation statement is deducible, then any weaker delegation statement is deducible within any longer length. Smaller depth and larger conjunctive delegatee set each weaken a delegation statement.

3. Every ground clause that has the form:
   $holds(A, pred, [params], l_0 + 1)$
   `if` $delegates(A, pred, [params], 1, BS, l_0)$,
   $holds(B_1, pred, [params], 1)$,
   $holds(B_2, pred, [params], 1)$,
   $\ldots$,
   $holds(B_n, pred, [params], 1)$,
   $l_0 < N$.
   Intuitively, this represents the deduction meta-rule that enforces the effect of depth-1 delegations.

4. Every ground clause that has the form:
   $delegates(A, pred, [params], \min(d, d_0 - l), CS, l_0 + l)$
   `if` $delegates(A, pred, [params], d_0, BS, l_0)$,
   $delegates(B_1, pred, [params], d, CS, l)$,
   $delegates(B_2, pred, [params], d, CS, l)$,
   $\ldots$,
   $delegates(B_n, pred, [params], d, CS, l)$,
   $l < d_0,\ l \leq (N - l_0)$.
   Intuitively, this represents the deduction meta-rule that enforces the effect of chaining of delegations. The depth of the deduced (head) delegation of A is bounded both by the depth of the delegation from A to BS and by the depth of the delegations from Bi's to CS. The depth of the delegation from A to BS has to cover the path lengths that have already been used in deriving delegations from Bi's to CS.

The $\mathcal{O}^I$ that results (from adding these further clauses to T_3^I) is a ground definite OLP. It thus has one or more *OLP-models*, *i.e.*, models in the usual OLP semantics [17]. In particular, it has a model $MinOLPModel(\mathcal{O}^I)$ that is minimal in the sense of the usual OLP semantics.

Proposition 1 *Given two interpretations $I \subseteq J$ of $\mathcal{LO}_\mathcal{P}$, if an interpretation K of $\mathcal{LO}_\mathcal{P}$ is an OLP-model of $\mathcal{O}^J$, then K is also an OLP-model of $\mathcal{O}^I$.*

Proof. See the expanded Research Report version for the full proof. **Overview**: Essentially, this is a logical-monotonicity property. The key observation is the following. The differences that may exist between $\mathcal{O}_J$ and $\mathcal{O}_I$ can only be caused by dynamic threshold structures, which are only allowed to appear in heads of clauses. Consider the normal forms of a dynamic threshold structure TS under I and J, *i.e.*, TS^I and TS^J. If we view them as propositional formulas, then TS^I implies TS^J, because $I \subseteq J$. This makes $\mathcal{O}^J$ at least as strong (in deduction power) as $\mathcal{O}^I$. ∎

Definition 2 *An interpretation I of $\mathcal{LO}_\mathcal{P}$ is an* **O-model** *of a D1LP program $\mathcal{P}$ if and only if I is an OLP-model of $\mathcal{O}^I = Trans^I(P)$.*

It turns out that every D1LP program $\mathcal{P}$ has at least one O-model, as we will show below in Theorem 7.

Theorem 3 *The intersection of any two O-models of $\mathcal{P}$ is also an O-model of $\mathcal{P}$.*

Proof. Given two O-models I and J of $\mathcal{P}$, one can conclude by the definition of O-models that I is an OLP-model of $\mathcal{O}^I$ and that J is an OLP-model of $\mathcal{O}^J$. Let $K = I \cap J$. Because $K \subseteq I$ and $K \subseteq J$, Proposition 1 implies that I and J are both OLP-models of $\mathcal{O}^K$. Because definite ordinary logic programs have the property that two models' intersection is still a model [17], K is an OLP-model of $\mathcal{O}^K$. By the definition of O-models, K is thus an O-model of P. ∎

Definition 4 *The* **minimal O-model** *of $\mathcal{P}$ is the intersection of all of its O-models. We write this as $MinOModel(\mathcal{P})$.*

It turns out that every D1LP $\mathcal{P}$ has a minimal O-model; below, in Theorem 7, we show how to construct it.

Ultimately, we are interested in models expressed in $\mathcal{LI}_\mathcal{P}$, the original D1LP language of $\mathcal{P}$. We define a simple reverse translation $ReverseTrans$ that maps each O-model I of $\mathcal{P}$ to its corresponding *D1LP-model* in $\mathcal{LI}_\mathcal{P}$, as follows.

- For each O-conclusion of the form
  $holds(A, pred, [params], length)$,
  include the D1LP-conclusion
  A `says` $pred(params)$.

- For each O-conclusion of the form $delegates(A, pred, [params], depth, Delegatee, length)$, include the D1LP-conclusion
  `A delegates` $pred(params)$`^`$depth$
  `to` $Delegatee$.

Notice here that (delegation path) length is ignored after the OLP conclusions are drawn.

We define the *Herbrand base* of $\mathcal{P}$, in $\mathcal{LI}_\mathcal{P}$, as the set of all ground statements of $\mathcal{P}$, restricted to require that every principal structure be a principal set. We define an *interpretation* of $\mathcal{P}$ to be an assignment of truth values ($true$ and $false$) to the Herbrand base of $\mathcal{P}$. Such an interpretation can also be viewed as a set of true ground statements, *i.e.*, as a *conclusion set*.

Definition 5 *An interpretation M of $\mathcal{LI}_\mathcal{P}$ is a* **model** *of a D1LP program $\mathcal{P}$ if and only if $M = ReverseTrans(I)$ and I is an O-model of $\mathcal{P}$. The* **minimal model** *of $\mathcal{P}$ is $ReverseTrans(MinOModel(P))$. We write this as $MinModel(\mathcal{P})$.*

Next, we show that $MinOModel(\mathcal{P})$ and thus its corresponding $MinModel(\mathcal{P})$ actually *exist*, by showing how to *construct* $MinOModel(\mathcal{P})$.

Definition 6 *Given $\mathcal{P}$, we define an* **operator** $\Psi_\mathcal{P}$ *that takes an interpretation I of $\mathcal{LO}_\mathcal{P}$ and returns another one: $\Psi_\mathcal{P}(I) = MinOLPModel(\mathcal{O}^I)$, where $MinOLPModel$ is the standard minimal model operator for OLP.*

Theorem 7 (Construct Minimal Model) *$MinOModel(\mathcal{P})$ is the* **least fixpoint of** $\Psi_\mathcal{P}$. *This fixpoint is obtained by iterating $\Psi_\mathcal{P}$ a* **finite** *number of times, starting from $\emptyset$. $MinModel(\mathcal{P})$ thus* **exists**, *for every D1LP $\mathcal{P}$.*

Proof. See the expanded Research Report version for the full proof. **Overview**: One key observation is that $\Psi_\mathcal{P}$ is a monotone operator, due to the monotonicity properties of Proposition 1 and of definite OLP's. Another key observation is that the domain of this operator, i.e., the space of interpretations, is finite due to the finite Herbrand base (largely because of the Datalog restriction). ∎

Inferencing: Because of the finiteness properties mentioned above, computing $MinModel(\mathcal{P})$ is decidable. Given the minimal model $MinModel(\mathcal{P})$, queries in D1LP can be translated as we did for the body of a clause, then answered using the model. We have a current implementation of restricted D1LP. It is written in Prolog and uses a top-down query-answering method.

4 Use of D1LP

In this section, we use the public-key infrastructure problem to demonstrate the use of D1LP. The trust-management approach views the PKI problem from one user's point of view. The user has trust beliefs and certificates from other principals, and it needs to decide whether a particular binding is valid according to its information. All of these beliefs, certificates, and decisions can be represented uniformly in D1LP.

D1LP can also be used to represent authorizations. Authorizing a principal to do something can be represented as a delegation to that principal. Whether to allow this principal to further grant this authorization to other principals can be controlled by delegation depth. An authorization request can be answered by deciding whether a delegation statement is true or false. Moreover, separation of duty [8] can be achieved by delegations to threshold structures.

We first show how certificates from different PKI proposals can be represented in D1LP. Pretty Good Privacy (PGP)'s certificates only establish key bindings; they have no delegation semantics. The delegations in PGP are expressed by trust degrees that are stored in local key rings. They all have depth 1. In PGP, a user can also specify threshold values for accepting a key binding. In D1LP, this can be achieved through dynamic threshold structures. One way is to use several predicates to denote different trust levels, for example, `fully_trusted` and `partly_trusted`. A user Alice may have the following policies:

```
Alice says fully_trusted(Bob).
Alice says fully_trusted(Sue).
Alice says partly_trusted(Carl).
Alice says partly_trusted(Joe).
Alice says partly_trusted(Peg).
Alice delegates is_key(_Key,_User)^1
    to threshold(1,fully_trusted/1).
Alice delegates is_key(_Key,_User)^1
    to threshold(2,partly_trusted/1).
```

Of course, one can also use *weighted* dynamic threshold structures.

In X.509 [6], certification authorities (CAs)' certificates are chained together to establish a key binding. For such delegation chains to be really meaningful, the certificates on such chains must also imply delegations. Since there is no limit on the length of delegation chains, all such delegations have depth '$*$'. Privacy Enhanced Mail (PEM) uses X.509's certificates but limits the CA hierarchy to three levels: IPRA, PCAs, and CAs. Thus PEM's trust model requires that every user give a depth-three delegation to IPRA.

A SPKI certificate does not establish key binding; it is a delegation from the issuer to the subject of the certificate.

It has one field that controls whether a delegation can be further delegated or not; this means that every delegation has depth 1 or '*'.

There are other proposals to use lengths of delegation paths as a metric for public-key bindings. The difference between these path lengths and our delegation depths is that, in the former, there is only one length, and it is specified by the trust root. However, every DL delegation statement can have a delegation depth limit. This has the effect of allowing every principal on the delegation path to specify how much further this path can go. Together, the set of delegation depths along the path determine whether the path is invalidly deep.

Next, we give an extended example of public key authorization with delegation. Consider a user Alice who wants to decide whether a public key `M_Key` is web site `M_Site`'s public key. There are many certification systems that may be relevant. In particular, Alice trusts three of them: systems X, Y, and Z. System X has three levels: `XRCA`, `XPCA`'s, and `XCA`'s, where `XRCA` is the root, `XCA`'s are CA's that certify users' public keys directly, and `XPCA`'s certify `XCA`'s public keys and are in turn certified by `XRCA`. System Y has two levels: `YRCA` and `YCA`'s. System Z has only one level: `ZRCA`, which certifies users' keys directly. Alice first translates (*i.e.*, represents) certificates of these systems into statements using the predicates `Xcertificate(`*signature_key*, *subject*, `...)`, `Ycertificate(...)`, `Zcertificate(...)`.[6] Then Alice asserts some rules that translate these into statements of a common certificate predicate, say, `is_site_key(_Key,_Site)`. For example:

```
_Issuer says is_site_key(_Key,_Site)
  if Xcertificate(_Issuer,_Key,_Site).
```

Next, Alice specifies the sense in which she trusts the three systems, by asserting the rule:

```
Alice delegates is_site_key(_K,_S)^3
    to {XRCA,{YRCA;ZRCA}}.
```

This means that Alice requires system X and one of system Y and system Z to certify a website public key. She does this with delegation depth 3 because she knows that 3 is the maximum number of levels in those certification systems. (Note that, for other purposes, Alice can use predicates other than `is_site_key` and trust these systems differently.) Suppose that `M_Key` is certified by both system Y and system Z, *i.e.*, there are certificates that translate into:

```
YRCA delegates is_site_key(_K,_S)^1
    to YCA1.
YCA1 says is_site_key(M_Key,M_Site).
ZRCA says is_site_key(M_Key,M_Site).
```

[6] The exact fields of these predicates are determined by Alice. They should be whichever elements of the certificates are relevant to Alice's policies.

Then the given information is not enough to deduce (*i.e.*, entail) that "`Alice says is_key(M_Key,M_Site).`", because there is no certification of that key from `XRCA`.

Now suppose that, in addition to these systems above, Alice has a friend Bob. For whatever reasons, Alice trusts Bob unconditionally to certify websites' public keys, *i.e.*,

```
Alice delegates is_site_key(_K,_S)^*
    to Bob.
```

Bob thinks that certification by system Z is itself enough for those sites that belong to association `assoc`, and he trusts `ASSOC` in deciding which sites belong to `assoc`, *i.e.*,

```
Bob delegates is_site_key(_K,_S)^1
    to ZRCA
  if I says belongs_to(_S,assoc).
Bob delegates belongs_to(_S,assoc)^1
    to ASSOC.
```

Alice stores these policies that she got from Bob earlier. Suppose that site `M_Site` also sent the following certificate issued by `ASSOC`:

```
ASSOC says belongs_to(M_Site,assoc).
```

With the above additional information, Alice can deduce the following:

```
Bob says belongs_to(M_Site,assoc).
Bob delegates
  is_site_key(M_Key,M_Site)^1
    to ZRCA.
Alice delegates
  is_site_key(M_Key,M_Site)^1
    to ZRCA.
```

Finally, Alice can deduce:

```
Alice says is_site_key(M_Key,M_Site).
```

5 Extension: Negations and Priorities

D1LP is (logically) monotonic. It cannot express negation or negative knowledge.

However, many security policies are non-monotonic or more easily specified as non-monotonic ones, *e.g.*, certificate revocation. In many applications, a natural policy is to make a decision in one direction, *e.g.*, in favor of authorizing H, if there is no information/evidence to the contrary, *e.g.*, no known revocation. Using *negation-as-failure* (a.k.a. *default negation* or *weak negation*) is often an easy and intuitive way to do this. Also useful in representation of many policies is *classical negation* (a.k.a. *explicit negation* or *strong negation*), which allows policies that explicitly forbid something. Classical negation in rules, especially in the consequents (heads) of rules, enables one to specify both the positive and negative *sides* of a policy, (*i.e.*, both permission and prohibition) using the expressive power of rules, *e.g.*, using inferential chaining. As argued in [14, 15], this allows more flexible security policies. Classical negation is particularly desirable for authorization in Internet scenarios, where the number of potential requesters is huge. For low-value transactions, users sometimes have security policies that give access to all except a few requesters. Without negations, it would be effectively impossible to do this.

Introducing classical negation leads to the potential for *conflict*: Two rules for opposing sides may both apply to a given situation. Care must be taken to avoid producing inconsistency. *Priorities*, which specify that one rule overrides another, are an important tool for specifying how to handle such conflict. *E.g.*, a known revocation overrides a general rule to presume trustworthiness. *E.g.*, one principal overrides another's decision/recommendation. Some form of prioritization is generally present in many rule-based systems; prioritization has also received a great deal of attention in the non-monotonic reasoning literature (see, *e.g.*, [12] for some literature review and pointers).

Prioritization information is naturally available. One common basis for prioritization is *specificity*: Often it is desirable to specify that more specific-case rules should override more general-case rules. Another basis is *recency*, in which more recent rules override less recent rules. A third common basis is relative *authority*, in which rules from a more authoritative source override rules from a less authoritative one. For example, a superior legal/bureaucratic/organizational jurisdiction or a more knowledgeable/expert source may be given higher priority. It is often useful to reason about prioritization, *e.g.*, to reason from organization roles or timestamps to deduce priorities. Reasoning about prioritization may itself involve conflict, *e.g.*, a less recent rule may be more specific or more authoritative.

To allow users to express non-monotonic policies in a natural and powerful fashion, we define **D2LP**, which stands for version 2 of Delegation Logic Programs. D2LP is (logically) non-monotonic. D2LP expressively extends D1LP to include negation-as-failure, classical negation, and partially-ordered priorities. Just as D1LP bases its syntax and semantics on definite ordinary LP's, D2LP bases its syntax and semantics on Courteous LP's. The version of Courteous LP's we use is expressively generalized as compared to the previous version in [12, 13].

In the rest of this section, we give an overview of D2LP. Full details will be given in a forthcoming companion paper.

Syntactically, each D2LP rule (clause) is generalized to permit each statement to be negated in two ways: by classical negation $\neg$ and/or by negation-as-failure (NAF) $\sim$. Each rule also is generalized to permit an optional *rule label*, which is a handle for specifying priority. Prioritization is specified via the predicate $overrides$. $overrides(label_1, label_2)$ means that every rule having rule label $label_1$ has strictly higher priority than every rule having rule label $label_2$. $overrides$ is treated specially in the semantics to generate the prioritization used by all rules. Otherwise, however, $overrides$ is treated as an ordinary predicate.

A D2LP direct statement has the form:

$$A \ \texttt{says} \ [\sim] \, [\neg] \, p$$

A D2LP delegation statement has the form:

$$A \ [\sim] \, [\neg] \ \texttt{delegates} \, p\hat{\ }d \ \texttt{to} \ PS$$

Here, as when we described D1LP, A is a principal, p is a base atom, d is a depth, and PS is a principal structure. Square brackets ("[...]") indicate the optionality of what they enclose. $\neg$ stands for classical negation and is read in English as "not". $\sim$ stands for negation-as-failure and is read in English as "fail".

When a statement does not contain $\sim$, we say it is *classical*; when it contains neither $\sim$ nor $\neg$, we say it is *atomic*.

Semantically, the negations' scope can be viewed as applying to the whole statement. Intuitively, $\neg s$ means that s is believed to be false. By contrast, $\sim cs$ means that cs is not believed to be true, *i.e.*, either cs is believed to be false, or cs is *unknown*. "Unknown" here means in the sense that there is no belief one way or the other about whether cs is true versus false.

A D2LP statement formula is defined as the result of conjunctions and disjunctions applied to D2LP statements, similarly to the way in which a D1LP statement formula is defined as the result of conjunctions and disjunctions applied to D1LP statements (*i.e.*, atomic statements). A D2LP rule (clause) is defined as:

$$\langle lab \rangle \ S \ \texttt{if} \ F.$$

Here, S is a *classical* statement. F is a statement formula. The rule label lab is an ordinary logical term (e.g., the constant $frau$ below) in the D2LP language. The rule label may optionally be omitted. Note that D2LP relaxes the D1LP prohibition on dynamic threshold structures in the body. Syntactically, a D1LP rule is a special case of a D2LP rule.

Next, we give a simple example that illustrates the use of classical negation and priorities. Let D2LP program $\mathcal{R}_1$ be the following set of rules:

$\langle cred \rangle$ A `says` $honest(\_X)$
    `if` B `says` $creditRating(\_X, good)$.
$\langle frau \rangle$ A `says` $\neg honest(\_X)$
    `if` C `says` $fraudulent(\_X)$,

D says $fraudExpert(C)$.
A says $overrides(frau, cred)$.
B says $creditRating(Joe, good)$.
D says $fraudExpert(C)$.

$\mathcal{R}_1$ entails the conclusion: A says $honest(Joe)$.

Continuing the example, suppose the following statement is added to $\mathcal{R}_1$ to form $\mathcal{R}_2$.

C says $fraudulent(Joe)$.

$\mathcal{R}_2$ instead entails the conclusion:

A says $\neg honest(Joe)$.

The semantics of a D2LP are defined via a translation $Trans2$ to a ground courteous LP that is roughly similar to D1LP's translation $Trans$ to a ground OLP. Courteous LP's expressively extend OLP's to include $\neg$ and $\sim$, as well as prioritization represented via an $overrides$ predicate on rule labels.

We impose some further expressive restrictions in D2LP, related especially to cyclicity of dependency between predicates, to ensure D2LP's well-behavior semantically and computationally. (Limited space prevents us from detailing these restrictions here.) The generalized version of Courteous LP's relies on the well-founded semantics [10], which is computationally tractable (worst-case polynomial-time) for the ground case.

Courteous LP's semantic well-behavior includes having a unique (minimal) model that is *consistent* (s and $\neg s$ are never both sanctioned as conclusions). D2LP inherits this same well-behavior. D2LP inferencing remains decidable; its finiteness properties are similar to those of D1LP.

In a forthcoming paper, we cover DL's treatment of negation in detail, as we have covered delegation in detail in this paper.

6 Discussion and Future Work

As explained in previous sections, our design of DL was primarily influenced by earlier work on trust management and on logic programming and knowledge representation. There is other, more tenuously related work in the computer security literature, and we briefly discuss some of it in this Extended Abstract. A longer discussion appears in the expanded, Technical Report version of this paper.

In [1, 19, 25], Abadi, Burrows, Lampson, Wobber, and Plotkin developed a logic for authentication in distributed systems. The central notion in their logic is delegation, which they express via the "*speaks for*" relation. They develop a system of reasoning about which principals speak for which other principals. But they didn't consider delegation-depth limits and threshold structures. In this sense, DL's treatment of delegation is more powerful.

Maurer [21] modelled public-key infrastructure via recommendations with levels and confidence values. Delegation in DL is very similar to recommendation in [21], but there are several differences. One is that Maurer's model supports direct statements and delegation statements but not clauses (rules). A second is that Maurer's model supports reasoning about the delegations and beliefs of what DL calls "Local," but it does not allow, say, Local A to reason about the beliefs of B (*e.g.*, about whether, in A's view, B delegates to C or B believes a particular statement). Thus, one cannot express, in Maurer's model, that "A says X if B says Y." This restriction permits delegation chaining to be much simpler than it is

in DL and eliminates the need to maintain "lengths." Thirdly, Maurer's model does not support delegation to lists, threshold structures, *etc.*. Finally, DL does not use confidence values.

Neither Abadi *et al.* nor Maurer consider negations and non-monotonicity. However, there is also previous work on authorization languages that consider negations. But these work is different from DL in that it does not consider delegation. The way these work handles negation is also different from D2LP. One well-known example is the language of Woo and Lam [26], which is based on Default Logic [22]. Woo and Lam do not guarantee that every program (or, in their terms, every "policy base") has a model; furthermore, when a model exists, it might not have a meaningful interpretation, because of potential inconsistency. Well-founded semantics and prioritized conflict handling allow D2LP to support a more expressive set of non-monotonic policies and give a unique and meaningful model to every program.

Jajodia *et al.* [14, 15] proposed a logical authorization language that is based on Datalog extended with two negations. They have only limited support for non-monotonic policies, however, via syntactic restrictions that ensure that policies are conflict-free and stratified. By contrast, D2LP is more expressive, via well-founded semantics and conflict handling. Programs written in Jajodia *et al.*'s language are syntactically restricted and delegation-free special cases of D2LP, and D2LP would give the same model for them.

Future work will address the computational complexity of compliance checking in DL, syntactically restricted classes of DL programs for which compliance can be checked very efficiently, implementation of the DL interpreter (for which we now have only a preliminary version for restricted D1LP), and deployment of DL in an e-commerce platform.

References

[1] M. Abadi, M. Burrows, B. Lampson, and G. Plotkin, "A Calculus for Access Control in Distributed Systems," *ACM Transactions on Programming Languages and Systems*, 15 (1993), pp. 706–734.

[2] C. Baral and M. Gelfond, "Logic Programming and Knowledge Representation", *Journal of Logic Programming*,

19,20(1994), pp. 73–148. Includes extensive review of literature.

[3] M. Blaze, J. Feigenbaum, J. Ioannidis, and A. Keromytis, "The KeyNote Trust-Management System," submitted for publication as an Internet RFC, March 1998. `http://www.cis.upenn.edu/~angelos/Papers/draft-keynote.txt`.

[4] M. Blaze, J. Feigenbaum, and J. Lacy, "Decentralized Trust Management," in *Proceedings of the Symposium on Security and Privacy*, IEEE Computer Society Press, Los Alamitos, 1996, pp. 164–173.

[5] M. Blaze, J. Feigenbaum, and M. Strauss, "Compliance-Checking in the PolicyMaker Trust Management System," in *Proceedings of Financial Crypto '98*, Lecture Notes in Computer Science, vol. 1465, Springer, Berlin, 1998, pp. 254–274.

[6] ITU-T Rec. X.509 (revised), *The Directory - Authentication Framework*, International Telecommunication Union, 1993.

[7] Y.-H. Chu, J. Feigenbaum, B. LaMacchia, P. Resnick, and M. Strauss, "REFEREE: Trust Management for Web Applications," *World Wide Web Journal*, 2 (1997), pp. 706–734.

[8] D. Clark and D. Wilson, "A Comparison of Commercial and Military Computer Security Policies," In *Proceedings of the IEEE Symposium on Security and Privacy*, IEEE Computer Society Press, Los Alamitos, 1987.

[9] C. Ellison, "SPKI Certificate Documentation," `http://www.pobox.com/~cme/html/spki.html`.

[10] A. Van Gelder, K. A. Ross, and J. S. Schlipf, "The Well-founded Semantics for Logic Programming," *Journal of the ACM*, 38 (1991), pp. 620-650.

[11] J. Gosling and H. McGilton, *The Java Language Environment, A White Paper*, Sun Microsystems, Inc., Mountain View, 1995.

[12] B. Grosof, "Courteous Logic Programs: Prioritized Conflict Handling for Rules," IBM Research Report RC20836, May 1997. This is an extended version of [13].

[13] B. Grosof, "Prioritized Conflict Handling for Logic Programs," in *Proceedings of the International Symposium on Logic Programming*, MIT Press, Cambridge, 1997, pp. 197–212.

[14] S. Jajodia, P. Samarati, and V. S. Subrahmanian, "A Logical Language for Expressing Authorizations," in *Proceedings of the Symposium on Security and Privacy*, IEEE Computer Society Press, Los Alamitos, 1997, pp. 31–42.

[15] S. Jajodia, P. Samarati, V. S. Subrahmanian, and E. Bertino, "A Unified Framework for Enforcing Multiple Access Control Policies," in *Proceedings ACM SIGMOD Conference on Management of Data*, 1997.

[16] S. T. Kent, "Internet Privacy Enhanced Mail," *Communications of the ACM*, 8 (1993), pp. 48–60.

[17] J. W. Lloyd, *Foundations of Logic Programming*, second edition, Springer, Berlin, 1987.

[18] M. Longhair (editor), "A P3P Preference Exchange Language (APPEL) Working Draft," W3C Working Draft 9, October 1998, `http://www.w3.org/P3P/Group/Preferences/Drafts/WD-P3P-preferences-19981009`.

[19] B. Lampson, M. Abadi, M. Burrows, and E. Wobber, "Authentication in Distributed Systems: Theory and Practice," *ACM Transactions on Computer Systems*, 10 (1992), pp. 265–310.

[20] M. Marchiori, J. Reagle, and D. Jaye (editors), "Platform for Privacy Preferences (P3P1.0) Specification," W3C Working Draft 9 November 1998, `http://www.w3.org/TR/WD-P3P/`.

[21] U. Maurer, "Modelling a Public-Key Infrastructure," in *Proceedings of the 1996 European Symposium on Research in Computer Security*, Lecture Notes in Computer Science, vol. 1146, Springer, Berlin, 1997, pp. 325–350.

[22] R. Reiter, "A Logic for Default Reasoning," *Artificial Intelligence*, 13 (1980), pp. 81–132.

[23] P. Resnick and J. Miller, "PICS: Internet access controls without censorship," *Communications of the ACM*, 39 (1996), pp. 87–93.

[24] R. Rivest and B. Lampson, "Cryptography and Information Security Group Research Project: A Simple Distributed Security Infrastructure," `http://theory.lcs.mit.edu/~cis/sdsi.html`.

[25] E. Wobber, M. Abadi, M. Burrows, and B. Lampson, "Authentication in the TAOS Operating System," *ACM Transactions on Computer Systems*, 12 (1994), pp. 3–32.

[26] T. Woo and S. Lam, "Authorization in Distributed Systems: A New Approach," *Journal of Computer Security*, 2 (1993), pp. 107–136.

[27] P. Zimmermann, *The Official PGP User's Guide*, MIT Press, Cambridge, 1995.

A Logical Framework for Reasoning on Data Access Control Policies

Elisa Bertino
Dipartimento di Scienze dell'Informazione
Università degli Studi di Milano
Via Comelico 39/41 - I20135 Milano, Italy
bertino@dsi.unimi.it

Francesco Buccafurri
Dipartimento DIMET
Università di Reggio Calabria
Feo di Vito - 89100 Reggio Calabria, Italy
bucca@ns.ing.unirc.it

Elena Ferrari
Dipartimento di Scienze dell'Informazione
Università degli Studi di Milano
Via Comelico 39/41 - I20135 Milano, Italy
ferrarie@dsi.unimi.it

Pasquale Rullo
Dipartimento di Matematica
Università della Calabria
Arcavacata di Rende 87030 Rende, Italy
rullo@si.deis.unical.it

Abstract

In this paper we propose a logic formalism that naturally supports the encoding of complex security specifications. This formalism relies on a hierarchically structured domain made of subjects, objects and privileges.

Authorizations are expressed by logic rules. The formalism supports both negation by failure (possibly unstratified) and true negation. The latter is used to express negative authorizations. It turns out that conflicts may result from a set of authorization rules. Dealing with such conflicts requires the knowledge of the domain structure, such as grantor priorities and object/subject hierarchies, which is used in the deductive process to determine which authorization prevails, if any, on the others. Often, however, conflicts are unsolvable, as they express intrinsic ambiguities.

We have devised two semantics as an extension of the well-founded and the stable model semantics of logic programming. We have also defined a number of access policies, each based on two orthogonal choices: one is related to the way how we cope with multiplicity of authorization sets in case of stable model semantics; the other is concerned with the open/closed assumption. A comparative analysis of the proposed authorization policies, based on their degree of permissivity, shows that they form a complete lattice.

1 Introduction

To date several access control policies have been developed to deal with controlling accesses to data by users and application programs [6, 11, 13, 20, 23]. Based on those policies, several authorization models have been formalized and corresponding access control mechanisms have been built, which are today in use in data management systems and research prototypes [2, 3, 5]. A major problem with current access control mechanisms is that each mechanism is based on a specific authorization model and it is thus based on a single specific policy, which is in fact built into the mechanism.

Several recent applications environments, such as distributed digital libraries, heterogeneous information systems, cooperative systems, workflow applications, groupware, have however articulated access control policy requirements which cannot be directly met by just a single access control policy. Those applications often need to deal with distributed objects of different types, like image and video data, relational data, object-oriented data, that often require to be administered under different policies. For example, complex objects may require a fine granularity for access control by which it must be possible to grant access authorizations on specific components of an object. Such requirement calls for positive and negative authorizations and exception mechanisms [23]. By contrast, relational data may not need such fine granularity in access control. However, even for such data there is the requirement of explicit denials [6]. Even different policies for authorization administration may need to coexist within the same system. For example, in a CSCW application environment, granting a user access to a data may require the joint authorization of several other users. In other applications, the authorization by a single administrator may suffice. It is thus clear that when an access control mechanism uses a specific policy, supporting requirements arising from different protection

1063-6900/99 $10.00

policies may became difficult if at all possible.

A possible solution is to develop access control mechanisms able to support multiple policies for different objects and users within the same system. It is obvious, however, that such a mechanism would have a more complex authorization model. The reason is that in several cases deciding whether allowing an access or not may be based on complex knowledge, such as information on grantor priorities, and may require quite articulated reasoning processes. It is therefore important that such a model be characterized by a formal semantics, ensuring that access control decisions be consistent and in accord with the application policies.

In this paper, we present a logic formalism that naturally supports the encoding of complex security specifications. This formalism relies on a hierarchically structured domain made of subjects, objects and privileges. Authorizations are expressed by logic rules; this allows us to condition the grant of an authorization to the presence and/or absence of other authorizations in the system. The formalism supports both negation by failure (possibly unstratified) and true negation, which is used to express negative authorizations (that is, authorizations expressing an explicit denial). The richness of our formalism implies that conflicts may arise from a set of authorization rules. Dealing with such conflicts requires the representation of complex knowledge about the considered domain, such as information on grantor priorities and on object and privilege hierarchies. Such knowledge is used in the deductive reasoning to decide which authorization prevails over the other. However, there are cases in which conflicts are unsolvable, since they express intrinsic conflicting requirements. For instance, consider two users Ann and Bob both having access to a document D_1. Suppose that their manager wishes to authorize Ann to read D_1 only when Bob does not have the right to modify it (and vice-versa). In this case, the domain knowledge is not enough to determine how to deal with the above specification, rather, there are a number of possible solutions (i.e., denying the access to both Ann and Bob, or to only one of them), each of which corresponds to a feasible interpretation of the specification.

To deal with these "structural" conflicts, we have devised two semantics as an extension of the well-founded and the stable model semantics of Logic Programming and Ordered Logic [7, 8, 15, 17], each of which corresponds to a possible conflict interpretation. The former defines a conservative approach whereby only "sure" authorizations are derived (that is, those authorizations which are not derived from ambiguous sources), whereas the latter goes beyond ambiguities by providing a number of authorization sets, each of which represents a consistent set of access authorizations. In the latter case, two alternative approaches can be used to decide whether an access can be authorized or not: one pessimistic, called *certainty reasoning*, where an access request is verified against the intersection of all the authorization sets; and one optimistic, called *possibility reasoning*, where the union is taken. If the possibility reasoning is adopted, the problem then arises of selecting the set of authorizations against which access control should be verified. To deal with such non-deterministic situation, we provide an innovative strategy to enforce access control where the choice of the authorization set is driven by the accesses currently in execution in the system.

A further aspect that should be taken into account when dealing with access control policies is whether authorization rules are used to specify denials (open assumption) or access rights (closed assumption). Under the open assumption an access is granted if the authorization rules do not allow the derivation of a denial for that access; under the closed assumption, an access is authorized only if the authorization rules allow the derivation of a (positive) authorization for that particular access.

The combination of the open/closed assumptions with the three semantics previously described gives rise to a number of authorization policies each of which can be useful for a particular context. To deal with such a multiplicity of policies, we provide a comparative analysis of the various access control policies, on the basis of their degree of *permissivity*, that is, on the basis of the number of accesses they allow. Based on this analysis, the System Security Officer can then decide the more suitable semantics for a specific application environment, without being forced to adopt a specific built-in policy.

We have presented a first proposal for an advanced authorization model based on a logic formalism in [4]. That model supports both positive and negative authorizations and derivation rules. The current paper extends our previous work by introducing different semantics for dealing with structural conflicts (in our previous proposal only the stable model semantics with possibility reasoning and the closed assumption is considered), and by providing a comparative analysis of the policies such semantics are able to express. This is a major extension, both for the practical relevance of supporting multiple access control policies and for the related theoretical issues.

From the side of logic formalisms for security specifications, Jajodia et al. [13, 14] propose a logic language for expressing authorization rules and show how this language can express most of the access control policies proposed so far. Programs that can be written in this language are a subset of stratified Datalog programs and therefore they are able to express only a limited set of authorization specifications. By contrast, in this paper we propose a very general language to express authorization specifications without syntactic restrictions (like stratification). Hence, we do not restrict ourselves to the consideration of programs having a unique model rather we allow a multiplicity of models to be associated with a given program and we show how different semantics can be used to deal with such multiplicity. A logic language, based on modal logic, has been proposed by Abadi et al. in [1]. However, their logic is mainly devoted to express concepts such as roles, delegation of authorizations, or the operation of certain protocols. A general logic language for expressing authorization rules has also been proposed by Woo and Lam in [26]. Although their language is very expressive, it suffers from several drawbacks. The most important is that no mechanisms are provided to deal with conflicting authorizations. By contrast, we have proposed both a general language to express authorization rules and a semantic framework to deal with conflicts that may arise from rule specifications.

The remainder of the paper is organized as follows. Section 2 introduces the basic components on which our logic framework relies. Sections 3 and 4 introduce the logic formalism, whereas Section 5 shows how different semantics can be used to model different access control policies. This section also provides a comparative analysis of the proposed policies. Section 6 deals with access control. Finally, Section 7 concludes the paper and outlines future work.

2 Basic Components

Our model relies on three basic components. The first component is a set $S = U \cup G$ of *subjects* to which authorizations are granted. Subjects can be either *users* (i.e., elements of U) or *groups* (i.e., elements of G).

Users are partially ordered according to their "importance". There are users, called *grantors*, that are allowed to specify authorizations. A group consists of a number of users. Groups are hierarchically organized into a group-subgroup relationship. Authorizations specified for a group will apply to all its subgroups/users.

The second basic component of our model is a set of objects O, denoting the resources to be protected. Objects to be considered depend on the underlying data model. Files and directories are examples of objects of an operating system, whereas if we consider a relational DBMS, resources to be protected are relations, views and attributes. To keep our authorization model general and thus applicable to the protection of information in different data models, we make no assumption on the underlying data model against which accesses must be controlled and on the privileges users can exercise in the system. Similarly to groups, objects are organized into a part-of hierarchy, called *object hierarchy*.

The last basic component of our model is a set of privileges P, denoting the access modes subjects can exercise on the objects in the system. In real situations, interactions exist among privileges. For instance, it is reasonable to assume that the `write` privilege is *stronger* than the `read` privilege (that is, it subsumes the `read` privilege). For this reason, also the set of privileges P is organized into a hierarchy, called *privilege hierarchy*.

The basic components of our model are formalized by the notion of *program domain*, defined next.

Definition 2.1 (Program Domain) A *(program) domain* consists of the following components:

1. **Subjects.** A countable set S of labels, called *subject identifiers*. This set is partitioned into two subsets, namely, G (*groups*), and U (*users*). S contains two special elements, namely, $\top_G \in G$ (the super group) and $\top_U \in U$ (the super user). The following hierarchies are defined:
   - *Group Hierarchy.* On S the partial order relation $\preceq_G$ is defined such that $\top_G \preceq_G s$, for all $s \in S$. $\preceq_G$ is such that $s \preceq_G s'$ implies that either $s \in G$ or $s = s'$ and represents both the group-subgroup hierarchy and the membership of users to groups. Given two groups $g_i, g_j \in G$, $g_i \preceq_G g_j$ we say that g_j is a *subgroup of* g_i. Moreover, given a user $u \in U$ and a group $g \in G$, $g \preceq_G u$ means that u *belongs to* g. As we shall see later in the paper, the super group $\top_G$ is used to define authorizations that hold for all subjects.
   - *User Hierarchy.* The set U of users is partially ordered by $\preceq_U$ in such a way that $\top_U \preceq_U u$, for all $u \in U$. We denote by $\prec_U$ the reflexive reduction of $\preceq_U$.[1] As we shall see later in the paper, the super user $\top_U$ is used to define strong authorizations, that is, authorizations that cannot be overridden.
2. **Objects.** A countable set O of labels, called *object identifiers*. O contains the special label $\top_O$, called *super object*. O is partially ordered by $\preceq_O$ in such a way that $\top_O \preceq_O o$, for all $o \in O$. The partial order $\preceq_O$ models a *part-of* relation among objects. We denote by $\prec_O$ the reflexive reduction of $\preceq_O$. Given two objects o_i and o_j, if $o_i \prec_O o_j$ we say that o_j is a *subobject* of o_i. $\top_O$ is used to define properties that must hold on all the elements of O.
3. **Privileges.** A countable set P of labels, called *privilege identifiers*. P is partially ordered by $\preceq_P$. We denote by $\prec_P$ the reflexive reduction of $\preceq_P$. We say that a privilege p_j *subsumes* privilege p_i if $p_j \prec_P p_i$.

3 Authorization Programs: Syntax

We assume that a domain D has been fixed. Over D, a set of authorization rules can be specified. These al-

[1] Given a partial order R, the reflexive reduction of R is $\{(a, b) \in R | a \neq b\}$.

low us to derive authorizations depending on the validity of some conditions as, for instance, the existence of other permissions or denials. Authorizations can be either positive or negative. A positive authorization states that a subject must be authorized for a given privilege on a given object, whereas a negative authorization states that a subject must be denied access to a given object. The set of specified authorization rules forms an *authorization program*.

Next we provide the syntax of an authorization program. Besides the domain D, from where constants are taken, we assume that the following sets are given:

1. A set Π of *predicate symbols* that are of two types: *built-in* and *user-defined*. There is a unique built-in predicate symbol, namely, $auth$, of arity 2, which has type $P \times U$ (i.e., the first term represents a privilege, whereas the second represents a user - actually the grantor of the authorization). User-defined predicate symbols are untyped and have a fixed arity.

2. A set Λ of *variable symbols*.

A *term* is either a constant (of D) or a variable (in Λ). A *reference* t is a pair in $(O \cup \Lambda \cup \{\mathbf{self}\}) \times (S \cup \Lambda \cup \{\mathbf{self}\})$. We denote by t_o the first element of t and by t_s the second one. If both $t_o \in O$ and $t_s \in S$ then t is a *bound* reference; if either t_o or t_s is **self** then t is a *self* reference.

An *atom* is a construct of the form: $p(\sigma_1, ..., \sigma_n)$, where p is a predicate symbol (in Π), n is the arity of p and $\sigma_1, ..., \sigma_n$ are terms. If p is built-in (i.e., $p = auth$), let $\tau_1 \times \tau_2$ denote its type; then, for each σ_i which is a constant, $\sigma_i \in \tau_i$ holds ($i = 1, 2$). A *simple literal* is either a *positive literal* Q or a *negative literal* $\neg Q$, where Q is an atom and $\neg$ is the *true negation symbol*. A *referential literal* is of the form $t.L$, where t is a reference and L is a simple literal. For instance, $(o, g).\neg p(X, Y)$, where o is an object and g is a group, is a referential literal. A *literal* is either a simple or a referential literal.

Two simple (resp. referential) literals are *complementary* if they are of the form Q and $\neg Q$ (resp. $t.Q$ and $t.\neg Q$). Given a literal L, we denote its complementary literal by $\neg.L$. Two literals are *conflicting* if they are of the form $t.auth(p, g)$ and $t.\neg auth(p', g')$ and $p = p'$.

A *rule* r is an expression of the form:

$$H \leftarrow A_1, ..., A_n, not\ B_1, ..., not\ B_m \quad n \geq 0, m \geq 0$$

where H, $A_1, ..., A_n$ and $B_1, ..., B_m$ are literals and not is the *negation by failure* symbol [19]. H is the *head* of r and $A_1, ..., A_n, not\ B_1, ..., not\ B_m$, $n \geq 0, m \geq 0$, is the *body* of r. Note that the head H may be a negative literal. We often denote the head literal of r by $Head(r)$ and the body of r by $Body(r)$. A rule whose head predicate symbol is $auth$ is called *authorization rule*, otherwise it is called *support rule*. In the head of an authorization rule, the second term (the one representing the grantor) is a constant (in U).

Definition 3.1 (Authorization Program) A *component identifier* (*c-identifier*, for short) is a bound reference (i.e., an element of $O \times S$). On the set of c-identifiers the partial order $\preceq_*$ is defined as follows: given two c-identifiers $\bar{t} = (\bar{t}_o, \bar{t}_s)$ and $\hat{t} = (\hat{t}_o, \hat{t}_s)$, $\bar{t} \preceq_* \hat{t}$ iff $\bar{t}_o \preceq_O \hat{t}_o$ and $\bar{t}_s \preceq_G \hat{t}_s$. We denote by $\prec_*$ the reflexive closure of the relation $\preceq_*$.

A *component* C is a pair $(t, \Sigma(t))$, where t is a c-identifier and $\Sigma(t)$ is a (possibly empty) set of rules with simple head literals.

An *(authorization) program* $\mathcal{P}$ is a finite set of components, one for each c-identifier. $\preceq_*$ induces a partial order on $\mathcal{P}$ in the obvious way, that is, given $C_i = (t_i, \Sigma(t_i))$ and $C_j = (t_j, \Sigma(t_j))$, $C_i \preceq_* C_j$ iff $t_i \preceq_* t_j$ (read "C_j is more specific than C_i").

Informally, an authorization rule, appearing in a component $(t, \Sigma(t))$, whose head is of the form $auth(p, g)$ (resp., $\neg auth(p, g)$), is used to express a positive (resp., negative) authorization for privilege p on object t_o granted by g to subject t_s. We recall that g identifies the user who specifies the rule.

Example 3.1 Consider the program consisting of the following component:

(o, s):
$\{r_1\colon auth(\texttt{read}, g) \leftarrow (o_2, s_1).\neg auth(\texttt{write}, g)$
$r_2\colon \neg auth(\texttt{write}, g') \leftarrow\}$

Informally, it states that, for object o and subject s, the following holds: 1) rule r_1: s is authorized by g to read object o provided that subject s_1 is denied (true negation) by g to write object o_2. Note that the literal $(o_2, s_1).\neg auth(\texttt{write}, g)$ is a referential literal addressing to the component with c-identifier (o_2, s_1); 2) rule r_2: s is denied by grantor g' to write o. Note that true negation is used in the head of r_2.

As another example, let us consider the following single-component program

(o, s):
$\{ r_1\colon auth(\texttt{write}, g) \leftarrow not\ any\_subj\_has\_auth$
$r_2\colon any\_subj\_has\_auth \leftarrow (\mathbf{self}, X).auth(\texttt{write}, Y),$
$X \neq s \}$

whose informal reading is the following: for object o and subject s it holds that s is authorized to write o if there is no authorization for anybody else to write o. Note that $any\_subj\_has\_auth$ is a user defined predicate symbol and that negation by failure is used. Further, in the body of r_2 there is a $self$ reference, that expresses a reference to object o. The reason why we use $self$ instead of o depends on the mechanism whereby rules are inherited along the subject/object hierarchy; indeed, while $self$ gets instantiated to the objects of the components where the rule is inherited, o keeps constant during inheritance (see Example 4.3).

Finally, the following program expresses that grantor g gives Bob the access to any object to which Ann is authorized by some grantor, and vice versa (recall that $\top_O$ is the super object).

$(\top_O, \texttt{Bob})$:
  $\{ \, auth(X, g) \leftarrow (\textbf{self}, \texttt{Ann}).auth(X, Y) \, \}$
$(\top_O, \texttt{Ann})$:
  $\{ \, auth(X, g) \leftarrow (\textbf{self}, \texttt{Bob}).auth(X, Y) \, \}$

In the examples above we have provided an "informal" meaning for authorization programs. The high declarativeness of the logic paradigm makes in general this task easy, at least for not complex programs. However, a formal definition of the semantics of an authorization program must be provided. This is the aim of the next section. As we will explain therein, the meaning of an authorization program is given by the authorizations that are derivable from it. As illustrated in Sections 5 and 6, access to the protected resources will be granted on the basis of the derivable authorizations.

We point out that semantic aspects (regarding both semantics of a program and access control policies) play a crucial role in our proposal, since they make the model innovative with respect to existing approaches. This matter will be deeply analyzed in the following sections. A crucial aspect we like to introduce here, just in an informal fashion, concerns the high expressiveness of the model. Indeed, due to unstratified negation by failure and explicit negation (negative authorizations), we allow the designer to (naturally) encode complex security specifications, not expressible in classical models. For instance, specifications (i.e., programs) entailing more than one alternative meaning, can be modeled in our framework. Here, we give an example of program expressing a mutual exclusion specification. As intuitively can be expected, the meaning of the program consists of two (alternative) sets of entailed authorizations.

Example 3.2 Consider the following program expressing that Ann and Bob cannot be simultaneously authorized to write object o.

$(o, \texttt{Ann})$:
  $\{ \, r_1\text{: } auth(\texttt{write}, \texttt{Tom}) \leftarrow not \; (\textbf{self}, \texttt{Bob}).auth(\texttt{write}, \texttt{Tom}) \, \}$
$(o, \texttt{Bob})$:
  $\{ r_2\text{: } auth(\texttt{write}, \texttt{Tom}) \leftarrow not \; (\textbf{self}, \texttt{Ann}).auth(\texttt{write}, \texttt{Tom}) \, \}$

In this program, the access to object o can be derived for Ann provided that Bob is not authorized (negation by failure) to access the same object, and vice versa. As a consequence, two sets of authorizations can be derived in this case, one in which only Ann has the permission to access o and the other in which only Bob has this permission.

4 Authorization Programs: Semantics

As we have seen in the previous section, an authorization program encodes the explicit knowledge concerning authorizations over a given domain. In this section, we provide the formal semantics of an authorization program, that is, the permissions that can be derived from its rules. To this end, two aspects are to be taken into account: first, the implicit knowledge coming from the hierarchical structure of the program domain and, second, possible contradicting authorizations arising from conflicting rules.

Some preliminary definitions are next given.

The *base* $B_{\mathcal{P}}$ of a program $\mathcal{P}$ is the set of all ground literals (both simple and referential) constructible from the predicate symbols in Π and the constants in the domain D. A set of literals is *consistent* if no conflicting literals occur in it. An *interpretation (for $\mathcal{P}$)* is any consistent subset of $B_{\mathcal{P}}$. Given an interpretation I, a ground (either base or referential) literal L is *true* (resp. *false*) *w.r.t.* I if $L \in I$ (resp., $\neg.L \in I$, that is, the complementary is true). Literals that are neither true nor false w.r.t. I are $undefined$ w.r.t. I. Let r be a ground rule of the form

$$H \leftarrow A_1, ..., A_n, not \; B_1, ..., not \; B_m \quad n \geq 0, m \geq 0$$

and I an interpretation. The body of r is *true w.r.t.* I if every A_i, $1 \leq i \leq n$, is true w.r.t. I and every B_j, $1 \leq j \leq m$, is not true w.r.t. I. The body of r is *false w.r.t.* I if some A_i $(1 \leq i \leq n)$ is false w.r.t. I or some B_j $(1 \leq j \leq m)$ is true w.r.t. I.

4.1 Rule Propagation along Hierarchies

We already said that the object (resp. group) hierarchy represents a part-of relationship. Thus, according to the object-oriented approach, rules defined for a given object (resp. group) are automatically inherited by all subobjects (resp. subgroups). This means that if, for instance, a user belongs to more than one group, he/she receives the authorizations specified for all the groups to which he/she belongs to. Similarly, if a user has an authorization to read a given directory, then he/she is by default authorized to read also all the files that belong to that directory, unless an explicit denial is specified. We note that authorization rules propagate regardless of the possibility of generating conflicts.

Definition 4.1 Given a component $(t, \Sigma(t))$, we define the *closure of* $\Sigma(t)$ *w.r.t.* $\preceq_*$ as follows: $\Sigma'(t) = \{\langle t', r\rangle \mid r \in \Sigma(t'), \; t' \preceq_* t\}$. We call each $\langle t, r\rangle \in \Sigma'(t)$ *referential rule*.

Example 4.1 Consider two objects o_1 and o_2 such that $o_1 \preceq_O o_2$ and a group G to which the u belongs (that is, $G \preceq_G u$ holds). Now, consider the program $\mathcal{P}_1$ consisting of the following (not empty) components:

(o_1, G):
$\{ auth(\texttt{write}, g) \leftarrow (\textbf{self}, u).\text{auth}(\texttt{execute}, g) \}$
(o_2, u):
$\{ \neg auth(\texttt{write}, g) \leftarrow$
$\neg auth(\texttt{execute}, g) \leftarrow \}$

(note that the components of $\mathcal{P}_1$ associated with the c-identifiers (o_1, u) and (o_2, G) are empty). Because of rule propagation along object and group hierarchies, each component is enriched by the inherited authorization rules as follows (note that $(o_1, G) \preceq_* (o_2, u)$, $(o_1, G) \preceq_* (o_2, G)$ and $(o_1, G) \preceq_* (o_1, u)$ hold):

$\Sigma'(o_1, G) = \Sigma'(o_2, G) = \Sigma'(o_1, u)$:
$\{ \langle\ (o_1, G), auth(\texttt{write}, g) \leftarrow (\textbf{self}, u).auth(\texttt{execute}, g)\ \rangle \}$

$\Sigma'(o_2, u)$:
$\{ \langle\ (o_1, G), auth(\texttt{write}, g) \leftarrow (\textbf{self}, u).auth(\texttt{execute}, g)\ \rangle$
$\langle\ (o_2, u), \neg auth(\texttt{write}, g) \leftarrow\ \rangle$
$\langle\ (o_2, u), auth(\texttt{execute}, g) \leftarrow\ \rangle \}$

We observe that each referential rule appearing above of the form, say, $\langle t, r\rangle$, holds the c-identifier t of the component which it comes from. For instance, the c-identifier (o_1, G) of the first rule of $\Sigma'(o_2, u)$ expresses that this rule is inherited from the component having (o_1, G) as c-identifier.

Authorizations propagate along the privilege hierarchy according to the following rules: *i)* a positive authorization for privilege p on object o implies a positive authorization on o for all the privileges following p in the privilege hierarchy; *ii)* a negative authorization for p on o implies a negative authorization on o for all the privileges preceding p in the privilege hierarchy.

The privilege propagation rules are based on the semantics assigned to the $\prec_P$ relation. Privileges at lower levels in the hierarchy are subsumed by privileges at higher levels. Thus, the first rule states that a positive authorization for a given privilege p implies a positive authorization for all the privileges subsumed by p. This means for instance, that if a subject has an authorization to write an object, then it has also an authorization to read it. The second rule states that a negative authorization for a given privilege p implies a negative authorization for all the privileges subsuming p. Thus, if a subject is denied to read an object, then it is also denied to write it.

Taking into account also privilege propagation, we next define the notion of closure of a component.

Definition 4.2 Given a component $(t, \Sigma(t))$, we define the *closure* $\Sigma^+(t)$ of $\Sigma(t)$ as illustrated in Figure 1.

Intuitively, $\Sigma^+(t)$, is the complete set of rules encoding the whole knowledge associated with t.

4.2 Conflict Resolution by Priority

In our model contradicting authorizations may arise due to the simultaneous presence of conflicting rules. However, we do not consider such a presence as an inconsistency; rather, we define a conflict resolution policy which determines which authorization, if any, should defeat the other. The basic idea is that authorization rules are assigned with different levels of reliability according to the hierarchical organization of the domain. In other words, hierarchies provide a means to implicitly assign priorities to authorizations rules, based on which the "preferred" ones are chosen (if any).

Informally, conflicts on authorizations are solved according to the following policy. First, the grantors of the conflicting rules are taken into account. To this end, the user hierarchy (see Definition 2.1) is considered. In particular, if one grantor prevails on the other, the conflict is solved in favor of the former (i.e., the rules which has been signed up by the stronger grantor prevail). Otherwise, i.e., grantors are incomparable, object and subject hierarchies are exploited. To this end, we rely on the following principle: the more specific is the component to which a rule r belongs to, the more reliable r is. Thus, the authorization defined by the most reliable rule prevails. However, it may happen that even components are incomparable; in such a case, we say that conflicts are *intrinsic* (or *unsolvable*) and conclude that there is no way to solve them: more alternative solutions there exist, none of which is preferable to the others. Thus, conflict resolution may entail more sets of possible authorizations.

Example 4.2 Consider the component (o_2, u) of program $\mathcal{P}_1$ of Example 4.1. Because of inheritance, this component contains two conflicting authorization rules (see $\Sigma'(o_2, u)$) in Example 4.1). Indeed, user u inherits an authorization to write object o_2 from the component (o_1, G), and a denial to write the same object from (o_2, u) (see $\Sigma'(o_2, u)$) in Example 4.1). Fortunately, this conflict can be easily solved. Indeed, although both authorizations are provided by the same grantor, we have that the source component (o_2, u) of the negative authorization is more specific than the other $((o_1, G))$ (indeed, both $o_1 \preceq_O o_2$ and $G \preceq_G u$ hold), so that the negative authorization prevails over the positive one. We say that the negative authorization *defeats* the positive authorization (the notion of *defeating* is formally defined in the following).

$$\Sigma^+(t) = \Sigma'(t) \cup \{\langle t', auth(\sigma_1, \sigma_2) \leftarrow B' \rangle \mid \langle t', auth(\sigma_3, \sigma_2) \leftarrow B \rangle \in \Sigma'(t), B' = B \wedge \sigma_1 \prec_P \sigma_3\}$$
$$\cup \{\langle t', \neg auth(\sigma_1 \sigma_2) \leftarrow B' \rangle \mid \langle t', \neg auth(\sigma_3, \sigma_2) \leftarrow B \rangle \in \Sigma'(t), B' = B \wedge \sigma_3 \prec_P \sigma_1\}$$

Figure 1. Closure of a component

Let us now consider a case in which hierarchies do not provide support to solve conflicts. Consider, for instance, a domain consisting of a user u and objects o_1, o_2 and o_3 such that $o_1 \prec_O o_3$ and $o_2 \prec_O o_3$. Suppose we have the following program $\mathcal{P}_2$:

(o_1, u):
  $\{ auth(\texttt{read}, g) \leftarrow (\textbf{self}, u).auth(\texttt{execute}, g')$
   $auth(\texttt{write}, g') \leftarrow (o_1, u).auth(\texttt{execute}, g) \}$
(o_2, u):
  $\{ \neg auth(\texttt{read}, g) \leftarrow \}$
(o_3, u):
  $\{ auth(\texttt{execute}, g') \leftarrow$
   $auth(\texttt{execute}, g) \leftarrow \}$

After inheritance and privilege propagation we have:

$\Sigma^+(o_3, u)$:
  $\{ \langle\ (o_1, u), auth(\texttt{read}, g) \leftarrow (\textbf{self}, u).auth(\texttt{execute}, g')\ \rangle$
   $\langle\ (o_1, u), auth(\texttt{write}, g') \leftarrow (o_1, u).auth(\texttt{execute}, g)$
   $\langle\ (o_2, u), \neg auth(\texttt{read}, g) \leftarrow\ \rangle$
   $\langle\ (o_3, u), auth(\texttt{execute}, g') \leftarrow\ \rangle$
   $\langle\ (o_3, u), auth(\texttt{execute}, g) \leftarrow\ \rangle \}$

Note that (o_3, u) contains two conflicting authorizations (both a permission and a denial for user u to read object o_3) granted by the same grantor g. Further, their source components are (o_1, u) and (o_2, u), that are incomparable. It turns out that such a conflict is not solvable by defeating, since the above program encodes an intrinsic ambiguity.

In our model, the conflict resolution policy is formalized by the concept of *defeating*, which we next define. To this end, however, we need some preliminary notation and definitions.

Notation Let a component identifier t and a reference $\hat{t}$ be given. $f_t(\hat{t})$ is the reference defined as follows: $f_t(\hat{t})_\gamma = t_\gamma$ if $\hat{t}_\gamma = \textbf{self}$, $f_t(\hat{t})_\gamma = \hat{t}_\gamma$, otherwise, where $\gamma \in \{o, s\}$. Further, given a rule r, and a component identifier t, we denote by $t.r$ the rule obtained from r by replacing each simple literal L by the referential literal $t.L$ and each referential literal $\hat{t}.L$ by $f_t(\hat{t}).L$. For instance, if r is $\neg p(a,b) \leftarrow q(a,b), (o, \textbf{self}).s(b)$, then $t.r$ is $t.\neg p(a,b) \leftarrow t.q(a,b), (o, t_s).s(b)$.

Definition 4.3 (Ground Program) We denote by $\mathcal{P}^*$ the set of all referential rules $\langle t, r \rangle$ such that $\langle t, r' \rangle \in \Sigma^+(t')$, for some component identifier t', and $r = t'.r'$. The *ground version* $G(\mathcal{P})$ of $\mathcal{P}$ is the set referential rules $\langle t, r \rangle$ obtained from each pair in $\mathcal{P}^*$ by replacing each variable appearing in it by each constant appearing in the program.

Example 4.3 The ground version of program $\mathcal{P}_2$ of Example 4.2 is:

$G(\mathcal{P}_2)$:
 $\{$ 1. $\langle\ (o_1, u), (o_1, u).auth(\texttt{read}, g) \leftarrow (o_1, u).auth(\texttt{execute}, g')\ \rangle$
 2. $\langle\ (o_1, u), (o_1, u).auth(\texttt{write}, g') \leftarrow (o_1, u).auth(\texttt{execute}, g)$
 3. $\langle\ (o_2, u), (o_2, u).\neg auth(\texttt{read}, g) \leftarrow (o_2, u).auth(\texttt{execute}, g')\ \rangle$
 4. $\langle\ (o_1, u), (o_3, u).auth(\texttt{read}, g) \leftarrow (o_3, u).auth(\texttt{execute}, g')\ \rangle$
 5. $\langle\ (o_1, u), (o_3, u).auth(\texttt{write}, g') \leftarrow (o_1, u).auth(\texttt{execute}, g)$
 6. $\langle\ (o_2, u), (o_3, u).\neg auth(\texttt{read}, g) \leftarrow (o_3, u).auth(\texttt{execute}, g')\ \rangle$
 7. $\langle\ (o_3, u), (o_3, u).auth(\texttt{execute}, g') \leftarrow\ \rangle$
 8. $\langle\ (o_3, u), (o_3, u).auth(\texttt{execute}, g) \leftarrow\ \rangle \}$

From this example it should be clear how the semantics of a self reference differs from that of an explicit reference to the object/subject with which the rule is associated. Indeed, self references are instantiated to the object/subject where the rule is inherited, while bound references keep constant during the inheritance process. To see this point, look at rules 4, 5 and 6 above.

Definition 4.4 (Conflicting Rules) Let $r_1 = \langle t_1, r \rangle$ and $r_2 = \langle t_2, r' \rangle$ be two referential rules in $G(\mathcal{P})$. r_1 and r_2 are *conflicting* if either

- they are support rules, and $Head(r)$ and $Head(r')$ are complementary literals, or
- they are authorization rules and $Head(r)$ and $Head(r')$ are conflicting literals.

We are now ready to formally define the conflict resolution policy.

Definition 4.5 (Defeating) Let I be an interpretation for $\mathcal{P}$ and let $r_1 = \langle \bar{t}, r \rangle \in G(\mathcal{P})$ be a referential rule. We say that r_1 is *defeated* in I if either

- r_1 is a support rule and there exists a support rule $r_2 = \langle \hat{t}, r' \rangle \in G(\mathcal{P})$ such that r_1 and r_2 are conflicting rules, the body of r' is true in I, and $\bar{t} \prec_* \hat{t}$ holds (see Definition 3.1), or
- r_1 is an authorization rule and there exists $r_2 = \langle \hat{t}, r' \rangle \in G(\mathcal{P})$ such that r_1 and r_2 are conflicting rules, the body of r' is true in I and (at least) one of the following conditions holds (next g and g' are the grantors appearing in $Head(r)$ and $Head(r')$, respectively):
  - $g' \prec_U g$, that is, g' is a grantor stronger than g;
  - g and g' are incomparable w.r.t. $\prec_U$ (i.e., neither $g' \prec_U g$ nor $g \prec_U g'$) and $\bar{t} \prec_* \hat{t}$;

Remark (Strong Authorizations). We have seen in the above definition that grantors play a crucial role in conflict resolution. Indeed , the more "important" a grantor is, the higher is the priority of the specified authorization. However, in order to prevent a possible complete loss of control, our model allows the possibility of defining properties with an *absolute* validity. This is the mechanism of *strong authorizations* [23]. Conceptually, we can see a strong authorization as an authorization provided by a sort of *super user*, that is, a user which is more important than any other (denoted by $\top_U$ in our model- see Definition 2.1).

4.3 Stable Authorization Sets

Assigning a meaning to a program is not a simple task at all. Indeed, we have seen that conflicts coming from true negation are not solvable, in general, in a single way; rather, a number of possible (equivalent) solutions often exist. In addition, as in (traditional) logic programming, the presence of unstratified negation by failure [25] is a source of further complexity, as other possible ambiguities may arise. Thus, we expect that, in general, more sets of entailed authorizations are associated with a given program. (This is not a novelty in logic programming, where a widely accepted semantics is that based on stable models [12] which assigns to a logic program a number (possibly zero) of alternative models, each representing a possible solution.)

We next define a semantics for authorization programs which relies on the classical notion of stable model. To this end, we need to extend some classical concepts to take into account the peculiarities of our language.

Definition 4.6 (Rule Satisfaction) A referential rule $\langle \bar{t}, r \rangle \in G(\mathcal{P})$ is *true w.r.t.* an interpretation I if either the head of r is true w.r.t. I or its body is not true w.r.t. I. A referential rule $\langle \bar{t}, r \rangle \in G(\mathcal{P})$ is *satisfied w.r.t.* an interpretation I if either it is true w.r.t. I or it is defeated in I.

Definition 4.7 (Authorization Program Model) A *model* for $\mathcal{P}$ is an interpretation M such that every referential rule in $G(\mathcal{P})$ is satisfied in M.

Definition 4.8 (Reduction of an Authorization Program) Given an interpretation I for $\mathcal{P}$, the *reduction* of $\mathcal{P}$ w.r.t. I, denoted $G_I(\mathcal{P})$, is the following set of ground rules:

$G_I(\mathcal{P}) = \{\ r \mid \exists\ \langle t, r \rangle \in G(\mathcal{P})$ not defeated in I and $Body(r)$ is true w.r.t. $I\ \}$.

Note that $G_I(\mathcal{P})$ can be regarded as a Datalog program (with negation by failure) [18, 25] simply by considering each referential literal of the form, say, $t.p(t_1, ..., t_n)$ (resp. $t.\neg p(t_1, ..., t_n)$), as a simple literal with predicate symbol $t.p$ (resp. $t.\neg p$). Thus, given a set X of rules, the immediate consequence operator $T_{\mathcal{P}}$ is defined in the usual way (see Figure 2).

Definition 4.9 (Stable Authorization Set) Let M be a model of $\mathcal{P}$. M is an *(stable) authorization set* for $\mathcal{P}$ if $M = T^{\infty}_{(G_M(\mathcal{P}))}(\emptyset)$.

Example 4.4 Consider the program $\mathcal{P}$ of Example 3.2 and let the domain consisting of object o, subjects `Ann`, `Bob` and `Tom`, and privilege `write`. Let $A_1 = \{(o,\texttt{Ann}).auth(\texttt{write},\texttt{Tom})\ \}$, be an interpretation for $\mathcal{P}$. The reduction of $\mathcal{P}$ w.r.t. A_1 is $G_{A_1}(\mathcal{P}) = \{(\mathrm{o}, \mathrm{Ann}).\mathrm{auth}(\texttt{write}, \mathrm{Tom}) \leftarrow\}$. Clearly, $A_1 = T^{\infty}_{(G_{A_1}(\mathcal{P}))}(\emptyset)$ and, thus, A_1 is an authorization set for $\mathcal{P}$. It can be easily shown that $A_2 = \{(o,\texttt{Bob}).auth(\texttt{write},\texttt{Tom})\ \}$ is also a stable authorization set of $\mathcal{P}$ (see comments in Example 3.2).

In the above example, multiplicity of authorization sets is determined by unstratified negation by failure. However, also conflicts (i.e., true negation) may cause multiple authorization sets.

Example 4.5 Consider program $\mathcal{P}_2$ of Example 4.2 whose ground version has been shown in Example 4.3. As we have seen, component (o_3, u) inherits two conflicting authorizations, none of which prevails on the other (since both their grantors and components are incomparable). As a consequence, two possible ways of solving this conflict exist, each corresponding to a possible authorization set. It easy to verify that $A_1 = \{\ (o_3,u).auth(\texttt{read},g),\ (o_3,u).auth(\texttt{execute},g'),\ (o_3,u).auth(\texttt{execute},g)\ \}$ and $A_2 = \{\ (o_3,u).\neg auth(\texttt{read},g),\ (o_3,u).auth(\texttt{execute},g'),\ (o_3,u).auth(\texttt{execute},g)\ \}$ are the authorization sets of the program. The reason for that is the presence in the program of intrinsically ambiguous conflicts that cannot be solved by defeating.

We note that both positive and negative authorizations may occur in a stable model.

$$T_{\mathcal{P}}: \quad 2^{B_{\mathcal{P}}} \rightarrow 2^{B_{\mathcal{P}}}$$
$$I \mapsto \{L \in B_{\mathcal{P}} | \exists r \in X \ s.t.\ Head(r) = L,\ and\ Body(r)\ is\ true\ w.r.t.\ I\}$$

Figure 2. $T_{\mathcal{P}}$ operator

4.4 The Well-Founded Authorization Set

Like in traditional logic programming, it may happen that a program does not admit any stable authorization set. To solve this problem, we define the notion of *well-founded authorization set* that is defined for all programs. The definition we are giving extends that proposed for Ordered Logic [16] to take into account negation by failure.

Definition 4.10 (Unfounded Set) Let $\mathcal{P}$ be a program and I an interpretation for $\mathcal{P}$. A subset $X \subseteq B_{\mathcal{P}}$ is an unfounded set of $\mathcal{P}$ w.r.t. I if for each $L \in X$, for each rule $\langle t, r\rangle \in G(\mathcal{P})$ of the form $L \leftarrow A_1, ..., A_n, notB_1, ..., notB_m$, at least one of the following conditions holds:

1. $Body(r)$ is false w.r.t. I;
2. there exists some A_i, $1 \leq i \leq n$, belonging to X (i.e., $Body(r) \cap X \neq \emptyset$);
3. $\langle t, r\rangle$ is defeated in I

It is easy to recognize that, like in both traditional logic programming and Ordered Logic, the union of two unfounded sets is an unfounded set, thus there exists the greatest unfounded set. We denote by $GUS_{\mathcal{P}}(I)$ the greatest unfounded set. We are now ready to define the $W_{\mathcal{P}}$ operator and then the well-founded authorization set.

Definition 4.11 ($W_{\mathcal{P}}$ Operator) $W_{\mathcal{P}}(I) = T_{\mathcal{P}}(I) \cap \neg GUSP(I)$, where

$$T_{\mathcal{P}}(I) = \{ L \in B_{\mathcal{P}} | \exists(t, r) \in G(\mathcal{P})\ s.t.\ H(r) = L, B(r) = L_1, ..., L_n, notP_1, .., notP_m, L_i \in I,\ 1 \leq i \leq n,\ P_j \in GUS_{\mathcal{P}}(I), 1 \leq j \leq m\}$$

Now, consider the following sequence of interpretations of $\mathcal{P}$

$$I_0 = \emptyset,\ I_1 = W_{\mathcal{P}}(I_0), ..., I_k = W_{\mathcal{P}}(I_{k-1}), ...$$

Since both $T_{\mathcal{P}}$ and $GUS_{\mathcal{P}}$ are monotonic operators, $W_{\mathcal{P}}$ is monotonic as well. Thus, since $B_{\mathcal{P}}$ is finite, the above sequence finitely converges to a fixpoint $W_{\mathcal{P}}^{\infty}$. It is easy to see that $W_{\mathcal{P}}^{\infty}$ is the least fixpoint of $W_{\mathcal{P}}$ and that $W_{\mathcal{P}}^{\infty} = \bigcup_{j \geq 0} I_j$.

Definition 4.12 (Well-founded Authorization Set) The *well-founded authorization set of* $\mathcal{P}$ is $W_{\mathcal{P}}^{\infty}$.

Clearly, every program has a unique well-founded authorization set.

Example 4.6 Let us consider a program consisting of the following unique component:

(o, u):
$\{\ auth(\texttt{append}, g) \leftarrow$
$auth(\texttt{read}, g) \leftarrow$
$\neg auth(\texttt{read}, g') \leftarrow \}$

where g and g' are incomparable and no interaction between privileges append and read exists. The well-founded authorization set $W = \{auth(\texttt{append}, g)\}$, whereas the stable authorization sets are $A_1 = \{\ (o, u).auth(\texttt{append}, g), (o, u).auth(\texttt{read}, g)\ \}$ and $A_2 = \{\ (o, u).auth(\texttt{append}, g), (o, u).\neg auth(\texttt{read}, g')\ \}$.

Intuitively, the well-founded semantics allows us to infer only "sure" authorizations, that is, authorizations that are undoubtly true as deriving from that portion of the program which is free from both unstratified negation (by failure) and conflicts (true negation) unsolvable by defeating.

Like in logic programming, the following property holds.

Proposition 4.1 *The well-founded authorization set is contained in the intersection of all stable authorization sets.*

The importance of the well-founded semantics for authorization programs lies in its tractability. Indeed, the operator $W_{\mathcal{P}}$ is computable in polynomial time.

5 Access Control Policies

As we have seen, a program $\mathcal{P}$ can be interpreted differently by using different semantics, namely, the well-founded or the stable semantics. However, once fixed a semantics, the problem as whether granting an access request remains still to be solved. Suppose, for instance, that two conflicting authorizations belong to distinct authorization sets. What should it be done in such a case? And what if an authorization does not occur in any authorization set either as positive or negative? To answer such questions, whether

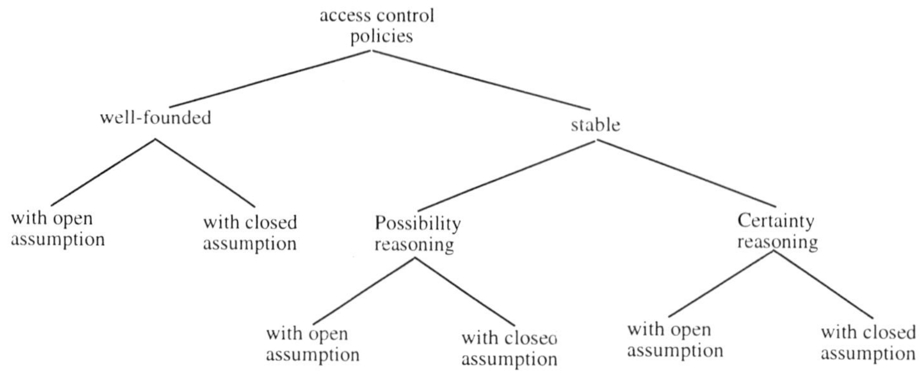

Figure 3. Access control policies' taxonomy

a program has been used to specify denials (*Open Assumption*) or to specify access rights (*Closed Assumption*) must be known.

For instance, assume that the well-founded semantics has been chosen. Deciding whether to grant or deny an access request is a quite simple task in such a case. Clearly, the result depends on whether the closed or the open assumption is taken. In the former case, a user is permitted an access only if a positive authorization is in the well-founded model. Otherwise, he/she is denied. If the open assumption is taken, a user is denied only if a negative authorization is in the well-founded authorization set. Otherwise he/she is authorized.

In case of stable semantics, the problem is how to deal with the multiplicity of authorization sets. Indeed, although each authorization set is consistent, conflicting authorizations may belong to different authorization sets. Thus, for an access request, the problem arises of whether it is to be accepted or denied. To this end, we consider the two modalities of *certainty* and *possibility* reasoning [21]. One is based on a pessimistic approach (certainty) whereas the other is based on an optimistic approach (possibility). Informally, in the former case, only the authorizations that are in *every* authorization set are taken into account. In particular, under the closed assumption, an access is granted only if it is "certain", that is, an authorization for it exists in every authorization set. Symmetrically, under the open assumption, an access request is accepted only if there is the certainty of not being denied, that is, there does not exist an authorization set containing a negative authorization for that access.

Under the possibility semantics, "possible" authorizations are allowed. In such case, under the closed assumption, an access request is granted if there exists a positive authorization authorizing it in *some* stable authorization set. Symmetrically, under the open assumption, an access request is accepted if there is the possibility of not being denied, that is, there exist some authorization set not containing an explicit denial. Figure 3 summarizes all the above access control policies.

Notation We denote by $Poss$, $Cert$ and Wf the three semantics of Possibility, Certainty and Well-founded, respectively. Further, $Sem = \{Poss, Cert, Wf\}$ and $Opt = \{Open\_ass, Closed\_ass\}$.

Definition 5.1 (Policy) An *authorization policy* (often simply "policy") is any pair $(\omega, \sigma) \in Opt \times Sem$.

Definition 5.2 (Access Request) An *access request* is a triple (u, p, o), with $u \in U$, $p \in P$, and $o \in O$.

Access request (u, p, o) states that user u requires to exercise privilege p on object o.

Definition 5.3 (Access Request Satisfaction) Let $\alpha = (u, p, o)$ be an access request on $\mathcal{P}$ and (ω, σ) an authorization policy. Further, let $W_{\mathcal{P}}^{\infty}$ be the well-founded authorization set of $\mathcal{P}$ and $\Gamma_{\mathcal{P}}$ the family of stable authorization sets of $\mathcal{P}$. We say that α is *satisfied*

1. *under* $(Closed\_ass, Wf)$ if $\exists$ a grantor g s.t. $(o, u).auth(p, g) \in W_{\mathcal{P}}^{\infty}$
2. *under* $(Open\_ass, Wf)$ if $\neg\exists$ a grantor g s.t. $\neg(o, u).auth(p, g) \in W_{\mathcal{P}}^{\infty}$
3. *under* $(Closed\_ass, Cert)$ if $\forall A \in \Gamma_{\mathcal{P}}$, $\exists$ a grantor g s.t. $(o, u).auth(p, g) \in A$
4. *under* $(Open\_ass, Cert)$ if $\forall A \in \Gamma_{\mathcal{P}}, \neg\exists$ a grantor g s.t. $\neg(o, u).auth(p, g) \in A$
5. *under* $(Closed\_ass, Poss)$ if $\exists\, A \in \Gamma_{\mathcal{P}}$ and a grantor g s.t. $(o, u).auth(p, g) \in A$

6. *under* $(Open\_ass, Poss)$ if $\exists\ A \in \Gamma_{\mathcal{P}}$ s.t. $\neg\exists$ a grantor g s.t. $\neg(o,u).auth(p,g) \in A$

In case of possibility reasoning we say that α is *satisfied in* A.

Remark (Nondeterminism). It is worth noting that the possibility semantics entails a form of don't care nondeterminism, as *any* authorization set satisfying a given request can (nondeterministically) be chosen as the meaning of the program.

Remark (Open/Closed Assumptions). It is easy to see that for authorization programs expressing only explicit denials the closed assumption coincides with the classical closed access control policy [20]. Similarly, for programs expressing only explicit positive authorizations the open assumption coincides with the classical open policy. Thus, the classical open and closed policies can be easily modeled in our framework simply by imposing semantic restrictions on the types of rules that can be specified in an authorization program.

Having defined different authorization policies, it is interesting to see how they can be compared from the point of view of their level of "permissivity".

Proposition 5.1 *Let ω^σ denote the set of all access requests that are satisfied under policy (ω,σ) and $\Omega = \{\omega^\sigma$ s.t. (ω,σ) is a policy$\}$. Then, the following holds:*

1. $Closed\_ass^{Wf} \subseteq Closed\_ass^{Cert} \subseteq Closed\_ass^{Poss} \subseteq Open\_ass^{Poss} \subseteq Open\_ass^{Wf}$
2. $Closed\_ass^{Cert} \subseteq Open\_ass^{Cert} \subseteq Open\_ass^{Poss}$

Thus, $(\Omega,\subseteq)$ is a complete lattice (shown in Figure 4) whose bottom element is $Closed\_ass^{Wf}$ (the most restrictive policy) and whose top element is $Open\_ass^{Wf}$ (the most permissive policy).

Example 5.1 Consider the following program (for simplicity, we assume that no relationships among privileges append, write, read and execute exist).

$$
\begin{array}{l}
(o,u):\\
\quad \{\ auth(\texttt{append},g) \leftarrow\\
\quad\ \ auth(\texttt{read},g) \leftarrow\\
\quad\ \ \neg auth(\texttt{read},g') \leftarrow\\
\quad\ \ auth(\texttt{execute},g) \leftarrow \neg auth(\texttt{read},g')\\
\quad\ \ auth(\texttt{write},g'') \leftarrow auth(\texttt{execute},g)\\
\quad\ \ auth(\texttt{write},g'') \leftarrow auth(\texttt{read},g)\ \}
\end{array}
$$

where g and g' are incomparable grantors. The well-founded model of this program is $W = \{auth(\texttt{append},g)\}$, as $auth(\texttt{append}$ is the only authorization not depending on any form of conflict. By contrast, the program has two stable models, namely,

$$
\begin{array}{rl}
A_1 = \{ & (o,u).auth(\texttt{append},g),\\
& (o,u).auth(\texttt{read},g),\\
& (o,u).auth(\texttt{write},g'')\ \}
\end{array}
$$

and

$$
\begin{array}{rl}
A_2 = \{ & (o,u).auth(\texttt{append},g),\\
& (o,u).\neg auth(\texttt{read},g'),\\
& (o,u).auth(\texttt{execute},g),\\
& (o,u).auth(\texttt{write},g'')\ \}
\end{array}
$$

Now, we have the following sets of satisfied requests:

1. $Closed\_ass^{Wf} = \{(u,\texttt{append},o)\}$,
2. $Closed\_ass^{Cert} = \{(u,\texttt{append},o), (u,\texttt{write},o)\ \}$,
3. $Closed\_ass^{Poss} = \{(u,\texttt{append},o), (u,\texttt{write},o), (u,\texttt{execute},o), (u,\texttt{read},o)\ \}$,
4. $Open\_ass^{Wf} = \{(u,\texttt{append},o), (u,\texttt{write},o), (u,\texttt{execute},o), (u,\texttt{read},o)\ \}$.
5. $Open\_ass^{Cert} = \{(u,\texttt{append},o), (u,\texttt{write},o), (u,\texttt{execute},o)\}$,
6. $Open\_ass^{Poss} = \{(u,\texttt{append},o), (u,\texttt{write},o), (u,\texttt{execute},o), (u,\texttt{read},o)\ \}$.

Consider, for instance, the access request $(u,\texttt{read},o)\}$ which is satisfied by $Open\_ass^{Wf}$, $Closed\_ass^{Poss}$ and $Open\_ass^{Poss}$. Let us consider first the $Open\_ass^{Wf}$ policy. In the well-founded model, both $(o,u).auth(read,g)$ and $(o,u).\neg auth(read,g)$ are undefined (i.e., they are neither true nor false). In absence of other information, this policy makes permission to prevail on denial. The other two policies behave likewise. Indeed, although $(o,u).auth(read,g)$ and $(o,u).\neg auth(read,g)$ both occur in distinct stable authorization sets, both policies take the positive authorization. By contrast, the reverse reasoning applies to the remaining policies, all of which make denials prevailing on permissions.

Remark (Conflict Resolution) The above example outlines how our authorization policies behave w.r.t. conflict resolution. In particular, we have that: $Open\_ass^{Wf}$, $Closed\_ass^{Poss}$ and $Open\_ass^{Poss}$ entail a "Permissions take precedence" resolution policy, while $Closed\_ass^{Wf}$, $Open\_ass^{Poss}$ and $Closed\_ass^{Poss}$ entail a "Denials take precedence" resolution policy [13].

6 The Access Control Mechanism

In this section we describe the access control mechanism which enforces the previous authorization policies.

Implementing the well-founded semantics in not a problem, as any access request just needs to be verified against

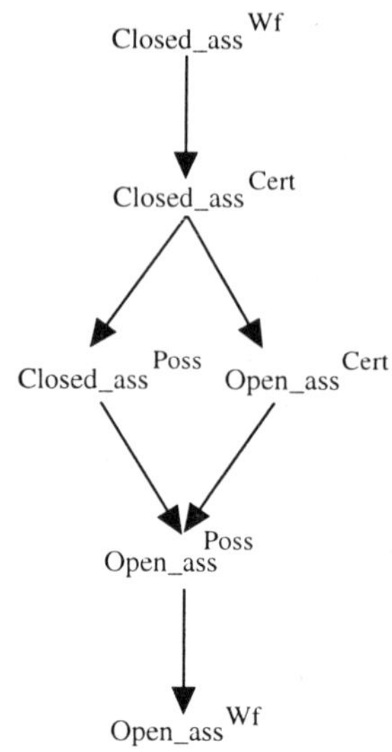

Figure 4. Access control policies' lattice

the well-founded authorization set and, according to the open/closed assumption, accepted or denied. Similarly, in case of certainty semantics, it is just required to verify whether α is satisfied or not (against the set of all authorization sets). The task when the semantics of the possibility is taken. In such a case, the choice of the stable authorization set against which access requests must be verified is driven by the privileges the subjects are exercising on the objects in the system when the access request is issued. Given an access request α, the access control mechanism selects an authorization set which: *i)* satisfies α and *ii)* satisfies all the current accesses. If such an authorization set exists, the access is authorized; otherwise, it is denied (at least for the moment). Clearly, enforcing this policy requires the system to maintain information on the set of accesses that are currently in execution.

The algorithm implementing our access control policy is illustrated in Figure 5. Here, the validity of the access request α is checked according to the selected semantics (well-founded, or certainty or possibility). In case of possibility semantics, the algorithm checks if α is satisfied by the current authorization set ($Current\_Auth\_Set$) of $\mathcal{P}$. If so, the access request is authorized. Otherwise, the algorithm looks for another authorization set A in $\Gamma_{\mathcal{P}}$ according to which both the submitted request and all the current accesses ($Current\_Access$) are satisfied. If this is the case, the access request is authorized. In both cases, α is added to $Current\_Access$.[2] If such an authorization set (satisfying both α and the elements in $Current\_Access$) does not exist, the request is rejected.

[2]We assume that the DBMS automatically updates $Current\_Access$ each time a subject finishes to access a given object.

Note that, if the well-founded semantics or the certainty semantics is adopted, then the access requests that can be authorized by the system coincide with the set of satisfied requests computed according to Definition 5.3. This means that an access request is authorized iff it is satisfied. By contrast, when the semantics of the possibility is chosen access request satisfaction is a necessary but not sufficient condition for the access to be granted. In such a case, the set of satisfied requests represent the set of access requests that can be potentially authorized. The ones actually authorized also depend on the accesses currently in execution.

Example 6.1 Consider the program $\mathcal{P}$ of Example 3.2, over the domain defined in Example 4.4. Suppose that the component (o, Ann) is enriched by a further authorization, namely $auth$(execute, Tom) $\leftarrow$. It easy to verify that the program so obtained admits two authorization sets, that are A_1 = {(o,Ann).$auth$(write, Tom), (o,Ann).auth(execute, Tom) }, and A_2 = {(o,Bob).auth(write, Tom), (o,Ann).auth(execute, Tom) }. Suppose now the closed assumption under certainty reasoning is fixed, and consider the access request (Bob, write, o). Since Bob is not authorized in *every* authorization set to write object o, the request is rejected. On the contrary, the access request (Ann, execute, o) is authorized, since Ann has a "certain" authorization (i.e., occurring in every authorization set) to execute object o.

Consider now the case of possibility reasoning. Assume that $Current\_Auth\_Set$ = A_1 and $Current\_Access$ = { (Ann, execute, o) }. Let α = (Bob, write, o) be a new access request. Clearly, α is not satisfied in A_1. However,

Algorithm 6.1 Access Control Algorithm

INPUT: 1) An access request $\alpha = (s, p, o)$
2) An authorization program $\mathcal{P}$

OUTPUT: 1) $AUTHORIZE$ if the access request can be authorized,
2) return $REJECT$, otherwise.

METHOD:

1. **if** $CERTAINTY$ or $WELL\_FOUNDED$ **then**
    if α is $satisfied$ **then**
        return $AUTHORIZE$
    else return $REJECT$
   endif
2. **else** (* **if** $POSSIBILITY$ **then** *)
3. Let $Current\_Access$ be the set of current accesses
    if α is $satisfied\ in\ Current\_Auth\_Set$ **then**
        $Current\_Access := Current\_Access \cup \{\alpha\}$
        return $AUTHORIZE$
    endif
4. **if** $\exists A \in \Gamma_{\mathcal{P}}$ such that each $\beta \in \{\alpha\} \cup Current\_Access$ is satisfied in A **then**
        $Current\_Authorization\_Set := A$
        $Current\_Access := Current\_Access \cup \{\alpha\}$
        return $AUTHORIZE$
    endif
5. return $REJECT$

Figure 5. Access Control Algorithm

the authorization set A_2 which satisfies both α and the current access is found. Then, the access request is authorized. Now $Current\_Auth\_Set$ is A_2 and $Current\_Access = \{$ (Ann, execute, o), (Bob, write, o)$\}$. If a new request (Ann, write, o) is submitted, it is denied, since there is no possibility to find an authorization set satisfying both the new request and those in $Current\_Access$.

A few concluding remarks on the complexity of the proposed access control algorithm. It is well known in logic programming that, under data complexity, computing the well-founded semantics is a polynomial task, while certainty and possibility reasoning are CoNP-complete and NP-complete, respectively [21]. It could be shown that such results hold for our authorization model. We note that, in principle, the complexity of stable model semantics is not a drawback, as it means that it is possible to express some NP-complete problems. At the same time, a number of efficient techniques have recently been proposed to drastically improve its computation [24, 9, 22, 10]. For instance, the *dlv* system [10], which supports the stable model semantics of (disjunctive) logic programs, is able to solve hard problems, such as *prime implicant*[3], very efficiently. For example, a problem instance with 202 clauses and 47 variables is solved in 0.3 seconds on a SUN Ultra 1/143 under Solaris 2.5.1. Based on these results, we believe that the proposed access control policies could result of practical interest in most concrete security applications, even in those exploiting the expressive power of unstratified negation. We plan to investigate such issues in the near future.

7 Final Remarks

We have proposed a logic formalism that naturally supports the encoding of complex security specifications. This formalism relies on a hierarchically structured domain made of subjects, objects and privileges and supports both negation by failure (possibly unstratified) and true negation. We have devised two semantics as an extension of the well-founded and the stable model semantics of logic programming. The former represents a very conservative approach whereby only "sure" authorizations are derived, that is, authorizations that do not depends either on unstratified negation or on conflicts not solvable by defeating. The stable model semantics goes a step forward, by solving possible ambiguities coming from both unstratified negation by failure and true negation. Such an approach entails a

[3]**Prime Implicants**: Find the prime implicants of a propositional CNF formula $\Phi = \bigwedge_{i=1}^{n}(d_{i1} \vee \ldots \vee d_{ic_i})$, where the $d_{i,j}$ are literals over the variables $x_1, \ldots, x_m$. Recall that a *prime implicant* of Φ is a consistent conjunction I of literals such that $I \models \Phi$ and for no subformula I' of I we have $I' \models \Phi$. As easily seen, a prime implicant exists if and only if Φ is satisfiable. Thus, finding a prime implicant, is a NP-hard problem, as it subsumes the satisfiability problem

form of non-determinism due to the multiplicity of authorization sets w.r.t. which an access request is to be checked. Based on the proposed semantics, a number of authorization policies have been defined by combining them with the open/closed assumption. A comparative analysis of such policies has been carried out from the point of view of their "permissivity".

We now comment on some characteristic of the proposal. By combining inheritance (from groups to subgroups/users, from object to subobjects) with true negation, our model supports exceptions and, thus, nonmonotonic reasoning. This allows the designer to capture the semantics of very complex application domains. From the point of view of authorization specification, our model is clearly hybrid (as both positive and negative authorizations can be specified). However, is the open/closed assumption which determines how a program must be interpreted, that is, as either defining denials or access rights.

We plan to extend this work along several directions. First we are developing more articulated conflict resolution policies, taking into account other aspects of the considered domain, such as the presence of roles. Moreover, we plan to investigate the use of heuristics for selecting the current model against which access requests must be checked when the possibility reasoning is adopted. A further direction concerns implementation issues. In particular, the logic language we have presented here is not intended as the end-user language to express authorizations and rules. Rather this language is used by the system to enforce our authorization policy. On top of this language, we plan to develop a visual programming environment to be directly used by the end-user.

References

[1] Abadi, M., Burrows, M., Lampson, B.W., Plotkin, G. A Calculus for Access Control in Distributed Systems. *ACM Trans. on Programming Languages and Systems*, 15(4):706–734, 1993.

[2] Bertino, E., Bettini, C., Ferrari, E. Samarati, P. A Temporal Access Control Mechanism for Database Systems. *IEEE Trans. on Knowledge and Data Engineering*, 8(1):67–80, February 1996.

[3] Bertino, E., Bettini, C., Ferrari, E. Samarati, P. An Access Control Mechanism Supporting Periodicity Constraints and Temporal Reasoning. *ACM Trans. on Database Systems*, to appear.

[4] Bertino, E., Buccafurri, F., Ferrari, E. Rullo, P. An Authorization Model and its Formal Semantics. In *Proc. of the 5th European Symposium on Research in Computer Security (Esorics'98)*, pages 127–142, LNCS 1495, Springer, September 1998.

[5] Bertino, E., Ferrari, E. Administration Policies in a Multipolicy Authorization System. *Proc. 11th IFIP Working Conference on Database Security*, Lake Tahoe (CA), August 1997, pp.15-26.

[6] Bertino, E., Jajodia, S., Samarati, P. Supporting Multiple Access Control Policies in Database Systems. *Proc. of the IEEE Symposium on Research in Security and Privacy*, Oakland (CA), 1996.

[7] Buccafurri, F., Leone, N., Rullo, P. Stable Models and their Computation for Logic Programming with Inheritance and True Negation. *Journal of Logic Programming* 27(1):5–43, April 1996.

[8] Buccafurri, F., Leone, N., Scarcello, F. On the Expressive Power of Ordered Logic. *AI Communications*, 9:14-13, 1996.

[9] W. Chen, D.S. Warren. Computing of Stable Models and its Integration with Logical Query Processing. *IEEE TKDE*, 17:279-300, 1995.

[10] Eiter, T., Leone, N., Mateis, C., Pfeifer, G., Scarcello, F., A Deductive System for Nonmonotonic Reasoning, *Proc. of the 4th Int. Conf. on Logic Programming and Nonmonotonic Reasoning (LPNMR '97)*, LNAI 1265, Berlin, 1997.

[11] E. Fernandez, E.B. Gudes and H. Song. A Model for Evaluation and Administration of Security in Object-Oriented Databases. *IEEE TKDE*, 6:275–292, 1994.

[12] Gelfond, M., Lifschitz, V. The Stable Model Semantics for Logic Programming. *Proc. 5th Int. Conf. on Logic Programming*, MIT Press, pp. 1070-1080, 1988.

[13] Jajodia, S., Samarati, P., Subrahmanian, V.S., Bertino, E. A Unified Framework for Enforcing Multiple Access Control Policies, *Proc. of ACM-SIGMOD*, May 1997.

[14] Jajodia, S., Samarati, P. Subrahmanian, V.S. A Logical Language for Expressing Authorizations. *Proc. IEEE Symposium on Research in Security and Privacy*, Oakland (CA), pp. 31–42, 1997.

[15] Laenens, E., Saccá, D., Vermeir, D. Extending Logic Programming. *Proc. of ACM SIGMOD*, May 1990.

[16] Leone, N., Rossi, G., Well-founded Semantics and Stratification for Ordered Logic Programs, *New Generation Computing*, Vol. 12, N. 1, Springer-Verlag, November 1993, pp. 91-121.

[17] Leone, N., Rullo, P. Ordered Logic Programming with Sets. *Journal of Logic and Computation*, 3(6):621–642, Oxford University Press, December 1993.

[18] Lifschitz, V. On the Declarative Semantics of Logic Programs with Negation. *Foundation of Deductive Database and Logic Programming* Minker, J. (ed.), Morgan Kaufman, 1987, pp. 89-148.

[19] Lloyd, J. W. *Foundations of Logic Programming*, Springer-Verlag, 1987.

[20] Lunt, M.T. Access Control Policies for Database Systems. *Database Security II: Status and Prospects*, pages 41–52, North-Holland, 1989.

[21] Marek, W., Truszczyński, M., Computing Intersection of Autoepistemic Expansions, *Proc. of the 1st Int. Workshop on Logic Programming and Non Monotonic Reasoning*, pp. 37-50, 1991.

[22] Niemelä, I., Simons, P., Efficient Implementation of the Well-founded and Stable Model Semantics. *Proc. of the 1996 Joint Int. Conf. and Symposium on Logic Programming*, pp. 289–303, Bonn, Germany, 1996.

[23] Rabitti, F., Bertino, E., Kim, E., Woelk, D. A Model of Authorization for Next-Generation Database Systems. *ACM Trans. on Database Systems*, 16(1):88–131, March 1991.

[24] Subrahmanian, V.S., Nau, D. and Vago, C. WFS + Branch and Bound = Stable Models. *IEEE Transactions on Knowledge and Data Engineering*, 7(3):362-377, 1995.

[25] Ullman, J.D. *Principles of Database and Knowledge-Base Systems, Vol. 1 and 2*, Computer Science Press, 1989.

[26] Woo, T.Y.C, Lam, S.S. Authorizations in Distributed Systems: A New Approach. *Journal of Computer Security*, 2(2 & 3):107–136, 1993.

Advances in Automated Security Protocol Analysis

Athena: a New Efficient Automatic Checker for Security Protocol Analysis *

Dawn Xiaodong Song
Computer Science Department
Carnegie Mellon University
5000 Forbes Avenue, Pittsburgh, PA 15213
skyxd@cs.cmu.edu

Abstract

We propose an efficient automatic checking algorithm, Athena, for analyzing security protocols. Athena incorporates a logic that can express security properties including authentication, secrecy and properties related to electronic commerce. We have developed an automatic procedure for evaluating well-formed formulae in this logic. For a well-formed formula, if the evaluation procedure terminates, it will generate a counterexample if the formula is false, or provide a proof if the formula is true. Even when the procedure does not terminate when we allow any arbitrary configurations of the protocol execution, (for example, any number of initiators and responders), termination could be forced by bounding the number of concurrent protocol runs and the length of messages, as is done in most existing model checkers.

Athena also exploits several state space reduction techniques. It is based on an extension of the recently proposed Strand Space Model [25] which captures exact causal relation information. Together with backward search and other techniques, Athena naturally avoids the state space explosion problem commonly caused by asynchronous composition and symmetry redundancy. Athena also has the advantage that it can easily incorporate results from theorem proving through unreachability theorems. By using the unreachability theorems, it can prune the state space at an early stage, hence, reduce the state space explored and increase the likely-hood of termination. As shown in our experiments, these techniques dramatically reduce the state space that needs to be explored.

*This research is sponsored by the National Science Foundation under Grant No. CCR-9803774. Views and conclusions contained in this document are those of the authors and should not be interpreted as representing the official policies, either expressed or implied, of the United States Government.

1. Introduction

A security protocol is a communication protocol that uses cryptography to achieve goals such as authentication and key distribution. Because of the subtlety of security protocols, experience has shown that the protocols can be flawed even when designed carefully. Thus, it is necessary to develop rigorous ways to analyze these protocols.

Many researchers have worked on applying formal techniques to the analysis of security protocols. They have developed logics of knowledge and belief such as BAN logic [2] and GNY logic [7]; semi-automatic and fully automatic tools such as the NRL Analyzer [14], the Interrogator Model [16], FDR [12], Murφ [17], Brutus [5], and Revere [9]; and theorem provers such as Isabelle [19]. Automatic checkers have the practical advantage that they are easy to use and do not need the assistance of experienced users. Unfortunately, current automatic checkers suffer from the state space explosion problem, mainly due to asynchronous composition and symmetry redundancy. Most automatic checkers are also limited to checking the properties of a security protocol under certain configurations of the protocol execution, e.g. with two initiators and two responders.

Thayer, Herzog and Guttman recently proposed the Strand Space Model (*SSM*) and demonstrated how to use *SSM* to prove certain security properties manually, for example authentication and secrecy [25]. *SSM* has the advantage that it contains the exact causal relation information which makes proofs concise. Inspired by their work, we have developed a new algorithm, *Athena*, for analyzing security protocols automatically.

We have designed a logic based on SSM that can express formally various security properties including authentication, secrecy and properties related to electronic commerce. We have also developed an automatic procedure for evaluating well-formed formulae in this logic. We provide

1063-6900/99 $10.00 © 1999 IEEE

a way of formally reduce the infinite-state-space problem into a finite-state-space problem which can be verified using model checking. Hence, for a well-formed formula, if the evaluation procedure terminates, then it will generate a counterexample if the formula is false, or provide a proof if the formula is true. Although the evaluation procedure is not guaranteed to terminate, experience shows that it does terminate for many useful protocols. In those cases when the procedure does not terminate for arbitrary configurations of the protocol execution, termination can always be forced by bounding the number of concurrent protocol runs and the length of messages. This is similar to the bounds in current model checkers such as FDR, Murφ and *Brutus*.

Athena also exploits several state space reduction techniques. First, the state transition is not asynchronously composed of independent process transitions, hence, avoid the state space explosion caused by asynchronous composition. Second, the state structures and state transitions capture exact causal relations, hence, achieve compact and efficient state representations. Third, Athena takes advantage of symbolic state transitions instead of explicit state search, by allowing a state to contain free variables. A state $s(\vec{x})$ with free term variables, $\vec{x}$, represents a class of variable-free states, $\{[\vec{\sigma}/\vec{x}]s(\vec{x})\}$, where $\vec{\sigma}$ is a substitution of term values. A state transition between two states which contain free variables represents a set of state transitions between two variable-free states. Thus, Athena can represent states and state transitions much more efficiently. As a special case of this, it naturally avoids the symmetry redundancy problem. Finally, Athena uses backward search instead of forward search. With forward search, all the participating principals have to be pre-stated. Our approach starts with a simple initial strand and then add new strands only when necessary according to exact causal relations. As demonstrated in our experiments, these techniques greatly reduce the state space that needs to be explored comparing with other current approaches.

Athena also has the advantage that it can easily incorporate results from theorem proving through unreachability theorems. By using the unreachability theorems, we can prune the state space at an early stage, hence, reduce the state space explored even further and increase the likelyhood of termination.

The paper is organized as follows. We first review some basic notions and properties of strand spaces (section 2). We then introduce a logic to reason about strand spaces and show how to use this logic to specify security properties (section 3), and explain the automatic evaluation procedure (section 4). Next, we discuss the advantages of our approach and compare it with other approaches (section 5). Finally, we conclude in section 6. Proof sketches of most propositions in this paper are omitted and can be found in [23].

2. Background

This section is a review of concepts developed by Thayer, Herzog and Guttman [25]. First, we explain the notion of *terms* that are used to represent the messages in the protocols. Then, we explain the notion of *strands, strand spaces* and *bundles*, and show how to represent protocols using strands. Finally, we give the formal description of the *penetrator model*.

2.1. Message Terms

The set of atomic terms is the union of a set of "*Text*" terms T and a set of "*Key*" terms K, where

- Text terms T contain several different types of terms, such as *Principal-names*, *Nonces*, or *Bank-account-number*.
- Key terms K contains a set of keys disjoint from T. In asymmetric crypto systems, K^{-1} represents K's opposite member in a public-private key pair. In a symmetric key system, $K^{-1} = K$.

The set of *terms* (A) is defined inductively as follows:

- If m is a Text term or a Key term, then m is a term.
- If m is a term, k is a Key term, then $\{m\}_k$ is a term. (This represents encryption.)
- If m_1 and m_2 are terms, then $m_1 \cdot m_2$ is a term. (This represents concatenation.)

We use the *free encryption* assumption, where

$$\{m\}_k = \{m'\}_{k'} \Leftrightarrow m = m' \wedge k = k'.$$

Thayer, Herzog and Guttman defined the *subterm relation* $\sqsubseteq$: a term a_1 is a *subterm* of term a_2 if a_1 appears in a_2; We define the *interm relation* $\Subset$, such that a_1 is a *interm* of a_2 if a_1 can be extracted from a_2 without the application of the decryption operation. The formal definition of the two relations are as follows.

- *subterm relation* $\sqsubseteq$
  - $a \sqsubseteq t$ *for* $t \in T$ *iff* $a = t$;
  - $a \sqsubseteq k$ *for* $k \in K$ *iff* $a = k$;
  - $a \sqsubseteq \{g\}_k$ *iff* $a \sqsubseteq g \vee a = \{g\}_k$;
  - $a \sqsubseteq g \cdot h$ *iff* $a \sqsubseteq g \vee a \sqsubseteq h \vee a = g \cdot h$.
- *interm relation* $\Subset$
  - $a \Subset t$ *for* $t \in T$ *iff* $a = t$;
  - $a \Subset k$ *for* $k \in K$ *iff* $a = k$;
  - $a \Subset \{g\}_k$ *iff* $a = \{g\}_k$;
  - $a \Subset g \cdot h$ *iff* $a \Subset g \vee a \Subset h$.

2.2. SSM : Strands, Strand spaces and Bundles

The notions in this subsection are mainly from the paper [25]. We extend them slightly to make them applicable to electronic commerce protocols.

Actions. The set of actions *Act* that principals can take during an execution of a protocol include extermal actions such as *send* and *receive*, and user-defined internal actions such as *debit*, *credit*, etc.. In the rest of the paper, we will only use *send* and *receive* for simplicity.

Events. An *event* is a pair $\langle action, argu\rangle$, where *action* is in *Act*, and *argu* is in (A) and is the argument of the action. For simplicity, we denote $\langle send,\ a\rangle$ and $\langle receive,\ a\rangle$ respectively as *signed terms* $\langle +a\rangle$ and $\langle -a\rangle$. We represent the set of finite sequences of signed terms as $(\pm A)^*$.

Strands and Strand Spaces. A *protocol* defines the sequence of events for each role of the participant. A *strand* represents a sequence of actions of an instance of a role.

A strand space is a set Σ with a trace mapping tr: $\Sigma \rightarrow (\pm A)^*$.

1. A *node* is a pair $\langle s, i\rangle$, with $s \in \Sigma$ and *i* an integer satisfying $1 \leq i \leq$ length(tr(s)). We say $n = \langle s, i\rangle$ belongs to the strand *s*, denoted as $n \in s$. Clearly, every node belongs to a unique strand. The set of nodes is denoted by N.

2. If $n = \langle s, i\rangle \in N$, then index$(n) = i$ and strand$(n) = s$. If $(tr(s))_i = \langle \sigma a\rangle$, where σ is one of the symbols $+, -$, then term$(n) = a$.

3. If $n_1, n_2 \in N$, then $n_1 \rightarrow n_2$ means that term$(n_1) = +a$ and term$(n_2) = -a$. This represents that n_1 sends a message *a* and n_2 receives the message.

4. If $n_1, n_2 \in N$, then $n_1 \Rightarrow n_2$ means that n_1, n_2 occur in the same strand with index(n_2) = index$(n_1) + 1$. This represents an event n_1 followed immediately by n_2 in the same strand.

5. A term *t originates* from a node $n \in N$ *iff sign(n)*$= +$; $t \sqsubseteq$ *term(n)*; and whenever n' precedes *n* on the same strand, $t \not\sqsubseteq$ *term(n')*.

6. A term *t uniquely-originates* from node *n iff t originates* on a unique $n \in N$. Nonces and other freshly generated terms are usually uniquely-originated.

We will also use N to refer to the directed graph (N, E) whose vertices are nodes and $E = (\rightarrow \cup \Rightarrow)$ is the set of edges that combines both types of relations $n_1 \rightarrow n_2$ and $n_1 \Rightarrow n_2$.

Bundles. A bundle represents the protocol execution under some configuration.

A bundle $C = (N_C, E)$ is a subgraph of N, where $E \subseteq (\rightarrow \cup \Rightarrow)$ is the set of the edges and $N_C \subseteq N$ is the set of nodes incident with the edges in E, and the following properties hold:

- C is non-empty and finite;
- If $n_1 \in C$ and *sign*$(n_1) = -$, then there is a unique n_2 such that $n_2 \rightarrow n_1 \in C$;
- If $n_1 \in C$ and $n_2 \Rightarrow n_1$, then $n_2 \Rightarrow n_1 \in C$;
- C is acyclic.

We say a strand $s \in C$ if for every node $n \in s$, $n \in C$.

Causal Precedence. Let *S* be a strand space, nodes n_1,$n_2 \in$ S. Define $n_1 \preceq_S n_2$ *iff* there is a sequence of zero or more edges of type $\rightarrow$ and $\Rightarrow$ leading from n_1 to n_2 in *S*. The relation $\preceq_S$ expresses a *causal precedence*.

Lemma 2.1. *Suppose C is a bundle, then* $\preceq_C$ *is a partial order, i.e. a reflexive, antisymmetric, transitive relation. Every non-empty subset of the nodes in C has* $\preceq_C$*-minimal members.*

The proof of this lemma can be found in [25].

2.3. Protocol specification using strands

A protocol usually contains several *roles*, such as *initiators, responders* and *servers*. The sequence of actions of each role is predefined by the protocol with a list of parameters, such as principal names and nonces. This can be specified as a *trace type*, denoted as *role[parameter list]*. A binding of the role and the parameter list gives an instance-trace of the role. A legal execution of a protocol forms a bundle, in which the strands of the legitimate principals are restricted to the predefined trace types, *role[parameter list]*. The strands of the legitimate principals are referred to as *regular strands*. The bundle also contains strands which are mapped to penetrator traces. These strands are referred to as *penetrator strands*. We explain them in more details in the next subsection. We now give an example of the Needham-Schroeder protocol [18] with the fix given by Gavin Lowe in [12]. We will refer to this protocol as *NSL* in the rest of the paper. Using the standard notation, the protocol is defined as follows:

1. $A \rightarrow B : \{N_a \cdot A\}_{K_B}$
2. $B \rightarrow A : \{N_a \cdot N_b \cdot B\}_{K_A}$
3. $A \rightarrow B : \{N_b\}_{K_B}$

There are two roles in this protocol: initiator and responder. The strands of the two roles are the following :

$$\underline{Resp[A, B, N_a, N_b]} \qquad\qquad \underline{Init[A, B, N_a, N_b]}$$

$$1 : \langle -\{N_a \cdot A\}_{K_b} \rangle \qquad\qquad 1 : \langle +\{N_a \cdot A\}_{K_b} \rangle$$

$$\Downarrow \qquad\qquad \Downarrow$$

$$2 : \langle +\{N_a \cdot N_b \cdot B\}_{K_a} \rangle \qquad\qquad 2 : \langle -\{N_a \cdot N_b \cdot B\}_{K_a} \rangle$$

$$\Downarrow \qquad\qquad \Downarrow$$

$$3 : \langle -\{N_b\}_{K_b} \rangle \qquad\qquad 3 : \langle +\{N_b\}_{K_b} \rangle$$

where the parameter list contains A and B as principal names, N_a and N_b as nonces. N_a *uniquely-originates* on the first node of the initiator's strand $Init[A, B, N_a, N_b]$. N_b *uniquely-originates* on the second node of the responder's strand $Resp[A, B, N_a, N_b]$. A responder's strand with the binding of $[A_0, B_0, N_{a0}, N_{b0}]$ is the following :

$$\underline{Resp[A_0, B_0, N_{a0}, N_{b0}]}$$

$$\langle -\{N_{a0} \cdot A_0\}_{K_{b0}} \rangle$$

$$\Downarrow$$

$$\langle +\{N_{a0} \cdot N_{b0} \cdot B_0\}_{K_{a0}} \rangle$$

$$\Downarrow$$

$$\langle -\{N_{b0}\}_{K_{b0}} \rangle$$

2.4. The Penetrator Model

We use the same penetrator model as the one in [25]. The penetrator P has a set of initial knowledge *init-info(P)* which usually contains the principal names and the keys that are known initially to the penetrator, denoted as K_p. K_p usually contains all the public keys, all the private keys of the penetrator, and all the symmetric keys K_{px}, K_{xp} initially shared between the penetrator and principals playing by the protocol rules. It can also contain some keys to model known-key attacks.

A penetrator can intercept messages, generate messages that are computable from its initial knowledge and the messages it intercepts. These actions are modeled by a set of *penetrator strands*.

A penetrator strand is one of the following, where g and h are *terms*:

- M[t]. Atomic message: $\langle +t \rangle$ where t $\in$ *init-info(P)* and t $\in$ T.
- F[g]. Flushing: $\langle -g \rangle$.
- T[g]. Tee: $\langle -g, +g, +g \rangle$.
- C[g,h]. Concatenation: $\langle -g, -h, +g \cdot h \rangle$.
- R[g,h]. Separation into components: $\langle -g \cdot h, +g, +h \rangle$.
- K[k]. Key:$\langle +k \rangle$ where $k \in K_p$.
- E[k,h]. Encryption: $\langle -k, -h, +\{h\}_k \rangle$.
- D[k,h]. Decryption: $\langle -k^{-1}, -\{h\}_k, +h \rangle$.

The different types of the penetrator traces are called *penetrator roles*, which ranges over {M,F,T,C,S,K,E,D}. It is also possible to extend the set of penetrator traces to model some special ability of the penetrator if needed.

3. The Logic

We first introduce a logic to reason about strand spaces and bundles. Then we show how to use this logic for formal specification of various security properties.

3.1. Syntax

The syntax of the terms consists of *node constants* $(n, n_1, \ldots)$, *strand constants* $(s, s_1, \ldots)$, *bundle constant* $(c, c_1, \ldots)$, and *bundle variable* $(C, C_1, \ldots)$.

Propositional formulas are defined as follows:

- $n \in s$, $n \in c$, $n \in C$, $s \in c$, $s \in C$ are (atomic) propositional formulas;
- $\neg f_1$ and $f_1 \wedge f_2$ are propositional formulas if f_1 and f_2 are propositional formulas.

Finally, well-formed formulas (wffs) are:

- $f, \neg F_1, F_1 \wedge F_2$;
- $\forall C.f$, where f is a propositional formula, which doesn't contain any other free variable than C;

where f is a propositional formula, F_1 and F_2 are wffs, and C is a bundle variable.

Notice, that in a wff $\forall C.f$, f needs to be a propositional formula and cannot contain any other variables than C. We also use the obvious abbreviations:

$$\begin{array}{rcl@{\qquad}rcl} f_1 \vee f_2 & \equiv & \neg(\neg f_1 \wedge \neg f_2) & f_1 \Rightarrow f_2 & \equiv & \neg f_1 \vee f_2 \\ f_1 \Leftrightarrow f_2 & \equiv & f_1 \Rightarrow f_2 \wedge f_2 \Rightarrow f_1 & \exists C.f & \equiv & \neg \forall C.\neg f \end{array}$$

3.2. Semantics

Let the set of nodes be $\mathcal{N}$. For a given protocol, the set of the regular strands and the penetrator strands is $\mathcal{S}_p$; the execution traces of a protocol p form a set of bundles, denoted as $\mathcal{D}_p$. Thus, for a given protocol p, the model M is a pair $(\{\mathcal{N}, \mathcal{S}_p, \mathcal{D}_p\}, \mathcal{I})$, where $\mathcal{I}$ is the interpretation. The semantics of the logic is given as follows :

- $\mathcal{I}(n), \mathcal{I}(s), \mathcal{I}(c)$ are a node, a strand and a bundle in $\mathcal{N}, \mathcal{S}_p, \mathcal{D}_p$ respectively.

- $M \models n \in s$ *iff* $\mathcal{I}(n) \in \mathcal{I}(s)$. We can similarly define $M \models n \in c$, $M \models s \in c$ as well.

- If f is a propositional formula or a wff, then $M \models \neg f$ *iff* $M \not\models f$.

- If f_1 and f_2 are propositional formulas or wffs, then $M \models f_1 \wedge f_2$ *iff* $M \models f_1$ and $M \models f_2$.

- $M \models \forall C.f$ *iff* $M \models [C/c_0]f$ for any bundle c_0 in the model.

3.3. Specifying security properties in the logic

Our logic can specify a variety of security properties including electronic commerce properties. However, here we mainly focus on the authentication and secrecy properties. The properties are presented in a similar way as in the paper [25] except that we formalize the properties into the wffs in our logic.

Authentication

Gavin Lowe [13] proposed agreement properties for authentication protocols. A protocol guarantees a participant B (say, as the responder) *agreement* for certain binding $\vec{x}$ if each time a principal B completes a run of the protocol as a responder using $\vec{x}$, supposedly with A, then there is a unique run of the protocol with the principal A as initiator using $\vec{x}$, supposedly with B.

A weaker *non-injective agreement* does not ensure uniqueness, but requires only each time a principal B completes a run of the protocol as responder using $\vec{x}$, supposedly with A, then there exists a run of the protocol with the principal A as initiator using $\vec{x}$, supposedly with B.

The non-injective agreement property can be specified using the logic as:

$$\forall C.Resp(\vec{x}) \in C \Longrightarrow Init(\vec{x}) \in C,$$

where $Resp(\vec{x})$ and $Init(\vec{x})$ are the responder and the initiator strand with binding $\vec{x}$. For example, in the *NSL* protocol, the *non-injective agreement* property can be specified as

$$\forall C.Resp[A, B, N_a, N_b] \in C \Longrightarrow Init[A, B, N_a, N_b] \in C.$$

Because of the freshness of the nonces generated in the protocol run, usually the agreement property can be proved after the non-injective agreement property is proved, with the argument that there can't be two strands $Init(\vec{x}) \in C$ since the nonces in $Init(\vec{x})$ are uniquely originated from only one strand, i.e. in *NSL* protocol, N_a is *uniquely-originated* in the strand $Init[A, B, N_a, N_b]$.

Secrecy

A value v is secret in a strand space S if, for every bundle C that contains S, there does not exist a node $n \in C$ such that $term(n) = v$. For example, when S is a responder strand, we can specify the secrecy property as :

$$\neg \exists C.(Resp(\vec{x}) \in C \wedge node(+v) \in C)$$

4. The Model Checking Algorithm

This section introduces a model checking algorithm for wffs. We focus on the most interesting case: how to evaluate a wff of the form $\forall C.f$.

Lemma 4.1. *If $\mathcal{H}$ is an algorithm that decides the validity of any wff of the form $\forall C.f_1 \Rightarrow f_2$ in a model M in finite steps, where f_1 is a conjunction and f_2 is a disjunction of the atomic propositions, then there exists an algorithm to evaluate any formula of the form $\forall C.F$ in the model M in finite steps, for any propositional formula F.*

The proof sketch of this lemma can be found in the appendix.

Hence, it is sufficient to just explain the procedure $\mathcal{H}$. Due to the space limit, we only show the procedure $\mathcal{H}$ for two cases:

$$\mu_1 = \forall C.s_1 \in C \Rightarrow s_2 \in C, \text{ and}$$
$$\mu_2 = \exists C.s_1 \in C,$$

where s_1 is a strand constant, s_2 is a regular strand constant. These cases can be used for evaluating agreement properties and secrecy properties as mentioned in section 3. The other cases are simple extensions from them.

In the following subsections, we first introduce the notions and state structures used in the model checking algorithm. We then explain formally how we can reduce a problem in an infinite space to a problem of model checking which is restricted to a finite state space. We then describe in more details the model checking algorithm, in particular the *next state transition function*. We will also point out various techniques we exploit for state space reduction. Finally, we explain how we can use *unreachability theorems* to further reduce state space explored.

4.1. Goals and Goal-bindings

Intuition: We start with a strand space graph which only contains s_1, and then try all possibilities of adding nodes and strands to complete a bundle (an exhaustive search). To complete a bundle, the graph needs to be backward closed under $\Rightarrow$ and $\rightarrow$, and acyclic. To make the graph backward closed under $\rightarrow$, it means that any term that is received by a node must have been sent by another node in the same graph. Thus, we introduce a notion of a *goal* to represent the received terms, and a notion of a *goal-binding* to represent that a goal term is first sent by a node. We apply unification to search for all possible goal-bindings. When all goals are bound, all received terms are connected to their first senders. Hence, the graph will be backward closed under $\to$. For any node in the graph, we add all the nodes, that precede it in the same strand, to the graph. Thus, the graph is backward closed under $\Rightarrow$. Simple cycle-detection can check whether a graph is acyclic.

Goals. A *goal* is a pair (t, n), where $sign(n) = -$, $t \Subset Term(n)$ and t is not a concatenation of other two terms. The *goal-set* of a bundle C is the set of all the *goals* in C, denoted as $G(C)$.

Goal Binding. Suppose that C is a bundle, then a goal (t, n) is *bound* to node n' if n' is a $\preceq_C$-minimal member of the set

$$\psi = \{m \in C \mid t \Subset term(m),\ sign(m) = +, \text{ and } m \preceq n\}.$$

We say that $((t, n), n')$ is the *goal binding* for (t, n) and denote it as $n' \overset{t}{\twoheadrightarrow} n$. The node n' is called a *binder* of *(t,n)*. We will also write $n' \twoheadrightarrow n$ to denote $n' \overset{t}{\twoheadrightarrow} n$ for some t, or, formally, $\twoheadrightarrow = \bigcup_{t \in T} \overset{t}{\twoheadrightarrow}$.

Proposition 4.2. *Let C be a bundle. For any goal $(t, n) \in G(C)$, there exists a node $n' \in C$ where the goal (t, n) is bound.*

Proof sketch. Since *sign(n)* $= -$, and $n \in C$, there must exist a node n'', where $n'' = \langle -Term(n) \rangle$ and $n'' \in C$. So $t \Subset Term(n'')$. Therefore, the set ψ is not empty, where

$$\psi = \{m \in C \mid t \Subset Term(m) \text{ and } sign(m) = + \text{ and } m \preceq n\}.$$

As shown in Lemma 2.1, ψ has at least a $\preceq_C$-minimal member n'. Hence, (t, n) can be bound to n'. □

A bundle contains the information about the sequence of actions of each principal ("$\Rightarrow$") and the information about who sends messages to whom ("$\to$"). Because the penetrator can always intercept a message from a principal and forward it to another principal, the information about who sends messages to whom ("$\to$") is not important any more. Given a received term, it is not important who sends it but rather who sends it first. Therefore, only the goal-binding information ("$\twoheadrightarrow$") is necessary. This is the intuition why we introduce the relation "$\twoheadrightarrow$". In the state structure, we do not keep the information about the relation "$\to$" but only the goal-binding relation "$\twoheadrightarrow$".

4.2. State Structures

Semi-bundles. A semi-bundle $h = (N_h, E_\Rightarrow)$ is a subgraph of N, where $E_\Rightarrow \subseteq \Rightarrow$ is the set of edges, N_h is the set of nodes incident to the edges in $E_\Rightarrow$, and the following properties hold:

- N_h is non-empty and finite;
- If $n_1 \in N_h$ and $n_2 \Rightarrow n_1$, then $n_2 \Rightarrow n_1 \in E_\Rightarrow$;
- h is acyclic.

Notice that the notion of a semi-bundle differs from the notion of a bundle in the aspect that a semi-bundle is backward closed under $\Rightarrow$, and not necessarily backward closed under $\to$.

States. A state is a tuple $\langle S, G, \twoheadrightarrow, \precsim \rangle$, where

- S is a semi-bundle containing strands of the principals;
- G is the set of unbound goals of S;
- $\twoheadrightarrow$ is the relation for the goal-bindings;
- $\precsim = (\twoheadrightarrow \cup \Rightarrow)^*$ — a reflexive and transitive closure of $\twoheadrightarrow$ and $\Rightarrow$ together.

  In other words, $n_1 \precsim n_2$ *iff* there exists a sequence of nodes $\{n'_i\}_{i=1}^k$, such that $n_1 = n'_1$, $n_2 = n'_k$, and for any $i \in [1, k-1]$, $n'_i \Rightarrow n'_{i+1}$ or $n'_i \twoheadrightarrow n'_{i+1}$. Hence, the relation $\precsim$ is a partial order on the nodes in S.

Mathematically, G and $\precsim$ can be computed from S and $\twoheadrightarrow$, but we keep them in the state structure for efficiency reasons.

If $l = \langle S_l, G_l, \twoheadrightarrow_l, \precsim_l \rangle$ is a state and c is a bundle, we say $l \in c$ *iff* $S_l \in c$.

Proposition 4.3. *If G is empty in a state $\langle S, G, \twoheadrightarrow, \precsim \rangle$, then there exists a bundle C such that $S \in C$, and S and C contain the same strands except that C might contain some more penetrator strands of type R or T than S.*

4.3. The Model Checking Algorithm

Bundle Sets. We define the *bundle set* of a state l to be the set of bundles that contain l, denoted as $\Psi(l) = \{c : bundle \mid l \in c\}$.

Next State Transition. If l is a state, the next state transition, $\mathcal{F}$: *state* $\to$ *a set of states*, is a function which maps l to the set of its next states, denoted as $L' = \mathcal{F}(l)$.

We say $\mathcal{F}$ is *complete-inclusive* if for any state l it satisfies the following properties :

1. L' is finite.
2. $\Psi(L') = \Psi(l)$, where $\Psi(L') = \bigcup_{l' \in L'} \Psi(l')$.

Unreachable states. If $\mathcal{F}(l)$ is empty for a state l, we say that l is *unreachable*. This means that there is not any bundle containing l, usually because l contains unsolvable goals.

As was mentioned earlier, we focus on explaining the algorithm for evaluating two simple wffs:

$$\mu_1 = \forall C.s_1 \in C \Rightarrow s_2 \in C, \text{ and}$$
$$\mu_2 = \exists C.s_1 \in C,$$

where s_1 is a strand constant, s_2 is a regular strand constant. The initial step of the model checking algorithm is to compute the initial state $l_0 = \langle S_0, G_0, \twoheadrightarrow_0, \precsim_0 \rangle$, where S_0 is the semi-bundle which only contains s_1, G_0 is the goal set of S_0, the relation $\twoheadrightarrow_0$ is empty, and $\precsim_0$ is the corresponding partial order on S_0. From the definition of $\Psi(l_0)$, we can derive:

$$\forall C.s_1 \in C \Rightarrow s_2 \in C \Leftrightarrow \forall c \in \Psi(l_0).s_2 \in c. \quad (4.1)$$
$$\exists C.s_1 \in C \Leftrightarrow \exists c.c \in \Psi(l_0). \quad (4.2)$$

The main procedure is a reachability analysis with a given next state transition $\mathcal{F}$. We will explain the next state transition $\mathcal{F}$ in the next subsection. *searchI* is the procedure for evaluating the formula μ_1, and *searchII* for μ_2. We give the pseudo code for *searchI* as follows. *searchII* is similar to *searchI*, and the pseudo code can be found in [23].

```
proc searchI(initialState){
    L = {initialState};
    while(¬empty(L)) do{
        l = choose(L);
        L = L \ l;
        L' = F(l);
        if ¬empty(L') then{
            for each l' = ⟨S', G', ↠', ≾'⟩ ∈ L'{
                if s2 ∉ l' then{
                    if empty(G') then return false;
                    else L = add(l', L);
                }
            }
        }
    }
    return true;
}
```

choose(L) is a function which returns an element in the set L. We always pick a state which contains the least number of strands in the set L first.

We now give some intuition how we can reduce an infinite-state-space problem to a problem in a finite state space. First, from the Equation 4.1, we transform μ_1 into the equivalent formula,$\forall c \in \Psi(l_0).s_2 \in c.$, where $\Psi(l_0)$ is the set of bundles which contain l_0, as defined before. Then μ_1 is true, if we can find a set of states L, which satisfies the following property:

- $\forall l \in L.s_2 \in l;$
- $\Psi(l_0) = \Psi(L).$

Thus, we reduce the problem in the infinite state space $\Psi(l_0)$ into a finite state space L. The reachability analysis is a way of searching for L. Once the search procedure terminates, the non-empty leaves of the search tree comprise the set L. We formalize these arguments into the correctness theorem below.

Theorem 4.4. *Let l_0 be an initial state, and $\mathcal{F}$ be a* complete-inclusive *next state transition function. If* searchI(l_0) *terminates and returns* true, *then the formula μ_1 is true; if it returns* false, *then μ_1 is false. The same holds for* searchII *and μ_2.*

Proof sketch. We only give the proof for *searchI* on μ_1. The proof for *searchII* on μ_2 can be derived similarly.

1. If *searchI*(l_0) returns false, then there exists a state $l = \langle S, G, \twoheadrightarrow, \precsim \rangle$ such that G is empty and $s_2 \notin l$. According to the Proposition 4.3, we can obtain at least a bundle which contains S and has the same regular strands as S. Therefore we find the counterexample C, $s_1 \in C$ and $s_2 \notin C$. Hence, μ_1 is false.

2. When *searchI*(l_0) returns true, the reachability analysis explores a state search tree T. An example of the state tree is in Figure 1. The root is the initial state l_0. The children of a tree node n is the next states $\mathcal{F}(n)$. Let L be the set of non-empty leaves of T. If L is empty, then there is no bundle which contains s_1, so μ_1 is true. If L is not empty, from the pseudo code we can see that for any $l \in L$, $s_2 \in l$. So for any $l \in \Psi(L)$, $s_2 \in l$. According to the complete-inclusive property of the next state transition $\mathcal{F}$, $\Psi(l_0) = \Psi(L)$. So $\forall l \in \Psi(l_0).s_2 \in l$. Finally, according to the Equation 4.1, we can see that μ_1 is true.

□

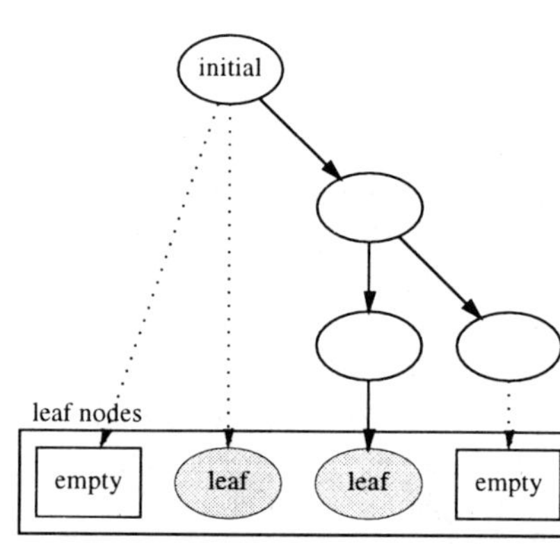

A solid arrow represents the next state transition relation, whereas the dashed arrow stands for a sequence of next state transition relations.

Figure 1. State Search Tree.

4.4. The next state transition algorithms

We first give the intuition of the next state function $\mathcal{F}$. For a state $l = \langle S, G, \rightarrow, \precsim \rangle$, we pick a goal $g = (t, n) \in G$ from the unbound goal set. We then find all possible ways of binding g to a node. For each way of binding, we construct a new *next state*. The value of $\mathcal{F}(l)$ is the set of all such next states. If there is no possible way of binding g, then the state l is unreachable and $\mathcal{F}(l)$ returns an empty set.

Now we give a more detailed description of $\mathcal{F}$. To find all possible ways of binding a goal g, we use a unification procedure U. For a *goal term t*, $U(t)$ returns all possible positions that can bind t, and the corresponding most general substitutions, denoted as $\{([r, i], \gamma_{[r,i]})\}$. $[r, i]$ denotes a *position*, which represents the node of index i in a strand of role r. Role r can be any regular role or penetrator role. Each position $[r, i]$ can be bound to a strand s', either an existing strand in S or a new strand, with the substitution $\gamma_{[r,i]}$. Hence, a node $n' = \langle s', i \rangle$ will bind the goal g. For each of such n', we construct a new *next state* $l' = \langle S', G', \rightarrow', \precsim' \rangle$, where $\rightarrow'$ is the same as $\rightarrow$ with the added binding $n \xrightarrow{t} n'$. If s' is already in S, then S' is the same as S with the added n' and its preceding nodes in strand s', if they are not already in s' yet. If s' is a new strand, then S' is the same as S with the added strand s', which contains all the nodes up to n'. Then G' and $\precsim'$ can be updated appropriately. If there is a conflict in updating G' and $\precsim'$, e.g. there is a cycle in $\precsim'$, then l' is an unreachable state and will not be returned as a next state. The value of $\mathcal{F}(l)$ is the set of all such next states l'.

Because we only add (and never delete) nodes and strands in the next state transition, and since the next state transition covers all possibilities of binding a goal, we can see that $\mathcal{F}$ is *complete-inclusive*. The proof sketch can be found in [23].

Notice that due to the most general substitution in a goal-binding, the nodes and strands in a state can contain free variables. A semi-bundle $S(\vec{x})$ in a state s with free variables, $\vec{x}$, represents a set of variable-free semi-bundles, $\{[\vec{\sigma}/\vec{x}]s(\vec{x})\}$, where $\vec{\sigma}$ is a substitution of values. Thus, the state $s(\vec{x})$ represents a set of variable-free states. Hence, we can represent states and state transitions much more efficiently Also, notice that we only add nodes and strands when necessary due to the exact causal relation, which reduces the state space even further.

4.5. Unreachability Analysis

In order to reduce the search space even further, we can use *unreachability theorems* to prove early that a state is unreachable. Recall that a state is unreachable if there is no bundle containing it. For practical purposes, we need to be able to express such theorems as computable predicates θ, that is, if $\theta(s)$ is true, then the state s is unreachable. Thus, we can simply eliminate s from the set of states immediately.

The unreachability theorems can be specific to a particular protocol, or can be general theorems that are not restricted to any concrete example. The latter can be proven once and for all and included in the core of the tool. This let the model checker easily incorporate results from theorem proving techniques and greatly reduce the state space explored. We give two examples of the unreachability theorems as follows.

Proposition 4.5. *Let C be a bundle, let $k \in K \setminus K_p$. If k never originates in a regular node, then $k \not\sqsubseteq$ term(p) for any penetrator node $p \in C$.*

The proof of this proposition is in [25].

If a protocol is well-typed, in other words, all messages specified in a protocol have fixed types, we can always compute a number which is the maximum number of nested encryption operations in a message that can be generated by a legitimate principal, denoted as E_m. Then the following proposition holds.

Proposition 4.6. *If a state l contains the following nodes as shown in the figure:*
n_1 is the binder of a term t_1, n_1 is on a penetrator strand $s_1 = D[k_1, h_1]$, $t_1 \in h_1$;
t_1 contains a number of nested encryptions which is greater than or equal to E_m.
Then l is unreachable, which means there is no any bundle which will contain l.

This proposition is used to eliminate an infinite expanding of type D strand.

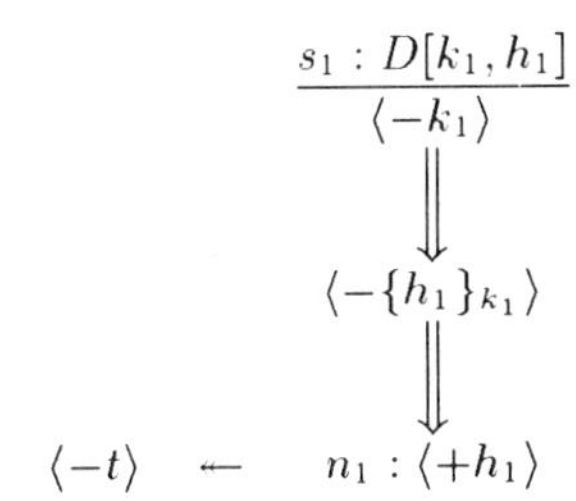

5. Discussion

Our approach has a number of advantages over previous techniques for automatic analysis of security protocols.

First, unlike most model checkers, our approach can reason about problems of infinite state space. When the evaluation procedure terminates, it will have found a mapping from the infinite state space to a finite state space while preserving the validity of well-formed formulae. The mapping is from the set of bundles to the non-empty leaf states of the search tree as described in section 4.3. Thus, by analyzing the finite state space, Athena can derive a proof that a security property holds under any configuration of the protocol execution.

Second, the state transition in Athena is not asynchronously composed of independent process transitions, but based on goal-bindings. Therefore, we avoid the state space explosion caused by asynchronous composition, while others suffer severely from this problem. Most other approaches are based on a trace-based model, where the global state is a list of independent local processes of the principals, and the global state transition is the asynchronous composition of the local process transitions. Hence, concurrent events are modeled by allowing all possible interleaving, and the state space grows exponentially with the number of principals in the protocol execution [20, 21]. In practice, these approaches have difficulties handling protocol executions with more than two initiators and responders. Although some researchers have explored observations that reduce the number of states and paths to be checked [22], and others are pursuing partial order reduction techniques, these techniques will still require a large number of states and paths to be checked unnecessarily.

Third, our states and state transitions, especially the goals and goal-bindings, capture the exact causal relations. By eliminating unnecessary information in state structures, our state representation is more compact and efficient than most other approaches. Each state in our model actually represents a set of traces in a trace-based model by linearizing the paths in the graph of the state.

Forth, unlike most other approaches, Athena takes advantage of symbolic state transitions instead of explicit state search. In explicit state search, state transitions have to be made from one explicit state to another. With security protocols, however, explicit states can be naturally grouped. A group of states can transit to the next group of states, similar to symbolic state transitions. In our approach, we allow a state to contain free variables. A state $s(\vec{x})$ with free term variables, $\vec{x}$, represents a class of variable-free states, $\{[\vec{\sigma}/\vec{x}]s(\vec{x})\}$, where $\vec{\sigma}$ is a substitution of term values. A state transition between two states which contain free variables represents a set of state transitions between two variable-free states. Thus, Athena can represent states and state transitions much more efficiently. As a special case of this, we naturally avoid the symmetry redundancy problem [3], while others suffer from it. For example, in most approaches, the model is composed of a number of replicated components, i.e. two initiators and two responders. A state can be identical to a second state up to a substitution of names and variable values. Thus, it is enough to just analyze one of the states because the analysis will produce the same outcome for both. Although some researchers are pursuing symmetry reduction techniques for explicit state search, it is still difficult to do aggressive symmetry reduction.

#init.	*#resp.*	*Murφ*	*Brutus (Red off)*	*Brutus (Red on)*	*Athena*
1	1	1,706	1,208	146	19
2	2	514,550	***	186,340	19

Brutus (Red on) means Brutus with partial order and symmetry reduction.

Brutus (Red off) means Brutus without partial order and symmetry reduction.

Table 1. Number of states explored in analyzing NSL protocol.

Fifth, Athena uses backward search instead of forward search. With forward search, all the participating principals have to be pre-stated. Our approach starts with a simple initial strand and then add new strands only when necessary according to the exact causal relation. Hence, we reduce the state space explored by avoiding the exploration of many unnecessary states and paths.

Sixth, our approach can use unreachability theorems to prove early that a state is unreachable, hence, prune the state space. The unreachability theorems can be specific to a particular protocol, or can be general theorems that are not restricted to any concrete example. The latter can be proven once and for all and included in the core of the tool. This let the model checker incorporate results from theorem proving techniques easily and systematically.

Our experimental results demonstrate the advantages of using Athena. For the NSL protocol, Athena explored 19 states and proved the agreement property of the protocol under any configuration. The sketch of the analysis can be found in the appendix. As shown in table 1, the number of states explored by Murφ and *Brutus* grows rapidly as the number of initiators and responders increase. For example, with two initiators and responders, Murφ and *Brutus* explore over 10,000 times as many states as Athena. We have also used Athena to find the known attacks in the Needham-Schroeder protocol [18] and the TMN protocol [24]. We have also used Athena to prove certain properties of the 1KP protocol [1] and the Kerberos protocol [10, 11]. Detailed results about these experiments can be found in [23].

6. Conclusions

We propose an efficient automatic checking algorithm, Athena, for analyzing security protocols. Athena incorporates a logic that can express security properties including authentication, secrecy and properties related to electronic commerce. We have developed an automatic procedure for evaluating well-formed formulae in this logic. For a well-formed formula, if the evaluation procedure terminates, it will generate a counterexample if the formula is false, or provide a proof if the formula is true. Athena also exploits several state space reduction techniques. It naturally avoids the state space explosion problem commonly caused by asynchronous composition and symmetry redundancy. It also has the advantage that it can easily incorporate results from theorem proving through unreachability theorems to further reduce the state space explored and increase the likely-hood of termination. As shown in our experiments, we successfully rediscover known flaws or provide proofs of properties for protocols with exploring only tens of states.

Acknowledgements

This research has benefited from discussions with other members of Ed Clarke's research group. The author also thanks Jon Millen for his helpful suggestions.

References

[1] M. Bellare, J. Garay, R. Hauser, A. Herberg, H. Krawczyk, M. Steiner, G. Tsudik, and M. Waidner. *i*KP - a family of secure electronic payment protocols. In *Proceedings of the 1st USENIX Workshop on Electronic Commerce*, July 1995.

[2] M. Burrows, M. Abadi, and R. Needham. A logic of authentication. Technical Report 39, DEC Systems Research Center, February 1989.

[3] E. Clarke, R. Enders, T. Filkorn, and S. Jha. Exploiting symmetry in temporal logic model checking. *Formal Methods in System Design*, 9(1/2):77–104, 1996.

[4] E. Clarke, O. Grumberg, and D. Peled. *Model Checking*. MIT Press, 1999.

[5] E. Clarke, S. Jha, and W. Marrero. Using state space exploration and a natural deduction style message derivation engine to verify security protocols. In *In Proceedings of the IFIP Working Conference on Programming Concepts and Methods (PROCOMET)*, 1998.

[6] D. Dolev and A. Yao. On the security of public key protocols. *IEEE Transactions on Information Theory*, 29(2):198–208, March 1989.

[7] L. Gong, R. Needham, and R. Yahalom. Reasoning about belief in cryptographic protocols. In *In Proceedings of the IEEE Symposium on Research in Security and Privacy, Oakland, California*, May 1990.

[8] N. Heintze and J. Tygar. A model for secure protocols and their compositions. *IEEE Transactions on Software Engineering*, 22(1):16–30, January 1996.

[9] D. Kindred and J. M. Wing. Fast, automatic checking of security protocols. In *USENIX 2nd Workshop on Electronic Commerce*, 1996.

[10] J. Kohl and B. Neuman. The kerberos network authentication service. Internet Request For Comment RFC-1510, 1993.

[11] J. Kohl, B. Neuman, and T. Ts'o. The evolution of the kerberos authentication service. IEEE Computer Society Press, 1994.

[12] G. Lowe. Breaking and fixing the Needham-Schroeder public-key protocol using FDR. In *Tools and Algorithms for the Construction and Analysis of Systems*, volume 1055 of *Lecture Notes in Computer Science*, pages 147–166. Springer-Verlag, 1996.

[13] G. Lowe. A hierarchy of authentication specifications. In *Proceedings of the 1997 IEEE Computer Society Symposium on Research in Security and Privacy*, pages 31–43, 1997.

[14] C. Meadows. A model of computation for the NRL protocol analyzer. In *Proceedings of the 1994 Computer Security Foundations Workshop*. IEEE Computer Society Press, June 1994.

[15] C. Meadows. Formal verification of cryptographic protocols: A survey. In *Advances in Cryptology - Asiacrypt '94*, volume 917 of *Lecture Notes in Computer Science*, pages 133–150. Springer-Verlag, 1995.

[16] J. Millen. The Interrogator model. In *Proceedings of the 1995 IEEE Symposium on Security and Privacy*, pages 251–260. IEEE Computer Society Press, 1995.

[17] J. C. Mitchell, M. Mitchell, and U. Stern. Automated analysis of cryptographic protocols using murφ. In *Proceedings of the 1997 IEEE Symposium on Security and Privacy*. IEEE Computer Society Press, 1997.

[18] R. Needham and M. Schroeder. Using encryption for authentication in large networks of computers. *Communications of the ACM*, 21(12):993–999, 1978.

[19] L. Paulson. Proving properties of security protocols by induction. In *Proceedings of the 1997 IEEE Computer Society Symposium on Research in Security and Privacy*, pages 70–83, 1997.

[20] D. Peled. All from one, one for all: on model checking using representatives. In C. Courcoubetis, editor, *Proceedings of the Fifth Workshop on Computer-Aided Verification*, volume 697 of *Lecture Notes in Computer Science*, pages 409–423, Elounda, Greece, June 1993. Springer-Verlag.

[21] D. Peled. Combining partial order reductions with on-the-fly model-checking. In D. L. Dill, editor, *Proceedings of the Sixth Workshop on Computer-Aided Verification*, volume 818 of *Lecture Notes in Computer Science*, pages 377–390, Stanford, CA, USA, June 1994. Springer-Verlag.

[22] V. Shmatikov and U. Stern. Efficient finite-state analysis for large security protocols. In *Proceedings of the 11th IEEE Computer Security Foundations Workshop*, 1998.

[23] D. Song. Inside Athena. Technical Report. Carnegie Mellon University. CMU-CS-99-125, 1999.

[24] M. Tatebayashi, N. Matsuzaki, and D. Newman. Key distribution protocol for digital mobile communication systems. In *Proc. CRYPTO'89*, 1990.

[25] F. Thayer, J. C. Herzog, and J. D. Guttman. Strand spaces: Why is a security protocol correct? In *Proceedings of 1998 IEEE Symposium on Security and Privacy*, 1998.

[26] T. Y. C. Woo and S. S. Lam. A semantic model for authentication protocols. In *Proceedings of the IEEE Symposium on Research in Security and Privacy*, 1993.

Appendix A : Proofs of the Propositions

Lemma 4.1. If $\mathcal{H}$ is an algorithm that decides the validity of any wff of the form $\forall C.f_1 \Rightarrow f_2$ in a model M in finite steps, where f_1 is a conjunction and f_2 is a disjunction of the atomic propositions, then there exists an algorithm to evaluate any formula of the form $\forall C.F$ in the model M in finite steps, for any propositional formula F.

Proof sketch. Since F is a propositional formula, it can always be transformed into a Conjunctive Normal Form: $F = f_1 \wedge f_2 \wedge \ldots \wedge f_n$, where $f_i, i = 1, \ldots, n$, are disjunctions of the atomic propositions and their negations. Because universal quantifiers distribute over conjunctions,

$$\forall C.F \equiv (\forall C.f_1) \wedge (\forall C.f_2) \wedge \cdots \wedge (\forall C.f_n).$$

For each $i \in (1, \ldots, n)$, f_i can be written as $(\vee_k \alpha_k) \vee (\vee_l \neg \alpha_l)$, where α_k and α_l are atomic propositions. This is equivalent to $(\wedge_l \alpha_l) \Rightarrow (\vee_k \alpha_k)$. So f_i can be evaluated in finite steps by $\mathcal{H}$. Hence, it is easy to see that we can decide F in finite steps. □

Appendix B : The NSL Example

We show a sketch how to prove the agreement property of the NSL protocol using Athena. Due to the space restriction, we omit some steps. The formula that needs to be checked is

$$\forall C.Resp[A_0, B_0, N_{a0}, N_{b0}] \in C \Longrightarrow Init[A_0, B_0, N_{a0}, N_{b0}] \in C.$$

The initial state l_0 is as

$$\begin{array}{c}
\underline{Resp[A_0, B_0, N_{a0}, N_{b0}]} \\
n_1 : \langle -\{N_{a0} \cdot A_0\}_{K_{b0}} \rangle \\
\Downarrow \\
n_2 : \langle +\{N_{a0} \cdot N_{b0} \cdot B_0\}_{K_{a0}} \rangle \\
\Downarrow \\
n_3 : \langle -\{N_{b0}\}_{K_{b0}} \rangle
\end{array}$$

To bind the goal $(n_3, \langle -\{N_{b0}\}_{K_{b0}} \rangle)$, there are three possibilities as follows.

1. l_1 :

$$\begin{array}{ccc}
\underline{Resp[A_0, B_0, N_{a0}, N_{b0}]} & & \underline{Init[A_x, B_0, N_{ax}, N_{b0}]} \\
\langle -\{N_{a0} \cdot A_0\}_{K_{b0}} \rangle & & \langle +\{N_{ax} \cdot A_x\}_{K_{b0}} \rangle \\
\Downarrow & & \Downarrow \\
\langle +\{N_{a0} \cdot N_{b0} \cdot B_0\}_{K_{a0}} \rangle & & \langle -\{N_{ax} \cdot N_{b0} \cdot B_0\}_{K_{ax}} \rangle \\
\Downarrow & & \Downarrow \\
\langle -\{N_{b0}\}_{K_{b0}} \rangle & \leftarrow & \langle +\{N_{b0}\}_{K_{b0}} \rangle
\end{array}$$

2. l_2 :

$$\begin{array}{ccc}
\underline{Resp[A_0, B_0, N_{a0}, N_{b0}]} & & \underline{E[K_{b0}, N_{b0}]} \\
\langle -\{N_{a0} \cdot A_0\}_{K_{b0}} \rangle & & \langle -K_{b0} \rangle \\
\Downarrow & & \\
\langle +\{N_{a0} \cdot N_{b0} \cdot B_0\}_{K_{a0}} \rangle & & \langle -N_{b0} \rangle \\
\Downarrow & & \Downarrow \\
n_4 : \langle -\{N_{b0}\}_{K_{b0}} \rangle & \leftarrow & \langle +\{N_{b0}\}_{K_{b0}} \rangle
\end{array}$$

3. l_3 :

$$\begin{array}{ccc}
\underline{Resp[A_0, B_0, N_{a0}, N_{b0}]} & & \underline{D[K_I, t_1 \cdot N_{b0} \cdot t_2]} \\
\langle -\{N_{a0} \cdot A_0\}_{K_{b0}} \rangle & & \langle -K_I \rangle \\
\Downarrow & & \\
\langle +\{N_{a0} \cdot N_{b0} \cdot B_0\}_{K_{a0}} \rangle & & \langle -\{t_1 \cdot \{N_{b0}\}_{K_{b0}} \cdot t_2\}_{K_I} \rangle \\
\Downarrow & & \Downarrow \\
\langle -\{N_{b0}\}_{K_{b0}} \rangle & \leftarrow & \langle +t_1 \cdot \{N_{b0}\}_{K_{b0}} \cdot t_2 \rangle
\end{array}$$

where t_1, t_2 are free term variables.

Later steps will show that l_1 lead to the correct execution of the protocol which contains the strand $Init[A_0, B_0, N_{a0}, N_{b0}]$. According to proposition 4.6, we can see that there is no bundle that can contain l_3 since in this protocol $E_m = 1$. We now compute the next states of l_2.

l_4 :

$$\begin{array}{ccccc}
\underline{Resp[A_0, B_0, N_{a0}, N_{b0}]} & & \underline{E[K_{b0}, N_{b0}]} & & \underline{D[K_I, t_3 \cdot N_{b0} \cdot t_4]} \\
 & & & & \langle -K_I \rangle \\
\langle -\{N_{a0} \cdot A_0\}_{K_{b0}} \rangle & & \langle -K_{b0} \rangle & & n_5 : \langle -\{t_3 \cdot N_{b0} \cdot t_4\}_{K_I} \rangle \\
\Downarrow & & & & \Downarrow \\
\langle +\{N_{a0} \cdot N_{b0} \cdot B_0\}_{K_{a0}} \rangle & & \langle -N_{b0} \rangle & \leftarrow & \langle +t_3 \cdot N_{b0} \cdot t_4 \rangle \\
\Downarrow & & \Downarrow & & \\
\langle -\{N_{b0}\}_{K_{b0}} \rangle & \leftarrow & \langle +\{N_{b0}\}_{K_{b0}} \rangle & &
\end{array}$$

where t_3, t_4 are free term variables. Later steps will show that l_4 is unreachable. Finally, we finish the proof after exploring 19 states with the conclusion that NSL protocol preserves the non-injective agreement property. Hence, the agreement property holds as well, as mentioned in section 3. The more detailed analysis of this example can be found in [23].

CVS: A Compiler for the Analysis of Cryptographic Protocols *

Antonio Durante[1] Riccardo Focardi[2] Roberto Gorrieri[1]

[1]Dipartimento di Scienze dell'Informazione,
Università di Bologna
Mura Anteo Zamboni 7, 40127 Bologna, Italy
e-mail: {durante,gorrieri}@cs.unibo.it

[2]Dipartimento di Informatica,
Università Ca' Foscari di Venezia
Via Torino 155, I - 30173 Venezia (Italy)
e-mail : focardi@dsi.unive.it

Abstract

The Security Process Algebra (SPA) is a CCS-like specification language where actions belong to two different levels of confidentiality. It has been used to define several non-interference-like security properties whose verification has been automatized by means of the tool CoSeC. In recent years, a method for analyzing security protocols using SPA and CoSeC has been developed. Even if it has been useful in analyzing small security protocols, this method has shown to be error-prone as it requires the description by hand of the protocol and of the environment in which it will execute. This problem has been solved by defining a protocol specification language more abstract than SPA, called VSP, and a compiler CVS that generates in an automatic way the SPA specification for a given protocol described in VSP. The VSP/CVS technology is very powerful and its usefulness is shown with the case-study of the Woo-Lam one-way authentication protocol, for which an attack undocumented in the literature is found.

1 Premise

Many security protocols, using cryptographic techniques, have been proposed in the literature to achieve several goals, e.g. authentication. They are supposed to succeed even in presence of malicious agents, sometimes called intruders or enemies, that can interfere with their correct execution. Unfortunately, many of them may fail when an intruder intercepts some messages and exploits the information they contain in order to introduce new messages into the network.

The approach based on verifying Non-Interference properties (NI for short), used for analyzing computer security, has been recently applied in [6, 5, 7] to find attacks upon some cryptographic protocols, such as the Needham-Schroeder public key authentication protocol [15] and the ISO SC27 [9]. Analyzing a security protocol using NI consists of the following steps. We specify the whole system (protocol and enemy) in the Security Process Algebra (SPA [6]). We then define the observable actions, i.e. those actions that are relevant for security and that can reveal if the enemy has interfered with the correct execution of the protocol. The tool CoSeC [6] takes as input the SPA specification that represents the system that we want to analyze and checks a particular NI property, called SNNI, on that process. If the system verifies SNNI, then we are sure that the enemy cannot interfere with the correct execution of the protocol in the analyzed session; otherwise we observe some enemy interferences, i.e., execution traces that were not possible without enemy's intervention. These extra-traces may reveal some possible attacks to the protocol.

Hence, we do not specify any specific property that the protocol must satisfy; we only observe if the intruder is able to modify (in some way) the flow of information among the honest participants. The task of understanding what are the interferences that correspond to attacks is not hard; the real problem is to specify the system (protocol and enemy) in SPA. In this paper we show the solution to this problem and how to apply the method based on NI verification in an automatic way.

*This work has been partially supported by the MURST, Progetto *Tecniche Formali per la Specifica, l'Analisi, la Verifica, la Sintesi e la Trasformazione di Sistemi Software*.

2 Making fully automatic the approach

We have briefly described how to analyze a protocol using NI according to [7]. It is important to note that if we want to analyze a protocol, we have to fix in advance the *context of analysis*, i.e. the session. Indeed, what we analyze is actually one particular session at a time. As a user can be potentially engaged in a infinite number of different sessions, with this method it is not possible to guarantee that the protocol is correct for all possible sessions.

In general if there is some flaw in the analyzed session we can conclude that the protocol is insecure; on the contrary, we cannot say that the the protocol is secure because we have no guarantee that the correctness result scales to more complex sessions. [1]

As mentioned above, the process of producing the SPA specification of the system (protocol and enemy) presents some drawbacks; as a matter of fact, it is:

- time-consuming: to produce a SPA specification for a small system (usually consisting of more than one thousand lines), we need some days of work. Moreover, when we change the session, the system is modified and we have usually to rewrite the SPA specification;
- only possible for a few expert people: although SPA could be used to describe any concurrent system, it is a really low level language; hence only well trained people can program easily in SPA;
- error-prone: when we specify the system by hand it is likely to forget some actions or to add unnecessary ones. In the first case the specification is incomplete and could miss to represent some important aspects of the real system; in the second case, the specification may be incoherent, because something that never happens in the real system may show up.

Another problem consists of the generation of an *enemy agent*; no standard method to build a powerful enemy which depends on the analyzed protocol was proposed in [6, 7].

These problems have been solved in the following way:

1. a notation more abstract than SPA was defined, called VSP notation;
2. a set of rules to build automatically an enemy was defined;
3. a compiler CVS to translate the VSP notation into SPA (also generating automatically the enemy) was implemented.

[1] For the particular case of secrecy properties, some preliminary results which permit to extend the proofs over small sessions to more complex ones have been proposed in [11]. We do not address this issue here.

In the next sections we give a brief overview on the VSP notation, we explain how the enemy can be made more or less powerful (defining suitably some parameters), we show how to use CVS and finally an application of VSP and CVS for the Woo-Lam one-way authentication protocol [21] is presented.

3 Overview on the VSP notation

VSP is an extension of SPA extended to accommodate value-passing in the usual way [14]. Moreover it requires to fully specify the parameters of the analysis. In the VSP notation, the specification of a protocol is composed of four parts:

1. *Declaration of types (e.g.: Agent, Nonce, Key) and their values, declaration of the structure of the protocol messages, declaration and definition of roles;* in this part we define abstractly the protocol, leaving unspecified the actual session and the other parameters for the analysis.
2. *Definition of the session;* this is done by considering a particular combination (sequential and/or parallel composition) of roles, each one instanced by assigning actual values (e.g. agent names, nonce values) to its parameters.
3. *Setting of the parameters of the enemy;* in this part we specify the features of the enemy, its initial knowledge and capability (e.g. ability to store intercepted values).
4. *Definition of visible actions;* the actions specified in this section are those used to observe and detect enemy interferences.

After the first and second parts of the VSP specification, CVS is able to build the SPA code of the whole protocol. If, in the session definition, the enemy instance appears, then CVS also builds the SPA code for the enemy according to the parameters specified in the third part. A more detailed description of these specification phases, is reported in Section 6 where we propose the VSP specification for the Woo-Lam one-way authentication protocol.

4 The Enemy

In order to analyze the protocol, it is necessary to study its behaviour when it is attacked by a malicious user, often called enemy. In particular, the enemy should be able to:

- intercept any sent message;
- store the information contained in intercepted messages for later uses;

- introduce new messages into the system using information he knows.

An enemy with the above features is able to use the information gained in the last intercepted message when he introduces new messages into the system or he can store stolen information and reuse it in future messages. It is important to note that an enemy with memory can store both *atom* information (like a single nonce) and structured information as *encrypted blocks* even if he cannot decrypt them. We assume that the encryption algorithm used is secure: the enemy is able to decrypt a message only if he knows the key that, hence, can be his own private key or one that he has learnt from an intercepted message.

It is possible to generate an enemy (for a given protocol) in an automatic way and, in principle, we can do it by generating the "most powerful" enemy. However the exponential nature of the enemy generation could prevent to complete the analysis, as we could not check SNNI in a reasonable amount of time or even run out memory very soon. For this reason we have given the possibility to restrict the enemy in some way. In VSP it is possible to set suitably the parameters of the enemy. These parameters are:

- *the initial knowledge*: the enemy can know a set of facts, such as the names of the participants or the agent public keys. The initial enemy knowledge should be the same as a real enemy on the net can know of. Nonetheless, in some cases, it is possible to reduce this set to speed-up the analysis or to see which pieces of information are strictly necessary for the attack.

- *memory*: the enemy in the session could learn new pieces of information and store them if the clause *memory* is true. When we define an enemy with memory we can choose the number of encrypted blocks that the enemy can store. An enemy without memory can reuse stolen information just after its interception, then forgetting it.

By setting these parameters, CVS is able to generate enemies of different power. These parameters can be set (by the user) depending on the kind of the analysis and of the features of the analyzed protocol.

5 Using CVS

The compiler CVS is written in standard C^{++} to facilitate the portability to different development environments and works under UNIX (as well as Windows). CVS compiles a VSP file to SPA code. The command sequence to compile a VSP file is:

```
cvs filename.vsp filename.spa
```

where the first *filename* is the source, and the second one the destination. With this command CVS first compiles the source file, checking if it contains syntax errors; in this case the compilation is interrupted and a suitable diagnostic message is generated. If there are no syntax errors, then CVS creates the output file denominated with the destination name, that can be directly loaded by CoSeC [6]. CVS generates also the log file, consisting of two kinds of information: the correspondence between the process names in VSP notation and those in the SPA code, as well as the knowledge that could be learnt by the enemy during a session.

Once CVS has generated the SPA code, CoSeC analyzes the protocol by checking SNNI on the SPA code. A protocol E is SNNI if and only if $E/H \approx_T E \setminus H$ where H represents the set of actions that correspond to the enemy activity; E/H is the process where we "hide" actions in H, this means that we leave the intruder act indiscriminately; $E \setminus H$ is the process where we "restrict" actions in H, i.e., we forbid the execution of the enemy. SNNI requires that these two processes are trace equivalent (written $\approx_T$). So if SNNI holds the protocol composed with the enemy (E/H) and the protocol without the enemy $(E \setminus H)$ must be equivalent. This has indeed the effect of checking if the enemy is able to interfere in some way with the protocol.

The usefulness of the tool has been tested with several case-studies of different protocols and for some of these protocols, we have found new (at least undocumented, to the best of our knowledge) attack sequences. In the next section we show how the methodology works, with a specific case-study, i.e., the Woo-Lam one-way authentication protocol [21].

6 The Woo and Lam one-way Authentication protocol

We consider the Woo and Lam one-way authentication protocol [21], that was already shown incorrect by Abadi (as reported in [22]). The aim of the Woo-Lam protocol is to establish one-way authentication between two users, say Alice (A) and Bob (B), using an authentication Server (S). Woo and Lam state that the protocol is correct if: "whenever a responder finishes execution of the protocol, the initiator of the protocol is in fact the principal claimed in the initial message".

Woo and Lam start with an initial version of the protocol and progressively simplify it. The version that we are going to analyze is the final version of the protocol. We will denote with K_{US} a key shared between a generic user U and the Server S. The protocol uses *nonces*, which are random numbers generated with the purpose of being used in a *single* run of the protocol. In general, N_U will represent a nonce generated by user U. The protocol is composed of five steps:

Message 1. $A \to B : A$
Message 2. $B \to A : N_B$
Message 3. $A \to B : K_{AS}(N_B)$
Message 4. $B \to S : K_{BS}(A, K_{AS}(N_B))$
Message 5. $S \to B : K_{BS}(N_B)$

Intuitively, *Message 1* represents the authentication request from *A* to *B*. In this message *A* sends her name in plain to *B*. In *Message 2*, *B* replies to *A* by sending the new nonce N_B in plain. Once *A* has received the nonce N_B, she encrypts it with the key K_{AS} and sends the result to *B*. In *Message 4*, *B* encrypts the name of the initiator *A* and $K_{AS}(N_B)$ with the key K_{BS} and sends the result to *S*. The Server receives a message of the form $K_{BS}(U, C)$, decrypts the cipher text C with the key K_{US} encrypts the result with K_{BS} and sends the result to B. When *B* receives the last message, he checks that it contains the nonce N_B and, in such a case, he concludes that was really talking to *A*, since only *S* could have decrypted the fourth message and checked the identity of the initiator.

Now we show how to specify the protocol using the VSP notation.

6.1 First phase of the VSP Specification

As we said above, a VSP protocol specification is divided into four parts. The first part consists of four sections and defines abstractly the protocol.

Name declarations. In the first section we define identifiers (e.g. agent names) that can belong either to built-in types or to user-definable ones. We have two kinds of built-in types: those where the identifiers have to be declared explicitly (i.e. **Agent**, **Key**), and those where the identifiers are implicitly generated by the compiler (i.e. **AsimKey**, **SimKey**). For the Woo-Lam protocol the identifiers declared explicitly are *A*, *B*, *S*, *E* of (built-in) type **Agent**, and *NB*, *NE* of (user-defined) type **Nonce**.

This protocol requires two shared keys between each of the honest users and the Server. These keys belong to a built-in type **SimKey**; their identifiers in SPA code are automatically generated by the CVS compiler hence we do not need to declare them. The built-in type **AsimKey** models the public and private keys used in asymmetric cryptographic algorithms. If we want to represent other key values, exchanged or shared between the agents, we can use the built-in type **Key** which permits to explicitly declare them.

```
#Names
Agent: A,B,E,S;
Nonce: NB,NE;
```

The identifiers *A*, *B*, are the names of the two honest agents; *S* is the name of the Server; *E* is enemy's name. *NB*, *NE* are the nonces generated by the agents *B* and *E*.

Action declarations. In the second section of the first part, the structure of the actions is declared. They can be divided into two sets. The first one contains the actions which are necessary to define the protocol, i.e., the actions representing the messages exchanged between the agents during a run of the protocol. The second one contains the actions used to observe the execution of the protocol and are necessary for the analysis.

Each action is composed by an action name with possibly one or more arguments, whose types are declared in the previous section. We have two kinds of argument: clear (or in plain text), crypted (or cipher text). A crypted block argument is enclosed between two brackets that are preceded by the word *crypt*. The first argument of a crypted block must be a key-type (e.g. **SimKey**, **AsimKey**, **Key**), the other arguments are the pieces of information to be crypted.

For every action it is possible to express some conditions on the values of the parameters. There are two kinds of condition: *equal to*, *different from*. For instance, "I_request(Agent,Agent) cond(0!1)" denotes the fact that the first argument of the action I_request must be different from the second one. These conditions are important to avoid senseless operations (e.g. self-request).

The VSP specification of the messages for the Woo-Lam protocol is:

```
#ActionDec
msg1(Agent)
msg2(Nonce)
msg3(crypt(SimKey,Nonce))
msg4(crypt(SimKey,Agent,crypt(SimKey,Nonce)))
msg5(crypt(SimKey,Nonce))
I_request(Agent,Agent)   cond(0!1)
R_running(Agent,Agent)
I_Connect(Agent,Agent,Number)
R_Connect(Agent,Agent,Number)
```

Note that it is possible to define actions parameters with many levels of nested encryption (e.g. action msg4). In this way it is possible to model also the mechanism of *digital signature*. Besides message declaration, we have specified five actions that we will use to observe the protocol executions. I_request(A1,A2) (R_running(A1,A2)) corresponds to the start of a session between agent A1 and agent A2, where A1 is the initiator (responder). The last two actions are used to observe the correct termination of the initiator and of the responder, respectively. In such actions, the special built-in type `Number`, is used whose aim will be explained in Section 7.

Roles declaration. In this section we declare the "roles" that the agents can play in a single session of a given protocol. The name of the enemy role is predefined as to be "Enemy". In the Woo-Lam protocol there are three roles: *Initiator, Responder, Server.* In a session the agents may play more than one role and more times the same role; in such a case we call it a "multiple session". In VSP the roles are simply declared as follows:

```
#RolesDec
Initiator
Responder
Server
Enemy
```

Processes definition. In this section we define the body of each role as a VSP process. Every VSP process consists of three parts (with the exception of the enemy that is generated automatically by CVS):

1. *a list of parameters*: this represents the declaration of the formal parameters of the process. For example, the VSP notation for the Responder in the Woo-Lam protocol is the following:

   ```
   #ProcessesDef
   Responder(dst: Agent, nonr: Nonce)
   ```

   Typically the first parameter (dst in this case) is used for the name of the agent that is playing the role. The other parameters strictly depend on the analyzed protocol. For the responder of the Woo-Lam protocol the second parameter is a nonce; indeed the responder has to generate a different nonce for every run.

2. *A set of variables*: these represent *the local environment* of the process. Every variable will appear in the list of parameters of the actions used in the process. It is possible to define some restrictions on the values that every variable can assume. For example the VSP notation for the Initiator of the Woo-Lam protocol is:

   ```
   Var
   Agent: dst1;     cond(Responder,Enemy)
   Nonce: nonr1;
   ```

   The side condition expresses that the variable dst1 can only assume the values in the set {Responder,Enemy}. For example if the name of the agent, playing the Responder role is *B* and the Enemy is *E*, then the variable dst1 can only hold *B* or *E*. The meaning of these variables will be clear when the body of the initiator process will be defined.

3. *A sequence of instructions*: it is the body of the VSP process. Instructions can be:

   - *Actions*: they can only be those previously declared in *#ActionDec*. They can be either input actions or output ones. Output actions are prefixed by a character `'` . Communication takes place by synchronous hand-shake.
   - *Conditional instructions*: VSP offers an if-then-else construct.

The bodies of the VSP processes are reported in Table 1.

As we explained, for some built-in types, CVS automatically generates their SPA values. In the Woo-Lam protocol this happens for the shared keys. We use the function of the form KA(A1), where A1 is a variable that belongs to type **Agent**. This function represents a key which is suitably generated for agent $A1$. This is useful when modelling situations where there is a trusted server that shares a key with every agent in the system. Indeed, we can refer to such keys directly through the KA function, as done in the Woo-Lam protocol specification. For example, the key used for encryption in msg3 of the Initiator is KA(src), which represents the key it shares with the server.

Another function used in the process body is `NUMB`; it is only used for the analysis and we will explain how in Section 7.

Besides, the specification for the enemy has to be given. This definition only fixes the strictly necessary parameters allowing the enemy to act as a honest user.

```
Enemy(e_id:Agent,n_id:Nonce)
Begin
End
```

As for Initiator and Responder, the needed pieces of information are the agent name (enemy) e_id and one nonce n_id.

6.2 Second phase of the VSP Specification

Session definition. Here we have to generate a mapping between the agent names and the roles; this mapping is not required to be injective (the same agent can be active in different roles), neither the inverse (several agents can be contemporaneously active in the same role). The actual agents may be composed either in parallel or in sequence. [2] Hence, complex sessions can be defined not only by generating more instances of each role, but also with a mixed composition (parallel/sequential) of processes. This specification phase is very important as it defines the actual structure of the (possibly multiple) session, hence of the whole SPA specification. A VSP process can be instantiated using the names declared in the section `#Names`. For the Woo-Lam protocol, we have decided to study a simple single session with one initiator (namely A), one responder (B), one

[2] In the latter case, the second agent can start its execution only after the first one has finished.

```
#ProcessesDef
Initiator(src : Agent)
Var
Agent: dst1;     cond(Responder,Enemy)
Nonce: nonr1;

Begin
        I_request(src,dst1).
        'msg1(src).
        msg2(nonr1).
        'msg3(enc(KA(src),nonr1)).
        'I_Connect(src,dst1,NUMB)
End

Responder(dst: Agent, nonr: Nonce)
Var
Agent: src1;     cond(Initiator,Enemy)
Agent: src4;     cond(Initiator,Enemy)
Nonce: nonr2,nonr1;

Begin
        msg1(src1).
        'R_running(dst,src1).
        'msg2(nonr).
        msg3(enc(KA(src4),nonr2)).
        'msg4(enc(KA(dst),src1,enc(KA(src4),nonr2))).
        msg5(dec(KA(dst),nonr1)).
        if (nonr1=nonr) then
         'R_Connect(dst,src1,NUMB)
endif
End

Server(ser: Agent)
Var
Agent: dst2;     cond(Responder,Enemy)
Agent: src2;     cond(Initiator,Enemy)
Agent: src3;     cond(Initiator,Enemy)
Nonce: nons;

Begin
        msg4(dec(KA(dst2),src2,dec(KA(src3),nons))).
        if (src2=src3) then
                'msg5(enc(KA(dst2),nons))
        endif
End
```

Table 1. The bodies of Initiator, Responder and Server

server (S) and the enemy (E), all composed in parallel. In the VSP notation, this is written as follows:

```
#Processes
Initiator(A)
Responder(B,NB)
Server(S)
Enemy(E,NE)
```

If we want to analyze a session where two or more processes are composed in sequence we use the `;` operator. For example, the VSP specification for the representation of two initiators in sequence, and a responder in parallel is the following:

```
Initiator(A);Initiator(B)
Responder(B,NB)
```

Channel definition. In this section we specify which are the actions that can be sent and received on the communication channel, i.e., that represent the protocol messages. They are a subset of the actions declared in `#ActionDec`. For our example:

```
#RestrictionOn
channel(msg1,msg2,msg3,msg4,msg5)
```

The actions which are not declared as protocol messages are called *visible actions*, as they are the actions observed in the analysis; we explicitly declare them in the last part of the VSP specification.

6.3 Third phase: the Enemy

In this section we specify the enemy parameters. CVS then builds in an automatic way a SPA specification of the enemy according to the chosen parameters. We have already explained in Section 4 what are the enemy parameters that can be set up; now we show how they are set for the Woo-Lam protocol.

```
#EnemyKnowledge
Agent: All;
Memory:False;
```

This specification means that the enemy initially knows all the agent names. Moreover, it has no memory, so when he introduces new messages in the system, besides the agent names he can additionally use only the information gained in the last intercepted message. It is possible to create a more powerful enemy with the clause: "Memory:True;", but in this case-study an enemy without memory is sufficient.

We could want to give to the enemy the knowledge of only a subset of the identifiers of a particular type. This can be done by specifying the type followed by the identifiers list. For example, to represent that the enemy knows only the agent names A and B, we can write: `Agent:A,B;` .

Note that in the Woo-Lam protocol double encrypted messages are present; CVS is able to generate an enemy that also deals with this kind of messages in a correct way.

6.4 Fourth phase of the VSP: the Visible Actions

In the last part of the protocol specification, we explicitly specify the set of visible actions. If the enemy modifies their execution then property SNNI is not verified; as we will see this could correspond to the presence of one (or more) flaw(s) in the protocol.

When we analyze a protocol through SNNI, the choice of visible actions is very relevant. Typically, we observe the starts and the correct termination of the parties, since we have seen that these are sufficient to detect the attacks in all the protocols we have analyzed. Indeed, in most protocols we can simply observe the correct terminations but this does not hold in general, e.g., in the Woo-Lam protocol this is not sufficient. For the Woo-Lam protocol the chosen visible actions are:

```
#Observe
R_running(Responder,Initiator)
I_request(Initiator,Enemy)
R_Connect(Responder,Initiator,Number)
I_Connect(Initiator,Enemy,Number)
```

As said above the first two actions represent the start of the protocol for the responder and the initiator respectively; while the last two actions represent their correct termination.

The presence of an interference is not a guarantee that an attack is presented in the protocol session (as we will see in the next session); on the other hand the absence of interference ensures that no security flaw is present in the protocol session according to the observed actions. In this sense the approach offers a sufficient, but not necessary, condition to correctness.

7 Interpreting the Interference Traces

By analyzing the VSP specification of the Woo-Lam protocol, we find out that it is not SNNI. The result of this analysis consists of a list of all interference traces, which do not necessary correspond to an attack. Indeed some of them are permitted commits between the enemy and the honest agents; some other traces can be part of an enemy request that the enemy cannot conclude; the rest of the traces may correspond to attacks. We explain how to interpret the output of CoSeC showing the list of interferences obtained for the Woo-Lam protocol, when observing the actions defined above.

We can divide the set of interference traces found for this protocol into three different sets. The first set is:

```
(1) I_request_A_E 'I_Connect_A_E_3
(2) I_request_A_E 'I_Connect_A_E_4
```

These two traces correspond to two requests made by the initiator A to the enemy E, followed by two commits between them. These do not correspond to an attack: they appear simply because we consider the enemy as a normal user, so he can perform a normal run with some other user.

The second set is:

```
(1) I_request_A_E 'R_running_B_A
    'I_Connect_A_E_4
(2) 'R_running_B_A I_request_A_E
    'I_Connect_A_E_4
```

These two traces are similar to the previous ones; the only difference is that the enemy does a request to the Responder (pretending to be A), but B is not able to finish this second run.

The third set is:

```
(1) I_request_A_E 'R_running_B_A
    'I_Connect_A_E_3 'R_Connect_B_A_1
(2) I_request_A_E 'R_running_B_A
    'R_Connect_B_A_1 'I_Connect_A_E_3
```

These two last sequences correspond to an attack. We can understand this because the Responder B is able to do a commit with the Initiator A (action `'R_Connect_B_A_1`) without a request made by the Initiator A. These two interferences represent the same attack. Indeed they differ only in the order of the two `Connect` actions. As a matter of fact, when the initiator and the responder have finished the protocol, they can emit their respective `Connect` actions in any order.

The number that appear on the end of a `Connect` action is generated by CVS when the function NUMB is an argument of an action in the VSP body. It basically labels, with a different number, every possible execution "branch" that can be taken in the SPA-code. This is very helpful when we have to reconstruct an attack sequence performed by the enemy. Indeed, given a certain `Connect` labelled with a number we can see exactly in the SPA-code what the enemy has done. [3] In this way we can understand all the steps of the attack that can be written as follows:

1.a $A \rightarrow E : A$
1.b $E(A) \rightarrow B : A$
2.b $B \rightarrow E(A) : N_B$
2.a $E \rightarrow A : N_B$
3.a $A \rightarrow E : K_{AS}(N_B)$
3.b $E(A) \rightarrow B : K_{AS}(N_B)$
4.b $B \rightarrow S : K_{BS}(A, K_{AS}(N_B))$
5.b $S \rightarrow B : K_{BS}(N_B)$

The initiator A begins a first session with the enemy E; when the enemy receives the message 1.a, it sends a request to the responder B (message 1.b) starting another session where it pretend to be A. The responder answers and sends his nonce N_B to A. The message 2.b is intercepted by E that reuses the nonce N_B in the first session, sending it to A; A encrypts N_B and sends it to E which simply forwards it to B, (message 3.b). Now B can conclude the protocol with the server S. At the end of the protocol, the responder B thinks to be connected to the initiator A, while A has never begun a run with B!

The SPA specification represents a single session of the protocol, where every participant plays just one role at a time, but the attack found occurs in a multiple session. This happens because the enemy plays two different roles: the responder in session a and the initiator in session b.

This particular attack sequence is new, even if it is not the first one found for this protocol. All the other attacks reported in literature are available in [3]. However it is the only one which can be carried out in a single session; all the other attacks reported in [3] occurring in multiple sessions, were discovered through CVS by choosing an appropriate session. In particular we have: the attack by Abadi and Needham (as reported in [22]) where a participant plays two times the responder role; the attack by Woo and Lam in [22] where a participant plays the responder role and the initiator role.

8 Conclusion and future research

In this work we have presented a new notation, called VSP, which permits to define security protocols at a level more abstract than SPA. The VSP specifications are compiled to SPA code through the CVS compiler. The main advantages of VSP are (i) the possibility of giving very compact value passing specifications and (ii) the high level of parameterization in the analysis. In particular we have shown that it is possible to set up a number of parameters which reduce significantly the state space of the analyzed system. This permits to start the analysis with a simplified enemy, which is still generated automatically, and then proceed with more complex ones. In this way we can start with very fast checks which could already reveal some simple attacks on the protocol. Moreover this "gradual" approach is useful to understand how much power the enemy needs in order to be able to attack the protocol.

Once the SPA code is obtained, it can be analyzed using a Non-Interference based technique. This is what mainly differentiate our compiler from other existing ones. For ex-

[3] We do not show here the details of this analysis since we should report the whole SPA-code.

ample, the CASPER compiler [12] translates protocols defined in a language similar to VSP to CSP [8] specifications. It is very similar to our CVS if observed at the specification level. However, the way protocols are analyzed is completely different. The Non-Interference check can be seen as a sufficient condition to the absence of every kind of (not only authentication) attacks on the particular session we are analyzing. Indeed it checks that the presence of the enemy does not change in any way the behaviour of the protocol with respect to a set of "relevant" actions. These actions are the only things we have to fix in the analysis and represent what we want to observe of the protocol. We do not have to define a particular property on such actions. If the check is successful, we can conclude that the enemy is able to do nothing (good or evil) on such observable actions. For example, we can easily check the authentication properties verified by CASPER by simply considering as relevant the actions that are observed by such particular properties (e.g., the run and commit actions). If the Non-Interference check is unsuccessful we obtain a set of interferences that can be easily analyzed in order to understand which interferences are "dangerous" and which are not. The CVS tool has been developed with the aim of supporting this Non-Interference based approach for the analysis of cryptographic protocols which has been first studied and shown flexible enough to reveal different attacks in [6, 5].

Before the implementation of CVS, only few protocols were analyzed using such a technique. This tool has permitted us to successfully analyze many more protocols. This has in a sense confirmed that the Non-Interference based analysis of security protocols is profitable. We report here some of them containing well-known attacks: the Yahalom protocol presented [2] and shown insecure in [19]; the Andrew protocol [18] with the attack presented in [10]; the Otway-Rees [16] shown flawed in [17] and the TMN protocol [20] with the attacks reported in [13]. All the attacks on these protocols presented in the literature have been captured by CVS. Moreover, in the TMN we have found an attack which seems new. The Otway-Rees is particularly interesting since it is requires an enemy with memory in order to attack it. In all of the checks on these protocols we have keenly exploited the high parameterization level of our tool, that has permitted to obtain quite fast analysis and detection of attacks.

As a future work, we are considering other techniques based on the introduction of some auxiliary information which could allow a more efficient and "local" analysis of some properties (see, e.g., [4, 1]). We are also trying to enhance the tool with some feature for cryptographic analysis in order to detect some attacks based on particular properties of the cryptographic algorithms adopted. Another possible improvement is a graphical interface that accepts as inputs the roles of the protocol, the handshake message between the participants (in a symbolic form) and the observable actions.

References

[1] C. Bodei, P. Degano, R. Focardi, and C. Priami. "Authentication via localized names". in this volume. June 1999.

[2] M. Burrows, M. Abadi, and R. Needham. "A Logic of Authentication". *Proceedings of the Royal Society of London*, 426:233–271, 1989.

[3] J. Clark and J. Jacob. "A Survay of Authentication Protocols Literature: version 1.0". November 1997. http://www.cs.york.ac.uk/~jac/papers/drareview.ps.gz.

[4] R. Focardi. "Using Entity Locations for the Analysis of Authentication Protocols". In *Proceedings of Sixth Italian Conference on Theoretical Computer Science (ICTCS'98)*, November 1998.

[5] R. Focardi, A. Ghelli, and R. Gorrieri. "Using Non Interference for the Analysis of Security Protocols ". In *Proceeding of the DIMACS Workshop on Design and Formal Verification of Security Protocols (H. Orman and C. Meadows Ed.)*, DIMACS Center, Rutgers University, September 1997.

[6] R. Focardi and R. Gorrieri. "The Compositional Security Checker: A Tool for the Verification of Information Flow Security Properties". *IEEE Transactions on Software Engineering*, 23(9), September 1997.

[7] R. Focardi and R. Gorrieri. "Analysis of Authentication Protocols using Non-Interference". Technical Report CS98-18, University of Venice, October 1998.

[8] C. A. R. Hoare. *Communicating Sequential Processes*. Prentice-Hall, 1985.

[9] "Entity Authentication Using Symmetric Techniques". Report ISO/IEC JTC1.27.02.2 (20.03.1.2), June 1990.

[10] G. Lowe. "Some New Attacks upon Security Protocols". *IEEE Computer Security Workshop 1996*, pages 164–165, 1996.

[11] G. Lowe. "CASPER: A Compiler for the Analysis of the security protocols". In *Proceedings Tenth IEEE Computer Security Foundation Workshop, (CSFW'97)*, pages 18–30, Rockport Massachusetts (USA), June 1997. IEEE Press.

[12] G. Lowe. "Towards a Completeness Result for Model Checking of Security Protocols". In *Proceedings of Eleventh IEEE Computer Security Foundation Workshop, (CSFW'98)*, Rockport Massachusetts (USA), June 1998. IEEE Press.

[13] G. Lowe and B. Roscoe. "Using CSP to detect errors in the TMN protocol". *IEEE Transaction on Software Engineering*, 23 (10), October 1997.

[14] R. Milner. *Communication and Concurrency*. Prentice-Hall, 1989.

[15] R. Needham and M. Schroeder. "Using encryption for authentication in large networks of computers". *Communications of the ACM*, 21(12):993–999, 1978.

[16] D. Otway and O. Rees. "Efficient and timely mutual authentication". *Operating system review*, 21, Jennuary 1987.

[17] L. C. Paulson. "The Inductive Approach to Verifying Cryptographic Protocols". In *Proceedings Tenth IEEE Computer Security Foundation Workshop, (CSFW'97)*, Rockport Massachusetts (USA), June 1997. IEEE Press.

[18] M. Satyanarayanan. "Integrating Security in large distribuited system". *ACM Transactions on Computer Systems*, 7(3):247–280, 1992.

[19] P. Syverson. "A Taxonomy of replay attacks". In *Proceedings Seventh IEEE Computer Security Foundation Workshop, (CSFW'94), (Li Gong Ed.)*, Franconia (NH), June 1994. IEEE Press.

[20] M. Tatebayashi, N. Matsuzaki, and D. B. Newman Jr. "Key distribution protocol for digital mobile communication system". *Advances in Cryptology: Proceedings of Crypto '89*, 435:324–333, 1990.

[21] T. Woo and S. Lam. "Authentication for distributed systems". *Computer*, 25:10–10, March 1992.

[22] T. Woo and S. Lam. "A lesson on authentication protocol design". *Operating system review*, pages 24–37, 1994.

Noninterference Using Process Algebras

Process Algebra and Non-interference

P Y A Ryan
Defence Evaluation and Research Agency
St Andrews Road, Malvern, UK

S A Schneider
Royal Holloway, University of London
Egham, Surrey, UK, TW20 0EX

Abstract

The information security community has long debated the exact definition of the term 'security'. Even if we focus on the more modest notion of confidentiality the precise definition remains controversial. In their seminal paper [4], Goguen and Meseguer took an important step towards a formalisation of the notion of absence of information flow with the concept of non- interference. This too was found to have problems and limitations, particularly when applied to systems displaying non-determinism which led to a proliferation of refinements of this notion and there is still no consensus as to which of these is 'correct'.

We show that this central concept in information security is closely related to a central concept of computer science: that of the equivalence of systems. The notion of non-interference depends ultimately on our notion of process equivalence. However what constitutes the equivalence of two processes is itself a deep and controversial question in computer science with a number of distinct definitions proposed in the literature. We illustrate how several of the leading candidates for a definition of non-interference mirror notions of system equivalence. Casting these security concepts in a process algebraic framework clarifies the relationship between them and allows many results to be carried over regarding, for example, composition and unwinding.

We also outline some generalisations of non-interference to handle partial and conditional information flows.

1. Introduction

It is a source of mild embarrassment that the information security community has not yet reached a consensus as to the precise meaning on the term 'security' or even to the simpler question of what is meant by confidentiality. It is clear that confidentiality boils down to the absence of certain undesirable information flows, but this begs the question of what constitutes an information flow or its absence. The thesis of this paper is that the characterisation of the absence of information flow reduces to characterising the equivalence of systems. The latter is of course a central concept in computer science and here too we find that there is no single agreed definition of what constitutes equivalence. Instead we again find a proliferation of definitions and it seems that which is appropriate depends on the particular application. Indeed, as we will show in detail in the later sections of this paper, there is a close correspondence between formulations of non-interference and formulations of process equivalence. It appears that by and large the proponents of the various forms of non-interference were unaware of the analogies with notions in the process algebra community and were independently reinventing these concepts in the security context.

A number of attempts to unify the various formulations of non-interference have been published recently, notably McLean [8] and Foccardi and Gorrierri [2]. These are very elegant and illuminating. We believe that identifying the analogies between the concepts in the security and the process algebra communities sheds further light on the notion of confidentiality and in particular helps explain the proliferation of definitions of confidentiality. Indeed the security community can perhaps derive some solace from the observation that the problem of defining non-interference is equivalent in difficulty to one of the central problems of computer science and so it should not be a source of surprise that consensus has eluded us.

Process algebras, in particular CSP, provide a general framework for describing interacting systems. Many of the formulations of confidentiality that one finds in the literature are presented in rather specialised and often specially tailored models of computation, so recasting them in a process algebra allows them to be generalised and compared. Another advantage of using a process algebraic framework is that it allows us to apply a number of established results, such as the completeness of unwinding rules, and compositionality.

We start with a brief overview of those aspects of CSP that we use in this paper. We then present a number of formulations of non-interference in a CSP style. In Section 4 we discuss some generalisations of non-interference designed to encompass a richer class of security policies.

2. Process algebra

Process algebras provide a particular approach to the study of concurrency and interaction. This paper bases its discussion within the framework of the process algebra CSP (Communicating Sequential Processes). A full account of this process algebra can be found in [11, 15]. It provides a language for describing interacting systems, together with a semantic theory for understanding them. This section provides a brief reminder of those aspects most relevant to this paper.

The language of CSP is constructed around *events*: instantaneous synchronisations which provide the communication primitive. Events may have some structure, the most common communication being a channel communication of the form $c.v$, where c is the channel name, and v is the value communicated. For the purposes of this paper we will divide Σ, the set of all events, into two classes: H (high) and L (low). The set H will be further divided into high inputs HI and high outputs HO.

Processes are used to describe possible patterns of interaction. In CSP, a process has an alphabet, or interface: the set of events it is able to synchronise on. The process $c!v \rightarrow P$ describes a process which is prepared to output v on channel c, and behave subsequently as P. The input $c?x \rightarrow P(x)$ may take in some value v along channel c and behave subsequently as $P(v)$. The choice $P \sqcap Q$ may behave non-deterministically either as P or as Q. Processes may be put in parallel: $P \parallel Q$ behaves as P running concurrently with Q, synchronising on events in their common alphabets, and performing other events independently. An interleaving of two processes, $P \mid\mid\mid Q$, simply executes P and Q concurrently without any communication occurring between them. Values are passed between parallel processes by means of synchronisations on the channels, linking an output channel of one to an input channel of another. The abstraction mechanism $P \setminus A$ describes the process P with all occurrences of A occurring internally in the resulting process. The process $STOP_A$ has alphabet A and can perform no events at all. Thus $P \parallel STOP_A$ behaves as the process P with all occurrences of A blocked. This is different from $P \setminus A$ in which all occurrences of events in A are made internal.

The process RUN_A also has alphabet A, and it is always ready to perform any event from the set A. The process $CHAOS_A$ also has alphabet A, and can perform or refuse to perform any such event at any stage during an execution—it is the most nondeterministic (divergence-free) process with alphabet A. Processes may also be recursively defined, by giving equations which contain the name of the process being defined as a subterm of the process expression. For example, the process

$$COPY = in?x \rightarrow out!x \rightarrow COPY$$

defines a buffer process $COPY$ as one which repeatedly alternates input and output. Indexed processes may also be recursively defined using families of equations.

The semantics of processes are given in terms of observations. A process is identified with the set of behaviours that may possibly be observed of it, where the kind of behaviour considered determines the nature of the model.

The *Traces Model* is concerned with the traces of a process: the (finite) sequences of events that it can perform during some execution. For example,

$$\begin{aligned} &traces(COPY) = \\ &\quad \{\langle\rangle, \} \\ &\quad \cup \{\langle in.v\rangle \mid v \in V\} \\ &\quad \cup \{\langle in.v, out.v\rangle \mid v \in V\} \\ &\quad \cup \{\langle in.v, out.v, in.w\rangle \mid v \in V, w \in V\} \\ &\quad \vdots \end{aligned}$$

where V is the type of the channels *in*, *out*.

If tr is a possible trace of a process P, then P/tr (pronounced 'P after tr') denotes the process that P becomes after executing the trace tr. For example, $COPY/\langle in.7\rangle = out!7 \rightarrow COPY$.

The traces model is sufficient for many applications but it is not able to fully distinguish different non-deterministic behaviours. To deal with non-determinism we must turn to the failures model of CSP: a *failure* of a process is a trace together with a *refusal set* which describes a set of events that the process might refuse to engage in after performing the trace. For example, $(\langle in.3\rangle, \{in.5, in.6\})$ is a failure of $COPY$. A *divergence* of a process is a trace after which it may perform an infinite sequence of internal actions. In this paper, we are assuming that the systems modelled do not diverge.

A process is *deterministic* whenever, given an arbitrary trace $tr ^\frown \langle a\rangle$, it could not have refused the last event instead of performing it: $(tr, \{a\})$ should not be a failure. Thus given any trace, there is only one possible response for each potential next event. In the failures model a process Q is a refinement of another process P when the set of Q's failures are a subset of P's failures. This means that Q is more deterministic. Thus $CHAOS_A$ is refined by any process with alphabet A, and deterministic processes cannot be further refined: no process is a strict refinement of a deterministic process.

Processes are considered equivalent in a semantic model if they have the same set of behaviours in that model. Thus if P and Q have the same traces, then they are equivalent in the traces model, written $P =_{traces} Q$. This means that if only their traces are examined, then they cannot be distinguished. Similarly, if P and Q have the same failures, then this is written $P =_{failures} Q$. The subscript to the equality symbol can be dropped if it is clear from the context.

Process semantics may also be described in terms of operational semantics, which describe transitions between states (process descriptions). Thus $P \xrightarrow{\mu} P'$ describes the performance by P of a single μ event, reaching the state P'. If s is a sequence of events, then $P \stackrel{s}{\Longrightarrow} P''$ describes a sequence of steps between successive processes, each step labelled by the corresponding event in the sequence s. Operational semantics allows alternative approaches to comparing processes.

One approach to comparing processes is in terms of *testing*. A test T is a particular kind of process, with some *SUCCESS* states. We consider the execution of T in conjunction with a process P and if $P \parallel T$ can reach a success state then 'P may T'. If P may T whenever Q may T and vice versa for all possible tests T, then P and Q are equivalent under may testing. For further information on testing see [5].

Strong bisimulation [9] identifies processes if the states in their execution graphs match. This will be the case if there is a symmetric *bisimulation relation* R such that if PRQ and $P \xrightarrow{\mu} P'$ then $\exists\, Q'.(P'RQ' \wedge Q \xrightarrow{\mu} Q')$, where μ is any transition label. This is the strongest useful equivalence between processes, and implies equivalence in any of the CSP semantic models. As well as requiring traces to match, bisimulation also requires the points at which choices are made within processes to match.

This can be relaxed by not requiring the two processes to match hidden (τ) events. Here we allow a visible event a in P to be matched by a sequence $\hat{a}$, for some $\hat{a} \in \tau^*.\alpha.\tau^*$, the set of all sequences of τ actions interleaved with a single a. This is known as weak-bisimulation.

P and Q are weakly bisimilar with respect to the symmetric relation $\approx$ if and only if whenever $P \approx Q$ then $P \xrightarrow{a} P' \Rightarrow \exists\, Q'.Q \stackrel{\hat{a}}{\Longrightarrow} Q' \wedge P' \approx Q'$.

In [3] Gardiner proposes a further weakening introduces an equivalence relation on the power set of states, known as power-bisimulation. This allows sets of states of P to be related to sets of states of Q. This has the effect of abstracting out the effect of the point at which non-deterministic choices are made. This allows the construction of a form of bisimulation that is precisely equivalent to failures equivalence and will be discussed more fully in section 3.3.

3. Non-interference

3.1. Goguen/Meseguer

Confidentiality policies are concerned with restricting classes of information flows. In the early days of the subject such policies were typically constructed by analogy with the paper world and so involved assertions such as: information should not flow from an object of higher classification to one of lower classification. Thus information flows are treated in a binary fashion: it is either allowed to flow or not, and the objects of the policy were typically fairly gross: data bases, files, agents etc. Such analogies now look rather dated in the light of the capabilities provided by current information processing systems and we will address the question of constructing more elaborate policies, with finer granularity of objects and more subtle controls of information flows, in Section 4. For the moment we will stick to this traditional viewpoint as, even in this comparatively simple context, there are a number of subtleties to be considered.

A central problem is to characterise the absence of information flow between objects, which in effect means across interfaces or along channels. The Bell and La Padula model takes the notions of *read* and *write* as primitives and so makes no attempt to formalise them. A number of critiques of Bell and La Padula are based on this observation. An early attempt to formalise the absence of information flow was the concept of non-interference proposed in the seminal paper by Goguen and Meseguer, [4].

Intuitively the idea is as follows: to establish that information does not flow from object A to object B it is sufficient to establish that A's behaviour has no effect on what B can observe. Put differently: B's view of the system is independent of A's behaviour. This latter suggests an appropriate way of capturing this mathematically: for any pair of behaviours of the system that differ only in A's behaviour, B's observations of the system cannot distinguish these two systems. This makes it clear that the notion of indistinguishability of behaviours is central. For systems that are deterministic it is fairly straightforward to make such equivalence precise and indeed it is deterministic systems that Goguen and Meseguer originally considered.

Casting the Goguen/Meseguer formulation into a more CSP like notation for ease of comparison with later formulations:

Assume that High interacts with the system S via the interface H and Low via the interface L and further that these two interfaces partition the full interface of S. Then High is said to be non-interfering with Low via S if:

$$\forall\, tr : I^*, c : I. \qquad Output_L S(tr, c) = Output_L S(tr \upharpoonright L, c) \tag{1}$$

where I is the set of inputs to S, and I^* the set of sequences of I's. $Output_L S(tr, c)$ denotes the output to Low from the system when it is in the state resulting from the sequence of inputs tr and when it receives a further input c. Finally, the projection to L $tr \upharpoonright L$ is the trace tr with all occurrences of H events removed (given that H and L partition the alphabet of S).

In other words, whatever inputs High has performed the output that Low sees is the same as he would see if High had done nothing. Note that for a system in which the Low output is uniquely determined this equality is straightforward to define.

Even in this seemingly straightforward definition a number of subtleties lurk, for example: it depends on drawing a distinction between 'inputs' and 'outputs' without making the semantics of this distinction clear. This is a bit like the failure of the Bell La Padula model to give a precise semantics to the terms 'read' and 'write'.

More significant is the point that for systems displaying non-determinism characterising the equality of Equation 1 turns out to be rather delicate. Thus the seemingly innocent phrase '...B's observations of the system cannot distinguish...' actually conceals some subtle problems. The question of deciding when two processes should be regarded as equivalent is a difficult one and one to which a number of answers have been proposed. It is far from clear which of these is to be regarded as 'correct'. Indeed it seems reasonable to suppose that there is in fact no 'correct' notion; which is appropriate depends on the context and application in question.

The diversity of notions of system equivalence shows up most clearly in the process algebra community where we find, for example, traces or failures equivalence, various flavours of bi-simulation as well as various forms of testing equivalence.

3.2. CSP Formulations

In an attempt to resolve the problems associated with drawing input/output distinctions as well as address the issue of non-deterministic systems, one of the authors proposed a recasting of the Goguen/Meseguer formulation into CSP [14]. Again the notation is tweaked slightly from the original 1990 presentation to make it more compatible with the rest of this paper.

$$\forall\, tr, tr' : traces(S).(tr \approx tr' \Rightarrow \\ refusals(S/tr) \cap L = refusals(S/(tr')) \cap L) \quad (2)$$

where $tr \approx tr' \Leftrightarrow tr \upharpoonright L = tr' \upharpoonright L$. $refusals(S/tr)$ denotes the sets of events the process S can refuse after the trace tr. A refusal is a set of events that the process may choose to refuse if the environment offers one of them. Different refusals sets can result after a given trace corresponding to different non-deterministic choices, hence the set of sets. It thus encodes the non-determinism of a system. $tr \upharpoonright L$ denotes the restriction of the trace tr to the set L. We take the distributed intersection of the refusal sets with L to get the Low level view.

CSP does not draw a distinction between inputs and outputs, both are regarded simply as 'events'. There is a danger in wrongly categorising events as input or output which is avoided, though arguably at the cost of a characterisation of confidentiality that errs towards being too strong. A simple example, due to Millen, serves to illustrate this.

Consider a system with high and low inputs but only high outputs. Naively we would regard such a system as secure and yet it could fail the CSP characterisation. Whether or not this system really is secure depends critically on the semantics of the term 'input'. If 'input' is taken to mean an event wholly under the control of the environment that cannot be refused or delayed by the system then we probably would accept this system as being secure. However if there is any possibility of the system influencing the occurrence (even if not the value) of the 'input' event in any way we immediately have a channel from high to low. Any event that is wrongly characterised as an input in this sense could slip through and lead to a system incorrectly being deemed secure.

The CSP approach is thus a much safer criterion but could lead to some secure systems being rejected. If you are to draw such input/output distinctions and use them in the definition of security then they must be precisely defined.

In fact it turns out that, although CSP doesn't draw such distinctions, we can nonetheless use the framework, given in equation 2, to distinguish at least the High (abstracted) input/output events.

This ability to distingiush inputs/outputs in CSP arises from our use of the more symmetric formulation of [14] instead of the more traditional form in which an arbitrary trace is compared to its purge. A consequence of this is that in this formulation it is not guaranteed that the purge of an arbitrary trace is itself a valid trace of the system. At first glance this appears to be a flaw as it seems to allow Low to deduce in some cases the occurrence of certain events at the high level. It actually turns out to be an advantage: the failure of the purge of a trace to be a trace is due to the occurrence of high signal events, i.e. events that cannot be refused or delayed by High. An example of such an event might be an alarm signal to alert High of some low-level activity. This clearly does not constitute a flow from High to Low and yet Low can deduce that such an alarm event has occurred.

For example, the process

$$S = l \rightarrow h \rightarrow l_2 \rightarrow STOP$$

has traces $\{\langle\rangle, \langle l\rangle, \langle l, h\rangle, \langle l, h, l_2\rangle\}$. The $purge_H$ of $\langle l, h, l_2\rangle$ is $\langle l, l_2\rangle$ which is not a trace of S. Thus when Low sees l_2

he knows h has occurred, but if High has no control over the occurrence of h it does not provide a means for High to signal to Low.

If we do not want h to be modelled as a signal event we should use the process

$$\begin{aligned} S = \;& l \rightarrow h \rightarrow l_2 \rightarrow STOP \\ & \Box \\ & l \rightarrow l_2 \rightarrow STOP \end{aligned}$$

which allows High to refuse h without deadlocking the system. Now when Low sees l_2 he cannot tell if h has occurred.

Using the purge formulation would be equivalent to assuming that all events are refusable.

The issue of 'input totality' that was a concern for many of the early formulations is another manifestation of this difficulty, i.e. the problem of what happens if an invalid input sequence is presented to the system. This is dealt with automatically in a CSP approach: invalid inputs are simply refused by the system.

The approach of [14] deliberately tried to stay as close as possible to the spirit of the original Goguen/Meseguer formulation. In particular it sticks to quantifying over traces and comparison of the next events. It is interesting to consider how one might alter it to cast it in a more conventional CSP style. Firstly rather than just comparing next events we can compare the subsequent behaviours, i.e. assert equivalence as processes and use the conventional CSP hiding operator rather than having to use (distributed) set intersection:

$$\begin{aligned} &\forall\, tr, tr' : traces(S).tr \approx tr' \Rightarrow \\ &\qquad ((S/tr) \upharpoonright L =_{failures} (S/tr') \upharpoonright L) \end{aligned} \tag{3}$$

where $S \upharpoonright L$ is the projection of the set of failures of S to the set L: each failure (tr, A) is projected to $(tr \upharpoonright L, A \cap L)$.

In fact we can think of the earlier formulation as a kind of partial unwinding of this. Thus we can perform an inductive proof that Equation 2 implies Equation 3. It is also immediate that Equation 3 implies Equation 2, and hence that the two equations give the same characterisation.

In order to avoid the need to explicitly quantify over traces we might try expressing a characterisation directly as a CSP equivalence:

$$S \setminus H =_{failures} (S \parallel STOP_H) \setminus H \tag{4}$$

At first glance one might think that this is equivalent to Equation 3. Putting *STOP* in parallel with S over the alphabet H has the effect of preventing all traces with H events. We thus appear to be asserting that the process with all the H events enabled is equivalent to that with H events prevented. In fact it differs in some subtle but significant senses. Firstly this is really the purge formulation and so, in particular, it implies that the purge of any trace is itself a trace. Furthermore, the standard CSP semantics of such an equation asserts equality over stable states, that is states that cannot perform any internal (i.e. high level) events. For any state in which internal events can occur the refusal set might alter as the result the occurrence of such these transitions. It is therefore rather hard to make sense of the equality of refusal sets over unstable states, hence the decision to deal just with stable states in the standard CSP semantics. The quantification of Equation 3 however does force equality for all traces, not just traces leading to stable states (i.e. traces that can not be immediately extended by tau events). Equation 3 is therefore strictly stronger that Equation 4.

For example, the process

$$S = h \rightarrow STOP \Box (l \rightarrow STOP \sqcap STOP)$$

meets Equation 4. On the other hand it fails Equation 3, since its failures after $\langle\rangle$ are not the same as its failures after $\langle h \rangle$, despite the low level views of both these traces being the same.

It turns out that we can cast Equation 3 in a form resembling Equation 4 and equivalent to it by using a different approach to concealing the High events. In Equation 3 we have concealed them by the rather obvious device of simply hiding them. An alternative is not to hide them but to camouflage them:

$$S \;|||\; RUN_H \quad =_{failures} \quad (S \parallel STOP_H) \;|||\; RUN_H \tag{5}$$

Here we interleave the two systems with RUN_H on the high level events. Now whenever Low sees an H event he cannot tell if it was performed by S or by RUN_H. By avoiding the use of hiding we have side-stepped the restriction to stable states. This form of abstraction was introduced by Roscoe et al [12], in which Equation 5 is shown to be equivalent to Equation 3.

The use of hiding to abstract certain events in this way provides us with another way of modelling signal events. Roscoe et al refers to this form of abstraction as 'eager' to reflect the idea that events abstracted in this way are thought of as occurring at the earliest opportunity. Correspondingly the interleaving abstraction is referred to as 'lazy'. These forms of abstraction have also been characterised in a testing framework [16] which has the added advantage of allowing input/output distinctions to be drawn over the low-level events as well as the high-level.

These abstractions and variants of them are discussed in detail in chapter 12 of [11].

3.3. Unwinding

It is usual when presenting a notion of non-interference to also present a so-called unwinding result. The idea is to present some constraints on the transitions of the system that together are equivalent to, or at least imply, the original property. Proving that a system obeys such constraints is more tractable than showing that it satisfies the original property.

In accordance with this tradition [14] presents such unwinding rules.

- Rule 1:

$$\forall Y_i, Y_j : States(S).Y_i \approx Y_j \Rightarrow Refusals(Y_i) \setminus H = Refusals(Y_j) \setminus H$$

- Rule 2:

$$\forall Y_i, Y_j : States(S).Y_i \approx Y_j \wedge \forall e : Initials(Y_i), e* : Initials(Y_j). \; e \upharpoonright L = e* \upharpoonright L \Rightarrow Y_i/\langle e \rangle \approx Y_j/\langle e* \rangle$$

We have introduced an equivalence relation over states of the system. The first rule asserts that for two equivalent states Lows view of the possibilities for the next step of the system is identical.

The second rule has the effect of ensuring that the equivalence is exactly that induced by purging High events. That is, if we let Y_i denote a state reached after trace tr_i, then rule 2 implies: $tr_i \upharpoonright L = tr_j \upharpoonright L \Rightarrow Y_i \approx Y_j$.

Proving that these imply the original non-interference is a fairly straightforward induction style proof. Showing that these are also necessary is a bit more delicate and this is proved in a rather cumbersome fashion in an appendix of [14].

A far more elegant and instructive proof of completeness can be obtained by noticing that these rules bear a remarkable resemblance to a statement of bi-simulation equivalence as used in process algebras.

In fact bi-simulation is subtly stronger than failures equivalence as it insists on the bi-similarity of individual states and draws distinctions between processes on the basis of where non-determinism is resolved. A simple example (pictured in Figure 1) illustrates this:

$$\begin{aligned} P &= (a \rightarrow b \rightarrow STOP) \sqcap (a \rightarrow c \rightarrow STOP) \\ Q &= a \rightarrow (b \rightarrow STOP \sqcap c \rightarrow STOP) \end{aligned}$$

The non-deterministic choice is made earlier in P than in Q and as a result it is easy to show that no bisimulation relation can be found for them. However an environment that can only observe the a, b and c events cannot distinguish between them. They are failures equivalent and testing equivalent.

Gardiner, [3], introduces the notion of a power bisimulation specifically to address this point and constructs a bisimulation-like equivalence that is exactly as discriminating as failures equivalence. [3] gives an extremely elegant formulation and proof in terms of predicate transformers.

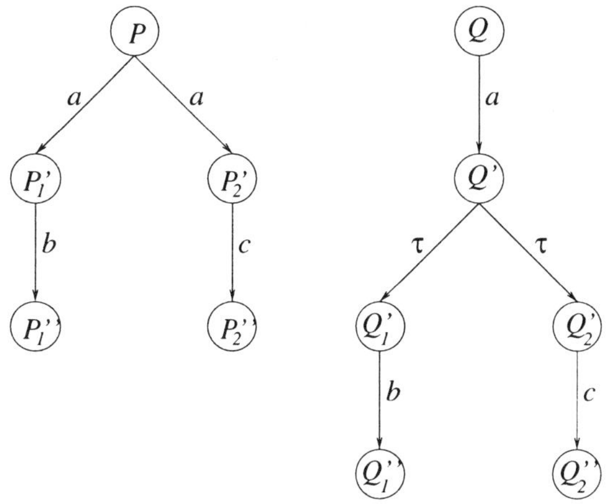

Figure 1. Processes P and Q

We notice that the unwinding rules already use the notion of an equivalence relation on the power set of states suggesting that we may be able to find a power bisimulation relation equivalent to them.

We proceed as follows: firstly we introduce what we call a 'loose-bisimulation'. This is in fact entirely analogous to weak-bisimulation except that here we require matching on τ events and treat the High events as abstracted (hidden) events. Thus we require the two processes to stay in step on the Low and τ events but allow arbitrary interleaving with high events.

We define the relation $\sim_S$ on states of S induced by purging the H events (but leaving L and τ's).

$$\sim_S \;=\; \{(S/tr, S/tr') \mid \; tr, tr' : traces(S) \wedge tr \upharpoonright L_\tau = tr' \upharpoonright L_\tau\}$$

where $L_\tau = L \cup \{\tau\}$

Given a state S and an event a define $[S]_a$ as:

$$[S]_a \;=\; \{S' : States(S) \mid \exists \hat{a} \in H^*.a.H^*.S \stackrel{\hat{a}}{\Longrightarrow} S'\}$$

where $H^*.aH^*$ is the set of sequences of elements of H interleaved with a.

We now assert that S is loosely-bisimilar with respect to $\sim_S$ if and only if for all a

$$S_1 \sim S_2 \;\Rightarrow\; [S_1]_a \sim [S_2]_a$$

We now define a power bisimulation relation $\approx_S$ induced by purging H's and τ's:

$$\approx_S \;=\; \{(\{S' \mid S \stackrel{tr}{\Longrightarrow} S'\}, \{S' \mid S \stackrel{tr'}{\Longrightarrow} S'\})$$

$$| \quad tr, tr' : traces(S) \wedge$$
$$tr \upharpoonright L = tr' \upharpoonright L\}$$

and for S and a define $\langle[S]\rangle_a$ by:

$$\langle[S]\rangle_a = \{S' : States(S) \mid \exists \tilde{a} \in H_\tau^*.a.H_\tau^*.S \overset{\tilde{a}}{\Longrightarrow} S'\}$$

We can then easily prove the following:

Lemma 3.1 If S satisfies the loose-bisimulation then it satisfies a power-bisimulation with respect to $\approx_S$:

$$S_1 \approx_S S_2 \Rightarrow \langle[S_1]\rangle_a \approx \langle[S_2]\rangle_a$$

□

We can further prove the following:

Lemma 3.2 If $S_1 \approx_S S_2$ then for all $s_1 : S_1$ there exists $s_2 : S_2$ such that $s_1 \sim_S s_2$, and vice versa.

□

Lemma 3.3

$$s_1 \sim_S s_2 \Rightarrow AcceptSet_L(s_1) = AcceptSet_L(s_2)$$

□

These two lemmas prove the following:

Lemma 3.4

$$S_1 \approx S_2 \Rightarrow AcceptSet_L(S_1) = AcceptSet_L(S_2)$$

□

It is worth examining this result more carefully. We see that there are two sources of potential non-determinism in Low's view: High's activity and the occurrence of τ events. We are in effect asserting that for a non-interfering system all of the non-determinism that Low sees is attributable to the internal τ activity. Furthermore we see that a corollary of the loose-bisimulation property is that High is non-interfering with the τ's, i.e. High cannot influence the occurrence of τ events. We will see the significance of this observation when we discuss the interaction of flavours of non-determinism in section 3.5.

To return to our simple example, we see that the power-bisimulation relation:

$$\{ \; \{P\} \approx \{Q\}, \\ \{P_1', P_2'\} \approx \{Q', Q_1', Q_2'\}, \\ \{P_1'', P_2''\} \approx \{Q_1'', Q_2''\}\}$$

establishes the power-bisimilarity of the P and Q above.

[3] shows how to construct a power bi-simulation that is is equivalent to failures equivalence. It now suffices to show that the power-bisimulation that we have defined above corresponds to that of the Gardiner approach. Proof of this is beyond the scope of this paper but is presented in a technical report in preparation. The completeness of the unwinding rules, i.e. that they are necessary as well as sufficient thus follows immediately.

The relevance of the notions of bisimulation to defining confidentiality was proposed by Foccardi and Gorrieri in, for example, [2], apparently without reference to analogies with unwinding. The use of the notion of power-bisimulation in security is, to our knowledge, new.

3.4. Composability

[14] contains proofs of the composability of this formulation of non-interference with respect to various CSP operators. In fact we see that such composability follows trivially from the composability of failures equivalence (or alternatively from the composability of power bi-simulation) with respect to the CSP operators.

Note however that composability depends on the property and the operators in question. The property of determinacy, for example, defined by Milner in [9] turns out not to be composable with respect to all the CCS operators, which prompts him to introduce the closely associated concept of confluence, which is. Again there appear to be analogies here with some of the quests for composability in the security community and indeed confluence appears to bear some resemblance to the notion of forward correctability. The details of the correspondence are complex however and will not be addressed here.

3.5. Non-deducibility

Sutherland's theory of non-deducibility, [18] characterises the lack of information flow in terms of an inability to deduce anything about high level behaviour from a low level view. A system M is said to exhibit this property if every low level view tr of an system execution is compatible with every high level view of inputs tr' (in the sense that there is some execution tr'' which presents both views). This captures the idea that no high-level behaviour can be ruled out by any low-level observation. It is described in process- algebraic terms as follows:

$$\forall tr \in traces(M \upharpoonright L), tr' \in traces(M \upharpoonright HI). \\ \exists tr'' \in traces(M). \\ (tr'' \upharpoonright L = tr \wedge tr'' \upharpoonright HI = tr') \tag{6}$$

This may also be characterised in a testing framework. A low level user may be considered as testing the system, attempting to elicit information concerning the high level inputs. Thus for non-deducibility to be present, such a low level user should not be able to rule out any possibility for $tr \upharpoonright HI$—the low level behaviour should be compatible with any high level user inputs.

Suppose that the test T has an alphabet L, and some distinguished *SUCCESS* states. A process may pass a test if there is some execution of the process together with the test which may reach a success state. A process P with its own success states may pass a test T through a system M if there is some execution of $P \parallel M \parallel T$ in which both P and T may reach a success state.

Then a system M exhibits non-deducibility if no test T through M may differentiate any two high level users $U1$ and $U2$ (drawn from the space of all possible high level users) which have alphabet HI, whose traces are only those of M restricted to HI, and which have some success states.

The restriction to alphabet HI corresponds to the requirement that any low level information is required to be compatible only with any sequence of high level inputs. This means essentially that no information at the low level is available about the high level input to the system—it is all masked by the system S. In other words, for any test T and any two high level users $U1$ and $U2$, $U1 \,|[\, HI \,]|\, S$ may pass T if and only if $U2 \,|[\, H1 \,]|\, S$ may pass T.

In the state machine formulations of the original definitions, all processes must always be able to accept any input values and provide outputs. This characterises an important subclass of CSP processes. If the space of high level users is restricted to such processes, then the testing formulation is equivalent to Sutherland's. However, CSP allows the consideration of more general classes of process if appropriate.

For example, the system

$$S \quad = \quad in_h?x \rightarrow (out_l!0 \rightarrow S \sqcap out_l!1 \rightarrow S) \qquad (7)$$

apparently passes no information from high to low. However, the high level process *STOP* can be distinguished from $in_h!1 \rightarrow STOP$ because a low level test will receive an output when the second is tested, but not when the first is tested. It depends whether *STOP* is considered a valid description of a high level user or not as to whether S is considered to permit information flow. The characterisation is thus dependent on the space of processes over which the high level users U can range—the kind of activity which must be indistinguishable.

It is observed in [19] that Sutherland's definition has some unwanted consequences. A system meeting this property still permits a high level user to communicate information to a low level user, essentially because high level outputs (which are ignored in the definition) may have a bearing on later high level inputs. It is instructive to recast their example in CSP terms. The system $M(k_1, k_2)$ is parametrised by two one-bit keys k_1 and k_2. It takes a high level input h_i, and offers a high level output h_o and a low level output l. On a high level input x of 0 or 1, it outputs that value xor'ed with the key k_1. Both keys are then randomly reset. On any other high level input (the original example uses a special value q) the second key k_2 is output to the low level and randomly reset, and the first key k_1 is output to the high level.

$$\begin{array}{l} M(k_1, k_2) = \\ \qquad h_i?x \rightarrow \ \textbf{if}\ x \in \{0,1\} \\ \qquad\qquad\qquad \textbf{then}\ \ h_o!0 \rightarrow l!(x \oplus k_1) \rightarrow \\ \qquad\qquad\qquad\qquad\qquad \prod_{k_1, k_2 \in \{0,1\}} M(k_1, k_2) \\ \qquad\qquad\qquad \textbf{else}\ h_o!k_1 \rightarrow l!k_2 \rightarrow \prod_{k_2 \in \{0,1\}} M(k_1, k_2) \end{array}$$

It is easily checked that this system allows any high level inputs with any low level view, and hence M exhibits non-deducibility.

However, a high level user can use this system to communicate to the low level, by employing a particular strategy. If the high level wishes to transmit a particular bit b, then he first learns the value of k_1 by inputting q, and then inputs $k_1 \oplus b$, which will result in the transmission of b to the low level. Based on this, a transmitter wishing to communicate a sequence $\langle b \rangle \frown u'$ of bits behaves as follows:

$$\begin{array}{l} T(\langle b \rangle \frown u') = \\ \qquad h_i!q \rightarrow h_o?k \rightarrow h_i!(k \oplus b) \rightarrow h_o?k' \rightarrow T(u') \end{array}$$

The CSP formulation in terms of HI draws attention to the weak point of Sutherland's definition. The only high level activity it is concerned with is high level input. However, high level users also interact with the system by receiving output, and in this case the output received can influence later input. Thus the definition does not capture all the ways in which the high level user can interact with the system.

The example of [19] can be replaced with a rather more intuitive and immediate example that we believe shows up the essence of the problem.

Consider a system in which high level data is encrypted and the encrypted form transmitted over a low channel. Thus far we have the classic scenario that arises in many security architectures and yet has proved so difficult to capture in a non-interference style framework. Assuming that the encryption scheme is itself 'secure' (in a cryptanalytic sense) then we would tend to accept that such a system is secure.

Suppose now that the high user can in fact observe or predict the key stream before he submits his plain-text for encryption. We can easily imagine this occurring in a number of ways and in fact Wittbold et al's example achieves essentially this. Then High can modify the plain-text in such a way as to communicate it to Low, in particular he can simply xor the predicted bits into the plain-text before submitting it to the encryption resulting in raw plain-text being broadcast over the low channel.

This is not too surprising so far but let us examine it more closely as it is a pointer to the root of the problem. The example involves two kinds of non-determinism: external (under the control of the users or processes, in particular High) and probabilistic, arising, in this case, from the cipher stream. In the above example we have allowed these to interact: we have allowed High to resolve his non-determinism basing his decisions on observations of how the probabilistic non-determinism is being resolved. If we were to force High to resolve all his non-determinism at the outset, before any of the cipher stream has been generated, or in the absence of any knowledge of this source of non-determinism, then he could not exploit this channel.

We see that this discussion touches on the points made earlier regarding the loose-bisimulation. The loose- bisimulation property implied that High should not be able to interfere with the τ events. If we can think of the τ events as representing the non-determinism associated with the cipher stream then we see that this is asserting that High cannot interfere with the cipher stream. The situation is a little delicate as the bisimulation does not prevent flow from the τ's to High which potentially could allow the scenario described above. In fact High xor'ing the cipher stream to the data stream is tantamount to interfering with the stream but it is not immediately clear that this has been formally captured. This will be a topic for further investigation. An obvious solution is to also require that the *tau*'s do not interfere with High but this seems a bit heavy handed.

Constructing semantic models for a process algebra to accurately capture the distinction between the various forms of non-determinism has proved difficult. A number of probabilistic process algebras have been proposed, for example Morgan [7] and Lowe [6]. These assume that non-determinism is resolved at the outset and so do not allow for the possibility of delaying choices and making decisions on the basis of observations of how non-deterministic choices are resolved 'at run time'. We thus see why it has proved so difficult to model this scenario in a non-interference style.

Currently we do not appear to have theories rich enough to fully capture the distinction between the various flavours of non-determinism. Indeed it is not clear that it would be particularly effective to try to develop and apply such extended theories as the greater complexity would probably render them unusable. For the crypto example at least it would seem more effective to use arguments outside the model to establish that the crypto is wholly independent of the rest of the system. In fact a well designed crypto device appropriately incorporated in a secure architecture will have precisely these characteristics: the cipher stream will be unobservable and unpredictable by High (or indeed any other user or process). High may of course be able to deduce the cipher stream after the event if he can observe the cipher-text stream but, crucially, this is too late to exploit. Furthermore an ideal encryption algorithm will have the property that observing an arbitrary length of the stream should not enable further bits to be predicted, i.e. the stream is effectively random. We of course have to take care that any implementations maintain these assumptions. Conventional refinement techniques will not preserve the non-determinism so from a refinement point of view this non-determinism has to be handled differently.

Such a situation is not entirely satisfactory but appears quite workable, at least for a large class of systems. Of course it might be that we encounter systems for which the flavours of non-determinism cannot be so conveniently isolated. This could probably by regarded as a symptom of a poorly designed system.

3.6. Non-deducibility on strategies

To avoid the problem with Non-deducibility outlined in the previous section, the notion of Non-deducibility on strategies was introduced [19]. In this formulation, any low view needs to be compatible with any high transmitter strategy, where a strategy describes what a high level user will input depending on previous inputs and outputs. Any low level trace view should thus be compatible with any high level view that is possible for the system.

Non-deducibility on strategies for a system S requires that $(U \parallel S) \setminus H$ should give the same set of (low level) traces whatever deterministic high level user U is used. (Note that the example $M(k_1, k_2)$ above does not have this property.)

Non-deducibility on strategies can be cast in testing terms very similar to the characterisation for non-deducibility above: a system S exhibits non-deducibility on strategies if no test T through S may distinguish between any two high level users who have alphabet H. It is essentially a simple variation on Equation 6.

$$\begin{aligned} &\forall\, tr \in traces(M \upharpoonright L), tr' \in traces(M \upharpoonright H). \\ &\quad \exists\, tr'' \in traces(M). \\ &\qquad (tr'' \upharpoonright L = tr \wedge tr'' \upharpoonright H = tr') \end{aligned} \tag{8}$$

This definition incorporates all possible high level interactions between the system and the high level users, because they can interact on the entire high level interface H and not simply on *HI* as in Equation 6. This means essentially that no information at the low level is available about any high level activity of the system at all. In other words, for any test T and any two high level users $U1$ and $U2$ meeting the same restrictions as previously, $U1 \,|[\, H \,]|\, S$ may pass T if and only if $U2 \,|[\, H \,]|\, S$ may pass T.

When high level users are restricted to the subclass of non-deterministic state machines, then this definition coincides with non-deducibility of strategies. In that case, the system S of equation 7 meets the definition. However, if U can range over all possible CSP processes, then S does not meet the definition: a low level user could distinguish between $STOP$ and $in_h!0 \rightarrow STOP$.

It is immediate that in the testing formulation Equation 8 implies Equation 6: if a test distinguishes the inputs of two high level users, then the same test will distinguish their high level activity.

3.7. A deterministic approach to Non-interference

An alternative definition of non-interference in the process algebra context was proposed by Roscoe, Woodcock and Wulf [12]. In their approach, a system S does not allow information flow from high to low if the system

$$Abstract_H(CHAOS_H \parallel S) \tag{9}$$

is deterministic. $Abstract_H$ denotes an appropriate abstraction of the H events to obtain a Low view of the system. Typically it will involve a mix of lazy and eager abstraction depending on whether the high events are considered delayable on not. This system presents events only at the low level, and its determinism means that there is only one possibility for each event at any stage (offer, or refusal), however the non-determinism in the system is resolved. Since any high level user will be a refinement of $CHAOS_H$, and since all CSP operators preserve the refinement relation, this means that any particular high level user U_H in parallel with the system will have to be a refinement of $CHAOS_H$ is parallel with the system. Since the result (when H is hidden) is already deterministic, this means that it cannot be further refined so it must remain unchanged. This is true for any high level user U_H, so all possible high level users must give the same result at the low level. Hence, no low level test can distinguish between them. It follows that this formulation implies non-deducibility on strategies. In a sense, $CHAOS_H$ embodies all possible strategies, and the requirement that the resulting system is deterministic states that all such strategies must always give the same result.

Advantages of this approach are that it side-steps much of the debate about what is the appropriate notion of process equivalence, virtually all the process algebras agree on what processes are deterministic. It is compositional, it is preserved by conventional refinement and it is automatically checkable (using for example using the built in determinism checking facility of FDR).

It is clear that where is can be applied this is an extremely effective characterisation of absence of information flow. The drawback is that there appears to be a large class of systems for which this property is too strong: for which some degree of low-level non-determinism is unavoidable. Perhaps such systems are best handled by isolating such essential non-determinism and showing that the property is preserved by refinement of the rest of the system.

An example will be instructive:

$$\begin{aligned} S &= in_h?x \rightarrow ((out_l!0 \rightarrow S) \sqcap (out_l!1 \rightarrow S)) \\ &\quad \sqcap (out_l!0 \rightarrow S) \sqcap (out_l!1 \rightarrow S) \end{aligned}$$

As it stands, this system does not allow information to flow from the high to the low level. This will remain the case if the non-determinism in the system is essential, and cannot be removed or subverted in some way, (perhaps by a poor implementation of random choice). However, different runs with the same high level user (say $in_h!1 \rightarrow STOP$) can result in a number of different possible low level behaviours. Thus S system does not meet definition 9, since it is non-deterministic at the low level.

However, if the system S can be refined when it is implemented, then it is not clear that the result will retain the nondeducibility on strategies. In particular, $S' = in_h?x \rightarrow out_l!x \rightarrow S'$ is a refinement of S.

If we are dealing with such a situation, where the non-determinism in the system is not guaranteed to all be retained, or where there is some doubt over its eventual form when the system is implemented, then a definition of non-interference which allows some measure of refinement will be useful. In this case definition 9 is useful, since it is preserved by refinement: any refinement of S will have to result in a refinement of $Abstract_H(CHAOS_H \parallel S)$, which must therefore be deterministic.

On the other hand, if the random choices in S can be guaranteed to be retained, we might say that the non-determinism in the system is essential. In this case refinement of S is not a concern and the CSP formulation of non-deducibility on strategies is sufficient to establish a lack of information flow.

It may be that we can establish a link between the determinism approach and the power-bisimulation approach presented in section 3.3. If we think of all the non-determinism observed by Low as resulting from different τ activities then we could assert that to be non-interfering an abstraction of the system that obscures the High events but retains the τ's should be deterministic. This would have many of the advantages of the deterministic approach whilst allowing some non-determinism to manifest itself in Low's view, allowing for example the encrypted channel examples.

The difficulty is that τ's are not really part of the CSP framework and that further non-determinism could arise from ambiguous τ transitions: two distinct transitions from a given state that are both labelled by a τ. Both of these problems can addressed by not labelling them as τ events but simply regarding them as another set of events hidden from Low and disjoint from High.

4. Generalisations of Non-interference

4.1. Motivation

The idea of non-interference is clearly a central one in information security. It is however often argued that in practice it is too strong, that no real policy ever calls for total absence of information flow over any channel and that in any case it is not achievable. For example even the so-called one-way regulators in fact allow for a very low bandwidth feedback from high to low to regulate the upward flow and prevent buffer overflows etc.

Even for the comparatively straightforward MLS style policies simple non-interference runs into problems, for example the encryption problem discussed earlier and the need to incorporate downgrades.

As information processing systems steadily grow more sophisticated and distributed the old paper world analogies look increasingly dated. The demand for security in the commercial sector as well as trends in the military sector are prompting the need for more flexible policies, with a finer granularity of objects and more subtle controls of flows. New paradigms like object orientation, hypertext, virtual machines, mobile code and agents etc allow a far greater granularity of objects to be considered as the elements of a security policy. More sophisticated styles of policy often call for history or location based access decisions and these again cannot be reduced to predicates on the classification labels of individual events or interfaces.

All of these suggests the need to investigate ways in which we might generalise non-interference to allow for partial, conditional flows etc.

4.2. Formalisation

We use as our starting point the formulation given in Section 3. The most liberal generalisation of this appears to be:

$$\forall\, tr, tr' : traces(S).tr \approx tr' \Rightarrow Abs_H((S \parallel Constrain)/tr) \equiv Abs_H((S \parallel Constrain/tr') \qquad (10)$$

where Abs_H denotes an appropriate form of abstraction to model the low-level view. We have a number of abstraction operators available to us, for example the various flavours of lazy and eager hiding. Another abstraction that has been used in formalising notions of anonymity but hitherto not confidentiality is 'projection', renaming a set of events to a single event. We will see later how this operator is useful in addressing the encryption problem.

$\approx$ denotes an equivalence relation between behaviours. Hitherto this has typically been defined in terms of some kind of purge function on traces but there seems to be no reason to restrict ourselves to such equivalences.

$\equiv$ denotes an appropriate process equivalence. Which is appropriate depends on the system and policy in question but failures or testing equivalence would seem most likely. In particular using a testing equivalence framework makes it possible to tailor the class of tests to the system and policy in question.

'*Constrain*' defines a set of high-level behaviours for which we wish to restrict the flow of information. The influence of behaviours of S that fall outside this envelope on the low-level will be unconstrained by Equation 10. We are regarding them as innocuous and we do not care how they interfere with Low. Presumably a policy might be formulated as the complement of this: stating what behaviours must not interfere, in which case Constrain might not itself be a process, i.e. might not satisfy the closure axioms for a process. How useful a degree of freedom this represents is unclear without trying it out against a sample of policies but we have included it for completeness.

A policy might be encoded as the conjunction of a set of equations of the form of Equation 10.

We can see how various forms of partial or constrained non- interference could be captured in this way. Such a formulation allows Low to determine High's behaviour up to the $\approx$ equivalence. That is, Low can determine which equivalence class High's behaviour belongs to but not where it lies within that class. We can thus define partial information flows and indeed we can arrange to have 'non-transitive partial flows': for which information flows from A to B and from B to C yet none flows from A to C.

Consider a data space that can be covered by the coordinates (x, y). Our $A \rightarrow B$ projection loses the y information so projects to (x, y'), for some arbitrary y'. The $B \rightarrow C$ projection loses the x information so we get $(x, y) \rightarrow (x', y)$. Putting these two projections together one after the other then gives a projection $A \rightarrow C : (x, y) \rightarrow (x', y')$, i.e. loss of all information about the original point in the A space.

This example is a bit simplistic as one could easily capture it in a simple labelling formulation. It does serve to illustrate the idea and one can easily construct something more elaborate. A more realistic instance would be a policy that allows for automatic downgrading of certain statistical information from a data base.

Another example in which a more general notion of equivalence seems appropriate is where we consider a high level process editing a file. In general many edit sequences could result in the same final text (we are assuming here that the editor is such that all the details of changes are forgotten and only the final resulting text retained, i.e. there is no mark-up facility). We thus want to regard all edit sequences resulting in the same final text as equivalent. Here again the idea of confluence crops up: that different sequences of actions give rise to equivalent states, im particular that certain pairs of actions may be commutative. Thus we might define an equivalence on traces w.r.t. certain permutation groups on actions.

Turning now to the problem of modelling high-level data being encrypted and send out over a low-level channel. Suppose that we take $\approx$ to be defined by:

$$tr \approx tr' \Leftrightarrow \#(tr \upharpoonright H) = \#(tr' \upharpoonright H)$$

and for our abstraction on the encrypted channel we rename the 0's and 1's of the enciphered stream to * say. Then we see that L can figure out the length but not the content of the H string. This would appear to accurately model the encrypted channel scenario. We have of course to carefully justify the projection on the cipher channel, presumably using cryptanalytic arguments.

There remains an issue of how to capture the effect of breaches of the crypto system in such a framework, particularly the retrospective effect (previously concealed information is revealed). This remains an open issue, though it does appear to bear a curious resemblance to the downgrading problem.

Notice also that the notion of confidentiality introduced in this example appears to be analogous to some of the notions of anonymity introduced in, for example, [17]. Here of course we are thinking of anonymity over the message space rather than an agent space.

4.3. Non-transitive non-interference

Another class of application that is amenable to this approach is that of so-called non-transitive non- interference and channel control policies addressed by Rushby in [13] . A couple of examples are presented for motivation: downgrading and a crypto device. The essence of the problem appears to be that though we want to allow flow from H to L it must be regulated, or at the very least audited, by an intermediary. Thus if a high-level data item is to be downgraded and issued to Low this can only happen if accompanied by appropriate actions by a Downgrader process. Similarly high-level data should only be passed to a low-level channel via the crypto device.

Rushby captures this by introducing a more elaborate purge function that, rather than acting in a purely pointwise fashion on the traces, takes account of the affect of downgrade events on the security labels of high events. Clearly we can capture such a policy in our framework with a suitable choice of equivalence, in particular that induced by Rushby's 'ipurge' will do. However we could envisage capturing different forms of intransitive policies to those considered by Rushby by exploiting the full generality of the $\approx$.

A later paper by Pinsky [10] presents an algorithm to construct, where it exists, a minimal equivalence and associated unwinding rule for a downgrading policy. The details are quite complex but it does appear that the algorithm presented by Pinsky can be thought of as an algorithm to construct the appropriate bisimulation relation. Indeed it seems probable that many of the unwinding results presented in the security literature can be interpreted in this way. A number of algorithms for establishing bisimulation relations between putatively equivalent processes are known in the process algebra community and it is probable that they could be usefully applied in the security context.

Note that for a policy encoded in Equation 10 the equivalence relation used can be used to induce a (power) bisimulation relation so establishing an unwinding result. Similarly the composability of such a property follows directly from the composibility of the process equivalence.

4.4. Encapsulation

The problem that Rushby addresses in [13] appears to boil down to one of encapsulation: We need to be sure that flows can only occur over certain known channels and that flows that do occur obey certain constraints.

Considering the first aspect: where the process P has no internal sources of non-determinism we can assert that if it looks deterministic over some interface I then I constitutes the entire interface. Where there are internal sources of non-determinism, a process Z say, the problem is more delicate: we presumably need some way of checking that all non-determinism observed over I can be ascribed to Z. Naively one could imagine freezing the non-determinism of Z, i.e. replacing it by some deterministic implementation. This is not adequate in general however; if there are other sources of non-determinism apart from Z them a particular freezing of Z might eliminate block them whilst other freezings might enable them. This suggests the need to examine all possible freezings but it is not clear that this would really be practical apart from in certain special cases, particularly if we are thinking of applying model-checking techniques. This is a topic of ongoing research.

The second aspect concerns that control of information flows over the channels that have been identified and this appears best done using the framework of equation 10.

5. Conclusions/Discussion

The central thesis of this paper is that the problem of formalising the notion of confidentiality boils down to that of formalising the equivalence of processes. The latter is a central and difficult question at the heart of computer science to which there is no unique answer. Which notion of equivalence is appropriate depends on the context and application. Consequently we should not be surprised that the information security community has failed to come up with a consensus on which constitutes confidentiality. Indeed, in this paper we have shown a close correspondence between various proposals for definitions of confidentiality in the security literature and forms of process equivalence in the process algebra literature. Where the system's security can be characterised as the determinism of the low-level view we are in better shape as the definition of determinism is fairly uncontroversial. It is not currently clear how large a class of real systems can be handled in this way.

Viewing security from a process algebraic framework brings with it a number of ready-made results and insights, particularly regarding composition and unwinding. It also helps to pin-point and isolate the source of many of the problems that have been encountered in the security literature, for example regarding the encryption problem, the lack of compositionality of certain formulations etc.

The usefulness of the concept of testing equivalence has also emerged for this viewpoint. This concept seems to have been curiously neglected in the context of defining non-interference though it has recently been used in the analysis of security protocols, see for example Abadi et al, [1]. The philosophy is strikingly similar: in [1] tests can be understood as encapsulating all possible attacks, and equivalence under testing establishes that no such attack can succeed in distinguishing a real system from an ideal one. In our context, tests might be understood as encapsulating all possible ways in which information may flow from high to low, either as a result of High attempting to communicate information, or from the point of view of Low attempting to elicit it, or indeed involving some collusion. Equivalence under testing establishes that no such way can succeed.

It seems very natural to think of two systems as being equivalent if no test can distinguish them. Of course the problem then becomes one of what class of tests is appropriate. In particular the generalised notion of testing introduced in [16] may prove useful in drawing a distinction between delayable and undelayable events at the low-level. Furthermore we have shown the significance of the notion of power-bisimulation. It establishes a correspondence between the testing, bisimulation and denotational styles of defining process equivalence.

We have proposed a generalised form of non-interference and shown that it can encompass a number of systems and policies of interest: with encrypted channels, partial and conditional flows, downgraders etc.

We have only addressed the so-called 'possibilistic' notions of non-interference, i.e. whether High can influence the possibility of Low performing certain observations. In other words we are abstracting away from issues of probability and time, in particular. Clearly these are important and need to be addressed. However it is also clear that even in the comparatively simple context of possibilisitic models there are many subtleties lurking. We hope that this paper has served to identify and shed some more light on these subtleties.

5.1. Acknowledgements

Much of the research reported here was carried out during a collaborative visit at Royal Holloway, and the first author is grateful to the Royal Holloway Department of Computer Science for their hospitality. We would also like to thank Bill Roscoe, Michael Goldsmith, Sylvan Pinsky, Paul Gardiner, Martin Abadi and Nick Moffat as well as the reviewers for useful discussions and comments.

References

[1] M. Abadi and A. Gordon. A calculus for cryptographic protocols: the spi calculus. *Information and Computation*, 1999.

[2] R. Focardi, A. Ghelli, and R. Gorrieri. Using non-interference for the analysis of security protocols. In *DIMACS workshop on Design and Formal Verification of Security protocols*, 1997.

[3] P H B Gardiner. Power simulation and its relation to failures refinement. DERA/FSEL technical report, to appear, 1999.

[4] J. A. Goguen and J. Meseguer. Security policies and security models. In *IEEE Symposium on Security and Privacy*, 1982.

[5] M. Hennessy. *Algebraic Theory of Processes*. MIT press, 1988.

[6] G. Lowe. *Probabilities and Priorities in Timed CSP*. D. Phil thesis, Oxford University, 1993.

[7] A. McIver, C. Morgan, K. Seidel, and J. Sanders. Refinement-oriented probability for CSP. *Formal Aspects of Computing 8(9)*, 1996.

[8] J McLean. A general theory of composition for trace sets closed under selective interleaving functions. In *IEEE Symposium on Research in Security and Privacy*, 1994.

[9] R. Milner. *Communication and Concurrency*. Prentice-Hall, 1989.

[10] S. Pinsky. Absorbing covers and intransitive non-interference. In *IEEE Symposium on Research in Security and Privacy*, 1995.

[11] A. W. Roscoe. *The theory and practice of concurrency*. Prentice-Hall, 1997.

[12] A. W. Roscoe, J. Woodcock, and L. Wulf. Non-interference through determinism. In *ESORICS*, 1994.

[13] John Rushby. Noninterference, transitiivity and channel-control security policies. Technical report, SRI, 1992.

[14] P. Y. A. Ryan. A CSP formulation of non-interference and unwinding. *Presented at CSFW'90 and published in Cipher Winter90/91*, 1990.

[15] S. A. Schneider. *Concurrent and Real time systems: the CSP approach*. John Wiley, 1999. (to appear).

[16] S. A. Schneider. Testing and abstraction. Technical Report TR-99-02, Royal Holloway, University of London, 1999.

[17] S. A. Schneider and A. Sidiropoulos. CSP and anonymity. In *ESORICS*, 1996.

[18] D. Sutherland. A model of information. In *9th National Computer Security Conference*, 1986.

[19] J. T. Wittbold and D. M. Johnson. Information flow in nondeterministic systems. *Proceedings of the 1990 Symposium on Research on Security and Privacy*, 1990.

What is intransitive noninterference?

A.W. Roscoe
Oxford University Computing Laboratory
Wolfson Building, Parks Road
Oxford OX1 3QD, UK

M.H. Goldsmith
Formal Systems (Europe) Ltd
Keble Court, 26 Temple Street
Oxford OX4 1JS, UK *

Abstract

The term "intransitive noninterference" refers to the information flow properties required of systems like downgraders, in which it may be legitimate for information to flow indirectly between two users but not directly. We examine the usual definition of this property in terms of a modified purge function, and show that this is a distinctly weaker property than an alternative we derive from considerations of determinism.

1 Introduction

The term "noninterference" (closely analogous to, and often synonymous with, others such as "noninference" and "independence") refers to a situation in which a system has a number of users, and it is desired that the actions of one of these users have no effect on what another sees. The main motivating application is usually multi-level security (MLS) in which we are presented with a *security policy*: a relation between the users setting out which information flows are permissible (generally from low to high level) and thereby which are not (from high to low). In this domain, we end up trying to specify and prove that high-level users cannot "interfere" with low-level ones. In slightly different circumstances we might be concerned about potential disruption of a high-level user by low-level ones[1], so that the direction of undesirable interference gets reversed. For simplicity, in this paper we will, except when specifically stated otherwise, concentrate on the former, and assume we are attempting to prevent high-level information being revealed to low-level users.

A wide range of theories have been developed to support reasoning about noninterference, with a view to giving precise mathematical characterisations of the security and other properties that arise. Directly or indirectly these always involve studying how the range of low-level behaviours is affected by high-level actions. The semantic arenas in which these have been developed include the following:

- State machines [5] that make (possibly null) inputs and outputs with users on each cycle; the definitions of noninterference usually being based on *purge* functions that project behaviours into low-level actions only, or on the idea of *unwinding* in which each individual high-level action is specified to have no effect on the low-level view.
- Process algebras offer a more free-form model of interaction, often with *handshaken* communications, but noninterference properties are sometimes presented as complex-looking predicates on semantic models with no obvious route to automation.
- Trace theory [12], represents something of a compromise.

The authors have always preferred the process-algebra approach, since the essence of noninterference (or the lack of it) is in the interactions between a system and its users, and process algebras provide highly-developed theories specifically developed to handle the subtleties of interaction and communication. In [16] (and see also [14, 17]), the first author and others proposed a definition of noninterference based on the *determinism* of the low-level view: the actions of higher-level users are turned into nondeterministic choices by means of *abstraction* mechanisms, and if the low-level view is then deterministic we can conclude that it does not depend on anything that the high-level users do. This formulation (which has well-understood links with other process algebra versions, but avoids the difficulty that the refinement of a secure process may not be secure) has been the key to successful automated checking on FDR [3], as it is possible to automate efficient decision procedures for the CSP formulation of determinism. It is also possible, by varying the form of abstraction used on high-level behaviour, to make distinctions between the influences of

*Email: Bill.Roscoe@comlab.ox.ac.uk, michael@fsel.com

[1] These might be the actions of an untrusted user, or even events representing the random occurrence of system faults.

1063-6900/99 $10.00 © 1999 IEEE

high-level inputs and high-level outputs (a criticism that had previously been made of process algebra formulations). The most extensive study of the compositional and other properties of this type of noninterference can be found in [20].

Just about every initial approach to this subject begins by simplifying the problem to one where there are just two users -- one high and one low -- and analysing potential flows from one to the other. This is quite sufficient when the relation between users that defines permitted information flow -- $A \leadsto B$ if information from A can flow to B -- is *transitive* (i.e., $A \leadsto B \wedge B \leadsto C \Rightarrow A \leadsto C$). (We will always assume the relation is reflexive, namely that $A \leadsto A$ for all A.) Fixing A, we can then be confident that no information-flow is allowed from the set of users $\{B \mid B \not\leadsto A\}$ to any of the users in $\{C \mid C \leadsto A\}$ (or else such a C would provide a link between the given B and A in an application of the transitive rule). It follows that in order to check potential information flows to A we can divide up the alphabet of interaction of our system into two compound ''users'', one for each of these two sets.

Since the partition of the interface of a system for security purposes may well not exactly coincide with the division into users, we will usually refer to the members of these partitions as ''domains''. In the case where we are considering a CSP process P with alphabet A, these domains will just be subsets of A which partition it. A security policy $\mathcal{V}$ is then a specification of what these domains are plus the information flow relation $\leadsto$.

It seems intuitively obvious that the relation $\leadsto$ must be transitive: how can it make sense for A to have lower security level than B, and B to have lower level than C, without A having lower level than C? But this argument misses a crucial possibility, that some high-level users are trusted to *downgrade* material or otherwise influence low-level users. Indeed, it has been argued that no large-scale system for handling classified data would make sense without some mechanism for downgrading information after some review process, interval (e.g., the U.K. 30-year rule) or defined event (the execution of some classified mission plan, for example). Largely to handle this important problem, a variety of extended theories proposing definitions of ''intransitive noninterference'' have appeared, though we observe that this term is not really accurate, as it is in fact the *interference* rather than the *noninterference* relation which is not transitive. Perhaps the best way to read the term is as an abbreviation for ''noninterference under an intransitive security policy''.

The objective of this paper is to understand what is meant by intransitive noninterference, and to place it in the context (both theoretical and automation) of our existing determinism-based work.

The rest of this paper is constructed as follows: in the next section we summarise the CSP/determinism formulation of noninterference and put it context. We then survey previous work on intransitive noninterference, and build determinism-based analogues of some as well as a condition inspired directly by the intuition underlying the determinism formulation of noninterference. We show how these conditions can be checked automatically using techniques similar to those developed for earlier ''transitive'' properties.

2 A review of noninterference conditions

Definitions of noninterference based on state machines are usually in terms of either or both of the ideas of *purging* and *unwinding*. Purging involves applying a function to the history of the system up to some point which removes all those parts (typically communications with high-level agents) that should not influence what a given agent A sees. Usually the definition of noninterference can be paraphrased by the statement that the purged history is still a valid history of the system, and leads to a state which looks identical to A. Unwinding, on the other hand, looks at individual steps and asserts that each high-level action leaves the aspects of the system which affect A unchanged. It is frequently claimed that purge-based definitions are more intuitive, and that unwinding-based definitions are more amenable to automated proof. Therefore many theorems have been proved showing that a given notion of unwinding implies a corresponding purge-based definition. These definitions are generally unproblematic in the context of *deterministic* machines (where the machine's behaviour is completely determined by its initial state and inputs to date) but can generate debating points when they are applied to nondeterministic systems. In particular it is then quite likely that, where a purge definition of security is formulated in terms of behaviours from a fixed initial state rather than from all states, it will pass more processes than the corresponding unwinding one thanks to essentially the same example as the $Chaos \sqcap LEAK$ one discussed below for CSP.

As discussed in the introduction, many researchers have chosen to formulate noninterference properties in the world of process algebra. The most frequently used process algebra for this purpose has been CSP (e.g., [9, 19, 7]), perhaps because it offers semantic models that apparently lend themselves well to definitions which mimic the above. For example we can specify conditions (essentially those of [19, 7]) on the set *traces*(P) of a process's finite communication sequences which closely mimic the purge and and unwinding definitions for state machines quoted above (H and L being respectively the sets of high and low level actions):

- $\forall s \in traces(P) \,.\, s \setminus H \in traces(P) \wedge (P/s)^0 \cap L = (P/(s \setminus H))^0 \cap L$

- $\forall s \in traces(P) . \forall h \in H . s \frown \langle h \rangle \in traces(P) \Rightarrow traces(P/s) \cap L^* = traces(P/s \frown \langle h \rangle) \cap L^*$

where L^* is the set of finite sequences formed from L, $s \setminus H$ is the trace s with all members of H deleted, P/s represents the process that behaves like P after it has performed the trace s, and $(P/s)^0$ is the set of events P can perform immediately after completing the trace s. The first of these (purge) says that the set of events that P offers the low-level user are exactly the same as though the high-level user had never communicated anything. The second (unwinding) says that a high-level action never changes how the process looks to the low-level user (in this formulation on the assumption that no further high-level action occurs). These definitions, as well as several alternative formulations, are equivalent.

The study of nondeterminism is inherent in concurrency, as it arises naturally from the ways in which parallel combinations of processes behave. Nondeterminism can be said to arise in a communicating system when, after a given trace, the set of options that the process offers its environment might be different on different occasions. In particular, a potentially nondeterministic system is not adequately described by its set of traces. Therefore all process algebras employ semantic devices to make more subtle distinctions than those offered by traces, and in the case of CSP this is done using *failures* (combinations (s, X) of a trace s and a set of events X that the process can refuse to communicate after s) and *divergences* (traces s on which the process can engage in an infinite unbroken sequence of invisible (τ) actions).

It is straightforward to reformulate the definitions given above into these more sophisticated models, as was done for example in [19]. Doing so, however, creates problems both of a practical and intellectual nature. The practical problem (in fact shared by the trace definitions given above) is that we end up with conditions which do not appear to be easily addressable on the automated model checkers (like CSP's FDR) which have been so successful in recent years in making process algebras usable. The intellectual problem comes from the fact that we encounter the *refinement paradox*: it is possible to have a process P which is secure and a refinement Q of it which is not. Consider for a moment the most nondeterministic divergence-free CSP process $Chaos_{H \cup L}$, where H and L are respectively the high and low alphabets. Most theories would deem this secure, but since every divergence-free process refines it there are evidently many insecure processes that do. While we might not worry about the abstract process $Chaos_{H \cup L}$, we might well worry about the equivalent process

$$Chaos_{H \cup L} \sqcap LEAK$$

where $\sqcap$ is the nondeterministic choice operator and $LEAK$ is any insecure process such as a perfect channel from high to low. Certainly the conventional understanding of what nondeterminism means in process algebras makes it far more natural to consider this insecure than secure. The trouble is that a theory which makes one process secure must also make all equivalent ones secure! Subtly different problems appear if we consider the process $Chaos_L \sqcap LEAK$, which never communicates anything with H at all unless it chooses the leaky alternative. For extensive discussion of these issues, see [14].

It is perhaps true to say that nondeterminism creates difficulties for formulations of noninterference in either a state-machine world or that of process algebra, but that the difficulties are less escapable in the latter mainly because it comes with more fixed notions of what things like refinement and process equivalence mean.

In [16], an alternative CSP formulation of security was proposed, based explicitly on process algebraic ideas rather than being a translation of ones from elsewhere. This was to create, using abstraction operators, a process $\mathcal{A}_H(P)$ that represents what a process P looks like to a user who cannot see the events H, and to define that P is secure if $\mathcal{A}_H(P)$ is deterministic. The intention is that the abstraction procedure should turn all the choices that the high-level user makes into nondeterministic choices internal to $\mathcal{A}_H(P)$. If any nondeterminism is visible at the outside this might well be as a result of these new choices and represent a way of transmitting information from high to low. On the other had, if $\mathcal{A}_H(P)$ is deterministic, then we can be sure that nothing high does will (at least in the terms described by the semantic model being used) affect what low sees.

Two different abstraction operators are used, the choice depending on whether it is assumed that the handshaken model of communication applies to all high actions (specifically, whether these are all delayable by the user) or whether some *signal* or output actions S (such as indicator lights or information being printed on a screen) are not delayable. These are respectively *lazy abstraction* $\mathcal{L}_H(P)$ and *mixed abstraction* $\mathcal{M}_H^S(P)$. The definitions of these operators given in [16, 14], in terms of masking H actions by interleaving, evolved in [15] to the following, equivalent for all the security definitions but superior for other purposes. For a divergence free, finitely nondeterministic and non-terminating (i.e., without the event ✓) process P:

- $\mathcal{L}_H(P) = (P \underset{H}{\|} Chaos_H) \setminus H$

- $\mathcal{M}_H^S(P) = (P \underset{H \setminus S}{\|} Chaos_{H \setminus S}) \setminus H$

The effect of the hiding operator $\setminus H$ is to conceal the high actions that occur from the environment, as we are forming the view of what the process looks like without them. The role of the parallel compositions with *Chaos* is to reflect the fact that the high-level user need not offer any of the actions he or she can delay. If the high action h can be delayed, then the process $h \to l \to STOP$ might look to low either like $STOP$ or at least the availability of l might be much delayed, in either case conveying information to low about high behaviour. The above definitions are actually those from the stable failures model $\mathcal{F}$ for CSP, though the lazy abstraction of allowed P is always divergence-free and mixed abstraction is only allowed when $P \setminus (S \cap H)$ is divergence-free. We give these because they are the most practical for automation purposes; for alternatives and a discussion of the relationship between abstraction and choice of model, see [15].

These two definitions immediately give rise to definitions of noninterference: P is respectively lazily ($\mathcal{L}IND_H(P)$) or mixed independent ($\mathcal{M}IND_H^S(P)$) if the processes $\mathcal{L}_H(P)$ and $\mathcal{M}_H^S(P)$ are deterministic. Lazy independence is precisely equivalent to the purge and unwinding definitions given above when P is deterministic, but much more severe when P is nondeterministic. Our new definitions are closed under refinement, and thereby avoid the refinement paradox. What this means is that they only pass processes which *must* behave securely, and therefore fail some secure processes because there are semantically equivalent processes whose security, like that of $Chaos_{H \cup L} \sqcap LEAK$, is questionable. In other words, our conditions err on the side of caution.

It is certainly the case that in order to assess the security of nondeterministic CSP processes accurately, it is necessary to use semantic models that are significantly finer than those traditionally used for CSP. The best-known attempts at using finer models are those of Focardi and Gorrieri [1, 2] (in a modified CCS) which again have the property of coinciding with all the other definitions on deterministic processes, and use the transition system models of CCS with weak and strong bisimulation equivalences as their methods of determining process equivalence (e.g., BNDC, BSNNI and SBSNNI). Unfortunately even these conditions pass some questionable processes related to the $Chaos_L \sqcap LEAK$ example, as shown by Forster [4] who goes on to offer some stronger conditions. But the latter can again be accused of over-caution, since the standard transition system model does not contain sufficient information to tell us the source of nondeterminism. It seems certain that any model that is capable of giving a proper treatment of this subject must retain many more details about nondeterministic choices (for example the form they take and what mechanism resolves each) than we have been used to recording.

Because of this continuing uncertainty about the right formulation for nondeterministic P, and because the $\mathcal{L}IND_H(P)$ and $\mathcal{M}IND_H^S(P)$ conditions are efficiently decidable on FDR, we decided to address intransitive noninterference properties by looking for analogues of these. Since these conditions are based on a binary partition of the alphabet, a simplification which, as discussed in the introduction, fails in the case of intransitive security policies, we certainly do have some work to do.

From here on we will concentrate on formulations of conditions within the language of CSP, to make direct comparisons easier. We are, however, confident that the basic issues we raise are independent of this choice.

3 A critique of *ipurge*

The main motivating examples for intransitive noninterference are *downgrading*, in which a trusted individual is permitted to move files from high to low classification, and other similar cases in which agent A can only influence B through a highly defined route (an *assured pipeline*) such as an encrypter[2] or a certification service (one which is allowed to determine whether or not B can see the information).

In order to understand how different theories relate to this, let us examine a pair of simple example processes of this type. First, a file system with a downgrader: let's suppose we have a set of users U, and a function *clearance* from this set to a partial order of security levels $(L, \leq)$. Similarly, there is a set F of filenames, and a mapping (which we are going to allow to vary) from F to L. We will assume that users may only *write* to files at their own level, and may *read* from files that are at their own level or below. A realistic operation which will be interesting later on is the *copy* operation which allows a user to copy data between files at his or her own level. In addition, there is a special interface for a trusted downgrader agent (though, in general, one could imagine there being a family of downgrading agents with different privileges) which can inspect files and decide to reclassify them to lower security levels. A simple CSP description of this process is given below:

$$
\begin{aligned}
& FS(cl, fv) = \\
& readreq?(u,f) : \{(u,f) \mid clearance(u) \geq cl(f)\}!fv(u) \\
& \qquad \to FS(cl, fv) \\
& \Box\ write?(u,f) : \{((u,f) \mid clearance(u) = cl(f)\}?v \\
& \qquad \to FS(cl, fv[v/f]) \\
& \Box\ copy?(u,f1,f2) : \{((u,f1,f2) \mid clearance(u) = cl(f1) \\
& \qquad\qquad\qquad\qquad = cl(f2)\} \\
& \qquad \to FS(cl, fv[fv(f1)/f2]) \\
& \Box\ dgread?f!fv(f) \to FS(cl, fv) \\
& \Box\ downgrade?f?c : \{c \mid c < cl(f)\} \to FS(cl[c/f], fv)
\end{aligned}
$$

Our second example is of a process that guards a channel ensuring that only suitable data gets through: it is assumed that it has some internal mechanism by which it decides, but we have implemented this by a nondeterministic choice. Data is input on channel *in*, then either sent on via channel

[2] The motivation here is that a high-level agent who encrypts data effectively downgrades it, even though in most mathematical senses the information content remains the same.

out or returned to its sender if deemed unsuitable

$$GUARD = in?x \to \quad (out!x \to GUARD \\ \sqcap\; return!x \to GUARD)$$

This process really only represents the intermediary; questions of noninterference will arise best once it is connected to a producer, and a consumer, of the information.

The formal definitions (e.g,[13, 21]) of intransitive noninterference in the literature that we have discovered all have their roots in that of [18] (which was itself influenced by [6, 8]) are all based on the state-machine model, and are very similar to each other. They are all based on *purge* functions in which all actions are retained that have a transitive causal link through the trace under consideration to the agent whose view is being considered. In other words, if $A \rightsquigarrow B$ and $B \rightsquigarrow C$ but $A \not\rightsquigarrow C$, then the purge (frequently termed *ipurge*) from C's perspective of the trace $\langle a, b, a\rangle$ would, with the obvious assignments of agents to actions, be $\langle a, b\rangle$ since there is a legitimate route for the first a but not the second to influence C. This, *prima facie*, seems very reasonable, as plainly the a before b may have influenced it (and hence C), and the one after has no legitimate route for influencing C. We believe that the motivation for this definition may well have been the fact that it is reasonable to specify that the resulting purge function does actually generate a trace of any reasonable process meeting the noninterference requirements. For example, consider the following trace of our downgrader process in which there are just two security levels and two users, and a file f with initial data 0 and initial security level *hi*.

$write.(hugh,f).1$
$downgrade.f.lo$
$read.(lois,f).1$

This is a perfectly legitimate trace, and *ipurge*-ing it with respect to level *lo* does not change it. If, however, the purge function had removed the initial event things would have been different, as

$downgrade.f.lo$
$read.(lois,f).1$

is not a trace of the system. In other words, this *ipurge* function retains enough information fully to explain the events seen at low level in terms of the overall behaviours of the system.

But this definition also has its problems. Let us suppose that our implementation of the file system were erroneous, and the event intended to downgrade the level *hi* file f_1 to level *lo* has the effect of downgrading another f_2 as well.

Then our system would have the trace

$write.(hugh,f_2).1$
$downgrade.f_1.lo$
$read.(lois,f_2).1$

which we would regard as generating an unwanted information flow. However, the *ipurge* function would, on the assumption that the only security domains were the security classifications (plus the downgrader) leave this trace alone and the definition of noninterference based on *ipurge* would fail to catch the leak. The problem here is that the interference that this trace causes to Lois is certainly accountable for by things Hugh did before the downgrader acted, but unfortunately not the things that were intended by the downgrader to influence him. In other words, anything the downgrader does is permitting all information which can influence it to pass on to Lois, irrespective of what the downgrader actually intended. Thus we have failed to capture the essence of what downgrading is all about.

This particular problem can be repaired by dividing the security domains into many pieces. It is simplest if we ignore two of the channels of our file system: *copy* and *dgread*. It is then necessary to have two for each file/classification pairing, one $U_{c,f}$ for the users at that level's operations on the file, and one $D_{c,f}$ for downgradings of the file *to* that level. The appropriate security policy is then that no information flow is allowed between any pair of domains associated with different files, or directly from $U_{c1,f}$ to $U_{c2,f}$ unless $c2 \geq c1$. $U_{c1,f} \rightsquigarrow D_{c2,f}$ for all $c1$ and $c2$, and $D_{c1,f} \rightsquigarrow U_{c2,f}$ just when $c2 \geq c1$. The misbehaviour discussed above then violates the *ipurge*-based security condition because it contains information flow between files.

To include the *dgread* actions (which plainly should not, in themselves, influence any ordinary user) we can introduce a further, domain (or perhaps one for each file) which can be influenced by all others (of that file) but influence no others. The *copy* action clearly generates an information flow between files: it is possible to deal with this by allowing these to provide the same sort of intransitive bridge between files as the downgrading actions do between levels. Thus we have apparently been forced to divide up the security levels into subdomains, and to have a part of the security policy that is intransitive quite apart from the pieces directly concerned with the downgrader.

Unfortunately, even the complicated security policy described above is not adequate for ensuring that a system with the given alphabet does not generate undesired information flows. Suppose that some bug in the system means that downgrading a file reverts the value of the file to the most recent back-up (and that a back-up occurs at every write).[3] Then we would have the trace

$write.(hugh,f).secret$
$write.(hugh,f).public$

[3] A more complex, but perhaps more plausible, instance of the same type of behaviour would be in a distributed file system in which files can temporarily have multiple values during an update. One can imagine a file might be downgraded during such a time, perhaps temporarily making an out-of-date and still secret value available at some points in the network.

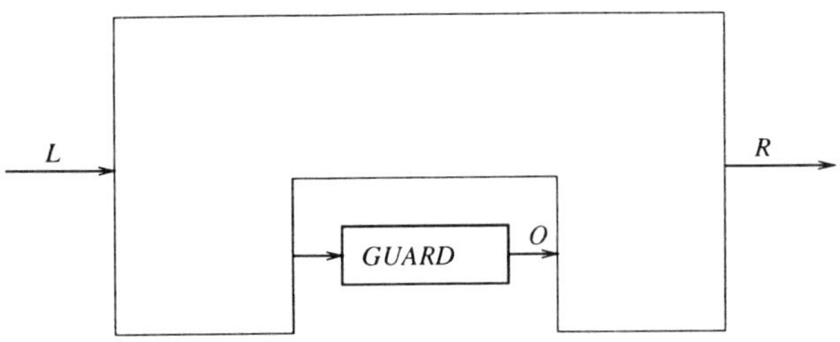

Figure 1. Network with intended assured pipeline

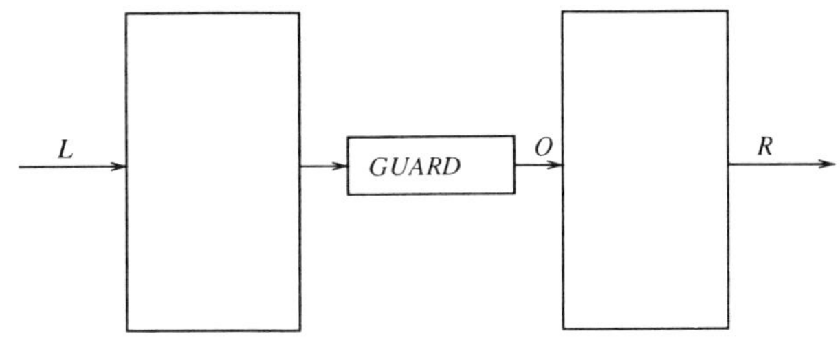

Figure 2. Assured pipeline by construction

downgrade.f.lo
read.(lois,f).secret

which seemingly carries undesired information flow: presumably the downgrader wanted to downgrade the contents of the file at the point of the *downgrade* action. However, because there is no information flow between files, this trace would be left alone by *ipurge* in even the refined policy, and this behaviour would be passed. This illustrates the fact that this definition of security permits *all* information contained in the trace of high-level actions prior to downgrading to be passed to low level, rather than the much more controlled information flow desired. We cannot see how the security domains could reasonably be re-worked to catch this type of flow.

We would argue that the *ipurge* definition makes sense as an explanation of the behaviour of a downgrading system which we already fully understand, in the sense that it represents a natural generalisation of the definition of transitive noninterference that it will satisfy. However, it has deficiencies when it comes to deciding whether the information flows contained in a process purported to be a downgrading system are limited to what we might expect.

The situation is rather similar with the other example. If it is part of a network as shown in Figure 1, we might reasonably require that no information passes from the users on the left to those on the right other than via *GUARD*. The natural thing to do is to study the relationship between the views of the system in the set L and R of events used by these two classes respectively, and the outputs O of *GUARD*. Plainly it is legitimate for L to influence O, and O to influence R, but not for L to influence R directly.

Now if the network were actually built as in Figure 2, we would have nothing to worry about: *GUARD* has the above property by construction. So the information flow analysis is only an issue when the more complex picture of Figure 1 is at hand, and physically, at least, there are other potential channels that we want to ensure either are not there or convey only information in any case allowed by *GUARD*. The problem with the *ipurge* definition here is that again each time *GUARD* does anything it permits all information contained in all preceding L interactions to be passed (via some other route) to R, even if only a small proportion of this is contained in the O history.

In both cases the problem is simply that the *ipurge* definition does not allow for the possibility that the intermediary may want to be selective about which of the information that has influenced it is passed on.

4 A determinism-based formulation

One of the advantages of the determinism-based formulation of information flow is that it gives an entirely different perspective on the problem. Thus, when we were thinking about how to formulate intransitive noninterference in terms of determinism we attempted to create the most natural specification from this different viewpoint though initially we expected that (as had been the case with transitive noninterference) that we would end up with a definition that would coincide for many cases. As we shall see, we end up with a rather different notion.

For simplicity, let us initially consider the case of a process P with three users A, B and C, with information allowed to flow between any pair of them except $A \not\rightsquigarrow C$. In trying to detect the potential for information flow from A to C through P there are two obvious views of the process we could consider.[4] The first is $\mathcal{L}_{A\cup B}(P)$ which is the view of C alone, and the second is $\mathcal{L}_A(P)$ in which just the actions of A, whose actions are not meant to create any nondeterminism in C's view are abstracted. The first is not really much use to us, because the act of creating the abstraction identifies nondeterminism created by A (which is forbidden) with that created by B (which is not). The second process may well be nondeterministic since we are allowing information flow from A to B, which would manifest itself in nondeterminism visible to B.

[4]The particular abstraction operator used is not the issue: we have used lazy abstraction here because it is, as discussed earlier, the most appropriate in a pure CSP context, but if the ways in which the abstracted user(s) interact with P included signal/output events, it would again be right to use mixed abstraction.

The specification that suggested itself to us, therefore, was that when we abstract away the events in A, the process has no nondeterminism visible to C:

$$\forall s \in traces(\mathcal{L}_A(P)) \,.\, \forall c \in C \,.$$
$$\neg(s \frown \langle c \rangle \in traces(\mathcal{L}_A(P)) \wedge (s, \{c\}) \in failures(\mathcal{L}_A(P))$$

This is a straightforward generalisation of the usual definition of determinism in CSP (we might phrase it "$\mathcal{L}_A(P)$ is *locally deterministic* in C") and says that after no trace s of the abstraction might C see either the acceptance or refusal of an event c in its alphabet.

The natural generalisation of this to an arbitrary (reflexive) security policy $\mathcal{V}$ is that, for each domain C, we abstract the union of the alphabets of the processes that are not allowed to influence C, which we can define:

$$noflow(C) = \bigcup\{A \mid A \not\rightsquigarrow C\}$$

and insist that, in just the same sense as above, the process

$$\mathcal{L}_{noflow(C)}(P) \quad \text{is locally deterministic in } C.$$

If this is true (for all the users C) we will say that P *obeys the (lazy) policy* $\mathcal{V}$. Given a subset S of events of the alphabet of P that are signals, it is clear how to define a corresponding notion using mixed abstraction. However, for the rest of the present paper we will concentrate solely on lazy abstraction and omit the bracketed *lazy* from the phrase above.

The following lemmas set out some basic desirable properties of this definition.

Lemma 1 *If P obeys policy $\mathcal{V}$ and $P' \sqsupseteq P$, then P' obeys $\mathcal{V}$ also.*

This is because the abstraction operators used are monotone and if $Q' \sqsupseteq Q$ has nondeterminism visible in a subset X of its alphabet, so does Q.

Lemma 2 *If $\mathcal{V}$ is transitive, then P obeys $\mathcal{V}$ if and only if it does so in the alternative definition we can infer in the way described in the introduction (in terms of multiple binary partitions of the alphabet) using concept of lazy independence discussed in Section 2.*

Lemma 3 *If the policies $\mathcal{V}$ and $\mathcal{V}'$ are based on the same partition of P's alphabet into domains, and $A \rightsquigarrow B$ in $\mathcal{V}$ implies $A \rightsquigarrow B$ in $\mathcal{V}'$, then if P obeys $\mathcal{V}$ it obeys $\mathcal{V}'$ as well.*

Evidently much of the underlying intuition in our definition is similar to that discussed for independence in Section 2. In particular we must expect to get sometimes over-pessimistic assessments in the case where the original process P has some nondeterminism visible to a low-level user.

An obvious question that arises is: what does our definition mean in terms of trace-sets when applied to a deterministic process P? Returning to the three user case, nondeterminism of $\mathcal{L}_A(P)$ can occur precisely when there are (necessarily different) traces s and s' of P, and $c \in C$, such that

$$\begin{array}{ll} s \setminus A = s' \setminus A & \text{and} \\ s \frown \langle c \rangle \in traces(P) & \text{and} \\ (s', \{c\}) \in failures(P) & \end{array}$$

This easily leads to the following alternative characterisation of our property.

Theorem 1 *Suppose P is deterministic and $\mathcal{V}$ is a security policy. Then P obeys $\mathcal{V}$ if and only if, for all domains C and $s, s' \in$ traces(P),*

$$s \setminus noflow(C) = s' \setminus noflow(C)$$
$$\Rightarrow (P/s)^0 \cap C = (P/s')^0 \cap C$$

This new characterisation has obvious similarities with the purge style discussed earlier. As in the purge-based trace definition in Section 2, we are stating that the choices C is offered by P are independent of any events that have occurred in the part of the alphabet that is not meant to pass information to C. Unlike the earlier definition, we are not demanding that the 'purged trace' $s \setminus noflow(C)$ is a trace of P. This is, of course, closely related to the discussion at the beginning of Section 3 where we showed that a simple definition of purge would not, in the case of an intransitive policy, produce a trace. What has happened is that the intuition of determinism has led us back to this simple purge function and produce ways of specifying noninterference that do not rely on *purge*(s) being a trace.

For the simple reason that the equivalence relation on traces induced by *ipurge* is (often strictly) finer than than produced by $s \setminus noflow(C)$, the above theorem allows us to deduce the following result.

Theorem 2 *Suppose P is deterministic and $\mathcal{V}$ is a security policy. Then if P obeys $\mathcal{V}$ in our new sense, it satisfies the ipurge definition of noninterference with respect to $\mathcal{V}$.*

(The assumption of P being deterministic is not in fact necessary here.) In other words, our new definition is less tolerant than the old one. As we shall soon see, sometimes it is strictly less tolerant.

It is interesting to consider how the examples discussed in Section 3 behave under this new definition. Let us first consider the case of the downgrader with just two users Hugh and Lois, and again we start by considering the situation where there are three domains for the security policy, the two users plus the downgrader, and the events *copy* and *dgread* are removed from the definition. The result is the opposite of last time: instead of a situation where leaky version of the system satisfies the property, we now find that even the apparently reasonable implementation given at the start of Section 3 does not. For we have the two traces

write.(*hugh*,*f*).0
downgrade.*f*.*lo*

and

write.(*hugh*,*f*).1
downgrade.*f*.*lo*

which are the same once the high-level actions ($noflow(Lois)$) are deleted, but after which Lois obviously gets different events offered by the system when she attempts to read f. What has happened is that the downgrading action does not contain enough information to explain the value that Lois can now see: we actually seem to need some of Hugh's history of interaction (as retained by *ipurge*) to explain this. But as we saw in the last section, this can allow the passing of far too much information, so what is the solution?

The most satisfactory answer we have found comes by looking more carefully at the definition of the downgrader. As presently defined, the agent controlling the *downgrade* actions can perform them without having seen what he or she is downgrading, and even if we assume that the file has always been read first via *dgread*, there is nothing in our definition to stop Hugh from writing a secret into the file between these two actions. From the point of view of responsibility and attribution, we argue that the definition of the downgrader would be greatly improved by adding a further field to the *downgrade* channel, namely the contents of the file at the point of downgrading. By doing so we would have created a "log" which identifies precisely what information has been downgraded. And by doing so we immediately remove the above problem, since the pair of traces above now become ones which are still different after Hugh's actions are removed. We have created a system in which it makes sense to claim that it is only the actions of the downgrader that affect Lois, not some actions of Hugh predicated upon intermediate actions of the downgrader. We believe that being forced to consider the tighter definition of noninterference produced a clearer and better description of the downgrader.

If there are more than two security levels (or, more precisely, more than one level to which it is possible to downgrade a file), it is still necessary to divide the *downgrade* events into multiple domains This is because we need to be able to determine from the security policy alone what users are to be influenced by a given $downgrade.f.c.v$ (noting the extra field v); unless c is the lowest classification this will not be them all. There is, however, no need to divide either the user or downgrader domains by filename as well (as we experimented with earlier). The security domains for our downgrader are then two for each level c: U_c containing all the events of the users with that classification, and D_c containing all event of the form $downgrade.f.c.v$ for the given c. The security policy is that $U_c \leadsto U_d$ if and only if $c \leq d$, $U_c \leadsto D_d$ for all c and d, and $D_d \leadsto U_c$ if and only if $d \leq c$. The modified definition of the downgrader obeys this policy, and if we introduced any of the potential errors into it discussed earlier that contain security flaws then the result would not obey it.

There is no problem in incorporating the *copy* events into this scheme, as they no longer cross the borderlines of domains. The *dgread* channel, if we wish to include it in the security policy, should be handled as before: putting it into a separate top domain which is influenced by all others but influences none other than itself. It is arguably better however, for a channel like this along which we are happy for any information to flow and which has a peripheral role in the analysis anyway, simply to abstract it away before we form the security policy. If, by doing so, nondeterminism were introduced at lower domains (which does not occur with the present example), it would provide the same warning of potential information flow resulting from use of such a channel that including it in the policy generates.

With our other example, the *GUARD* process, it would normally be appropriate to make the outputs of this process play the intermediary (downgrader-like) role in the security policy, probably abstracting away its inputs if these are not overall inputs to the system. Our new definition of noninterference then says unequivocally that the information flow to the downstream side must be accountable for purely in terms of what *GUARD* chooses to output. Again we regard this as more satisfactory than the definition that allows anything which has occurred prior to a *GUARD* output to be transmitted in a way that bypasses this component process.

5 Automation

The key to making the determinism characterisation of (transitive) noninterference practically useful has been the existence of efficient decision procedures for the determinism of a finite-state CSP process. Aside from normalising (see, for example, [15]) the complete process value, and then inspecting the result, which in many cases is likely to be relatively slow, we are aware of two different algorithms for this. The more elegant (also described in [15]) exploits the fact that the deterministic processes are the maximal elements of the failures/divergences model of CSP under the refinement order. The algorithm involves extracting an arbitrary deterministic refinement P' of our target process P: P is then deterministic if and only if P refines P'. The alternative method, developed by Lazic [10] for the purpose of extending ideas of data independence to determinism checking, involves running two copies of P in parallel with each other in such a way that the first is always allowed to choose any communication it likes, and only then is the second offered it (and only it). The process is deterministic just when this second offer is never refused, and this is something that can easily be checked by a refinement check.

The unconventional parallel composition used in the last of these methods is achieved by renaming each event a of one (say the second) copy of P to a distinct "shadow" event a' (which is different both from all events of P and all other b'), and linking the two by the process

$$TEST = ?a : A \to a' \to TEST$$

where A is the alphabet of P. Because we are combining two copies of P in parallel, this method is, in the worst case, quadratic in the state-space size of P, though it is unlikely to be this bad in practice. In the type of example we are considering, where P is produced by applying abstraction operators to a (usually) deterministic process, there are often substantial advantages to be had in applying state-compression operators to P prior to this type of check.[5]

For the generalised concept of noninterference introduced in this paper we need to be able to check for *local* determinism in a set of events C, so it is natural to ask how the above methods extend to it. The one which involves checking over the normal form is little different: the main effort is in the normalisation (unchanged from the previous case), but the check that has to be done on each normal form node is slightly different. We have to discover if any node has both c as an initial event and $\{c\}$ as a refusal set for any $c \in C$. The method based on the maximality of deterministic processes does not work, as locally deterministic processes are not necessarily maximal, and we cannot see a reasonable fix[6]

This leaves the method in which P is run in parallel with itself. This is easy to amend: all we have to do is change the renaming and *TEST* process a little. Shadow events are only created for events in C, so the second copy P' of P has all its other events left unchanged by the renaming. The *TEST* process allows P and P' to synchronise as they please on these other events, except that after P has performed an event in C it insists that P' does its shadow and nothing else: if B are the events of P less the set C,

$$\begin{aligned} TEST &= ?x : B \to TEST \\ &\quad \Box ?c : C \to c' \to TEST \end{aligned}$$

The resultant combination (in which all three processes must synchronise on events in B, P and *TEST* on C, and *TEST* and P' on C') can deadlock immediately after an event in C if and only if P is not locally deterministic in C.

We conclude that the generalised noninterference condition is decidable in the same spirit as the original determinism-based one, but what was, in some ways, the most attractive option is not now available to us. We have performed a number of experiments with the parallel method described above for the type of example process discussed in this paper, but it is obviously desirable that larger case-studies, where the results are less easily predictable, are carried out.

It is also possible to decide the *ipurge* definition of noninterference in the context of CSP and FDR, by carefully combining a renamed version of the target process with a monitor process whose role, essentially, is to decide which events need to be abstracted. This, in fact, uses only ordinary, as opposed to local, determinism checking, but is complex to formulate for security policies with many failures of transitivity.

6 Conclusions

It was a great surprise to us to discover how the previously published definitions of intransitive noninterference behaved when we considered them in the context of our examples. We assume that these definitions were driven somewhat by the desire to have traditional-looking definitions based on the purge function and on unwinding, but our conclusion is that they are worryingly liberal in the sense that they fail to catch potential security leaks. (The *ipurge* definition does, as several of the references cited at the start of Section 3 demonstrate, yield useful definitions of unwinding.)

The advantage of our new definition, which as can be seen from the trace reformulation given in Theorem 1 is in some way closer to those of ordinary noninterference, is that it clearly establishes the principle that the only permitted influences on the low-level process are by the intermediary (even though the latter may well have been influenced in what it said by the high-level process). We do not have to find some way of formulating which high-level information the intermediary intended through or make the bold assumption (seemingly made by the various authors who have used *ipurge*) that it was all to be allowed. As we saw, the new definition forced us to create what was really a better downgrading system in which the blame for any (managerially) undesired information flow is directly attributable to

[5] Compressing an abstracted process can often itself be more efficient by abstracting all events as early as possible as the process is built up and using the compression operators hierarchically.

[6] In fact, the formulation of lazy abstraction given earlier also causes problems with this algorithm in checking ordinary determinism thanks to the way it handles divergence. In that case, however, there is a convenient fix, but not one which is valid for local determinism. That is to use a specific implementation of $\mathcal{L}_A(P)$, namely the one in which H behaves as *STOP*, as a reference.

something the downgrader does. We expect that further case study work will help to determine whether the rigours of satisfying our stronger formulation of noninterference are generally helpful or turn out to be unreasonably onerous. Faced with a choice of two conditions, one of which is demonstrably too weak and the other arguably too strong, it is surely better to aim to satisfy the latter rather than being happy with the former.

As stated earlier, in this work we have concentrated on the deterministic P case of systems described in CSP. Theorem 1 easily points to how analogous definitions could be formulated in state-machine models or other paradigms with similar notations of traces, but it is not quite so easy to see how the decision procedures we have developed for CSP would carry over to the usual frameworks these use. We imagine that work currently under way to help understand ordinary noninterference in the context of nondeterministic CSP should extend to the intransitive context we have set out. However, as discussed earlier, the right answer for how to handle this issue is still uncertain.

The CSP characterisations given in [15] of (transitive) noninterference and fault tolerance are closely related to each other. This is because a system is obviously fault tolerant if the occurrence of faults (which we can code as being triggered by specific events) has no effect on what the user sees. The definition, in fact, is that the system with fault events lazily abstracted refines the one in which the faults are prevented (by parallel composition with *STOP* synchronising on the fault events) from occurring. While this definition is intuitively appealing, its use is limited to circumstances under which the system is sufficiently robust that the user never sees any negative effect from faults. One can imagine wanting to analyse systems in which faults can affect the user's view, but hopefully only in a controlled way. We believe that the same ideas used here to reason about intransitive noninterference may provide a means by which such systems can be analysed. The fault actions are again analogous to the high-level actions of MLS, and the user's view is again analogous to the low-level ones. But this time we might have a fault recovery system or operating system playing a downgrader-like role, and want to show that the only effects the user can see resulting from faults are those s/he is warned about by this intermediary. This will be a topic for future research.

Acknowledgements

We would like to thank Sylvan Pinsky and Peter Ryan for advice and discussions about intransitive noninterference.

The work reported in this paper was funded by DERA Malvern and the US Office of Naval Research.

References

[1] R. Focardi, Comparing two information flow security policies, Proceedings of CSFW IX, IEEE Computer Society Press, 1996.

[2] R. Focardi and R. Gorrieri, A classification of security policies for process algebras, Journal of Computer Security, **3**, 1, pp5-33, 1994.

[3] Formal Systems (Europe) Ltd. *FDR2 manual*, 1998. `http://www.formal.demon.co.uk/fdr2manual/`.

[4] R. Forster, Non-interference properties for nondeterministic processes, Dissertation for transfer to D.Phil status, Oxford University Computing Laboratory 1997.

[5] J.A. Goguen and J. Meseguer. *Security policies and security models*, in Proceedings of the 1982 IEEE Symposium on Security and Privacy, pp 1 1-20. IEEE Computer Society Press, 1982.

[6] J.A. Goguen and J. Meseguer. *Inference control and unwinding*, in Proceedings of the 1984 IEEE Symposium on Security and Privacy, pp 75-86. IEEE Computer Society Press, 1984.

[7] J. Graham-Cumming, *The formal development of secure systems*, Oxford University D.Phil Thesis, 1992.

[8] J.Haigh and W. Young, Extending the non-inference model of MLS for SAT, in Proceedings of the 1986 IEEE Symposium on Security and Privacy, pp 232-239, IEEE Computer Society Press, 1986.

[9] J.L. Jacob, Specifying Security Properties, in *Developments in Concurrency and Communication*, C.A.R. Hoare (ed.) Addison-Wesley 1990.

[10] R.S. Lazic and A.W. Roscoe. Verifying determinism of concurrent systems which use unbounded arrays. Technical report, Oxford University Computing Laboratory, April 1998. Full version of [11].

[11] R.S. Lazic and A.W. Roscoe. Verifying Determinism of Data Independent Systems with Labellings, Arrays and Constants. In *Proceedings of Infinity'98*, 1998. To appear; full version issued as [10].

[12] J. MacLean Proving noninterference and functional correctness using traces, Journal of Computer Security **1**: 37-57 (1992).

[13] S. Pinsky, Absorbing covers and intransitive noninterference, Proceedings of 1995 IEEE Symposium on Security and Privacy.

[14] A.W. Roscoe, CSP and determinism in security modelling, Proceedings of 1995 IEEE Symposium on Security and Privacy.

[15] A.W. Roscoe. *The Theory and Practice of Concurrency*. Prentice Hall, 1998. ISBN 0-13-6774409-5, pp. xv+565.

[16] A.W. Roscoe, J.C.P. Woodcock, and L. Wulf. Noninterference through determinism. *Journal of Computer Security*, 4(1), 1996. Revised from Proceedings of the European Symposium on Research in Computer Security (ESORICS) 1994, LNCS 875.

[17] A.W. Roscoe and L. Wulf, Composing and decomposing processes under security properties, Proceedings of CSFW VIII, IEEE Computer Society Press, 1995.

[18] John Rushby. Noninterference, transitivity, and channel-control security policies. Technical Report csl-92-2, SRI, 1992.

[19] P.Y.A. Ryan, A CSP formulation of non-interference, Cipher, pp 19-27. IEEE Computer Society Press, 1991.

[20] Lars Wulf. *Interaction and Security in Distributed Computing*. DPhil, Wolfson College, University of Oxford, Hilary 1997.

[21] W. Young and W. Bevier, A state-based approach to non-interference, Proceedings of CSFW VII, IEEE Computer Society Press, 1994.

Index of Authors

IEEE COMPUTER SOCIETY

Press Activities Board

1/29/99